THE INTERNATIONAL HANDBOOK OF ANIMAL ABUSE AND CRUELTY: THEORY, RESEARCH, AND APPLICATION

THE INTERNATIONAL HANDBOOK OF ANIMAL ABUSE AND CRUELTY: THEORY, RESEARCH, AND APPLICATION

EDITED BY FRANK R. ASCIONE

Purdue University Press
West Lafayette, Indiana

First paperback printing, 2010. ISBN 978-1-55753-565-8.

Printed in the United States of America.

ISBN: 978-1-55753-463-7

Library of Congress Cataloging-in-Publication Data

The international handbook of animal abuse and cruelty: theory,
research, and application / edited by Frank R. Ascione.
       p. cm.
   ISBN 978-1-55753-463-7
1. Animal welfare. 2. Cruelty. 3. Violence—Psychological aspects.
4. Human—animal relationships. I. Ascione, Frank R.

HV4708.I57 2008
179'.3—dc22

                                  2007051801

For Fernando Tapia and Alan R. Felthous whose pioneering research opened new pathways to understanding the etiology and significance of animal abuse

Contents

Foreword

Criminal justice literature is replete with references to the "violent triad." This concept suggests that anyone who has a background that includes the three characteristics of animal abuse, fire-setting, and enuresis has a greater potential for violence. Years ago, Dr. Sigmund Freud insightfully, if only intuitively, asserted that a connection existed between fire-setting and aggressive behavior. He further explained the unconscious process by which urination became the regressive gratification of infantile pleasure among fire-setters. Most notably among other writers, Dr. H. Yarnell, then of Bellevue Hospital in New York City, took Freud's work and applied it to her own clinical experiences with juveniles. Dr. Yarnell began to see a connection not only with fire-setting and enuresis but also with animal abuse. The violent triad of animal abuse, fire-setting, and bed-wetting that predicted future violence was born and has been used in clinical, forensic, and law enforcement communities since the 1940s.

Upon examining much of the literature in which this violent triad has been applied, a major issue emerges: how the terms *animal abuse*, *fire-setting*, and *enuresis* are defined and what criteria are used to make differential diagnoses among the more significant levels of these activities. Two scenarios involving different boys can illustrate the importance of uniform definitions and accepted criteria to measure the degree of seriousness or significance. With simple definitions of animal abuse, both boys could, and in some jurisdictions would, be labeled deviant and criminal. However, even a cursory reading of these scenarios indicates both qualitative and quantitative differences between these boys. Although the results of their actions—animals killed for no good reason—are similar and most regrettable, the differences in their reactions to their behaviors are remarkable and significant.

In the first scenario, Bobby has asked for a pellet gun for a number of years, but his parents have resisted. Now that he has turned 14 and seems both old and mature enough in his parents' view, they have agreed to entrust him with a pellet gun. Also he has attended a safety course in the use of the gun and cannot remove it from the house without supervision. On a warm spring day, however, he decides to take the pellet gun, without permission, into the woods for some practice shooting. He sets up a number of cans and rocks on a ridge and fires his pellet gun, zeroing in on the makeshift targets. Then, he notices a mother duck with several ducklings in a nearby pond. Without much thought, he places one of the little ducks in his sights and pulls the trigger. Nothing happens, so he shoots again. This time, a small duck is struck. He quickly moves his sights to another, fires, and hits that one. By this time, the other ducks have swum away. As Bobby walks home, his thoughts turn to the little ducks in the pond. He sees them struggling to maintain life and then succumbing to the trauma of the pellets. He cannot get the image out of his mind. Now, he begins to struggle, too, with the guilt of having killed these little ducks. He is unable to eat that evening and has trouble sleeping because every time he closes his eyes, he sees the struggling ducklings.

In another scenario, Johnny's best friend, Martin, received a pellet gun for his birthday. Friends since they met in junior high school and now 15 years old, they spend a good deal of time together. When Johnny learns about Martin's new pellet gun, he persuades Martin to lend it to him. Johnny has decided that he wants to shoot out windows in an abandoned building in the woods behind their school. When he gets to the building, Johnny's attention is drawn quickly to several ducks walking through the woods toward a pond. He systematically fires at them, trying to kill each one. As they disperse, he follows them, firing until all are dead. He tells

Martin the following day that he wants to keep the gun for a while. He has seen several newborn rabbits in the area.

Depending on the definition of animal abuse and the criteria used to determine the level and nature of it, both Johnny and Bobby can be labeled as "animal abusers." Although in some sense both deserve these labels, of what value are they diagnostically and prognostically? Is there a sense that these labels, as used here, will tell us anything about Johnny or Bobby, especially about the potential they may have for future violent behavior?

Probably nowhere more is there a need to clearly define the terms and plainly and unmistakably state distinguishing criteria than in the study of animal abuse. Terms such as *animal abuse*, *zoophilia*, and *bestiality* are used sometimes with nuanced differences and sometimes interchangeably. Where differences exist among these terms, they do so from author to author, making it difficult to extrapolate from multiple studies what the commonalities are. The person who monthly engages an animal in sexual ways that do not involve physical or apparent emotional abuse of the animal may well be considered engaging in animal abuse. How different is this person from the individual who not only engages in sexual contact with the animal, but also tortures the creature during the sexual activity? How different from these two individuals is the person who once—and only once—was caught dropping large rocks on turtles with a group of fellow teenagers? The use of the violent triad may prove helpful in identifying these individuals and bringing all of them into the mental health arena for assessment. But the real danger of stopping at this level is labeling children as potentially violent who really are not. Recording an incident of animal abuse without clear definitions and criteria and without an understanding of the context in which the incident occurred and the physical and emotional effects it had on the individual might well be meaningless.

The first step in meaningful reporting of incidents of animal abuse is the development of uniform, clearly articulated, and generally accepted definitions. This is a difficult process but certainly not an impossible one. For example, in the 1980s, law enforcement agencies throughout the United States began to collect information regarding crimes motivated by hate or bias. The definition of a hate- or bias-motivated crime lacked uniformity when varying jurisdictions attempted to measure the frequency of these acts. In 1990, the Uniform Crime Reporting (UCR) Program of the Federal Bureau of Investigation expanded to include the category of hate crimes. A standardized definition of a hate crime came about through the cooperation of local, state, and federal law enforcement agencies, along with various human interest groups. A model policy was then developed that included recommendations for law enforcement agencies to consider when investigating and submitting hate crime statistics to the UCR Program, which began compiling and distributing the data to law enforcement via an annual publication. This marked the first time that the UCR Program asked law enforcement agencies to examine offenders' motivations for committing a crime. Perhaps a government agency, such as the Centers for Disease Control or the National Institute for Mental Health, could become the lead organization in formulating a similar effort for developing clear definitions and accepted criteria for animal abuse and the other two characteristics of the violent triad, fire setting and enuresis.

Dr. Frank Ascione has been working for decades attempting to clarify and resolve many of these clinical and research issues. His work, along with that of many of the contributors to this anthology, examines and clearly articulates the various forms of human and animal interaction. He has introduced a second generation of research into the entire question of animal abuse. Dr. Ascione and his collaborators from around the world in the mental and physical health disciplines, veterinary science, social work, and criminal justice are bringing into clearer focus the multiple causes and implications of animal abuse. Most important, they are doing this in a way that has meaningful applications to clinicians, as well as to law enforcement officers.

Anthony J. Pinizzotto, Ph.D.
Senior Scientist
Forensic Psychologist
FBI, Behavioral Science Unit
Quantico, VA

Preface

When it became clear that the time had come for assembling a compendium of papers reflecting the current state of scholarly work on animal abuse and cruelty, I realized that the easiest part of such a task would be identifying prominent scientists from diverse disciplines whose recent research and conceptual analyses illuminated our understanding of these topics. So the first individuals to whom I express my appreciation are the contributors to this volume.

My vision for this handbook would never have been realized without the essential support of the Kenneth A. Scott Charitable Trust, a foundation that has been instrumental in facilitating my research and writing on a number of past and current projects. Dr. H. Richard Obermanns, Executive Director of the Trust, shepherded this project through the grant approval process and offered encouragement and affirmation over the lengthy gestation period from chapter outlines to finished handbook.

During this editorial project, I greatly benefited from a sabbatical year (2006) provided by Utah State University and by a number of international colleagues. The late Phil Donohoe introduced me to the rich cultural heritage of and current challenges facing the indigenous peoples of Australia. Although I knew him only a short time before his untimely death, we became fast friends. Phil and his family opened their hearts and lives to me, and I will be forever grateful. The majestic landscapes and vistas of Kakadu National Park will always remind me of Phil's spirit and dedication to enhancing the lives of Aboriginal Australians.

Dr. Camilla Pagani and Dr. Francesco Robustelli arranged for me to spend a week with them in Rome, Italy, at the National Research Center, during which time we developed an Italian version of an animal abuse assessment instrument. Camilla and Franco's work on children and animals is unique in their country, and I have been privileged to be their collaborator and friend. My friend and colleague, Dr. Eleonora Gullone, cordially hosted a month at Monash University in Melbourne, Australia. My thanks to Eleonora for providing me space and quiet time to devote to writing and editing. Dr. Akimitsu (AKI) Yokoyama also arranged a remarkable month for me in Japan, during which I learned of the commonalities of the animal abuse issues across cultures as well as culturally unique challenges. The supreme host, AKI toured with me throughout Japan as I lectured on animal abuse and publicized AKI's Japanese translation of my book, *Children and Animals: Exploring the Roots of Kindness and Cruelty* (Purdue University Press). AKI's cadre of students was a constant source of support and affirmed for me the vibrancy of this scientific field of study in Japan. A return trip to Japan in 2007 allowed me to directly experience the growing interest in animal welfare issues. My deepest thanks also go to Rumiko Tanaka and her family in Ena, Japan, for a refreshing and restful break from my lecture tour.

This handbook is my fourth project with Purdue University Press. Tom Bacher and Margaret Hunt have provided excellent editorial guidance, and Rebecca Corbin has been a fantastic author liaison. Becki, along with Bryan Shaffer, designed and developed marketing materials and were diligent in responding to my numerous requests for assistance throughout this project. Sharon Anderson at BookMasters turned e-mailed drafts of chapters into meticulously copyedited versions and created the final layout of this handbook.

Rebecca Scharton, a psychology graduate student at Utah State University, prepared the index for the handbook. Many thanks!

Thanks, once again, to my family for keeping me focused on the bright side of human nature. My wife, Debbie, provided encouragement when this project seemed never ending, and my children, Matthew, Cathy (and husband, Matt), and David and grandsons, Calvin and Luca, give me the reasons for devoting attention to human and animal welfare.

Frank R. Ascione
Logan, Utah
December 2007

Introduction

Animal Abuse and Scholarly Research: Reflections on the Past and a Contemporary View

Frank R. Ascione

Animal welfare issues have been the focus of my professional research for over two decades. These issues have included programs to promote humane attitudes toward animals in children (Ascione, 1992) and the problem of animal abuse (Ascione, 1993). When I began to study animal maltreatment more intensively, I quickly realized that the existing literature was relatively meager, especially empirical studies from psychology, psychiatry, and social work. In addition to scattered references to animal abuse in psychoanalytic and anthropological publications (see Ascione, 1993, 2005), a few classic studies paved the way for those of us interested in pursuing this topic in a more systematic fashion. Among these classic studies, I include Fernando Tapia's work with children who abuse animals (Rigdon & Tapia, 1977; Tapia, 1971), Alan Felthous's studies of criminal samples (e.g., Felthous & Yudowitz, 1977), the pioneering study of animal abuse in the context of child maltreatment by Randy Lockwood and his colleagues (DeViney, Dickert, & Lockwood, 1983), and James Hutton's (1983) examination of animal abuse and family dysfunction.

By the end of the 1990s, Randy Lockwood and I (Lockwood & Ascione, 1998) were able to include, in a roughly 500-page compendium, most of what have been considered the significant published articles on the topic of animal abuse (Rowan, 2006). Phil Arkow and I followed with a compendium of original papers examining the links among animal abuse, child maltreatment, and domestic violence (Ascione & Arkow, 1999). Since the publication of these books, the resurgence, growth, and maturation of scholarly interest in this topic have been dramatic. I hope this international handbook is clear evidence that the study of animal abuse is now an established field of scholarly inquiry that cuts across and intertwines multiple scientific disciplines and

attracts respected professionals from a number of continents. Collectively, these chapters illustrate the numerous ways in which animal welfare and human welfare are often linked.

In the following paragraphs, I briefly highlight the focus of each chapter provided by the contributing authors who represent the diversity of professional fields addressing animal abuse. The first section of the handbook deals with historical analysis as well as theoretical and research issues particular to the varied disciplines dealing with animal abuse (e.g., veterinary medicine, law, clinical child psychology, adult mental health, sociology, social work). The second section is devoted to emerging research within the international community, and the final section concentrates on applications and practical considerations from clinical, forensic, law enforcement, and psychiatric perspectives.

This handbook opens with **Unti's** historical analysis of the movement against animal cruelty in the United States. He traces early philosophical treatises linking animal abuse to other social problems and outlines the common roots of child protection and animal protection programs in the United States. Unti provides a compelling history of the development of societies for the prevention of cruelty to animals in the late 1800s and notes how, early in the history of this movement, some humane societies included not only animals but women, children, and the elderly in their efforts to protect vulnerable members of society. He provides hypotheses to account for the lack of social science interest in human–animal relations during the first half of the twentieth century and then suggests characteristics of U.S. society that led to a new focus on the human–animal bond. After a consideration of factors that may have contributed to increased research attention to animal abuse in the 1990s and beginning of the twenty-first century, he predicts that attention to animal abuse is likely to continue in future scholarly efforts.

Arkow and **Munro** focus on the veterinary profession's roles in addressing animal abuse. Describing animal abuse as a public health issue similar to other forms of violence, Arkow and Munro speculate on reasons that may account for veterinarians' reluctance to query their human clients (pet owners) about animal abuse and other forms of family violence. They include results from a number of surveys of veterinarians in the United States, United Kingdom, Canada, and Australia demonstrating that veterinarians are likely to encounter animal abuse at some time in their professional careers. An extensive elaboration of the concept of "non-accidental injuries in animals" is provided, as well as clinical examples of such injuries and suggestions for differential diagnosis. The authors offer extensive recommendations related to veterinary training, issues related to confidentiality and litigation, and the need for close collaboration between veterinarians and other human welfare professionals.

Recent evolution and advances in animal abuse legislation in the United States are outlined by **Frasch**. She notes dramatic increases in the number of states with felony-level provisions for certain forms of animal abuse and reports on a unique study of law enforcement officials and their evaluation of the effects of these legislative modifications on prosecutorial practices. This study was based on extensive interviews with prosecutors and other law enforcement officers and addresses definitions of animal abuse in state statutes, inconsistent treatment of animal abuse cases by different courts, and the advantages of felony-level statutes for certain types of animal abuse crimes. Frasch closes her chapter with recommendations for future research of this kind that would include additional states and the need for better data collection within law enforcement agencies and prosecutors' offices.

Tracking crimes against animals is the topic explored by **Lockwood**, who outlines a number of compelling reasons why such tracking is needed (animal abuse is a crime, a potential sign of community problems, an indicator crime that may be related to family violence, and a potential predictor crime for other criminal offenses). He describes the relevance of forensic analysis and appropriate attention from the criminal justice system for preventing and intervening in cases of animal abuse. In addition to considering parallels between tracking animal abuse and

related social problems, such as child maltreatment and domestic violence, he suggests ways that systemic change could occur to enhance our understanding of the prevalence of animal abuse in the United States. He does this effectively by considering the major crime data collection systems currently used in the United States, systems that do not currently include specific records of animal abuse.

Dadds brings his expertise in clinical child psychology to an analysis of how animal abuse may be embedded within the more general category of disruptive behavior disorders. He examines the relation of animal abuse to Conduct Disorder, including the recently discussed callous/unemotional subtype of this disorder that may have special relevance for some children and adolescents who display antisocial behaviors. Dadds provides an extensive discussion of the motivations that may underlie animal abuse and describes a number of important new assessments (including one of his own) that promise more effective ways to measure both parent/guardian reports and self-reports of young people's animal abuse histories. He effectively frames his chapter within theories of developmental psychopathology and outlines an agenda for future clinical research.

The potential psychobiological aspects of animal abuse are explored by **Maiuro, Eberle, Rastaman, and Snowflake** in a chapter focusing on attachment issues. They discuss both healthy and maladaptive attachments between humans and animals and apply adult attachment theory to an understanding of pet abuse that may occur in the context of domestic violence. Further depth to these issues is provided by the authors' analysis of cortical, psychophysiological, and hormonal factors that have been implicated in studies of human-perpetrated violence. Their clinical experience also supports the routine assessment of animal abuse in protocols used to interview both victims and perpetrators of intimate partner violence.

Flynn contributes a comprehensive sociological analysis of animal abuse that covers issues related to chronological age, gender, childhood socialization, and cultural factors. As a sociologist, he outlines studies of animal abuse and its relation to corporal punishment and family violence, research on dog fighting and cock fighting, and theoretical frames that may facilitate our understanding of animal abuse. The theoretical frames include both feminist theory and symbolic interactionism. Flynn completes his contribution with a detailed agenda for future sociological research, including a call to examine "socially acceptable" forms of animal abuse.

A perspective from the field of social work is provided by **Faver** and **Strand**, who emphasize the important place that pets hold within family ecology across the life span. They note how the history of the social work movement has close ties with the development of programs fostering animal welfare and they elaborate on the varied contexts within which social workers may encounter the abuse of animals (e.g., child maltreatment, intimate partner violence, abuse of the elderly, cases of animal hoarding and self-neglect). They close their chapter with recommended action strategies that relate to education, assessment, the development of community coalitions, and agency programs for cross-training and cross-reporting.

Beetz illustrates the complex theoretical, psychological, and criminological issues that pervade the topic of bestiality. She defines bestiality, suggests a typology of these acts that includes consideration of its varied motivations, notes the difficulties in accurately gauging the prevalence of this phenomenon, and discusses the veterinarian's role in addressing cases of bestiality. In addition to rich historical analysis, including religious and legal views on bestiality, Beetz summarizes a number of recent surveys that attempt to shed light on the nature of this practice and the characteristics (e.g., personality, attachment) and attitudes of people who have sexual interactions with animals.

The hoarding of animals affects significant numbers of pets and **Patronek** focuses on this form of maltreatment. After defining hoarding, he makes a compelling case for distinguishing hoarding from active abuse of animals and other types of neglect. His research and that of his colleagues provide prevalence estimates of this phenomenon as well as the demographic characteristics of perpetrators who have come to the attention of animal and human welfare agencies. Patronek suggests theoretical models that may need to be enlisted to understand hoarding (e.g., cognitive behavioral, psychiatric, developmental, sociological) and intervention/treatment approaches that should be considered by law enforcement and mental health professionals. He concludes with recommendations for future analyses of this problem and includes a hoarding monitoring form valuable for tracking hoarding cases.

In the first of three chapters with an international focus, **Pagani, Robustelli,** and **I** explore the issue of animal welfare in contemporary Italian society. The chapter is written from a global perspective on the general problem of violence and incorporates discussion of attitudes toward diversity and its relation to empathy and cultural factors. Recent changes in Italian law and in Italians' interest in animal welfare issues serve as a backdrop for describing a major study of animal welfare issues with a large sample of Italian schoolchildren. This study assessed youths' attitudes and experiences related to both socially acceptable and socially unacceptable forms of animal abuse as well as young people's views on the motivations that may have led to such acts.

Maruyama and **I** address recent and dramatic changes in Japan's efforts to address animal welfare, juvenile crime, child maltreatment, and domestic violence through legislation and the activities of enforcement agencies. We elaborate on the historical, social structural, and religious/philosophical factors related to Japanese people's views of animals, especially pets, in the context of contemporary social problems in Japan. Juvenile crime, school violence and bullying, and associated legal and psychiatric issues are discussed with reference to recent, high-profile cases where animal abuse appeared to be a prelude to serious violence against humans. Laws related to animal welfare and abuse have been modified a number of times in recent years, in a very progressive manner, and the ramifications of such changes are described along with parallel examinations of domestic violence, child maltreatment, and elder abuse. We describe research in Japan, spearheaded by Maruyama, on children's attitudes toward pets and other animals and programs in Japan aimed at humane education and the use of animals to assist therapeutic processes.

Australian perspectives and initiatives related to animal abuse are the themes to which **Gullone** and **Clarke** bring their expertise as a developmental psychologist and forensic psychologist, respectively. Their topics include the history of the development of the Royal Society for the Prevention of Cruelty to Animals, changes in animal welfare laws, investigation of and penalties for animal abuse, and emerging discussions on the role of veterinarians as mandated reporters of animal abuse. There is rich material in this chapter on pet ownership in Australia, a model program to prevent dog bites in children, and the results of a survey of Australian veterinarians on animal abuse issues. Gullone describes a study conducted in Victoria that confirms how common pet abuse is in families confronted with domestic violence and Clarke presents the first-of-its-kind police data on the overlap between animal abuse and other serious criminal activity based on law enforcement records from New South Wales. Case studies that highlight the value of considering animal abuse a sentinel for serious crimes against people are included. Gullone and Clarke close their chapter with insightful recommendations for future research and agency collaboration on animal abuse.

Magid[1] brought his extensive experience as a clinician and as an international authority on relationship disorders in children to his chapter on animal abuse and attachment. For those unfamiliar with attachment theory, Magid's chapter provides an excellent introduction, especially in relation to the human–animal bond. He blends the components of current attachment theory with topics as diverse as animal hoarding, severe trauma in humans, ecological aspects of psychopathology related to animal abuse, and reactive attachment disorder. Magid's own breadth of expertise is illustrated when he discusses phenomena at the behavioral/psychological level, neural/cortical/anatomic levels, and the evolutionary level. He includes discussion of child maltreatment and emerging research on the neuroanatomical correlates of abuse and how these factors are potentially related to emotion regulation and the development of empathy. His recommendations for future multidisciplinary research are complemented by his insightful clinical perspective.

Given recent changes in the characterization of animal abuse offenses in many U.S. states, **Schlueter's** chapter, written from the perspective of a long history of law enforcement experience, is a timely contribution. Schlueter begins with a history of her own personal journey directed toward more effective law enforcement responses to animal-related crimes. She shares insights that can emerge only after extensive professional experience in the field of law enforcement, and dispels a number of myths that, at times, are unfortunate obstacles to considering animal abuse a significant crime in its own right as well as a crime that may be related to the victimization of humans. Her chapter is enriched by a detailed set of recommendations for investigators as well as practical considerations relevant for other law enforcement professionals.

The roles of the clinical child psychologist, social worker, and prosecutor in animal abuse cases in the context of child maltreatment, and how they can be effectively blended, are carefully outlined in the chapter by **Boat, Loar,** and **Phillips**. Boat emphasizes the importance of asking children about their experiences and relations with pets and discusses issues related to attachment, loss, and related traumas involving animals. In addition to examining the role of animals in the therapeutic process, she presents her important assessment model whose value is illustrated with a compelling case study. Loar speaks from the perspective of child protective services and contributes a family-based risk assessment demonstrating the parallels between characteristics of children and pets who are at risk of neglect and/or maltreatment. She describes how information from such an assessment can be valuable in guiding therapeutic interventions. Phillips concentrates on animal abuse in child maltreatment and domestic violence cases. She elaborates effective procedures for conducting forensic interviews with children and adolescents and urges courts to take animal abuse seriously as a potential impediment to family safety (e.g., threats to women and children's pets). Following a discussion of sentencing issues for those convicted of animal abuse crimes, she presents a number of examples from case law that will be of interest to other prosecutors and members of the judiciary.

Lewchanin and **Randour** approach the issue of animal abuse by elaborating on assessment and intervention issues, the need for community education and agency policy development, and suggested improvements in gathering animal-related crime statistics. The importance of the human–animal bond in childhood and adolescence serves as a backdrop for reviewing research on animal abuse with juvenile offenders, the critical need to explore motivations for animal abuse, and the value of referring to successful prevention and intervention programs designed for juvenile fire setters as models for dealing with juvenile-perpetrated animal abuse. Lewchanin and Randour outline essential components of successful programs and provide models for assessment and intervention, including the AniCare Child protocol (which includes a focus on self-management and the development of empathy). They close their chapter with policy recommendations for state and federal jurisdictions as well as advice for improving the training of counselors and other therapists on animal abuse issues that may emerge in therapeutic contexts.

Yokoyama speaks from the perspective of a Japanese psychiatrist who has conducted research on animal-facilitated education and therapy and who has emerged as a national expert on animal abuse issues. Using fascinating clinical examples,

Yokoyama explores animal abuse in the content of the major categories of psychiatric disorders contained in the DSM-IV-TR (American Psychiatric Association, 2000). Here, he shows the reader how animal abuse may be a significant factor not just in Conduct Disorders but for major mental health problems covering the life span. Since it is only within the past decade that Japan has begun to systematically address animal welfare, child maltreatment, and domestic violence as challenging social problems, his analyses suggest an agenda for the future as Japan acknowledges the potential overlap among these forms of maltreatment. In addition to incorporating important Japanese clinical case material and studies reported in Japanese scholarly publications, Yokoyama outlines emerging animal abuse problems, including animal abuse depicted on the Internet, the hoarding of animals, and the benefits and risks of robotic pets as substitutes for live companion animals.

I believe that each of these chapters represents a significant facet of a comprehensive attempt to understand animal abuse in its various forms. The authors have summarized extant research and thoughtfully provided research agendas for the future, agendas we all hope will be of value to other professionals and especially to students who are embarking on their scholarly careers.

Note

1. Ken Magid died tragically (August 13, 2005) in an airplane accident just weeks after completing his chapter.

References

American Psychiatric Association. (2000). DSM-IV-TR. Washington, DC: American Psychiatric Association.

Ascione, F. R. (1992). Enhancing children's attitudes about the humane treatment of animals: Generalization to human-directed empathy. *Anthrozoös, 5*, 176–191.

Ascione, F. R. (1993). Children who are cruel to animals: A review of research and implications for developmental psychopathology. *Anthrozoös, 6*, 226–247.

Ascione, F. R. (2005). *Children and animals: Exploring the roots of kindness and cruelty.* West Lafayette, IN: Purdue University Press.

Ascione, F. R., & Arkow, P. (Eds.). (1999). *Child abuse, domestic violence, and animal abuse: Linking the circles of compassion for prevention and intervention.* West Lafayette, IN: Purdue University Press.

DeViney, E., Dickert, J., & Lockwood, R. (1983). The care of pets within child abusing families. *International Journal for the Study of Animal Problems, 4*, 321–329.

Felthous, A. R., & Yudowitz, B. (1977). Approaching a comparative typology of assaultive female offenders. *Psychiatry, 40*, 270–276.

Hutton, J. S. (1983). Animal abuse as a diagnostic approach in social work: A pilot study. In A. Katcher and A. Beck (Eds.), *New perspectives on our lives with companion animals* (pp. 444–447). Philadelphia, University of Pennsylvania Press.

Lockwood, R., & Ascione, F. R. (1998). *Cruelty to animals and interpersonal violence: Readings in research and application.* West Lafayette, IN: Purdue University Press.

Rigdon, J., & Tapia, F. (1977). Children who are cruel to animals—a follow-up study. *Journal of Operational Psychology, 8*, 27–36.

Rowan, A. N. (2006). Animal cruelty: Definitions and sociology. *Behavioral and Brain Sciences, 29*, 238–239.

Tapia, F. (1971). Children who are cruel to animals. *Child Psychiatry and Human Development, 2*, 70–77.

Cruelty Indivisible:
Historical Perspectives on the Link Between Cruelty to Animals and Interpersonal Violence

Bernard Unti

For centuries, even before the emergence of organized animal protection, concern about cruelty to animals as a pathway to interpersonal violence has motivated calls for an ethic of kindness and compassion. Once anti-cruelty societies emerged in the nineteenth century, they amplified an extant discourse of concern over the link between animal cruelty and violence to human beings, and invoked that relationship as a central premise of the case for improved treatment of animals as well as for humane education. The strength of affinities between organized animal protection, temperance, and child protection, among other factors, reinforced a broadly shared belief in the indivisibility of cruelty.

Despite early gains, however, general social concern about the link between cruelty to animals and interpersonal violence in the United States did not endure beyond the first few decades after the humane movement's founding in 1866. Like organized animal protection itself, interest in that connection waned in the early decades of the twentieth century. It received virtually no attention in the professional literatures of criminology, psychology, sociology, and social work, and it did not become institutionalized within any of those fields.

Nor did awareness of the link flourish in the years immediately following World War II, a revitalization period for animal protection marked by the founding of the Animal Welfare Institute (1951) and The Humane Society of the United States (1954). There were occasional references to it in movement literature (Fleming, 1975), but, in a sense, the link even had to be "rediscovered" by organized animal protection during the 1980s, just as a few researchers were steadily asserting its importance within psychiatry, criminology, and social science.

By 1990, the link had resurfaced as a prominent element of humane outreach, and secured substantial legitimacy within relevant professional circles concerned with the metastasis of violence. That trend continues, and many have come to conceptualize the problem of cruelty to animals as part of a broader "ecology of violence" (Ascione, 1999). Today, arguably, the link has been permanently fixed within contemporary popular consciousness and professional knowledge, and it seems unlikely that it will ever again go unappreciated or undervalued. However, it is worth trying to account for and learn from its unsteady progress and variable status as a matter of broader social concern, as influenced by factors including the relative fortunes of feminism and other social movements, the rise of scientific philanthropy, the shifting intensity of societal preoccupation with violence, and the varying priorities of organized animal protection. Such a review underscores the significance of recent efforts to permanently institutionalize concerns about the link within appropriate professional networks.

Originary Ideas

The idea of a link between cruelty to animals and violent behavior toward humans is an old one. From the classical writers Pythagoras and Porphyry, to the medieval scholastic Thomas Aquinas, to the early modern philosophers Montaigne (1533–1592) and John Locke (1632–1704), the presumption of a nexus between cruelty to animals and intra-human violence was commonly invoked by moralists.

Locke's environmentalism, premised on the idea of the mind as a *tabula rasa* (blank slate) to be shaped through education and experience, was crucial to framing the link as a matter of social importance. Although others had sounded the theme before, in *Some Thoughts on Education* (1693/1989), Locke offered the most significant early statement of the need to chastise and correct youthful cruelty. "This tendency should be watched in them, and, if they incline to any such cruelty, they should be taught the contrary usage," he wrote. "For the custom of tormenting and killing other animals will, by degrees, harden their hearts even toward men; and they who delight in the suffering and destruction of inferior creatures, will not be apt to be very compassionate or benign to those of their own kind" (Locke, 1693/1989).

Locke's reflections provided both a framework for understanding the problem of unchecked cruelty as well as the possibility of addressing it. By offering a way forward—the inculcation of humane values through teaching and the encouragement of good example—Locke set forth the fundamental premise of humane education. By acknowledging the value of animals as an instrument of childhood socialization, Locke highlighted the domestic sphere as a crucial context—one in which the lessons and rituals of kindness could be practiced, cultivated, and reinforced. Finally, by underscoring the risk of letting such behavior go uncorrected, Locke established himself as the most significant early theorist of the relationship between the abuse of animals and human interpersonal violence.

It did not take long for Locke's insights to gain influence, and they were powerfully inscribed within popular culture by the British artist William Hogarth (1697–1764), whose widely circulated engraved series *The Four Stages of Cruelty* (1750–1751) conveyed its own narrative of progression from cruelty to animals to violence against human beings. Moreover, growing comprehension of the importance of childhood experience and its impact on youthful character sustained a robust transatlantic publishing industry devoted to the production of juvenile works infused with the kindness to animals didactic. In North America the first of these began to appear in the late 1790s and early 1800s. The genre quickly gained important American enthusiasts, including Lydia Maria Child and Harriet Beecher Stowe (Pickering, 1981; Unti, 2002).

As it happened, the kindness-to-animals ethic resonated well with the republican gender ideology of the post–Revolutionary United States, which assumed a set of paternalistic relationships within and outside the family, with special emphasis on the development of a virtuous citizenry devoted to republican principles of governance. Educating the boy was especially critical, since he would, as a man, assume responsibility for family, chattel, property, and social institutions. Women, assumed to be the

repositories of gentle virtue and compassionate feeling, were responsible for educating the child for his leadership role, and humane education would provide one means of inoculating boys against the infectious tendencies of tyranny that might set in and undermine the body politic were they to go unchecked. Animals were the perfect medium for instruction to impress upon the child his responsibilities toward those who were helpless and dependent upon him (Grier, 1999; Kerber, 1980; Unti, 2002).

The Nineteenth-Century Ecology of Cruelty and Violence

Seeking to provide an appropriate framework for considering the connection between cruelty to animals and interpersonal violence, recent scholarship has settled upon ecological theory, a way of looking at individual human development through patterns and contexts of social relationships, and the social and cultural values and practices that shape human development (Ascione, 1999). Although our understanding of human psychology is far better developed in the early twenty-first century, it is possible to "frame" the connection in a similar way for the mid-nineteenth century, the era in which organized animal protection first emerged. Humane advocates and others saw cruelty as an indivisible phenomenon, and sought to root it out through their support for related social movements, notably temperance and child protection, which shared organized animal protection's revulsion against the perpetrators of cruelty, violence, and neglect.

The animal protection movement was one of the most striking of post–Civil War reforms. After the organization of societies for the prevention of cruelty to animals in New York (1866), Philadelphia (1867), and Boston (1868), the concept spread rapidly throughout the United States. Animal advocates campaigned on a host of issues, including the mistreatment of horses in transportation and conveyance, the frightful roundup and destruction of dogs in summer, animal fighting, pigeon shooting, and the abysmal treatment of cattle en route to slaughter. Heightened sensitivity to suffering; emerging concepts of moral, religious, and legal obligation toward animals; revulsion at the sight of cruelty; and concern about the public health implications of animals' mistreatment all helped to spur the formation of anti-cruelty societies.

Today the complex associations between animal abuse and the socially maladapted personality have been established. During the nineteenth century, such links were assumed, though not typically empirically substantiated. Occasionally, however, humane advocates cited specific evidence to demonstrate the relationship between cruelty to animals and violence against humans. Animal protectionists Caroline Earle White and Mary F. Lovell, of the Women's Pennsylvania Society for the Prevention of Cruelty to Animals, for example, claimed there were at least three cases in Philadelphia where people arrested for cruelty later gained infamy as murderers (Unti, 2002).

Humane advocates did not perceive cruelty simply as a personal vice in need of correction. It was a moral problem for the whole society, as middle-class supporters of animal protection believed that unchecked cruelty had the potential to spread and corrupt the entire social body. Animal protectionists became "culture builders," promoting notions of the good and proper (Frykman & Löfgren, 1987). Caring for animals was certainly thought to make people better human beings. By extension, though, all benevolent efforts would improve society, and mark its civilized status.

There is little question that the strength of feminism during the immediate post–Civil War years helped to focus attention on the landscape of domestic violence, and its animal victims. Organized animal protection depended heavily upon the support of women. Like such manifestations of nineteenth-century social feminism as the club movement and the Women's Christian Temperance Union (WCTU), humane reform allowed women to extend their influence into public life without explicit rejection of prevailing doctrines concerning their proper place as the guardians of the private domestic sphere. If anything, animal protection benefited from views of women as the natural protectors of private and public morality. In most instances, too, humane work provided critical space for female institution-building activity.

The conspicuous participation of women in post–Civil War anti-cruelty work rested in part upon their earlier engagement with the kindness-to-animals ethic as an element of domestic education ideology. In the antebellum era, many mothers tried to inculcate the values of benevolence, mercy, and kindness in their children, on the assumption that the moral sensibility they encouraged would in turn ensure the ethical progress of the republic. In the postbellum setting, women strove to project these same values into the public sphere, promoting humane education

outreach, supporting legal restraints against cruelty, endowing horse fountains, and participating in animal rescue and relief.

Women demonstrated a special commitment to the humane education of children, and comprised the majority of those who participated in Band of Mercy work, organizing kindness clubs in schools and other institutions, and exposing children to stories, poems, illustrations, and practical information about animals and the need to treat them with tender regard. As producers of didactic literature incorporating the humane ethic, women outnumbered men, codifying the kindness-to-animals theme in numerous works. In the minds of humane advocates, instruction in kindness was essential to the ultimate elimination of cruelty. The properly educated child would have due regard for animals, avoid the temptations of vice, and grow up as a well-socialized individual who treated his dependents—women, children, and animals—with kindness and loving regard.

The fact that the majority of individuals arrested for cruelty to animals were men provided a compelling reason for women's commitment. Many came to believe that the problem arose directly from male propensities toward violence. For Lydia Maria Child, such cruelty foretold the mistreatment of women by the men in their lives. "Wherever I have seen men gentle, patient, and considerate toward animals I have always observed that such men were good sons, husbands, and fathers," Child wrote. "A woman had better beware how she marries a man that kicks his dog, beats his oxen, and stands talking while his horse is left unblanketed in the cold wind, or in summertime tied fast, helplessly in the power of tormenting flies" (Unti, 2002).

Shared Affinities: Temperance and Child Protection

Apart from its intrinsic appeal, the fortunes of organized animal protection during the Gilded Age rested in some measure on its relationships with two other reforms—temperance and the prevention of cruelty to children. All three movements reflected concerns about the ramifications of cruelty and violence—for individuals, the family, and the social order. Each addressed issues that straddled the line between private and public spheres. These affinities, which reflect the sociocultural landscape in which the problem of cruelty, especially domestic cruelty, was embedded, helped to sustain animal protection during the last quarter of the nineteenth century.

Animal protection proved a congenial complement to temperance, linked as they were by bourgeois assumptions and common tactics. Both depended on female constituencies concerned with reshaping the behavior of men. Each proceeded on the assumption that children were tractable subjects who could be led to genteel patterns of conduct (even if their parents could not). The two causes also shared what temperance historian Jack Blocker has termed "the theme of self-control that lay at the core of middle-class identity in the nineteenth century" (Blocker, 1989).

Most societies for the prevention of cruelty to animals handled cases in which drunkenness played a part in cruelty or neglect. Humane advocates understood that the suffering of animals, especially horses, often resulted from vicious beatings by intoxicated drivers and caretakers. Sometimes, a groggery might be the venue for a dogfight. On other occasions, humane agents might find a badly neglected animal outside a saloon with its dissolute owner inside on a binge (Unti, 2002).

Humane work greatly benefited when the WCTU embraced kindness to animals as a platform during its "Do Everything" phase under Frances Willard. After its formation in 1874, the WCTU rapidly became the largest and most influential women's organization in the country. Focused on promoting standards of respectable behavior rather than acquisition of the vote, the WCTU significantly expanded the base of women's social activity. With its broad and growing constituency, the WCTU brought the anti-cruelty cause to a far greater audience than the humane movement could have reached on its own, and temperance advocates frequently drew the connection between cruelty to animals and criminal behavior (Pearson, 2004; Unti, 2002).

Humane education, as a preventive reform, appealed to supporters of temperance, who, like animal protectionists, targeted their efforts at the socialization of boys. Temperance also provided useful strategic examples; the English movement's Bands of Hope, in which children pledged themselves to purity of thought and action, served as models for the American Bands of Mercy. The founder of the Massachusetts Society for the Prevention of Cruelty to Animals (MSPCA), George Angell, made extensive use of the WCTU's network of activists to promote and distribute humane education materials, and many WCTU propagandists employed such literature in their work. It was largely due to such

collaboration that, by 1893, *Black Beauty*, a book Angell heavily promoted, had been translated into numerous languages and shipped all over the world. There was a clear relationship in this and other works between the values of humaneness and the temperance habit. The villains in *Black Beauty, Beautiful Joe* (its canine analogue), and other anti-cruelty novels were drunkards, while their protagonists were pious, gentle, and abstemious. Such characterizations gave these novels "crossover" appeal and reinforced the link between the two movements (Unti, 2002).

Mary F. Lovell (1843–1932), Caroline Earle White's colleague in Pennsylvania humane work, played the critical role in linking temperance and humane organizations. In 1891, with Frances Willard's blessing, Lovell established the WCTU's Department of Mercy, authoring numerous leaflets and articles under its banner. The *Union Signal* commonly highlighted anti-cruelty work through Department of Mercy reports, humane issue alerts, book reviews, fiction, photography, artwork, and advertisements (Unti, 2002).

The two causes shared a number of prominent adherents and some of the same strategies for inscribing their values within the public sphere. The erection of public fountains, for example, was an important point of confluence. Water had important symbolic and practical meanings within the ideology of temperance. For WCTU members, sponsorship of fountains was an act of civic concern, since the availability of safe drinking water in public places gave thirsty people an alternative to alcoholic beverages. Humane advocates also felt confident, as one annual report from the American Society for the Prevention of Cruelty to Animals (ASPCA) noted, that "a large proportion of the human beings who thus slaked their thirst, were deterred from taking into their mouths an enemy, to steal away their senses." In addition, easy access to drinking water for horses reduced the appeal of watering troughs set up outside saloons and drinking establishments to lure customers (Unti, 2002).

The nexus between animal protection and child protection is a more complicated one, resting not only upon some shared affinities or networks, but upon practicality, contingency, and precedent. The so-called child rescue movement emerged directly from SPCA work, and the correlation between animal and child protection should be understood in part as a matter of shared organizational form and the underdeveloped administrative capacities of local, state, and national governments in the arena of child welfare during the late nineteenth century. Child protection adopted the organizational models and some of the statutory precedents of animal protection and, fatefully, humane societies in some communities actually incorporated the protection of children into their missions, because this seemed for a time to be the most viable way to advance both causes.

Importantly, however, the child rescue movement does not fit within the rubric of social feminism. Certainly, women cared about the domestic violence that child protection societies uncovered and confronted. In many cases, too, these groups enjoyed solid support from women. However, men dominated most societies for the prevention of cruelty to children, and these organizations sometimes pursued goals and policies that undercut women's interests. Ultimately, women and feminists gave their energy and support to other child welfare initiatives, some of which were at variance with the philosophy of the child protection societies. Organized child protection was driven more by class than by gender concerns (Gordon, 1988).

The fact that the animal protection laws of the late 1860s preceded certain kinds of laws protecting children is not indicative, as has been suggested, of a lower social tolerance for animal abuse than for child abuse (Boat, 1995). Rather, it reflects the fact that, from the perspective of legislators, courts, and other social actors, statutory authority for intervention against cruelty to animals was easier to agree upon than similar intervention in the case of children over whom someone might make a claim of guardianship. As it turned out, sympathy for animals produced someone who was willing to cross legal and other boundaries dividing private matters from public concern—Henry Bergh, founder of the ASPCA—before sympathy for the plight of children did (Pearson, 2004).

Nor was general philanthropic concern for children underdeveloped in the 1860s. From the earliest years of the nineteenth century, there had been a lengthy tradition of "child saving," which centered on poor, orphaned, runaway, and abandoned children who were considered dependents of the community. These children were placed in apprenticeships and asylum homes, and later in the century with "boarding mothers." In the years leading up to and following the Civil War, a number of philanthropic societies, including the Children's Aid Society (1853) in New York, tried to address the

misfortune of abandoned and homeless children. On occasion, police might make an arrest in a case of severe neglect, and the press condemned many other forms of cruelty to children. However, direct intervention in the lives and intrusion into the homes of poor families that were otherwise intact were not common, and the agencies involved concentrated mainly on dealing with the fallout of family instability and trouble (Pearson, 2004; Unti, 2002).

In the immediate post-war years, however, the phenomenon of cruelty to children, encompassing both abuse and neglect, began to capture broad notice. Attention focused increasingly on the absence of effective public or philanthropic agencies ready to confront and remedy children's exploitation and mistreatment. Law enforcement authorities, preoccupied with other crimes, were not inclined to investigate and prosecute parents or guardians who could plausibly claim the right to discipline children over whom they had authority. At the same time, existing charities devoted to the care of children were in a position to assume control over their lives only after gaining legal custody (Pleck, 1987; Steele, 1942).

Early in their histories, societies for the prevention of cruelty to animals began to receive complaints about cruelty to children in private and public contexts. George Angell tried to discourage the Boston citizenry from bringing such pleas for intervention to the MSPCA. "Our hands are quite full of the work we have undertaken, and we cannot consistently open the door to other reforms," Angell wrote. "At the same time, we believe if our theories for the humane treatment of animals could prevail, cruel treatment of children would constantly decrease, so that our work indirectly accomplishes what is sought by those who ask our aid in special cases" (Unti, 2002).

Within a year of the ASPCA's formation in 1866, both *Harper's Weekly* and the *New York Tribune* called for the establishment of a similar organization devoted to the children of New York. Bergh's very success in using the law and the ASPCA's statutory power to reach cruelty and injustice that had heretofore been out of reach if not out of sight led many to wonder why the same approach could not be taken to assist children in distress. Whenever people approached Bergh to intervene in such cases, he declined on the grounds that the mistreatment of children was outside the ASPCA's domain. In several instances, the newspapers specifically chided him for this restraint. In fact, the reproaches Bergh suffered for excessive devotion to the interests of animals reinforced a steady association in the national press between cruelty to animals and cruelty to children (Unti, 2002).

The pressure to take consistent action when such cases surfaced had further intensified by early 1874, when Bergh and Elbridge Gerry, the ASPCA's general counsel, chose to intervene in the case of Mary Ellen Wilson, a decision that had fateful consequences for the course of the humane movement. As Bergh later recalled, the fact that Etta Wheeler, the social worker who had discovered Mary Ellen's situation, had already approached the Children's Aid Society without satisfaction greatly influenced his decision to intervene. Bergh elected to petition the court for Mary Ellen's removal in his capacity as a private citizen, and not on behalf of the ASPCA, and Gerry determined to secure a writ of habeas corpus in the Court of Special Sessions (Unti, 2002).

Although scholarly and public confusion continues on this point, Bergh and Gerry did not intervene in Mary Ellen's case under an animal protection statute. After Bergh and Gerry petitioned Judge Abraham Lawrence, presenting him with the evidence they had collected, the judge issued a special warrant under the Habeas Corpus Act, permitting officers of the ASPCA to take Mary Ellen into custody. Once in court, the little girl told of her own dire circumstances, and displayed the welts and cuts that Mrs. Connolly's whip and scissors had caused. Mrs. Connolly was convicted and received a jail sentence (Unti, 2002).

After the case concluded, Gerry, Bergh, and Quaker merchant John D. Wright incorporated a separate organization, the New York Society for the Prevention of Cruelty to Children (NYSPCC), to focus on child protection. Wright assumed the presidency, but Gerry secured the enabling legislation and handled all other formalities. From that point on, child welfare became the central focus of his life, and after Wright died Gerry took over the presidency, serving in that capacity from 1876 to 1901 and (after 1879) devoting himself more or less full-time to its management. Bergh served on the NYSPCC's board of managers until his death in 1888, and occasionally played a role in specific cases (Unti, 2002).

While some critics attacked the interventionist ideology and Protestant sectarian bias of the NYSPCC, others expressed strong approval of its efforts to ensure compliance with relevant statutes and to punish violators through prosecution. "There

are in this city today eight or ten excellent institutions for the benefit of friendless children, but they have power only over those legally entrusted to their care," the New York Post noted. "The laws passed by the New York legislature for the protection of little children and the prevention of cruelty to them are ample in scope, but hitherto it has been nobody's business to enforce them." The state deputized the NYSPCC to represent the public interest in court proceedings relating to crime, abuse, and misconduct involving children. The NYSPCC sought to identify situations in which children were being cruelly treated, to secure their removal from such situations, and to prosecute, convict, and punish those responsible for such mistreatment (Unti, 2002).

What happened next offered a stunning parallel to the SPCA phenomenon less than a decade earlier. The developments in New York sparked a nationwide proliferation of like-minded societies committed to the passage and enforcement of statutes protecting children. At first, they concentrated on cases of physical abuse, but over time the SPCCs became active in a range of cases. During the last quarter of the nineteenth century, the SPCCs steadily gained importance, concomitant to the revolution in jurisprudence that Michael Grossberg has called "judicial patriarchy"—nineteenth-century judges' increasing appropriation of family law power, including authority over child placement. Through judicial agency, the state came to play a primary role in constructing and carrying out the principles and policies of family law, and the courts became the keystone of an institutional complex legitimating state intervention in family life (Grossberg, 1985).

Many of the new societies elsewhere modeled themselves after the NYSPCC. In Boston, New York, Philadelphia, and San Francisco, concerned citizens formed separate anti-cruelty organizations devoted entirely to children. However, in many smaller communities and states away from the East Coast, another organizational form emerged, that of the dual-function humane society. Some of these were SPCAs responding to appeals to become active in the protection of children. Where appropriate or necessary, they modified their charters. Occasionally, as in the case of the Albany-based Mohawk and Hudson River Humane Society, animal protection was added to the responsibilities of an established child protection organization. The Connecticut Humane Society represented still another model, addressing cruelty to animals, child rescue, and the abandonment and neglect of the elderly.

A fourth variation was the state-sponsored agency or bureau, which straddled the boundary between government agency and private philanthropy (Unti, 2002).

In Chicago, this consolidation of purposes proved eventful. In May 1877, Illinois passed its first legislation prohibiting cruelty to children. Only two months later, the Illinois SPCA, which had been operating under an animal protection statute approved in 1869, took steps to change its name to the Illinois Humane Society and to incorporate children into its sphere of concern. The organization had contemplated such a name change for several years prior to the addition of child protection work because, as its president John L. Shortall explained some years later, the term "humane" encompassed a general commitment to the identification, relief, and prevention of suffering wherever it lay. The Illinois society's decision to carry the designation "humane" as an organizational title helped to solidify the word's use as a descriptive for the larger movement. Numerous societies subsequently adopted it for themselves (Covotsos, 1981).

The desire of reformers in many communities to combine child and animal protection work crucially altered the evolution of the American Humane Association (AHA), which originally formed in connection with efforts to secure passage of the Twenty-Eight Hour Law to reduce the suffering of cattle in transit. When the original AHA delegates assembled in 1877, the subject did not come up, but at its conference the following year, a debate ensued over the incorporation of child protection into the organization's mission. Interestingly, the three leading figures of animal protection—Bergh, White, and Angell—while supportive of the goals of child protection, all believed it problematic to join the two concerns. Bergh noted that there were numerous private and state-subsidized institutions for the protection of children but virtually none for the protection of animals. White expressed her view that "if the subjects were united, very soon after all the efforts would be for the children and the animals would not be thought of." The majority of delegates present disagreed, however. Elbridge Gerry, by now an enthusiastic child rescue advocate, made a motion to revise the charter, and it carried (Unti, 2002).

Consequently, quite a number of the AHA constituent organizations evolved as dual- and sometimes triple-function societies, a few taking on the third issue of neglect and abuse of the elderly. Over the years, the AHA annual meetings were bifurcated, with child and animal protection each taking up separate days of the conference. The multifunctional humane society was an important organization in those communities where no relevant government agencies existed, as well in those areas where such agencies were relatively undeveloped. Moreover, these societies all operated under the assumption that there was a definite connection between cruelty to children and to animals and that they could be addressed by some of the same law enforcement solutions.

The Decline of Animal Protection and the Diminution of the Link in the Early Twentieth Century

In the early years of the twentieth century, the forces of modernization reshaped the contexts of animal use, making it more difficult for the humane movement to accomplish its goals. The rise of Fordism—the collective social institutions of mass production and mass consumption—ushered in a series of technical and scientific changes that profoundly transformed the human–animal relationship. Cruelty to animals began to manifest itself in a range of new and unprecedented forms, and an extraordinary intensification and diversification of animal use ensued. Animal protection, with limited resources and political influence, was no match for powerful opponents in agriculture, transportation, fashion, and industrial and medical research. Many of the new cruelties were institutional, not individual in nature, and special exemptions placed some of them outside the ambit of animal protection statutes. The humane movement's focus also shifted as the burden of municipal animal control supplanted the relief of working horses as its principal concern.

As important as these developments were, however, they did not comprise the only impediment to the progress of organized animal protection. In the Progressive era, the strength of the movement's connections to other reforms diminished. Over time, animal protection fell out of step with the general shift toward scientific and professional reform that characterized the period 1890–1920. It did not recover until a post–World War II renaissance saw the movement's fortune rise once again (Unti & Rowan, 2001).

To some extent, the humane movement's cautious attitudes about science, and its strained relationships with members of the scientific, medical, and veterinary communities, lay behind this development. The cultural authority of science as an instrument of social progress surged during the Progressive era, gaining enthusiasts in almost every realm of reform. Other movements of the early twentieth century acted quickly to align themselves with scientific methods, and the goals of professionalization, rationalization, and administrative efficiency that characterized so many reform causes rested firmly on the assumption that all social problems could be resolved through the application of systematic, logical, and informed analysis. Suffrage advocates embraced practical arguments based on social science and assumptions of rational efficiency for according women the vote. Temperance advocates squarely aligned themselves with the Progressive era's cult of efficiency, successfully identifying alcohol with increased risk and lower productivity in the workplace, serious health problems, family destabilization, widespread political corruption, and the scourge of prostitution. Like suffragists, anti-alcohol campaigners also threw themselves single-mindedly into political work in support of a constitutional amendment. After 1913, national prohibition became their principal preoccupation (Buettinger, 1997; Link & McCormick, 1983).

Humane advocates had a more ambivalent feeling about science and its values, for they did not see it being deployed in the interests of animals' basic psychological and biological needs. A range of interests put scientific knowledge to use to more efficiently exploit animals in agriculture, medical research, fur production, and other fields. For the most part, medical scientists and veterinarians worked to raise animal productivity, not to enhance animal well-being, and there was little interest in animals' natural behavior and psychology. Drawing back from what they believed to be Darwin's anthropomorphic tendencies, scientists in many disciplines followed the example of behaviorism, which objectified animals, presupposed mental discontinuity between humans and other species, and reduced the study of animals and especially of animal mind to an investigation of physiological facts (Costall, 1998).

The divisive effects of debates over vivisection and access to impounded animals for experiments limited the potential for cooperation between the scientific and humane communities. That polarization very likely delayed the development of the science of animal welfare—the qualitative and quantitative measurement of animals' behavior, physiology, and psychological and physical well-being—that has become so pivotal to modern humane work.

During the post-1920 years, even the survival of strong affinities or alliances with feminism or temperance would not likely have helped animal protection, as both of these movements also faltered. Feminism fractured into competing camps, became an important target for reactionary forces, and grew weaker during the interwar period. For its part, temperance foundered on the shoals of the nation's failed experiment with Prohibition.

In any case, with respect to the link between cruelty to animals and interpersonal violence, the most telling marker of the waning fortunes of animal protection was its divergence from child welfare. This differentiation resulted both from heightened social interest in the welfare of children and a change in the philosophy and practice of child welfare during the first two decades of the twentieth century.

The child, as several generations of scholars have noted, was at the center of Progressive era social reform, in large part because of enhanced appreciation for the importance of children as the key to any society's future health and well-being. With this recognition of their status as fundamental figures in the social structure, children began to claim a far greater share of public concern than animals, then being increasingly objectified as commodities within that same structure (Pearson, 2004; Wiebe, 1967).

The practical distancing of the two movements came about as the philosophy and practice of child welfare activities moved away from the law enforcement model it had shared with animal protection. With the contemporaneous emergence of professional altruism, a major split within child protection developed. This pitted "strict constructionists," faithful to the narrow mission of child rescue, against a more liberal faction committed to the principles of modern social work. Most of the strict constructionists remained within the orbit of the AHA, whose president, William O. Stillman, was part of an older generation of child rescue advocates who believed that the societies should restrict their work to law enforcement. The NYSPCC, under the enduring influence of Elbridge T. Gerry, led the organizations that embraced this view. Such groups laid emphasis on the swift removal of children from homes in which they were found to be suffering from cruelty (Carstens, 1921; Unti, 2002).

Members of the other faction, led by Carl Carstens and the Massachusetts Society for the Prevention of Cruelty to Children (MSPCC), allied themselves with the broader environmentalist approach of modern social work, including a commitment to study all of the many social conditions affecting child welfare. Gradually, most child protection societies, including many SPCCs, embraced this perspective (Carstens, 1921; Gordon, 1988; Shultz, 1924). The new paradigm emphasized preventive and remedial measures that addressed the circumstances in which children were raised, taking into account ethnicity, family stability, poverty, education levels, and other factors. The family and the home environment became subjects of study and the focus of treatment. The old approach of child removal came into question. In the evolving debate over child welfare, the AHA and its member societies associated themselves with an archaic paradigm that eventually went out of favor. The historic links between the causes of child protection and animal protection unraveled, even as concern for children greatly eclipsed concern for animals as a matter of popular attention and public policy.

Even before the advent of the new paradigm, the attempt to combine child and animal protection had frequently proved awkward. Disagreement over how to allocate the Rochester Humane Society's limited resources resulted in the formation of separate organizations in 1897. After political trouble with Mayor Victor Berger, the Wisconsin Humane Society abandoned its child protection function. In Chicago, the Illinois Humane Society's increasing preoccupation with the problems of children led to the 1899 formation of the Anti-Cruelty Society, specifically devoted to animals. A few years later, a similar schism within the Ohio Humane Society sparked the formation of the Hamilton County Society for the Prevention of Cruelty to Animals (Unti, 2002).

The unwieldy and undesirable character of dual-purpose work was evident in the responses gathered by Columbia University's Roswell McCrea for his 1910 survey of humane organizations. A large number of respondents complained that it was no longer possible to combine the two missions. The humane society model, one SPCA official noted, was mainly useful in those smaller cities and towns "where the volume of business is small or the support not strong enough to operate two distinct societies successfully." Similar considerations governed the state board model, employed in Colorado, Minnesota, Montana, Washington, West Virginia, Wisconsin, and Wyoming (McCrea, 1910; Shultz, 1924; Unti, 2002).

Unwilling or slow to adapt, humane societies steadily diverged from the mainstream of Progressive Era child welfare. Some humane society leaders fought against the establishment of the United States Children's Bureau, an idea that emerged from the

settlement house community, was taken up by the National Child Labor Committee in 1906, and was a reality by 1912 (Muncy, 1991). William O. Stillman of the AHA, John D. Lindsay of the NYSPCC, and other humane movement leaders were suspicious of what they perceived to be the Bureau's focus on research, its diversion of attention from the practical problems of the neglected and abused child, and the potential threat of a centralized federal agency that might one day come to dominate and control the nation's child welfare work.

They were in the minority. Very few of the child welfare organizations that formed after 1910 joined the AHA; most opted instead to affiliate with the National Conference of Social Work, which had a division devoted to children. After 1912, the Children's Bureau itself became the center of child welfare work. These developments curtailed relationships between humane societies that incorporated child and animal welfare and the preponderance of child-centered organizations. Ultimately, child welfare was incorporated into professional social work, and into the bureaucratic structures of the state. Animal protection never was. The child protection function of many humane societies began to atrophy, and they focused exclusively on animal protection, if they survived at all. The divergence between the two movements occurred swiftly (Hall, 1999; Muncy, 1991; Shulz, 1924).

The cause of animal protection arguably lost more from the bifurcation than did child welfare. For one thing, the emerging field of modern social work showed very little recognition for the seriousness of cruelty to animals as a problem in domestic family life, or as a question in child development. In addition, animal protection would never enjoy the benefit of the expertise and insights that a more integrated approach within social work might have generated. That would have to wait for many decades more.

Anthropocentrism and Philanthropy

The responsibility for failing to develop information and insights concerning the link between cruelty to animals and interpersonal violence does not lie solely with organized animal protection. Philanthropy became more rigidly anthropocentric in the first quarter of the twentieth century than it had been in the last quarter of the nineteenth. Philanthropy-driven social science and social work, moreover, did not treat cruelty to animals as a substantial problem or one worthy of serious inquiry. This did not help the prospects for closer collaboration between those with an interest in cruelty to animals and those with an interest in human social problems, including violence.

An especially telling episode concerned the fate of a $100,000 donation made to Columbia University in 1907, specifically earmarked for promoting humane education and kindness to animals. President Nicholas Murray Butler, on the advice of social scientists Edward T. Devine and Samuel M. Lindsay, used it to support Lindsay's faculty position at Columbia in Social Legislation. Lindsay and Devine were both leaders in the field of child welfare, but much less enthused about the mistreatment of animals as a social problem. Apparently, they saw no future in a program for studying children's ideas and attitudes toward animals and the proper methods and techniques for encouraging humane values. In fact, Lindsay disparaged this approach with his remark to the 1913 AHA convention that the university was not fitted "to carry on propaganda." With a little imagination and will, research on humane education as well as efforts to test the correlation between cruelty to animals and other antisocial behavior could easily have been undertaken within Columbia University's Teachers College. Ultimately, the funds disappeared into Columbia's general account and, with the exception of several historical studies of animal protection, no serious efforts toward the goal of the donor were ever made (Unti, 2002).

The status of animal protection vis á vis the Progressive era's most ambitious attempt to rationalize charitable giving is also instructive. The drive to make social philanthropy less wasteful and thus more attractive to corporate constituents led to the coordinated intensive, centralized fundraising approach of the Community Chest, a precursor to the United Way, which sought to coordinate philanthropic support through federated solicitation and allocation of funds in the interests of efficiency. But this consolidation did not benefit societies for the prevention of cruelty to animals. In some cases, they made no attempt to gain inclusion, believing they could garner more support through independent appeals. In most instances, however, animal organizations were specifically excluded from participation on the grounds that societies providing aid to people were superordinate (Unti, 2002).

Animal protection did not fare any better as a beneficiary of foundation philanthropy or the social science work it funded. Margaret Olivia Sage (1828–1918), widow of railroad magnate Russell Sage, was one of the anti-cruelty movement's strongest backers in the early years of the twentieth century. However, the broad scope of her interests was characteristic of nineteenth-century evangelical sentiment, and she generally funded religious work, hospitals, and colleges. Discovering animal causes, she became a significant donor to the AHA, the ASPCA, and the New York Women's League for Animals. Among other things, Sage provided funds for an animal hospital, fountains and watering stations maintained by New York groups, and an animal ambulance. In 1907, she created a foundation in her late husband's name to support analysis and action for "the improvement of social and living conditions in the United States of America," and recruited the best minds of American social science to assist her. The foundation they set up operated according to the most modern, Progressive-era principles of social philanthropy. While the trustees were given broad latitude to decide how its money would be used, the Russell Sage Foundation did not carry on or propagate its founder's support for animal protection (Crocker, 1996; Hammack, 1994; Unti, 2002).

Mrs. Sage was, ironically, one of the last of her kind. In the latter decades of the nineteenth century, humane advocates and others saw concern for animals as part of a larger "social religion," an aggregate of wide-ranging but coincident reforms that aimed to assist the helpless, the vulnerable, and the disadvantaged. But once professional social work and philanthropy, guided by scientific assumptions, came to dominance in the twentieth century, animal protection lost its cognizable position in the network of American social reform. Social science showed no interest in the relationship between the mistreatment of animals and other social issues, or in applying its insights to the relief of animals. Cruelty to animals did not appear to raise interesting questions. Animal protection was marginalized, not strengthened, by the advent of scientific philanthropy.

The Lack of Institutionalization

Although the animal protection movement continued its own efforts to advance awareness of the link, understanding and awareness of the connection between cruelty to animals and interpersonal violence within the relevant professional networks that would have made a meaningful difference did not progress. Just as humane education did not gain the lasting attention of teacher-training institutions (Unti & DeRosa, 2003), the putative links between such cruelty and the violent personality did not gain the serious attention of social work, psychology, or criminology during the early decades of the twentieth century.

Above all, this era witnessed a striking lack of academic attention paid to animals as a factor in children's self-development and to the exploration of children's empathy for animals and its implications for their interactions with others. Both were areas of inquiry that might have rendered useful insights and future avenues for research and professional intervention. Save for a handful of studies that hewed to the recapitulation theory of G. Stanley Hall, or the rare and undeveloped reference to cruelty and juvenile delinquency, this line of inquiry lay undeveloped (Burt, 1925; Myers, 1998).

This lack of attention is all the more remarkable in light of the "medicalization" of cruelty wrought by Kraft Ebbing's *Psychopathia Sexualis* (1892/1965) and the work of other scientists who focused on cruelty as an element of deviant pathological criminality, as well as Freud's admonition that childhood cruelty to animals, reflecting a child's lack of empathy toward others, "brings with it a danger that the connection between the cruel and the erotogenic instincts, thus established in childhood, may prove unbreakable in later life." This trend may have undermined the humane movement's preference for focusing on cruelty as a moral and ethical problem, as Susan Pearson suggests, but there is no reason why it should have impeded research in child development (Freud, 1905/2000; Kraft Ebbing, 1892/1965; Pearson, 2004).

Another possibility is suggested by the occasional reference in this period to juvenile cruelty as a normative process that was not socially problematic. "It is thought to be the propensity of all boys from the age of five to the age of fourteen," an anonymous contributor wrote in *Current Literature*, "to inflict every kind of cruelty upon insects and animals." These "so-called cruel children," the writer continued, "will cease their cruelties in time through a development of their intellectual capacities in other directions" (Anonymous, 1907).

One of the singular exceptions to the dearth of research in the pre–World War II era occurred in England, where Susan Isaacs studied children's interactions with animals during the mid-1920s. Isaacs conducted her research in a small Cambridge school, where she paid special attention to the conflicting tendencies toward cruelty and kindness to animals that she observed in children. "The problem

of dealing with the contradictory impulses of the child is more difficult because of the great inconsistencies of grown-up standards," Isaacs wrote. "They are surprisingly confused and contradictory, and it is worth while trying to realize what effect they may have on the minds of children who are struggling to order and control their own conflicting impulses" (Isaacs, 1931; Unti & DeRosa, 2003).

Isaacs proposed that educators seek "to make a positive educational use of the child's impulses" so that children could be helped to reach "a more satisfactory psychological solution for their own internal conflicts." This method of instruction, she argued, would become "an active influence in the building up of a positive morality of behavior toward animals, going beyond the mere negative standard of not being unkind to them" (Isaacs, 1930).

Isaacs's investigation yielded some compelling results, based on her willingness to challenge dogmas surrounding what facts children should be taught, and by what means. She focused on children's exposure to the death of animals and to dissection. The children "showed greater sympathy with the living animals, and more consistent care, after they had 'looked inside' the dead ones, and fewer lapses into experimental cruelty," Isaacs reported. "In other words," she continued, "the impulse to master and destroy was taken up into the aim of understanding. The living animal became much less of an object of power and possession, and much more an independent creature to be learnt about, watched and known for its own sake." Isaacs found that the children moved steadily toward the non-interfering, observational attitude of many modern naturalists, and developed a humane outlook and sense of responsibility toward their pets and toward animals in general (Isaacs, 1930).

While perhaps not broadly representative or conclusive, Isaacs's work certainly demonstrated that for those who cared to do so, there were ways to investigate children's attitudes and behaviors, and insights to be gained. Yet fruitful research on children's psychological development and the methods by which a caring attitude could be inculcated had to wait for the attention of late-twentieth-century researchers.

If humane education itself had made greater inroads during the early twentieth century, it might have catalyzed academic and professional interest in the link. Yet despite the Progressive era's intense focus on the building of character, and the animal protection movement's success in securing the passage of compulsory humane education laws, humane education gained little hold. The movement's resources were too limited and there simply was not commensurate effort in any quarter to see these laws honored, or to see the principles of humane education enshrined in the curriculum of teacher training institutes and colleges.

Moreover, like nature study, with which it shared a preoccupation with character development, humane education did not withstand the challenge posed by the emergent field of science education, which was strongly utilitarian in its focus and in some cases actively resistant to the perceived dogmas of humane education, particularly its apparent sentimentality (Unti, 2002).

In several instances, efforts to promulgate the humane ethic as well as an awareness of the link met with some success. During the Progressive era, one element of the kindness ethic found its way into the chivalric code of the scouting movement, one of the era's most important character-building initiatives. Scout Rule No. 6 made humane conduct a standard of behavior: "A Scout is kind. He is a friend to animals. He will not kill or hurt any living creature needlessly, but will strive to save and protect all harmless life" (Unti, 2002).

A basic understanding of the link between cruelty to animals and interpersonal violence also influenced one of the highest profile humane initiatives of the 1920s, the Jack London Clubs, which campaigned against the degrading influence of animal acts upon the character of the children who witnessed either training sessions or performances. The campaign drew its momentum from Jack London's *Michael Brother of Jerry*, which centered on the appalling cruelties suffered by the book's canine protagonist (Unti, 2002).

In their way, anti-vivisectionists and advocates for the regulation of vivisection also raised the implications of the link, underscoring the desensitization that could occur when students were allowed to witness and participate in classroom vivisection and dissection. The worst form of graduation to interpersonal cruelty this process might produce, they asserted, was the abuse of human patients by doctors who had overcome their scruples by experimenting first upon animals—a phenomenon critics documented in several controversial instances. The occasional anti-vivisectionist pamphlet went so far as to identify classroom vivisection as "one of the agencies in the alarming increase in juvenile and other crimes." In the late 1920s, anti-vivisectionists

made much of a psychologist's statement that kidnapper killers Leopold and Loeb had progressed to their crime after becoming "crazed with ideas of research" after conducting unspecified "scientific work" (Lederer, 1995; Ryan Shapiro, personal communication, July 28, 2005).

As late as the 1940s, there were a few animal advocates, such as Alice Morgan Wright and Edith J. Goode, who publicly argued that cruelty to animals went hand in hand with cruelty to people (Birke, 2000). But animal protection in the middle decades of the twentieth century was a devitalized movement, overwhelmed by the urban animal overpopulation problem, and unable to focus much energy and attention on humane education or outreach with social work.

In any case, most of these initiatives, though important, were rooted in fairly simple principles of encouraging kindness and avoiding desensitization to cruelty. None matched Isaacs's work for its originality and conceptualization of the link as a question in child development, and none anticipated the modern track of reading the link as a sign of prospective sociopathic behavior. In pursuing the course of inquiry that she did, Isaacs was wrestling with the ambiguities of social attitudes toward killing, sanctioned in many contexts. This was the same question to which Margaret Mead would make reference in her address to the Midcontinent Psychiatric Meeting in 1963. One could draw a straight line connecting the two women's observations, but one wouldn't find any substantive research in between. Until the 1980s, the link between cruelty to animals and interpersonal violence would stand largely as an anecdotal tradition, unverified by either qualitative or empirical study.

The Post–World War II Period

Although organized animal protection experienced an impressive renaissance in the decade following World War II, this had few immediate implications for recognition of the link. Even after formation of The Humane Society of the United States (HSUS), the one organization determined to intervene against cruelty on a broad, national scope, not much occurred on this front. A small organization focused on the great national cruelties of slaughterhouse practices and absence of regulation in laboratories, the HSUS had neither the time nor the resources to devote to popularizing the link. Even with respect to humane education, a related concern where its expressed interest was strong, the HSUS developed no substantive programs until the late 1960s, and conducted no professional curriculum development research until the mid-1970s (Unti, 2004).

Still, it seems clear that an appreciation for the link was not entirely lost at mid-century. Mead certainly appreciated it, observing that "one of the most dangerous things that can happen to a child is to kill or torture an animal and get away with it." Mead's conclusion that failure to correct the malicious killing of animals set the stage for the emergence of violent impulses that violate social norms led her to call for humane education and for child therapists to be on the alert to cruelty as a diagnostic sign. She was also one of the first to point out that the mistreatment or abuse of socially valued animals was an especially troubling harbinger of potential predisposition to harm human beings (Mead, 1964).

During this era, interest in the link did gain currency within a small circle of researchers in child psychiatry and developmental psychology, beginning in the mid-1960s and remaining steady for a decade or so. Several of their case studies, with a strong Freudian focus, led to recognition of the triad, showing that cruelty to animals might present itself in conjunction with other symptoms, specifically bed wetting and fire setting, as manifestations of aggression. These studies drew little popular attention, but they helped to turn professional focus to the possibility that together or separately, the presentation of such symptoms might prove useful in predicting children's future violent antisocial behavior (Hellman & Blackman, 1966; MacDonald, 1963).

The same was true for Fernando Tapia's case study work and follow up (1971; Rigdon & Tapia, 1977), which demonstrated that antisocial children known to abuse animals continued to be abusive some years later, and confirmed the point that cruelty to animals frequently appears alongside other indications of psychological problems as well as other disturbing forms of domestic violence. Other researchers also advanced the possibility that cruelty to animals might indicate the presence of other forms of family violence, and the significant finding that 60% of families who met the legal criteria for child abuse and neglect in one community also abused or neglected their companion animals formed the basis of one of the era's landmark studies (DeViney, Dickert, & Lockwood, 1983; Fucini, 1978).

The field also gained from several studies that demonstrated overlap between offender populations, showing that households that produced cases for SPCAs were often known to child protection agencies (Hutton, 1983; Walker, 1980).

More typical of the research from this era were the four retrospective studies conducted by Alan Felthous and co-authors, all of which set the standard for more sophisticated studies of the topic. Felthous (1980) studied psychiatric patients, focusing on more severe forms of animal cruelty and using a nonpsychiatric comparison group. Kellert and Felthous (1985) compared criminal and noncriminal populations, revealing that more violent and assaultive individuals reported higher rates of "substantial cruelty to animals" in childhood. They also identified a range of factors that might motivate acts of cruelty to animals, and expanded their frame of reference to include the broader dynamics of aggression, control, and violence within the domestic environment. Kellert and Felthous concluded that frequency of acts of cruelty against animals was decisive in distinguishing aggressive from nonaggressive criminals, and also identified frequency as a factor in the escalation or graduation cycle on the part of some individuals studied. Felthous and Yudowitz (1977) had found a similar distinction in their study of assaultive and nonassaultive female offenders.

In this and subsequent research, the challenges of verification of acts of cruelty and violence became clear, as did the problems created by lack of cross-reporting, appropriate information gathering, and excessive reliance on self-reporting. All of these factors would frustrate early attempts to corroborate the link between cruelty to animals and interpersonal violence.

Still, such studies represented initial efforts to posit serious questions about cruelty, human development, and the maladapted personality. Some were specific to the relationship between cruelty to animals and violence, while others focused on cruelty to animals as part of a complex of factors relevant to the understanding of violent behavior. Moreover, they laid the foundation for future work that examined the question of the link from a variety of theoretical and applied perspectives.

The two studies by Felthous and Kellert in the mid-1980s produced important conceptual advances. They introduced a more sophisticated typology of cruelty, focusing on motive as a way of differentiating individual actions. This was one of the earliest studies that specifically identified the problems caused by poor definitions of cruelty, a theme upon which others would elaborate in the future (Kellert & Felthous, 1985).

Kellert and Felthous also captured the state of the field in this era with a frank assessment that, "Until credible and scientific documentation occurs, most societal decision-makers will regard animal cruelty as a relatively minor issue. At present, most judicial authorities minimize the importance of animal cruelty among children if unaccompanied by violent or aggressive conduct toward human beings." This, too, was an observation that others would make in assessing the attitude of law enforcement and social services community in the United States and other nations (Kellert & Felthous, 1985; Vermeulen & Odendaal, 1993).

Several years later, Felthous and Kellert summarized the current literature on the link, noting the inconsistencies and contradictory findings in nine selected studies, underscoring the inadequacy of the evidence concerning the association between cruelty to animals and interpersonal violence, highlighting the impact of poor record-keeping and limited diagnostic work, and arguing for better methodologies and conceptual rigor in future research. Significantly, the two researchers observed that half of the studies that did not find a strong association between cruelty and later violence relied on testing instruments that did not prompt for relevant information concerning maltreatment of animals, convincing them that direct interviews about involvement with animals were essential to a sound study. Studies that were inconclusive also employed definitions of cruelty that were overbroad and imprecise (Felthous & Kellert, 1987).

Despite the limitations of this scholarship, increased attention within professional networks did have an effect. A significant benchmark was reached when cruelty to animals gained its place in the 1988 revision of the Diagnostic and Statistical Manual of Mental Disorders (DSM) as a symptom of conduct disorder. The DSM revision is a largely political process, and what brought this about is unclear. However, one might speculate that the cumulative effect of research on the triad, the impulse to make the symptom list for conduct disorder as objective as possible, the "gut reactions" some clinicians held about behaviors indicative of conduct disorder, and the emergence of Achenbach's Child Behavior Checklist—which includes an item about cruelty to animals—in the early 1980s may all have influenced the appearance of the cruelty to animals "symptom" in DSM IIIR (F. R. Ascione, personal communication, July 26, 2005; R. Lockwood, personal communication, July 26, 2005).

Importantly, in the 1988 DSM, cruelty to animals was grouped with symptoms relating to the "destruction of property" rather than interpersonal violence. However, its classification would change some years later as broader understanding of the complexity of cruelty to animals took hold in relevant professional networks.

A crucial impetus to the broader recognition of the link was the manifestation of interest within criminology—a field open to insights from both the soft and the hard sciences. As one of its raisons dêtre, criminology was focused on a fundamental question: Where do violent people come from? How do we spot them earlier? And how do we stop them from developing in the first place? Criminological reviews, focused on offender populations, raised many practical and theoretical questions about violence, its origins, and its dynamics.

An important source of legitimacy came with the serious attention given to the subject by researchers associated with the FBI's behavioral sciences unit, which first began to quantify cruelty to animals as a factor in its criminal profiles during the late 1970s. The unit's focus on psychological understanding of the offender as part of developing an accurate profile led researchers to embrace the correlation between cruelty to animals and interpersonal violence as a useful law enforcement tool. FBI studies of criminal populations also revealed significant rates of childhood animal abuse, bestiality, and severe physical animal abuse in the backgrounds of serial perpetrators of sexual homicide (Lockwood & Church, 1996; Ressler, Burgess, & Douglas, 1988; Ressler, Burgess, Hartman, Douglas, & McCormack, 1998).

The Broader Social and Political Context

If the real momentum for increased recognition of the link came in the 1980s, there were a number of social trends that helped to make that decade a decisive one. It was a decade of strong feminism, in which a broader understanding of domestic violence took hold. The 1980s also marked the maturation of human–animal bond studies, which focused on the importance of animals to the physical and psychological well-being of those humans who care for them. This trend helped to legitimate the increased attention given to the crime of cruelty.

The 1980s also saw a wider social recognition of the problem of violence, as heightened gang bloodshed, "wilding," and the specter of the marauding "superpredator" came into public consciousness. Pointed concerns about violence produced a renewed determination on the part of professionals to confront and devise strategies to reduce and mitigate its impact, in part by broadening their own spheres of practice through collaboration with those in other fields. During the decade extending from 1983 to 1993, arrests of youths for serious violent offenses surged by 70%; more alarmingly, the number of young people who committed homicides nearly tripled over the course of that deadly decade. During the same period, law enforcement agencies launched a more concerted effort to identify and track serial killers, laying increased emphasis on the investigation of particularly vicious, unusual, or repetitive crimes (Lockwood & Church, 1996; U.S. Surgeon General, 2001).

The vitality of organized animal protection in the 1980s was also influential. A strong humane movement with its own professional cadre chose to make corroboration of the link a serious priority. Groups such as the American Humane Association and the Latham Foundation sponsored symposia and scholarship on the subject, but an especially catalytic factor was the attention given to it by HSUS. There, in the mid-1980s, staff members Phyllis Wright and Randall Lockwood began to discuss the need for a comprehensive campaign to ensure that law enforcement and social services agencies took individual cases of cruelty to animals seriously, for their inherent viciousness as well as for what they might say about the perpetrator's potential for further misdeeds, including further violence against animals or other human beings (Unti, 2004).

After years of experience in conducting raids, HSUS investigators were in a position to confirm that law enforcement officers took dog fighting very seriously in states where it was a felony. This led the organization to push harder for felony upgrade campaigns in respect to animal fighting. Investigators and others testified before many state legislatures and were key figures in the assignment of felony status to such crimes (Unti, 2004).

Wright watched these developments with interest, for she had been having a lot of trouble getting law enforcement agencies to treat individual cases of cruelty discovered by local humane society investigators with gravity. On occasion, she noted, even the most shocking instances of cruelty failed to move local authorities, and they frequently failed to pursue such cases. This was enormously frustrating,

and, worse, it was actively undermining the work of local humane societies, which needed and wanted law enforcement authorities to conceptualize animals as victims as well as to take animal cruelty seriously as a crime (Unti, 2004).

Staff members agreed that a thorough campaign would involve education, legislative initiatives, and enhanced networking with law enforcement agencies. In 1986, Lockwood and Guy Hodge authored an award-winning piece in *HSUS News* that highlighted "The Tangled Web of Animal Abuse"—"the link between cruelty to animals and other forms of violent or anti-social behavior." This landmark article marked a significant early step in the campaign to sensitize the humane movement to the need for serious efforts to integrate its concerns with those of law enforcement and social service agencies (Lockwood & Hodge, 1986). Lockwood and other members of the Training Initiatives staff at HSUS then initiated a program of outreach to law enforcement and social services agencies. The HSUS hired a social worker to coordinate some of these relationships, and Lockwood undertook a heavy schedule of lectures, training, and documentation efforts designed to support the program.

Within a decade of its initial efforts on this front, the HSUS was in regular contact with congressional offices, representatives of the Federal Bureau of Investigation and the Department of Justice, and other law enforcement agencies, collaborating in efforts to promote awareness and education within law enforcement circles, which began to view prosecution of animal cruelty cases as an important part of threat assessment and another way of getting dangerous individuals into the legal system. With more successful animal cruelty prosecutions on the record, humane societies and law enforcement personnel would find themselves better equipped to address future threats to animals or people by the same individuals (Lockwood & Church, 1996).

Staff members from government affairs, regional offices, companion animals, and other HSUS divisions also worked to support the program, pushing for legislation to upgrade deliberate animal cruelty to felony status. In 1999, seven such laws were passed, and by 2004 collective efforts on the part of the national humane movement had pushed the total number of states in which such acts can be prosecuted as felonies to 41, up from just 4 states in 1990. In 1998, in a related trend, California became the first state to make psychological counseling a condition of probation for anyone convicted of cruelty to animals. Several others have followed suit. All of these legislative campaigns benefited from a high level of public interest and concern about animal cruelty (Livingston, 2001; Lockwood, 1999).

The humane movement continued to play an important role throughout the 1990s, as more organizations began to emphasize the link as part of their public outreach. Scholars with close links to animal protection helped to advance understanding by bringing together relevant scholarship in accessible form (Ascione & Arkow, 1999; Lockwood & Ascione, 1998) and by providing training that gave professionals in other fields an orientation to these issues. At century's end, the link was a strong priority for half a dozen movement organizations, some of which hired psychologists and social workers to coordinate their programs of outreach to the human services community.

The logic of the link was certainly made durable by the evidence concerning perpetrators of the schoolyard shootings that came to public attention in the 1990s. A study of nine incidents revealed that 5 of 11 perpetrators had histories of alleged animal abuse, including Luke Woodham, who months before killing his mother and two classmates had tortured and killed his own dog (Verlinden, 2000; Verlinden, Hersen, & Thomas, 2000).

Trends in Post-DSM Research

If the recognition of cruelty to animals as a diagnostic benchmark in the 1988 DSM was a significant juncture in the maturation of research on the link, it did not resolve the lingering questions that had plagued research since the 1970s. However, its inclusion within the DSM did coincide with a new generation of studies, more sophisticated, more richly detailed, and better grounded in an expanding scholarship on domestic violence, criminal psychology, and related fields. The appearance of this scholarship marked the maturation of the field.

The subsequent revision of the DSM in 1994 reflected a broader understanding of cruelty to animals, listing it with other symptoms of "violence against others," taking account of the fact that animals are more than simply property and that the motivations for harming them may be quite different from those associated with vandalism or property damage. Physical cruelty to animals was now listed among the symptoms grouped under the heading "Aggression toward People and Animals,"

an implicit recognition that the abuse of animals involves causing pain, suffering, or death to sentient creatures and that it may be a sign of an individual's impaired capacity for empathy (DSM IV, 1994).

The DSM revision owed much to the refinement of professional understanding concerning cruelty and the emergence of typologies that followed in the wake of the one offered by Kellert and Felthous in 1985. Even at this writing, scholars and professionals continue to grapple with suitable definitions of cruelty to animals, a complex phenomenon that involves diverse cultural, societal, and individual standards for its interpretation. For those in law enforcement, humane investigations, and the social services community, this is not just a conceptual problem because—simply stated—those who are responsible for confronting cruelty need to have a good understanding of what it is (Ascione, 1993; Kellert & Felthous, 1985; Merz-Perez & Heide, 2004; Vermeulen & Odendaal, 1993, Rowan, 1993).

Studies of prior animal abuse in convicted offenders continued in the post-DSM era. Miller and Knutson (1997) reported that prisoners incarcerated for various felony offenses were more likely to have harmed or killed a pet than a comparison group of undergraduate psychology students. In a survey of offenders in a South African prison, Schiff, Louw, and Ascione (1999) found a much higher percentage of childhood animal abuse among those who had committed crimes of aggression. Other analyses of incarcerated child molesters, sex offenders, and murderers suggest that animal abuse is prominent within the developmental experience of 25% to 33% of violent adult offenders (Ascione, 2005).

In the wake of the DSM listing, professional research also focused on the relationship between animal abuse and conduct disorder (CD), in part because there is considerable overlap between CD symptoms and behaviors associated with serious violent juvenile offenses. Studies of assessment instruments, the relative significance of patterns of chronic behavior, the relationship between cruelty to animals and CD subcategories and related disruptive disorders, and the importance of cruelty to animals as an early symptom of CD all reflect this preoccupation. Its position within the diagnostic schema was further strengthened by a study that confirmed cruelty to animals as one of the earliest of CD's symptoms (Ascione, 2005; Frick et al., 1993).

Arluke, Levin, Luke, and Ascione (1999) shifted conventional debate over the link with their attempt to test the "graduation to violence" hypothesis in a population of 153 animal abusers and 153 control participants. They found that the progression was not necessarily sequential from animal abuse to interpersonal violence, but argued that it might be better to focus on the correlation found between cruelty to animals and a range of antisocial behaviors. In their study, individuals prosecuted for animal abuse were more likely to have an adult arrest in such crime categories as property offenses, drug offenses, and public disorder offenses than comparison group members did.

Wright and Hensley (2003) found stronger support for the escalation thesis, seconding a point made by Arluke et al. (1999) and Hickey (2002) that appropriate definitions and measurements would likely establish the validity of the graduation hypothesis.

In another approach defined by increased nuance, Ressler, Burgess, Hartman, Douglas, and McCormack (1998) sharpened their focus to the particular value of cruelty to animals as a predictor of extremely violent crimes.

Interest in animal abuse within the context of family violence remained an important arena for research, and a number of studies laid greater emphasis on cruelty to animals as a major variable. In findings significant for the future of institutional response to animal abuse, Ascione and his colleagues conducted interviews and examined intake questioning practices at shelters for battered women to determine that 71% of women seeking shelter reported threats or actual harm to their pets, and that 62% of women who were battered reported that their children had also witnessed animal abuse. Similar findings emerged in studies by Flynn and Quinlisk (Ascione, 1997; Ascione, 2005; Ascione, Weber, & Wood, 1997; Flynn, 2000; Quinlisk, 1999).

As Ascione (2005) noted, additional studies within the period 1995–2005 identified animal cruelty as a comorbid symptom in studies of bullying, pervasive development disorder not otherwise specified, juvenile fire setting, antisocial personality disorder, adult criminal offending, sex offending by children and adults, sexual homicide, and serial murder.

An expanding number of studies called attention to the need for examining multiple forms of victimization, finding higher percentages of cruelty to animals among boys who lived in households where both physical abuse and domestic violence were present (Ascione, 2005). Similar concerns led to heightened focus on using cruelty to animals as a possible means for proving child abuse and a tool for risk assessment in at-risk children, as well as to the positive notion of prevention of animal abuse as a device for mitigating the general phenomenon of family violence (Boat, 1999; LaCroix, 1998).

Another area of expanding interest was the sexual abuse of animals, either in the form of bestiality or as associated with child sexual abuse. Half a dozen studies conducted between 1997 and 2003 provided evidence for a relationship between sexual abuse victimization and bestiality. Among other outcomes, this led to calls for the redefinition of bestiality as a form of sexual assault (Ascione, 2005; Beirne, 1997).

Professional literature also increased its focus on the role that empathy may play in the prevention of animal abuse. Empathy appears to have its roots in early infancy, and its absence may make it easier for humans to harm others. Magid and McKelvey (1987) suggested that children who lack empathy may be more likely to abuse animals, and Quinlisk (1999) cited the need for research concerning empathy. The value of humane education as an instrument of childhood socialization has yet to be convincingly and empirically established, but the humane movement has nevertheless found it valuable to frame its commitment to humane education through the character connection and empathy connection frameworks (Unti & DeRosa, 2003).

A number of studies focused on the production and refinement of measuring and screening instruments for cruelty. Quinlisk (1999) and Lewchanin and Zimmerman (2000) produced manuals for mental health clinicians to use in evaluating children and adolescents suspected of animal cruelty. Ascione et al. (1997) employed a structured interview protocol called the Cruelty to Animals Assessment Instrument (CAAI), while Guymer, Mellor, Luk, and Pearse (2001) developed the Children's Attitudes and Behaviors toward Animals (CABTA) screening instrument, which distinguished between typical and malicious cruelty to animals. Ascione and Weber (1997a, 1997b) used instruments tailored to assessments of those who enter shelters after leaving situations where domestic violence was present.

The drive to identify arenas in which signs of animal abuse might be easily observed has led to greater focus on the responsibility of veterinarians for reporting cruelty. Munro and Thrusfield focused on a variety of nonaccidental physical injuries to dogs and cats presenting at veterinary practices, and introduced the concept of the "battered pet" (Munro, 1996; Munro & Thrusfield, 2001a, 2001b, 2001c, 2001d; Patronek, 1997).

Building upon Susan Isaacs's consideration of children and conflicting social values, efforts by the humane movement to highlight apparently contradictory attitudes and behaviors, and Margaret Mead's 1964 expression of concern over socialization to violence, a number of recent studies have explored the challenges posed by the ambiguity of societal attitudes toward the killing of animals. Children and adults alike have to negotiate significant moral complexities in working out questions associated with the killing of animals in various sanctioned contexts. At least one scholar, Grandin, has suggested that there are ways to discuss what may be unacceptable cruelty within the context of socially sanctioned uses, and ways to address the issues involved. Ascione also addressed this question, suggesting that the ecological framework is relevant because it takes into account all social and cultural relationships in which animals are present. Still others called for a broader sociological analysis including a broader definition of what constitutes animal abuse (Ascione, 1999; Flynn, 2001; Grandin, 1988; Hirschberg, 1953; Mead, 1964).

Conclusion

The evolution of understanding concerning the link between cruelty to animals and interpersonal violence, from early modern human development theory to movement platform to psychological and criminological standard to social commonplace, has been a contingent and unsteady development. In recent years, however, it has definitively moved from the realm of the anecdotal notion to that of the empirically tested principle. With respect to both qualitative and quantitative studies, we are, it seems, increasingly comfortable in making the point that our nineteenth-century forebears intuitively understood, that cruelty to animals can be a reliable sign not only of those who might pose the risk of harm to others, but also of those who are at risk of becoming victims of violence themselves. As in the nineteenth century, animals are again integrated into our understanding of family and our conceptualization of domestic violence.

To the extent that those who work to reduce interpersonal violence are inclined to welcome anything that illuminates its sources and its remedies, it seems unlikely that society will lose its interest in cruelty to animals as a potential sentinel. However, even if history does not repeat itself, with awareness of the link again losing its cultural currency and

influence, one cannot assume that continued integration of the link will proceed without difficulty, and efforts to cultivate still stronger institutional responses may meet resistance. With so much serious interpersonal violence occurring, it will remain a challenge to see that animal abuse is taken seriously. Society faces many other problems, and social work and law enforcement are already overburdened professions. In the face of competing pressures and claims, calls for mandated cross-reporting by social work agencies, veterinarians, law enforcement agencies, and others, or for the creation of a national registry or centralized reporting system, or for the inclusion of cruelty to animals in testing instruments, may not find a willing audience. Legislation to require such reporting will be met with scrutiny and possible resistance.

The best progress of all is that which is institutionalized, and in this respect, there is reason for optimism about the future of the link. Multidisciplinary approaches to the prevention of family violence and cruelty to animals have proliferated, and continue to take root in communities throughout the United States as coalitions based upon inter-professional cooperation bring humane society personnel together with the human services community, law enforcement, the veterinary profession, and other stakeholders. This has led to some very concrete program work, including the creation of "safe haven" sites for the companion animals of those in flight from abusive domestic relations, and training for prosecutors and other law enforcement officials. Moreover, our enhanced ability to examine, classify, and understand cruelty to animals as an objectively definable behavior will make it possible for relevant professionals and agencies to better fulfill their responsibilities. There is no shortage of good ideas about prevention, intervention, how research might proceed, or how further practical advances might be made (Ascione & Arkow, 1999; Arluke & Lockwood, 1997; Lockwood & Ascione, 1998).

Both felonization and increased enforcement ensure that a great deal more information now makes it into the record-keeping systems of both law enforcement and human services, and this holds great benefits to society, even as it makes the crime of cruelty to animals more visible as a matter of public knowledge. Egregious cases of cruelty occupy a lot of media attention now, helping to solidify public understanding of the seriousness of animal cruelty and (often) the implications of the link. Awareness of the topic continues to spread within veterinary medicine, law enforcement, social work, and other professional networks.

While cruelty to animals, in and of itself, may not be a definitive predictor of violence against humans, on the basis of the research available, we can at least say it is significantly linked to interpersonal violence and other criminal behavior. Moreover, in juveniles, it is a behavior that is alarming enough to demand intervention. Few would dispute that aggressive acts against animals constitute an early diagnostic indicator of future psychopathology that may escalate in range and severity against other victims, that children's witnessing of animal abuse may desensitize them to violence, that animals in violent households are victims especially vulnerable to batterers who know that hurting a pet is a way to coerce and hurt others, and that animal abuse is a reliable indicator of other problems in a given household (Arkow, 1999).

In the end, the ecological approach will serve our communities better by helping to shift society's response from a focus on how to identify the potential for criminal behavior to a broader and deeper set of questions about what motivates offenders, how such behavior emerges, and what steps can be taken to minimize the likelihood of violence against those at risk. Such alertness to violence in all of its forms, and to all of its potential victims, human and non-human, will make possible the creation of appropriate mechanisms by which offenders can be held to account, by identifying offender populations whose potentially harmful tendencies can be addressed through appropriate counseling, education, and training, and, when necessary, enforcement, prosecution, and punishment. By taking cruelty to animals more seriously as a social problem, and conceptualizing animal abusers as individuals who might later become dangerous to others, human and non-human, we can create a greater sense of security and a greater level of safety in every community, worthwhile goals in any era.

References

Anonymous. (1907). Bloodthirstiness in children. *Current Literature* (January) XLII, 98.

Arkow, P. (1999). The evolution of animal welfare as a human welfare concern. In F. R. Ascione & P. Arkow (Eds.), *Child abuse, domestic violence, and animal abuse: Linking the circles of compassion for prevention and intervention* (pp. 19–37). West Lafayette, IN: Purdue University Press.

Arluke, A., Levin, J., Luke, C., & Ascione, F. (1999). The relationship of animal abuse to violence and other forms of antisocial behavior. *Journal of Interpersonal Violence, 14,* 245–253.

Arluke, A., & Lockwood, R. (Eds.). (1997). Special Theme Issue: Animal Cruelty. *Society and Animals, 5,* 183–194.

Ascione, F. R. (1993). Children who are cruel to animals; a review of research and implications for developmental psychopathology. *Anthrozoös, 6,* 226–247.

Ascione, F. R. (1997). Final Report: Animal welfare and domestic violence (Geraldine R. Dodge Foundation). Logan, Utah: Department of Psychology, Utah State University.

Ascione, F. R. (1998). Battered women's reports of their partners' and their children's cruelty to animals. *Journal of Emotional Abuse, 1,* 119–133.

Ascione, F. R. (1999). The abuse of animals and human interpersonal violence: Making the connection. In F. R. Ascione & P. Arkow (Eds.), *Child abuse, domestic violence, and animal abuse: Linking the circles of compassion for prevention and intervention* (pp. 50–61). West Lafayette, IN: Purdue University Press.

Ascione, F. R. (2005). Children, animal abuse, and family violence. In *Child victimization: maltreatment, bullying and dating violence, prevention and intervention* (pp. 1–27). Kingston: Civic Research Institute.

Ascione, F. R., & Arkow, P. (Eds.). (1999). *Child abuse, domestic violence, and animal abuse: Linking the circles of compassion for prevention and intervention.* West Lafayette: Purdue University Press.

Ascione, F. R., & Weber, C. V. (1997a). Battered partner shelter survey (BPSS). Logan, UT: Utah State University.

Ascione, F. R., & Weber, C. V. (1997b). Children's observation and experience with pets (COEP). Logan, UT: Utah State University.

Ascione, F. R., Weber, C., & Wood, D. S. (1997). The abuse of animals and domestic violence: A national survey of shelters for women who are battered. *Society and Animals, 5,* 205–218.

Beirne, P. (1997). Rethinking bestiality: Towards a sociology of interspecies sexual assault. *Theoretical Criminology, 1,* 317–340.

Birke, L. (2000). Supporting the underdog: Feminism, animal rights and citizenship in the work of Alice Morgan Wright and Edith Goode. *Women's History Review, 9*, 693–719.

Blocker, J. (1989). *American temperance movements: Cycles of reform*. Boston: Twayne.

Boat, B. (1995). The relationship between violence to children and violence to animals: An ignored link? *Journal of Interpersonal Violence, 10*, 229–235.

Boat, B. (1999). Abuse of children and abuse of animals: Using the links to inform child assessment and protection. In F.R. Ascione & P. Arkow (Eds.), *Child abuse, domestic violence, and animal abuse: Linking the circles of compassion for prevention and intervention* (pp. 83–100). West Lafayette, IN: Purdue University Press.

Buettinger, C. (1997). Women and anti-vivisection in late nineteenth-century America. *Journal of Social History, 30*, 857–872.

Burt, C. (1925). *The Young Delinquent*. New York: Appleton.

Carstens, C. (1921). Development of social work for child protection. *Annals of the American Academy of Political and Social Science, 98*, 138, November.

Costall, A. (1998). Lloyd Morgan, and the rise and fall of "animal psychology." *Society and Animals, 6*, 13–29.

Covotsos, J. (1981). *The Illinois Humane Society, 1869–1979*. River Forest, IL: Rosary College Graduate School of Library Science.

Crocker, R. (1996). From widow's mite to widow's might: The philanthropy of Margaret Olivia Sage. *Journal of Presbyterian History, 74*, 253–264.

DeViney, E., Dickert, J., & Lockwood, R. (1983). The care of pets within abusing families. *International Journal for the Study of Animal Problems, 4*, 321–329.

Felthous, A. R. (1980). Aggression against cats, dogs, and people. *Child Psychiatry and Human Development, 10*, 169–177.

Felthous, A. R., & Kellert, S. R. (1987). Childhood cruelty to animals and later aggression against people: A review. *American Journal of Psychiatry, 144*, 710–717.

Felthous, A. R., & Yudowitz, B. (1977). Approaching a comparative typology of assaultive female offenders. *Psychiatry, 40*, 270–276.

Fleming, D. S. (1975). Cruelty to animals as predictive of psychopathologic behavior. *NAAHE Journal* (Fall), 11–14.

Flynn, C. P. (2000). Woman's best friend: Pet abuse and the role of companion animals in the lives of battered women. *Violence Against Women, 6*, 162–177.

Flynn, C. P. (2001). Acknowledging the zoological connection: A sociological analysis of animal cruelty. *Society and Animals, 9*, 71–87.

Freud, S. (2000). *Three essays on the theory of sexuality*. New York: Perseus Books. (Original work published 1905)

Frick, P. J., Van Horn, Y., Lahey, B. B., Christ, M. A. G., Loeber, R., Tannenbaum, L., & Hanson, K. (1993). Oppositional defiant disorder and conduct disorder: A meta-analytic review of factor analyses and cross-validation in a clinic sample. *Clinical Psychology Review, 13*, 319–340.

Frykman, J., & Löfgren, O. (1987). *Culture builders: A historical anthropology of middle-class life*. New Brunswick: Rutgers University Press.

Fucini, S. (1978). The abuser: First a dog then a child? *National Humane Review, 5*, 14–15.

Gordon, L. (1988). *Heroes of their own lives: The politics and history of family violence*. New York: Viking.

Grandin, T. (1988). Behavior of slaughter plant and auction employees toward the animals. *Anthrozoös, 1*, 205–213.

Grier, K. C. (1999). Childhood socialization and companion animals: United States, 1820–1920. *Society and Animals, 7*, 95–120.

Grossberg, M. (1985). *Governing the hearth: Law and the family in nineteenth century America*. Chapel Hill: University of North Carolina Press.

Guymer, E. C., Mellor, D., Luk, E. S. L., & Pearse, V. (2001). The development of a screening questionnaire for childhood cruelty to animals. *Journal of Child Psychology and Psychiatry, 42* (8), 1057–1063.

Hall, R. P. (1999). The link's direct connection to child protective services. In F. R. Ascione & P. Arkow (Eds.), *Child abuse, domestic violence, and animal abuse: Linking the circles of compassion for prevention and intervention*. West Lafayette, IN: Purdue University Press.

Hammack, D. C. (1994). A center of intelligence for the charity organization movement: The foundation's early years. In D. C. Hammack & S. Wheeler (Eds.), *Social sciences in the making: Essays on the Russell Sage Foundation, 1907–1972*. New York: Russell Sage Foundation.

Hellman, D., & Blackman, N. (1966). Enuresis, fire-setting, and cruelty to animals: A triad predictive of adult crime. *American Journal of Psychiatry, 122*, 1431–1435.

Hickey, E. W. (2002). *Serial murderers and their victims*. Belmont, CA: Wadsworth/Thomson Learning.

Hirschberg, J. C. (1953). Psychological aspects of cruelty. *National Humane Review* (November), 11–13.

Hutton, J. S. (1983). Animal abuse as a diagnostic approach in social work: A pilot study. In A. H. Katcher & A. M. Beck (Eds.), *New perspectives on our lives with companion animals* (pp. 444–447). Philadelphia: University of Pennsylvania Press.

Isaacs, S. (1930). *Intellectual growth in young children*. London: George Routledge and Sons.

Isaacs, S. (1931). Humane education of young children. In *Conference of Educational Associations Report*. London: College of Preceptors, 78–81.

Kellert, S., & Felthous, A. R. (1985). Childhood cruelty toward animals among criminals and non-criminals. *Human Relations, 38*, 1113–1129.

Kerber, L. (1980). *Women of the republic: Intellect and ideology in revolutionary America*. Chapel Hill: University of North Carolina Press.

Krafft-Ebing, R. von. (1965). *Psychopathia sexualis, with especial reference to contrary sexual instinct: A medico-legal study*. New York: Stein and Day. (Original work published 1892)

LaCroix, C. (1998). Another weapon for combating family violence: Prevention of animal abuse. *Animal Law, 4*, 1–32.

Lederer, S. (1995). *Subjected to science: Human experimentation before the second world war*. Baltimore: Johns Hopkins University.

Lewchanin, S., & Zimmerman, E. (2000). *Clinical assessment of juvenile animal cruelty*. Brunswick, ME: Biddle Publishing.

Link, A., & McCormick, R. L. (1983). *Progressivism*. Arlington Heights, IL: Harlan Davidson.

Livingston, M. (2001). Desecrating the ark: Animal abuse and the law's role in prevention. *87 Iowa L. Rev. 1:* 1–73.

Locke, J. (1989). *Some thoughts concerning education* (5th ed) (J. W. & J. S. Yolton, Eds.). Oxford: Clarendon Press. (Original work published 1693)

Lockwood, R. (1999). Animal cruelty and societal violence: A brief look back from the front. In F. R. Ascione & P. Arkow (Eds.), *Child abuse, domestic violence, and animal abuse: Linking the circles of compassion for prevention and intervention* (pp. 3–8). West Lafayette, IN: Purdue University Press.

Lockwood, R., & Ascione, F. (Eds.) (1998). *Cruelty to animals and interpersonal violence*. West Lafayette, IN: Purdue University Press.

Lockwood, R., & Church, A. (1996). Deadly serious: An FBI perspective on animal cruelty. *HSUS News* (Fall), 27–30.

Lockwood, R. & Hodge, G. (1986). The tangled web of animal abuse: The link between cruelty to animals and human violence. *HSUS News* (Summer), 10–15.

MacDonald, J. M. (1963). The threat to kill. *American Journal of Psychiatry, 8*, 125–130.

Magid, K., & McKelvey, C. A. (1987). *High risk: Children without a conscience*. New York: Bantam Books.

McCrea, R. (1910). *The humane movement: A descriptive survey*. New York: Columbia University Press.

Mead, M. (1964). Cultural factors in the cause and prevention of pathological homicide. *Bulletin in the Menninger Clinic, 29*, 11–22.

Merz-Perez, L., & Heide, K. M. (2004). *Animal cruelty: Pathway to violence against people*. Walnut Creek: Altamira Press.

Miller, K. S., & Knutson, J. F. (1997). Reports of severe physical punishment and exposure to animal cruelty by inmates convicted of felonies and by university students. *Child Abuse and Neglect, 21*, 59–82.

Muncy, R. (1991). *Creating a female dominion in American reform 1890–1935*. New York: Oxford University Press.

Munro, H. (1996). Battered pets. *Irish Veterinary Journal, 49*, 712–713.

Munro, H., & Thrusfield, M. V. (2001a). Battered pets: Features that raise suspicion of non-accidental injury. *Journal of Small Animal Practice, 42*, 218–226.

Munro, H., & Thrusfield, M. V. (2001b). Battered pets. Non-accidental physical injuries found in dogs and cats. *Journal of Small Animal Practice, 42*, 279–290.

Munro, H., & Thrusfield, M. V. (2001c). Battered pets. Sexual abuse. *Journal of Small Animal Practice, 42*, 333–337.

Munro, H., & Thrusfield, M. V. (2001d). Battered pets. Munchausen syndrome by proxy (fictitious illness by proxy). *Journal of Small Animal Practice, 42*, 385–389.

Myers, G. (1998). *Children and animals: Social development and our connections to other species*. Boulder: Westview Press.

Patronek, G. (1997). Issues for veterinarians in recognizing and reporting animal neglect and abuse. *Society and Animals, 5*, 267–280.

Pearson, S. (2004). The rights of the defenseless: Animals, children, and sentimental liberalism in nineteenth-century America. Unpublished doctoral dissertation, University of North Carolina.

Pickering, S. F. (1981). *John Locke and children's literature in eighteenth-century England*. Knoxville: University of Tennessee Press.

Pleck, E. (1987). *Domestic tyranny: The making of social policy against family violence from colonial times to the present*. New York: Oxford University Press.

Quinlisk, J. A. (1999). Animal abuse and family violence. In F. R. Ascione & P. Arkow (Eds.), *Child abuse, domestic violence, and animal abuse: Linking the circles of compassion for prevention and intervention* (pp. 168–175). West Lafayette, IN: Purdue University Press.

Ressler, R. K., Burgess, A. W., & Douglas, J. E. (1988). *Sexual homicide: Patterns and motives*. Lexington, MA: Lexington Books.

Ressler, R. K., Burgess, A. W., Hartman, C. R., Douglas, J. E., & McCormack, A. (1998). Murderers who rape and mutilate. In R. Lockwood & F. R. Ascione (Eds.), *Cruelty to animals and interpersonal violence* (pp. 179–193). West Lafayette, IN: Purdue University Press.

Rigdon, J. D., & Tapia, F. (1977). Children who are cruel to animals—a follow-up study. *Journal of Operational Psychiatry, 8*, 27–36.

Rowan, A. (1993). Cruelty to animals. *Anthrozoös, 6*, 218–220.

Schiff, K., Louw, D., & Ascione, F. R. (1999). Animal relations in childhood and later violent behavior against humans. *Acta Criminologica, 12*, 77–86.

Shultz, W. J. (1924). *The humane movement in the United States*. New York: Columbia University Press.

Steele, Z. (1942). *Angel in top hat*. New York: Harper and Brothers.

Tapia, F. (1971). Children who are cruel to animals. *Child Psychiatry and Human Development, 2*, 70–77.

Unti, B. (2002). The quality of mercy: Organized animal protection in the United States, 1866–1930. Unpublished doctoral dissertation, American University, Washington, DC.

Unti, B. (2004). *Protecting all animals: A fifty-year history of the humane society of the United States*. Washington: Humane Society Press.

Unti, B., & DeRosa, B. (2003). Humane education past, present and future. In D. Salem & A. Rowan (Eds.), *The state of the animals: 2003* (pp. 27–50). Washington: Humane Society Press.

Unti, B., & Rowan, A. (2001). A social history of animal protection in the post-world war II period. In D. Salem & A. Rowan (Eds.), *The state of the animals: 2001* (pp. 21–37). Washington: Humane Society Press.

U.S. Surgeon General. (2001). Youth violence: A report of the surgeon general. Accessed online at http://www.surgeongeneral.gov/library/youthviolence/.

Verlinden, S. (2000). Risk factors in school shootings. Unpublished doctoral dissertation, Pacific University, Forest Grove, OR.

Verlinden, S., Hersen, M., & Thomas, J. (2000). Risk factors in school shootings. *Clinical Psychology Review, 20*, 3–56.

Vermeulen, H., & Odendaal, J. S. (1993). Proposed typology of companion animal abuse. *Anthrozoös, 6*, 248–257.

Walker, J. R. (1980). A study on the relationship of child abuse and pet abuse. Unpublished professional project, University of Pennsylvania School of Social Work, Philadelphia.

Wiebe, R. (1967). *The search for order 1877–1920*. New York: Hill and Wang.

Wright, J., & Hensley, C. (2003) From animal cruelty to serial murder: Applying the graduation hypothesis. *International Journal of Offender Therapy and Comparative Criminology, 47*, 71–88.

A Timeline of Benchmarks Relating to the Link

1579–1580 Michel de Montaigne's essay "Of the Education of Children"

1693 John Locke, *Some Thoughts on Education* published

1750 Hogarth produces The Four Stages of Cruelty

1798 John Lawrence writes "If cruelty be allowable … towards brutes, it also involves human creatures; the gradation is much easier than may be imagined."

1808 Lord Erskine invokes the link while introducing his bill against animal cruelty

1809 Philippe Pinel reports on a case of cruelty to animals by a child

1824 Royal Society for the Prevention of Cruelty to Animals [RSPCA]

1829 New York State anti-cruelty statute

1850 Fugitive Slave Act

1852 Harriet Beecher Stowe, *Uncle Tom's Cabin*

1866 American Society for the Prevention of Cruelty to Animals [ASPCA]

1867 Pennsylvania Society for the Prevention of Cruelty to Animals [PSPCA]

1868 Massachusetts Society for the Prevention of Cruelty to Animals [MSPCA]

1874 Women's Christian Temperance Union [WCTU]

1875 Henry Bergh and Elbridge T. Gerry launch New York Society for the Prevention of Cruelty to Children

1877 Anna Sewell, *Black Beauty*

1877 American Humane Association [AHA]

1882 Band of Mercy concept introduced to United States

1886 MSPCA spurs humane education mandate in Massachusetts

1889 American Humane Education Society [AHES]

1890 AHES edition of *Black Beauty* appears

1892 Albert Leffingwell spurs AHA campaign against classroom vivisection

1893 Marshall Saunders, *Beautiful Joe*

1893 ASPCA, *Kindness to Animals: A Manual for Use in Schools and Families*

1894 MSPCA secures a ban on classroom vivisection in Massachusetts

1904 William O. Stillman assumes presidency of the AHA

1905 Oklahoma and Pennsylvania pass compulsory humane education laws

1905 Stillman and Stella Preston form Humane Education Committee in New York State

1906 Krafft-Ebing's *Psychopathia Sexualis* discusses sadistic behavior toward non-human animals

1907 Henry Bergh Foundation for the Promotion of Humane Education established at Columbia University

1909 Compulsory humane education legislation in Illinois

1910 Flora Helm Krause, *Manual of Moral and Humane Education*

1915 Be Kind to Animals Week launched

1915 AHA votes to seek compulsory humane education in every state

1916 Sandor Ferenczi, "A Little Chanticleer" (case study of a boy's cruelty toward humans and non-human animals)

1916 AHES produces the first humane education film, "The Bell of Atri"

1916 ASPCA creates humane education department

1917 Compulsory humane education laws passed in Maine, Wisconsin, and New York

1919 Harriet C. C. Reynolds, *Thoughts on Human Education: Suggestions on Kindness to Animals*

1920 Kentucky approves compulsory humane education law

1923 Florida approves compulsory humane education law

1924 William J. Shultz, *The Humane Movement in the United States*, judges humane education the most important development of the past decade

1924 Frances E. Clarke, *Lessons for Teaching Humane Education in the Schools*

1925 Alexander Ernest Frederick, *The Humane Guide: A Manual for Teachers and Humane Workers*

1931 Susan Isaacs, *Intellectual Growth in Young Children*

1971 case study (Tapia)

1985 Typology of Abuse (Kellert and Felthous)

1986 Hodge and Lockwood

1993 Taxonomy of cruelty (Rowan)

1994 Ethology and Taxonomy (Odendaal)

1996 Battered Pet (Munro)

1997 Women in shelters (Ascione, Weber, and Wood)

1998 Animal care and condition scales (Patronek)

The Veterinary Profession's Roles in Recognizing and Preventing Family Violence: The Experiences of the Human Medicine Field and the Development of Diagnostic Indicators of Non-Accidental Injury

Phil Arkow and Helen Munro

Introduction

Critical to the institutionalization of medical responses to the public health problems of child abuse and domestic violence were the increased awareness among medical professions that these issues were medical conditions worthy of professional response, and the overcoming of practice management and ethical concerns that served as barriers to professional involvement. One such barrier was the recognition and dissemination of diagnostic clinical indicators that differentiate non-accidental injury (NAI) from other types of traumas and that lead physicians to include physical or sexual abuse in differential diagnosis. As a result of the first promulgation of such indicators in the landmark "Battered Child Syndrome" article (Kempe, Silverman, Steele, Droegenmuller, & Silver, 1962), the United States launched one of its most rapid responses to a public health crisis, an institutional model of recognition and reporting that has been imitated widely throughout the world.

An earlier paradigm of what previously had been considered "accident-prone" children has been replaced with a widespread recognition of child abuse and a national system of mandatory reporters and child protective services (CPS) agencies. Training manuals are now readily available to help medical personnel identify telltale spiral fractures; immersion or cigarette burns; characteristic bruises caused by slaps, electric cords, or coat hangars; and other markers of child abuse (e.g., Kessler & Hyden, 1991). The human health care profession codified its responsibility to evaluate suspected child abuse and, later, domestic violence and to act accordingly.

In contrast, more than 69,000 practitioners of veterinary medicine in the United States have been largely excluded from reporting systems for child abuse, domestic violence, and animal abuse. The veterinary profession has long been recognized for its public health responsibilities and as caregivers who see more human clients than animal patients (McCulloch, 1976). The failure to include veterinary medicine among its human medicine counterparts is a significant barrier to achieving full community recognition of the seriousness of animal abuse and its implication for animal well-being and human health and safety.

In order to integrate veterinary medicine into human medicine recognition and response systems, four issues must be addressed:

1. Veterinary professionals must learn how to approach clients in order to gather additional information to assist in a more accurate diagnosis and a more effective response that protects the interests of the patient, other animals in the household, and persons in the family.
2. Veterinary professionals must be trained and supported by their peers to undertake appropriate steps once they suspect that abusive behaviors may be a cause of the patient's condition.
3. A wide array of practice management concerns must be resolved to make veterinary involvement in the prevention of various forms of family violence an institutional norm.
4. Veterinarians and their staffs must be trained to identify the clinical conditions that indicate a differential diagnosis of NAI.

These issues have been largely resolved by the human medical fields. The experiences of the human health care professions will prove helpful to veterinarians as they enter these uncharted waters (Munro & Thrusfield, 2001b).

Reasons for Involvement

As early as 1985, the U.S. Surgeon General emphasized that sociological, law enforcement, and criminal justice systems interventions had led to "unmitigated failure" in addressing violence (Koop & Lundberg, 1992). Authorities began calling for an interdisciplinary, epidemiologically based response that focused on violence as a public health matter.

Calling violence "a public health emergency," the U.S. Surgeon General said, "Physicians and other health professionals are firsthand witnesses to the consequences of violence. We see, diagnose, treat, mend, patch, console, and care for the victims of violence and their families thousands of times each day." In encouraging all health care professionals to open and maintain channels with other disciplines, the Surgeon General concluded, "As health professionals, the prevention of violence by using public health methods in our communities is as much our responsibility as is the treatment of its victims" (Novello, Shosky, & Froehlke, 1992). Failure to provide medical intervention has been described as "iatrogenic retraumatization"—abuse caused by the profession itself when unassisted victims feel hopeless with no practical alternative to escape (Skolnick, 1995).

All medical professionals have taken oaths to protect well-being and the public's health. The inclusion of the veterinary profession in this effort is required given their professional mandate as public health practitioners, the profession's oath to prevent suffering, and veterinarians' interactions with families (Arkow, 2004).

Veterinarians are frequently the best qualified to determine if an animal is suffering unnecessary and excessive pain or if an injury or death was unjustifiable. Confidences may be revealed if the veterinarian is required to do so by law or if the health or welfare of others is endangered. Veterinarians are largely given full immunity from civil or criminal liability for reporting suspected abuse to appropriate authorities in good faith. Consequently, veterinary involvement in violence prevention is indicated (Phillips, 1994).

Animal abuse frequently coexists with domestic violence and serves as a barrier to prevent many battered women from leaving abusive partners out of fear for the welfare of the animals in the household. Several studies (Doherty, 2002; Hornosty & Doherty, 2002; Lembke, 1999) have identified this to be a par-

ticular concern in rural areas, where the veterinarian who makes "house calls" may be in an advantageous position to recognize and assist victims of abuse.

Veterinarians are ideally placed as sentinels to identify and deal with animal abuse, and where this is severe or cannot be dealt with effectively by the veterinarian, to report it to appropriate authorities. Given the clear links between abuse perpetrated on animals and that perpetrated on humans (Ascione & Arkow, 1999), pro-activity by veterinarians in respect to animal abuse has the potential to save human life and reduce suffering along with animal life and suffering (Lawrie, 2002).

Sharing information can prevent future maltreatment. The community has delegated the responsibilities of protecting animals, children, elders, and battered women to officials in a variety of professions. Health care officials are unable to meet these duties if they do not know that abuse is occurring (Vulliamy & Sullivan, 2000). Veterinarians are considered part of the community health care system's response to domestic violence prevention (Community Crisis Center, undated).

Other factors prompting veterinary involvement include:

- Failure to intervene perpetuates public health problems and puts patients and others at risk
- Veterinarians are well-trained to identify and correct substandard care
- Veterinarians should be at the forefront of setting the highest standards for animal welfare
- Participation in family violence prevention programs is an opportunity to build bridges between veterinary medicine and other professions
- To elevate the status of the profession and the status and well-being of animals

Prevalence

Veterinarians frequently voice the opinion that as animal professionals they are unlikely to encounter human abuse, are untrained to recognize and respond to it, and that pet owners who care enough about their animals to provide veterinary care are unlikely to be abusive. These assumptions need to be reexamined. Munro and Thrusfield (2001a) have shown unequivocally that perpetrators do indeed present abused animals for veterinary examination.

Three market research studies from the American Veterinary Medical Association (AVMA) describe the primary market niche for small-animal practitioners to be those populations that are most at risk of family violence victimization. In 72.8% of pet-owning households, the primary caregiver is a female. Parents with children are the dominant market for companion animals: 64.1% of households with children under age 6, and 74.8% of households with children over age 6, have pets. Moreover, nearly half—46.9%—of American pet owners consider pets to be "members of the family," while slightly more than half—50.9%—consider their animals to be companions and pets with whom they presumably have emotional ties. Only 2.2% of pet owners consider these animals to be "property" (American Veterinary Medical Association, 2002).

Households with histories of child abuse are as likely to take their animals to veterinarians as are non-abusive families. Further, an additional public health issue exists in child-abusing households in that the incidence of dog bites in violent homes was reportedly 11 times greater than in the normal population (DeViney, Dickert, & Lockwood, 1983).

In a survey of 15 randomly selected small- and large-animal practitioners in Indiana, Landau (1999) reported that 87% of veterinarians interviewed had treated abused patients, with 50% of veterinarians treating one to three abused patients per year; 60% of respondents had treated an animal who they suspected had been severely or intentionally abused or neglected. In addition, 20% of those surveyed stated they had worked with clients whom they suspected were themselves being abused.

Sharpe (1999) described a national random survey of 368 small-animal practitioners who reported an annual mean number of 5.6 animal abuse cases per 1,000 patients. Only 2.4% of respondents believed that a veterinarian should do nothing if animal abuse is suspected and only 14.9% said veterinarians should do nothing if child abuse or spouse abuse is suspected.

In a survey of 1,000 veterinarians in the United Kingdom, Munro and Thrusfield (2001a, 2001b, 2001c, 2001d) reported that 91.3% of respondents acknowledged NAI, and 48.3% had either suspected or seen NAI in their practices (see Appendix for a copy of the survey). Of 448 reported cases of NAI, 6% were sexual in nature and nine suspected cases of fabricated or induced illness (FII) (synonyms: factitious induced illness and Munchausen syndrome by proxy) were reported.

In replicating the Munro and Thrusfield study, the Colorado Veterinary Medical Association reported that 100% of 214 veterinarians responding to a survey acknowledged the existence of NAI and 61.7% had seen cases of NAI in pets in their practice (American Humane, 2003).

In a survey of 300 Canadian practitioners, Kovacs, Adams, and Carioto (2004) reported 50% of respondents had seen one to five cases of unintentional maltreatment in the past year, and 46% had seen one to five cases of intentional animal maltreatment in the past year. Only 10% of respondents had never seen a case of intentional animal maltreatment. About 90% agreed that part of the veterinarian's job is to respond to animal maltreatment and that learning how to recognize and report it should be part of the curriculum. About 70% felt competent to report suspicions to authorities, but only 50% felt qualified to discuss their suspicions with clients. Fewer than 17% felt that reporting unintentional animal maltreatment should be mandatory, but more than 80% felt that reporting intentional animal maltreatment should be mandatory.

Similarly, an Australian study by Peter Green reported that 185 participating veterinarians divided abuse into two categories: deliberate harm and acts of omission. The average rate of suspected abuse seen in Australian veterinary practices was 0.12%. In 5.8% of cases where animal abuse was suspected, human abuse was known to occur, and in a further 17.8% of cases of suspected animal abuse, human abuse was suspected. In 53.8% of cases of known or suspected human abuse the target was a spouse; in 15.4% of cases it was a child. When asked if veterinarians have a moral responsibility to intervene where they suspect animal abuse, 96.1% answered yes (Sherley, 2004).

Challenges Facing the Veterinary Profession

The Lack of Consistent Systems

The child protection field's 40-year history of protective systems has been enabled in part by statutory language that includes specific definitions of physical, sexual, and emotional child abuse and child neglect.

By contrast, animal anti-cruelty statutes, which trace their ancestry to century-old provisions to protect draft horses, are vague, archaic, and offer minimal protection for animals and little deterrent effect (Lacroix & Wilson, 1998). It was not until 2003, for example, that New York State enacted legislation requiring animals to have adequate shelter.

Although more than 43 states in recent years have made some forms of serious or intentional animal abuse felonies, anti-cruelty laws vary widely from state to state. Prosecutors are generally willing to prosecute only the most egregious animal cruelty cases due to real or perceived limited resources, inexperienced staff, incomplete investigations, pressure from the community to focus on other crimes, and bias against taking animal abuse seriously as a violent crime (Frasch, Otto, Olsen, & Ernest, 1999; Tannenbaum, 1995).

Animal protection laws are enforced haphazardly by municipal and nonprofit agencies with no national coordinating authority. Municipal animal control and law enforcement agencies have varying levels of interest in cruelty enforcement, and nonprofit humane societies and SPCAs often lack enforcement powers (Frasch et al., 1999; LaCroix, 1999). This is in stark contrast to the system of child protection, which has model legislation, federal funding, federally collected statistics, and 50 state agencies that supervise over 3,100 county child protective services departments.

Attempts to replicate elements of the child protection paradigm in animal protection have been sporadic. The term "battered dogs" apparently first entered print in a 1983 article in *Dog World* magazine by dog writer and trainer Job Michael Evans (1983). The term "battered pets" entered the professional literature in 1996 (Munro, 1996) and Munro and Thrusfield went on to describe non-accidental injury in animals as "Battered Pet Syndrome" in 2002. Diagnostic manuals similar to those in child protection that depict stereotypical NAI consistent with child abuse have not been developed for the animal protection field, although standardized body condition scoring assessments are used by equine welfare investigators in the United States, Canada, United Kingdom, Australia, and elsewhere to objectively evaluate a horse's welfare (Carroll & Huntington, 1988; Henneke, 1995; Kohnke, 1992). Patronek (1998) devised the comparable Tufts Animal Care and Condition scales to numerically evaluate dogs' and cats' body conditions and environmental risks to give cruelty investigators objective means of determining threats to animals. Diagnostic and treatment guidelines such as those used by child protection agencies (e.g., American Medical Association,

1992) have not been replicated in animal protection in the United States. Only a handful of guides (e.g., Arkow, 2003a; Humane Society of the U.S., 2003; Maxwell & O'Rourke, 2000; Olson, 1998) have provided competency-based training for professionals to recognize animal abuse and its links with child abuse, domestic violence, and elder abuse. However, diagnostic guidelines for non-accidental injury were described by Munro & Thrusfield (2002) and further refined in a recent publication (Thrusfield & Munro, 2007). In addition, a number of texts, published in the last three years (Merck, 2007; Cooper & Cooper, 2007; Sinclair, Merck, & Lockwood, 2006; Miller & Zawistowski, 2004), may provide guidance for practitioners presented with suspected animal maltreatment of all types.

Reluctance Within the Profession

There is growing awareness that veterinarians' attentiveness to possible animal abuse, domestic violence, and child abuse may improve the well-being of the patient and of others in the household (Arkow, 1992, 1994). However, such involvement presents troubling ethical, legal, economic, and personal challenges to practitioners. The ethical dilemma was articulated by Rollin (1988): Is the veterinarian's primary obligation to the animal (patient) or to the owner (client)?

The experiences of human medical professionals and their efforts to acknowledge and respond to Battered Child Syndrome and domestic violence parallel the challenges faced by veterinarians today. For example, many physicians fail to respond adequately to reports of domestic violence battering for several reasons:

- Physicians' close identification with their patients precludes them from considering the possibility of domestic violence in their differential diagnosis;
- Fear of offending patients by discussing areas culturally defined as private or by violating the physician/patient relationship;
- A sense of powerlessness and inadequacy in identifying appropriate interventions;
- Frustration that the ultimate outcome is outside their hands and that unless the client is motivated to change, medical attempts at intervention are useless; and
- The overwhelming roles asked of a professional complicated by the time constraints of

a busy practice, particularly if incidents are of such a low prevalence in a patient population that pursuit is not seen as a good investment of time. (Sugg & Inui, 1992)

In response to these concerns, Dr. Carol Warshaw said:

Time is a real factor, but when we compare the time it would take to ask about abuse and make appropriate referrals with the time spent on repeated visits, multiple workups, and treating the long-term sequelae of unrecognized abuse, not having time loses its validity as a reason not to intervene....In an area where competence and mastery are highly valued, it's difficult to risk venturing into subjects that make us feel less confident. We often find it easier to focus on problems we know we can solve. Feelings of discomfort can be overcome the same way we overcome feelings of discomfort when asking a patient about his or her sexual history—by understanding that these questions are legitimate and important. (Skolnick, 1995)

Similarly, physicians may fail to report suspected child abuse due to:

- Inadequate training to diagnose the problem
- Risk of alienating or stigmatizing the family
- Lack of confidence that local officials will respond adequately
- Unwillingness to experience personal, legal, and financial risks
- Discomfort with being a "policeman" or in interviewing hostile clients
- Inconsistent definitions of child abuse (Morris, Johnson, & Clasen, 1985)

The Lack of Adequate Training

Even in the human medicine field, training is notoriously lax in equipping clinicians to deal with the complex dynamics of abuse cases and attendant painful social and personal issues (Chiodo, Tilden, Limandri, & Schmidt, 1994; Skolnick, 1995; Sugg & Inui, 1992). "As dentists, we're very well trained to identify and treat caries or an abscess, but child abuse is more nebulous," said a New Jersey state dental official (Mark, 1994). The dearth of time spent in medical school studying child abuse and neglect encourages the notion that child abuse is of marginal importance (Vulliamy & Sullivan, 2000).

The amount of professional education dedicated to addressing family violence has increased in recent years. Dentists and dental hygienists who graduated since 1980 have had more exposure to elder abuse and child abuse education than those who graduated in earlier years. However, dentists and dental hygienists also widely agreed that their training was inadequate to help them determine whether a patient had been abused. If physical indicators are equivocal, dental health care workers express a lack of confidence in their abilities to engage in this type of sensitive dialogue and to define the suspected situation (Chiodo et al., 1994).

Similarly, veterinary practitioners who graduated more than 15 years ago agree that they were not formally trained to recognize and address the issue of violence. "My four years of veterinary school and four years of residency had not prepared me for the story my client was about to tell," wrote Dr. Sharon Fooshee (1998), describing a cat that had been doused with rubbing alcohol, thrown into a fireplace, set on fire with a cigarette lighter, and then had its leg broken and rectum slit with a knife. Previously, the cat had been dunked in a sink and set outdoors in winter to freeze to the pavement. The cat's sister was also thrown out a window and fell three stories to a parking lot.

Numerous authorities have recommended that veterinary school curricula include additional training on the subject of abuse. Dr. Patty Olson noted that forensic pathology and toxicology screening are not as advanced in the veterinary field as they are in human medicine, making detection of poisons— "a huge cause of animal suffering"—a challenge. "We are a long way from where we need to be," she said (Reisman & Adams, 1996).

Landau (1999) described the extent of veterinary training in a 1997 survey of the deans of all 31 veterinary colleges in North America. The survey achieved a 100% response rate. She reported that 97% of schools strongly agreed or agreed that veterinarians will encounter severe animal abuse during their careers; 75% of schools addressed the topic of recognizing and reporting animal abuse; 31% had a hospital policy for reporting suspected severe abuse; and 17% made their students aware of that policy. Also, 63% of schools strongly agreed or agreed that veterinarians will encounter human abuse, but only 21% addressed the recognition and reporting of severe human abuse. Only two schools at the time had a hospital policy for reporting suspected severe human abuse, and both schools made their students aware of this policy.

This training, however, was constrained by the exigencies of the curriculum. Each student received, on average, only 76 minutes of training on animal abuse and 8 minutes on client abuse.

The extent of abuse training in veterinary schools currently is not clear, but a number of veterinary colleges include abuse issues in ethics classes. Several veterinary teaching hospitals have instituted policies for reporting suspected abuse in client animals (Ontario Veterinary College, 2003; Veterinary Hospital of the University of Pennsylvania, 1998).

There appears to be support for more training. A survey of veterinarians in Massachusetts (Donley, Patronek, & Luke, 1999) reported that 76.4% of veterinarians expressed concern about being inadequately trained to distinguish between suboptimal care and legal neglect; 70% indicated that published criteria would make them more likely to report suspicions of a "battered pet." Over 84% believed that training about recognizing and reporting animal abuse should be part of veterinary education.

Veterinarians are not alone in noting the absence of formal training regimens: Many professions mandated to report suspected child abuse and neglect have also experienced this constraint. Numerous professionals admitted that during their careers they failed to report suspected maltreatment to appropriate authorities because they lacked training about legal obligations and reporting procedures (National Clearinghouse on Child Abuse and Neglect Information, 1999).

Dental educators have observed that increasing the content of family violence training in curricula alone will not serve the needs of health care workers. Rather, curriculum and continuing education must approach abuse holistically in collaboration with other health care and community workers (Chiodo et al., 1994). The most effective training can come not from books and videos, but rather from professional dental associations on the state and district level (Mark, 1994).

Fear of Litigation

Jack (2000) has described the role of the veterinarian as evolving to that of a "health care professional." This new role will likely lead to greater public accountability and to increased liability exposure when society's expectations are not met.

In a litigious society, veterinarians are concerned about the legal implications of reporting family violence, as physicians were during the early years of implementing child abuse reporting procedures. The American Academy of Pediatrics (1966) reported that although physicians were fearful of legal action and patient criticism, mandated reporting laws would reduce or remove parents' resentment against reporters. Physicians were advised to consult with other professionals so a report would come from a group rather than from an individual; this would result in more accurate diagnoses and help to defuse legal action. King (1998) wrote that veterinarians can similarly defuse retaliatory actions by obtaining consultation support from state diagnostic laboratories, radiologists, and other professionals.

Dental professionals have been hesitant to intervene in abuse cases because they fear subsequent litigation and because they want to ensure that more good than harm will come from the intervention (Chiodo et al., 1994).

Veterinarians have voiced concerns regarding possible civil and criminal exposure should they make a false report, a good-faith report that proves to be unfounded, or fail to make a report as prescribed by law. The experiences of the child protection field may prove helpful.

Similar to laws requiring the reporting of certain infectious diseases, interests of public safety can override physician–patient rights of confidentiality, thereby removing one source of potential litigation. To encourage reporting, all states provide mandated child abuse reporters with immunity from liability. This immunity may be absolute (in effect even when reports are made negligently or fraudulently) or qualified (protects those who report in good faith even when no abuse or neglect is revealed). However, immunity provisions cannot prevent a costly lawsuit from being filed (American Medical Association, 1992). Many states and provinces today offer veterinarians absolute or qualified immunity for reporting suspected animal abuse (Patronek, 1998).

Of greater concern to mandatory reporters are provisions that expose them to civil lawsuits for failure to report suspected child abuse. The financial liability for further injury of a child whose maltreatment should have been detected and prevented by a timely report can be quite extensive. At least six states statutorily prescribe civil liability for failure to report (National Clearinghouse on Child Abuse and Neglect Information, 1999). Prosecutions for failure to report, however, have been rare. Whether failure-to-report sanctions would be enacted regarding the reporting of abuse of animals—which are considered property without legal standing—remains undetermined.

In the domestic violence field, a woman or her family may seek legal action against a person who reports her to be a victim, or who fails to identify and intervene, especially if she suffers injury or death. Physicians are encouraged to routinely screen all women for domestic violence, to maintain good liability coverage, and to work with their state medical association's legal department to reduce this risk (Salber & Taliaferro, 1995).

Veterinarians can reduce exposure by maintaining liability insurance and signing "hold harmless" agreements with government and nonprofit agencies (King, 1998). Maintaining comprehensive medical records—including health assessment, medical history, statements made, observed behaviors, detailed description of injuries, an opinion as to whether injuries are adequately explained, results of laboratory tests and diagnostic procedures, and photographs and imaging studies—may reduce the exposure to liability.

Fear of Adverse Economic Impact

The possible erosion of the client base is a concern that has been voiced by veterinarians. Again, the experiences of human medicine may resolve this concern. There is no conclusive evidence that physicians have suffered significant economic adversity from being part of the mandated reporter system. In one series of interviews with 58 pediatricians and family physicians in Ohio, four respondents who had reported cases of child abuse were surprised to find that many families whom they reported continued to visit their offices for medical care. Only 3% of respondents believed that "some" physicians were concerned about being sued by families for reporting a suspicion (Morris et al., 1985).

A national survey of 907 psychotherapists reported that the breach of confidentiality consequent to reporting suspected child maltreatment did not inevitably collapse the therapeutic relationship. Although 25% of clients were reported to discontinue treatment as a result of mandated reports, most were retained and many overcame initial negative reactions. Further, most of the therapists who filed reports believed that their actions resulted in a cessation of the abuse (Steinberg, Levine, & Doueck, 1997).

Economic concerns cannot override the mandate to report suspected abuse because this can endanger the child. By citing the necessity to report as specified by statute, physicians may more easily explain their actions to parents (American Medical Association, 1992). This strategy would appear to apply to veterinarians as well.

The Perception That No Action Will Be Taken

A perception among pediatricians and psychotherapists is that mandated reports will not be acted upon by overworked, underfunded child protection officials. Physicians are unlikely to report suspected child abuse if they lack confidence in the CPS agency, cannot predict a favorable outcome, or do not receive feedback after they have made their report (Steinberg et al., 1997; Vulliamy & Sullivan, 2000).

A significant number of child protection reports are not investigated and many are dismissed when reports cannot be substantiated. The CPS agency may elect to pursue referrals to community resources or educational strategies rather than prosecutorial interventions as the most appropriate intervention (Chiodo et al., 1994).

The veterinary field has followed this line of reasoning, although whether the practitioner should pursue a client educational strategy rather than referring an incident for possible prosecution is still undetermined. In the absence of mandates requiring veterinarians to report suspected abuse, professional codes of ethics in several countries have taken several varying positions.

The newest such code is in Canada, where in 2005 the Canadian Veterinary Medical Association (CVMA) adopted a new strategic approach to the issue of animal abuse. An earlier position statement declared that in situations of animal abuse that cannot be resolved through education, it is the veterinarian's responsibility to report such observations to the appropriate authorities (Arkow, 2003b). The CVMA's new position statement declares that "veterinarians have a moral obligation to report suspected cases"; in return, "society has an obligation to support those veterinarians who report in good faith using their professional judgment." CVMA recognizes that moral obligation is not legal obligation, and legal obligation and questions regarding immunity are the jurisdiction of Canadian provinces. The CVMA encourages provincial veterinary associations "to lobby their provincial governments to develop legislation to make mandatory the reporting of animal abuse by veterinarians and to provide immunity to those who do so using their professional judgment and in good faith. Other health professionals who are required to report suspected abuse cases have such protection. Veterinarians deserve similar immunity," says the CVMA. The CVMA further encourages veterinary schools to discuss animal abuse and reporting so that graduating veterinarians are better able to recognize the signs of abuse and know the appropriate steps in documenting and reporting it (Canadian Veterinary Medical Association, 2005).

New Zealand's Code of Professional Conduct for Veterinarians (Veterinary Council of New Zealand, 2004), enacted in 1998, notes that veterinarians have "a special responsibility for animal welfare." A veterinarian who becomes aware of an animal "suffering unreasonable or unnecessary pain or distress must take action to ensure that the matter is effectively dealt with." This action may include conducting a thorough examination of all mitigating circumstances in the case, and offering professional advice. If the situation still shows no sign of being remedied and the animal is still suffering unreasonable or unnecessary pain or distress, the New Zealand veterinarian must report the case to an inspector under the Animal Welfare Act.

The Royal College of Veterinary Surgeons in the United Kingdom issued guidelines in 2003 (Veterinary Record, 2003), which encourage veterinarians to include NAI in the differential diagnosis. If the examination of the animal leads to a suspicion of abuse, the veterinarian should first attempt to discuss his or her concerns with the client; "in cases where this would not be appropriate or where the client's reaction increases rather than allays concerns," the veterinarian should contact the relevant authorities.

The American Veterinary Medical Association's guidelines, first issued in 1995, were amended in 1999 to read that when "animal abuse or neglect as defined by federal or state laws or local ordinances" cannot be resolved through client education, AVMA considers it the responsibility of the veterinarian to report such cases to appropriate authorities to protect the welfare of animals and people (American Veterinary Medical Association, 1999a).

The Conscientious and Caring Veterinary Personality

It is common for veterinarians to feel that responsibility falls on them to "prove" a case of abuse. Nevertheless, it is important for them to accept that this is not their remit, which is confined to evidence on veterinary matters. All case investigations, it should be remembered, are multidisciplinary (see page 393 for chapter by Boat, Loar, and Phillips), involving a variety of groups: for example, animal welfare organizations, police, and legal personnel. There may also be actual witnesses of the abuse. In those cases that do reach the courts, the final decision remains—correctly—a legal one. Some veterinarians are relieved to realize that their evidence is only part of the case—albeit an important one—because it goes some way to assuage these feelings of professional responsibility, which can be very deep.

In addition, the caring personality of the veterinarian may lead to concerns that there are extenuating circumstances with regard to the *people* who have been accused of animal abuse. Again, it should be remembered that the veterinarian's duty is to the animal, not to the person, and that others should be left to take responsibility in such matters. The case may well have aspects of which the veterinarian is unaware, and is certainly not competent to judge.

Inadequate Definitions

Veterinarians are challenged by conflicting professional, personal, public, and legal standards. Ascione (1993) defined cruelty to animals as "socially unacceptable behavior that intentionally causes unnecessary pain, suffering, or distress to and/or death of an animal," but the child protection field does not require *intent* as a criterion to prove that maltreatment occurred (English, 1998). One veterinary dictionary (Blood & Studdert, 1999) defines cruelty as "the infliction of pain or distress unnecessarily," astutely observing that "the definition of unnecessary varies between countries and from time to time in one country. Determination of the prevailing standard of cruelty can only be decided by the courts."

It can be noted that, in Great Britain, it is irrelevant whether or not there is *intention* to cause suffering, because *lack of intent* is not a defense under animal welfare laws. There is therefore no necessity to sub-define abuse as "intentional" or "non-intentional." It is up to the court to judge whether the actions of the accused have been those of a "reasonable person" in the particular circumstances of the case (Radford, 2001).

The new Canadian veterinary position statement defines animal abuse as "the active maltreatment or passive neglect of animals and staged animal fighting. Animal hoarding is neglect on a large scale" (Canadian Veterinary Medical Association, 2005).

In 1974, the U.S. Congress passed Public Law 93–247, the Child Abuse Prevention and Treatment Act (CAPTA), to provide a national definition of child abuse and neglect and prescribe actions states should take to protect children. This law established a broad definition of maltreatment as "the physical and mental injury, sexual abuse, neglected treatment or maltreatment of a child under age 18 by a person who is responsible for the child's welfare under circumstances which indicate the child's health and welfare is harmed and threatened thereby, as determined in accordance with regulations prescribed by the Secretary of Health, Education, and Welfare." CAPTA sets minimum standards, but the details of defining physical abuse, sexual abuse, emotional abuse, and neglect falls to the states, and specific definitions vary considerably (English, 1998).

While each state has its own definitions, there appears to be more statutory consistency in child protection than in animal protection, and, as suggested by Munro and Thrusfield (2001a), child protection terminology can serve as a model for the animal protection field. In any event, legal definitions of animal maltreatment may conflict with public perceptions, and enforcement and judicial interpretation in any incident are also dependent upon case law, common sense, sound judgment, local policy, and previous experience (Arkow, 2003a).

Confidentiality Concerns

Like physicians, veterinarians have concerns about client confidentiality. Courts in some states have explicitly refused to recognize a veterinarian–client privilege; other states allow it, either in veterinary practice acts, administrative rules, or statutes affecting a variety of health professionals. There are circumstances where confidentiality requirements are explicitly waived to protect the health and welfare of the individual, the animals, or others who may be endangered (Patronek, 1998).

Some textbooks on veterinary ethics emphasize that clients are not just consumers but animal owners who entrust to the veterinarian property in which they may invest significant emotional importance.

Ethical concerns regarding confidentiality are often described more in terms of the veterinarian's responsibility to inform the client of maltreatment that occurred to animals under care, rather than the practitioner's obligation to discuss clients' maltreatment of animals (Tannenbaum, 1995).

Confidentiality is a challenge for numerous professions. For example, child protection caseworkers who observe animal abuse are restricted by state laws from revealing the names of their clients to animal welfare officials, who, in turn, are reluctant to pursue a report made anonymously. The veterinary profession may be ahead of the curve in this area, as national veterinary associations in the United States, Canada, and the United Kingdom waive doctor–client confidentiality when public health and safety are jeopardized.

The most explicit such protocol is the United Kingdom's Royal College of Veterinary Surgeons Guide to Professional Conduct (RCVS, 2007). This declares that "the public interest in protecting an animal overrides the professional obligation to maintain client confidentiality" (Veterinary Record, 2003). British veterinarians are advised to discuss their concerns with clients, to consider whether child abuse or domestic violence might be present (with or without the presence of animal abuse), and to consider reporting their concerns to appropriate animal protection, child protection, or law enforcement authorities.

While the American Veterinary Medical Association's (1999a) Animal Welfare Position Statement does not specifically mention confidentiality, it does say that "disclosure may be necessary to protect the health and welfare of animals and people." AVMA's Principles of Veterinary Medical Ethics (1999b) further declares that while veterinarians and their associates should protect the personal privacy of patients and clients, they "should report illegal practices and activities to the proper authorities" and "should not reveal confidences unless required to by law or unless it becomes necessary to protect the health and welfare of other individuals or animals."

Mary Beth Leininger, past president of the AVMA, said:

> Confidentiality holds for personal privacy of clients unless the veterinarian is required to reveal the confidences of a medical record because of the health or welfare of either the

person or animal. As an organization and as a group of professionals, we feel an obligation to safeguard the health and well-being of not only the animals we care for, but of the need to care for society, as well. (King, 1998)

There May Be Gender Bias Within the Profession

Gender- and age-based biases against reporting suspected family violence have been described in the human medicine literature. Younger physicians are more willing to report suspected child abuse than older physicians, perhaps because of inclusion of child abuse training into medical schools and residency programs in recent years (Morris et al., 1985).

Similarly, there may be more interest in this subject among younger veterinarians, an increasing percentage of whom are female. Currently, 55% of AVMA's members are male and 45% are female; among the student AVMA membership, the ratio is 30% male to 70% female (A. J. Shepherd, personal communication, October 24, 2003).

Chiodo et al. (1994), in a survey of Oregon dental health care workers, reported that the possibility of gender bias must be considered in a profession in which 92% of responding dentists were male and 99.2% of responding dental hygienists were female. While both dentists and hygienists listed reporting as a relatively remote choice for intervention, dental hygienists were earlier identified as having a significant role in being aware of possible family violence, recognizing trauma, documenting injuries, providing follow-up care, and mandatory reporting (ten Bensel, King, & Bastein, 1977). This may have implications in the veterinary field, in which the veterinary assistant and technician populations are predominantly female.

Sugg and Inui (1992) reported that many male physicians were reluctant to broach the subject of domestic violence for fear of being viewed as betraying the patient's trust, but no female physicians surveyed believed that discussing domestic violence with female patients would jeopardize the physician–patient relationship.

An informal survey of veterinarians at several conferences by C. A. Lacroix (personal communication, 2000) found that both male and female veterinarians were willing to display information about domestic violence in their clinics and wanted more information about animal abuse and family violence. The ratio of females to males responding to the survey was 2:1, and it cannot be determined whether this suggests that females were more likely than males to respond to the questionnaire, or were overrepresented as participants in the workshops.

The Need for Consistent Terminology

As noted earlier in this chapter, there is an unfortunate lack of accepted standard terminology with regard to what exactly is meant by "animal abuse," "animal cruelty," or "animal maltreatment." This causes difficulties—not only for veterinarians, but also for other bodies of people, such those working in animal welfare societies or in legal circles. Compounding this lack of clear terminology is the inescapable fact that human society maintains several animal groups for differing purposes. For example, humans rear, kill, and eat farmed animals, and laboratory animals are used to test products for human (and animal) use. However, acceptable animal husbandry standards common in these industrial uses may not be acceptable to a companion animal. It is therefore an unavoidable fact that what is generally accepted as tolerable in the treatment of one group of animals might well be regarded as "cruel" or "abusive" in another group. This muddies the water even further, the result being much debate on definitions (Rowan, 1993; Vermeulen & Odendaal, 1993).

Nevertheless, for companion animals, adopting the tried and tested terminology developed by the medical profession for children can solve the problem very easily. (And it can also be used in appropriate cases in non-companion animals.) This terminology, which is accepted and used worldwide, has two considerable advantages:

- First, in a subject area that crosses both animal and human boundaries, it achieves a common language between veterinarians and other health professionals;
- Second, it promotes consensus on *consistent* terminology—an important factor in avoiding confusion, particularly where research is involved.

Using this terminology, there are four basic types of abuse, any of which may co-exist:

1. Physical abuse

- *Synonyms*: non-accidental injury (NAI), Battered-Child Syndrome, Battered-Pet Syndrome.

- Includes physical actions such as beating, punching, kicking, shaking, burning, throwing (e.g., against walls, downstairs, out of windows, etc.). A weapon, such as a hammer or baseball bat, may be used. Physical abuse also includes the administration of drugs or poisons, and gunshot wounds.

2. Sexual abuse

- Any use of an animal or child for sexual gratification.
- This term is preferable to "bestiality" or "zoophilia" because each of these terms focuses primarily on the perpetrator. Sexual abuse conveys the sense of the physical harm that may occur to the animal.

3. Emotional abuse

- For example, habitual verbal harassment by threats and/or threatening behavior.
- Although some people put forward the view that animals do not possess "emotions," this is at variance with modern thought (Webster, 2005).

4. Neglect

- Failure to provide the basic physical and/or emotional necessities of life, for example, food, water, shelter, medical or veterinary attention, companionship, and affection. Abandonment of an animal is therefore an obvious example of neglect. Leaving a collar to tighten and constrict the neck of a growing puppy is another.

In the more than 45 years since courageous Dr. Kempe and his colleagues published their groundbreaking "Battered-Child Syndrome" paper, a substantial body of knowledge has grown up on all four types of child abuse, and continues to develop. The veterinary profession can make use of this knowledge because it provides a significant head start on how to approach the same subject in animals. The circumstances, the acts involved, the excuses offered, and the resulting injuries are remarkably similar, be the victim animal or child. This is quite simply because there is a common denominator—the human perpetrator.

This common denominator is neatly illustrated by examination of the explanations presented by clients to account for animals' injuries, because the excuses

> **Case example 1**
> A young adult springer spaniel was presented with fractured ribs, bruising of the eyes, and bleeding from the mouth. The owner stated that the dog had "*fallen downstairs*." The veterinarian considered that the injuries were too severe to be explained by this story, and confronted the owner, who then admitted violence. The dog was euthanized because of the injuries.

> **Case example 2**
> A dog over 2 years of age died of injuries which the owner said had been caused by "*falling downstairs.*" The dog had suffered massive axillary haemorrhage, rib fractures, and haemothorax.

offered are strikingly similar for pets and children. For example, pediatric texts consistently record that a history of a "fall" is commonly offered to explain the injuries in cases of NAI in babies and small children (Hobbs, Hanks, & Wynne, 1999a). A similar excuse may be offered to explain an injury in a pet.

Physical Abuse: Diagnostic Pointers to a Non-Accidental Injury

The term non-accidental injury may at first seem strange, but it simply means an injury that has been inflicted deliberately. However, a non-accidental injury in a *child* is generally understood to mean an injury inflicted by a parent, a member of the child's family, or a person looking after the child. In a *pet*, the perpetrator may live in the pet's home, but unlike small children, the pet may be allowed to roam freely, so the perpetrator may be outside the family group.

There are no definite rules for diagnosis of non-accidental injury, but there are pointers that raise suspicion. These are sometimes also referred to as "diagnostic features" or "diagnostic guidelines."

It must be emphasized that none of the following pointers is diagnostic per se. It is a combination that raises suspicion and, as case examples will illustrate, this combination is variable. (This is the same as in child physical abuse.)

Aspects in the History

- The history is inconsistent with the injuries (i.e., the injury does not "fit" the history—usually, the injuries are too severe to be explained by the history supplied)
- The history is discrepant (i.e. changes in the telling, or from person to person)
- A previous injury or death has occurred in another animal in the same household, or

belonging to the same owner, particularly when the incident is unexplained
- No explanation is offered for the injury
- Lack of motor vehicle accident (MVA) or any other possible accident
- Family violence is known or suspected

Implication of a Particular Person as the Perpetrator

- Owner may actually admit injuring the animal himself or herself
- Owner may name husband/boyfriend/partner/child as the culprit
- Owner may state the injuries are due to NAI but refuses to give a name
- Lodger/neighbor/stranger may be blamed

Type of Injury

- Repetitive injury is highly suspicious
- Certain injuries may cause suspicion because they are unusual, or because they do not "fit" with the owner's explanation

The Behavior of the Owner Arouses Concern

- May be aggressive on questioning
- May show a lack of concern for the pet
- May behave oddly

The Behavior of the Animal Arouses Concern

- May be frightened of owner
- May be happier when separated from the owner (e.g. when hospitalized)

Case example 3
Inconsistent history
A Yorkshire terrier was taken to the veterinarian with extensive, severe burns to the chest and abdomen. The explanation given was that "the dog sat too close to the radiator." The veterinarian was not the owner's usual veterinarian and the consultation was out of hours.

Case example 4
Repetitive injury
A cat was presented with abdominal muscle rupture. The veterinarian assumed the injury was caused by a motor vehicle accident. Ten days later the cat was brought back with a severe pelvic injury, but this time the veterinarian was surprised to find out that the cat never went outside. No explanation was forthcoming to explain either injury, and the cat was presented to a different veterinarian's office two weeks later, with a fractured femur.

Risk Factors for NAI in a Pet

In addition to the features that raise suspicion of NAI, certain risk factors should also be taken into account.

Domestic Abuse

Until relatively recently, the relevant groups dealing with child abuse and domestic violence (which is generally taken to mean violence against women) were compartmentalized, with little or no sharing of knowledge and information. For example, it would have been most unlikely that a pediatrician, presented with a suspected case of NAI in a child, would have considered whether or not the mother lived in a violent relationship. However, it is now universally acknowledged that domestic violence is a high-risk factor for NAI in children, and it is perfectly clear that such violence is a risk factor for the family pets also (Munro & Thrusfield, 2001a).

Case example 5
An adult domestic shorthaired cat with head and eye injuries was taken to the veterinarian. The female owner stated that her partner had been abusive to the cat and also to herself.

Case example 6
A small mixed breed dog was presented with a fractured tibia. The owner's ex-partner, who had a history of violence toward the owner, had thrown the dog against the wall.

Other Owner-Associated Risk Factors

Factors such as alcoholism, drug abuse, and mental illness are important.

Age, Gender, and Breed of Animal

Male dogs under the age of two years, and all cats of this age, are particularly at risk (Munro & Thrusfield, 2001b).

Crossbred dogs and domestic shorthaired cats have been shown to be at increased risk in the United Kingdom, as have Staffordshire bull terriers. A possible explanation for the latter is that in the United Kingdom Staffordshire owners of a pugnacious disposition may especially favor bull terriers.

Animals with Disabilities

It is recognized that children with disabilities are vulnerable to abuse (Hobbs, Hanks, & Wynne,

1999b), and it is quite possible that animals with a disability may similarly be disadvantaged. One has only to think of undiagnosed deafness in, for example, a Dalmatian puppy, to realize what might result when a controlling owner, frustrated by the puppy's apparent misbehavior, loses his temper.

Socio-Economic Group of the Owner

It would seem plain common sense that the risk of animal abuse (using the term in its widest sense, and therefore including *neglect*) is higher in areas of social deprivation and poverty. However, it can be found in all social groups, including those of affluence. People who are better off are also usually more articulate, enabling them to avoid detection more easily.

Animal Sexual Abuse

The term "animal sexual abuse" derives from the modern term "child sexual abuse," and is preferable to "bestiality" or "zoophilia," both of which focus on the human perpetrator without conveying any sense of the physical harm that may happen to the animal (see page 201 for chapter by Beetz). It is the very fact that the physical actions center on the sexual organs, and/or the anus and rectum, which distinguishes the abuse as sexual in nature. As in children (and adults), both sexes may be abused.

For many people, animal sexual abuse is deeply embarrassing, and indeed some regard the activity almost as a last taboo. Even veterinarians can find the subject difficult, which may go some way to explain the apparent absence of descriptions of sexual abuse injury in textbooks on veterinary gynecology.

However, it needs to be accepted that sexual abuse of animals does occur, that physical injury to both

---

Case example 7
An adult female border collie with vaginal injuries was presented for examination. The owner had found her husband having sex with the dog.

Case example 8
A young male domestic shorthaired cat was taken by his owner for examination. Four equidistant radial splits, consistent with the insertion of a large object, were present in the cat's anus. Suspicion was aroused because the lesions were considered inexplicable, and it also was noted that the owner was angry when questioned.

---

sexes may result, and that the injuries—depending on the actual type of sexual act (the spectrum is wide) and the size of the animal—can be very severe (Munro & Thrusfield, 2001c).

Fabricated or Induced Illness (FII)

Currently, this is the latest term that has been adopted for an uncommon form of abuse that by convention has been given a separate chapter in pediatric texts. It has also been called *factitious illness by proxy* and *Munchausen syndrome by proxy*.

In pediatric terms, this type of abuse involves the falsification of illness in a child. The perpetrator is usually the child's mother, and the motive is to gain the sympathy and attention that surround the child's illness. The symptoms may be very varied, and laboratory tests contradictory and confusing. The person presenting the child for treatment may be very plausible and manipulative, making case detection and management extremely difficult.

In the veterinary context, it is the owner who fabricates, or induces, injury in an animal. Feldman (1997) described a case in which an owner eventually admitted that she had starved her dog, and fabricated signs, to gain the concern of others for herself. Repetitive injury is sometimes employed, and the prognosis may be poor if the animal remains with the owner (Munro & Thrusfield, 2001d).

Differential Diagnosis of NAI

Naturally Occurring Conditions

Investigation of a suspected case should include standard checks (e.g., radiography, hematology) for naturally occurring conditions, such as skeletal disorders (e.g., metabolic bone disease) and blood clotting factor deficiencies. (However, it should be remembered that the fact that an animal has a naturally occurring condition does not *exclude* the animal from abuse.)

Motor Vehicle Accidents (MVAs)

MVAs may be a cause for concern for veterinarians when considering the differentiation of injuries caused in such accidents and those associated with NAI. This is an area where more research is urgently needed, but at the present time several factors can be considered.

On clinical examination, the claws of an animal that has been hit by a vehicle are often "tattered,"

Case example 9

A litter of baby ferrets was found abandoned in a wood. The animals were in extreme pain, and each had multiple limb fractures. NAI was considered in the differential diagnosis, but X-ray examination revealed that the fractures were caused by severe nutritional bone disease. The owner was traced, given a formal warning on neglect (lack of veterinary treatment and abandonment), and advice on correct nutrition of other ferrets.

Case example 10

An adult dog was presented with bilateral subconjunctival haemorrhages. There was no history of an MVA and lab tests for bleeding disorders were negative. The couple's other dog had died under unexplained circumstances one month before. The owner admitted her boyfriend had shaken her dog.

---

there may be dirt in the hair coat, and there may be skin abrasions.

With regard to fractures—common both in MVAs and NAI—Kolata and Johnson (1975) demonstrated that the greatest number of skeletal injuries in dogs involved in an MVA occurred in the body backward from the last rib (i.e., the hind part), with the pelvic bones being the most frequently affected. Munro and Thrusfield (2001b) accordingly suggested that a pelvic fracture in the dog is more likely to indicate MVA, but pointed out that this should be considered "with other supporting evidence" (i.e., other features of NAI, such as an inconsistent history). Unfortunately, currently there are no comparative data (such as Kolata and Johnson's) available for MVAs in cats.

It is wise not to assume MVA—particularly when other features of the case may suggest otherwise—so there is a need to ascertain whether the animal is actually allowed out of the house. Many cats, for example, are housebound, making an MVA impossible. (See case example 4.)

Other Injuries

The demonstration that repetitive injuries are highly suspicious of NAI in the dog and cat (Munro & Thrusfield, 2001b) was a significant advance in veterinary knowledge, but further research on other deliberate injuries is urgently required. Here again, veterinarians can benefit from their medical colleagues, because injuries found in children demonstrate the possibilities. In the years since Kempe, many textbooks have been penned and journals established, all solely concerned with every type of child abuse. There is even a specialist textbook on diagnostic imaging of child abuse (Kleinman, 1998). As a result, information is available on the many injuries associated with NAI in children, their level of "suspicion" ("suspicious" or "highly suspicious"), and their differentiation from natural disease.

A simple example is that of cigarette burns. Few veterinarians will be aware of the detailed descriptions of these burns available in all textbooks on child abuse—including details of the (differing) patterns that permit differentiation of deliberate and accidental burns. Such descriptions are absent in veterinary texts, although it is known that cigarettes are used to inflict burns on animals.

Fractures are common in both child and animal abuse, but physicians have extensive knowledge of the fracture types that may be particularly associated with child abuse. One such fracture is the spiral fracture of the humerus. In infants, this pattern of fracture is now known to be highly associated with the forces involved when the infant is swung violently by the arm (Hobbs, Hanks, & Wynne, 1999c). A similar fracture, also associated with violent swinging, occurs in the tibia. It is quite possible that spiral limb fractures in young pets may sometimes have the same origin, but as yet this is unproven.

Developmental Factors

Milestones in a child's normal physical development are now well documented and play a part in knowing what is possible, and what is not possible, when a child's injuries are stated to be accidental. For example, a parent may claim that the reason why a 2-month-old baby has fractured limbs is because the infant "rolled away from the middle of the bed and fell onto the floor." In the past, many have believed such a story, being unaware (or unable to face up to the fact) that this was physically impossible, because the average age of attainment of an infant's ability to roll is actually 6.5 months (Behrman, Kliegman, & Jenson, 2000). Thus, the parent's explanation cannot be acceptable.

Knowledge of developmental milestones may also be helpful in the investigation of suspected NAI in animals. Turner and Bateson (2000), citing the work of Martin (1982), point out that development of the kitten's ability to right the body in mid-air while falling (the air-righting reaction) begins at four weeks of age and is complete by six weeks. Consequently, grave doubt must be expressed when, for example, severe head injuries in an eight-week-old kitten are blamed on "a fall from the top of a door." The air-righting reaction means that kittens land on their feet, making severe head injury extremely unlikely. Clearly, developmental milestones of both the dog and the cat need to be examined further as knowledge of NAI in these animals expands.

Responses to Veterinary Needs

In addition to the national animal welfare position statements and veterinary codes of ethics previously discussed, state legislative activity has begun to codify veterinary response to suspected abuse. California and Colorado require veterinarians to report suspected child abuse. Veterinarians in Alabama, Arizona, Illinois, Minnesota, West Virginia, Alberta, and Quebec are required to report suspected aggravated cruelty, animal torture, animal fighting, or dog fighting. Arizona, California, Florida, Georgia, Idaho, Maryland, Massachusetts, Michigan, New Hampshire, New Jersey, Oregon, Pennsylvania, and Rhode Island provide veterinarians with immunity from civil or criminal liability if they make reports in good faith of suspected animal cruelty.

Federal legislation has been repeatedly introduced into the Canadian Parliament that would redefine animal abuse as a crime of violence rather than a crime against property. Federal funds have been made available for interdisciplinary domestic violence prevention teams that include animal protection agencies in the United States through the Department of Justice's Office of Community Oriented Policing Services (COPS), and in Canada through the National Crime Prevention Strategy.

Research Agenda for the Future

As research and programmatic responses into what is popularly called the "Link" between animal abuse and other forms of family violence mature, and as efforts in this area begin to gain some traction, some apparent patterns for future growth and development are beginning to emerge. General public awareness of the "Link," and more detailed involvement by the various professions involved, are continuing and accelerating. The growing interest in this topic among veterinary associations is mirroring similar developments in schools of social work, the field of animal law, prosecutors, law enforcement, agencies working in mental health interventions, and other professions that work with animals and people.

Veterinarians will continue to be on the leading edge of this issue, particularly in regard to several areas that have been identified (Arkow, 2006) as trends for the near future.

1. **Development of diagnostic indicators**: As practitioners require more specific training on identifying the clinical signs of NAI, more diagnostic guidelines will be developed by veterinarians for veterinarians. Similarly, as practitioners discover needs for additional practice management skills to approach clients about suspicious cases, training materials will be made available.

2. **Animal shelters**: Animal care and control facilities that investigate and prosecute animal abuse will need reliable, institutionalized systems of reporting animal abuse data to law enforcement agencies and the courts. Veterinarians can be invaluable in helping to objectify and classify animal abuse and to provide expert witness testimony. Systems are already in place in many areas for the reporting of zoonotic public health concerns, and perhaps these can serve as models for animal abuse reporting.

3. **Animal-assisted interventions**: Much of the field of animal-assisted therapy and animal-assisted activities has shifted in recent years toward targeted interventions directed at violence-prone youth. Many dog training programs have been developed (Duel, 2004) that provide at-risk teens with opportunities to resolve conflicts nonviolently by using positive-reinforcement behavior modification to make shelter dogs more adoptable. What is unknown is the effectiveness of these programs. Veterinarians can provide valuable assistance in organizing these programs, ensuring the welfare of the animals involved, and conducting research to evaluate the long-term successes and failures of these strategic interventions.

4. **Community coalitions**: Many local groups have organized to provide inter-agency cross-training and cross-reporting protocols, linking child protection, domestic violence, animal protection, and elder abuse agencies. But few of these coalitions have achieved the critical mass, infrastructure, or institutionalization necessary for widespread

sustainability. Few coalitions seem to take advantage of the federal funding available. It is critical for the veterinary profession to be represented in these coalitions.

5. **Advocacy**: The increase in the number of states that have made some forms of serious animal abuse felonies is impressive, but there are no indications yet that these states are experiencing either a decrease in animal abuse or an increase in reporting or prosecutions. As veterinary medicine is one of several professions becoming involved in mandates to report suspected family violence, ongoing research will be needed to evaluate the efficacy of these legislative strategies.

6. **Training**: Colleges of veterinary medicine have begun to introduce training in the "Link" into the curricula; it is anticipated that law schools, schools of social work, and law enforcement training academies should be the next venues for this instruction.

Conclusion

Preventing cruelty to animals is the founding mission of the SPCA movement, and protecting animal health is the founding mission of the veterinary profession. But despite over a hundred years of dedicated work, animal abuse persists with disheartening regularity.

Our understanding of the causes of animal abuse has increased somewhat, but there is still much to be done to address these causes. As we examine the triggers involved, it is becoming increasingly clear that we cannot separate violence against companion animals from the broader issues of violence in our families and communities (RSPCA Australia, 2004). Engaging the veterinary profession in this effort is a priority.

Veterinary involvement can be many-faceted. Veterinarians can provide medical care for abused pets; assist SPCAs and humane societies with investigation, documentation, and forensics in cruelty investigations and serve as expert witnesses in prosecutions; participate in multidisciplinary response teams; train animal shelter staffs and cross-train human services officials in the intricacies of cruelty investigations; provide animal-based therapeutic opportunities for at-risk youth and convicted animal abuse offenders; and provide resource and referral information about child abuse, animal abuse, elder abuse, and domestic violence to their clients. When discussions with clients fail to resolve concerns of suspected abuse, or when such consultations increase rather than allay concerns, the veterinarian should consider referring cases of suspected abuse to appropriate authorities.

Human medicine's crossing of many of these thresholds years ago resulted in increased reporting of cases of child abuse, domestic violence, and elder abuse. The time has come for veterinary medicine to join the human medicine field in assuming public health responsibilities in the prevention of violence.

When animals are abused, people are at risk; when people are abused, animals are at risk (Arkow, 1996). Although the etiology and symptoms of family violence are not completely understood and there are no obvious solutions, family violence may be abated through a multidisciplinary approach that includes the veterinary profession.

The veterinarian is not only a public health authority, but also a type of family practitioner. As the human health care field did earlier, the veterinary profession now has the responsibility to identify and promulgate standardized diagnostic criteria and clinical and environmental indicators of NAI to animals, and to be engaged in community programs that prevent family violence.

Veterinary consideration for the protection of all family members will elevate the status of animals and of the veterinary profession, protect all family members who are at risk, make intervention strategies more effective, and set the highest standards of animal well-being. As professionals with long-standing and committed humane interests, veterinarians are well positioned to find creative approaches that abate violence and help heal animals of many species—including the human one (Lockwood, 2000).

References

American Academy of Pediatrics Committee on Infant and Pre-School Child. (1966). Maltreatment of children: The physically abused child. *Pediatrics, 37*(2), 377–382.

American Humane. (2003). *Non-accidental injury in dogs and cats in Colorado: Final report to Animal Assistance Fund.* Englewood, CO.

American Medical Association. (1992). *Diagnostic and treatment guidelines on child physical abuse and neglect.* Chicago.

American Veterinary Medical Association. (1999a). *Animal welfare position statements: Animal abuse and animal neglect.* Schaumburg, IL.

American Veterinary Medical Association. (1999b). *Principles of veterinary medical ethics of the American Veterinary Medical Association.* Schaumburg, IL.

American Veterinary Medical Association. (2002). *U.S. pet ownership & demographics sourcebook.* Schaumburg, IL.

Arkow, P. (1992). The correlations between cruelty to animals and child abuse and the implications for veterinary medicine. *Canadian Veterinary Journal, 33*, 518–521.

Arkow, P. (1994). Child abuse, animal abuse, and the veterinarian. *Journal of the American Veterinary Medical Association, 204*(7), 1004–1007.

Arkow, P. (1996). The relationships between animal abuse and other forms of family violence. *Family Violence & Sexual Assault Bulletin, 12*(1–2), 29–34.

Arkow, P. (2003a). *Breaking the cycles of violence: A guide to multi-disciplinary interventions.* Alameda, CA: Latham Foundation.

Arkow, P. (2003b). Groundbreaking legislation in Great Britain: British vets take major step forward in reporting suspected family violence. *Latham Letter, 24*(2), 12–13.

Arkow, P. (2004). The veterinarian's role in preventing family violence: The experience of the human medical profession. *Protecting Children, 19*(1), 4–12.

Arkow, P. (2006). Introduction: Making the link. In P. Carlisle-Frank & T. Flanagan (Eds.), *Silent victims: Recognizing and stopping abuse of the family pet.* Lanham, MD: Rowman & Littlefield.

Ascione, F. R. (1993). Children who are cruel to animals: A review of research and implications for developmental psychopathology. *Anthrozoös, 6*(4), 226–247.

Ascione, F. R., & Arkow, P. (Eds.). (1999). *Child abuse, domestic violence and animal abuse: Linking the circles of compassion for prevention and intervention.* West Lafayette, IN: Purdue University Press.

Behrman, R. E., Kliegman, R. M., & Jenson, H. B. (Eds.). (2000). The First Year. In *Nelson Textbook of Pediatrics* (16th ed.) (pp. 34–35). London: W.B. Saunders Co.

Blood, D. C., & Studdert, V. P. (1999). *Saunders Comprehensive Veterinary Dictionary* (2nd ed.). London: W.B. Saunders.

Canadian Veterinary Medical Association. (2005). *Online from 339: Animal Abuse: New Strategic Approach/New Position Statement,* (Issue 3). Retrieved April 10, 2005, from www.canadianveterinarians.net

Carroll, C. L., & Huntington, P. J. (1988). Body condition scoring and weight estimation of horses. *Equine Veterinary Journal, 20*(1), 41–45.

Chiodo, G. T., Tilden V. P., Limandri, B. J., & Schmidt, T. A. (1994). Addressing family violence among dental patients: Assessment and intervention. *Journal of the American Dental Association, 125*, 69–75.

Community Crisis Center. (undated). Domestic violence: A community problem. Elgin, IL.

Cooper, J.E., & Cooper, M.E. (2007). *Introduction to Veterinary and Comparative Forensic Medicine.* Oxford: Blackwell.

DeViney, E., Dickert, J., & Lockwood, R. (1983). The care of pets within child abusing families. *International Journal for the Study of Animal Problems, 4*, 321–329.

Doherty, D. (2002). *Making family violence law information available to people in rural areas: An inventory of promising practices.* Fredericton, New Brunswick: Muriel McQueen Fergusson Centre for Family Violence Research.

Donley, L., Patronek, G. J., & Luke, C. (1999). Animal abuse in Massachusetts: A study of case reports at the MSPCA and attitudes of Massachusetts veterinarians. *Journal of Applied Animal Welfare Sciences, 2*(1), 59–73.

Duel, D. (2004): *Violence prevention & intervention: A directory of animal-related programs.* Washington, DC: Humane Society of the U.S.

English, D. J. (1998). The extent and consequences of child maltreatment. *The Future of Children: Protecting Children from Abuse and Neglect, 8*(1), Spring, 39–53.

Evans, J. M. (1983). Battered dogs: A private violence. *Dog World*, December, 12.

Feldman, M. D. (1997). Canine variant of factitious disorder by proxy. *American Journal of Psychiatry, 154*, 1316–1317.

Fooshee, S. (1998). Cleopatra's story. *Animal Sheltering, 21*(1), 32.

Frasch, P. D., Otto, S. K., Olsen, K. M., & Ernest, P. A. (1999). State animal anti-cruelty statutes: An overview. *Animal Law, 5*, 69–80.

Henneke, D. R. (1995). A condition scoring system for horses. *Equine Practitioner, 7*, 14–16.

Hobbs, C. J., Hanks, H. G. I., & Wynne, J. M. (1999a). Physical abuse. In *Child Abuse and Neglect: A Clinician's Handbook* (2nd ed.) (p. 80). London: Churchill Livingstone.

Hobbs, C. J., Hanks, H. G. I., & Wynne, J. M. (1999b). Abuse of children with disability. In *Child Abuse and Neglect: A Clinician's Handbook* (2nd ed.) (pp. 273–282). London: Churchill Livingstone.

Hobbs, C. J., Hanks, H. G. I., & Wynne, J. M. (1999c). Physical abuse. In *Child Abuse and Neglect: A Clinician's Handbook* (2nd ed.) (pp. 82–84). London: Churchill Livingstone.

Hornosty, J., & Doherty, D. (2002, March). *Responding to wife abuse in farm and rural communities: Searching for solutions that work.* Paper presented at Rural Canada: Moving Forward or Left Behind? Saskatchewan Institute of Public Policy and The Centre for Research and Information on Canada, Regina, Saskatchewan, Canada.

Humane Society of the U.S. and State of Wisconsin Dept. of Health & Family Services, Div. of Disability & Elder Services, Bureau of Aging & Long Term Care Resources. (2003). *Creating Safer Communities for Older Adults and Companion Animals.* Washington, DC.

Jack, D. C. (2000). Horns of dilemma: The vetrilegal implications of animal abuse. *Canadian Veterinary Journal, 41*, 715–720.

Kempe, C. H., Silverman, F. N., Steele, B. F., Droegenmuller, W., & Silver, H. K. (1962). The battered-child syndrome. *Journal of the American Medical Association, 181*, 17–24.

Kessler, D. B., & Hyden, P. (1991). Physical, sexual and emotional abuse of children. *Clinical Symposia, 43*(1).

King, M. (1998). Red flag: Signs of animal abuse. *Veterinary Product News, 10*(6), 17–21.

Kleinman, P. K. (Ed.). (1998) *Diagnostic imaging of child abuse* (2nd ed.). St. Louis: Mosby Yearbook Inc.

Kohnke, J. (1992). *Feeding and Nutrition: The Making of a Champion.* Rouse Hill, NSW, Australia: Birubi Pacific.

Kolata, R. J., & Johnson, D. E. (1975). Motor vehicle accidents in urban dogs: A study of 600 cases. *Journal of the American Veterinary Medical Association, 167*, 938–941.

Koop, C. E., & Lundberg, G. D. (1992). Violence in America: A public health emergency: Time to bite the bullet back. *Journal of the American Medical Association, 267*(22), 3075–3076.

Kovacs, S. J., Adams, C. L., & Carioto, L. (2004). Attitudes, opinions and experiences of veterinary practitioners regarding animal maltreatment: A survey of Southwestern Ontario and the Atlantic Provinces. Presentation at 10th International Conference on Human-Animal Interactions, International Association of Human-Animal Interaction Organizations, Glasgow, Scotland.

Lacroix, C. A. (1999). Another weapon for combating family violence: Prevention of animal abuse. In F. R. Ascione & P. Arkow (Eds.), *Child abuse, domestic violence and animal abuse: Linking the circles of compassion for prevention and intervention.* (pp. 62–80). West Lafayette, IN: Purdue University Press.

Lacroix, C. A., & Wilson, J. F. (1998). State animal anti-cruelty laws. In P. Olson (Ed.), *Recognizing & reporting animal abuse: A veterinarian's guide.* (pp. 20–24). Englewood, CO: American Humane Association.

Landau, R. (1999). The veterinarian's role in recognizing and reporting abuse. In F. R. Ascione & P. Arkow (Eds.), *Child abuse, domestic violence and animal abuse: Linking the circles of compassion for prevention and intervention.* (pp. 241–249). West Lafayette, IN: Purdue University Press.

Lawrie, M. (2002). The mandatory reporting of animal abuse. Veterinary Surgeons Board of Western Australia: Current Issues, Autumn. Retrieved December 5, 2004, from www.vetsurgeonsboardwa.au.com

Lembke, L. (1999). Animal abuse and family violence in a rural environment. In F. R. Ascione & P. Arkow (Eds.), *Child abuse, domestic violence and animal abuse: Linking the circles of compassion for prevention and intervention.* (pp. 228–240). West Lafayette, IN: Purdue University Press.

Lockwood, R. (2000). Animal cruelty and human violence: The veterinarian's role in making the connection—the American experience. *Canadian Veterinary Journal, 41*, 876–878.

Mark, A. M. (1994). Taking a stand against child abuse. *Journal of the American Dental Association, 125*, 74.

Martin, P. (1982). *Weaning and behavioural development in the cat.* Unpublished doctoral thesis, University of Cambridge, Cambridge, UK.

Maxwell, M. S., & O'Rourke, K. S. (2000). *Domestic violence: A competency-based training manual for Florida's animal abuse investigators.* Tallahassee: Florida State University Institute for Family Violence Studies.

McCulloch, M. J. (1976, June). Contributions to mental health. In R. K. Anderson, et al. (Eds.), *A description of the responsibilities of veterinarians as they relate directly to human health* (pp. 9-1–9-20). Minneapolis: University of Minnesota School of Public Health.

Merck, M. (2007). *Veterinary Forensics—Animal Cruelty Investigations.* Ames, IA: Blackwell.

Miller, L., & Zawistowski, S. (2004). *Shelter Medicine for Veterinarians and Staff.* Ames, IA: Blackwell.

Morris, J. L., Johnson, C. F., & Clasen, M. (1985). To report or not to report: Physicians' attitudes toward discipline and child abuse. *American Journal of Diseases of Children, 139*(2), 194–197.

Munro, H. M. C. (1996). Battered pets. *Irish Veterinary Journal, 49,* 712–713.

Munro, H. M. C., & Thrusfield, M. V. (2001a). Battered pets: Features that raise suspicion of non-accidental injury. *Journal of Small Animal Practice, 42,* 218–226.

Munro, H. M. C., & Thrusfield, M. V. (2001b). Battered pets: Non-accidental physical injuries found in dogs and cats. *Journal of Small Animal Practice, 42,* 279–290.

Munro, H. M. C., & Thrusfield, M. V. (2001c). Battered pets: Sexual abuse. *Journal of Small Animal Practice, 42,* 333–337.

Munro, H. M. C., & Thrusfield, M. V. (2001d). Battered pets: Munchausen syndrome by proxy. *Journal of Small Animal Practice, 42,* 385–389.

Munro, H. M. C., & Thrusfield, M. V. (2002). The Battered-Pet Syndrome. *Veterinary Times, 32*(13), 26–28.

National Clearinghouse on Child Abuse and Neglect Information. (1999). *Current trends in child maltreatment reporting laws* (pp. 20–22). Washington, DC.

Novello, A. C., Shosky, J., & Froehlke, R. (1992). From the Surgeon General, U.S. Public Health

Service: A medical response to violence. *Journal of the American Medical Association, 267*(22), 3007.

Olson, P., Ed. (1998). *Recognizing & reporting animal abuse: A veterinarian's guide.* Englewood, CO: American Humane Association.

Ontario Veterinary College. (2003). *Ontario Veterinary College and Laboratory Services Division Procedure for Reporting Suspected Abuse in Client Animals.* Guelph, ON, Canada: University of Guelph.

Patronek, G. (1998). Issues and guidelines for veterinarians in recognizing, reporting and assessing animal neglect and abuse. In P. Olson (Ed.), *Recognizing & reporting animal abuse: A veterinarian's guide* (pp. 25–39). Englewood, CO: American Humane Association.

Phillips, T. (1994). Cruelty: To report or not to report? *Large Animal Veterinarian, 49*(4), 34.

Radford, M. (2001). Cruelty, culpability and consequences. In *Animal welfare law in Britain* (pp. 221–258). Oxford University Press.

Reisman, R., & Adams, C. A. (1996). Should vets tell? *ASPCA Animal Watch,* Summer, 18–21.

Rollin, B. E. (1988). Veterinary and animal ethics. In J. F. Wilson (Ed.), *Law and ethics of the veterinary profession* (pp. 24–49). Yardley, PA: Priority Press.

Rowan, A. N. (1993). Editorial. Cruelty to animals. *Anthrozoös,* Volume VI, 218–220.

Royal College of Veterinary Surgeons (2007). Guide to Professional Conduct. Part 3. Annexes. *Animal Abuse, Child Abuse and Domestic Violence.* Retrieved May 1, 2007, from www.rcvs.org.uk

RSPCA Australia. (2004). Cruelty to animals—a human problem: First announcement. Retrieved December 5, 2004, from www. rspca.org.au

Salber, P. R. & Taliaferro, E. (1995). *The physician's guide to domestic violence: How to ask the right questions and recognize abuse … another way to save a life* (p. 78). Volcano, CA: Volcano Press.

Sharpe, M. (1999). A survey of veterinarians and a proposal for intervention. In F. R. Ascione & P. Arkow (Eds.), *Child abuse, domestic violence and animal abuse: Linking the circles of compassion for prevention and intervention* (pp. 250–256). West Lafayette, IN: Purdue University Press.

Sinclair, L., Merck, M., & Lockwood, R. (2006). *Forensic investigation of animal cruelty: A guide for veterinary and law enforcement professionals.* Washington, DC: Humane Society Press.

Sherley, M. (2004). Animal cruelty and interpersonal violence. [Review of presentation, "Knowledge and attitudes of Australian veterinarians to animal abuse and human interpersonal violence," July 21, at Delta Society Australia National Seminar, Sydney.] Retrieved December 5, 2004, from www.vsbsa.org.au

Skolnick, A. A. (1995). Physician, heal thyself—then aid abused women. *Journal of the American Medical Association, 273*(22), 1744–1745.

Steinberg, K. L., Levine, M., & Doueck, H. J. (1997). Effects of legally mandated child-abuse reports on the therapeutic relationship: A survey of psychotherapists. *American Journal of Orthopsychiatry, 67*(1), January, 112–122.

Sugg, N. K., & Inui, T. (1992). Primary care physicians' response to domestic violence: Opening Pandora's Box. *Journal of the American Medical Association, 267*(23), 3157–3160.

Tannenbaum, J. (1995). *Veterinary ethics: Animal welfare, client relations, competition and collegiality* (2nd ed.). St. Louis: Mosby.

ten Bensel, R. W., King, K. J., & Bastein, S. A. (1977). Child abuse and neglect: History, identification and reporting. *Dental Hygiene*, March, 51119–51125.

Thrusfield, M.V., & Munro, H. M. C. (2007). Abuse. In E. Coté (Ed.), *Clinical Veterinary Advisor: Dogs and Cats.* (pp. 14–16). St. Louis: Mosby Elsevier.

Turner, D. C., & Bateson, P. (2000). Behavioural development in the cat. *In The domestic cat: The biology of its behaviour* (2nd ed.) (p. 11), Cambridge, UK, Cambridge University Press.

Vermeulen, H., & Odendaal, J. S. (1993). Proposed typology of companion animal abuse. *Anthrozoös, VI*, 248–257.

Veterinary Council of New Zealand. (2004). *Code of professional conduct for veterinarians: Animal welfare.* Wellington, NZ.

Veterinary Hospital of the University of Pennsylvania. (1998). *Policy regarding suspected animal abuse and neglect.* Philadelphia: University of Pennsylvania.

Veterinary Record. (2003). RCVS issues guidance on dealing with abuse in animals and humans, *15* (15), 446–447.

Vulliamy, A. P., & Sullivan, R. (2000). Reporting child abuse: Pediatricians' experiences with the child protection system. *Child Abuse & Neglect, 24*(11), 1461–1470.

Webster, J. (2005). Sentience, sense and suffering. In *Animal welfare: Limping towards Eden*. Universities Federation for Animal Welfare Series (pp. 46–76). Oxford: Blackwell Publishing Ltd.

Appendix

This survey is supported by

FACULTY of VETERINARY MEDICINE

Royal (Dick) School of Veterinary Studies
The University of Edinburgh
Summerhall
Edinburgh EH9 1QH

February, 1998

Non-accidental injury in the dog and cat

Dear Colleague,

Please help us with this survey.

What is this survey about?

The survey is about **non-accidental injury (NAI)** in the dog and cat. Non-accidental injury is also sometimes known as *physical abuse*. In children, you may also know it as the *"Battered Child Syndrome"*. In dogs and cats it therefore can be called the *"Battered Pet Syndrome"*.

Why study NAI?

First: although non-accidental injury is known to occur in companion animals, recognition and diagnosis can be very difficult for veterinary surgeons. There is no published comprehensive account of the circumstances, clinical signs, and pathology of the "battered pet". In *child* physical abuse, which has been recognised for over 30 years, guidelines are available for recognising the condition and for helping to **differentiate** between *accidental* and *non-accidental* injury. For example, unexplained subdural haematomata and retinal haemorrhages are highly suggestive of NAI and a torn frenulum is virtually diagnostic.

The experiences of veterinary surgeons who complete this questionnaire will help to ascertain the extent of NAI in the dog and cat, as seen in clinical practice, and to formulate guidelines to differentiate between accidental and non-accidental injury.

Secondly: a diagnosis of NAI is important because there is evidence that the occurrence of physical abuse to animals may indicate that similar abuse is being directed against other family members, such as the children. It may also be an early indicator of future violent behaviour by the perpetrator.[†]

Will your answers be anonymous?

Yes. Your name and address are not requested.

[†] Arkow, P. (1994) Child abuse, animal abuse and the veterinarian. *Journal of the American Veterinary Medical Association*, **204**, 1004-1007.

51

Note: this questionnaire may be completed collectively by all members of the practice, both veterinary surgeons and nurses.

Section 1

1.1   Do you acknowledge NAI? (please tick)   Yes ☐

                                                       No   ☐

1.2   Have you ever suspected, or seen, NAI? (please tick)

        Yes ☐   No   ☐
         ↓   ↓
        Please go to Section 2   *Please go to Section 3, on the back page*

Section 2
Details of suspected or known cases of NAI

To make it straightforward to fill in the questionnaire, case sheets have been provided for *five* cases. Do not worry if you have fewer - just leave the pages blank. Please feel free to give as much detail as you can. Thank you.

If you feel that you have seen more than 5 cases, please tick here ☐

If you have ticked the box, we would be most grateful if you supplied details of these further cases. More case-sheets will be sent to you, on request. (This will result in loss of your anonymity **BUT all information will be treated as strictly confidential.**)

Name:

Address:

Please move now to Case 1.

2.1

Case 1

Approximate date:

Species (please tick)   Dog ☐   Cat ☐

Breed (please specify)

Sex (please tick)   male ☐   female ☐   male neuter ☐   female neuter ☐   unknown ☐

Age (please tick)   under 12 weeks ☐   3-6 months ☐   7 months-2 years ☐   over 2 years ☐

unknown ☐

What made you suspect, or allowed you to recognise, NAI? (please specify)

Did this involve :   a single episode ☐   **or**   more than one episode ☐

What injuries did you see on the:

Head	Eyes
Thorax	Abdomen
Limbs	Other site (please specify)

Please tick one of the following:

Patient: Survived ☐   Died of injuries ☐   Euthanased because of severity of injuries ☐

If this is your last case, please go to section 3 (back page).

2.2

Case 2

Approximate date:

Species (please tick)   Dog ☐   Cat ☐

Breed (please specify)

Sex (please tick)   male ☐   female ☐   male neuter ☐   female neuter ☐   unknown ☐

Age (please tick)   under 12 weeks ☐   3-6 months ☐   7 months-2 years ☐   over 2 years ☐

unknown ☐

What made you suspect, or allowed you to recognise, NAI? (please specify)

Did this involve :   a single episode ☐   **or**   more than one episode ☐

What injuries did you see on the:

Head	Eyes
Thorax	Abdomen
Limbs	Other site (please specify)

Please tick one of the following:

Patient: Survived ☐   Died of injuries ☐   Euthanased because of severity of injuries ☐

If this is your last case, please go to section 3 (back page).

2.3

Case 3

Approximate date:

Species (please tick)   Dog ☐   Cat ☐

Breed (please specify)

Sex (please tick)   male ☐   female ☐   male neuter ☐   female neuter ☐   unknown ☐

Age (please tick)   under 12 weeks ☐   3-6 months ☐   7 months-2 years ☐   over 2 years ☐

unknown ☐

What made you suspect, or allowed you to recognise, NAI? (please specify)

Did this involve :   a single episode ☐   **or**   more than one episode ☐

What injuries did you see on the:

Head	Eyes
Thorax	Abdomen
Limbs	Other site (please specify)

Please tick one of the following:

Patient: Survived ☐   Died of injuries ☐   Euthanased because of severity of injuries ☐

If this is your last case, please go to section 3 (back page).

2.4

Case 4

Approximate date:

Species (please tick)   Dog ☐   Cat ☐

Breed (please specify)

Sex (please tick)   male ☐   female ☐   male neuter ☐   female neuter ☐   unknown ☐

Age (please tick)   under 12 weeks ☐   3-6 months ☐   7 months-2 years ☐   over 2 years ☐

                       unknown ☐

What made you suspect, or allowed you to recognise, NAI? (please specify)

Did this involve :   a single episode ☐   **or**   more than one episode ☐

What injuries did you see on the:

Head	Eyes
Thorax	Abdomen
Limbs	Other site (please specify)

Please tick one of the following:

Patient: Survived ☐   Died of injuries ☐   Euthanased because of severity of injuries ☐

If this is your last case, please go to section 3 (back page).

2.5

Case 5

Approximate date:

Species (please tick)   Dog ☐   Cat ☐

Breed (please specify)
Sex (please tick)   male ☐   female ☐   male neuter ☐   female neuter ☐   unknown ☐

Age (please tick)   under 12 weeks ☐   3-6 months ☐   7 months-2 years ☐   over 2 years ☐

                       unknown ☐

What made you suspect, or allowed you to recognise, NAI? (please specify)

Did this involve :   a single episode ☐   **or**   more than one episode ☐

What injuries did you see on the:

Head	Eyes
Thorax	**Abdomen**
Limbs	**Other site (please specify)**

Please tick one of the following:

Patient: Survived ☐   Died of injuries ☐   Euthanased because of severity of injuries ☐

If this is your last case, please go to section 3 (back page).

Section 3

Have you seen or experienced any of the following in your patients? (please tick)

3.1   unexplained injuries (if yes, please specify)   Yes ☐   No ☐

3.2   more than one fracture, of differing ages, in same animal   Yes ☐   No ☐

3.3   unexplained old rib fractures   Yes ☐   No ☐

3.4   history not consistent with injury (if yes, please specify)   Yes ☐   No ☐

3.5   previous history of unexplained injury/death, with the
        same owner/family   Yes ☐   No ☐

Please now complete Section 4, below.

Section 4

Please use this space for any further comments you may wish to make.

**Thank you very much for completing this questionnaire.
A *Freepost* envelope is provided in which to return it.
Your help is greatly appreciated.**

Helen C. Munro   Michael Thrusfield
Research Fellow   Senior Lecturer
Departments of Veterinary Clinical Studies/Pathology   Department of Veterinary Clinical Studies
Royal (Dick) School of Veterinary Studies   Royal (Dick) School of Veterinary Studies
Summerhall, Edinburgh EH9 1QH   Easter Bush Veterinary Centre
                                                    Roslin, Midlothian EH25 9RG
☎   0131 650 7997   ☎   0131 650 6223
Fax   0131 650 6511   Fax   0131 650 6588
Email   Helen.Munro@ed.ac.uk   Email   M.Thrusfield@ed.ac.uk

The Impact of Improved American Anti-Cruelty Laws in the Investigation, Prosecution, and Sentencing of Abusers

Pamela D. Frasch[1]

Introduction

Before 1993, only seven states in the United States had some form of felony[2] anti-cruelty law.[3] Of those original seven states, three had first passed their felony laws more than a century ago.[4] Between 1993 and October 2004, however, 34 additional states and the District of Columbia added a felony anti-cruelty law to their state statutes.[5] Why there has been such dramatic recent growth in the number of felony anti-cruelty provisions is up for debate. Some would argue that a growing awareness of the link between animal abuse and human violence has played a key role. Others may argue that our society has evolved to recognize that violence in any form is abhorrent and must be punished appropriately. Still others may argue that increasing penalties for animal abuse is consistent with this nation's recent trend toward tougher treatment of violent offenders, as evidenced by "three strikes" legislation, and the criminalization of activity that had previously been viewed as generally benign behavior, such as drunk driving.

Whatever the reason, the fact remains that dramatic growth in the number of felony anti-cruelty provisions is a recent phenomenon. But whether it has had much impact on the overall quality or quantity of actual abuse prosecutions remains a question. This chapter explores that question.

Methodology

Reliable national or even regional statistics on the number, type, and disposition of animal abuse cases do not exist. In some instances, local or state statistics are available, but are generally incomplete and confusing. Thus, we relied on extensive interviews of key law enforcement officials in targeted jurisdictions in addition to any appropriate statistics we were able to locate.[6] We chose six states in geographically diverse locations and focused on at least one small and one large county for each state.

California – Marin County and Los Angeles County
New York – New York County, Westchester County, and Albany County
Florida – Hillsborough County (Tampa) and Santa Rosa County
Texas – Harris County (Houston) and Smith County
Colorado – Denver County and El Paso County
Illinois – Cook County (Chicago), Madison County, and Sangamon County

Several primary issues were discussed with each interviewee:

- Have there been any trends in the number of prosecutions since the most recent amendments to the felony statutes? Have there been any overall trends in the last few years?
- Are law enforcement officials (e.g., animal control, police, prosecutors, judges) more likely to investigate, prosecute, or convict an offender if there is a felony-level crime versus a misdemeanor-level crime?
- Are there any problems with the current wording of the statutes and, if so, can you offer any suggestions?
- Are there any other problems, issues, or general impressions outside of the statutory language that are relevant to investigations or prosecutions regarding animal abuse?

We attempted to contact the appropriate prosecutor(s), police officer(s), judge(s), and humane investigator(s) in each jurisdiction. Overall, we were successful in our efforts. In some instances, however, particularly in California, whether because of vacations, workload, or other scheduling conflicts, complete responses to inquiries were not received prior to publication of this paper. We have included, in Appendix E, a complete list of the individuals and organizations from which we received the information included in this paper. We did not include the names of those we attempted to contact without success or those who did not provide complete responses prior to publication of this paper.

The information we received through statistical research and interviews highlights the differences between jurisdictions in their prosecutorial approach, statistical record-keeping habits, and interest and commitment in tackling the problem of animal abuse via the criminal justice system. It is our hope that this information will motivate individuals and jurisdictions concerned about animal abuse to work to establish standardized record keeping for purposes of informing future legislative efforts in this area.

General Impressions

Overall

Most interviewees stated that having a felony-level anti-cruelty statute was a positive development from the perspective of attaching greater importance to the crime. There was general agreement among all interviewees that police officers and prosecutors are more likely to invest time and resources into investigating and prosecuting felony-level crimes than misdemeanors. This greater interest in pursuing felony-level animal abuse did not, however, necessarily translate into a greater amount of total attention and resources devoted to animal abuse cases whether they be misdemeanors or felonies.

The statistics that were available tended to be incomplete and thus were not a reliable source for precise interpretation. Nonetheless, the statistical and anecdotal information we received from the interviewees generally do not indicate a meaningful increase in the overall number of animal abuse cases that have been processed since the felony laws in the targeted jurisdictions were first added.[7] Rather, the cases charged as felonies tended to have more sensational fact patterns that would have attracted media, community and law enforcement attention even if they had been charged as misdemeanors. The biggest difference noticed by interviewees is that with a felony charge, a defendant, if convicted, potentially faces stiffer sentencing and will have a felony conviction on his or her permanent record.

Advantages to Felony-Level Convictions

From a law enforcement perspective, interviewees agreed that there are several advantages to having a felony on a perpetrator's permanent record: (1) convicted felons cannot own guns; (2) in some jurisdictions, the conviction cannot be wiped clean from the record absent a full pardon; (3) a felony conviction gives judges the ability to impose more meaningful sanctions; (4) the outcome of restraining orders, child custody disputes, and similar civil proceedings likely will be impacted; (5) in "three strikes" states, the animal abuse felony conviction sometimes counts as one of the strikes; and (6) a felony conviction can keep a perpetrator from getting into positions of special public trust, such as becoming a legal guardian, schoolteacher, or police officer.

Statistics

None of the jurisdictions targeted in this report could boast of maintaining excellent statistical records on animal cruelty reports, investigations, or prosecutions. When statistics were available, they were generally incomplete and confusing. Virtually all interviewees agreed, however, that maintaining statistics on animal abuse cases would be invaluable for targeting "hot spots" within the community, conducting comparative analysis of similar types of cases, and assessing the appropriateness of future legislative proposals to amend the anti-cruelty statutes.

Specialization of Law Enforcement

Larger jurisdictions were more likely to have either specialized police officers or former police officers as animal control personnel. The general consensus was that specialization aids in coordination and evidence gathering, making it more likely that a criminal charge would be filed at the prosecutorial levels. In smaller jurisdictions, where specialization was not as common, animal control officers (who were associated with humane society–type shelters) complained that it could be difficult to get prosecutors to "pay attention" to their investigations. Yet prosecutors from these same jurisdictions expressed overall satisfaction with the process by which animal abuse cases were brought to their attention.

Many interviewees stated that the lack of consistent personal contact between the various agen-

↳ *Interesting – the disconnect by DA's...*

cies was a problem. As an example, very few animal control officers could name a prosecutor with whom they had regularly worked, and none of the animal control officers or prosecutors could name a judge with whom they had regularly worked on animal abuse cases. This was especially the case in the larger jurisdictions where cases sometimes are randomly assigned to different courts and divisions. There was a strong perception that these inefficiencies have a negative impact on the conviction rate. Some argued that if the cruelty cases could be heard in a single court (such as the domestic violence, juvenile, or family court in a particular county), then the same judge would be able to develop expertise in the field, create consistent court practices for animal abuse cases, and become familiar with repeat offenders.

Statutory Language

In all jurisdictions, interviewees commented on the "definitions" sections within the anti-cruelty statutes. The consensus was that clearer and broader definitions would aid prosecutors and, ideally, would categorize more forms of cruel behavior as illegal. Interestingly, civil penalties and forfeiture procedures often were mentioned as perhaps the most effective tool to halt acts of cruelty.

Training

From our interviews, it seems the most critical aspect of animal anti-cruelty enforcement that must be addressed is training. Interviewees consistently emphasized the importance of (1) developing community support for law enforcement to take animal abuse cases seriously and (2) providing adequate training for police and prosecutors on how to investigate and prosecute cruelty cases effectively.

More specifically, interviewees stated:

- There is a belief that law enforcement officials, judges, and the general public respond more aggressively when they understand the link between animal cruelty and crimes against people. The interviewees not only accepted this proposition theoretically but also had seen it in their work:
  - "Drug dealers are dog fighters."
  - "Animal abusers also abuse wives and children."
- Police and prosecutors cannot investigate or prosecute laws they do not know or understand. They already have limited resources and believe they cannot invest the time and

energy necessary to learn unfamiliar laws. Training is perceived as essential so that recognizing and investigating animal abuse cases becomes second nature.

- Train police to look at the whole picture. Often, animal cruelty is not the only crime being committed. When investigating animal cruelty, look for dog fighting, domestic abuse, child endangerment, and drugs. When investigating these other crimes, look for animal cruelty.
- Prosecutors will not bring a charge without proper evidence. Teach the police how to recognize the telltale signs of abuse and how to gather and document evidence for animal cruelty cases.
- Police need help with these cases. For example, they need to know where they can bring seized animals for safekeeping, whether and how animals can be removed from harm's way when investigating domestic violence complaints, and how state anti-cruelty laws apply to juvenile offenders. Provide the proper resources so they can do their jobs.
- Community support is crucial. Police, prosecutors, judges, and lawmakers respond to public pressure.

State-by-State Summaries—

Florida

State Law. Florida Statute section 828.12 (last amended in 2002) is the primary anti-cruelty law in Florida. Certain activities bring misdemeanor liability (e.g., providing inadequate shelter) while others are felonies (e.g., intentionally causing a cruel death). The most recent amendments added subsections (2)(a) and (2)(b). The new language provides that a person convicted of knowingly torturing an animal must pay a minimum fine of $2,500 and undergo psychological counseling. Furthermore, a second violation for a similar offense now brings a minimum fine of $5,000 and at least a six-month jail sentence with no early release. Also relevant is the felony dog-fighting statute found at Florida Statute section 828.122. The first felony anti-cruelty law in Florida was added in 1989. (See Appendix A for relevant anti-cruelty sections.)

Statistics. Available Florida statistics as well as our interviews indicate that the arrest rate of animal abusers has been on the rise since the felony law was passed. (See Appendixes B and C.) Statewide arrests rose from 669 between 1972 and 1989 to 2,567 between 1989 and June 2004. Statistics regarding the disposition or further processing of those arrests were not available. However, enhanced penalties relating to an anti–dog-fighting statute (§ 828.122) appear to be principally responsible for the dramatic increase in the number of arrests. (See Appendix C.) Some interviewees stated their belief that the overall increased number of cases is due to better investigative work and awareness rather than any recent change in the law.

Interviews. Interviewees suggested several language changes for section 828.12, primarily within the definition section to make the statute more effective. For example, without clear definitions for terms such as *shelter, necessary sustenance*, and *health*, it is difficult to enforce adequate living conditions for animals. In addition, two separate interviewees felt that the statute uses somewhat outdated terms to describe prohibited behavior. They pointed to the terms *overloads*, and *overdrives*, which have their origins in the early anti-cruelty laws that were passed in New York more than a century ago to target overworking of draft animals. Interviewees stated that these situations rarely are encountered in present-day cruelty cases.[9]

Interviewees drew a connection between these current difficulties in prosecuting animal abuse cases and what they perceived to be inadequate public and law enforcement education and awareness. As an example, interviewees cited a recent case in which a disc jockey was acquitted of felony charges for castrating and killing a pig without anesthesia as part of a cookout event (D. Carter, personal communication, June 29, 2004; C. Guestring, personal communication, July 29, 2004; D. McCullough, personal communication, June 29, 2004; C. Oster, personal communication, July 12, 2004; R. Pechow, personal communication, August 6, 2004; K. Vetel, personal communication, June 30, 2004).

Texas

State Law. Texas Penal Code section 42.09 (last amended in 2001) is the primary anti-cruelty law in Texas. Certain activities bring misdemeanor liability (e.g., not providing necessary food or shelter) while others are felonies (e.g., torturing animals). The 2001 amendments added subsection (i) which increased the felony grade and fine for repeat offenders. The first felony law in Texas was added in 1997. (See Appendix A for relevant anti-cruelty statutes.)

Statistics. The only statistics made available were from Harris County and showed an overall increase in the number of arrests between 2001 and 2004, particularly with felony arrests, but a fairly steady rate of felony convictions (see Appendix B). The interviewees did not attribute the increase in arrests or any other recent trend specifically to changes in the felony statute, but rather to (what they perceived as) heightened efforts by the relevant government agencies to pursue animal abuse cases. They would not speculate, however, whether the increased effort was a result of the increased penalties. There was some consensus that felony cases are more likely to be investigated and pursued but the belief is that any increased interest is in part due to the publicity that comes with more serious crimes. Some of the interviewees stated that they have learned to utilize the media to their advantage to highlight serious cases. Some noted a direct link between media exposure of serious cases and successful prosecutions.

Interviews. Several problems with the felony language were noted by interviewees. Some suggested that sections of the law could be combined more comprehensively to protect all animals and prohibit a wider range of cruel acts. For example, some interviewees complained that the phrase "food, care or shelter … required to maintain the animal in a state of good health" is unnecessarily vague and difficult to enforce. They stated that they are aware of an individual in Tyler who "hoards" cats and keeps them in a house. No humans live in the house, but the owner stops by to feed them from time to time. While the cats are probably in "good health" as required by section 42.09, they are also living in several inches of their own waste. Interviewees expressed frustration because of their belief that under current law there is no mechanism to address this situation.

In addition, for a defendant to be convicted of a felony under the anti-cruelty statute, the prosecutor must show that the accused perpetrator intentionally[10] tortured the animal. The interviewees thought this was an unreasonably high burden.

Another problem cited by interviewees related to wild animals. Currently, the statute covers animals owned or captured, so either the owner is charged or the state can press cruelty charges against another when the animal is harmed by someone other than the owner. Wild animals not owned or captured by an individual receive no protection under the statute, even though such cruelty cases occur from time to time.

Interviewees pointed to education and publicity as important to improving public awareness and fostering better cooperation among law enforcement agencies. Information relating specifically to the link between animal abuse and human violence was viewed as particularly critical for the purpose of encouraging the public to take animal abuse seriously. All agreed that police and prosecutor training on how to investigate and prosecute animal abusers would likely improve arrest and prosecution rates.

Some interviewees expressed frustration that so few animal abusers end up in court. One interviewee suggested handling this problem by treating lower level animal abuse cases much like traffic tickets—simply issue a citation and require the abuser to make a court appearance. Some interviewees also noted that enhanced civil penalties and orders can make effective weapons against abuse, at least for the animals in question, since court orders can be used either to remove animals from abusive situations more quickly or force the animals' owners to change their living conditions (G. Chambers, personal communication, July 12, 2004; K. Downs, personal communication, July 15, 2004; V. George, personal communication, July 2004; M. Timmers, personal communication, July 21, 2004).

California

State Law. California Penal Code section 597 is the primary anti-cruelty law in California. The statute provides for prosecutorial discretion to charge most abusive acts as either a misdemeanor or a felony (§597(b)), requires automatic forfeiture of seized animals upon conviction (§597(f)), and requires psychological testing and treatment (§597(g)). Sanctions for violation of California's anti-cruelty law include imprisonment in the state prison and/or a fine of not more than $20,000 or, alternatively, imprisonment in a county jail for not more than one year and/or a fine of not more than $20,000. The first felony anti-cruelty law for California was added in 1988. (See Appendix A for relevant anti-cruelty statutes.)

Statistics. Interviewees could not identify any source from which statistics could be accessed either for California on a statewide basis or for the targeted counties. In Marin County in particular, one interviewee speculated that the dearth of animal abuse cases filed implied that statistics simply were not kept.

Interviews. The interviewees did not perceive any meaningful change in the number of animal abuse prosecutions since the felony law was passed. Indeed, one interviewee expressed cynicism about what he assumed was the underlying assumption of this report—that is, if more animal cruelty cases were treated as felonies, more miscreants would be serving serious time in prison and more potential wrongdoers would be dissuaded from engaging in bad acts. This interviewee argued that the political tide in California is going against increasing jail time given the enormous cost to build and administer additional prisons and jails. Therefore, he suggested, it will become increasingly more difficult to prosecute and incarcerate criminals for animal abuse, a crime that is generally perceived as not as important, and as occurring less frequently, than other types of violent crime.

No interviewee we talked with had additional suggestions with regard to possible statutory language changes. Nor did any interviewee have specific concerns about current practices for investigating or prosecuting animal abuse cases (B. Ballenger, personal communication, July 29, 2004; S. Koenig, personal communication, July 2004; K. O'Hare, personal communication, July 2004).

New York

State Law. New York Agriculture & Markets Code sections 353 and 353a are the principal anti-cruelty laws in New York. Certain abusive acts bring misdemeanor liability (e.g., depriving any animal of "necessary sustenance") while others bring felony liability (e.g., "aggravated cruelty" intended to cause "extreme physical pain"). Misdemeanor violations of section 353 are punishable by imprisonment for not more than one year and/or by a fine of not more than $1,000. Felony violations of section 353a are punishable as other felonies under Penal Law section 55.10, except that any term of imprisonment may not exceed two years. The first felony anti-cruelty law for New York was added in 1999. (See Appendix A for relevant anti-cruelty statutes.)

Statistics. Limited statewide statistics for arrests and dispositions from late 1999 through 2003 under section 353(a) (Aggravated Cruelty to Animals) were available from the Division of Criminal Justice Services. (See Appendix B.) Those statistics demonstrate a slight overall rise in the arrest rates between 2000 and 2004 with conviction rates of 70% to 88% of those charged.[11] In Albany County, statistics older than 18 months were not available. Over the past 18 months, the records show only two arrests (both resulting in convictions). (See Appendix B.)

Interviews. Interviewees perceived that a significant problem with the anti-cruelty laws in New York is the archaic misdemeanor language contained in section 353. Interviewees stated that it is extremely difficult to prosecute under this section because the language and legislative history are vague. The consensus, however, is that the relatively recent passage of the felony anti-cruelty law (§ 353a) has made a significant difference in how animal cruelty cases are perceived by the public and law enforcement, despite the fact that it generally excludes farmed animals. Additionally, the omission of "reckless" behavior from section 353a was noted as problematic because it makes it difficult to prosecute many serious crimes. Examples of reckless behavior included failing to provide food and thus starving an animal to death or leaving an animal in subzero weather to freeze to death.

One interviewee believes that animal abuse cases receive little attention from police departments because police lack adequate training and education and are less likely to be familiar with laws, like the anti-cruelty laws, that are located in the agricultural code. To her, training and engaging the support of police are as important as changing the actual laws. Interviewees noted that local attorneys and activists have worked diligently to address this issue by, among other things, producing and distributing "palm cards" to police officers as handy, easily accessible guides to the anti-cruelty laws; training current police officers as well as new recruits at the police academy; and fielding calls from police who need advice in an attempt to raise officers' familiarity with the rules and improve their handling of animal cruelty cases.

Another perceived problem is that New York has a thriving agricultural industry that sometimes is at odds with the purpose and intent of the anti-cruelty laws. For example, some interviewees believe that the Farm Bureau and rural legislators "feel bad" for farmers who struggle economically and claim they cannot afford to feed their animals. This results in a perceived reluctance to provide the support prosecutors and investigators need to move forward with cruelty charges. Interviewees stated that adding a felony-level penalty has increased awareness of animal cruelty laws for everyone, including the police, but that there still exists a big difference between urban and rural areas as to whether anti-cruelty cases will be investigated and prosecuted. For example, in upstate New York, interviewees stated that people are concerned about how the laws

will affect their farming lifestyle. Therefore, the anti-cruelty laws tend to be overlooked. In addition, misdemeanors generally are heard by a city/county board where the judge is not necessarily a lawyer, while the felonies go to the Supreme Court[12] where the judge is a lawyer. The city/county board judges are elected officials with other vocations such as farming who may have a different perspective and place less emphasis on (1) animal cruelty, (2) the link between animal abuse and human violence, and (3) the details of the anti-cruelty statutes (L. Charbonneau, personal communication, September 2004; T. Clingan, personal communication, July 19, 2004; J. Schenkerman, personal communication, July 20, 2004; S. Wolf, personal communication, July 30, 2004; New York State Division of Criminal Justice services, personal communication, July 20 ,2004).

Colorado

State Law. Colorado Revised Statute Annotated section 18-9-202 criminalizes a broad range of cruel acts, such as tormenting or cruelly beating an animal or depriving an animal of necessary sustenance, as misdemeanors. Violation of section 18-9-202 is a class 1 misdemeanor, and a second or subsequent violation is a class 6 felony. The first felony anti-cruelty law in Colorado was added in 2002. (See Appendix A for relevant anti-cruelty statutes.)

Statistics. We received starkly conflicting information regarding available statistics. For example, at least one interviewee indicated that some statewide and county felony statistics might be available but would require the payment of a fairly significant research and analysis fee. Another interviewee indicated that it is impossible to track accurately any change in anti-cruelty prosecutions since the felony law was passed. He noted anecdotally, however, that to his knowledge only a handful of felony charges have been filed throughout the entire state of Colorado since the felony law was enacted in 2002. The Colorado Department of Agriculture, Animal Welfare Department, was able to supply us with only one month of statistics, July 2004. But even these statistics are inaccurate because they represent only 16.22% of statewide agencies reporting. (See Appendix B.) Another interviewee stated that there is not an official database from which to acquire information pertaining to outcomes of anti-cruelty prosecutions. Animal shelters do not maintain uniform information, information from the Colorado District Attorney's Council would be limited in that it would only show cases filed on the state level, and information compiled by law enforcement would not likely include disposition data. Interviewees pointed out that funding for public agencies has been cut drastically in recent years and, without a statute requiring agencies to report animal cruelty, it is virtually impossible to maintain accurate statistics.

Interviews. Despite the above-noted confusion, the recent addition of a felony-level penalty was generally perceived to be positive, as it provides broader discretion to law enforcement and judges on how best to prosecute and sentence animal abusers. Interviewees, however, noted that legislative changes were not enough: "[A] significant challenge is the long-held attitude of minimizing the seriousness of these offenses," one interviewee said. "The days of ignoring these cases as 'boys will be boys' or 'it's just a dog' must end. One hurdle is changing the attitude among some police officers, prosecutors, juries and judges." "Link" education and collaboration among agencies were seen as important solutions to this problem.

Although interviewees were reasonably satisfied with the current anti-cruelty language, they indicated that changes worth considering would be to require "reasonable veterinary care" and a "sanitary environment" as fundamental to minimum care standards. One interviewee stated that the Colorado anti-cruelty laws are "actually quite easy to work with" and easily understood by most law enforcement officials. One disconcerting comment made by the same interviewee is that "even though humane officers do not have full police powers, it is not an issue because people are never arrested on the first offense for a misdemeanor." Her experience showed that only when cruelty rises to a felony level is the perpetrator arrested regardless of whether it is a first offense (D. Balkin, personal communication, June 24, 2004; S. Dutcher, personal communication, September 2004; T. Hake, personal communication, July 2004; J. Zender, personal communication, August 2, 2004).

Illinois

State Law. The principal criminal law protecting animals in Illinois is found at Illinois Statute Chapter 510, Act 70, the "Humane Care for Animals Act" ("HCAA"). The HCAA was significantly amended in 2002 and 2003. The following provides relevant highlights of those amendments:

Amendments. In 2002, Illinois became the first state to enact a new law making recording an act of animal cruelty a Class A misdemeanor and requiring psychological counseling for companion animal hoarders. Other changes to the state's cruelty laws in 2002 and 2003 included:

- Increased penalties for neglect, cruel treatment, aggravated cruelty, and animal torture.
- Required psychological counseling for juveniles convicted of animal cruelty.
- Law enforcement authority to seize vehicles used in dog fighting.
- The opportunity for humane societies to ask courts for security to be posted when they are caring for impounded animals.
- Civil damages in aggravated cruelty or torture cases that may include out-of-pocket expenses, emotional distress, and punitive damages up to $25,000.
- The establishment of The Illinois Animal Abuse Investigation Fund to help pay for investigation of cruelty and neglect complaints.
- Sentencing in which convicted animal abusers will either go to jail or be sentenced to probation; mere "court supervision" no longer being a sentencing option for judges.

The first felony anti-cruelty law for Illinois was added in 1999. (See Appendix A for relevant sections of the HCAA.)

Statistics. We received statistics from three different sources. Although some statistics seem to indicate a steady increase in the number of offenses, arrests, and convictions since the passing of the felony anti-cruelty laws, the specific figures are highly inconsistent with each other, thus making it virtually impossible to know exactly how effective the felony laws have been in increasing the number of arrests and convictions. (See Appendix B.)

Interviews. As noted above, there has been tremendous recent legislative activity relating to anti-cruelty laws in the state of Illinois. Consequently, we were successful in speaking to numerous people about the efficacy of the state statutes and the mechanisms by which those statutes are enforced. Since passage of higher penalties in cruelty cases, the perception among most interviewees is that there has been a rise in the number of prosecutions in Illinois. The interviewees believed this was due in part to the new laws, better education opportunities for police officers on animal cruelty laws, an increase in the number of prosecutors willing to pursue animal cruelty cases vigorously, more awareness within the general public on how to report a crime, and better cooperation between investigators and prosecutors.

Interviewees stated that information on investigating and prosecuting animal cruelty cases has become more accessible to law enforcement generally. For example, one interviewee posts information on the animal cruelty and dog-fighting laws on the state prosecution's bar association website. Another interviewee runs a court advocacy program in the Cook County area to recruit volunteers from the community to attend court proceedings. The purpose of the program is to let judges and prosecutors know that the community has a stake in how animal abuse cases are handled and will hold law enforcement officials accountable for failure. The interviewee stated that this program has proven to be an effective tool because it forces all involved to take the case more seriously. Other interviewees co-wrote a manual to educate police, prosecutors, and humane investigators on animal cruelty laws. Interviewees have also learned to exploit media opportunities to aid community members by teaching them how to avoid activity that will harm animals and where to report animal cruelty when it occurs. For example, one interviewee regularly contacts local television stations on hot days and asks meteorologists to provide viewers relevant information such as, "It's hot today—make sure your pets have plenty of shade and water."

Interviewees stated that the Chicago Police Department has taken significant steps toward ensuring that violation of animal cruelty laws are dealt with appropriately. Among other things, the police department trains officers to look for animal abuse when they are on a domestic violence or child endangerment call and works with local organizations to relay information to its officers about the relationship between gangs, domestic violence, and animal abuse. For officers who do not have time to attend a live training session, local organizations use the Internet to conduct presentations, allowing officers to sit down and view them when police work is slow. The police department also conducts training specifically on investigative techniques for animal cruelty cases and recently distributed a palm card, which serves as a quick reference for the animal laws and crimes to all of Chicago's approximately 10,000 police officers. Finally, the police department has worked with Animal Care and Control to create a manual of state and municipal laws that serves as an additional reference about the laws and how to put a case together. Such attention from

the Chicago Police Department gives the issue of animal cruelty much needed focus and credibility within the community. Other police departments in Illinois are beginning to follow suit, thus shedding more light on animal abuse cases and the link between animal abuse and human violence.

One unintended result of such visible community education and outreach has been the dramatic decrease in the number of felony dog-fighting arrests and convictions from 2002 to 2003. Dogfighters apparently became a lot more careful and "went underground" rather than continuing to stage fights in alleys and parks. Additionally, public information on the new laws has helped educate some violators on how best to evade arrests.

Notwithstanding the recent positive legislative developments, interviewees stated that there continue to be some problems with the HCAA. For example, section 13 of the HCAA states that whenever the HCAA conflicts with the wildlife code, the wildlife code controls. Another perceived serious problem with the HCAA is the cost of care/forfeiture provisions. These provisions generally provide a mechanism to allow for the legal transfer of ownership of an animal seized in a cruelty case to a humane society, or other appropriate person or agency, who can then take immediate action to place the animal into a permanent home as appropriate. In the alternative, the defendant can post a bond that will cover the costs of care for the animal during the pendency of the criminal proceeding. Without a forfeiture provision, animals seized in a cruelty case can linger for months and even years in an agency kennel until the case has been resolved one way or another. This can prove to be expensive to the agency and extremely stressful for the animal. The HCAA provision provides only 14 days within which to file a forfeiture petition. In practice, this has proved to be not enough time.

Despite these and other problems with the HCAA, the overall impression by most interviewees is that the HCAA has many positive elements. The definition of "animal," for example, protects a broader range of animals (including wildlife) than do other states' laws. Additionally, because the HCAA no longer allows violators of the HCAA to get court supervision, offenders can no longer get their record expunged after 12 months of good behavior, thus making increased second-offense penalties more likely.

Interviewees made several recommendations that they believed would improve the overall process of investigating and prosecuting animal cruelty cases. For example, jury members, prosecutors, police officers, and judges throughout the state should be educated about the link between animal abuse and human violence. Another perceived problem is how to effectively navigate the overburdened misdemeanor courts. One suggested solution is to dedicate a specific prosecutor or unit to handle all animal cruelty cases so that each matter receives appropriate attention from an experienced team.

Interviewees supported the notion of using alternative approaches to battle the problem of animal cruelty. For example, one interviewee introduces his investigators to the prosecutors to help build a stronger working relationship, which in turn helps the prosecutorial process. Another supports the idea of creative sentencing by judges as a way to educate perpetrators. And yet another interviewee would like to see even stricter penalties for all forms of animal cruelty in the belief that stronger penalties will deter future bad acts.

Overall, interviewees agreed that in order to continue building on the important steps already taken by local welfare organizations, police departments, and prosecutors around the state, Illinois must allot further funds to continue to educate police officers, better train prosecutors, hire additional parole officers, and create a way to maintain meaningful statistics (C. Bathurst, personal communication, June 25, 2004 and July 14, 2004; A. Breyer, personal communication, July 5, 2004; S. Brody, personal communication, June 30, 2004; S. Brownstein, personal communication, July 9, 2004; J. Burton, personal communication, June 24, 2004; C. Imig, personal communication, June 25, 2004; M. James, personal communication, June 29, 2004; K. Kavanagh, personal communication, June 22, 2004; T. Lavery, personal communication, June 16, 2004; J. McBride, personal communication, July 1, 2004; N. Proutsos, personal communication, July 2004; L. VanKavage, personal communication, June 16, 2004; A. Wilkins, personal communication, July 2004; D. Williams, personal communication, June 29, 2004; N. Williamson, personal communication, July 2004).

Recommendations

As we have seen, a number of similar concerns about how animal abuse cases are investigated, processed, and prosecuted were expressed by most interviewees regardless of jurisdiction. These concerns can be addressed by exploring and, when possible, adopting the following recommendations:

Training

All interviewees agreed that more aggressive training of police officers, prosecutors, humane investigators, and judges would be beneficial. Training should include information on how to analyze and interpret the language and different elements of the anti-cruelty laws, how to investigate cruelty cases, how to collect and handle evidence, how to prosecute cases, how to recognize related types of crimes (such as domestic violence, child abuse, and elder abuse), and how to encourage the court to impose appropriate and creative penalties.

Definitions

Many interviewees expressed concern about the vague and confusing language used in the definitions sections of the anti-cruelty laws. Because each state has a unique anti-cruelty law, it is recommended that attorneys with expertise in criminal law and animal law review these sections. The Animal Legal Defense Fund has model language that can be used as a starting point for proposed statutory revisions. (See Appendix D.)

Dedicated Prosecutor/Police Officer/Judge/Court

Many interviewees expressed frustration over the lack of cooperation between the agencies charged with investigating and prosecuting animal abuse cases and the random assignment of different police officers, prosecutors, and judges to new cases. Interviewees felt strongly that assigning all cruelty cases to the same police officer(s), prosecutor(s), and court would increase efficiencies, create meaningful expertise, and result in more cases being successfully prosecuted.

Public Education

Information about the "link" between animal abuse and human violence was seen as critical for purposes of creating community support for taking animal abuse seriously as a violent crime. Some interviewees also urged public education about the basics of the anti-cruelty laws and how the average person can spot abuse and report it effectively.

Felony Laws in All States

Although there was some confusion and disagreement about whether the actual number of prosecutions increased after the passage of a felony law, virtually all interviewees agreed that felony laws receive more attention and resources on every level—police, prosecutor, judge, the public, and the media—and that the implications for a defendant charged and convicted on a felony were vastly different than if the same crime had been charged as a misdemeanor. Thus, interviewees generally agreed that the inclusion of a felony level anti-cruelty law was an important step in the ultimate goal of reducing animal abuse in the community.

Education About/Improvement of Cost of Care and Forfeiture Laws

Some interviewees were concerned that existing cost of care and forfeiture laws were not being utilized to the full extent because of short deadlines to file forfeiture petitions or from a general lack of awareness of forfeiture as a mechanism to gain legal custody of the abused animals before the completion of the criminal case. Attorneys concerned about this problem should review their states' forfeiture law to ensure that it is working properly within the system. If no cost of care/forfeiture provision exists, attorneys should consider working with the legislature to add one. (See Appendix D for an example of suggested language.) Finally, when working with the police or prosecutor on an animal abuse case, activists and caseworkers should make sure law enforcement is aware of the forfeiture provision and assist them in taking advantage of it.

Statistical Database

Very few statistics on animal abuse cases exist, and those that do exist are confusing and incomplete. All interviewees agreed that creating a standardized method of collecting and maintaining animal abuse statistics would be extremely beneficial for the purposes of analyzing the effectiveness of specific anti-cruelty statutes, identifying which types of animal abuse are more common, and responding more effectively in those areas where the most animal abuse is occurring. Interviewees also stated that the most effective way of ensuring that statistics will be kept and maintained in an appropriate manner is to create a law that requires agencies to do so. Securing legislative appropriations to fund the technical infrastructure for such a database was also perceived as being critically important.

Notes

1. Pamela D. Frasch is an attorney for and Vice President of Legal Affairs for the Animal Legal Defense Fund. In addition, she is an adjunct professor of law at Northwestern School of Law of Lewis & Clark College in Portland, Ore., and is the co-editor of *Animal Law—Cases and Materials, 3rd Ed.* (Carolina Academic Press, 2006).

2. U.S. states generally categorize crimes into two principal groups—felonies and misdemeanors. The difference between the categories usually depends on the severity of the punishment. In most states, felony penalties provide for incarceration of a year or longer. If less than a year, then it is considered a misdemeanor. Some states also categorize certain crimes as "wobblers," meaning that the crime can be viewed as either a misdemeanor or a felony. In that case, the convicted defendant may be incarcerated for more or less than a year, depending on the details of the particular case.

3. California, Florida, Louisiana, Massachusetts, Oklahoma, Rhode Island, and Wisconsin.

4. Massachusetts (1804), Oklahoma (1882), and Rhode Island (1896).

5. In total, 41 states plus the District of Columbia now have some form of felony anti-cruelty law. The remaining jurisdictions without felony anti-cruelty provisions are Alaska, Arkansas, Hawaii, Idaho, Kansas, Mississippi, North Dakota, South Dakota, and Utah.

6. The author thanks Cara Frisbie, Russell Cole, and Terence Woodsome for their assistance in conducting these interviews. All of the interviews were conducted during the summer of 2004 while Ms. Frisbie, Mr. Cole, and Mr. Woodsome were summer law associates at the law firm of Latham & Watkins in Menlo Park, California.

7. One exception is Florida, which shows a dramatic increase in the number of *arrests* on a statewide basis. (See Appendix C.) Statistics regarding whether those arrest resulted in prosecutions were not available.

8. The statutory laws referenced in this chapter were current as January 1, 2006. There has been much legislative activity in the field since that time, so please check for the latest legislative developments in the referenced jurisdictions before relying on the provisions set forth in this chapter.

9. According to one interviewee, however, this "antiquated" language has been used successfully very recently in prosecuting individuals for holding dogsled races on city streets.

10. In order to prove a crime, a prosecutor must generally prove four elements: (1) that the defendant engaged in some conduct (2) while having a particular mental state (3) which resulted in (4) a prohibited consequence. The second element (mental state) generally falls under three categories: (1) knowingly, (2) negligently, or (3) intentionally. In this case "intentionally" means that the defended purposefully engaged in the prohibited conduct.

11. The statistics did not include information on all misdemeanor arrests or convictions. As a result, the statistics falsely give the impression that more felony than misdemeanor arrests have been made under New York's anti-cruelty laws.

12. The New York Supreme Court is the trial court of unlimited original jurisdiction that generally hears cases outside the jurisdiction of other trial courts of more limited jurisdiction, and that exercises jurisdiction over felony charges.

Appendix A
Relevant State Anti-Cruelty Laws

California Penal Code
§ 597 – Cruelty to Animals

(a) Except as provided in subdivision (c) of this section or Section 599c, every person who maliciously and intentionally maims, mutilates, tortures, or wounds a living animal, or maliciously and intentionally kills an animal, is guilty of an offense punishable by imprisonment in the state prison, or by a fine of not more than twenty thousand dollars ($20,000), or by both the fine and imprisonment, or, alternatively, by imprisonment in a county jail for not more than one year, or by a fine of not more than twenty thousand dollars ($20,000), or by both the fine and imprisonment.

(b) Except as otherwise provided in subdivision (a) or (c), every person who overdrives, overloads, drives when overloaded, overworks, tortures, torments, deprives of necessary sustenance, drink, or shelter, cruelly beats, mutilates, or cruelly kills any animal, or causes or procures any animal to be so overdriven, overloaded, driven when overloaded, overworked, tortured, tormented, deprived of necessary sustenance, drink, shelter, or to be cruelly beaten, mutilated, or cruelly killed; and whoever, having the charge or custody of any animal, either as owner or otherwise, subjects any animal to needless suffering, or inflicts unnecessary cruelty upon the animal, or in any manner abuses any animal, or fails to provide the animal with proper food, drink, or shelter or protection from the weather, or who drives, rides, or otherwise uses the animal when unfit for labor, is, for every such offense, guilty of a crime punishable as a misdemeanor or as a felony or alternatively punishable as a misdemeanor or a felony and by a fine of not more than twenty thousand dollars ($20,000).

(c) Every person who maliciously and intentionally maims, mutilates, or tortures any mammal, bird, reptile, amphibian, or fish as described in subdivision (d), is guilty of an offense punishable by imprisonment in the state prison, or by a fine of not more than twenty thousand dollars ($20,000), or by both the fine and imprisonment, or, alternatively, by imprisonment in the county jail for not more than one year, by a fine of not more than twenty thousand dollars ($20,000), or by both the fine and imprisonment.

(d) Subdivision (c) applies to any mammal, bird, reptile, amphibian, or fish which is a creature described as follows:

(1) Endangered species or threatened species as described in Chapter 1.5 (commencing with Section 2050) of Division 3 of the Fish and Game Code.
(2) Fully protected birds described in Section 3511 of the Fish and Game Code.
(3) Fully protected mammals described in Chapter 8 (commencing with Section 4700) of Part 3 of Division 4 of the Fish and Game Code.
(4) Fully protected reptiles and amphibians described in Chapter 2 (commencing with Section 5050) of Division 5 of the Fish and Game Code.
(5) Fully protected fish as described in Section 5515 of the Fish and Game Code.

This subdivision does not supersede or affect any provisions of law relating to taking of the described species, including, but not limited to, Section 12008 of the Fish and Game Code.

(e) For the purposes of subdivision (c), each act of malicious and intentional maiming, mutilating, or torturing a separate specimen of a creature described in subdivision (d) is a separate offense. If any person is charged with a violation of subdivision (c), the proceedings shall be subject to Section 12157 of the Fish and Game Code.

(f)(1) Upon the conviction of a person charged with a violation of this section by causing or permitting an act of cruelty, as defined in Section 599b, all animals lawfully seized and impounded with respect to the violation by a peace officer, officer of a humane society, or officer of a pound or animal regulation department of a public agency shall be adjudged by the court to be forfeited and shall thereupon be awarded to the impounding officer for proper disposition. A person convicted of a violation of this section by causing or permitting an act of cruelty, as defined in Section 599b, shall be liable to the impounding officer for all costs of impoundment from the time of seizure to the time of proper disposition.

(2) Mandatory seizure or impoundment shall not apply to animals in properly conducted scientific experiments or investigations performed under the authority of the faculty of a regularly incorporated medical college or university of this state.

(g) Notwithstanding any other provision of law, if a defendant is granted probation for a conviction under this section, the court shall order the defendant to pay for, and successfully complete, counseling, as determined by the court, designed to evaluate and treat behavior or conduct disorders. If the court finds that the defendant is financially unable to pay for that counseling, the court may develop a sliding fee schedule based upon the defendant's ability to pay. An indigent defendant may negotiate a deferred payment schedule, but shall pay a nominal fee if the defendant has the ability to pay the nominal fee. County mental health departments or Medi-Cal shall be responsible for the costs of counseling required by this section only for those persons who meet the medical necessity criteria for mental health managed care pursuant to Section 1830.205 of Title 7 of the California Code of Regulations or the targeted population criteria specified in Section 5600.3 of the Welfare and Institutions Code. The counseling specified in this subdivision shall be in addition to any other terms and conditions of probation, including any term of imprisonment and any fine. This provision specifies a mandatory additional term of probation and is not to be utilized as an alternative in lieu of imprisonment in the state prison or county jail when such a sentence is otherwise appropriate. If the court does not order custody as a condition of probation for a conviction under this section, the court shall specify on the court record the reason or reasons for not ordering custody. This subdivision shall not apply to cases involving police dogs or horses as described in Section 600.

Colorado Revised Statutes Annotated Section 18-9-202—Cruelty to Animals; Aggravated Cruelty to Animals

(1)(a) A person commits cruelty to animals if he or she knowingly, recklessly, or with criminal negligence overdrives, overloads, overworks, torments, deprives of necessary sustenance, unnecessarily or cruelly beats, allows to be housed in a manner that results in chronic or repeated serious physical harm, carries or confines in or upon any vehicles in a cruel or reckless manner, or otherwise mistreats or neglects any animal, or causes or procures it to be done, or, having the charge or custody of any animal, fails to provide it with proper food, drink, or protection from the weather consistent with the species, breed, and type of animal involved, or abandons an animal.

(b) Any person who intentionally abandons a dog or cat commits the offense of cruelty to animals.

(1.5)(a) A person commits cruelty to animals if he or she recklessly or with criminal negligence tortures, needlessly mutilates, or needlessly kills an animal.

(b) A person commits aggravated cruelty to animals if he or she knowingly tortures, needlessly mutilates, or needlessly kills an animal.

(1.6) As used in this section, unless the context otherwise requires:

(a) "Serious physical harm" means any of the following:

(I) Any physical harm that carries a substantial risk of death;

(II) Any physical harm that causes permanent maiming or that involves some temporary, substantial maiming; or

(III) Any physical harm that causes acute pain of a duration that results in substantial suffering.

(1.8) A peace officer having authority to act under this section may take possession of and impound an animal that the peace officer has probable cause to believe is a victim of a violation of subsection (1) or (1.5) of this section or is a victim of a violation of section 18-9-204 and as a result of the violation is endangered if it remains with the owner or custodian.

(2)(a) Except as otherwise provided in paragraph (b) of this subsection (2), cruelty to animals is a class 1 misdemeanor.

(a.5)(I)(A) In addition to the sentence imposed pursuant to this subsection (2), any person convicted of aggravated cruelty to animals pursuant to subsection

(1.5) of this section shall pay a surcharge of up to four hundred dollars to the clerk of the court in the county in which the conviction occurs or in which a deferred sentence is entered. Each clerk shall transmit the moneys to the court administrator of the judicial district in which the offense occurred for credit to the fund.

(B) This subparagraph (I) is repealed, effective July 1, 2005.

(II) In addition to any other sentence imposed for a violation of this section, the court may order an offender to complete an anger management treatment program or any other appropriate treatment program.

(III) The court shall order an evaluation to be conducted prior to sentencing to assist the court in determining an appropriate sentence. The person ordered to undergo an evaluation shall be required to pay the cost of the evaluation, unless the person qualifies for a public defender, then the cost will be paid by the judicial district. If the evaluation results in a recommendation of treatment and if the court so finds, the person shall be ordered to complete an anger management treatment program or any other treatment program that the court may deem appropriate.

(IV) Upon successful completion of an anger management treatment program or any other treatment program deemed appropriate by the court, the court may suspend any fine imposed, except for a five hundred dollar mandatory minimum fine which shall be imposed at the time of sentencing.

(V) In addition to any other sentence imposed upon a person for a violation of any criminal law under this title, any person convicted of a second or subsequent conviction for any crime, the underlying factual basis of which has been found by the court to include an act of cruelty to animals, shall be required to pay a mandatory minimum fine of one thousand dollars and shall be required to complete an anger management treatment program or any other appropriate treatment program.

(VI) Nothing in this paragraph (a.5) shall preclude the court from ordering treatment in any appropriate case.

(VII) This paragraph (a.5) does not apply to the treatment of pack or draft animals by negligently overdriving, overloading, or overworking them, or the treatment of livestock and other animals used in the farm or ranch production of food, fiber, or other agricultural products when such treatment is in accordance with accepted agricultural animal husbandry practices, the treatment of animals involved in activities regulated pursuant to article 60 of title 12, C.R.S., the treatment of animals involved in research if such research facility is operating under rules set forth by the state or federal government, the treatment of animals involved in rodeos, the treatment of dogs used for legal hunting activities, wildlife nuisances, or to statutes regulating activities concerning wildlife and predator control in the state, including trapping.

(b)(I) A second or subsequent conviction under the provisions of paragraph (a) of subsection (1) of this section is a class 6 felony. A plea of nolo contendere accepted by the court shall be considered a conviction for the purposes of this section.

(II) In any case where the court sentences a person convicted of a class 6 felony under the provisions of this paragraph (b) to probation, the court shall, in addition to any other condition of probation imposed, order that:

(A) The offender, pursuant to section 18-1.3-202(1), be committed to the county jail for ninety days; or

(B) The offender, pursuant to section 18-1.3-105(3), be subject to home detention for no fewer than ninety days.

(III) In any case where an offender is committed to the county jail or placed in home detention pursuant to subparagraph (II) of this paragraph (b), the court shall enter judgment against the offender for all costs assessed pursuant to section 18-1.3-701, including, but not limited to, the cost of care.

(c) Aggravated cruelty to animals is a class 6 felony; except that a second or subsequent conviction for the offense of aggravated cruelty to animals is a class 5 felony. A plea of nolo contendere accepted by the court shall be considered a conviction for purposes of this section.

(2.5) It shall be an affirmative defense to a charge brought under this section involving injury or death to a dog that the dog was found running, worrying, or injuring sheep, cattle, or other livestock.

(3) Nothing in this part 2 shall be construed to amend or in any manner change the authority of the wildlife commission, as established in title 33, C.R.S., or to prohibit any conduct therein authorized or permitted.

Florida Statute § 828.12—Cruelty to Animals

(1) A person who unnecessarily overloads, overdrives, torments, deprives of necessary sustenance or shelter, or unnecessarily mutilates, or kills any animal, or causes the same to be done, or carries in or upon any vehicle, or otherwise, any animal in a cruel

or inhumane manner, is guilty of a misdemeanor of the first degree, punishable as provided in s. 775.082 or by a fine of not more than $5,000, or both.

(2) A person who intentionally commits an act to any animal which results in the cruel death, or excessive or repeated infliction of unnecessary pain or suffering, or causes the same to be done, is guilty of a felony of the third degree, punishable as provided in s. 775.082 or by a fine of not more than $10,000, or both.

(a) A person convicted of a violation of this subsection, where the finder of fact determines that the violation includes the knowing and intentional torture or torment of an animal that injures, mutilates, or kills the animal, shall be ordered to pay a minimum mandatory fine of $2,500 and undergo psychological counseling or complete an anger management treatment program.

(b) Any person convicted of a second or subsequent violation of this subsection shall be required to pay a minimum mandatory fine of $5,000 and serve a minimum mandatory period of incarceration of 6 months. In addition, the person shall be released only upon expiration of sentence, shall not be eligible for parole, control release, or any form of early release, and must serve 100 percent of the court-imposed sentence. Any plea of nolo contendere shall be considered a conviction for purposes of this subsection.

(3) A veterinarian licensed to practice in the state shall be held harmless from either criminal or civil liability for any decisions made or services rendered under the provisions of this section. Such a veterinarian is, therefore, under this subsection, immune from a lawsuit for his or her part in an investigation of cruelty to animals.

(4) A person who intentionally trips, fells, ropes, or lassos the legs of a horse by any means for the purpose of entertainment or sport shall be guilty of a third degree felony, punishable as provided in s. 775.082, s. 775.083, or s. 775.084. As used in this subsection, "trip" means any act that consists of the use of any wire, pole, stick, rope, or other apparatus to cause a horse to fall or lose its balance, and "horse" means any animal of any registered breed of the genus *Equus*, or any recognized hybrid thereof. The provisions of this subsection shall not apply when tripping is used:

(a) To control a horse that is posing an immediate threat to other livestock or human beings;
(b) For the purpose of identifying ownership of the horse when its ownership is unknown; or
(c) For the purpose of administering veterinary care to the horse.

Florida Statute § 828.24—Prohibited Acts; Exemptions

(1) No person shall kill an animal in any way except by an approved humane method.

(2) No person shall shackle or hoist with intent to kill any animal prior to rendering the animal insensitive to pain.

(3) Nothing in this section precludes the enforcement of s. 828.12 relating to cruelty to animals.

Florida Statute § 828.122—Fighting or Baiting Animals; Offenses; Penalties

(1) This act may be cited as "The Animal Fighting Act."

(2) As used in this section, the term:

(a) "Animal fighting" means fighting between roosters or other birds or between dogs, bears, or other animals.
(b) "Baiting" means to attack with violence, to provoke, or to harass an animal with one or more animals for the purpose of training an animal for, or to cause an animal to engage in, fights with or among other animals. In addition, "baiting" means the use of live animals in the training of racing greyhounds.
(c) "Person" means every natural person, firm, copartnership, association, or corporation.

(3) Any person who knowingly commits any of the following acts commits a felony of the third degree, punishable as provided in s. 775.082, s. 775.083, or s. 775.084:

(a) Baiting, breeding, training, transporting, selling, owning, possessing, or using any wild or domestic animal for the purpose of animal fighting or baiting;
(b) Owning, possessing, or selling equipment for use in any activity described in paragraph (a);
(c) Owning, leasing, managing, operating, or having control of any property kept or used for any activity described in paragraph (a) or paragraph (b);
(d) Promoting, staging, advertising, or charging any admission fee to a fight or baiting between two or more animals;
(e) Performing any service or act to facilitate animal fighting or baiting, including, but not limited to, providing security, refereeing, or handling or transporting animals or being a stakeholder of any money wagered on animal fighting or baiting;

(f) Removing or facilitating the removal of any animal impounded under this section from an agency where the animal is impounded or from a location designated by the court under subsection (4), subsection (5), or subsection (7), without the prior authorization of the court;

(g) Betting or wagering any money or other valuable consideration on the fighting or baiting of animals; or

(h) Attending the fighting or baiting of animals. Notwithstanding any provision of this subsection to the contrary, possession of the animal alone does not constitute a violation of this section.

(4) If a court finds probable cause to believe that a violation of this section or s. 828.12 has occurred, the court shall order the seizure of any animals and equipment used in committing the violation and shall provide for appropriate and humane care or disposition of the animals. This subsection is not a limitation on the power to seize animals as evidence at the time of arrest.

(5) If an animal shelter or other location is unavailable, a court may order the animal to be impounded on the property of its owner or possessor and shall order such person to provide all necessary care for the animal and to allow regular inspections of the animal by a person designated by the court.

(6) If a veterinarian finds that an animal kept or used in violation of this section is suffering from an injury or a disease severe enough that it is not possible to humanely house and care for the animal pending completion of a hearing held under s. 828.073(2), final disposition of the criminal charges, or court-ordered forfeiture, the veterinarian may euthanize the animal as specified in s. 828.058. A veterinarian licensed to practice in this state shall be held harmless from criminal or civil liability for any decisions made or services rendered under this subsection.

(7) If an animal can be housed in a humane manner, the provisions of s. 828.073 shall apply. For the purpose of a hearing provided pursuant to s. 828.073(2), any animal baited, bred, trained, transported, sold, owned, possessed, or used for the purpose of animal fighting or baiting shall be considered mistreated.

(8) In addition to other penalties prescribed by law, the court may issue an order prohibiting a person who is convicted of a violation of this section from owning, possessing, keeping, harboring, or having custody or control over any animals within the species that are the subject of the conviction, or any animals kept for the purpose of fighting or baiting, for a period of time determined by the court.

(9) This section shall not apply to:

(a) Any person simulating a fight for the purpose of using the simulated fight as part of a motion picture which will be used on television or in a motion picture, provided s. 828.12 is not violated.

(b) Any person using animals to pursue or take wildlife or to participate in any hunting regulated or subject to being regulated by the rules and regulations of the Fish and Wildlife Conservation Commission.

(c) Any person using animals to work livestock for agricultural purposes.

(d) Any person violating s. 828.121.

(e) Any person using dogs to hunt wild hogs or to retrieve domestic hogs pursuant to customary hunting or agricultural practices.

(10) This section shall not prohibit, impede, or otherwise interfere with recognized animal husbandry and training techniques or practices not otherwise specifically prohibited by law.

Illinois Statute Chapter 510, Act 70 § 3.01—Cruel Treatment

No person or owner may beat, cruelly treat, torment, starve, overwork or otherwise abuse any animal.

No owner may abandon any animal where it may become a public charge or may suffer injury, hunger or exposure.

A person convicted of violating this Section is guilty of a Class A misdemeanor. A second or subsequent conviction for a violation of this Section is a Class 4 felony. In addition to any other penalty provided by law, upon conviction for violating this Section, the court may order the convicted person to undergo a psychological or psychiatric evaluation and to undergo any treatment at the convicted person's expense that the court determines to be appropriate after due consideration of the evidence. If the convicted person is a juvenile or a companion animal hoarder, the court must order the convicted person to undergo a psychological or psychiatric evaluation and to undergo treatment that the court determines to be appropriate after due consideration of the evaluation.

Illinois Statute Chapter 510, Act 70 § 3.02—Aggravated Cruelty

No person may intentionally commit an act that causes a companion animal to suffer serious injury or death. Aggravated cruelty does not include euthanasia of a companion animal through recognized methods approved by the Department of Agriculture.

A person convicted of violating Section 3.02 is guilty of a Class 4 felony. A second or subsequent violation is a Class 3 felony. In addition to any other penalty provided by law, upon conviction for violating this Section, the court may order the convicted person to undergo a psychological or psychiatric evaluation and to undergo any treatment at the convicted person's expense that the court determines to be appropriate after due consideration of the evaluation. If the convicted person is a juvenile or a companion animal hoarder, the court must order the convicted person to undergo a psychological or psychiatric evaluation and to undergo treatment that the court determines to be appropriate after due consideration of the evaluation.

Illinois Statute Chapter 510, Act 70 § 3.03—Animal Torture

(a) A person commits animal torture when that person without legal justification knowingly or intentionally tortures an animal. For purposes of this Section, and subject to subsection (b), "torture" means infliction of or subjection to extreme physical pain, motivated by an intent to increase or prolong the pain, suffering, or agony of the animal.

(b) For the purposes of this Section, "animal torture" does not include any death, harm, or injury caused to any animal by any of the following activities:

(1) any hunting, fishing, trapping, or other activity allowed under the Wildlife Code, the Wildlife Habitat Management Areas Act, or the Fish and Aquatic Life Code;

(2) any alteration or destruction of any animal done by any person or unit of government pursuant to statute, ordinance, court order, or the direction of a licensed veterinarian;

(3) any alteration or destruction of any animal by any person for any legitimate purpose, including, but not limited to: castration, culling, declawing, defanging, ear cropping, euthanasia, gelding, grooming, neutering, polling, shearing, shoeing, slaughtering, spaying, tail docking, and vivisection; and

(4) any other activity that may be lawfully done to an animal.

(c) A person convicted of violating this Section is guilty of a Class 3 felony. As a condition of the sentence imposed under this Section, the court shall order the offender to undergo a psychological or psychiatric evaluation and to undergo treatment that the court determines to be appropriate after due consideration of the evaluation.

New York Agriculture & Markets Code § 353—Overdriving, Torturing and Injuring Animals; Failure to Provide Proper Sustenance

A person who overdrives, overloads, tortures or cruelly beats or unjustifiably injures, maims, mutilates or kills any animal, whether wild or tame, and whether belonging to himself or to another, or deprives any animal of necessary sustenance, food or drink, or neglects or refuses to furnish it such sustenance or drink, or causes, procures or permits any animal to be overdriven, overloaded, tortured, cruelly beaten, or unjustifiably injured, maimed, mutilated or killed, or to be deprived of necessary food or drink, or who wilfully sets on foot, instigates, engages in, or in any way furthers any act of cruelty to any animal, or any act tending to produce such cruelty, is guilty of a misdemeanor, punishable by imprisonment for not more than one year, or by a fine of not more than one thousand dollars, or by both.

Nothing herein contained shall be construed to prohibit or interfere with any properly conducted scientific tests, experiments or investigations, involving the use of living animals, performed or conducted in laboratories or institutions, which are approved for these purposes by the state commissioner of health. The state commissioner of health shall prescribe the rules under which such approvals shall be granted, including therein standards regarding the care and treatment of any such animals. Such rules shall be published and copies thereof conspicuously posted in each such laboratory or institution. The state commissioner of health or his duly authorized representative shall have the power to inspect such laboratories or institutions to insure compliance with such rules and standards. Each such approval may be revoked at any time for failure to comply with such rules and in any case the approval shall be limited to a period not exceeding one year.

New York Agriculture & Markets Code § 353A—Aggravated Cruelty to Animals

1. A person is guilty of aggravated cruelty to animals when, with no justifiable purpose, he or she intentionally kills or intentionally causes serious physical injury to a companion animal with

aggravated cruelty. For purposes of this section, "aggravated cruelty" shall mean conduct which: (i) is intended to cause extreme physical pain; or (ii) is done or carried out in an especially depraved or sadistic manner.

2. Nothing contained in this section shall be construed to prohibit or interfere in any way with anyone lawfully engaged in hunting, trapping, or fishing, as provided in article eleven of the environmental conservation law, the dispatch of rabid or diseased animals, as provided in article twenty-one of the public health law, or the dispatch of animals posing a threat to human safety or other animals, where such action is otherwise legally authorized, or any properly conducted scientific tests, experiments, or investigations involving the use of living animals, performed or conducted in laboratories or institutions approved for such purposes by the commissioner of health pursuant to section three hundred fifty-three of this article.

3. Aggravated cruelty to animals is a felony. A defendant convicted of this offense shall be sentenced pursuant to paragraph (b) of subdivision one of section 55.10 of the penal law provided, however, that any term of imprisonment imposed for violation of this section shall be a definite sentence, which may not exceed two years.

Texas Penal Code § 42.09—Cruelty to Animals

(a) A person commits an offense if the person intentionally or knowingly:

(1) tortures an animal;
(2) fails unreasonably to provide necessary food, care, or shelter for an animal in the person's custody;
(3) abandons unreasonably an animal in the person's custody;
(4) transports or confines an animal in a cruel manner;
(5) kills, seriously injures, or administers poison to an animal, other than cattle, horses, sheep, swine, or goats, belonging to another without legal authority or the owner's effective consent;
(6) causes one animal to fight with another;
(7) uses a live animal as a lure in dog race training or in dog coursing on a racetrack;
(8) trips a horse;
(9) injures an animal, other than cattle, horses, sheep, swine, or goats, belonging to another without legal authority or the owner's effective consent; or
(10) seriously overworks an animal.

(b) It is a defense to prosecution under this section that the actor was engaged in bona fide experimentation for scientific research.

(c) For purposes of this section:

(1) "Abandon" includes abandoning an animal in the person's custody without making reasonable arrangements for assumption of custody by another person.
(2) "Animal" means a domesticated living creature and wild living creature previously captured. "Animal" does not include an uncaptured wild creature or a wild creature whose capture was accomplished by conduct at issue under this section.
(3) "Cruel manner" includes a manner that causes or permits unjustified or unwarranted pain or suffering.
(4) "Custody" includes responsibility for the health, safety, and welfare of an animal subject to the person's care and control, regardless of ownership of the animal.
(5) "Necessary food, care, or shelter" includes food, care, or shelter provided to the extent required to maintain the animal in a state of good health.
(6) "Trip" means to use an object to cause a horse to fall or lose its balance.

(d) An offense under Subsection (a)(2), (3), (4), (9), or (10) is a Class A misdemeanor, except that the offense is a state jail felony if the person has previously been convicted two times under this section.

(e) It is a defense to prosecution under Subsection (a)(5) that the animal was discovered on the person's property in the act of or immediately after injuring or killing the person's goats, sheep, cattle, horses, swine, or poultry and that the person killed or injured the animal at the time of this discovery.

(f) It is a defense to prosecution under Subsection (a)(8) that the actor tripped the horse for the purpose of identifying the ownership of the horse or giving veterinary care to the horse.

(g) It is a defense to prosecution for an offense under this section that the person had a reasonable fear of bodily injury to the person or to another by a dangerous wild animal as defined by Section 822.101, Health and Safety Code.

(h) It is an exception to the application of this section that the conduct engaged in by the actor is a generally accepted and otherwise lawful:

(1) use of an animal if that use occurs solely for the purpose of:
(A) fishing, hunting, or trapping; or
(B) wildlife control as regulated by state and federal law; or

(2) animal husbandry or farming practice involving livestock.

(i) An offense under Subsection (a)(1), (5), (6), (7), or (8) is a state jail felony, except that the offense is a felony of the third degree if the person has previously been convicted two times under this section.

Texas Penal Code § 42.10—Dog Fighting

(a) A person commits an offense if he intentionally or knowingly:

(1) causes a dog to fight with another dog;
(2) for a pecuniary benefit causes a dog to fight with another dog;
(3) participates in the earnings of or operates a facility used for dog fighting;
(4) uses or permits another to use any real estate, building, room, tent, arena, or other property for dog fighting;
(5) owns or trains a dog with the intent that the dog be used in an exhibition of dog fighting; or
(6) attends as a spectator an exhibition of dog fighting.

(b) In this section, "dog fighting" means any situation in which one dog attacks or fights with another dog.

(c) A conviction under Subdivision (2), (3), or (4) of Subsection (a) may be had upon the uncorroborated testimony of a party to the offense.

(d) It is a defense to prosecution under Subdivision (1) or (2) of Subsection (a) that the actor caused a dog to fight with another dog to protect livestock, other property, or a person from the other dog, and for no other purpose.

(e) An offense under Subdivision (1) or (5) of Subsection (a) is a Class A misdemeanor. An offense under Subdivision (2), (3), or (4) of Subsection (a) is a state jail felony. An offense under Subdivision (6) of Subsection (a) is a Class C misdemeanor.

Appendix B
Summary of Available Statistics from All Jurisdictions

Location	Provided by	Felony law implemented	Arrests before felony law implemented	Arrests after felony law implemented	Convictions/ Acquittals	Dismissed/ Other
California (Marin County)	Marin County Deputy District Attorney	1988	Statistics not kept	N/A	N/A	N/A
Colorado (Statewide)	Colorado Dept. of Agriculture	2002	Total Impounds for July 2004 = 91 Total Investigations for July 2004 = 699 Total Warnings/ Summons for July 2004 = 385	N/A	N/A	N/A
Florida (Hillsborough County)	County Animal Services	1989	N/A	2000: 2 2001: 15 2002: 2 2003: 9 as of 6/30/04: 19	Convictions 2000: 2 2001: N/A 2002: 2 2003: 6 2004: 1 Acquittals 2000: 0 2001: N/A 2002: 0 2003: 0 2004: 0	2001: 2 dismissed, 7 no charges filed 2003: 1 no charges filed, 1 wanted, 1 trial set 2004: 1 wanted, 1 trial set, 12 filed, 4 hearing/ arraignment set
Illinois (Chicago)	Dog Advisory Working Group (DAWG)	1999	N/A	2001: 32 misd., 14 fel. 2002: 42 misd., 8 fel. 2003: 80 misd., 29 fel.	Convictions 2001: 25 (5 fel.) 2002: 23 (6 fel.) 2003: 38 (6 fel.) Acquittals 2001: 3 2002: 6 (1 fel.) 2003: 5 (1 fel.)	2001: 2 dismissed, 1 violation of parole, 1 extradited to TX 2002: 9 dismissed 2003: 13 dismissed, 2 violations of parole

Location	Provided by	Felony law implemented	Arrests before felony law implemented	Arrests after felony law implemented	Convictions/ Acquittals	Dismissed/ Other
Illinois (Chicago)	Chicago Police Dept. reports gathered by DAWG	1999	N/A	2001: 49 misd. arrests, 18 fel. arrests 2002: 151 offenses, 49 misd. arrests, 18 fel. arrests 2003: 409 offenses, 107 misd. arrests, 13 fel. arrests 2004: 135 offenses, 33 misd. arrests, 6 fel. arrests	N/A	N/A
Illinois (Chicago)	Chicago Police Dept.'s Research and Dev. Division	1999	N/A	2001: 49 misd., 18 fel. 2002: 90 misd., 19 fel. 2003: 107 misd., 13 fel. through 6/30/04: 3 misd., 6 fel.	N/A	N/A
Illinois (Sangamon County)	Clerk of Circuit Court	1999	N/A	47	1994: 0 not guilty 1995: 0 not guilty 1996: 0 not guilty 1997: 0 not guilty 1998: 0 not guilty 1999: 0 not guilty 2000: 1 not guilty 2001: 1 not guilty 2002: N/A 2003: N/A 2004: N/A	1994: 4 dismissed, MOS 1995: 3 dismissed, MOS, 1 w/hold judgment/state 1996: 0 1997: 2 dismissed, MOS 1998: 2 dismissed, MOS 1999: 1 dismissed, MOS 2000: 1 dismissed, MOS, 1 w/hold judgment/ state 01: 2 dismissed, MOS, 1 terminated unsatisf 01: 2 dismissed, MOS, 1 terminated unsatisf

Location	Provided by	Felony law implemented	Arrests before felony law implemented	Arrests after felony law implemented	Convictions/ Acquittals	Dismissed/ Other
						02: 2 w/hold judgment unsatisf 03: 3 w/hold judgment/state 04: N/A
New York (Albany County)	Albany County Animal Control	1999	N/A	Only 2 on record – anything older than 18 months is not accessible	Convictions 2 guilty	N/A
New York (Statewide)	New York State Division of Criminal Justice Services	1999	N/A	1999: 2 2000: 30 2001: 40 2002: 65 2003: 47	1999: 2 (1 served time) (1 fel.) 2000: 17 (10 served time) (12 fel.) 2001: 28 (11 served time) (22 fel.) 2002: 40 (11 served time) (28 fel.) 2003: 22 12 served time) (19 fel)	Dismissed: 1999: 0 2000: 6 2001: 4 2002: 12 2003: 2 Acquitted: 1999–2001: 0 2002: 1 2003: 0
Texas (Harris ounty)	Houston Animal Control	1997	N/A	N/A	Convictions 2001: misd. 26, fel. 2 2002: misd. 4, fel. 5 2003: misd. 12, fel. 11 2004: misd. 7, fel. 6 Acquittals 2001: misd. 1, fel. 0 2002: misd. 0, fel. 1 2003: misd. 1, fel. 3 2004: misd. 6, fel. 2	2001: misd. 3, fel. 0 2002: misd. 16, fel. 7 2003: misd. 12, fel. 5 2004: misd. 6, fel. 0

Key:

Misd.: Misdemeanor
Fel.: Felony
N/A: Not Available
MOS: Motion of State

Appendix C

Statewide Arrests under Florida Statute § 828.12 and Related Offenses*

Statute	1972	1973	1974	1975	1976	1977	1978	1979	1980	1981	1982	1983	1984	1985	1986	1987	1988
§ 828.12	6	10	23	29	19	28	16	28	45	46	49	37	45	106	47	50	20
§ 828.12(1)	0	0	0	0	0	0	0	0	0	0	0	0	0	0	0	0	0
§ 828.12(2)	0	0	0	0	0	0	0	0	0	0	0	0	0	0	0	0	0
§ 828.12(4)	0	0	0	0	0	0	0	0	0	0	0	0	0	0	0	0	0
§ 828.122	0	0	0	0	0	0	2	2	2	2	60	3	2	2	6	25	10
§ 828.122(3)(a)	0	0	0	0	0	0	0	0	0	0	0	0	0	0	0	0	0
§ 828.122(3)(b)	0	0	0	0	0	0	0	0	0	0	0	0	0	0	0	0	0
§ 828.122(3)(c)	0	0	0	0	0	0	0	0	0	0	0	0	0	0	0	0	0
§ 828.122(3)(h)	0	0	0	0	0	0	0	0	0	0	0	0	0	0	0	0	0
§ 828.122(3)(h)	0	0	0	0	0	0	0	0	0	0	0	0	0	0	0	0	0
§ 828.122(4)	0	0	0	0	0	0	0	0	0	0	1	0	0	0	0	0	0
§ 828.122(4)(a)	0	0	0	0	0	0	0	0	0	0	0	0	0	0	0	0	0
§ 828.122(4)(b)	0	0	0	0	0	0	0	0	0	0	0	0	0	0	0	0	0
§ 828.123	0	0	0	0	0	1	0	0	0	0	0	0	0	0	0	0	0
§ 828.123(2)	0	0	0	0	0	0	0	0	0	0	0	0	0	0	0	0	0
§ 828.125	0	0	0	0	0	0	0	0	0	0	0	0	0	0	0	0	0
§ 828.125(1)	0	0	0	0	0	0	0	0	0	0	0	0	0	0	0	0	0
§ 828.125(3)	0	0	0	0	0	0	0	0	0	0	0	0	0	0	0	0	0
Total	**6**	**10**	**23**	**29**	**19**	**29**	**18**	**30**	**47**	**48**	**110**	**40**	**47**	**108**	**53**	**75**	**30**

* § 822.122 is an anti-fighting/baiting statute, § 828.123 prohibits killing of dogs and cats for pelts, and § 828.125 prohibits abuse of horses and cattle.

Statute	1989	1990	1991	1992	1993	1994	1995	1996	1997	1998	1999	2000	2001	2002	2003	6/2004	Total
§ 828.12	65	69	79	73	90	81	124	161	162	152	103	62	46	26	37	19	1953
§ 828.12(1)	0	0	0	0	0	0	0	0	0	12	48	76	108	120	153	70	587
§ 828.12(2)	0	0	0	0	0	0	0	0	0	20	62	96	116	128	188	83	693
§ 828.12(4)	0	0	0	0	0	0	0	0	0	0	0	0	1	1	1	0	3
§ 828.122	22	12	9	48	13	20	14	26	27	32	5	18	24	1	9	9	405
§ 828.122(3)(a)	0	0	0	0	0	0	0	0	0	7	11	35	72	23	108	21	277
§ 828.122(3)(b)	0	0	0	0	0	0	0	0	0	1	0	6	2	1	8	51	69
§ 828.122(3)(c)	0	0	0	0	0	0	0	0	0	0	0	0	0	0	1	0	1
§ 828.122(3)(h)	0	0	0	0	0	0	0	0	0	0	0	0	0	0	0	44	44
§ 828.122(3)(h)	0	0	0	0	0	0	0	0	0	0	0	0	0	0	0	42	42
§ 828.122(4)	0	0	0	0	0	0	0	0	0	0	0	0	0	0	0	0	1
§ 828.122(4)(a)	0	0	0	0	0	0	0	0	0	0	2	4	0	0	3	11	20
§ 828.122(4)(b)	0	0	0	0	0	0	0	0	0	2	2	36	26	0	27	1	94
§ 828.123	0	0	0	0	0	0	0	0	0	0	0	0	0	0	0	0	1
§ 828.123(2)	0	0	0	0	0	0	0	0	0	0	0	0	0	0	0	2	2
§ 828.125	3	8	4	2	4	0	3	0	2	1	2	0	0	0	0	0	29
§ 828.125(1)	0	0	0	0	0	0	0	0	0	1	3	3	1	1	0	0	9
§ 828.125(3)	0	0	0	0	0	0	0	0	0	1	0	1	0	0	0	0	1
Total	90	89	92	123	107	101	141	187	191	228	238	337	396	301	535	353	4231

Appendix D
Animal Legal Defense Fund
Model State Animal Protection Laws

Definitions

A. ANIMAL

"Animal" means any nonhuman living creature.

B. GUARDIAN

"Guardian" means a person who has control, custody, possession, title, or other legal interest in an animal.

C. MINIMUM CARE

"Minimum care" means care sufficient to preserve the health and well-being of an animal and, except for emergencies or circumstances beyond the reasonable control of the guardian, includes, but is not limited to, the following requirements:

1. Food of sufficient quantity and quality to allow for normal growth or maintenance of body weight.
2. Open or adequate access to potable water of a drinkable temperature in sufficient quantity to satisfy the animal's needs.
3. Access to a barn, house or other enclosed structure sufficient to protect the animal from wind, rain, snow, or sun, and which has adequate bedding to protect against cold and dampness.
4. Veterinary care deemed necessary by a reasonably prudent person to relieve distress from injury, neglect, or disease.
5. Continuous access to an area:
   a. With adequate space for exercise necessary for the health of the animal. Inadequate space may be indicated by evidence of debility, stress, or abnormal behavior patterns.
   b. With air temperature suitable for the health of the animal.
   c. With adequate ventilation.
   d. With regular diurnal lighting cycles of either natural or artificial light.
   e. Kept reasonably clean and free from excess waste or other contaminants that could affect the animal's health.

D. PERSON

"Person" means an individual, corporation, trust, partnership, association, or any other legal entity.

E. PHYSICAL INJURY

"Physical injury" means physical trauma, impairment of condition, or pain inconsistent with reasonable handling or training techniques.

F. PHYSICAL TRAUMA

"Physical trauma" means fractures, cuts, burns, punctures, bruises, or other wounds or illnesses produced by violence or by a thermal or chemical agent.

G. POSSESSION

"Possession" means to have physical custody or to exercise dominion or control over an animal.

H. SERIOUS PHYSICAL INJURY

"Serious physical injury" means physical injury that creates a substantial risk of death or that causes protracted disfigurement, protracted impairment of health, or protracted loss or impairment of the function of a limb or bodily organ.

I. TORTURE

"Torture" means an action taken for the primary purpose of inflicting or prolonging pain.

Costs of Care Bonds

A. The guardian of an animal that has been impounded pending outcome of a criminal action charging a violation of the [animal protection statutes] may prevent disposition of the animal by an animal shelter, humane society, or other animal care agency that has temporary custody of the animal, by posting a bond with the court in an amount the court determines is sufficient to provide for the animal's minimum care for at least thirty days, including the day on which the animal was taken into custody. Such bond shall be filed with the court within ten days after the animal is impounded. If a bond is not so posted, the custodial animal care agency shall determine final disposition of the animal in accordance with reasonable practices for the humane treatment of animals. At the end of the time for which expenses are covered by the bond, if the guardian desires to prevent disposition of the animal by the custodial animal care agency, the guardian shall post a new bond with the court within ten days following the prior bond's expiration. If a new bond is not so posted, the custodial animal care agency shall determine final disposition of the animal in accordance with reasonable practices for the humane treatment of animals. However, nothing in this subsection shall prohibit the immediate disposition of the animal by euthanasia if, in the opinion of a licensed veterinarian, the animal is experiencing untreatable extreme pain or suffering. The guardian shall be liable for all costs of providing minimum care, or disposal of the animal.

B. If a bond has been posted in accordance with subsection (1) of this section, the custodial animal care agency may draw from the bond the actual reasonable costs incurred by the agency in providing minimum care to the impounded animal from the date of initial impoundment to the date of final disposition of the animal in the criminal action.

Forfeiture

In addition to any other sentence it may impose, a court shall require a defendant convicted under [any animal protection statute] to forfeit all legal interest of the defendant in the animal subjected to the violation. The court shall award all such interest to the animal to a humane society, animal shelter, or other organization that has as its principal purpose the humane treatment of animals.

Appendix E
Contact List

The following are the individuals and organizations interviewed for this report:

The Anti-Cruelty Society (Illinois)

Balkin, Diane—Deputy District Attorney, Denver County District Attorney's Office (Colorado)

Ballenger, Bob—Legal Officer, Los Angeles County Department of Animal Care and Control (California)

Bathurst, Cynthia—Co-Founder and Director, DAWG. (Illinois)

Breyer, Amy—Attorney (Illinois)

Brody, Sandy—Chicago Police Department (Illinois)

Brownstein, Steve—Sergeant, Chicago Police Department (Illinois)

Burton, Jim—Deputy Chief of Administrative Services, Springfield Police Department (Illinois)

Carter, Donald—Animal Control Officer, Santa Rosa County Animal Control (Florida)

Chambers, Gary—Field Officer, City of Tyler, Smith County (Texas)

Charbonneau, Leonard—Animal Control Officer, Albany County Animal Control (New York)

Clingan, Thomas—Judge, Albany County (New York)

Downs, Keith—District Attorney, Smith County (Texas)

Dutcher, Scot—Chief Investigator for Animal Cruelty, Colorado Department of Agriculture (Colorado)

George, Vicki—Supervisor, Criminal Data Auditing, Harris County District Court (Texas)

Guestring, Craig—Attorney, State Attorney's Office, Santa Rosa County (Florida)

Hake, Tonya—Colorado Integrated Criminal Justice Information System, Colorado District Attorney's Council (Colorado)

Imig, Carroll—Director of the Bureau of Animal Welfare, Department of Agriculture (Illinois)

James, Michael—Office of the Chief Deputy Clerk, Clerk of the Circuit Court, Criminal Department, Cook County (Illinois)

Kavanagh, Kathy—Assistant State Attorney, Cook County State Attorney's Office (Illinois)

Koenig, Sheri—Lieutenant and Chief Investigator, Los Angeles County Department of Animal Care and Control (California)

Lavery, Timothy—Research and Development Division, Cook County Sheriff's Office (Illinois)

Mayer, Amy—Assistant State Attorney, Madison County State Attorney's Office (Illinois)

McBride, Jane—Board President of Illinois Humane and Illinois Assistant Attorney General (Illinois)

McCullough, Dennis—Investigations Supervisor, Hillsborough County Animal Control (Florida)

New York State Division of Criminal Justice Services, Bureau of Justice Research and Innovation Statistical Services Unit (New York)

O'Hare, Kelly—Deputy District Attorney, Marin County District Attorney's Office (California)

Oster, Cindy—County Attorney, Hillsborough County (Florida)

Pechow, Robert—Attorney, State Attorney's Office, Hillsborough County (Florida)

Proutsos, Nikki—Executive Director, Chicago Department of Animal Care and Control (Illinois)

Records Department, Clerk of the Circuit Court of Sangamon County, 7th Judicial Circuit Court (Illinois)

Schenkerman, Jodine, Attorney (New York)

Timmers, Mark—Sergeant, Harris County Constable's Office, Houston Humane Society Animal Control Division (Texas)

VanKavage, Ledy—Attorney and Midwest Legislative Affair Director, ASPCA (Illinois)

Vetlel, Ken—Animal Services Investigator, Hillsborough County Animal Control (Florida)

Wilkins, Andrew—Animal Control Officer Supervisor, Sangamon County Animal Control Center (Illinois)

Williams, Darlene—Public Defender, Cook County Public Defender's Office (Illinois)

Williamson, Neil—Sheriff, Sangamon County Sheriff's Office (Illinois)

Wolf, Stacy—Attorney and Director of Legislative Services, ASPCA (New York)

Zender, Jessica—State Court Administrator's Office (Colorado)

Counting Cruelty: Challenges and Opportunities in Assessing Animal Abuse and Neglect in America

Randall Lockwood
Senior Vice President/Anti-Cruelty Initiatives and Legislative Services
The American Society for the Prevention of Cruelty to Animals

The question that I am asked most frequently by the media and by professionals in law enforcement and animal protection is "Is cruelty to animals on the rise?" My answer has to be "We really don't know." Certainly public and professional concern about animal abuse and neglect *is* on the rise and thousands of media stories each year address specific incidents of cruelty or general alarm about the topic. Reporters and others are often surprised that there is, as yet, no formal state or national tracking of this particularly disturbing crime.

In this essay I will take a closer look at that common question and review why it is important to try to get a more satisfactory answer. I will review the ongoing history of efforts to provide answers to similar questions about the incidence of crime, child abuse, family violence, and certain animal issues. Tracking crime and violence in the United States has been a massive 80-year undertaking, involving expenditure of hundreds of millions of dollars by many federal agencies and thousands of local entities. There are potential lessons to be learned in seeing the obstacles that have hampered those efforts. I will outline a few preliminary attempts to quantify and analyze animal cruelty and the barriers that might exist to establishing systems that can meet this need at a national level. Finally, I will suggest some approaches, based on past efforts in law enforcement, that might move us toward the goal of being able to provide a satisfactory answer to the question.

Why Do We Need to Know About Animal Cruelty Offenses?

What would be the advantage of having consistent and reliable information about the incidence and prevalence of animal abuse and neglect? The arguments for gathering such information are clear:

1. **Cruelty to animals *is a crime*.** We are a society of laws. The prevailing attitudes and beliefs in a society form the basis of the laws that are proposed and passed and these laws set the standards for proper behavior in society. The prevention of unnecessary animal suffering has been at the core of laws in Western society for centuries (Favre & Tsang, 1993; Frasch, Waisman, Wagman, & Beckstead, 2000; Wise, 2003). If we want to know the state of our society, an essential measure is the extent to which our laws are obeyed or violated. This is why so many resources have been dedicated to constantly monitoring the state of society by looking at the incidence of criminal activity in great detail. However, there has, as yet, been little effort to formally integrate information about animal-related crimes into this picture.

2. **Cruelty to animals destabilizes communities**. Law enforcement officials often express surprise at the reactions of communities to incidents of animal abuse. High-profile cases involving animal victims often result in substantial offers of rewards and hundreds or even thousands of letters to local officials demanding action. Many people see animals as truly innocent victims, so their victimization may be more disturbing than person-on-person crimes in which all parties may share some responsibility.

Crimes involving animal cruelty can be seen as a classic example of "broken window" crimes. These are actions that may be officially considered "minor" crimes, but members of the communities in which they occur view a lack of response as a sign that no one cares about violence and decay in their neighborhood. The notion of broken window crimes was first introduced by Wilson and Kelling (1982) and expanded on by Skogan (1992) and Kelling and Skogan (1997). These authors advocated the importance of building confidence in local law enforcement through increased attention to minor crimes such as vandalism, turnstile jumping, and aggressive panhandling. They do not make specific mention of crimes against animals in their analyses, but it is clear to those of us in humane law enforcement that there is great public concern over animal abuse and neglect and more organized abuses such as dog fighting. Although the broken window concept has come under recent criticism (Harcourt, 2001), public response to animal cruelty shows that these crimes are clearly seen as reflecting the general level of lawlessness in a community and the ability of law enforcement to respond. Measuring trends in a community's ability to detect and respond to such crimes is important for building a more complete picture of the effectiveness of law enforcement.

3. **Cruelty to animals can be an *indicator crime*.** A large and growing body of literature (including this volume) has documented the co-occurrence of animal cruelty and interpersonal violence, particularly domestic violence and child abuse (Ascione, 1998; Ascione & Arkow, 1999; Ascione & Lockwood, 2001; DeViney, Dickert, & Lockwood, 1983; Lockwood & Ascione, 1998; Ponder & Lockwood, 2000, 2001). Paying attention to the victimization of animals can often lead to the discovery of people who have been harmed by the same perpetrator, or who are at high risk of being harmed. Animal cruelty investigators and humane agents are now seen as important sentinels for the detection of many forms of abuse and in some areas are key mandated reporters of suspected child and elder abuse. Improved tracking of crimes against animals, and the degree to which these crimes co-occur with acts against people, can provide a valuable tool for identifying the circumstances that are most indicative of situations where people and animals are both at risk.

Serious animal *neglect* can also be an indicator of a variety of social problems that need to be addressed. Recently, much attention has been given to the problem of animal hoarding, the accumulation of large numbers of animals in extremely unsanitary conditions, often resulting in the death of many animals and potentially serious health consequences for the people who are living with them (Berry, Patronek, & Lockwood, 2005; Patronek, 1999, 2001, see also Patronek, *Animal Hoarding: A Third Dimension of Animal Abuse*, in this text). Although animal hoarders are rarely likely to be involved in serious interpersonal crimes, they are often in need of social and/or mental health services (Hoarding of Animals Research Consortium, 2000; Lockwood, 2002). Such services are more likely to be effective if provided before conditions have deteriorated. In addition to animal care costs, if serious animal hoarding cases go undetected until they have resulted in property damage and condemnation, this can have significant impact on a community's financial resources (Prejean, 2003).

4. **Cruelty to animals can be a *predictor crime*.** An equally impressive collection of literature substantiates the commonsense opinion that those who have a history of repeated acts of intentional violence toward animals are at higher risk for exhibiting similar violence or lawlessness toward others in the future (Arluke, Levin, Luke, & Ascione, 1999; Ascione, 1993; Becker, Stuewig, Herrera, & McClosky, 2004; Felthous & Kellert, 1987b; Merz-Perez & Heide, 2003). This can be particularly important in identifying juvenile offenders with a potential for serious violence, offering the possibility of appropriate intervention at an age or stage of the offender's history where such intervention is more likely to be effective. The emphasis in contemporary prosecution is on a balanced approach that addresses community safety, offender accountability, and competency development (Harp, 2002). Responding to early acts that involve animal cruelty can be an effective tool in identifying offenders who may benefit most from attending to these issues. We need good long-term data on early offense histories and the consequences to be able to evaluate which of these offenses may be most predictive of future problems, and which community responses provide the best results in the most cost-effective way.

Tracking animal cruelty and other offenses will improve our ability to conduct true longitudinal studies of the relationship between animal cruelty and other anti-social behaviors. If expending resources to investigate and prosecute animal cruelty can reduce the social and economic costs by helping to prevent later crimes or other social problems, then that is something well worth documenting.

What Do We Need to Know About Animal Cruelty Offenses and Offenders?

Ideally, as with other crimes, we want to be able to capture the complete story of each incident of animal cruelty. We would like to know "who did what to whom, where, when, and how, and what happened as a result?"

The Offenders – The demographics of animal cruelty offenders is a primary interest. Several surveys (see below) have suggested that perpetrators of intentional animal cruelty are predominantly male and under 30, while those involved in animal hoarding are generally female and over 60. However, as with crime in general, there may be a trend toward greater involvement of women in more violent crimes. The demographics of the offender population will have an effect on the programs and services that would be needed to respond appropriately. Such an analysis could also help reveal whether certain offenses are not making it into the criminal justice system. For example, if juvenile offenders make up 50% to 60% of arrestees for vandalism and arson, but only 20% of intentional animal cruelty arrests, it could indicate that many juvenile acts of animal abuse may go undetected or unreported.

The Victims – Recent analyses of crimes against humans have placed great emphasis on describing the victim population as a way of assessing the impact of crime and planning for the needs of victims (Kindermann, Lynch, & Cantor, 1997). Similarly, agencies that respond to animal cruelty need good information on animal victim populations to be able to respond appropriately. For example, communities dealing with a proliferation of dog-fighting activity or animal hoarders may not be able to respond effectively if there are no adequate facilities to house animals that might be seized in responding to such problems.

The Offense – A third important measure is the actual nature of the offense. Certain forms of cruelty, such as neglect, will be treated differently than intentional abuse, torture, or animal sexual assault. Precise descriptions of the act or acts involved are needed to suggest appropriate charges and responses. Several systems for categorizing animal cruelty offenses have been proposed (see below and Vermuellen & Odendaal, 1993). As we will see, inconsistencies in descriptions of crimes were a significant obstacle to standardized reporting of crimes against people. Efforts to improve tracking of ani-

mal cruelty will require improved standardization of descriptions of these crimes as well.

Interactions – Improved reporting and tracking of animal cruelty will substantially increase our ability to see patterns of offenders, victims, and offense types. Such an analysis will provide a valuable forensic tool in investigating cases where suspects have not yet been identified. Felthous and Kellert (1987a) describe certain offender "preferences" in their choice of animal victims, such as the preference for victimization of cats by young male offenders with histories of physical or sexual assaults. Similarly, we are more likely to see certain forms of intentional abuse of small companion animals (e.g., throwing and kicking) in animal cruelty cases that co-occur with domestic violence. Having a better understanding of such interactions can aid in profiling possible perpetrators in unsolved cruelty cases, and in better understanding possible underlying motives and appropriate responses.

Time and Space – Law enforcement agencies are placing greater emphasis on community-oriented policing, which strives to be more responsive to external stakeholders such as citizens, community groups, and elected officials. This has placed new demands on law enforcement to analyze crime in the context of when and where it occurs and the community characteristics associated with different law enforcement problems (Harries, 1999; O'Shea & Nicholls, 2003). Response to animal cruelty cases often requires the coordination of several agencies, including animal care and control, police, state veterinarian, health department, child protective services, and adult protective services. It is important to have an accurate picture of when and where these services are most needed to adequately respond to such cases.

Response of the Criminal Justice System – Finally, we want to be able to review the progression of society's response to incidents of animal cruelty. The flow of typical cases through the criminal justice system is outlined in Figure 1. Most of this chart is applicable to *any* reports of animal abuse and neglect as well, whether they are first investigated by humane agents or regular law enforcement. Such cases will begin with an incident of animal cruelty being observed. Some (hopefully most) of these events will be reported and a percentage of these will be investigated, with a percentage of these leading to arrest. At this point, the pathways for adult and juvenile offenders can diverge. If charged, those cases charged as felonies may follow a slightly

Figure 1: The Progress of a Case through the Criminal Justice System

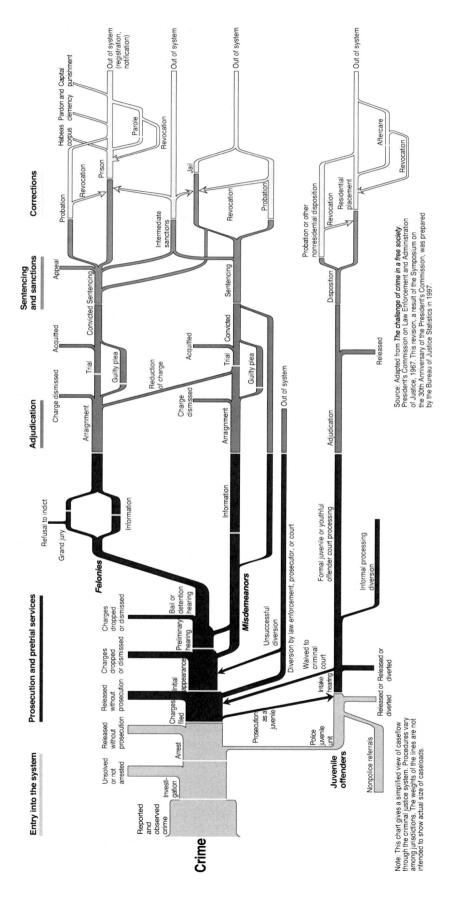

Note: This chart gives a simplified view of caseflow through the criminal justice system. Procedures vary among jurisdictions. The weights of the lines are not intended to show actual size of caseloads.

Source: Adapted from *The challenge of crime in a free society*, President's Commission on Law Enforcement and Administration of Justice, 1967. This revision, a result of the Symposium on the 30th Anniversary of the President's Commission, was prepared by the Bureau of Justice Statistics in 1997.

different path. Knowing the pathways taken by different offenses and offenders tell us much about how society views these incidents and provides a wealth of information about the resources we need to handle such cases effectively. This information allows us to plan for the needs of the various agencies (police, prosecution, corrections, social service, animal care and control, etc.) that will ultimately be involved in the case.

I have described the information needs that would be met in an ideal world. Since animal cruelty has traditionally been considered a relatively low priority by law enforcement agencies, it is unlikely that all these needs could be met. However, the growing interest in preventing and responding to such crimes offers the hope that many of these needs will be addressed. It is therefore helpful to briefly examine the history of counting *crime* in general in the United States as a way of identifying potential obstacles to counting *animal cruelty* and reviewing the processes that have helped overcome those obstacles. I will also look at attempts to track other forms of interpersonal violence, including child abuse and domestic violence.

Counting Crime: A Brief History

Tracking and tabulating incidents of crime in the United States has historically been done in ways that try to serve at least three different purposes. These can sometimes have competing requirements in the kind of information that is kept and the way it is collected, organized, accessed, and disseminated. The earliest systems were designed primarily to assist in the *tracking of known or suspected offenders* and any property (e.g., stolen vehicles) that might be associated with their crimes. Later systems added the function of attempting to tabulate the *incidence of crime* and its *victims*. The third generation of data gathering added a new dimension—tracking crime in ways that could be analyzed in connection with *social and economic variables* such as employment, education and poverty levels, law enforcement staffing, availability of social services, and many other demographic and community variables. A comprehensive history of these efforts is reviewed in a report by the Search Group (1993).

Formal police departments did not exist in America until the establishment of the first full-time police force in Boston in 1835, followed by New York City in 1844. Their records were kept in a police blotter, which primarily maintained descriptions and arrest histories of repeat offenders. The rising popularity of photography and fingerprinting in the late 19th century led the International Association of Chiefs of Police (IACP) to establish a "national" system in Chicago in 1896 to keep names, photographs, and other records of habitual criminals.

In 1908, the U.S. Department of Justice formed the Identification Bureau, the forerunner of the FBI, to maintain fingerprint and criminal history records. In 1924 Congress directed the newly restructured FBI to create an identification division, merging its records with those of the IACP and other agencies.

In response to rising crime in the early 1960s, the FBI created a Committee on Uniform Crime Reports and worked with the IACP and the Department of Commerce to review the technology that could be used for storing and exchanging criminal history records. The National Crime Information Center (NCIC) came online in 1967 (FBI, 1996). In 1971 the NCIC implemented an interstate computerized criminal history (CCH) record system. This was dropped in the early 1980s in favor of a decentralized national criminal history record system—the Interstate Identification Index (III).

Today the purpose of the FBI's NCIC system is to maintain fingerprints and criminal history records for people arrested for federal offenses and maintain state offender records (the III) that essentially duplicate records of the state repositories from approximately 80,000 law enforcement agencies. These records are maintained in 17 different files with over 10 million records, with an additional 24 million criminal history records in III.

The NCIC files hold information on:

1. Individuals with outstanding federal warrants
2. Individuals who have committed or are associated with a felony or serious misdemeanor, including probation and parole violations
3. Juveniles adjudicated delinquent who have escaped or absconded
4. Violent felons with three or more convictions
5. Missing persons, including those missing after a catastrophe
6. Members of violent criminal gangs
7. Unidentified persons

Other files maintained by NCIC include stolen vehicles, boats, license plates, guns, securities, and other property. The system was further upgraded in 2000 to include individuals on sex offender registries and people on probation or parole. The budget for the NCIC system in 2000 was $180 million (FBI, 1999).

Since animal cruelty offenses may be considered felony or serious misdemeanor offenses, it is likely that some animal abusers are currently in the system in files 2, 3, or 4 as described above, but, as we will see, there is currently no coding system that allows easy identification of these offenders.

Reporting the Incidence of Crime in America

The NCIC system and its predecessors were primarily developed as a way of sharing information on criminals and missing persons across state lines to aid in the apprehension of offenders and the recovery of stolen property. These systems were *not* designed to provide a statistical picture of the incidence of crime or the socioeconomic aspects of crime. The IACP formed a Committee on Uniform Crime Records during the 1920s, developing a system for tracking crimes that were considered *serious, frequent, pervasive, nationwide, and likely to be reported to law enforcement*. This was formalized into the Uniform Crime Reporting (UCR) Program in 1930, and the FBI was designated to serve as the clearinghouse for these data (FBI, 2005). As of 2004, the UCR system gathers reports from more than 17,000 federal, state, county, city, tribal, and university law enforcement agencies representing about 94% of the population.

Despite extensive participation, the UCR Program is not a comprehensive tabulation of crime in America. The emphasis is on tracking aggregate reports of eight major offenses: murder, forcible rape, robbery, aggravated assault, burglary, motor vehicle theft, larceny, and arson. The first seven are tracked in a hierarchical fashion, that is, if an offense involves more than one of these crimes, only the top one is counted. Arson was added to the list by Congressional mandate in 1979 and is tracked independently (FBI, 2005). Many other crimes are recorded in the system, but only *if they result in arrest* (see Table 1).

Although the Uniform Crime Reporting System strives to create a comprehensive picture of crimes that are of concern to policy makers and the general public, animal cruelty is completely overlooked as a crime classification. Some of the crimes tracked by UCR may include animal cruelty (as noted in Table 1). The 164-page UCR Reporting handbook (FBI, 2004)

designates farm animal theft as a specific form of larceny. Companion animals are mentioned only in the context of larceny, under theft of miscellaneous property. In this catch-all category they are lumped together with other property such as books, bicycles, and cell phones (p. 88).

The Uniform Crime Report continues to provide the major snapshot of serious and violent crime in the United States and is the most frequently cited data for national, state, and local crime trends in this country. However, in the 1980s many legislators, social scientists, and criminal justice professionals felt that the value of the UCR was limited for policy and planning decisions and that changes were needed (Justice Research and Statistics Association, 1996). The UCR focuses on aggregate data for the eight major crimes described above, with an emphasis on murder and property crimes and inadequate coverage of many interpersonal crimes of concern to public and legislators, particularly family violence, hate crimes, and financial crimes (fraud, extortion, embezzlement). A major criticism was that the UCR approach ignores the fact that crime often comes in clusters with multiple offenses and more than one victim. A robbery may include use of a weapon and a physical or sexual assault and several victims at one time. This same flaw was seen in state systems contributing to the III. Finally, the UCR format provides little usable social information—for example, it overlooks offender and victim demographics and the relationship between victim and offender.

In 1985 the UCR program underwent a five-year period of redesign into the National Incident-Based Reporting System (NIBRS). The NIBRS system looks at *each incident* of crime in more than 20 categories (see Table 1). For each offense known to police within these categories, detailed information about the incident, victim, property, offender, and arrestee is gathered when available (see Table 2). Many state programs have expanded the reporting within their states beyond the core requirements for the NIBRS program, adding as many as 75 data elements to the 53 required for NIBRS participation. Usually this has been in response to demands for additional information by state legislatures on such topics as domestic violence (Bureau of Justice Statistics, 1997).

Although NIBRS offers the prospect of a far more comprehensive picture of crime in America, state participation is this more advanced and complex system has been lagging. As of August 2005, 29 states have been certified to report NIBRS data

Table 1 Offense Categories for Summary Uniform Crime Reports (UCR) and National Incident-Based Reporting System (NIBRS).

Summary UCR	NIBRS
Offenses and arrests reported for the following, in hierarchical order:	*Offenses and arrests are reported for the following without application of a hierarchy:*
Murder	*Arson
Forcible rape	Assault offenses
Robbery	Bribery
Aggravated assault	Burglary, breaking and entering
Burglary	Counterfeiting/forgery
Motor vehicle theft	*Destruction/damage/vandalism of property
*Larceny	Drug/narcotic offenses
*Arson (not subject to hierarchy rule)	Embezzlement
	Extortion/blackmail
ARRESTS ONLY are reported for:	Fraud offenses
Curfew and loitering law violations	Gambling offenses
*Disorderly conduct	Homicide offences
Driving under the influence	Kidnapping/abduction
Drug abuse violations	*Larceny/theft offenses
Drunkenness	Motor vehicle theft
Embezzlement	*Pornography/obscene material
Forgery and counterfeiting	Prostitution offenses
Fraud	Robbery
Gambling	*Sex offenses, forcible
Liquor laws	*Sex offenses, nonforcible
*Offenses against family and children	*Stolen property offenses
Other assaults	Weapon law violations
Prostitution	
Runaways	*ARRESTS ONLY are reported for the following:*
*Sex offenses (other than rape and prostitution)	Bad checks
Stolen property (buying, selling, receiving)	Curfew/loitering/vagrancy
Suspicion	*Disorderly conduct
Vagrancy	Driving under the influence
*Vandalism	Drunkenness
Weapons (carrying, possessing)	*Nonviolent family offenses
*All other offenses (except traffic)	Peeping tom
	Runaways
	Trespassing
	*All other offense

Source: Bureau of Justice Statistics Special Report (NCJ 178890), *Effects of NIBRS on Crime Statistics*, July 2000.
*Note: Categories marked * might include animal cruelty incidents*

to the FBI, covering only about 23% of the U.S. population and 18% of the nation's reported crime. Ten states are in the testing phase, six are in development, and six have no plan to participate (Justice Research and Statistics Association, 2005).

There have been several reasons for the slow adoption of NIBRS (Bureau of Justice Statistics, 1997), which may also suggest possible barriers to attempts to develop more universal reporting of animal cruelty crimes:

1. *Funding* – Participation in NIBRS is viewed by some agencies as creating significant additional costs for data entry staff and the level of quality control required by the FBI. To begin regular submission of NIBRS data to the FBI, the state UCR/NIBRS system must be certified by the FBI based on error rate, statistical reasonableness, and updating capability

2. *Uncertainty of benefits* – Some law enforcement agencies do not see any advantage to them

Table 2   Primary Information That NIBRS Records on Each Crime Incident

Administrative Segment:	23. Type of victim
1. Incident number	24. Age of victim
2. Incident date/hour	25. Sex of victim
3. Clearance indicator and date	26. Race/ethnicity of victim
	27. Residential status of victim
Offense Segment:	28. Homicide/assault circumstances
4. UCR offense code	29. Justifiable homicide circumstances
5. Attempted/completed code	30. Type of injury
6. Alcohol/drug use by offender	31. Related offender number
7. Type of location	32. Relationship of victim to offender
8. Number of premises entered	
9. Method of entry	**Offender Segment:**
10. Type of criminal activity	33. Offender number
11. Type of weapon/force used	34. Age of offender
12. Bias crime code	35. Sex of offender
	36. Race of offender
Property Segment:	
13. Type of property loss	**Arrestee Segment:**
14. Property description	37. Arrestee number
15. Property value	38. Transaction number
16. Recovery date	39. Arrest date
17. Number of stolen vehicles	40. Type of arrest
18. Number of recovered vehicles	41. UCR arrest offense code
19. Suspected drug type	42. Arrestee armed indicator
20. Estimated drug quantity	43. Age of arrestee
	44. Sex of arrestee
Victim Segment:	45. Race/ethnicity of arrestee
21. Victim number	46. Residential status of arrestee
22. Victim UCR offense code	47. Disposition of arrestee under 18

Source: Bureau of Justice Statistics Special Report (NCJ 178890), *Effects of NIBRS on Crime Statistics,* July 2000.

for improving their day-to-day operations. NIBRS is seen as having more value to social science researchers than to law enforcement, and more beneficial at the macro level than at the local level.

3. *Policy concerns* – Improved reporting is usually associated with apparent increases in what is being reported (crime, disease, etc.). Conversely, a popular political tactic is to discourage reporting of troublesome events or to reduce funding for positions for staff to track such events. Officials express concern that NIBRS makes crime rates appear to rise simply by allowing reporting of multiple offenses within an incident. However, detailed comparisons of UCR and NIBRS data has shown that crime rates reported by the two systems differ only slightly (Rantala & Edwards, 2000).

4. *Administrative issues* – Participating agencies complain that too much time is spent by street officers on completing incident reports, suggesting a need for better-designed checklists and automated input systems. Lack of feedback has been another administra-

tive issue. Local agencies submit monthly reports but don't see aggregate reports until yearly tabulations.

5. *Data elements* – Frontline officers view some elements required by NIBRS reports as not having investigative value, for example, victim-offender relationship, multiple offense and multiple victims, and nature of substance abuse. There is also concern about inconsistent definitions of offenses between UCR, NIBRS, state statutes, and the NCIC definitions. Since NIBRS was designed as a statistical database, it intentionally lacks certain information items that help agencies with their operational needs such as geocodes to map crime data and fields to note offender physical characteristics, such as scars, marks, and tattoos, to identify specific criminals and to link previously unknown cases to particular suspects.

6. *Education* – Proponents of NIBRS have suggested that stakeholders (e.g., local law enforcement agencies) need improved education on the nature and objectives of NIBRS and the value of their contribution to the project.

There is a popular notion that we have a complete and detailed picture of the incidence of crime in America thanks to the ongoing surveillance of the FBI. Given the shortcomings on the Unified Crime Reports and the slow adoption of the National Incident-Based Reporting System, that is far from true. Any proposed attempt to get a better picture of the scope of animal cruelty should pay close attention to these difficulties.

Reporting Crime Victimization

The NCIC system is designed primarily to aid in apprehending criminals. The UCR and NIBRS programs were designed to provide policy makers with a better picture of the incidence of crime. None of these systems adequately addresses the greatest concern of the general public and their elected representatives, namely, the impact of crime on its *victims*. In addition, all of the above systems are dependent upon having data about crimes that have been reported or investigated. Since a major social concern is that many crimes go unreported or unresponded to, another system was needed to address these concerns.

In 1973 the Bureau of Justice Statistics began working with the U.S. Census Bureau to gather data on crime victimization, victim-offender relationships, and victim and offender demographics. The original program, the National Crime Survey (NCS), was redesigned in 1992 as the National Crime Victimization Survey (NCVS). The survey is conducted annually by staff of the Census Bureau, sampling 42,000 households (about 75,000 individuals) about their experiences related to victimization by rape, sexual assault, robbery, assault, theft, household burglary, and motor vehicle theft. Data are analyzed with attention to specific segments of the population such as women, the elderly, members of various racial groups, city dwellers, or other groups (Kindermann et al., 1997).

The redesign of the NCVS was driven, in part, by a desire to improve the measurement of assaults, sex crimes, and domestic violence. Questions were changed to better stimulate respondent's recall of victimizations and to clarify the concept of criminal victimization. The current survey instrument asks about exposure to certain specific acts (e.g., being grabbed, punched, choked, having a rock or bottle thrown, etc.) rather than relying on criminal code definitions of assault. The redesign yielded significantly higher estimates of crime rates. Reports of rape rose 157%, assaults rose 57%,

and thefts rose by 27%. Kindermann et al. (1997) suggest that a major cause of lower estimates of crimes under the old NCS system was that they did not conform to stereotyped views of what constitutes crime. Crimes committed by family members or non-strangers were underreported without the more detailed questioning allowed under the NCVS interview protocol. The new system is also much better at picking up disclosures of attempted crimes (uncompleted) and crimes that had not been reported to the police.

The NCVS is a powerful but costly tool. The 2005 budget for the Census Bureau projects with the Bureau of Justice Statistics was nearly $40 million. The lessons learned from this project provide suggestions for effective ways of gathering data about crimes that are disturbing to the public, but which may go unreported and unprosecuted, and thus may have particular application to the analysis of animal cruelty.

Counting Other Forms of Family Violence

Child Abuse

The structure of the nation's systems for tracking child abuse are different from those designed to assess other crimes. The complexity of child abuse and neglect and the many local and state agencies that can become involved in a child abuse case may provide a closer approximation of some of the issues that we would confront in attempting to provide national tracking of animal cruelty.

The key federal legislation addressing child abuse and neglect is the Child Abuse Prevention and Treatment Act (CAPTA), originally enacted in 1974 (P.L. 93–247). This Act was amended several times and was most recently amended and reauthorized as the Keeping Children and Families Safe Act of 2003 (P.L. 108–36). The 1988 amendments directed the U.S. Department of Health and Human Services to establish a national data collection and analysis program. The Children's Bureau in the Administration on Children, U.S. Department of Health and Human Services, collects and analyzes the data from the states. The data are entered into the National Child Abuse and Neglect Data System (NCANDS).

NCANDS collects case-level data on all children who received an investigation or assessment by a CPS agency. States that are unable to provide case-level data submit aggregate counts of key indicators. The NCANDS database consists of two components.

The Summary Data Component (SDC) compiles aggregate child abuse and neglect statistics from all states, including data on reports, investigations, victims, and perpetrators. The Detailed Case Data Component (DCDC) compiles case-level information from those child protective services agencies that are able to provide electronic child abuse and neglect records for substantiated or indicated cases of child maltreatment. The DCDC file contains 62 variables. In addition to basic information concerning the report and the child, this child victim's file also contains information about the type of maltreatment, support services provided to the family, and special problems that were identified for the child, caretaker, or family. Neither of the files contains data on the alleged perpetrators (National Data Archive on Child Abuse and Neglect [NDACAN], 2003).

The datasets produced by NCANDS are maintained in the National Data Archive on Child Abuse and Neglect at Cornell University, where they are available to qualified researchers for more detailed analyses (NDACAN, 2005a). The current Children's Bureau funding for this archive is $2.6 million for the next 5 years (NDACAN, 2005b).

NCANDS, like NIBRS, is a system that is designed to help social scientists better understand the dynamics of child victimization. The data do not constitute a statistically representative sample of maltreated children in the United States, but are considered representative.

A more comprehensive analysis of child abuse data is provided by the National Incidence Study (NIS). NIS is a periodic effort of the National Center on Child Abuse and Neglect (NCCAN), mandated by Congress. In contrast to NCANDS, the NIS design assumes that the children seen by Child Protective Services represent only the "tip of the iceberg," so this project seeks input from a much larger population of possible reporters.

To date, three NIS surveys have been conducted. The first NIS was mandated under P.L. 93–247 (1974) and conducted in 1979 and 1980. NIS-2 was conducted in 1986–1987 and NIS-3 data were collected in 1993–1994 and published in 1996.

The most recent iteration, NIS-4, is currently underway. It was mandated by the Keeping Children and Families Safe Act of 2003 and is being conducted by Westat Inc. (Details of the current project are available at www.NIS4.org.) The NIS-4 will gather data in a nationally representative sample of only 122 counties. The Child Protective Service agencies serving these counties will be asked to provide data about all children in cases they accept for investigation during one of two reference periods (September 4 through December 3, 2005 or February 4 through May 3, 2006). In addition, professionals working in the same counties in a variety of other agencies will be asked to serve as NIS-4 sentinels, including elementary and secondary public schools; public health departments; public housing authorities; short-stay general and children's hospitals; state, county, and municipal police/sheriff departments; licensed day care centers; juvenile probation departments; voluntary social services and mental health agencies; and shelters for runaway and homeless youth shelters or victims of domestic violence.

Like the analysis of crime currently available through the National Incident-Based Reporting System, the picture of child abuse in America provided by NCANDS and NIS is incomplete, but both systems are extremely useful in estimating trends and producing a better understanding of the social dynamics of child abuse and neglect. Thus it is beneficial to consider some of the strategies of these systems when designing a system for tracking and reporting animal cruelty.

Domestic Violence

Like other forms of family violence, domestic violence has proven difficult to systematically define and monitor. Although law enforcement officials feel that there is good tracking of homicides involving intimate partners, the Centers for Disease Control and Prevention has noted that data on nonfatal cases are less accessible and often inconsistent due to methodical differences (CDC, 2000). While acknowledging that violence against women is a great problem, the CDC report notes that there is little consensus as to whether data on domestic violence generated by the National Crime Victimization Survey overestimates or underestimates the seriousness of the problem.

There have been several comprehensive reviews of the quality of the data available on domestic violence. Section 40292 of Title IV—the Violence Against Women Act—of the 1994 Violent Crime Control and Law Enforcement Act specified that a study be conducted on "how the States may collect centralized data bases on the incidence of sexual and domestic violence offenses within a State." The Justice Research and Statistics Association (JRSA) was designated to undertake the study (Justice Research and Statistics Association, 1996).

Several of the key findings of this analysis are relevant to the collection of data concerning animal abuse. First, the report indicates that the federal government and a majority of states (35 for domestic violence; 30 for sexual violence) are currently collecting some statistics annually on these offenses. However, it is pointed out that (p.3): "there was a wide variation in how each State defines these offenses, determines what is counted, and measures or reports incidents. The variability also applies to the types of victims included in reports." Part of the problem comes from the statutory definitions of family and domestic violence. Some states have adopted family violence as opposed to domestic violence statutes, so their statistics may include child victims along with adults. In addition, some state statutes apply regardless of the gender of the victims and the offenders, while others are not inclusive of all possible relationships and living situations.

Second, this report to Congress concludes that the FBI's summary UCR system does not provide the detailed information needed to document the full extent of domestic violence-related events known to law enforcement agencies. It is suggested that the NIBRS *could* provide much needed detailed data for domestic violence-related offenses, but this has been hampered by the slow rate of adoption of the NIBRS data standard by state and local agencies.

Third, the study recognized that victimization surveys such as the NCVS can provide important insights, but continue to be controversial since they may generate higher crime estimates. In addition, victimization studies can be confounded by differences between what the public sees as violent or criminal behavior and how the state laws and the criminal justice system view the same incidents. Such a disconnect between public and legal definitions of offenses could be even more likely in assessments of animal cruelty based on victimization estimates.

Finally, the analysis noted that existing monitoring of family violence was plagued by failures of local agencies to provide complete and accurate data. This was reported to be a problem in 83% of states. Nonparticipation by some agencies in collecting family and sexual violence was reported in 70% of states. A lack of participation from law enforcement and animal control agencies in gathering and reporting animal abuse information is likely to be equally problematic.

An additional review of problems encountered in collecting information on violence against women was undertaken at a workshop conducted by the U.S. Department of Health and Human Services and the U.S. Department of Justice in 1998 (CDC, 2000). This gathering of more than 100 experts in the field of violence against women echoed the concerns raised by the earlier Congressional review. This group made many recommendations for future data gathering. Among the suggestions that have relevance to tracking violence against animals were the following:

1. *Definitions* – There is a need to develop uniform definitions associated with intimate-partner violence. These should focus on five major components— physical violence, sexual violence, threats of physical or sexual violence, stalking, and psychological/ emotional abuse. Data collection should allow for examination of co-occurrence of these different components and attention should be given to how they overlap. Definitions of data elements should be common across different surveys.

2. *Interviews* – It was suggested that personal interviews are a better tool for measuring violence against women than record reviews, but no single or existing tool (e.g., NCVS) was considered sufficient.

3. *Collaboration* – The group called for greater collaboration between service providers and researchers to improve the quality of data collected. Data should be integrated from nationally representative surveys, local health data, local criminal justice data, and nonnationally representative data from service providers

4. *Funding* – Participants suggested that there is a need for each state to provide funds for data collection and monitoring of violence against women.

5. *Comprehensive Coverage* – Concern was raised that many instances of violence against women go undetected or unreported. Also, there is a need to gather data on groups previously overlooked in surveys, including the homeless, women in the military, women in institutions, and women with disabilities.

Tracking Animal Issues Other Than Cruelty

Before we can begin to apply some of the lessons learned from attempts to quantify violence against people to questions about the nature and prevalence of cruelty to animals, it is instructive to review how well we have fared in asking other quantitative questions about human–animal interactions.

Pet and Shelter Populations

We cannot assess the extent of crimes against our animal companions unless we first have a basic idea of the nature of that population. Relatively accurate data on dog and cat populations are available from veterinary and pet-related industry sources (Clancy & Rowan, 2003), but different sampling methods produce estimates that can vary by 20% or more (Patronek & Rowan, 1995).

Tracking incidents of animal cruelty necessitates also having basic data on the agencies, other than police departments, that are likely to be the first recipients of reports of animal abuse and neglect. It has been frustratingly difficult to produce a reliable list of humane societies, animal care and control agencies, and "brick-and-mortar" shelters that can be used for this and other data-gathering purposes (Rowan, 1992).

Tracking companion animal issues such as surrender, adoption, and euthanasia rates through demographic analysis of the population of companion animals entering and exiting animal shelters has also been difficult. The 1994–1997 Shelter Statistics Survey conducted by the National Council on Pet Population Study and Policy (NCPPSP, 2000) attempted to collect such information via survey cards sent to more than 5,000 shelters. Although fewer than 20% of shelters responded, information was gathered on the handling of about 4 million animals for each year of the study. Because the responding shelters could not be assumed to represent a random sampling of facilities, the Council notes that "it is not possible to use these statistics to estimate the number of animals entering animal shelters in the United States, or the numbers euthanized on an annual basis." Other projects undertaken with a smaller number of shelters have attempted to get a clearer picture of the dynamics of the relinquishment of animals to shelters (Kass, 2001; New, 2000; New et al., 1999; Salman et al., 1998; Salman et al., 2000; Scarlett, 1999).

It is likely that the problems associated with identifying appropriate agencies to participate in any attempts to gather systematic information will be reduced by the growing presence of stable humane societies and animal care and control organizations on the Internet, and increased participation of such organizations in centralized networks such as Petfinder.com.

Dog Bites

One way to assess possible problems in documenting how often people are responsible for harm to animals is to look at how well we have been able to track the reverse—how often do animals harm people? Since monitoring public health issues has always been a politically higher priority than animal abuse, it is instructive to see how well this problem has been quantified. Like animal cruelty, this issue has been the subject of growing public and professional concern. The media and public officials frequently ask me "How many people are bitten by dogs each year and what percentage of those are due to specific breeds?" As with cruelty statistics, the answer has to be "We don't really know."

There are similarities between the Center for Disease Control's tracking of dog bites and its abilities to document violence against women. As with domestic violence homicides, the CDC reports that it can do a reasonably good job of documenting dog bite incidents that result in the death of a victim (Sacks, Lockwood, Hornreich, & Sattin, 1996; Sacks, Sinclair, Gilchrist, Golab, & Lockwood, 2000). However, nationwide tracking of non-fatal injury has been difficult since there is wide variety of state and local laws defining the problem and no uniform reporting procedures (Weiss, Friedman, & Coben, 1998).

The CDC largely abandoned efforts to collect aggregate dog bite data from the states in the 1970s. A partial solution was provided in the 1990s by the adoption of a uniform coding system for emergency departments (EDs) for the approximately 90 million ED visits each year (National Center for Health Statistics, 2005). The addition of an E-code (E906.0-"dog bite") allowed tracking from those EDs that participate in the system. There have been limits to this solution. As with NIBRS, workload and budget constraints have hampered universal adoption of E-codes by EDs. Also, an incident may not be coded as a bite if there are additional medical problems that override such coding. Likewise, this approach fails to capture incidents that go unreported or which are treated by family physicians or urgent care centers that might not file E-code data. These difficulties account for discrepancies between incident rates estimated from ED visits (334,000 cases per year), compared with estimates from public telephone survey techniques that indicate that there are 757,000 medically treated cases and 3.73 million non-medically treated bites per year (Sacks et al., 1996). Simply adding a reporting category to a national monitoring system does not guarantee comprehensive data collection, but it can improve our understanding of the dynamics of the problem.

Counting Animal Cruelty

In the United States, a major obstacle to the collection of standardized animal cruelty data has been the distribution of enforcement authority across thousands of federal, state, and local agencies. A few countries have benefited from having a long-standing interest in preventing cruelty to animals and a more centralized authority for the enforcement of anti-cruelty laws.

The oldest organization with well-developed animal cruelty law enforcement authority is England's Royal Society for the Prevention of Cruelty to Animals (RSPCA). Almost from its inception in 1824, the annual and monthly reports of the RSPCA have detailed the animal cruelty cases its inspectors have investigated and prosecuted under these laws. These reports contained very specific information about the animals that were abused and the precise nature of the maltreatment. For most of the first century of the RSPCA's existence, the majority of cases involved maltreatment of livestock and draft animals, but proponents of companion animal welfare recognized the growing concern about the abuse of dogs and cats. From 1857 to 1860, dogs and cats accounted for only 2% of the cruelty convictions, although 13% of the RSPCA's reports to the public focused on dog and cat cruelty cases (Brown, 1974).

The RSPCA continues to provide annual reports of its anticruelty activities (RSPCA, 2005a). The most recent summary reports that over one million animals were seen by inspectors between June 2004 and May 2005. There had been a 78% rise in cases of "animals' basic needs not being met" and a 96% rise in cases of animals not having access to water. The majority of complaints about neglect involved dogs. The RSPCA has used such data to support its call for legislation that would be more effective in addressing neglect (RSPCA, 2005b).

The first SPCA in Australia was founded in 1871 (Victoria), inspired by the formation of the RSPCA in England. Additional provinces and territories incorporated SPCAs between 1872 and 1965. In 1956, the Societies were given the Royal Warrant and became known as the Royal Societies for the Prevention of Cruelty to Animals. These societies were consolidated as RSPCA Australia in 1981 to promote unity and commonality in purpose. One outgrowth of that effort has been to attempt to provide regular accounting of the state of animal cruelty throughout the country. In 2000 there were 48,000 cases investigated by RSPCA Australia, almost 50% of them involving dogs, with 316 convictions for animal cruelty (Titelius, 2000). As in the United Kingdom, such statistics have been used to document the need for educating magistrates about the need for stronger penalties and have stimulated the

creation of task forces on animal cruelty and violent crime (Lawrence & Alexander, 2005).

Efforts to Count Animal Cruelty in the United States

As noted above, the responsibility for receiving and investigating complaints about animal abuse and neglect in the United States is distributed across many diverse law enforcement, animal control, and humane organizations. They are responsible for the enforcement of animal cruelty laws that are different in every state, with each state even having its own definition of "animal." Actions that might be prosecutable as felony animal cruelty in one state may not even be considered a crime in a neighboring state. There is also, as yet, no well-defined standard for record keeping for such cases. Even when cases are prosecuted and there are resulting convictions, it can be difficult to get accurate aggregate counts of such events even in a single state.

Despite these difficulties, there have been two major efforts to gather systematic data about animal cruelty cases in the United States to gain some insights into the scope of the problem, the nature of the victims and perpetrators, possible trends, and suggested courses of action.

The Humane Society of the United States (HSUS) has gathered accounts of high-profile cases for decades, often in response to inquiries by local animal protection groups or the media. These efforts were given a more formal structure in 2000, when The HSUS began to receive daily media clips from Cyberalert®, a service tracking more than 13,000 newspapers, magazines, journals, wire services, TV networks, and local TV stations. These clips were drawn from coverage of stories with any mention of animal abuse, cruelty, or neglect. These cases were supplemented with any additional reports received from local organizations requesting assistance. The reports were then reviewed, and data on the specifics of each case are entered into a Microsoft Access® database. The data recorded for each case are detailed in Table 3.

There are obvious limitations to this approach. The cases sampled are far from complete, representing only reported cases that have risen to the level of media awareness. However, since they reflect cases that are publicized, they provide a snapshot of the kinds of cases that the public is made aware of and which may help shape public policy.

Data collected in this way have proven useful to provide some analysis of the dynamics of animal abuse and neglect. For example, these data have

Table 3   Data Fields in the HSUS's Animal Cruelty Database and Pet-Abuse.com's Animal Abuse
Registry Database Administration System (AARDAS)

Administrative	**Offense Type (continued)**
+* Case #	neglect
+* Offense date	poisoning
+* Offense city, state	shooting
	+sanitary deprivation
Offender Information	stabbing
+* Offender name	theft
+* Age and age category (child <12, teen, adult)	throwing
+* Total number of offenders in case	unclassified
+* Flag if first or primary offender	*unlawful trade—smuggling
* Offender is public servant	*unlawful trapping/hunting
* Offender works in animal welfare	+veterinary deprivation
* Drugs/alcohol mentioned in offense	
	Offense Details
Victim Information	+* Narrative of event (from media or police report)
+* Species (coded)	+* Charges filed (Y/N)?
+* Type (companion, farm, wild, multiple)	+ Charged as felony?
+* Number animals abused in incident	+ Charged as misdemeanor?
+* Number killed in incident	
* Victim was loose	**Concurrent Crimes Against People**
	+* Flag for any concurrent interpersonal crime
Offense Type	+ Spouse witness?
+* Flags presence of each type of cruelty offense	+ Child witness?
including (in both unless noted):	+* Domestic violence?
abandonment	+* Child abuse?
beating	+* Elder abuse
bestiality	
burning (caustic substance)	**Case Outcome**
burning (fire/fireworks)	+* Status (convicted, acquitted, dismissed, failed to
choking, suffocation	appear
+dragging	+* Psychological evaluation?
drowning	+* Counseling ordered?
fighting	+* Jail sentence/time
hanging	+* Probation/length
hoarding	+* Fine/amount
kick/stomp	+ Restitution ordered?
mutilation	+* Community service?
	+ HSUS staff involved?

+ = in HSUS
* = in AARDAS

been "mined" to attempt to provide some insights into the specific issue of cruelty to cats (Lockwood, 2005; Sinclair & Lockwood, 2005).

This study reviewed records of reports on 4,695 cases of animal cruelty reported between January 2000 and May 2004. These cases involved 5,225 alleged offenders. Despite the higher incidence of cats in the companion animal population, they were underrepresented in these reports of cruelty. Of these cases, 51.8% reportedly involved dogs, 15.1% involved cats, 3.7% involved both cats and dogs,

3.7% involved cats and dogs and one or more other species, and 25.7% involved other species only—usually horses, livestock, fighting cocks, and wildlife.

Cases were broadly categorized as featuring "intentional cruelty" (e.g., traumatic physical injury), "neglect" (including malnourishment, abandonment, and starvation), or "collecting or hoarding" as defined by Patronek (1999). Overall, 62.7% of the cases were characterized as "intentional." This was significantly higher for cats (69.0%) than for dogs (60.8%, chi-square=15.43, p<.001). Animals were killed in 47.4%

of all cases involving cats or dogs. Cats were killed in significantly more cases in which they were victims (56.9%) of cruelty than were dogs (44.7%, chi-square=32.39, p<.001).

Although not necessarily representative of national trends, findings such as this allowed the authors to make specific policy recommendations, including:

- Strengthen and enforce laws protecting cats and other companion animals.
- Respond to individuals and organizations promoting abusive practices.
- Promote humane control of "problem" or feral cats.

The HSUS database project also served as the basis for several annual reports on animal cruelty in America that highlighted different aspects of the problem, such as the connection to other crimes. The report for 2000 (HSUS, 2001) noted that 21% of the reports of intentional cruelty that year also involved reports of some form of family violence. The report for 2001 cases drew attention to cases involving young offenders and the need for appropriate intervention and prevention programs (HSUS, 2002). The report for 2002 data emphasized the need for inclusion of animal cruelty concerns in "neighborhood watch" crime surveillance programs (HSUS, 2003). The report on data gathered in 2003 emphasized the incidence of animal abuse within the context of domestic violence (HSUS, 2004).

The HSUS cruelty database program was discontinued in 2004 due to the heavy demands it placed on staff. It was difficult to ensure standardization of data entry of the more than 1,500 cases entered each year. This effort also proved to be challenging for staff who faced the task of reading and reviewing dozens of disturbing stories of animal torment each day.

A second project, The Animal Abuse Registry Database Administration System (AARDAS) project, was launched in January 2002. It gathers information in much the same way as the HSUS cruelty database (see Table 3), relying on press clips and notification from local groups. It also incorporates data on animal sexual assault originally gathered by the Animal Sexual Abuse Information Resource Site (ASAIRS), which was officially discontinued in 2003. The information gathered by AARDAS is made continuously available to the general public at the website Pet-Abuse.com. The site provides a sophisticated search engine and crime-mapping capabilities, and allows user notification of the progress of specific cases through criminal justice system. Like the HSUS database, the system holds information on only a small proportion of cases. As of January 2006, there were about 6,500 cases in the database from a period of more than 15 years.

Like the HSUS database, AARDAS can be mined to explore data of relevance to public policy and legislation. For example, there has been growing concern that animal sexual assault has often been decriminalized in the process of overturning state sodomy laws, usually on the grounds of persecution of individuals based on their sexual orientation and the criminalization of behaviors transpiring between consenting adults (Sinclair, Merck, & Lockwood, 2006). More than 30 states have subsequently repealed their sodomy laws through legislative or court action.

Ironically, as these antiquated statutes were discarded, the prohibitions against bestiality that were subsumed in these statutes were also often thrown out (see Beetz, *Bestiality and Zoophilia: A Discussion of Sexual Contact With Animals*, in this text). This sometimes has had the effect of essentially decriminalizing animal sexual assault unless the act involved some other crime such as animal cruelty. This has been identified as a problem by veterinarians (Munro & Thrusfield, 2001) and criminologists (Beirne, 1997). In response to this unintended change, many state legislatures have re-enacted provisions specifically targeting bestiality as distinct from other traditional "crimes against nature." As of this writing, 29 states have laws specifically prohibiting sexual abuse of animals. Five states provide felony level penalties with imprisonment for up to 20 years and fines of up to $50,000.

The HSUS and AARDAS systems allow review of a cross-section of cases involving animal sexual assault. Of the 5,225 cases in the HSUS database for 2002–2004, only 46 (.88%) involved animal sexual assault. The majority of cases involved dogs (36%) or horses (21%), but reports included incidents involving cats, sheep, cows, rabbits, chickens, pigs, goats, llamas, sea gulls, and an elephant! Criminal charges were filed in 76% of cases. A third of these charges were for crimes other than animal sexual assault, including child abuse, theft, breaking and entering, and drug charges. The incidence of animal sexual assault cases in the Pet-Abuse.com database was low, but since the system includes data originally collected for ASAIRS, it is nearly double that of the HSUS sample, with 73 out of 4,440 cases from 1989 to 2005 (1.6%). As with the HSUS cases, the majority of the cases recorded involved dogs (52%) and horses (18%).

Victimological Studies

The NCVS does not ask any questions about crimes against animals, even if they occur in the context of interpersonal crimes such as domestic violence. Two representative national surveys commissioned by the HSUS included questions designed to get some preliminary data on people's exposure to such incidents. A telephone poll of a representative sample of the U.S. population was conducted in January 2003 by Penn, Schoen, and Berland (PSB survey). In July 2004, an Internet-based poll of a representative sample of 1,031 adults was conducted for the HSUS by Edge Research (Omnibus survey). Two questions regarding exposure to animal cruelty were included in both surveys:

1. Have you seen anyone intentionally or carelessly inflict pain or suffering on an animal during the last year?
2. IF YES: Did you report the incident to an animal agency, the police, or other authorities?

The percentage of respondents reporting that they had witnessed cruelty was the same in the Omnibus survey as in the PSB phone survey (14%). Those with dogs or cats were more likely to report witnessing cruelty than those without (15.6% vs. 6.9%). Exposure to animal cruelty was inversely associated with income, with the highest incidence reported by those with incomes under $20,000 (16.7%), declining to 14% in the $21,000–$75,000 ranges and 8% in the $76,000 + bracket. Reported witnessing of cruelty also declined with age, with 17% of those under 35 reporting witnessing cruelty, declining to 12% in the 35–49 group, 11% in the 50–64 group, and 7% in those over 65 (Lockwood, 2004).

More than half of the respondents in the Omnibus survey said they had reported the animal cruelty they had witnessed. This was comparable to the 60% of the PSB survey who reported. Reporting was significantly more likely among those with dogs and cats in the home (58% vs. 33% with no companion animals), those who donate to animal protection (66% vs. 39% among non-donors), women (64% vs. 44% in men), and those over 65 (75% vs. 37% in those under 35). There were no differences in reporting of abuse associated with education, income, or geographic region (Lockwood, 2004).

Although these two surveys were made using samples that are statistically representative of the U.S. population, we should not use the results to project precise estimates of the extent of animal maltreatment. These were not intended to be true victimological surveys and they employed open-ended interpretations of what acts the respondents considered to be "abuse." However, the 14% of the population who reported witnessing such acts, if projected to only one such observed event per household, would suggest that there may be more than 15 million such incidents annually. Thus the 1,200–1,500 incidents each year logged by the HSUS and AARDAS systems could represent less than 1 one-hundredth of 1% of all such occurrences!

Clearly animal cruelty is a widespread problem of great public concern with significant implications for law enforcement, social services, and public health. Access to information about incidents of animal abuse and neglect is a powerful tool for professionals in many disciplines. Despite this importance, our ability to identify victims and offenders, and to get a complete picture of these incidents, is limited.

Applying Lessons Learned from Counting Violence against People

Over the last 80 years, an enormous amount of time, money, and effort has been spent on the problem of tracking violence, abuse, and neglect involving human victims, with mixed success. Our ability to identify and apprehend the perpetrators of violence has dramatically increased and we have seen a steady improvement in our ability to document incidents of violence and the contexts in which they commonly occur. However, social scientists, law enforcement professionals, public health officials, policy makers, and the general public continue to express disappointment in the completeness, detail, and clarity of the picture of violence we are able to produce with these extensive resources. Several issues continue to be raised regarding attempts to track the interconnected problems of crime, child abuse, and domestic violence, and they are likely to be concerns that will have to be addressed as we attempt to develop much-needed assessments of the state of animal cruelty as well.

1. *Inconsistent definitions* – Studies of crime and family violence have been hampered by inconsistent definitions. When does a push or a shove become an assault? How do we determine the "primary offender" when two or more individuals are involved? When is a relationship considered "cohabitation"? The same

problem affects any analysis of cruelty to animals. There are 50 different state definitions of "animal" and of animal abuse and neglect. These are undergoing constant revision as laws are updated. However, there are certain core events and concepts that are central to nearly all of these definitions, including deprivation of food, water, shelter and care; inhumane killing; and infliction of unnecessary pain or suffering. These can be used to produce reasonable checklists of incidents that should be reported, counted, and tracked.

2. *Inconsistent laws and regulations* – As is the case with domestic and family violence, each state has its own laws addressing the problem of animal cruelty. States vary widely in the seriousness they attach to crimes against animals. In the case of crimes against people, it was hoped that systems based on tracking well-defined incidents, regardless of the applicable statutes, would provide a more consistent picture of the prevalence of such crimes. This is a guiding principle behind NIBRS. However, the reality is that if a state or local system views an incident as a minor crime—or not a crime at all—the incident is likely to be ignored and uncounted.

3. *Lack of participation by local or state agencies* – Any request for new data puts new time, money, and manpower demands on participating agencies. As we saw above, problems of missing or incomplete data and noncompliant agencies have hampered the effectiveness of NIBRS and attempts to gather data about violence against women. Animal care and control agencies have traditionally been at the bottom of the list to receive resources to support new initiatives, and they are frequently the first to see cuts when budgets must be reduced. Participation by these agencies in efforts to gather data on animal abuse and neglect must be made as simple and inexpensive as possible.

4. *Lack of appreciation of the value of data* – One of the reasons identified as an obstacle to the option of NIBRS by local and state agencies was a common sentiment that the data that agencies were being asked to provide were not directly related to solving or preventing crimes (Bureau of Justice Statistics, 1997). The street officer may not see the value of knowing whether a domestic violence offender is married to his or her victim has been in a substance abuse program, although crime analysts consider these to be important facts. Likewise, information on a suspect's prior history of animal torture may not be appreciated as relevant in an arson investigation,

but could prove important in tracing the pathways to violence. Greater training on the short- and long-term benefits of having such data could encourage participation in data gathering.

5. *Uncertain policy implications of data* – Even good data are subject to different interpretations about how they should shape public policy. As we noted above, there is often concern that improved reporting and tracking of social or health problems can create the impression that these efforts are associated with an apparent *increase* in the problem. Likewise, successful intervention and prevention programs run the risk of losing funding if they actually succeed in significantly reducing the problem they were designed to address. At the very least, improved tracking of animal cruelty issues can provide data that can reinforce the need for legislative or policy changes, and that can provide a tool for assessing the impact of those changes. If, for example, a community enacts stronger laws and more aggressive enforcement of provisions against animal fighting, it will be useful to track not only complaints or arrests for this crime, but also other related problems such as illegal gambling, dangerous dog complaints, and interstate traffic in fighting animals.

Possible Solutions

What steps can be taken to improve our ability to answer the question that began this essay? How can we get a better idea of the extent of animal cruelty and the nature of the victims and perpetrators of such crimes? Here are some suggested courses of action.

1. *Increase public awareness of animal cruelty issues* – Over the last decade, many animal protection and related groups have launched major efforts to educate the public about animal cruelty issues and the connections between animal cruelty and human violence (Ascione & Lockwood, 2001; Lockwood, 1999). Television programs such as *Animal Precinct*, which showcases the activities of the Humane Law Enforcement section of the American Society for the Prevention of Cruelty to Animals (ASPCA), have been extremely popular with the general public.

Public interest in and support for efforts to combat animal abuse are very high. In both the PSB phone and the Internet-based Omnibus surveys described above, 97% of the public considered "protecting animals from cruelty and abuse" to be important, with more than two-thirds of respondents saying that it was "very important." Eighty-five percent of the public agreed with the statement: "It has been demonstrated that people who repeatedly and intentionally harm animals are more likely to show violence towards people." Only 4% disagreed and 11% did not know (Lockwood, 2004). These findings suggest that these education efforts are succeeding, but some work is still needed to educate the public on animal cruelty issues, and that most people clearly would be supportive of efforts to further protect animals and identify those who are at risk for harming animals and people.

2. *Strengthen anti-cruelty laws* – Crimes against animals will not get "into the system" unless they are seen as significant events in the eyes of the law. Having the potential for felony-level penalties for some forms of abuse, as we now have in over 40 states, is a significant step (Ascione & Lockwood, 2001), but additional provisions are needed. Other provisions that facilitate the investigation and prosecution of cruelty to animals that have been instituted to varying degrees in some states include provisions that:

- Allow restitution to agencies that respond to animal abuse and neglect, including reimbursement of costs or financial bonding to cover costs of holding animals.
- Recognize the status of animal victims as more than mere property. Illinois has a statute that specifies that the owner of an animal that is a victim of an act of aggravated cruelty may seek monetary payment for the emotional pain that is suffered by the owner, and for any pain and suffering of the pet. Tennessee legislates that a person is entitled to seek monetary compensation for suffering and loss of companionship in cases where a person's pet has been killed or sustains injuries that result in death caused by the unlawful or negligent act of another or the animal of another.
- Strengthen requirements that allow or mandate the forfeiture of abused animals and provide for prohibitions of perpetrators having custody of animals in the future.
- Provide for psychological assessment and appropriate counseling or treatment of perpetrators at their expense.
- Facilitate cross-reporting of suspected animal and human abuse between animal care and control and human service agencies such as child protective services and adult protective services.
- Remove unnecessary exemptions from cruelty codes (e.g., Alabama's cruelty code

contains an exemption for "shooting a dog or cat with a BB gun for defecating/urinating on property"; Indiana's code contains an exemption for "discipline"; New Mexico exempts cockfighting and at least eight states specifically exempt rodeos from cruelty codes).

3. *Increase law enforcement training on animal cruelty issues* – We cannot track cases that are not reported, investigated, and charged. In the past, most training about animal abuse and neglect has targeted humane agents and animal control officers. Animal cruelty will not be taken seriously by all of the nation's 950,000 uniformed police officers until training on the subject is incorporated into standardized, certified training for such officers. This is a major objective of new efforts of the ASPCA, with such training being instituted in Illinois, and with programs under development for many additional states. The International Association of Chiefs of Police (IACP) and other law enforcement agencies have begun to distribute information on animal cruelty issues to a large audience (Lockwood, 1989; Ponder & Lockwood, 2000, 2001). Similarly, professional training on animal cruelty issues for prosecutors has been incorporated into the "Jumpstart" training program conducted regularly by the American Prosecutors Research Institute with the assistance of ASPCA staff.

4. *Enhance cruelty to animals data gathering at the local level* – Effective accounting of cases of animal abuse and neglect must begin at the local level. Some agencies, such as the Massachusetts SPCA, have attempted detailed analysis of their animal cruelty caseloads (Donley, Patronek, & Luke, 1999). As with the UCR the collection of aggregate data necessitates consistency in how such events are recorded. There is currently little uniformity in record keeping by the many different agencies that investigate and respond to animal abuse and neglect, although some popular shelter data management packages (e.g., Chameleon) have sections devoted to cruelty case tracking. Systems such as the discontinued HSUS database and AARDAS (Pet-abuse.com) have identified useful common data elements that should be captured (see Table 3). Part of the ASPCA's anticruelty initiative will be to develop simplified, uniform checklists that can be incorporated into existing data systems to provide for easier export and analysis of summary data from cruelty cases that are handled by a cross-section of agencies. This effort will also require identifying all agencies currently

having authority to respond to animal cruelty cases, a challenge similar to that faced by the National Council on Pet Population Study and Policy in its efforts to identify all animal shelters.

5. *Add cruelty to animals data elements to forms from other agencies* – Since animal abuse and neglect can often occur in the context of human victimization, it is important to add provisions for gathering such data to existing forms. For example, a number of agencies have added questions about animal cruelty to intake forms for people seeking orders of protection or reporting incidents of domestic abuse (e.g., Kings County, NY) and for high-risk domestic violence cases (Colorado Springs, CO). Likewise, some adult protective service agencies have been encouraged to routinely note and report evidence of animal abuse and neglect encountered in the course of working with vulnerable adults (Raymond, 2003).

6. *Enhance gathering of aggregate cruelty to animals data at the state level* – In reviewing the shortcomings of the tracking of violence against women, the JRSA suggested that "Since most laws and policies that deal directly with domestic and sexual violence offenses are passed by the States, it is appropriate that information systems are created or enhanced at this level of government" (JRSA, 1996, p. 6). The same argument can be applied to the tracking of animal cruelty, since each state has its own laws and definitions. However, attempts to mandate this under state law (e.g., in California) have thus far been unsuccessful. Renewed efforts to establish such mechanisms will be significantly enhanced if appropriate reporting systems are first improved at the local level, as described in suggestion 4.

Similar problems have affected states' ability to track dog bite injuries, but some states, such as Nevada, have successfully established local reporting mechanisms that can feed into a statewide report (Bureau of Health Planning and Statistics, 2003). Such programs demonstrate the need for good coordination of all potential reporters and stakeholders, including law enforcement, health departments, humane agencies, veterinarians, and social services.

7. *Enhance national tracking of cruelty to animals*

A. *Addition of animal cruelty to UCR/NIBRS* – The ideal, of course, would be to have the crime of animal cruelty counted in the same way that many other crimes are tracked at a national level. This is the approach that had been suggested by the JRSA to improve our understanding of violence against

women, which suggested that domestic violence could be added to the list of NIBRS offense codes (JRSA, 1996). Animal advocates, such as the Doris Day Animal Foundation, have pushed for the same approach to add "cruelty to animals" to the NIBRS coding (Randour, 2005).

Since NIBRS allows the states to add additional codes, this approach has been used for domestic violence in a few states (including Michigan and Kansas), but the JRSA notes several problems inherent in this approach. They indicate that expansion of these state additions into national tracking would create significant problems for federal, state, and local governments because they would have to reprogram software and reprint manuals and forms to accommodate this change (JRSA, 1996). Also, to begin regular submission of NIBRS data to the FBI, the state UCR/NIBRS system must be certified by the FBI based on error rate, statistical reasonableness, and updating capability. This is one of the reasons for the slow adoption of NIBRS by the states. Still, such efforts should be supported. As noted in Table 1, many crimes related to animal cruelty are already reportable under UCR/NIBRS, they simply do not have a unique coding. Since many of the miscellaneous crimes that are included are reported into the system only upon arrest, reporting of animal cruelty will be improved if there are more arrests for these crimes.

B. *Addition of animal care and control and humane agencies to list of UCR contributors* – The agencies that currently submit data to the FBI for UCR include fire marshals, alcohol beverage control agencies, regional and special-purpose task forces, federal agencies, and private college police departments.. Adding animal agencies to this system will require compiling a complete list of agencies with citation/charging authority and assigning Originating Reporting-agency Identifier (ORI) codes to those that do not already have them. This is being planned in conjunction with the ASPCA's initiatives.

C. *Creation of a process similar to the National Incidence Study* – The NIS system has proven to be very valuable in getting beneath the "tip of the iceberg" in documenting the dynamics of child abuse and neglect. A similar process that looked at the problems of animal cruelty in a representative sample of 100 or more communities would be equally valuable to the understanding of animal cruelty. Such a program would necessitate having some of the above elements already in place before it could generate reliable data. It would require coordination by Westat or an organization with similar organizational and statistical resources, and thus is likely to be a costly undertaking. As the other components of this process are put into place, we should begin identifying stakeholders and potential sponsors of such an undertaking.

8. *Collect victimization data* – The National Crime Victimization Survey (NCVS) is an important tool for identifying crimes that are more likely to fall through the cracks of the criminal justice system and go unreported, uninvestigated, or unprosecuted. Since this is currently often the case with animal abuse and neglect, the inclusion of questions regarding the victimization of animals could provide a useful measure of the extent of the problem and its connection to many demographic variables.

The inclusion of questions on animal abuse on the NCVS would face fewer hurdles than incorporation into NIBRS, but these efforts would likely encounter some organizational inertia. The NCVS survey is conducted in conjunction with the U.S. Census Bureau. Historically, this agency has been unresponsive to efforts to include even basic questions on pet ownership on the Census, despite strong support for such inclusion from humane and veterinary organizations and the pet industries (Clancy & Rowan, 2003). We should undertake efforts to put pressure on the Bureau of Justice Statistics and the Census Bureau to make this small addition to the NCVS.

In the meantime, animal advocates can continue to independently gather the best possible data on the victimization of animals. The inclusion of questions on animal victimization in other national surveys, such as the PSB and Omnibus surveys described above, is a relatively inexpensive way to begin to get a better understanding of the incidence of animal abuse and neglect. Well-crafted questions can usually be added to existing surveys at a relatively low cost (about $1,000 per question). Likewise, projects such as AARDAS/Pet-abuse.com deserve encouragement and support. While not necessarily reflective of the state of animal abuse nationwide, such efforts provide an important window in the lower depths of the human psyche and help provide insights into the cause and prevention of cruelty.

The ASPCA and other organizations have a strong commitment to facilitating many elements of the solutions I have outlined. Every incident of animal abuse is a tragedy in miniature, a story of a sentient creature who has suffered and possibly died. If we are to prevent violence in all its forms, these stories must count and be counted.

References

Arluke, A., Levin, J., Luke, C., & Ascione, F. (1999). The relationship of animal abuse to violence and other forms of antisocial behavior. *Journal of Interpersonal Violence, 14*, 963–975.

Ascione, F. R. (1993). Children who are cruel to animals: A review of research and implications for developmental psychopathology. *Anthrozoös, 6*, 226–246.

Ascione, F. R. (1998). Battered women's reports of their partners' and their children's cruelty to animals. *Journal of Emotional Abuse, 1*, 119–133.

Ascione, F. R., & Arkow, P. (Eds.). (1999). *Child abuse, domestic violence and animal abuse: Linking the Circles of compassion for prevention and intervention*. W. Lafayette, IN: Purdue University Press.

Ascione, F. A., & Lockwood, R. (2001). Cruelty to animals: Changing psychological, social, and legislative perspectives. In D. J. Salem & A. N. Rowan (Eds.), *The state of the animals: 2001* (pp. 39–53). Washington, DC: Humane Society Press.

Becker, K. D., Stuewig, J., Herrera, V. M., & McClosky, L. A. (2004). A study of firesetting and animal cruelty in children: Family influences and adolescent outcomes. *J. American Academy of Child and Adolescent Psychology, 43*(7), 905–912.

Beirne, P. (1997). Rethinking bestiality: Towards a concept of interspecies sexual assault. *Theoretical Criminology, 1*(3), 317–340.

Berry, C., Patronek, G., & Lockwood, R. (2005). Animal hoarding: A study of case outcomes. *Animal Law, 11*, 167–194.

Brown, A. (1974). *Who cares for animals? 150 years of the RSPCA*. London: Heinemann.

Bureau of Health Planning and Statistics. (2003). *Dog bite injuries and costs, Nevada, 1999–2002*. Nevada State Health Division, Carson City, NV.

Bureau of Justice Statistics. (1997). *Implementing the national incident-based reporting system: A project status report*. (Report NCJ-165581). Washington, DC: Bureau of Justice Statistics, U.S. Department of Justice.

CDC. (2000). Building data systems for monitoring and responding to violence against women: Recommendations from a workshop. *Morbidity and Mortality Weekly Report, 49*(RR-11), 1–18.

Clancy, E. A., & Rowan, A. N. (2003). Companion animal demographics in the United States: A historical perspective. In D. J. Salem & A. N. Rowan (Eds.), *The state of the animals II: 2003* (pp. 9–26). Washington, DC: Humane Society Press.

DeViney, E., Dickert, J., & Lockwood, R. (1983). The care of pets within child abusing families. *International Journal for Study of Animal Problems, 4*, 321–329.

Donley, L., Patronek, G. J., & Luke, C. (1999). Animal abuse in Massachusetts: A summary of case reports at the MSPCA and attitudes of Massachusetts veterinarians. *Journal of Applied Animal Welfare Science, 2*, 59–73.

Favre, D., & Tsang, V. (1993, Spring). The development of anti-cruelty laws during the 1800's. *Detroit College of Law Review, 1*, 1–35.

Federal Bureau of Investigation. (1996). National Crime Information Center: 30 Years on the beat. *The Investigator*, December 1996–January 1997 issue. Retrieved November 18, 2005 from http://permanent.access.gpo.gov/lps3213/ncicinv.htm

Federal Bureau of Investigation. (1999). Press Release. July 15, 1999. Retrieved November 18, 2005 from www.fbi.gov/pressrel/pressrel99/ncic2000.htm

Federal Bureau of Investigation. (2004). *Uniform Crime Reporting Handbook*. Clarksburg, WV: Uniform Crime Reporting Program. Retrieved November 18, 2005 from www.fbi.gov/ucr/ucr.htm

Federal Bureau of Investigation. (2005). *Crime in the United States 2004. Uniform Crime Reports*. Washington, DC: U.S. Department of Justice.

Felthous, A. R., & Kellert, S. R. (1987a). Psychosocial aspects of selecting animal species for physical abuse. *Journal of Forensic Sciences, 32*, 1713–1723.

Felthous, A. R., & Kellert, S. R. (1987b). Childhood cruelty to animals and later aggression against people: A Review. *American Journal of Psychiatry, 144*, 710–717.

Frasch, P., Waisman, S., Wagman. B., & Beckstead, S. (2000). *Animal Law*. Durham, NC: Carolina Academic Press.

Harcourt, B. E. (2001). *Illusions of order: The false promise of broken window policing*. Cambridge, MA: Harvard University Press.

Harp, C. (2002). *Bringing balance to juvenile justice*. Alexandria, VA: American Prosecutors Research Institute.

Harries, K. (1999). *Mapping crime: Principle and practice*. Washington, DC: National Institute of Justice.

Hoarding of Animals Research Consortium. (2000). People who hoard animals. *Psychiatric Times, 17*, 25–29.

HSUS. (2001). First Strike® Campaign 2000 report of animal cruelty cases. Press Release, Washington, DC: Humane Society of the U.S., April 13, 2001.

HSUS. (2002). First Strike® Campaign 2001 report of animal cruelty cases. Press Release, Washington, DC: Humane Society of the U.S., April 1, 2002.

HSUS. (2003). First Strike® Campaign 2002 report of animal cruelty cases. Press Release, Washington, DC: Humane Society of the U.S., March 28, 2003.

HSUS. (2004). First Strike® Campaign 2003 report of animal cruelty cases. Press Release, Washington, DC: Humane Society of the U.S., April 16, 2004.

Justice Research and Statistics Association. (1996). *Domestic and sexual violence data collection: A report to Congress under the Violence Against Women Act*. Washington, DC: National Institute of Justice and Bureau of Justice Statistics.

Justice Research and Statistics Association. (2005). *Status of NIBRS in the states*. Retrieved November 16, 2005 from www.jrsa.org/ibrrc/background-status/nibrs_states.shtml

Kass, P. (2001). Understanding animal companion surplus in the United States: Relinquishment of nonadoptables to animal shelters for euthanasia. *Journal of Applied Animal Welfare Science, 4*(4), 237–248.

Kelling, G. L., & Skogan, W. G.. (1997). *Fixing broken windows: Restoring order and reducing crime in our communities*. New York: Touchstone.

Kindermann, C., Lynch, J., & Cantor, C. (1997). *Effects of the redesign of victimization estimates*. Washington, DC: U.S. Department of Justice.

Lawrence, E., & Alexander, M. (2005, February 6). Worst year for animal cruelty. *Sunday*

Mail (Australia). Retrieved October 27, 2005 from www.news.com.au

Lockwood, R. (1989). Cruelty to animals and human violence. *Training Key #392* (pp. 1–4). Alexandria, VA: International Association of Chiefs of Police.

Lockwood, R. (1999). Animal cruelty and human violence: A look back from the front. In F. Ascione & P. Arkow (Eds.), *Child abuse, domestic violence and animal abuse: Linking the circles of compassion for prevention and intervention* (pp. 3–8). W. Lafayette, IN: Purdue University Press.

Lockwood, R. (2002). Making the connection between animal cruelty and abuse and neglect of vulnerable adults. *The Latham Letter, 23*(1), 10–11.

Lockwood, R. (2004). *Detailed analysis of July 2004 edge-research omnibus survey.* Unpublished Report for Humane Society of the United States, Washington, DC.

Lockwood, R. (2005). Cruelty towards cats: Changing perspectives. In D. Salem & A. Rowan (Eds.), *The state of the animals III: 2005.* Washington, DC: Humane Society Press.

Lockwood, R., & Ascione, F. R. (Eds.). 1998. *Cruelty to animals and interpersonal violence: Readings in research and application.* W. Lafayette, IN: Purdue University Press.

Merz-Perez, L., & Heide, K. M. (2003). *Animal cruelty: Pathway to violence against people.* Walnut Creek, CA: Altamira Press.

Munro, H. M. C., & Thrusfield, M. V. (2001). "Battered pets": sexual abuse. *Journal of Small Animal Practice, 42*, 333–337.

National Center for Health Statistics. (2005). *International classification of disease, ninth revision, clinical modification (ICD-9-CM).* Hyattsville, MD: U.S. Department of Health and Human Services, National Center for Health Statistics.

National Data Archive on Child Abuse and Neglect. (2003). *National child abuse and neglect data system (NCANDS) detailed case data component, 1998–1999. User's guide and codebook.* Ithaca, NY: Family Life Development Center, Cornell University.

National Data Archive on Child Abuse and Neglect. (2005a). *About NDACAN.* Retrieved May 7, 2005 from http://www.ndacan.cornell.edu/NDACAN/AboutNDACAN.htmlvw

National Data Archive on Child Abuse and Neglect. (2005b). NDACAN funding renewed. *The NDACAN Updata, 16,* 1.

NCPPSP. (2000). The shelter statistics survey, 1994–97. National Council on Pet Population Study and Policy. Retrieved June 5, 2005 from http://www.petpopulation.org/statsurvey.html

New, J. C., Jr. (2000). Characteristics of shelter-relinquished animals and their owners compared with animals and their owners in U.S. pet-owning households. *Journal of Applied Animal Welfare Science, 3*(3), 179–201.

New, J. C., Salman, M. D., Scarlett, J. M., Kass, P. H., Vaughn, J. A., Scherr, S., & Kelch, W. K. (1999). Moving: Characteristics of dogs and cats and those relinquishing them to 12 U.S. animal shelters. *Journal of Applied Animal Welfare Science, 2*(2), 83–96.

O'Shea, T. C., & Nicholls, K. (2003). *Crime analysis in America: Findings and recommendations.* Washington, DC: Office of Community Oriented Policing Services, U.S. Department of Justice.

Patronek, G. P. (1999). Hoarding of animals: An under-recognized public health problem in a difficult-to-study population. *Public Health Reports, 114,* 81–87.

Patronek, G. P. (2001). The problem of animal hoarding. *Municipal Lawyer*, May/June, 6–9, 19.

Patronek, G. P., & Rowan, A. N. (1995). Determining dog and cat numbers and population dynamics. *Anthrozoös, 8*(1), 31–43.

Ponder, C., & Lockwood, R. (2000). Recognizing the connection: Law enforcement's response to animal cruelty and family violence. *The Police Chief, 67*(11), 31–36.

Ponder, C., & Lockwood, R. (2001). Cruelty to animals and family violence. Training Key #526, Arlington, VA. *International Association of Chiefs of Police,* 1–6.

Prejean, R. (2003). Man bites dog! *North Central Texas American Planning Association News,* July/August, 2–7, 10–15.

Randour, M. L. (2005). *Why assigning animal cruelty its own classification under the FBI's crime data collection system will benefit communities.* Washington, DC: Doris Day Animal Foundation.

Rantala, R. R., & Edwards, T. J. (2000). *Effects of NIBRS on crime statistics.* Washington, DC: Bureau of Justice Statistics, U.S. Department of Justice.

Raymond, J. (Ed.). (2003). *Creating safer communities for older adults and companion animals.* Madison, WI: Department of Health and Family Services (Publication PDE-3181).

Rowan, A. N. (1992). Shelters and pet overpopulation: A statistical black hole. *Anthrozoös, 5*(3), 140–143.

RSPCA. (2005a). The faces of animal cruelty in Britain today. Press release, The Royal Society for the Prevention of Cruelty to Animals, August 25, 2005.

RSPCA. (2005b). *Do your duty: 25 reasons for a new animal welfare law.* London: Royal Society for the Prevention of Cruelty to Animals.

Sacks, J. J., Lockwood, R., Hornreich, J., & Sattin, R. W. (1996). Fatal dog attacks, 1989–1994. *Pediatrics, 97,* 1–5.

Sacks, J. J., Sinclair, L., Gilchrist, J., Golab, G., & Lockwood, R. (2000). Breeds of dogs involved in fatal human attacks in the United States between 1979 and 1998. *Journal of the American Veterinary Medical Association, 217*(6), 836–840.

Salman, M. D., Hutchison, J., Ruch-Gallie, R., Kogan, L., New, J. G. Jr., Kass, P., & Scarlett, J. (2000). Behavioral reasons for relinquishment of dogs and cats to 12 shelters. *Journal of Applied Animal Welfare Science, 3*(2), 93–106.

Salman, M. D., New, J. G. Jr., Scarlett, J. M., Kass, P. H., Ruch-Gallie, R., & Hetts, S. (1998). Human and animal factors related to the relinquishment of dogs and cats in 12 selected animal shelters in the United States. *Journal of Applied Animal Welfare Science, 1*(3), 207–226.

Scarlett, J. M. (1999). Reasons for relinquishment of companion animals in U.S. animal shelters: Selected health and personal issues. *Journal of Applied Animal Welfare Science, 2*(1), 41–57.

Search Group Inc. (1993). *Use and management of criminal history record information: A comprehensive report.* Washington, DC: Bureau of Justice Statistics, Office of Justice Programs, U.S. Department of Justice.

Sinclair, L., & Lockwood, R. (2006). Cruelty towards cats. In. J. R. August (Ed.), *Consultations in Feline Medicine.* Philadelphia: Elsevier.

Sinclair, L., Merck, M., & B. Lockwood, R. (2006). *Forensic investigation of animal cruelty: A guide for veterinary and law enforcement professionals.* Washington, DC: Humane Society Press.

Skogan, W. G. (1992). *Disorder and decline: Crime and the spiral of decay in American neighborhoods.* Berkeley: University of California Press.

Titelius, R. (2000, November 13). Dogs suffer most cruelty. *Herald Sun* (Australia). Retrieved June 5, 2005 from www.news.com.au

Vermeulen, H., & Odendaal, J. S. J. (1993). Proposed typology of companion animal Abuse. *Anthrozoös, 6*(4), 248–257.

Weiss, H. B., Friedman, D. I., & Coben, J. H. (1998). Incidence of dog bite injuries treated in emergency departments. *Journal of the American Medical Association, 279*(1), 51–53.

Wilson, J. Q., & Kelling, G. L. (1982). Broken windows. *Atlantic Monthly, 281*(3), 41–62.

Wise, S. M. (2003). The evolution of animal law since 1950. In D. J. Salem & A. N. Rowan (Eds.), *The state of the animals II: 2003* (pp. 99–106). Washington, DC: Humane Society Press.

Conduct Problems and Cruelty to Animals in Children: What Is the Link?

Mark R. Dadds

Cruelty to animals is not a necessary or sufficient condition for the diagnosis of any of the diagnostic categories of childhood behavioral disorders. Neither is it a symptom that has any empirically documented diagnostic or prognostic value over and above the other symptoms. Why then should one discuss it in relation to the behavioral disorders of childhood? The answer to this is speculative but may nonetheless help shed light on both the nature of behavioral disorders in children as well as the phenomena of cruelty to animals itself. In this chapter, I will discuss some examples of contemporary thinking about both the disruptive behavior disorders and cruelty to animals in children with the aim of drawing some tentative but potentially important conclusions about how they may be linked in ways that inform their overlapping scientific bases and practice implications.

The following questions guide the chapter: To what extent is cruelty to animals a concurrent or prognostic sign of pathology in a child and/or his or her family system? Can cruelty to animals be a specific predictor of concurrent and future violence (to humans) over and above other behavior associated with conduct problems in the child and family? If cruelty to animals is a distinctive marker for concurrent or future problems, how can its identification be used to reduce violence and other problems in our society? Can cruelty to animals, or conversely, concern and empathy for the welfare of other organisms, be modified by social interventions in the context of a children with generalised behavioral problems?

Definitions of Cruelty to Animals and Conduct Problems in Children

How cruelty and conduct problems are defined has important implications for understanding their links. The *Oxford English Dictionary* defines cruelty as "… a disposition to inflict suffering; delight or indifference to another's pain; merciless, hardheartedness. …" Clearly this definition considers cruelty to be an enduring trait. Other definitions, specific to animal cruelty, have emphasized a more behavioral dimension. Felthous and Kellert (1986) define "substantial cruelty to animals" as a "pattern of deliberately, repeatedly, and unnecessarily hurting vertebrate animals in a manner likely to cause serious injury" (p. 57). Brown (1988) and Vermeulen and Odendaal (1993) define animal cruelty as above but note that it can occur through acts of commission and omission, that is, failing to provide care.

A number of consistent dimensions of cruelty are raised by the above definitions. All definitions include a behavioral dimension ("inflicted"), whereby behavior is typically seen to include both acts of commission (e.g., beating a dog) and omission (e.g., neglecting to provide adequate food or water). The majority require a sense of purpose ("deliberate" or "knowingly"), however Vermeulen and Odendaal (1993) include accidental acts ("unintentional or ignorant"). The dimension of frequency is similarly controversial. Felthous and Kellert (1987) require repeated acts while Vermeulen and Odendaal (1993) suggest that a single act will suffice. There is somewhat more consensus on the issue of whether acts of cruelty are physical or psychological, with the majority of definitions accounting for both. Psychological abuse is considered to encompass the instillation of negative emotional states, such as fear and anxiety, as well as neglectful acts such as the deprivation of affection, or appropriate stimuli (Vermeulen & Odendaal, 1993). However, there is recognition that psychological abuse is somewhat subjective and harder to determine (Ascione, 1993; Vermeulen & Odendaal, 1993). Although not reflected in the final definitions, several researchers also provide comment on the affective dimension of obtaining pleasure from perpetrating or witnessing cruelty (Ascione, 1993; Felthous & Kellert, 1987). Finally, there is an implicit assumption in the definitions that the cruelty is proactive, that is, not solely occurring in response to provocation (as would be the case for a child who hits out at a dog who bites or scratches). For the purposes of this paper, then, cruelty to animals refers to repetitive and proactive behavior (or pattern of behavior) intended to cause harm to sentient creatures. The implications of this are that accidental, unknowing, and single occurrences, as would be expected from many young children, are not included.

Conduct problems is a generic expression used to encompass a range of "externalizing" behaviors, that is, behaviors that are distressing to those around the problem child. In current diagnostic parlance (the *Diagnostic and Statistical Manual of Mental Disorders* of American Psychiatric Association and the International Classification of Diseases), categories include conduct disorder (violation of the rights of others; antisocial behavior), attention deficits and hyperactivity, and oppositional behavior (aggression, non-compliance, rule breaking). The overlapping essence of these disorders is a persistent pattern of "undercontrolled" antisocial and aggressive behavior that, in its most severe form, begins early in childhood and is persistent through life. Many children show a marked but temporary increase in these behaviors around the adolescent years; however, these may be less virulent than the life-course persistent type. For this chapter, I will use the generic term conduct problems to refer to the broad class of externalizing problems that include aggression, violating the rights of others, rule breaking, and general antisocial behavior, unless there is a need to be more specific.

Contemporary models of the causes of specific conduct problems are varied but generally emphasize interacting risks of biological vulnerability in the child with exposure to environmental insults such as abusive and/or neglectful parenting and social disadvantage (Caspi & Moffit, 1995; Dadds, 1995). Interestingly, the notions of "intentionality" or "motives" for the behavior have not occupied a central part in these models. Conduct problems can stem from impulsivity that is not controllable by the child, through to deliberate "reward-driven" behavior that can be seen as instrumental in achieving one's goals. The motives for behavior are a crucial part of understanding cruelty, as noted above, and only recently have attempts been made to catego-

rize conduct problems using these dimensions. Here lies one aspect of how cruelty to animals may have heuristic value in refining our understanding of subtypes of conduct problems, and I will return to this throughout the chapter.

The significance of children's cruelty to animals as a symptom relevant for assessing a child's psychological health has been formally acknowledged in the last three revisions of the DSM (APA, 1987, 1994) specifically with reference to conduct disorder. Cruelty to animals was first included in the DSM-III-R (APA, 1987). In the DSM-IVTR, the essential feature of conduct disorder is "… a repetitive and persistent pattern of behavior in which the basic rights of others or major age-appropriate societal norms or rules are violated" (APA, 2000, p. 85). These behavior patterns fall into four major groupings, one of which is aggressive conduct that causes or threatens physical harm to people or animals. In this context, cruelty toward animals is considered indicative of a disturbed mental and/or emotional state in children. However, consistent with the trend in the DSM toward multiple diagnostic criteria (Spitzer, Davies, Russell, & Barkley, 1990), this is only the case when the cruelty is part of a larger pattern of antisocial behavior, that is, held to be a part of a symptom cluster. Current diagnostic systems have little to say about the individual contribution of any particular behavioral symptom. Thus, the role of cruelty to animals within the general diagnosis of conduct disorder is unclear and it is important to note that few large-scale studies of the specific clusters of behaviors making up conduct problems have typically failed to support a unique role for cruelty to animals.

On the positive side, Luk, Staiger, Wong, and Mathai (1999) examined persistent conduct problems in a clinic-referred sample of 141 children and a community sample of 36 children (aged 5–12 years). The children who showed cruelty to animals were found to have more severe conduct symptoms compared with the non-cruel group. The authors conclude that cruelty to animals is possibly a marker of a subgroup of conduct disorder that has a poor prognosis; however, the sample was small and cruelty was not examined in relation to alternative or coexisting symptoms. Becker, Stuewig, Herrera, and McCloskey (2004) examined the relationship between fire setting, cruelty to animals, and patterns of delinquency in high-risk families and controls. Cruelty to animals in children was associated with marital violence and harsh parenting, a diagnosis of conduct disorder for the child, and referral for violent offending. However, rates of conduct disorder (27%) and violent offending (25.8%) indicated that the majority of cruel children did not have these problems, and rates were actually higher in fire-setting children (31.3% and 40.6%, respectively). Thus, while the study further supports the association of cruelty to conduct problems and violence, it fails to support a powerful or unique role for cruelty to animals.

Loeber, Keenan, Lahey, Green, and Thomas (1993) developed an empirically driven diagnostic framework for oppositional defiant disorder (ODD) and conduct disorder (CD) in an effort to construct a developmentally based diagnostic system for these disorders. They found that a number of low base rate symptoms, including cruelty to animals, did not discriminate well between different diagnostic categories. Loeber et al. (1993) advocate the importance of retaining low base rate symptoms within the symptom list, however, arguing that the variety of early problem behavior is one of the best predictors of chronicity. In a meta-analysis of 60 factor analytic studies of the Child Behavior Checklist (CBCL) (Frick et al., 1993), cruelty to animals was one of several items that discriminated between subtypes, falling in the extremes of the destructive dimension. Frick et al.'s (1993) destructive/nondestructive dichotomy corresponds to a wealth of CD literature supporting subtypes based on an aggressive versus nonaggressive distinction. Aggressive behavior can be broken into reactive or proactive (e.g., see Dodge, Bates, & Pettit, 1990). The latter refers to premeditated, instrumental aggression, and would correspond most closely to the phenomena of intentional cruelty to animals.

These studies show that cruelty to animals may relate differently to clusters of behaviors within the broad category of conduct disorder; however, they fail to support the idea that cruelty to animals has diagnostic or prognostic value in and of itself. As noted, however, there are important methodological limitations in these studies in terms of the measure of cruelty; typically it was the one item on the CBCL. As previously noted, studies of offender groups have typically used more time-consuming and comprehensive measurement strategies. These studies have their own methodological limitations but have reached fairly similar conclusions about the importance of cruelty to animals as a prognostic factor.

Much of the early research into the prognostic value of childhood cruelty to animals examined it as part of a triad of behaviors (cruelty to animals, fire setting, and enuresis) proposed to be predictive of later violence/aggression and criminality. Heath, Hardesty, and Goldfine (1984) explored the historical basis to this behavioral cluster. They report that as early as 1905, Freud noted that it was common to warn children that playing with fire would lead them to wet the bed. Freud proposed a link between enuresis, fire setting, and sexual problems. Heath et al. (1984) report that while this relationship was maintained in the psychoanalytic literature, it was given a somewhat different direction by later authors who pointed to the importance of aggression in fire setting and bed-wetting.

Heath et al. (1984) and Felthous and Kellert (1987) review the early literature with respect to cruelty, fire setting, and bed-wetting as predictors of later criminality. At best, the relationship can be considered tenuous. Some studies found no significant relationships (e.g., MacDonald, 1968), whereas others found partially supportive relationships (e.g., Hellman & Blackman, 1966; Heller, Ehrlich, & Lester, 1984). For example, Hellman and Blackman (1966) retrospectively compared aggressive and nonaggressive criminals in an effort to determine whether fire setting, enuresis, and cruelty to animals were predictive of aggressive adult crimes. Seventy-four percent of the prisoners charged with aggressive crimes had a history of the symptom triad or part of the triad, while only 28% of non-aggressive criminals exhibited the triad or part of the triad. This was a statistically significant difference. However, Heller et al. (1984) retrospectively investigated the incidence of cruelty to animals, fire setting, and enuresis in the case reports of 1,935 offenders evaluated at a court psychiatric clinic. The incidence of the triad, or part of the triad, was found equally among violent and nonviolent criminals. Only cruelty to animals significantly differentiated between those charged with a violent crime and those charged with a nonviolent crime. In both of the previous studies, some subjects only exhibited a part of the triad. Indeed, there is no consensus within the literature that the component behaviors within the triad are related to each other. Some studies find no association between these behaviors (e.g., Michaels, 1955) while others find partial relationships (Kuhnley, Hendred, & Quinlan, 1982).

In an effort to determine if a relationship exists between fire setting, enuresis, and cruelty to animals, Heath et al. (1984) compared children exhibiting these behaviors on demographic variables and clinical measures of adjustment (internalizing and externalizing behavior, total pathology, and social competence). Participants were 204 consecutive outpatient admissions, aged 4–16 years (130 boys, 74 girls). Children were identified as enuretic, cruel to animals, or fire setting by parental identification on the Child Behavior Checklist (CBCL: Achenbach, 1991). Additional clinical information was gained from the clinic charts and a family information sheet. Findings indicated partial relationships, with enuresis and cruelty to animals being related to, and interacting with, only a portion of the total fire-setting population. Enuresis was significantly associated with non-cruel fire setters, and cruelty to animals was associated with non-enuretic fire setters. No significant associations were found between cruelty to animals, and Socio Economic Status, age, or sex. Heath et al. (1984) concluded that situational or environmental factors are likely to be more significant than individual behaviors (e.g., cruelty, fire setting, bed-wetting) in predicting future aggressive behavior.

Nonetheless, empirical study into the stability of cruelty from childhood to criminality in adulthood, the so-called "graduation hypothesis" (Arluke, Levin, Luke, & Ascione, 1999) or "escalation thesis" (Beirne, 1999) continued. The retrospective research conducted by Felthous and Kellert (1985, 1986) has been influential in establishing a link between childhood animal cruelty and later violence/aggression toward people. Using the previously reported studies for guidance, they began with several assumptions. First, repeated acts of serious cruelty to socially valued animals (e.g., dogs) are more likely to be associated with violence toward people than are isolated acts of cruelty, minor abuses, and victimization of less socially valuable species (e.g., rats). Second, if animal cruelty is associated with aggression against people, it is most likely associated with serious, recurrent personal violence. A single violent offence or act would not identify this core population with continuous aggression. Third, subjects must be interviewed directly because prison records and other documents do not contain systematically gathered and adequately detailed historical data. Fourth, if a positive history of cruelty to animals exists, it will most likely be elicited by inquiry into a number of areas wherein animal involvement is possible. One or two questions on cruelty to animals do not sufficiently tap the history of an individual's involvement with animals.

Felthous and Kellert (1986) defined substantial cruelty toward animals as "… a pattern of deliberately, repeatedly, and unnecessarily hurting vertebrate animals in a manner likely to cause serious injury" (p. 57). In addition, they defined adult aggression as that which is recurrent, impulsive, and injurious to other people. Two prisons were studied and counsellors were asked to rate their assigned prisoners on a scale of aggressiveness from 1–10. Aggressive behaviors ranged from threatening speech to violent acts, with high scores reflecting frequent, severe, and multiform aggressive behavior. Only those subjects with extremely high or low scores were asked to participate in the study. In addition to the prisoners, randomly selected men were interviewed as noninstitutional control subjects. A standard interview schedule was administered to each participant. The interview items pertained to antisocial behaviors, environmental background, and various aspects of animal involvement such as owning family pets, raising livestock, training animals, hunting, and attending organized fights (e.g., dog fights). The subjects were asked about 16 specific types of animal cruelty. A survey on attitudes toward animals was also administered. For each subject who consented, a parent or family member who knew him in childhood was contacted and interviewed.

Statistical analysis showed a significant association between acts of cruelty to animals in childhood and serious, recurrent aggression against people as adults. It was found that 25% of the aggressive criminals had abused animals five or more times in childhood, in contrast to 5.8% of the nonaggressive criminals, and 0% for noncriminals. The differences between the aggressive criminals and control subjects were significant, regardless of whether the control group comprised nonaggressive prisoners or randomly selected nonprisoners. Therefore, the hypothesis that recurrent serious animal abuse in childhood is related to a chronic violent disposition toward people was supported.

Arluke et al. (1999) provided evidence to suggest that it may be less appropriate to represent childhood or adolescent abuse of animals in terms of a "graduation hypothesis," and more appropriate to represent it in terms of a generalization of deviance whereby the abuse of animals by children is seen as one of a range of forms of antisocial behavior that becomes evident in childhood. Arluke et al. (1999) compared the criminal records of 153 animal abusers with the criminal records of the same number of controls who were matched on demographic characteristics. The results of the study indicated that while those who had abused animals were more likely to be interpersonally violent than were controls, they were also more likely than controls to engage in a range of antisocial behaviors, particularly property, drug, and public disorder offences. In addition, the authors concluded that instances of animal abuse were no more likely to precede than they were to follow violent offences. These findings suggest that rather than representing animal abuse as a discrete step in the development of criminal/violent behavior, it may be more appropriate to represent adolescent animal abuse as one of a cluster of antisocial behaviors from which both violent and nonviolent criminal behavior may result. A note of caution is that these data are based on official reports and exact sequences of events may be inaccurate.

Miller and Knutson (1997) used self-report data to investigate whether people charged with violent offences differed from people charged with nonviolent offences with respect to prior exposure to animal cruelty. This study concluded that prior animal abuse did not differentiate between the four groups (homicide, violent, sex, and other) of offenders they investigated. It should be noted, however, that this study included witnessing cruelty to animals as well as perpetrating it, and thus findings may be weakened in that regard. Contrary findings were reported by Merz-Perez, Heide, and Silverman (2001), who found that violent offenders were more likely to have a history of animal abuse, including cruelty to their own pets as children, than nonviolent offenders.

Felthous and Kellert (1986) propose that the above discrepancies within the literature may themselves have multiple determinants. For instance, the thoroughness with which historical information is obtained within different studies varies considerably. For example, their study involved a personal and in-depth historical interview, whereas others have used a single checklist criterion to ascertain animal cruelty. In the second part of the study, Felthous and Kellert (1986) isolated the subjects who had a pattern of substantial animal abuse in childhood. Of the 20 prisoners who gave this history, 16 belonged to the most aggressive category, and 4 fell into the nonaggressive category. Three of the 50 nonprisoners had shown a pattern of animal cruelty. Several other observations were made about abusive aggressive criminals (AAC) in comparison to abusive nonaggressive criminals, and abusive noncriminal subjects. AAC subjects tended to engage in a greater variety of abusive acts, tended to abuse a greater number of animal species, had been cruel to

cats and dogs, and showed less restraint during the act of abuse and less remorse afterwards.

These findings suggest that certain features of childhood cruelty to animals may be more meaningful in evaluating aggressive individuals. These features include direct involvement, lack of self-restraint, lack of remorse, variety of cruelty acts, variety of species victimized, inclusion of socially valued species (e.g., pets), and motivations for cruelty. Felthous and Kellert (1986) therefore concluded that cruelty to animals appears to be one of several behaviors (e.g., injurious assaults, window smashing, fire setting) that can represent a pattern of impulsive, diffuse aggression in childhood or adolescence. The pattern may or may not subside with attainment of adulthood. This interpretation is more consistent with Arluke et al. (1999), who suggest that animal abuse is one of a number of behaviors representative of a more general class of antisocial behavior, rather than a distinct step in the development of adult criminal or violent behavior.

This broader interpretation is in accordance with earlier studies (e.g., Hellman & Blackman, 1966) that suggest that childhood cruelty toward animals is a deviant interactional pattern that may operate as one component of a behavioral spectrum associated with violence and criminality in adolescence and adulthood. It must be concluded that while there are strong indications that cruelty to animals may have unique power in predicting later adult violence, no existing study has been able to unequivocally demonstrate that early animal cruelty is prognostically distinct from other aspects of early conduct problems and aggression.

If cruelty to animals has not so far been shown to be prognostically unique, why would we continue to question its links with broader conduct problems? In what follows, I will argue that the way conduct problems are conceptualized may overturn this negative finding. That is, conduct problems (or conduct disorder) may be a heterogeneous category that masks several important clusters that have as yet failed to be clearly delineated. It is possible that cruelty to animals may be one key to exploring a more differentiated model of conduct disorders with important implications for predicting later violence. To make this argument it is necessary to review some innovative ideas about conduct problems that have not been fully explored. In the next section, I will briefly review several ideas about conduct problems that open up new ways of thinking about and researching cruelty to animals as a diagnostic or prognostic heuristic. Most of these are based on distinctions made on the basis of differing goals of cruel and other antisocial/aggressive behavior.

Motivations for Cruelty

Given the definitions explored above, measurement of the phenomenon of cruelty stands to benefit by consideration of the various motivations or intentions that children have for engaging in acts of cruelty toward animals. While invoking unobservable mental states such as motivation and intentions raises some well-worn methodological problems, clearly there is a need for researchers to distinguish cruelty derived from developmental immaturity from cruelty that may be malicious.

Kellert and Felthous (1985) provide a preliminary classification of motivations for cruel behavior toward animals derived from their retrospective interviews with incarcerated criminals. They have proposed nine motivations for cruelty; however, they note that the motivation for any particular act is typically multidimensional. First, they propose the motivation to control an animal. This encompasses shaping an animal's behavior or eliminating undesirable characteristics of an animal (e.g., kicking a dog in the testicles when the dog barks in the house). The second motivation is retaliation, in which a perpetrator may use extreme punishment or revenge for a presumed wrong on the part of an animal (e.g., burning a cat for scratching the furniture). The third is satisfaction of a prejudice against a species or breed, whereby perpetrators designate a species as either good or bad (e.g., cat hatred). Kellert and Felthous (1985) note that extreme prejudice is frequently found against certain types of rodents, pests, or insects (e.g., cane toads, rats). There is an accompanying belief that such animals are not worthy of moral consideration.

A fourth and equally common motivation is proposed to be the expression of aggression through an animal (e.g., where dogs are trained to attack other animals or people). A fifth and similar motivation is the enhancement of one's own aggression. Kellert and Felthous (1985) report that perpetrators used cruelty to animals as a way of improving their own aggressive skills or to impress others with their capacity for violence (e.g., perpetrators used animals for target practice, or to impress fellow gang members). The sixth motivation encompasses shock value and amusement (e.g., burning cats and setting them to run around a tavern). Retaliation or exacting

revenge against other people by abusing their pets is proposed as the seventh motivation (e.g., castrating a neighbor's cat). The displacement of hostility and aggression from a person to an animal was the eighth and common motivation for criminals who had been abused as children. Displaced aggression typically involved authority figures that the subject hated or feared but was afraid to aggress against (e.g., perpetrators exacting revenge for beatings they suffered).

The final motivation is proposed to be nonspecific sadism. This encompasses the desire to inflict injury, suffering, or death on an animal in the absence of any particular provocation or especially hostile feelings toward the animal. The primary goal here is the pleasure derived from causing injury and suffering. Kellert and Felthous (1985) found that sadistic gratification was sometimes associated with the desire to exercise total power and control over an animal, and may have served to compensate for a person's feelings of weakness or vulnerability (e.g., snapping animals necks "for kicks and for fun"). Clearly, further empirical substantiation of these motivations for animal cruelty is needed as they are crucial to precision of assessment.

Ascione, Thompson, and Black (1997) also note a number of motives for cruelty to animals that are more relevant to child and adolescent samples, arguing that understanding motivations is critical to designing effective interventions. Ascione and Lockwood (2001) draw a parallel with models of intervention for juvenile fire setting that are based on typologies of fire-setting behavior. At the minimum, interventions could consider three important typologies in children: exploratory/curious animal abuse, pathological abuse, and animal abuse that is part of a broader pattern of delinquent/antisocial behavior (Ascione, 2001).

Cruelty as Callous/Reward-Driven Behavior

A recent approach to identifying subcategories of conduct disorder is a downward extension of the (adult) idea of psychopathy in which some forms of antisocial behavior are characterized by a callous/unemotional temperament. For children possessing a temperament that is less sensitive to others' emotions and punishment, and more prone to impulsive thrill seeking and anger, discipline-related socialization may be less effective (Kochanska, 1993) and the child may fail to learn appropriate inhibitory control and concern for others. On the other hand, children who possess highly emotional or arousable temperaments are thought to be more susceptible to the emotions of others and discomfort triggered by transgressions from behavioral standards. Therefore, these children respond to lower levels of punishment and learn to avoid particular behaviors quickly, including negative emotions in others (Dadds & Salmon, 2003; Hare & Schalling, 1978; Kochanska, 1997).

The paired notions of lack of inhibitory control (impulsivity) and lack of empathic or emotional arousal (callous/unemotional traits: CU) are synonymous with the traditional two-factor conceptualization of psychopathy in adults (e.g., Hare, Hart, & Harpur, 1991) and more recently in children and adolescents (Frick & Ellis, 1999). As shown in adult data, high scores on the CU factor are associated with more severe and proactive aggression, less responsiveness to cues of punishment, disrupted processing of emotional cues, a reward-dominant style, and less anxiety. These factors are thought to impede the development of conscience (Barry et al., 2000; Blair, Colledge, Murray, & Mitchell, 2001; Christian, Frick, Hill, Tyler, & Frazer, 1997; Lynam, 1997; O'Brien & Frick, 1996). While still in its early stages, there is emerging evidence that children with both conduct problems and a callous/unemotional temperament show more severe and chronic problems of aggression and antisocial behavior. The idea that such children may engage in aggression for proactive and even sadistic reasons alerts us to the possibility that cruelty to animals may be a marker of such traits.

This has only been the subject of one study to date. Dadds, Whiting, and Hawes (2006) tested the idea that cruelty is a callous aggression that will be more strongly associated with callous/unemotional traits than general externalizing problems. Results indicated that for both boys and girls, CU traits were associated strongly with cruelty. For boys, externalizing problems also added prediction in regression analyses. Family conflict was not associated with cruelty for either. These results suggest that cruelty to animals may be an early manifestation of the subgroup of children developing conduct problems associated with traits of low empathy and callous disregard, rather than the more common pathway of externalizing problems and parenting problems.

It is impossible to discern the precise relationship between CU traits and cruelty from the Dadds et al. study as the design was purely correlational. Parents could be rating children more highly on the CU measure in part because of their behavior toward animals; conversely, CU could truly be a causal

factor in cruelty. Further research is needed to test this; however, it can be seen that the trait variable of CU was associated with cruelty over and above the child's general pattern of conduct problems and family conflict. It thus holds potential for being a marker of child characteristics associated with intentional cruelty.

Cruelty as an Emotional Response— Biological Factors

It is not the place here to present a general discussion on the biological models of aggression; however, some specific observations have been made that, when integrated with psychosocial correlates, may bear fruit. The relationship between low serotonin levels and rage and aggression has long been noted and has recently culminated in a landmark paper showing that chronic antisocial behavior is associated with interacting risks of a polymorphism of the MAOA gene involved in serotonin activity and exposure to abusive parenting (Caspi, McClay, Moffitt, Mill, Martin, Craig, Taylor, Poulton, 2002. Typically, the type of aggression associated with serotonin problems is one of explosive rage rather than the callous/reward-driven type noted in the last section. Kruesi (1989) reported on the case of a 12-year-old girl, raised in a (presumed healthy) middle-class household, who had abnormally low cerebrospinal fluid concentrations of 5HIAA (5-hydroxyindoleacetic acid—a measure of serotonin turnover), and a distinct history of physically cruel behavior to animals by age 12. At a 4-year follow-up, the child was being held in a detention center and had begun to self-harm. Kruesi concludes that the case study suggests that relationships between cruelty to animals and low 5HIAA concentrations warrant further investigation and prospective follow-up; however, little has been done to pursue these suggestions.

Cruelty and Cognitive Errors

Dodge and colleagues' research on peer rejection and social maladjustment in boys (Crick & Dodge, 1994; Price & Dodge, 1991) has shown that aggressive children display deficits and distortions at various levels of social information processing. For example, in ambiguous social situations, these children underutilize pertinent social cues, misattribute hostile intent to neutral peer behavior, respond with aggression, and expect that aggressive responses will lead to reward (Crick & Dodge, 1994). Peers typically retaliate to such aggressive behavior with aggression in return. The aggressive child's belief in a hostile environment is reinforced, as is his own aggressive behavior. Ascione (1993) speculates that if such children can attribute hostile intentions to their peers, intention cues provided by animals would be even more ambiguous, and the child could easily respond to animals with aggression and cruelty. Ascione (1993) describes a boy's brutalization of a dog after the dog had barked at him. The boy interpreted the bark as personally directed aggression, without ever considering that the dog may have been startled or frightened. In this sense, the boy's cruelty would be seen as an emotional response based in part on cognitive errors. However, insufficient research has been done using this model to allow us to specify the actual mechanisms at work. Cognitive–attributional errors are themselves affected by the emotional state of the person, the behavior he or she is exposed to, and a host of other factors (e.g., Dadds, Mullins, McAllister, & Atkinson, 2003). At extremes, the cognitive errors may be epiphenomena that have little causal role themselves; that is, cognitions can only be assessed by self-report and may thus be post hoc self-justifications for one's behavior.

Despite this problem, there is evidence that a general cognitive style marked by a hostile attributional bias (for conduct problem children) and or attributions about low self-control (for parents) is predictive of high levels of aggression. A wealth of studies have shown that parents at risk for abusive parenting have low perceived control over child behavior relative to the power they ascribe to the child (e.g., Dadds et al., 2003). A recent study applied this model of attributions to parents' interactions with companion animals. Sims, Chin, Eckman, Enck, and Abromaitis (2001) showed that such attributions are also associated with greater negative affect during a brief interaction with a puppy. Similar to Ascione (1993), Sims et al. argued that cognitive schema associated with aggressive behavior may be generalized across caregiving situations that involve children and companion animals.

This research is provocative in terms of its substantive findings but also in that it suggests methodologies of studying cognitive constructions might be generalizable from parent–child studies with companion animals. A problem for this approach, however, is the idea that cruelty involves some degree of intentionality. In the child abuse literature, it is frequently pointed out that only a small (but highly visible) proportion of parents

deliberately abuse their children; most are themselves victims of overwhelming circumstances and hit out when unable to cope. Children who show reactive aggression only are typically the group with high levels of hostile attributional biases, and similarly hit out because they perceive threats with which they cannot cope. Children who display proactive aggression are generally not characterized by these hostile attributional biases (Crick & Dodge, 1994), and these may be the sample characterized by intentional cruelty that has higher prognostic value. Notwithstanding, there is potential here to further clarify clusters and specific mechanisms of conduct problems by considering the motives for cruelty against the backdrop of the child's cognitive and emotional style.

Cruelty and Nurturance/Empathy— Positive Interactions Between Children and Animals

It is important to note that a pattern of cruelty to animals can also mark a loss of opportunities for much positive learning in the child's life. A number of authors have pointed to the developmental importance of the relationship between children and companion animals (Agnew, 1998; Grier, 1999; Kellert & Felthous, 1985; Robin & ten Bensel, 1985; Wilson & Turner, 1998). Robin and ten Bensel (1985) argue that companion animals are a vital part of the healthy emotional development of children. They assert that the constancy of animal companionship can facilitate the child's mastery over a variety of developmental tasks, such as developing a sense of responsibility and competence, and developing feelings of empathy toward others. Some literature even suggests that pets may have a preventative effect on the development of mental disturbance. For example, Levinson and Mallon (1997) suggest on the basis of clinical experience that children who have pets evidence less separation anxiety than those who don't. Bodmer (1998) suggested that having a positive relationship with a pet can moderate the negative effects of family and other stressors on children's well-being.

Robin and ten Bensel (1985) review research that suggests that animals can have positive benefits by serving a variety of roles. Firstly, pets function as playmates and companions. Companion pets have a unique ability to create feelings of security within children. They are devoted, attentive, loyal, and noncritical, and they unconditionally love and accept a child. In this way, pets have the ability to function as transitional objects, assisting children in the developmental task of separation and individuation and helping children to feel safe within this process. Second, pets allow for the gradual introduction of responsibilities in a child, and allow the child to experience the pleasures associated with such responsibility. Much of the usual activity of children and pet animals resembles a parent/child relationship, with the animal representing the child as an infant. Consequently, children may treat their pets as they are treated, or as they want to be treated themselves. Pets have been found to elicit maternal and caring behavior in even very young children (Fogle, 1983; cited in Robin & ten Bensel, 1985). However, very little research of this type has been conducted. In fact, recent studies vary dramatically in terms of their support for a relationship between empathy and pet ownership. A recent study showed no relationship between pet ownership and empathy in children (Daly & Morton, 2003), while Paul (2000) found the opposite for adult reports of empathy and pet ownership. A high priority is for more experimental research to be conducted using direct observations of nurturance, care, and empathy versus aggression, neglect, and cruelty as measures of the ways children and their parents interact with animals.

Third, pets provide education and life experiences for children. For example, observation of animals can lead to education about the normal functions of sexuality and elimination. Similarly, pet loss provides experience for children in dealing with the process of death and bereavement, thus preparing them for later experiences with human life. It is common that children learn through pets that grief following death is a natural process that is painful, but is tolerable and does not last forever.

Finally, Robin and ten Bensel (1985) argue that pets function in a similar way to a new family member within the family system. With the arrival of a new pet, families undergo a variety of changes, both positive and negative. The role of the pet depends upon the emotional climate of the family, as well as the family structure. For example, pets may facilitate increased familial closeness as a result of playing together with the pet, or they may exacerbate family dysfunction as a result of disagreements over the rules and care of pets. Pets may also become a part of the families' pathology. For many disturbed and abused children, a pet may becomes a sole love object. Alternatively, for violent and abusive families, pets often serve as an object against which violence may be perpetrated.

To this list we would add the importance of developing empathy for the experiences of other organisms. A common occurrence in functional families is the parent modeling caregiving to a pet and educating the child about the pet's feelings and needs (Agnew, 1998). All young children will at one time accidentally or experimentally cause discomfort to a pet. Consider the differential effects on the child's development of empathy of the parent who shows concern and advocates the pet's feelings to the child compared with the parent who finds the discomfort amusing and encourages the child to continue. Little empirical work is currently being done in this regard; however, the idea has been around for some time. Bathurst (1933, cited in Baenninger, 1995) found that preschoolers who lived in houses with pets displayed more sympathetic responses to their peers than were preschoolers who came from homes without pets. This idea has important implications for community intervention models and will be reviewed in the next section.

Cruelty to Animals as an Assessment Tool

Measurement of cruelty to animals has only recently been given much empirical attention. Historically, two broad approaches have been used, and unfortunately these are partly responsible for the scarcity of overlap between research into cruelty to animals and conduct problems. In the field of conduct disorders, most investigators (e.g., Heath et al., 1984) have used the single checklist item "cruelty to animals" on the Achenbach CBCL. This item can be rated by parents and/or teachers; however, it is not included in the youth self-report version, and it simply asks about the occurrence of cruelty without providing a definition of the behavior. It is thus difficult to interpret any resulting findings. Clearly, parents could interpret such behavior in a variety of ways, including harm done to an animal unintentionally though impulsive over-exuberance or neglect due to attentional or other uncontrollable factors. Conversely, parents who are cruel and neglectful themselves may underreport important cruel behavior in a child.

In contrast to the area of conduct disorders, scientists looking at cruelty to animals in violent populations (usually incarcerated violent offenders) have generally assessed childhood animal cruelty in unstructured or semi-structured interviews, or by reviewing official files in order to determine if there is a history of cruelty. For example, Boat (1995) and Kellert and Felthous (1985) developed structured interview schedules for the purposes of their own clinical/research use. In an effort to overcome the lack of standardization in measurement, Ascione et al. (1997) developed the Children and Animals (Cruelty to Animals) Assessment Instrument (CAAI). The CAAI is a semi-structured interview developed for use with children over age 4 and their parents, to obtain information on animal maltreatment. The CAAI was field-tested with a community sample of 20 children (75% boys, 65% with a pet) and a clinical sample. The clinical sample included children in residential and day treatment programs for emotionally disturbed youth, incarcerated adolescents, and children accompanying their mothers to shelters for battered women. Interview questions were organized to assess witnessing and performing cruelty and kindness toward animals in four categories (farm, wild, pet, stray).

Ascione et al. (1997) included nine dimensions of cruelty: *Severity* is the degree of intentional pain or injury caused to an animal, as well as the sexual abuse of an animal. *Frequency* concerns the number of separate acts of cruelty noted in assessment results. *Duration* covers the period of time over which cruel acts occurred, while *Recency* is the dimension based upon the most current act(s) of cruelty. *Diversity* (across and within categories) concerns the number of different categories of animals harmed, as well as the number of individual animals harmed within categories. *Sentience* is an indication of animal's ability to experience pain. The *Empathy* dimension is concerned with the degree of the child's remorse for cruel acts or the child's concern for the animal's welfare. *Covert* is a dimension assessing the child's attempts to conceal cruel behavior, and finally, *Isolate* is whether the cruelty occurred alone or with other children and/or adults present. Inter-rater reliability for the CAAI ranged from 60%–83%.

On a qualitative note, the CAAI was found to be valuable for assessing some of the motivations that children may have for engaging in animal cruelty. For example, curiosity/exploration was a significant motivator, especially for younger children. Other motivations included peer reinforcement for cruel behavior (i.e., gang membership), cruelty as a means of altering the perpetrator's mood state, and imitation of the witnessed cruelty toward animals. Establishing the motivations for animal cruelty is extremely important as it assists in determining whether clinical intervention or remediation is required, and if so, of what nature.

Ascione et al. (1997) examined the relation between the CAAI and the "cruel to animals" item on the CBCL (Achenbach, 1991). Not surprisingly, they concluded that assessing cruelty by use of only one checklist item could provide misleading information or fail to fully capture the level of cruelty that some children displayed toward animals. While initial evaluations of the CAAI appear promising, one significant limitation to its widespread use is its length, which would typically exclude its use from anything except a research context.

Guymer, Mellor, Luk, and Pearse (2001) produced a parent-report questionnaire version (the CABTA) of Ascione's measure. Psychometric properties of their measure were encouraging; however, the study was limited by the use of small, highly selective samples. Further, their measure was only developed for parents. Given that acts of cruelty would be expected to occur under a level of secrecy, parental reports of children's cruelty may not be reflective of actual levels of cruel behavior. Prevalence rates for child cruelty increase dramatically when based on children's self-reports rather than parental reports on the CBCL (Offord et al., 1991). Another limitation was that the CABTA refers specifically to intentional behavior in one item only, with the possibility that high scores on the CABTA may reflect other non-intentional maladaptive behaviors in children.

A second brief version of the CAAI has recently been developed and validated that overcomes many of these problems. The Children and Animals Inventory (CAI: Dadds et al., 2004; see appendix) is a nine-item self- and parent-report measure of Ascione et al.'s (1997) nine parameters of cruelty that is reliable, stable, and readily usable in clinical or research settings. Of particular note, self- and parent-reports showed good convergence with independent observations of cruelty versus nurturance during free interactions with domestic animals.

The development of these measures should allow researchers to assess cruelty to animals in a way that is user-friendly with the large samples needed for predictive studies, but allows characterisation of the complex dimensional nature of cruelty that clearly cannot be measured with one item.

Cruelty as Learned Behavior—Family Functioning and Parent–Child Interactions

Multiple variables indicating dysfunctional family functioning have been implicated in the onset and maintenance of aggressive and antisocial behavior in children (see Dadds, 1995). Typically, however, they are mediated by dysfunctional parent–child interactions. Patterson (1982) identified coercive family processes as a major characteristic and contributor to child and family dysfunction marked by aggression. In brief, by failing to reinforce prosocial behavior, backing down from requests, and reinforcing a child's escalating demands, parents negatively reinforce a child's increasingly defiant and aggressive behavior. Similarly, harsh and abusive discipline practices, displayed when the child escalates to misbehavior, are rewarded by the child's temporary capitulation. Such interactions typically result in an explosive escalation of aggression, and these coercive interchanges, once established, become reinforcing and self-sustaining. Established aggressive interactions within the family serve to intensify aggressive behavior outside the family. Ascione (1993) speculates that children growing up in such families may learn to generalize aggressive and coercive control techniques and begin to apply such behaviors to animals. Flynn (1999) examined the relationship between corporal punishment inflicted by parents and the perpetration of animal abuse in 267 undergraduates. Males who committed animal cruelty in childhood or adolescence were physically punished more frequently by their fathers, both as preteens and teenagers, than males who did not perpetrate animal abuse. Over half of male teenagers who were hit by their fathers had perpetrated animal abuse. The social learning model has much to offer the study of childhood cruelty, both in terms of the proposed mechanisms (modeling, imitation, reinforcement theory, coercive processes) and its use of relatively rigorous methodologies. Particularly with young children, the potential for direct observational studies of parent–child interactions with pets should be noted.

In their retrospective study of aggressive and nonaggressive criminals who were cruel to animals, Kellert and Felthous (1985) found that domestic violence was frequent among subjects with cruelty histories (particularly extreme paternal violence and alcoholism) and this finding has been supported by numerous other studies. Boat (1995) reports on battered women who frequently describe how pets have been stabbed, shot, hung, or otherwise mutilated by abusive spouses. Gelles and Straus (1988; cited in Ascione, 1993) provide equally compelling evidence from children who were witness to parental violence. Deviney, Dickert, and Lockwood (1983) found that higher rates of animal abuse are found in families where child abuse or neglect is substantiated than in the general population. Deviney et al. (1983) studied 53 families who met New Jersey legal criteria for child abuse or neglect and who also had companion animals in their homes. Observations during home interviews revealed that pets were abused or neglected in 60% of these families. When the sample was categorized into physically abused (40%), sexually abused (10%), and neglected (58%), an alarming finding was that in 88% of families displaying child physical abuse, cruelty to animals was also present. Two-thirds of pets were abused by fathers, one-third by children.

A history of childhood sexual abuse is also associated with deviant interactions between children and animals. Ressler, Burgess, Hartman, Douglas, and McCormack (1986) explored the relationship of childhood sexual abuse to deviant interactions in 36 convicted sexually-oriented killers. Ressler et al. (1986) provide no methodological information regarding how they determined the presence of behavioral, emotional, and somatic symptoms in childhood or adolescence. However, those offenders who were sexually abused in childhood or adolescence were significantly more likely than non-abused offenders to report, among other psychiatric symptoms, cruelty to animals, cruelty to other children, and assaultive behavior toward adults. An analysis of the relationship between past sexual abuse and participation in certain sexual activities indicated that the sexually abused murderers were significantly more likely than non-abused murderers to engage in deviant sexual contact with animals (40% versus 8%).

Boat (1995) also cited anecdotal reports by several authors describing the sexual abuse of children in daycare settings and acts of bestiality. Forcing children to interact sexually with animals and ensuring children's silence by threatening to hurt or by actually maiming pets are noted in numerous case studies of sexually abused children. Therefore, the association between cruelty to animals and childhood sexual abuse clearly deserves further empirical attention.

Ascione, Friedrich, Heath, and Hayashi (2003) showed that cruelty to animals in 6- to 12-year-old children was associated with a history of abuse, with additive risk coming from physical abuse and domestic violence. The study was innovative in that it also measured history of sexual abuse and inappropriate sexual contact with animals. Cruelty to animals was significantly associated with sexual contact with animals for the group of children who had themselves been sexually abused. This points to the potential benefit of assessing cruel behavior using broader definitions than provided by many measures, and assessing the cruelty against a broader range of background variables.

On the basis of the evidence cited above, it appears reasonable for researchers and clinicians alike to be aware of the importance of childhood animal cruelty as a potential indicator of disturbed family relationships. The research clearly indicates relationships between the violent and abusive environments in which children are raised and children's own violent reactions toward animals. Indeed, Robin and ten Bensel (1985) reported that abused and disturbed youth suffered more pet loss, had their pets for less time, and were more likely to have had their pets killed accidentally or purposely than non-disturbed youth. While not directly addressing the reliability and utility of using pet abuse as an indicator of child problems, the foregoing studies certainly provide broad support for more communication between pet and child welfare agencies.

Developmental Stages in Cruelty

In the discussion above, a number of variations in the phenomena of both cruelty and conduct problems have arisen. In the literature on conduct disorders, contemporary models emphasize developmental change and growth of symptom clusters across the life span (e.g., Caspi & Moffit, 1995). However, little attention has been given to such developmental models in cruelty cf. Wright & Hensley, 2003), despite the interesting observation that one of the earliest depictions of cruelty to animals emphasized a developmental stage model. English artist William Hogarth condemned cruelty toward animals in his now famous series of four etching-engravings, *The Four Stages of Cruelty*, produced in 1751. The series depict a progression in four scenes: a boy being cruel toward animals; the same person, now a young man, beating a disabled horse; the young man killing a woman; and finally, the execution of the man himself.

It is likely that cruelty to animals follows a number of predictable developmental trajectories ranging from innocuous and temporary childhood experimentation through to a chronic pathway that shows gradual escalation in severity. However,

research into developmental pathways is in its infancy and there a few models to guide such a longitudinal perspective. A notable exception came from Goldberg (1995), who proposed a theoretical delineation of the development of the malevolent (cruel) personality, with references to his own clinical experiences. He proposes five stages to the development of the malevolent personality: (1) child of scorn: the shaming of the vulnerable child, (2) child of the devil: the inoculation of the "bad" self, (3) the transition from victim to perpetrator of insensitivity and disregard, (4) experimental malevolence, and (5) the forging of the malevolent personality.

Goldberg (1995) suggests that shame (stage 1) is one of the most devastating interpersonal weapons a person can use to influence or punish someone else. Each shaming experience, especially those that involve disregard and mistreatment, threatens to deplete a person's sense of personal identity. These experiences inform the sufferer in destructive and painful ways that he or she is inadequate. As such, they undermine the sufferer's interpersonal relationships and feelings of well being and security. Chronic shame prevents one from defining oneself constructively to others, leaving one vulnerable to further abuse and neglect, and resulting in the internalization of inadequacy (stage 2). People in stage 3, unlike earlier stages where shame and humiliation was passively tolerated, feel disregard and insensitivity toward others, both toward those who have mistreated them and toward anyone else who tries to get close. Everyone in the world is regarded as responsible for having permitted shame and humiliation. The sufferer then begins to experiment with malevolent actions (stage 4), and the relief/pleasure that such actions bring are subsequently internalized into the malevolent personality (stage 5). Thus Goldberg (1995) believes that people make their choices to behave in such a way by disregarding any positive/pleasurable experiences that result from acting in a non-malevolent manner. While it is easy to criticize these personality/analytic ideas as highly speculative, Goldberg's model is noteworthy in that it directs us to consider a developmental progression toward cruelty, and in terms of its stage specification, is testable through empirical studies.

Potential Strategies for Identification and Intervention

Clearly, the evidence that cruelty to animals has any prognostic over and above other symptoms of conduct problems is at present not strong enough to warrant alarm bells at every observed instance, nor special programs being set up to identify its occurrence. However, evidence of a pattern of cruelty should warrant further assessment of a child's general adjustment and family circumstances. It appears that a pattern of cruelty in a child with conduct problems may indicate a high risk for later delinquency, and may be a sign of violence within the child's environment.

Apart from family members, neighbors, and in some instances teachers, the professionals most likely to identify cruelty to pets are veterinarians. Research indicates they regularly detect abused animals, and feel ethically obliged to report, with nearly half believing that reporting should be mandatory (Donley, Patronek, & Luke, 1999).

Given that the evidence reviewed indicates that cruelty to animals is likely to be a part of a complex of conduct and family problems, the idea of working directly or specifically on the cruel behavior may not be indicated. Further, there is very little literature describing or evaluating direct interventions for cruelty. However, there are some indirect reasons for not entirely dismissing this idea. Recent reviews by Gullone (2003) and Katcher and Wilkins (1998) provide a detailed rationale for the inclusion of animal care into preventative and treatment programs for conduct disorder. Programs for children and adolescents who have committed sex offences (and who have usually been abused themselves) typically focus on the development of empathy as a prime target (Becker, 1996; Bunston, 2000; Rich, 1998). Similarly, interventions for victims of physical and emotional abuse typically target the experience of receiving and showing empathy as a major component. Recent articles from therapists have even discussed ways that pets can be utilized in therapy to aid children who have problems with empathy (Fine, 2000; Mason & Hagan, 1999).

We could locate only two trials, however, that directly worked with children's relationships with animals. Ascione and Weber (1996) assessed a year-long school-based humane education program on 4th graders' attitudes toward animals. Generalization to human-directed empathy was also measured. In a controlled trial, increases in humane attitudes relative to the control group was evident at the 2-year follow-up and had generalized to human-directed empathy. The study involved a community sample and so effects on the severe-end children showing cruelty is unknown. Zasloff, Hart, and Weiss (2003) evaluated a dog-training program (Teaching Love and Compassion) for inner-city youth. The results showed modest increases in the participants' understanding of pet care and comfort with pets; however, no measures of broader adjustment were taken. These studies are preliminary and as yet provide no evidence that working on relationships with animals can impact on a child's broader behavior and mental health; however, they pave the way for research looking at the effectiveness of such interventions used both preventively, as tertiary treatments, and as contexts in which children with major problems with cruelty can be identified.

Conclusions and Directions for Future Research

The last decade has seen an increase in research that will help develop a clearer picture of the phenomenon of childhood animal cruelty. This chapter focussed on its relationship to conduct problems in young people has highlighted several noteworthy points:

1. Child–animal relationships offer parents and children opportunities to learn nurturing, caregiving, and empathic behaviors toward subordinates. Studies so far of the relationship of pet ownership to empathic development had produced unclear results. However, very little research has been conducted into the developmental pathways associated with healthy child–pet relationships, or the microprocesses characteristic of parent–child interactions in this context.

2. Child–animal relationships characterized by cruelty commonly exist within a broader pattern of aggressive and antisocial behavior. Retrospective studies of violent criminals produce findings consistent with the idea that early cruelty to animals is predictive of later violence. Prospective studies are limited to evidence that the presence of proactive aggression in childhood, of which cruelty may be a part, is predictive of later delinquency. Whether the presence of early cruelty has predictive power that is unique over and above predictions that could be made by other early behavior problems (e.g., aggression to humans, truancy, stealing) has not been adequately studied.

3. Our understanding of the relationship between cruelty to animals and conduct dis-

orders will be greatly enhanced by adopting definitions and assessment strategies that embrace several dimensions, including the type and variety of cruel behaviors, the type and variety of targets (different species, different relationships to child), motives for the behavior (e.g., causing pain versus attracting a caregiver's attention), the child's potential for empathic and remorseful responding, and evidence of enjoyment of the animal's pain.

4. Further, the relationship between cruelty to animals and conduct problems will be clarified by refining our definitions of conduct problems and antisocial behavior. As reviewed, a number of different etiological factors may underlie these phenomena and lead to better distinctions in our categorizations. Thus, the emerging constructs of emotional versus callous/unemotional temperament, impulsivity and hyperactivity, cognitive–attributional errors, and abusive learning environments need to be parsed out in order to clarify how subtypes of conduct problems may differentially relate to different aspects of cruel behavior.

5. There is little evidence that cruelty to animals exists in a triad of uniquely predictive behaviors (i.e., with fire setting and bedwetting).

6. A problem with the inclusion of animal cruelty into the DSM system, and thus its specific role in categorization of the disruptive behavior problems, is that no attempt is made to build in assessment of the various dimensions of cruelty that may characterize its unique prognostic features (i.e., variety of cruel acts and targets, deriving pleasure from the pain of others). The recent development of multidimensional measures of cruelty to animals (e.g., the CAI; Dadds et al., 2004) will help incorporate more comprehensive measurement of cruelty into research.

7. Little work has been done on community and clinical procedures for identifying and helping children showing cruelty to animals. Given the strong associations found between cruelty and other behavioral and family problems, it would be premature to set up clinical programs that specifically target cruel behavior out of context from the child's general health and adjustment and family relationships. However, several innovative approaches were noted, specifically, community interventions in which empathy toward animals can be targeted with potential benefits to levels of human empathy, and clinical interventions which utilize pets as vehicles for learning about empathy and nurturance.

I would like to finish with some suggestions for research studies that would help clarify the role of cruelty to animals in the development of conduct disorders:

1. We desperately need epidemiological studies of child and adolescent cruelty to animals that adopt a developmental perspective, comprehensive definitions that involve important components of its characteristics and motivations, and consideration of contextual factors such as the broader adjustment of the child and family.

2. Research into the relationship of pet ownership and empathy has yielded mixed results. Experimental studies are needed of child behavior and caregiver–child interactions in the presence of pets and other animals that focus on the development of specific caregiving versus cruel behaviors and more general constructs such as empathy.

3. Given that cruelty is a relatively low-occurrence behavior, we need longitudinal studies of children already showing cruel behaviors. Specifically, subtyping models of conduct disorder need to be tested in which the predictive power of early cruelty is compared with that afforded by more general aspects of the child's adjustment.

4. Finally, we need prevention studies assessing the role of empathic pet-training on at-risk children, and intervention studies looking at the efficacy of reducing cruelty and increasing empathic and nurturing behaviors in children already showing signs of cruelty.

References

Achenbach, T. (1991). *Integrative Guide for the 1991 CBCL/4–18, YSR, & TRF Profiles*. Burlington: University of Vermont, Department of Psychiatry.

Agnew, R. (1998). The causes of animal abuse: A social-psychological analysis. *Theoretical Criminology, 2*(2), 177–209.

American Psychiatric Association (APA). (2000). *Diagnostic and statistical manual for mental disorders (4th ed., text revision).* Washington, DC: APA Press.

American Psychiatric Association (APA). (1994). *Diagnostic and statistical manual for mental disorders (4th ed.).* Washington, DC: APA Press.

American Psychiatric Association (APA). (1987). *Diagnostic and statistical manual of mental disorders: third edition, revised* (DSM-III-R). Washington, DC: APA.

Arluke, A., Levin, J., Luke, C., & Ascione, F. (1999). The relationship of animal abuse to violence and other forms of antisocial behavior. *Journal of Interpersonal Violence, 14*(9), 63–975.

Ascione, F. R. (1993). Children who are cruel to animals: A review of research and implications for developmental psychopathology. *Anthrozöos, VI*(4), 226–247.

Ascione, F. R. (2001). Animal abuse and youth violence. *Juvenile Justice Bulletin,* September. Washington, DC: U.S. Department of Justice.

Ascione, F. R., Friedrich, W. N., Heath, J., & Hayashi, K. (2003). Cruelty to animals in normative, sexually abused, and outpatient psychiatric samples of 6 to 12 year old children: Relations to maltreatment and exposure to domestic violence. *Anthrozöos, 16,* 194–212.

Ascione, F. R., & Lockwood, R. (2001). Cruelty to animals: Changing psychological, social, and legislative perspectives. In D. J. Salem & A. N. Rowan (Eds.), *State of the Animals 2000* (pp. 39–53). Washington, DC: Humane Society Press.

Ascione, F. R., Thompson, T. M., & Black, T. (1997). Childhood cruelty to animals: Assessing cruelty dimensions and motivations. *Anthrozöos, 10*(4), 170–177.

Ascione, F. R., & Weber, C. V. (1996). Children's attitudes about the humane treatment of animals and empathy: One-year follow up of a school-based intervention. *Anthrozöos, 9*(4), 188–195.

Baenninger, R. (1995). Some consequences of animal domestication for humans. *Anthrozöos, 8,* 69–77.

Barry, C. T., Frick, P. J., DeShazo, T. M., McCoy, M. G., Ellis, M., & Loney, B. R. (2000). The importance of callous-unemotional traits for extending the concept of psychopathy to children. *Journal of Abnormal Psychology, 109,* 335–340.

Becker, J. V. (1996). Outpatient treatment of adolescent male sexual offenders. In M. P. Andronico (Ed)., *Men in groups: Insights, interventions, and psychoeducational work* (pp. 377–388). Washington, DC: American Psychological Association.

Becker, K. D., Stuewig, J., Herrera, V. M., & McCloskey, L. A. (2004). A study of firesetting and animal cruelty in children: Family influences and adolescent outcomes. *Journal of the American Academy of Child and Adolescent Psychiatry, 43,* 905–912.

Beirne, P. (1999). For a non-speciesist criminology: Animal abuse as an object of study. *Criminology, 37,* 117–147.

Blair, R. J. R., Colledge, E., Murray, L., & Mitchell, D. G. V. (2001). A selective impairment in the processing of sad and fearful expressions in children with psychopathic tendencies. *Journal of Abnormal Child Psychology, 29,* 491–498.

Boat, B. W. (1995). The relationship between violence to children and violence to animals: An ignored link? *Journal of Interpersonal Violence, 10*(2), 229–235.

Boat, B. W. (1997). Commentary on childhood cruelty to animals: Assessing cruelty dimensions and motivations. *Anthrozöos, 10*(4), 178–179.

Bodmer, N. M. (1998). Impact of pet ownership on the wellbeing of adolescents with few familial resources. In C. C. Wilson & D. C. Turner (Eds.), *Companion animals in Human Health.* Sage Publications Inc: California

Brown, L. (1988). *Cruelty to animals: The moral debt.* London: Macmillan.

Bunston, W. (2000). Working with adolescents and children who have committed sex offences. *Australian and New Zealand Journal of Family Therapy, 21*(1), 1–7.

Caspi, A., & Moffitt, T. E. (1995). The continuity of maladaptive behavior: From description to understanding in the study of antisocial behavior. In D. Cicchetti & D. J. Cohen (Eds.), *Developmental psychopathology* (Vol. 2, pp. 472–511). New York: Wiley.

Caspi, A., McClay, J., Moffitt, T. E., Mill, J., Martin, J., Craig, I. W., Taylor, A., Poulton, R. (2002). Role of Genotype in the Cycle of Violence in Maltreated Children. *Science, 297 (5582),* 851–854

Christian, R. E., Frick, P. J, Hill, N. L., Tyler, L., & Frazer, D. R. (1997). Psychopathy and conduct problems in children: II. Implications for subtyping children with conduct problems. *Journal of the American Academy of Child and Adolescent Psychiatry, 36*, 233–241

Crick, N. R., & Dodge, K. A. (1994). A review and reformulation of social information processing mechanisms in children's social adjustment. *Psychological Bulletin, 115*, 74–101.

Dadds, M. R. (1995). *Families, children, and the development of dysfunction.* Newbury Park, CA: Sage Press.

Dadds, M. R., Mullins, M. J., McAllister, R. A., Atkinson, E. (2003). Attributions, affect, and behavior in abuse-risk mothers: A laboratory study. *Child Abuse & Neglect. 27(1)*, 21–45.

Dadds, M. R., Salmon, K. (2003). Punishment Insensitivity and Parenting: Temperament and Learning as Interacting Risks for Antisocial Behavior. *Clinical Child and Family Psychology Review. 6(2)*, 69–86.

Dadds M. R., Whiting, C., Bunn, P., Fraser, J. A., Charlson, J. H., Pirola-Merlo, A. (2004). Measurement of cruelty in children: The cruelty to animals inventory. *Journal of Abnormal Child Psychology, 32(3)*, 321–334.

Dadds, M. R., Whiting, C., & Hawes, D. (2006). Associations among cruelty to animals, family conflict, and psychopathic traits in childhood. *Journal of Interpersonal Violence, 21*, 411–429.

Daly, B., & Morton, L. L. (2003). Children with pets do not show higher empathy: A challenge to current views. *Anthrozoös, 16*, 298–314.

DeViney, E., Dickert, J., & Lockwood, R. (1983). The care of pets within child abusing families. *International Journal for the Study of Animal Problems, 4*, 321–329.

Dodge, K. A., Bates, J. E., & Pettit, G. S. (1990). Mechanisms in the cycle of violence. *Science, 250*, 1678–1683.

Donley, L., Patronek, G. J., & Luke, C. (1999). Animal abuse in Massachusetts: A summary of case reports at the MSPCA and attitudes of Massachusetts veterinarians. *Journal of Applied Animal Welfare Science, 2*(1), 59–73.

Felthous, A. R., & Kellert, S. R. (1986). Violence against animals and people: Is aggression against living creatures generalised? *Bulletin of the American Academy of Psychiatry and the Law, 14*, 55–69.

Felthous, A. R., & Kellert, S. R. (1987). Childhood cruelty to animals and later aggression against people: A review. *American Journal of Psychiatry, 144*, 710–717.

Fine, A. H. (2000). *Handbook on animal-assisted therapy: Theoretical foundations and guidelines for practice.* San Diego, CA: Academic Press, Inc.

Flynn, C.P. (1999). Exploring the link between corporal punishment and children's cruelty to animals. *Journal of Marriage and the Family, 61*, 971–981.

Frick, P. J., & Ellis, M. (1999). Callous-unemotional traits and subtypes of conduct disorder. *Clinical Child and Family Psychology Review, 2*, 149–168.

Frick, P. J., van Horn, Y., Lahey, B. B., Christ, M. G., Loeber, R., Hart, E. A. et al. (1993). Oppositional defiant disorder and conduct disorder: A meta-analytic review of factor analyses and cross validation in a clinic sample. *Clinical Psychology Review, 13*, 319–340.

Goldberg, C. (1995). The daimonic development of the malevolent personality. *Journal of Humanistic Psychology, 35*, 7–36.

Grier, K. C. (1999). Childhood socialization and companion animals: United States, 1820–1870. *Society and Animals, 7*, 95–120.

Gullone, E. (2003). The proposed benefits of incorporating non-human animals into preventive efforts for conduct disorder. *Anthrozoös, 16*, 160–174.

Guymer, E. C., Mellor, D., Luk, E. S. L., & Pearse, V. (2001). The development of a screening questionnaire for childhood cruelty to animals. *Journal of Child Psychology and Psychiatry, 42*, 1057–1063.

Hare, R. D., Hart, S. D., & Harpur, T. J. (1991). Psychopathy and the DSM IV criteria for antisocial personality disorder. *Journal of Abnormal Psychology, 100*, 391–398.

Hare, R. D., & Schalling, D. (1978). *Psychopathic Behavior: Approaches to Research.* London: Wiley.

Heath, G. A., Hardesty, V. A., & Goldfine, P. E. (1984). Firesetting, enuresis, and animal cruelty. *Journal of Child and Adolescent Psychotherapy, 1*, 97–100.

Heller, M. S., Ehrlich, S. M., & Lester, D. (1984). Childhood cruelty to animals, firesetting, and enuresis as correlates of competence to stand trial. *The Journal of General Psychology, 110*, 151–153.

Hellman, D. S., & Blackman, H. (1966). Enuresis, firesetting and cruelty to animals. *American Journal of Psychiatry, 122*, 1431–1435.

Katcher, A., & Wilkins, G. G. (1998). Animal-assisted therapy in the treatment of disruptive behavior problems in children. In A. Lundberg (Ed.), *The environment and mental health: A guide for clinicians* (pp. 193–204). Mahwah, NJ: Lawrence Erlbaum Associates Inc.

Kellert, S. R., & Felthous, A. R. (1985). Childhood cruelty to animals among criminals and noncriminals. *Human Relations, 38*, 1113–1129.

Kochanska, G. (1993). Toward a synthesis of parental socialisation and child temperament in early development of conscience. *Child Development, 64*, 325–347.

Kochanska, G. (1997). Multiple pathways to conscience for children with different temperaments: From toddlerhood to age 5. *Developmental Psychology, 33*, 228–240.

Kruesi, M. J. P. (1989). Cruelty to animals and CSF 5HIAA. *Psychiatry Research, 28*, 115–116.

Kuhnley, E. J., Hendren, R. L., & Quinlan, D. M. (1982). Firesetting by children. *Journal of the American Academy of Child Psychiatry, 21*, 560–563.

Levinson, B. M., & Mallon, G. P. (1997). *Pet-orientated child psychotherapy* (2nd ed.). Springfield, IL: Charles Thomas.

Loeber, R., Keenan, K., Lahey, B. B., Green, S. M., & Thomas, C. (1993). Evidence for developmentally based diagnoses of oppositional defiant and conduct disorder. *Journal of Abnormal Child Psychology, 21*(4), 377–410.

Luk, E. S. L., Staiger, P. K., Wong, L., & Mathai, J. (1999) Children who are cruel to animals: A revisit. *Australian and New Zealand Journal of Psychiatry, 33*(1), 29–36.

Lynam, D. R. (1997). Pursuing the psychopath: Capturing the fledgling psychopath in a nomological net. *Journal of Abnormal Psychology, 106(3)*, 425–438.

MacDonald, J. (1968). *Homicidal threats*. Springfield, IL: C.C. Thomas.

Mason, M. S., & Hagan, C. B. (1999). Pet-assisted psychotherapy. *Psychological Reports, 84*, 1235–1245.

Merz-Perez, L., Heide, K. M., & Silverman, I. J. (2001). Childhood cruelty to animals and subsequent violence against animals. *International Journal of Offender Therapy and Comparative Criminology, 45*, 556–573.

Micheals, J. (1955). *Disorders of character*. Springfield, IL: C. C. Thomas.

Miller, K. S. & Knutson, J. F. (1997). Reports of severe physical punishment and exposure to animal cruelty by inmates convicted of felonies and by university students. *Child Abuse and Neglect, 21*(1), 59–82.

O'Brien, B. S., & Frick, P. J. (1996). Reward dominance: Associations with anxiety, conduct problems, and psychopathy in children. *Journal of Abnormal Child Psychology, 24*, 223–240.

Offord, D. R., Boyle, M. H., & Racine, Y. A. (1991). The epidemiology of antisocial behavior in childhood and adolescence. In D. J. Pepler & K. H. Rubin (Eds.), *The development and treatment of childhood aggression*. Hillsdale, NJ: Lawrence Erlbaum Associates, Inc.

Patterson, G. R. (1982). *Coercive family process*. Eugene, OR: Castalia.

Paul, E. S. (2000). Empathy with animals and with humans: Are they linked? *Anthrozoös, 13*, 194–202.

Price, J. M., & Dodge, K. A. (1989). Peers' contributions to children's social adjustment. In T. J. Berndt & G. W. Ladd (Eds.), *Peer relationships in child development* (pp. 341–370). Wiley: New York.

Ressler, R. K., Burgess, A. W., Hartman, C. R., Douglas, J. E., & McCormack, A. (1986). Murderers who rape and mutilate. *Journal of Interpersonal Violence, 1*, 273–287.

Rich, S. A. (1998). A developmental approach to the treatment of adolescent sexual offenders. *Irish Journal of Psychology, 19*(1), 102–118.

Robin, M., & ten Bensel, R. (1985). Pets and the socialization of children. *Marriage and Family Review, 8*, 63–78.

Sims, V. K., Chin, M. G., Eckman, M. L., Enck, B. M., & Abromaitis, S. M. (2001). Caregiver attributions are not just for children: Evidence for generalized low power schema. *Journal of Applied Developmental Psychology, 22*, 527–541.

Spitzer, R. L., Davies, M. P. H., Russell, A., & Barkley, R. A. (1990). The DSM-III-R field trial of disruptive behavior disorders. *Journal of the American Academy of Child and Adolescent Psychiatry, 29*, 690–697.

Vermeulen, H., & Odendaal, J. S. J. (1993). Proposed typology of companion animal abuse. *Anthrozoös, 6*, 248–257.

Wilson, C. C., & Turner, D. C. (1998) Quality of life outcomes, Aspects of animal–human interactions. In C. C. Wilson & D. C. Turner (Eds.), *Companion Animals in Human Health*. New York: Sage.

Wright, J., & Hensley, C. (2003). From animal cruelty to serial murder. Applying the graduation hypothesis. *International Journal of Offender Therapy and Comparative Criminology, 47*, 71–88.

Zasloff, R. L., Hart, L. A., & Weiss, J. M. (2003). Dog training as violence prevention tool for at-risk adolescents. *Anthrozoös, 16*, 352–359.

Appendix
Children and Animals Inventory

- This set of questions talks about children and animals and how sometimes kids can hurt animals on purpose.
- Please answer these questions as **honestly** as possible, no one knows your name or can ever find out your answers so please don't be afraid of getting into trouble if you speak truthfully.

1. Have you ever hurt an animal on purpose? (tick):
   Never ☐
   Hardly ever ☐
   A few times ☐
   Several times ☐
   Frequently ☐

2. How many times have you hurt an animal on purpose? (tick):
   Never ☐
   Once or twice ☐
   Three to six times ☐
   More than six times ☐

3. **a)** What types of animals have you hurt in the past (tick as many boxes as needed):
   None ☐
   Wild animals ☐ How many? ——
   Stray animals ☐ How many? ——
   Farm animals ☐ How many? ——
   Pet animals ☐ How many? ——

3. **b)** Which of these animals have you been cruel to? (tick):
   None ☐
   Worms or insects ☐
   Fish, lizards, frogs, etc. ☐
   Birds or mammals ☐

4. How long did you do this for (on and off)? (tick):
   Never ☐
   For about one month ☐
   For about six months ☐
   Longer than six months ☐

5. When was the last time you hurt an animal on purpose? (tick):
   I have never hurt an animal ☐
   More than a year ago ☐

Less than 1 year ago but more than 6 months ago ☐
In the last 6 months (half a year) ☐

6. Do you treat animals cruelly in front of others or by yourself? (tick):
   I have never hurt an animal ☐
   In front of others ☐
   Alone ☐

7. **a)** If you hurt an animal with others, are they adults or friends? (tick):
   I have never hurt an animal ☐
   Adults who were also hurting the animal ☐
   Friends who join in ☐
   With friends who don't join in ☐

7. **b)** If you hurt an animal by yourself, do you try to hide what you have done?
   I have never hurt an animal ☐
   No, I don't try to hide it ☐
   Sometimes I try to hide it, not always ☐
   Yes, I do try to hide it ☐

8. If you purposely hurt an animal, how do you feel?
   I have never been cruel to an animal ☐
   I feel very sad for the animal ☐
   Sometimes I feel bad, not always ☐
   I do not feel bad for the animal ☐

9. How do you feel about people hurting animals?
   Very sad and upset ☐
   Don't know ☐
   They deserve it ☐
   It is fun ☐
   ONLY ANSWER THIS LAST QUESTION IF YOU HAVE HURT AN ANIMAL ON PURPOSE.

10. Can you tell us what happened when you hurt an animal on purpose or what you usually do if you hurt animals often? ————————
    ————————————————————
    ————————————————————
    ————————————————————
    ————————————————————

Cruelty to Animals Scoring Chart

Item	Response	Score
1. Frequency	Never	0
	Hardly ever	1
	A few times	2
	Several times	3
	Frequently	4
2. Frequency	Never	0
	Once or twice	1
	Three to six times	2
	More than six times	3
3. a) (i) Diversity: Across Categories	None	0
	One of four types (wild, pet, stray, farm) harmed	1
	Two of four types	2
	Three or four of four types	3
3. a) (ii) Diversity: Within Categories	None from any categories	0
	No more than two animals from any one category	1
	More than two but fewer than six from one category	2
	Six or more animals from any one category	3
3. b) Diversity	None	0
	Animal maltreated is an invertebrate (worm, insect)	1
	Animal is a cold-blooded vertebrate (fish, amphibian, reptile)	2
	Animal is a warm-blooded vertebrate (bird, mammal)	3
4. Duration	Never	0
	Maltreatment occurred in a one-month period	1
	Occurred in a six-month period	2
	Occurred in a period longer than six-months	3
5. Recency	Never	0
	Maltreatment occurred over one year ago	1
	Occurred over six months ago	2
	Occurred in the last six months	3
6. Covert	Never hurt an animal	0
	Child performs act in front of peers	1
	Child is alone	2
7. a) Isolate	Never hurt an animal	0
	Child is with one or more adults	1
	Child is with one or more peers who are participants	2
	Child is with peers who are not participants	3
7. b) Conceal	Never hurt an animal	0
	Don't try to hide it	1
	Sometimes hide it	2
	Always try to hide it	3
8. Emotional response	Never been cruel to an animal	0
	Child indicates remorse or sensitivity to animal's distress	1
	Oscillates between sensitivity and callous uncaring	2
	No evidence of caring or empathy	3

Item	Response	Score
9. Empathy	Very sad and upset	0
	Don't know	1
	They deserved it	2
	It is fun	3
10. Severity (free response)	If no instances of maltreatment or only one case of minor, teasing, non-destructive, or non-painful act is mentioned.	0
	More than one case of above acts. It is assumed that the acts would not cause physical harm, e.g., annoying, teasing, frightening, restraining, or interfering. Examples: loud noise to scare sleeping pet, bangs on birdcage, chases ducks, etc. No malicious intent.	1
	One or more acts of maltreatment assumed to result in pain or discomfort to the animal, may be accompanied by minor physical damage. No use of weapons or tools. Examples: twisting leg, throwing something at an animal, tying legs together with string, pressing jaws together.	2
	One or more instances of maltreatment considered to result in significant pain or discomfort to an animal, maybe accompanied by physical damage. Examples: deep cuts, loss of parts of limbs, prolonging suffering, torturing, using instruments (weapons, extremes of temperature, caustic agents), suffocation.	3

Pet Abuse: Relationships to Psychobiology, Attachment Processes, and Domestic Violence

Roland D. Maiuro
Moss Rehabilitation Research Institute
Albert Einstein Healthcare Network

Jane A. Eberle
Seattle Public Schools

Pooka Rastaman & Bianca Snowflake
Seattle, Washington

"Dogs love their friends and bite their enemies, quite unlike people, who are incapable of pure love and always have to mix love and hate in their object-relations."
— *Sigmund Freud (In Bonaparte, 1994)*

"Pre-man evolved into early man because he was out there competing with all the rest … he didn't take himself out of the competition … the place where natural selection is going on … he was still part of the general community of life."
— *Daniel Quinn (1992)*

Introduction

With some cultural exceptions, and where animals are used for work, hunting, and food sources, it is a major taboo to inflict violence on an animal. This is particularly true for animals that are domesticated as family pets. Violent abuse of a companion animal such as a dog or cat often elicits the response: "How could someone do that to a poor innocent animal?" Such a comment inherently questions just how perverse the motivation must be or how profoundly disturbed the individual must be who would perpetrate such an act. In very severe cases of animal abuse, some have wondered whether the explanatory framework goes beyond social, emotional, and environmental causes to include

biological bases such as faulty wiring or aberrant constitutional makeup (e.g., primary psychopathy).

For this reason, and since some of the other chapters in this volume already provide discussion of psychosocial perspectives, the present chapter will examine what is known about the psychobiological basis for violence directed toward an animal. Since a comprehensive clinical definition of family violence includes a consideration of violence and abuse toward family pets (Rosenbaum & Maiuro, 1989, 1990), we will also examine what is known about the interrelationship between abuse of human intimates and pet abuse. Attachment theory is proposed as a potentially useful psychobiological framework for examining and understanding the linkages between family violence and pet abuse.

Healthy Attachment to Animals in Children and Adults

Despite the commonality of pet ownership in studies of attachment to pets, most data collection has been anecdotal or relied on survey-based accounts of human and family experiences with dogs or cats. In a large-scale study of about 1,000 pet owners, Albert and Bulcroft (Albert & Bulcroft, 1988; Bulcroft, 1990) observed that many senior adults retained vivid memories of family pets that they had during their childhood years and were easily brought to tears and joy by such recollections. These authors also observed that pets appeared to play important roles across all of the developmental stages of a family, beginning as newlyweds, to the birth of children, to the parenting of teenagers, and then finally to the "empty-nest" stage. They found that families in which children were present were the most likely to own pets, with children often initiating the purchase or acquisition of a pet. The fact that pet ownership provides early nurturance training was aptly illustrated by the fact the child and the mother often shared the day-to-day duties associated with the care, feeding, and well-being of the animal.

However, Albert and Bulcroft also found that pet ownership did not always equate to attachment. Although more likely to own a pet, some children reported relatively lower levels of attachment. In fact, newlyweds, those never married, and those without children had the highest levels of attachment. The authors speculated that this was not only due to the increased amount of time the adult(s) might spend with the pet but that the companion animals might assume a role similar to that of children in such households. The fact that pets can assume such status is also supported by the fact that 87% of those questioned agreed that their pet was "part of the family." Since the time of the study, there have been shifting demographics that point toward single or reduced numbers of humans in households as a result of higher divorce rates, single parenting, remarriage, and smaller family size. Bulcroft, as well as many family scholars who have followed, now believe that more recent family structure lends itself to even higher levels of emotional attachment to pets, as the family, however defined, often functions as a "haven in a heartless world."

The early work of Albert and Bulcroft has been amplified by more recent studies that have made use of more formal measures of positive adjustment. Triebenbacher (1998) completed a survey of 94 boys and 80 girls in preschool through grade 5. These children described their pets as "special friends" and "important family members" as well as sources of social interaction, affection, and emotional support. Serpell (1999) provides perhaps the most detailed description of the many positive roles that animals play in children's lives. He reports that parental surveys indicate that the presence of companion animals not only provides companionship for the growing child but also promotes caring attitudes and behaviors. Additionally, the children's relationships with their pets teach responsibility for another living

being as well as being a source of security, affection, and amusement. Statistically significant links have been found between the strength of preschool children's companion animal bond and their capacity for empathy for other children (Poresky, 1996).

Unhealthy Attachment to Animals in Behaviorally Disordered Children

It is now well established in the field of mental health that conduct disorder in children and adolescents and antisocial personality disorder in adults are strongly associated with abuse of animals (Arluke, Levin, Luke, & Ascione, 1999; Bell, 2001; Henry, 2004; Hensley & Tallichet, 2005). Numerous studies have identified animal abuse as a common developmental feature in the lives of both criminal and psychiatric populations at high risk for violence (Merz-Perez, Heide, & Silverman, 2001; Skeem et al., 2004). Only recently have research studies (Foley, Eaves, Wormley et al., 2004) begun to explore the biopsychosocial and etiological pathways that may be related to this association.

The first work to suggest a possible biopsychosocial basis for animal abuse in children focused upon what was called the "ego triad." Originally studying conduct disordered children from a psychoanalytic perspective, Yarnell (1940) proposed a linkage between fire setting, cruelty to animals, and enuresis. Although initially interpreted in terms of its symbolic meaning, the "ego triad" was identified subsequently by other researchers as a co-morbid cluster that could predict serious maladjustment and later adult criminal behavior (Lester, 1975; Prentky & Carter, 1984; Robbins & Robbins, 1967; Rothstein, 1963; Wax & Haddox, 1974). The fact that primary enuresis is generally viewed as an indicator of a delay in neurological maturation in both sleep and arousal centers of the brain, and associated with a strong family history, lent support to the idea that constitutional abnormalities might exist in such children and contribute to their behavior (Byrd & Weitzman, 1996).

More recent multivariate studies that have employed more objective measures and sophisticated methods of analysis, however, have cast doubt on the validity of the ego triad. Although fire setting and cruelty to animals are often identified simultaneously in socially troubled juveniles, the presence of enuresis has often been confounded by the use of institutionalized samples of children in which overall developmental care and parental discipline have been in question (Quinsey, Chaplin, & Upfold, 1989; Sakheim & Osborn, 1999; Sakheim, Osborn, & Abrams, 1991; Saunders & Awad, 1991). In a detailed review of existing studies examining the relationship of the developmental triad of animal abuse, fire setting, and bed-wetting, Dadds (current volume) found some evidence supporting the predictive utility of cruelty to animals and fire setting during childhood as univariate risk factors for future violence and criminal acts. The relationship of bed-wetting to such outcomes, however, is less clear. The author concluded that there is little empirical evidence to support the theorized cluster of variables as a true predictive triad.

Brain-Behavior Correlates of Poor Attachment and Aggression in Children

Despite the failure to find an empirical basis for enuresis as a possible psychobiological marker for antisocial and violent behaviors, more recent studies have found support for a variety of other brain-behavior mechanisms. These include deprivation or traumatic experiences (Van voorhees & Scarpa, 2004) that could affect general brain development, the interconnections with the pre-frontal cortex, the amygdala, as well as excesses or deficits in mood and impulse regulatory hormones (e.g., serotonin and neuroandrogenic metabolism). These data suggest that there may be some type of psychobiological vulnerability or pathway at work, particularly in cases of repeated, non-instrumental, and/or severe violence and abuse toward other people and animals.

At birth, an infant's brain is not completely developed (Diamond, 2002). Thus, environmental influences can have a dramatic effect upon brain growth and development. The fact that children exposed to trauma, stress, and neglect are at risk for atypical brain development is now well established. These data have been derived from studies (De Bellis, 2005; Downey & Coyne, 1990; Duncan & Miller, 2005; Spitz, 1945) of brain-behavior relationships in orphans raised in institutional settings, children reported to Child Protective Services (CPS), families reported to legal agencies due to domestic violence, individuals who have sustained brain damage across the life span, and correctional populations.

The impact and potentially lasting impact of such deprivation and traumatic experiences upon infant development was first underscored by Harlow's classic work with monkeys (Harlow, Harlow, & Suomi, 1971). Rhesus monkeys reared in isolation or denied "contact comfort" from their mothers showed an enduring incapacity to relate with other monkeys. In short, those monkeys who experienced relatively brief periods of isolation during the first three months of life followed by normal care were able to re-adjust and learn essential social skills. However, those monkeys exposed to longer periods of deprivation (six months to a year) were adversely affected for life. Deviant behaviors observed included lack of appropriate social interactions, self-mutilation, eating and self-care problems, increased anxiety, and higher levels of aggression that developed while young and persisted into adulthood.

Macovei (1986), Johnson et al. (1992), and Kreppner et al. (2001) have replicated and extended such findings with human infants who were isolated, neglected, or subjected to malnutrition, lack of environmental stimulation, and poor medical care. In addition to high death rates and health problems, these children exhibited severe deficits in physical, cognitive, language, and social development. These children also evidenced symptoms of "reactive attachment disorder," a condition described in depth by Bowlby (1982).

The Psychobiology of Attachment

Bowlby (1969, 1982) and Ainsworth, Blehar, Waters, and Wall (1978) have provided the theoretical foundation for the development of early attachment with the primary caregiver as having a psychobiological impact on the development of the infant with long-lasting effects on affect (such as fear, anger, and despair) and interpersonal relationships. As Decety and Jackson (2004) indicate, human empathy develops through social interaction and emotional bonds with others, with self-other awareness and self-regulation of emotions being vital components. At 36 hours, human infants can discriminate several facial expressions (such as happy, angry, sad, and surprised) and by 2 to 4 months can imitate human actions and emotional resonance (Hoffman, 2000; Serrano, Iglesias, & Loesches, 1992). Moreover, studies that have compared facial recognition in infants of physically and emotionally abusive mothers to those of non-abusive mothers reveal that infants of abusive mothers are quick to detect cues of anger while being less accurate in their detection of other emotions such as sadness (Pollak & Sinha, 2002).

The early emergence of these abilities suggests that such attachment mechanisms may be biologically wired or a function of preexisting brain templates in humans during early development. In a special issue on brain development and caring, Levine (2002) describes research which supports that there is enormous risk of violence in individuals who lack secure attachments and, thereby, do not develop caring or empathic behaviors.

The infant's experience of positive and aversive responses by the parent/caregiver as well as the infant's response to the parent/caregiver ("mutual contingent reactions") form the foundation upon which later toddler and childhood relationships are built (Figure 1). The infant has limited options for communication of such basic needs of hunger or sleep and displaying emotions in reaction to joy or pain. In turn, the caregiver/parent reacts and tries to interpret the intent or purpose of the infant's cries, tantrums, and smiles. "Maternal sensitivity" is a term used to describe the skill of a parent to identify emotions in the infant and to respond with positive support. Within this interaction, deficits can occur in either mother or child, and can be psychobiologically transmitted from mother to child through differential conditioning. In his longitudinal work on conduct disorders in boys, Patterson (2002) similarly and independently concluded that the early developmental pathways to aggression are multifaceted and result from an interaction between biological processes and environmental variables dictated by the child–caregiver interaction.

Brain-Behavior Mechanisms

Building upon the work of Luria (1966, 1973), test batteries have been developed for clinical evaluation of brain-behavior relationships in humans. The 1970s and 1980s were notable for the emergence of the use of neuropsychological assessment methods (Lezak, 1983, 1995; Reitan & Davison, 1974; Rourke, Bakker, Fisk, & Strang, 1983) to evaluate brain-behavior relationships in children, adolescents, and adults. Developmental norms have been developed to evaluate the functioning of young children on such tests (Maiuro, Townes, Vitaliano, & Trupin, 1984). Since neuroimaging techniques were limited to computerized tomography (CT), these test results assisted the neuropsychologist in understanding the localization of brain function by examining performance, pathognomic signs, unexpected deviations in cerebral dominance and laterality, and asymmetrical patterns and relationships.

When damage occurs early in life, the brain is still developing and more flexible. Thus, it is felt that brain insults in utero or prenatally may result in better outcomes in terms of general physical functioning. However, Trauner, Nass, and Ballantyne (2001) conducted a study of 39 children with pre- or perinatal brain damage and compared them to a control group of 54 children on the Children Behavior Checklist (Achenbach & Edelbrock, 1983) at ages 4 to 15 years. There was a significant difference in full-scale intelligence scores with the age-relevant Wechsler Scales (Wechsler, 1974, 1989), with the

Figure 1
Biopsychosocial Model of Bowlby's Attachment System

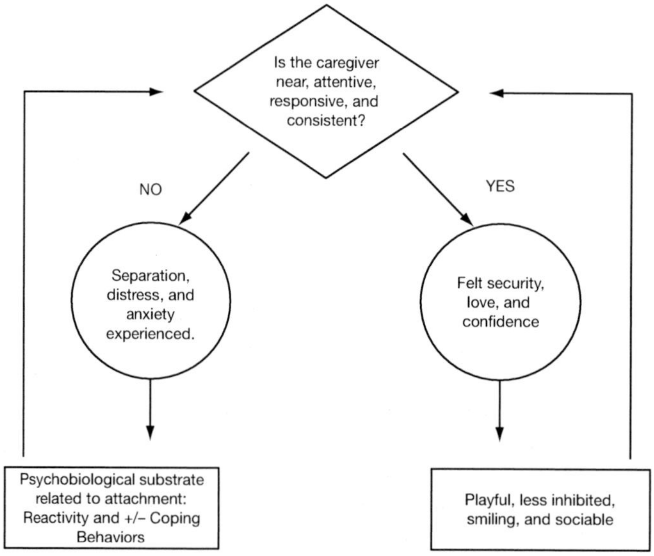

Table 1 Psychobiology of Attachment

Brain Structure or Mechanism	Behavioral-Emotional Process or Function	Adverse or Negative Exposure
Decreased # Brain Cells/Connections	General Intelligence (IQ)	Poor Nutrition, Prenatal Stress or Fetal Alcohol Effects
Neuronal Pruning & Myelination	Connectivity between Brain Structures	Chronic Stress in Infancy and Childhood
Shrunken or Degenerated Hippocampus	Facial Cue Recognition, Emotional or Traumatic Memory	Child Maltreatment; Chronic Stress
Amygdala	Fear Conditioning Emotional Reactivity	Poor Caregiver Bonding
Stress Hormones (cortisol levels)	Fight or Flight Responses	Abuse, Neglect, and Trauma Overstimulation
Androgenized Brain/High Testosterone	Sensation Seeking, Risky Behavior	Y Chromosome in Combination with Compromised Executive Functions
Hypothalamus-Pituitary-Adrenal (HPA) axis	Responding to Stress or Danger	Chronic Stressors such as Child Abuse and Sexual Abuse
Decreased Serotonin Level	Anxiety, Depression, Aggression, Mood Instability, Impulsivity	Chronic Stressors in Infancy and Childhood
Decreased Dopamine Levels	Attention, Vigilance, Learning New Material	Smoking during Pregnancy. Chronic Stressors in Infancy and Childhood
Frontal Lobe	Executive Functioning	Chronic Stressors in Infancy and Childhood
Pre-Frontal Area Orbitofrontal	Moral Reasoning and Judgment, Empathy	Chronic Stress, Child Abuse Sexual Abuse, Traumatic Brain Injury or Lesion, Faulty Attachment Experiences

brain damaged group's mean scores significantly lower than the control group. When intelligence scores were not used as a covariate, the brain-damaged group's scores were significantly higher than the control group on the Behavior Problem Scales of Social, Attention, and Thought Problems, although the scores did fall within the normal range for both groups. Retesting with the Child Behavior Checklist over an interval of four years revealed no significant increase in overall scores but a significantly higher mean score in Social Problems that persisted for the brain-damaged group at the second testing. Despite the limitations of the study (e.g., variability in site of lesions, report of problem behaviors only by parents, small sample [n = 18] of frontal lesions), it appears that behavioral-emotional functioning may be particularly sensitive to brain damage, even in the presence of significant brain reorganization associated with early age.

There is now evidence that the very architecture of the brain can be affected by exposure to unhealthy events and socialization experiences (Table 1). During the process of neurogenesis (the production of brain cells), about 200 billion neurons have been created by the 20th week of fetal life. Later, a massive neural "pruning" of these large numbers of cells occurs as the brain becomes functional and selective in terms of which connections should survive. Approximately six weeks later, during the third trimester, only 50 percent of those cells remain alive. The surviving 100 billion neurons are the ones that will aid the growth and development of the newborn child. This early overproduction of neurons and neural networks is the "plasticity mechanism" by which human beings are capable of adapting to the varied environmental challenges across climates and continents.

A fine-tuning of a child's emerging behavioral-emotional capacity occurs between three and six years of age. At approximately age 5 or 6, the brain has reached 90%–95% of its adult volume and is four times its birth size. From the age of 3, extensive internal rewiring takes place in the frontal lobes which house the cortical regions involved in organizing actions, focusing attention, and regulating impulses based upon foresight and perceived consequences. When children lack active healthy social encounters with others (compromised by threat, stress, and anxiety), the brain does not wire itself properly in the emotional centers and pathways. According to Perry (2002), the development of the cerebral cortex can be reduced by as much as 20% under these conditions, rendering many brain structures either underdeveloped or wired in a way that contributes to deviant and maladaptive behavior.

With the advent of more advanced blood assay and brain imaging techniques, the presence of a variety of forms of brain dysfunction have been detected that place a child at risk for faulty attachment and behavioral-emotional problems. When a pregnant woman experiences the effects of chronic stress in her body, she passes them along to the fetus. The cortisol in her bloodstream shunts blood away from the uterus, and this in turn squeezes off some of the fetus's supply of oxygen and nutrients—up to 60% in extreme cases. Diamond and Hopson (1999) reported that this crossover of hormones could act in the fetal brain as it does in the adult—by cutting the number of neurons that develop and by preventing some of their dendritic branches and spines from forming (Diamond & Hopson, 1999; Gunnar & Vasquez, 2001; Weinstock, 2001). The babies of mothers so exposed are more likely to be restless, irritable, and are more prone to a variety of adjustment problems.

The fact that overexposure to stress-related hormones can occur postnatally has also been demonstrated. One such study conducted by Cicchetti and Rogosch (2001) documented a variety of atypical cortisol regulation patterns exhibited among maltreated children. They investigated cortisol regulation in a sample of school-aged maltreated (n = 175) and demographically comparable low-income non-maltreated (n = 209) children drawn from a day camp research program. While overall group differences between maltreated and non-maltreated children were not found for average morning or average afternoon cortisol levels, significant variations were found that were based on the subtypes of maltreatment that the children had experienced. Maltreated children who had been both physically and sexually abused (as well as neglected or emotionally maltreated) exhibited substantial elevations in morning cortisol levels. Children who had high (>1 SD) cortisol levels in both the morning and afternoon were also overrepresented in the multiple abuse group. Developmental timing of

maltreatment did not account for these group differences, whereas the severity of abuse was significantly related to cortisol level.

Since severely conducted disordered youth often have histories of abuse and neglect, there has been considerable theoretical speculation that these youth may be operating with atypical and deviant emotional processing systems. Such research has generally focused upon the hypothalamic-pituitary-adrenal axis (HPA) which is responsible for releasing cortisol, adrenocorticotropin (ACTH), and corticotrophin-releasing hormone (CRH). In a study conducted by McBurnett, Lahey, Rathouz, and Loeber (2000), 38 school-aged boys were referred to a clinic for childhood onset of aggressive conduct disorder. Low hypothalamic-pituitary-adrenal axis activity was found to be a significant correlate of severe and persistent aggression. The chronically low cortisol levels observed over time suggested a psychobiological basis for such conduct. This idea is further supported by a recent study by Saltzman, Holden, and Holahan (2005), who found that children exposed to marital violence differed significantly with respect to sympathetic nervous system and HPA functioning when compared to a clinical comparison group that was not exposed to marital violence.

Research has shown that such over-activation can cause malfunctions in the hippocampus, a major part of the brain involved in learning and memory. In a stressful encounter, another part of the brain, the amygdala, instructs the hypothalamus to signal the pituitary and adrenal glands to secrete stress hormones. This action by the amygdala involves an emotional response to stimulation independent of higher cortical systems of the brain. The hippocampus is responsible for a cognitive appraisal of the stress situation. If the appraisal is benign, the hippocampus sends messages to counter the instructions of the amygdala. However, if the stress persists too long, the hippocampus has difficulty maintaining its ability to control the release of the stress hormones and the amygdala becomes dominant and poorly regulated. Severe but temporary, or merely constant, stress results in the shriveling of some dendrites in the hippocampus, while prolonged stress causes irreversible changes such that cells in the hippocampus begin to degenerate, leading to permanent memory loss that might otherwise be available to guide emotional adjustment and adaptation. LeDoux (1996) cited evidence of shrunken hippocampuses (found in autopsies) in children who have experienced repeated abuse similar to that seen in veterans who have suffered Posttraumatic Stress Disorder (Farran, 2001).

The biological predisposition to attachment problems and conduct disorder may not only be a trait acquired through neglect or trauma but also one in which there is a genetically based vulnerability. Herman, Philbeck, Vasilopoulos, and Depetrillo (2003) conducted a study of 204 male and female college students aged 17 to 23 years. They also analyzed each student's genotype with a focus on the 5-HTT gene, which is involved in recycling the chemical serotonin after it is secreted into the synapse of a cell. The researchers determined that students had either long or short versions of the serotonin transporter gene. The researchers found that the students who carried two copies of the short version of 5-HTT were more likely to report troublesome drinking patterns by more frequently engaging in binge drinking, drinking more often to get drunk, and consuming more alcoholic drinks per occasion than did students with the other genotypes. The authors speculated that individuals who are homozygous for the short version, and known to be at risk for higher levels of anxiety, may use alcohol to modify their mood and reduce tension.

Such an interpretation is supported by a similar study conducted by Caspi et al. (2004). In a longitudinal study of children who carried the "short" or stress-sensitive version of the serotonin transporter gene, 43% developed depression when confronted with multiple stressors, compared to only 17% with the longer version of the gene. Those with the short version of the gene were also at higher risk for depression if they also had been abused as children. In comparison, no matter how many stressful life events they endured, the participants with the "long" or protective version of the gene experienced no more depression than people who were totally spared from stressful life events.

In the same study, Caspi et al. further reported that there is a genetic vulnerability that modifies the action of the mood-regulating neurotransmitter norepinephrine (NE). This gene regulates the enzymes released from the nerve endings along with NE and is called monoamine oxidase (MAO-A). The authors believe there is an interaction between this genetic vulnerability and traumatic exposure such as frequent changes in primary caregiver, rejection by the mother, and physical or sexual abuse. Although only 12% of the maltreated children were found to have low activity levels of MAO-A, this subsample of children accounted for 44% of the group total

convictions for assault and other violent crimes. Moreover, when followed to adulthood, 85% of the severely maltreated children who also had the gene for low MAO-A activity developed antisocial outcomes, frequently marked by violent criminal behavior. Caspi et al (2004) concluded that the combination of maltreatment and the genetic variation magnified the odds of antisocial behavior by nine times. This level of risk is noteworthy from a public health perspective in that it is roughly equivalent to the relationship between high cholesterol and heart disease. However, the relationship of low MAO-A to aggression only emerged when combined with traumatic exposure, as the genotype alone did not predict later antisocial and violent behavior.

Gray (1975) theorized that there may be two primary biologic pathways to increased risk for antisocial or aggressive behavior. One biologic system, the Behavioral Inhibition System (BIS), serves to inhibit behavior in response to punishment and is mediated by the septo-hippocampal regions of the brain. The other system, the Behavioral Activation System (BAS), serves to activate behavior in response to reward or to escape punishment and is mediated by the amygdala and limbic system. Thus, aggression may develop as a function of a relatively underactive BIS (leading to poor socialization and emotional attachment from an inability to learn from cues of punishment) or a relatively overactive BAS (leading to impulsive aggression in situations of frustration or self-defense).

Behavioral Activation System theory has received support from a number of researchers. Gardner, Karmel, and Flory (2003) and Lynam (1996) have linked abnormalities in childhood reactivity, both hyperactivity and hypoactivity, to later behavioral problems. These problems have been described varyingly as conduct disorder and cruelty in children (Burke, Loeber, & Birmaher, 2004) and as psychopathy and antisocial traits when assessed in adulthood. As described by Hare (1996) and Lynam (1996), "psychopathy" refers to a constellation of traits that include being hot-tempered, cold-hearted, impulsive, irresponsible, impoverished in emotion, and manipulative, as well as lacking empathy, anxiety, guilt, and remorse. Moreover, cruelty to animals has been frequently documented in the developmental histories of individuals diagnosed as having antisocial personality disorder (Blair, 2001). In a carefully conducted study, Gleyzer, Felthous, and Holzer (2002) examined criminal defendants who had histories of substantial animal cruelty in comparison to matched defendants without this history. Data were systematically obtained from the files by using four specifically designed data retrieval outlines. A history of animal cruelty during childhood was significantly associated with Antisocial Personality disorder, antisocial personality traits, and polysubstance abuse. Mental retardation, psychotic disorders, and alcohol abuse showed no such association.

Given the now ancient historical timeline associated with various forms of violent and victimizing behavior, it is also possible that some individuals are predisposed to engage in cruel and "abnormally" violent and deviant conduct without disordered or traumatized developmental histories. Thus, as in the case of some so-called "lower animal forms" such as "rogue" elephants and other pack species, normally observed bonds and attachments could be weakly developed in some human beings and attended by high levels of predatory behavior simply as a result of the luck of the "genetic draw." As part of a gender-linked theory, Ellis (2005) suggests that the simple attribute of being male predisposes human beings to having a psychophysiology that is more prone to violent and victimizing behavior. Reviewing the biological correlates of criminal behavior, Ellis postulates an Evolutionary Neuroandrogenic theory (ENA) that male sex hormones influencing the human brain "increase the probability of competitive/victimizing behavior" over time. Several aspects of neurophysiological functioning are also cited as predisposing males to violent and victimizing behavior, including testosterone production, suboptimal arousal to pain, a need for elevated sensory stimulation, and limbic system vulnerability. When these factors are additionally combined with compromised or ineffective executive functioning, Ellis believes they can contribute to problems with moral reasoning and much higher rates of criminal behavior. The theory predicts that serious criminality, including violent behavior, will be more concentrated in adolescent and young adult males of low social status due to pressures to compete without the usual level of supports needed to promote pro-social behavior.

Although the findings specifically associating testosterone level and aggression in humans are modest, at best, official reports indicate that being male increases the risk of the most severe forms of interpersonal violence and abusive behavior (Barash, 2002; Lipton & Barash, 2005). In a comprehensive review of gender and animal cruelty, Gerbasi (2004)

observed that a consensus had formed among researchers that animal abuse is closely linked to conduct disorder in children, and that a link exists between human violence and animal abuse. Gerbasi further observed that aside from hoarding of animals by older females, clinical experience indicates that most animal abuse is perpetrated by males.

The Humane Society of the United States (2006) similarly reported descriptive statistics from 2003 that indicate the majority of animal cruelty cases are committed by men and boys. Based on a compilation of 1,373 reports obtained from a combination of media sources and animal welfare agencies, the demographic characteristics of 1,682 perpetrators were identified. The society reported that the vast majority of "intentional cruelty" cases were committed by adult and teenage males, with shooting being the most common form of violence. The most commonly victimized animals were companion animals or pets, with dogs outnumbering cats. Even in instances during which an animal was neglected, males outnumbered females. Males were also significantly more often the perpetrators when animal cruelty occurred in connection with family violence.

Pet Abuse and Domestic Violence

It is now known that animals may also be abused in the context of family violence or when abusive behavior occurs between intimate adult partners. In an early study of co-occurrence and co-morbidity, Ascione (1998) reported an interview study of 38 women who were battered and had sought shelter. Of this group 58% of the women had children and 74% had pets. When asked whether their adult partner had ever threatened or actually hurt or killed one or more of their pets, 71% of women with pets responded "yes." Whether it be through a "pecking order" effect, direct modeling, or a psychobiologically mediated process of faulty attachment, it was also found that 32% of the abused women who had children reported that their children had hurt or killed one or more family pets. In a replication study during which 100 women who were battered and had entered a shelter were compared to a comparison group of 117 non-battered women, all of whom had pets, Ascione et al. (2007) found that 54% of the battered women compared with 5% of the non-battered women reported that their partner had hurt or killed pets. Children's exposure to this animal abuse was reported by 62% of the battered women. The fact that concomitant pet abuse may also increase the risk to human family members is underscored by the fact that nearly one in four of the battered women reported that concern for their pets' welfare had prevented them from seeking shelter sooner.

Flynn (2000) reported similar findings in a study of 43 women with pets who had entered a South Carolina domestic violence shelter (28 of the women were also accompanied by children). Of these 43 women, 46.5% (n = 9) reported threats to or harm (n = 11) of their pets. Although only 7% of children were reported to be cruel to animals, 33.3% of women whose pets were abused reported that their children had also been abused. Of the women whose pets were not abused, 15.8% reported that child abuse had occurred by their partner. The figure reported for concomitant child abuse was somewhat less (10.5%) for women with no pets. Although the overall figures for overlapping abuse are lower than those reported by Ascione (1998), it is clear that exposure to one form of abuse significantly increases the risk for the presence of another form of abuse.

Becker, Stuewig, Herrerra, and McCloskey (2004) analyzed data obtained from 363 women and one of their children (6 to 12 years of age) over a 10-year period to examine the impact of marital violence on children's mental health. Subsequent interviews and court records indicated that exposure to marital violence, harsh parenting, and pet abuse by the father were associated with animal cruelty by the child. Children exposed to marital violence were 2.3 times more likely to be cruel to animals than those from nonviolent homes. Marital violence as well as pet abuse and drinking by the father were also related to fire setting. Self-reports of later violent crime by the adolescents were also related to animal cruelty.

In a controlled comparison group study, Duncan, Thomas, and Miller (2005) compared two residential samples of youth to determine what differentiated those who abused animals from those who did not. Files from a 10-year period from a residential program for boys who were diagnosed with conduct or oppositional defiant disorder were reviewed. Excluded were boys who had histories of psychosis or bipolar, neurological conditions, or low intellectual functioning. Two groups with 50 subjects in each were compared: those with documented histories of animal cruelty and those without such history. The chart reviews coded histories of physical child abuse, sexual child abuse, paternal

alcoholism, paternal unavailability, and domestic violence in addition to the animal cruelty. When the data were analyzed, exposure to domestic violence emerged as the most significant factor that differentiated the groups. As predicted, the boys exposed to domestic violence were significantly more likely to be cruel to animals. The boys who abused animals were 2 to 2 1/2 times more likely to have been physically and/or sexually abused and/or exposed to domestic violence. Paternal alcoholism and unavailability did not differentiate the two groups.

Despite the presence of data showing a significant relationship between pet abuse and other forms of family violence, relatively little is known about the psychological dynamics of such abuse. Case studies based upon work with battered women suggest that the abuse of family pets can be used as a tactic of intimidation and control by a perpetrator of spouse abuse. In this respect, perpetrators may abuse or kill a family dog or cat as an instrumental means of terrorizing or punishing an intimate partner or child for something they have done or for abandoning them. Such tactics may be used as a threat to instill fear for contacting police or legal authorities or as a symbolic reminder of what could happen to them (Browne, 1987). Violence and abuse directed at pets of women who have threatened to leave or have left a violent relationship can contribute to a victim's sense of having no way out and further reinforce feelings of hopelessness and helplessness as part of battered woman's syndrome (Flynn, 2000). In many cases, the well-being of animals may not be prioritized by law enforcement officials and domestic violence shelters may not have accommodations to allow victims to take their pets with them when they leave a violent relationship (Ascione, 2000).

In one of the few studies of pet abuse and family violence in which the perpetrator was assessed directly, Maiuro, Wachs, Tzovarras, Wu, and Vitaliano (2003) found evidence of threats and/or abuse of pets in 24% of a sample of DV perpetrators referred for treatment. When the sample was corrected for pet ownership, the percentage of pet-abusing cases observed was 63%, a figure similar to that reported by Ascione et al. (2007) in their studies of battered women. When the investigators compared spouse-abusing men who also committed pet abuse with spouse-abusing men who did not abuse the family pet, the presence of pet abuse was found to be associated with more frequent, more severe, and more different types of domestic violence. Pet abuse was also positively correlated with indices of generalized anger and aggression as well as with abusive forms of dominance and control.

Attachment Disorder, Relationships, and Domestic Violence

Although the formal diagnosis of attachment disorder within the formal DSM-IV nomenclature remains a narrowly defined entity requiring a clear, and often institutionally based history of profound parental deprivation during the first year of life, many researchers believe that there is a much broader spectrum of conditions related to faulty attachment. Hazan and Shaver (1987) were among the first researchers to explore Bowlby's attachment ideas in the context of adult romantic relationships. According to Hazan and Shaver, the emotional bond that develops between adult romantic partners is largely a function of the same psychobiological system that gives rise to the emotional bond between infants and their caregivers. Hazan and Shaver noted that both infants and caregivers and adult romantic partners share the following behavioral-emotional connections and action patterns:

- Both feel safe when the other is nearby and responsive
- Both engage in close, intimate, bodily contact
- Both feel insecure when the other is inaccessible
- Both share discoveries with one another
- Both caress each others' facial features and head as well as exhibit mutual fascination and preoccupation with one another
- Both engage in "baby talk" as a form of affective communication

On the basis of these parallels, Hazan and Shaver argued that adult romantic relationships, like infant–caregiver relationships, are bonded attachments, and that romantic love is a product of the same psychobiological systems that give rise to caregiving and empathy. It is of interest to further note that some of these same connections and action patterns occur between humans and their pets as part of the bonding process: Both feel safe when the other is nearby; both engage in intimate contact in the form of petting, sitting on the lap,

and, in some cases, sleeping together; and both are characterized by "baby talk" as a form of affective communication.

Bowlby (1988) theorized that individuals develop an internal working model based upon conditioning experiences relating to how caregivers responded to their needs as children. If the caregiver responds in a consistent manner to the child's needs, the child learns that the caregiver is responsive, available, and dependable. Consequently, the child will develop a positive sense of self-worth and feel that others are trustworthy. If the caregiver is not consistent in how he or she responds to the child, the child learns that the caregiver is unreliable, others are untrustworthy, and will very likely develop a negative sense of self-worth. The views and beliefs an individual develops, as a result of how the caregiver responded to him or her, underlies the internal working model of self and the internal working model of others that mediate the ability to form healthy attachments.

When Bowlby's original concepts are integrated and combined with the presently reviewed research on neurobiological and brain-behavior mechanisms associated with attachment, a dynamic interplay of biopsychosocial factors results (Figure 1). In this respect, there are a number of positive and negative feedback loops between the environment and psychobiological substrate of the developing child that have the capacity to reciprocally modify each other, changing both the "software" programming involved and the psychobiological "hardware" involved in the perception, processing, and reaction to relationships with both humans and animals.

Bartholomew and Horowitz (1991) took Bowlby's work further and postulated that an internal working model of self and an internal working model of others combine together and form four distinct adult attachment styles. These four styles are derived from an interaction of the self and other components together with positive and negative emotional dimensions. A positive view of others and a positive view of self constitute the *secure* attachment style. The secure attachment style is characterized by a sense of worthiness in the individual. Individuals with secure attachment expect others to be accepting and responsive and are comfortable with intimacy and autonomy. A positive view of others and a negative view of self is associated with the ***preoccupied*** (sometime referred to as anxious-ambivalent or anxious-avoidant) attachment style. Individuals characterized by the preoccupied attachment style have a sense of personal unworthiness but have positive expectations and positive views of others. Individuals with preoccupied attachment tend to develop anxious and dependent features and become absorbed and engrossed with others to a neurotic degree. A negative view of others and a positive view of self are associated with a *dismissing* attachment style. Perhaps the least common and least studied of all these attachment types, the dismissing attachment style is characterized by a narcissistic sense of personal worthiness while others are viewed untrustworthy and negative. In order to protect themselves, they avoid intimacy by remaining emotionally detached, interacting with others as objects in an instrumental fashion dictated by personal needs and impulses. The highest correlations observed for this subtype reflect emotional "coldness" and a lack of nurturing attitudes toward others. Finally, a negative view of others along with a negative view of self constitutes the *fearful* attachment style. Individuals characterized by the fearful attachment style view others as being untrustworthy and are socially avoidant to guard themselves against hurt and disappointment by others. They achieve such avoidance by blaming others; creating interpersonal tension; projecting and justifying their feelings of fear as perceived hostility on the part of others; and attacking others in an angry, counter-phobic fashion (Bartholomew, 1990; Bartholomew, Henderson, & Dutton, 2001; Bartholomew & Horowitz, 1991; Ward & Hudson, 1996).

In an attempt to bridge the developmental gap between infants and adults, Brennan, Clark, and Shaver (1998) have adopted a conceptual model of attachment

dynamics that is less cognitive and less reliant upon "self" and "other" identity formation. In this model there are two fundamental and observable dimensions: attachment-related *anxiety* and attachment-related *avoidance*. Within this system, a prototypical secure adult is low on both of these conflict dimensions. Figure 2 provides a multidimensional model of attachment typology based upon an integration of both Bartholomew and Horowitz's (1991) as well as the more recent empirically and psychometrically driven work of Brennan, Clark, & Shaver (1998).

Brennan's findings are critical because recent analyses of the statistical patterning of behavior among infants reveal two functionally similar dimensions: one that captures variability in the anxiety and resistance of the child and another that captures variability in the child's willingness to use the parent as a safe haven for support (Fraley & Spieker, 2003). Moreover, these dimensions have also been demonstrated as similar functionally to the two dimensions uncovered among adults, suggesting that similar patterns of attachment exist across different points in the life span. They are also compatible with taxometric research published by Fraley and Waller (1998) which conceptualizes the contribution of individual differences in attachment dimensionally rather than categorically.

In one of the earliest studies mentioning a possible relationship between attachment disorder and the perpetration of domestic violence, Maiuro, Cahn, Vitaliano, Wagner, and Zegree (1988) observed that as many as two-thirds of their sample of domestically violent men had Beck Depression Scale scores consistent with at least mild levels of

Figure 2
Multidimensional Model of Attachment Typology

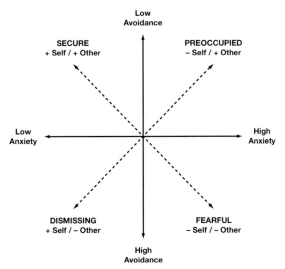

clinical depression. This result for spouse-abusing men contrasted with a significantly lower rate of depression in a comparison group of men who were assaultive toward strangers. The researchers suggested that the depression observed, along with high levels of anger and hostility assessed, might reflect preoccupation with possible loss of their romantic partners attended by angry and ambivalent behavior and attempts to control them.

To date, there are only a few research studies that have begun to explore the link between faulty attachment and the capacity for domestic violence and abuse. Dutton, Saunders, Starzomski, and Bartholomew (1994) explored these styles in abusive relationships in adult couples and found both *fearful* and *preoccupied* as significantly associated with abusive behavior. Using a community sample, Henderson, Bartholomew, Trinke, and Kwong (2005) studied whether secure and insecure attachment to the intimate partner could determine whether "attachment differentially predicts abuse receipt and perpetration." The four attachment prototypes (secure, fearful, preoccupied, and dismissing) as described by Bartholomew and Horowitz (1991) were examined for their relationship to abuse variables. Results indicated that *preoccupied* attachment was predictive of reciprocal abuse relationship dynamics. In contrast, and as would be predicted, little association was found between *secure* attachment and relationship abuse.

Discussion

The present chapter has presented findings that indicate that pet abuse is strongly related to other forms of family violence. This relationship exists as a form of co-morbidity in which one form of abuse is likely to coexist with the other, again in the transmission from parent to child, as well as a form of developmental trauma that might predispose a child to later interpersonal violence and antisocial behavior. As it stands, in developmental psychology and mainstream mental health, pet abuse has been articulated largely as a concomitant feature of other forms of pathology such as conduct disorder and fire setting. Given the convergence of findings that suggest that pet abuse is not only a symptom of immediate dysfunction but also a risk marker for future problems, it is reasonable to conclude that the abuse of animals is worthy of prioritization as a serious mental health and behavioral problem in its own right. The presently reviewed findings make a strong case for exactly that status.

Three potential theories were postulated by Duncan and Miller (2002) to explain why children abuse animals: social learning of angry and cruel parentally modeled behaviors as a means of resolving conflict, the psychoanalytic defense mechanisms of projection and introjection (or identification with the aggressor) related to identity development and control, and the lack of development of appropriate bonding and empathy. Although these theoretical pathways may not be mutually exclusive, there are probably subtypes of pet abuse with some being more malignant than others. Moreover, there are likely to be children at risk who in combination with other vulnerabilities act out by abusing animals.

As presently discussed, one form of vulnerability may be psychobiological in nature and related to the process and underpinnings of attachment and empathy. While social learning and modeling factors associated with aggressive behavior have been researched for many years, the advances in functional neuro-imaging and assessment (Bufkin & Luttrell, 2005; Frankie et al., 2005) are now permitting a more detailed and thorough understanding of the brain processes that might also affect the expression and behavioral inhibition of aggression. The research in this area has gone a long way from the early notion of the bed-wetting, fire setting, and pet abuse triad to suggest multiple forms of psychobiological risk.

The role of neuropsychological deficits as a possible vulnerability factor for perpetrators of domestic violence has also begun to receive attention. Rosenbaum and his colleagues conducted a series of studies linking marital aggression to head injury (Cohen, Rosenbaum, Kane, Warnken, & Benjamin, 1999; Cohen et al., 2003; Hershorn & Rosenbaum, 1991; Rosenbaum and Hoge, 1989; Rosenbaum et al., 1994). They found that many abusive men disclose personal histories of head trauma when asked and, in later work, that many men with head injury have been violent to family members. They discussed this correlation as a possible causal link in that brain dysfunction and neurological impairment resulting from head trauma can reduce impulse control, distort judgment, cause communication difficulties, and create hypersensitivity to the disabling effects of alcohol. Teichner, Golden, Van Hassel, and Peterson (2001) corroborated these findings in a comparative study of men who batter with a group of matched non-patient controls. Their results indicated that 48% of the male batterers exhibited cognitive dysfunction (defined by scores exceeding cutoffs on two or more indices of a commonly used battery of neuropsychological tests), as compared to only 4.3% of the non-patient controls. Inspection of individual neuropsychological measures indicated poorer performance across all subtests for domestically violent men with impaired test scores as compared to both non-impaired perpetrators and normal controls. These researchers concluded that the pattern of neuropsychological deficits observed in perpetrators of domestic violence was consistent with overall lower executive control over emotional processes.

Although the work of Rosenbaum et al. and Teichner et al. supports the presence of neuropsychological deficits in subsamples of men who are domestically violent, it is also clear that the majority of domestically violent men may have no identifiable history of head injury per se. Moreover, closer inspection of the data of these studies reveals impairment scores in the mild to moderate range for many participants. In many cases, the histories of head injury were intertwined with histories of having been personally subjected to physical and emotional abuse as a child. In addition, multivariate analyses reveal that such deficits are often manifested as difficulties in verbal and emotional expression and behavioral impulsivity. Such findings are consistent with an earlier study by Maiuro, Cahn, and Vitaliano (1986) who found a significant difference between domestically violent men (without documented histories of head injury) and nonviolent men on measures that tapped the ability to initiate assertive requests related to their wants and needs. The researchers also found a significant and negative correlation between initiating/request behavior and covert feelings of anger and hostility among the perpetrators of domestic violence. Taken together, these results suggest that the causal pathways between neuropsychological deficits and concomitant aggressive behavior may be more complex than those that could be attributed to head injury. Rather, a variety of etiological processes may be at work, including psychobiological changes in emotional pathways associated with attachment trauma in childhood, learning disabilities that compromise the development of verbal expression skills, as well as classic post-concussive irritability and impulsivity associated with physical head trauma (cf. Raine et al., 2005).

Attachment disorder is a relatively new term that was absent from most psychiatric textbooks as little as 10 years ago. As noted, companion animals are often intimately involved as part of the attachment history for many children and families. Although there have been no direct studies of perpetrators of pet abuse with formalized assessments of attachment, the developmental histories of such individuals are replete with case study material descriptive of poor parenting, trauma, and neglect that could disrupt and adversely affect the attachment system. Moreover, when one examines the descriptors and formal diagnostic criteria used for conduct disordered children and antisocial adults known to have abused animals, the terms are remarkably consistent with those used to delineate all three categories of faulty attachment (e.g., disturbed relationships; isolation from and/or rejection by others; lack of close friends or of lasting empathic, reciprocal relationships with others; relationships marked by discord, hostility, and resentment).

Pet-abusing individuals with histories of generally aggressive and impulsive behavior would likely have both *fearful* and *dismissing* attachment styles. Like the fearful offender, individuals with a dismissing attachment style would be expected to exhibit a high degree of hostility to avoid bonding with others. However, unlike the fearful offender, dismissing individuals do not experience a negative view of self, and may perceive potential victims as objects. The more cruel and sadistic forms of pet-abusing behavior would be congruent with the psychopathic characteristics of the dismissed or detached subtype. In fact, there is now preliminary evidence, based on recent studies of violent criminal populations, to suggest that antisocial personality features, sadistic traits, and the devaluation of other living beings are strongly associated with a dismissing attachment style (Meloy, 1992; Timmerman & Emmelkamp, 2006; Ward & Hudson, 1996). Attachment theory would appear to hold considerable promise for improving our understanding the etiology of violence and victimization of all types, including the specific linkages between family violence and pet abuse.

Despite current advances in our knowledge, our understanding of pet abuse has been limited by the lack of comprehensive diagnostic procedures and protocols used to interview or examine potential pet abusers. Current DSM-IV diagnoses have limited criteria directly having to do with animal abuse. In fact, since 1987, the only diagnosis in DSM (American Psychiatric Association, 1987) that includes animal abuse as a specified part of its criteria has been conduct disorder, "Has been physically cruel to animals." Even when one examines the most commonly used risk assessments for domestic violence (Campbell, 2004; Weisz, Tolman, & Saunders, 2000), one finds that they do not include pet abuse as a factor to consider (cf. Ascione, Weber, & Wood, 1997). Moreover, an empirical review of current state standards for domestic violence perpetrator treatment programs conducted by Maiuro and Eberle (in press) failed to find any state or jurisdiction that actually required a program to assess whether the batterer or any member of the family had harmed animals as part of intake or risk assessment process. The recent work of Maiuro et al. (2003) indicates the presence of pet abuse is associated with more frequent, more severe, and more different types of domestic—violence. These data support the need to include pet abuse in both routine and high-risk domestic violence assessment protocols.

As noted by Beirne (2003), research regarding the "cycle of violence" that includes the abuse of animals, as well as the possible progression from animal abuse to human violence, has been hindered by the lack of refined, reliably recorded, and longitudinal databases. As effective recognition and intervention with pet abuse requires an interdisciplinary approach, reliable diagnostic protocols need to be developed for use by a variety of professionals. There is no widely agreed upon standard for identifying an injury or other trauma-related condition in a veterinary patient as being the result of intentional abuse or neglect. Paradigmatically speaking, veterinary professionals are working in an environment similar to that of pediatricians prior to the seminal work of Kempe, Silverman, Steele, Droegmue, and Silver (1962) which defined the battered child syndrome. Further work is needed to delineate the common patterns of lacerations, contusions, and bone injuries in various stages of healing that would be associated with intentional injury in animals. Also, even more so than in the case of other vulnerable victims, an animal cannot provide a direct account of abuse. More work is required to assist frontline veterinarians to develop a reliable means for identifying incongruities between subjective presentations provided by humans and objective data resulting from examination of the animal (refer to the chapter in the current volume by Arkow and Munro).

Despite an established clinical literature on the relationship between childhood disorders and misconduct toward animals, there is a need to improve standardized measures of child behavior to include animal abuse and cruelty to animals. The Child

Behavior Checklist developed by Achenbach and Edelbrock (1983) only has one item that explicitly asks the parent to rate within the last 6 months whether their child is never, sometimes, or often "cruel to animals." The youth and teacher forms do not include the same item but instead ask whether the child "Fears certain animals, situations, or places other than school." Less directly, the youth is asked to what extent they "like animals" or are "mean to others" or "tease others." Teachers are asked to what extent the student exhibits "Cruelty, bullying, or meanness to others" but not toward animals. The youth is asked, however, about setting fires, acting like the opposite sex, and feeling suicidal. Although parents are perhaps the most reliable informants about conduct problems of their children, elementary teachers often have animals within their classrooms allowing for potential assessment and observation. The need to include multiple informants is clear when one considers the barriers involved for parents and children experiencing domestic violence in their homes to divulge accurate information.

It is encouraging to see two new specialized measures that show promise for enhancing our understanding of pet abuse in children. The "Physical and Emotional Tormenting Against Animals Scale (PET)" and the "Children's Treatment of Animals Questionnaire (CTAQ)" have both been developed recently (Baldry, 2003a, 2003b; Thompson & Gullone, 2003). These measures are self-report questionnaires to be completed by children and adolescents. The purpose of the CTAQ is to examine children's treatment of animals. Correlated significantly with measures of empathy, the CTAQ has 13 items that describe the child's levels of responsibility and communication, as well as negative interactions (such as teasing and yelling), with their companion animals. Although the norms for the measure are based on a small sample of 61 subjects, the CTAQ has demonstrated acceptable internal consistency and test-retest reliability. More work, however, is needed to validate the measure with larger samples and with convergent behavioral indices of socialization and empathy.

The PET was standardized on an Italian adolescent sample (n = 1,396) aged 11 to 17. Previous work by Baldry (2003a, b) reported that a child's animal abuse was associated with prior exposure to animal abuse and with having a father abuse the mother. The questionnaire consists of a nine-item scale that measures indirect or witnessed abuse of an animal perpetrated by another person as well as direct animal abuse by the informant rated on a 5-point Likert scale. Although preliminary validation indicated low scores for the general population that was assessed, the measure may have promise for assessing the degree of animal abuse exposure beyond simple presence or absence, and for use with adolescents at risk for conduct disorder or those exposed to domestic violence.

The realization that adverse and traumatic exposure may result in lasting psychobiological changes (Cohen, Perel, De Bellis, Friedman, & Putnam, 2002) that profoundly affect the ability to make healthy attachments has additional implications for treatment. In this respect, the most effective interventions may be preventive or during the early course of mother–infant or parent–child interaction. A number of researchers (Crockenberg, 1981; Elgar, Curtis, McGrath, Waschbusch, & Stewart, 2003; Martin, 1981; van den Boom, 1994, 1995) have examined the influence of infant temperament identified as "irritable" on responsiveness among mothers. Using a treatment and control group design, such research has demonstrated the dynamic interaction between improved sensitivity in maternal response to the infant's improved mood and adjustment. Thus, positive maternal relationships with the infant can result in increased sociability, self-soothing, and environmental exploration, as well as decreased crying or irritability in the child. Furthermore, it has been reported that such attachment-mediated, positive behavioral effects are sustained at 12 and 42 months of age for the child as evidenced by enhanced indices of child security, cooperation, and positive peer contact. The fact that there are psychobiological correlates and processes associated with the vulnerability to violent and abusive behavior also suggests that psychopharmacological intervention may play a role in modifying such behavior. Maiuro and Avery (1996) have proposed such intervention as an adjunctive treatment for select cases of domestic violence and abuse.

Given what we know about the role that healthy pet ownership plays in the attachment process for children, pet therapy might also be a way of remapping emotional learning with at risk or troubled youth. In this respect, what may be the symptom may also have potential for playing a role in the cure. Just as pets have been shown to be beneficial in the treatment and well-being of autistic and traumatized children, there may be potential for carefully conducted and therapeutically guided exposure to pets for those who have been previously abused and abusive to pets.

Although there is a dearth of data regarding the actual amenability of pet abuse cases to treatment, there is preliminary evidence that numerous types of animal assisted therapy (AAT) can be used to promote such positive human traits of empathy, acceptance, compassion, nurturance, and socialization with severely traumatized children. Barker (1999; Barker, Barker, Dawson, & Knisely, 1997; Barker & Dawson, 1998) showed the strong supportive role of pets in the childhood of sexual abuse survivors. In this retrospective study, they found that, in some cases, the pet was the only reported supportive entity during the survivor's childhood. In an unpublished clinical study, Nebbe (1998) claimed that survivors with a strong human–animal bond in childhood reported less abusive behavior as adults, and lower anger levels than those lacking a strong bond. In one of the few controlled studies to date, Katcher and Wilkins (1994) reported that an AAT/nature education program was therapeutic for children in residential treatment for attention deficit/hyperactive and conduct disorders. The program was specifically effective in decreasing agitated and aggressive behavior, improving cooperation with instructors, engaging students in learning, and in improving behavioral control in regular classrooms. Thus, AAT may also provide a less demanding bridge and an effective ramp to help some "at risk" and pet abusive individuals approach the more challenging task of successfully relating to human peers and adults.

References

Achenbach, T. M., & Edelbrock, C. (1983). *Manual for the child behavior checklist and revised child behavior profile*. Burlington, VT: Queen City Printers.

Ainsworth, M. D. S., Blehar, M. C., Waters, E., & Wall, S. (1978). *Patterns of attachment: A psychological study of the strange situation*. Hillsdale, NJ: Erlbaum.

Albert, A., & Bulcroft, K. (1988). Pets, families, and the life course. *Journal of Marriage and the Family, 50*, 543–552.

American Psychiatric Association. (1987). *Statistical and Diagnostic Manual (third edition revised) (DSM-III-R)*. Washington, DC: American Psychiatric Association.

Arluke, A., Levin, J., Luke, C., & Ascione, F. (1999). The relationship of animal abuse to violence and other forms of antisocial behavior. *Journal of Interpersonal Violence, 14*, 963–975.

Ascione, F. R. (1998). Battered women's reports of their partners' and their children's cruelty to animals. *Journal of Emotional Abuse, 1*, 119–133.

Ascione, F. R. (2000). *Safe havens for pets: Guidelines for programs sheltering pets for women who are battered.* Logan, UT: Utah State University.

Ascione, F. R., Weber, C. V., Thompson, T., Heath, J., Maruyama, M., & Hayashi, K. (2007). Battered pets and domestic violence: Animal abuse reported by women experiencing intimate violence and by non-abused women. *Violence Against Women, 13*, 354–373.

Ascione, F. R., Weber, C. V., & Wood, D. S. (1997). The abuse of animals and domestic violence: A national survey of shelters for women who are battered. *Society & Animals, 5*, 205–218.

Baldry, A. C. (2003a). The development of the P.E.T. scale for the measurement of physical and emotional tormenting against animals in adolescents. *Society & Animals, 12*, 1–17.

Baldry, A. C. (2003b). Animal abuse and exposure to interparental violence in Italy: Assessing of violence in youngsters. *Journal of Interpersonal Violence, 18*, 258–281.

Barash, D. P. (2002, May 24). Evolution, males, and violence. *The Chronicle of Higher Education*, 7–9.

Barker, S. B. (1999). Therapeutic aspects of the human-companion animal interaction, *Psychiatric Times, 16*(2).

Barker, S. B., Barker, R. T., Dawson, K. S., & Knisely, J. S. (1997). The use of the family life space diagram in establishing interconnectedness: A preliminary study of sexual abuse survivors, their significant others and pets. *Individual Psychology, 53*, 435–450.

Barker, S. B., & Dawson, K. S. (1998). The effects of animal-assisted therapy on anxiety ratings of hospitalized psychiatric patients. *Psychiatric Services, 49*, 797–801.

Bartholomew, K. (1990). Avoidance of intimacy: An attachment perspective, *Journal of Social and Personal Relationships, 7*, 147–158.

Bartholomew, K., Henderson, A., & Dutton. D. G. (2001). Insecure attachment and abusive intimate relationships. In C. Clulow (Ed.), *Adult attach-ment and couple psychotherapy* (pp. 43–61). Philadelphia: Taylor & Francis.

Bartholomew, K., & Horowitz, L. M. (1991). Attachment styles among young adults: A test of a four category model. *Journal of Personality and Social Psychology, 61*, 226–244.

Becker, K. D., Stuewig, J., Herrera, V. M., & McCloskey, L. A. (2004). A study of firesetting and animal cruelty in children: Family influences and adolescent outcomes. *Journal of the American Academy of Child & Adolescent Psychiatry, 43*, 905–912.

Beirne, P. (2003). From animal abuse to interhuman violence? A critical review of the progression thesis. *Society & Animals, 12*, 34–65.

Bell, L. (2001). Abusing children—abusing animals. *Journal of Social Work, 1*, 223–234.

Blair, R. J. R. (2001). Neurocognitive models of aggression, the antisocial personality disorders, and psychopathy. *Journal of Neurology, Neurosurgery and Psychiatry, 71*, 727–731.

Bowlby, J. (1969). *Attachment and loss: Vol. 1. Attachment* (2nd ed.). London: Hogarth Press.

Bowlby, J. (1982). *Attachment: Attachment and loss* (2nd ed.). New York: Basic Books.

Bowlby, J. (1988). *A secure base: Parent-child attachment and healthy human development.* New York: Basic Books.

Brennan, K. A., Clark, C. L., & Shaver, P. R. (1998). Self-report measurement of adult romantic attachment: An integrative overview. In J. A. Simpson & W. S. Rholes (Eds.), *Attachment theory and close relationships* (pp. 46–76). New York: Guilford Press.

Browne, A. (1987). *When battered women kill.* New York: Free Press.

Bufkin, J. L., & Luttrell, V. R. (2005). Neuroimaging studies of aggressive and violent behavior. *Trauma, Violence, & Abuse, 6*, 176–191.

Bulcroft, K. (1990). Pets in the American family. *People, Animals, Environment, 8*, 13–14.

Burke, J. D., Loeber, R., & Birmaher, B. (2004). Oppositional defiant disorder and conduct disorder: A review of the past 10 years, part II. *Focus, 2*, 558–576.

Byrd, R. S., & Weitzman, M. (1996). Bed-wetting in U.S. children: Epidemiology and related behavior problems, *Pediatrics, 98*, 414–420.

Campbell, J. C. (2004). *Danger assessment.* Baltimore: Johns Hopkins University, School of Nursing.

Caspi, A., Moffit, T. E., Morgan, J., Rutter, M., Taylor, A., & Arseneault, L. (2004). Maternal expressed emotion predicts children's antisocial behavior problems: Using monozygotic-twin differences to identify environmental effects on behavioral development. *Developmental Psychology, 40*, 149–161.

Cicchetti, G., & Rogosch, F. A. (2001). Diverse patterns of neuroendocrine activity in maltreated children. *Development and Psychopathology, 13*, 677–693.

Cohen, J. A., Perel, J. M., De Bellis, M. D., Friedman, M. J., & Putnam, F. W. (2002). Treating traumatized children: Clinical implications of the psychobiology of PTSD. *Trauma, Violence, & Abuse, 3*, 91–108.

Cohen, R. A., Brumm, V., Zawachi, T. M., Paul, R., Sweet, L., & Rosenbaum, A. (2003). Impulsivity and verbal deficits associated with domestic violence. *Journal of the International Neuropsychological Society, 9*, 760–770.

Cohen, R. A., Rosenbaum, A., Kane, R. L., Warnken, W. J., & Benjamin, S. (1999). Neuropsychological correlates of domestic violence. *Violence and Victims, 14*, 397–411.

Crockenberg, S. B. (1981). Infant irritability, mother responsiveness, and social support influences on the security of infant-mother attachment. *Child Development, 52*, 857–886.

De Bellis, M. D. (2005). The psychobiology of neglect. *Child Maltreatment, 10*, 150–172.

Decety, J., & Jackson, P. L. (2004). The functional architecture of human empathy. *Behavioral and Cognitive Neuroscience Review, 3*, 71–100.

Diamond, A. (2002). Normal development of prefrontal cortex from birth to young adulthood: cognitive functions, anatomy, and biochemistry. In D. T. Stuss & R. T. Knight (Eds.), *Principles of frontal lobe function* (p. 503). New York: Oxford.

Diamond, M., & Hopson, J. (1999). *Magic trees of the mind: How to nurture your child's intelligence, creativity, and health emotions from birth through adolescence.* New York: Penguin.

Downey, G., & Coyne, J. C. (1990). Children of depressed parents: An integrative review. *Psychological Bulletin, 108*, 50–76.

Dutton, D. G., Saunders, K., Starzomski, A. J., & Bartholomew, K. (1994). Intimacy-anger and insecure attachment as precursors of abuse in intimate relationships. *Journal of Applied Social Psychology, 24*, 1367–1386.

Duncan, A., & Miller, C. (2002). The impact of an abusive family context on childhood animal cruelty and adult violence. *Aggression and Violent Behavior, 7*, 365–383.

Duncan, A., Thomas, J. C., & Miller, C. (2005). Significance of family risk factors in development of childhood animal cruelty in adolescent boys with conduct problems. *Journal of Family Violence, 20*, 235–239.

Elgar, F. J., Curtis, L. J., McGrath, P. J., Waschbusch, D. A., & Stewart, S. H. (2003). Antecedent-consequent conditions in maternal mood and child adjustment problems: A four-year cross-lagged study. *Journal of Clinical Child and Adolescent Psychology, 32*, 362–374.

Ellis, L. (2005). A theory explaining biological correlates of criminality. *European Journal of Criminology, 2*, 287–315.

Farran, D. C. (2001). Critical periods in early intervention. In D. B. Bailey, Jr., J. T. Bruer, F. J. Symons, & J. W. Litchman (Eds.), *Critical thinking about critical periods* (pp. 233–266). Baltimore, MD: Paul H. Brookes.

Flynn, C. P. (2000). Battered women and their animal companions: Symbolic interaction between human and animals. *Society & Animals, 8*, 99–127.

Foley, D. L., Eaves, L. J., Wormley, B., Silberg, J. L., Maes, H. H., Kuhn, J., & Riley, B. (2004). Childhood, adversity, monoamine oxidase A genotype, and risk for conduct disorder. *Archives of General Psychiatry, 61*, 738–744.

Fraley, R., & Spieker, S. (2003). Are infant attachment patterns continuously or categorically distributed? *Developmental Psychology, 39*, 387–414.

Fraley, R. C., & Waller, N. G. (1998). Adult attachment patterns: A test of the typological model. In J. A. Simpson & W. S. Rholes (Eds.), *Attachment theory and close relationships* (pp. 77–114). New York: Guilford Press.

Frankie, W. G., Lombardo, I., New, A. S., Goodman, M., Talbot, P. S., Huang, Y., et al. (2005). Brain serotonin transporter distribution in subjects with impulsive aggressivity: A positron emission study with [^{11}C]McN 5652. *The American Journal of Psychiatry, 162*, 915–923.

Freud, S. In M. Bonaparte (1994). *Topsy: The story of a golden-haired chow* (p. 3). Somerset, NJ: Transaction Books.

Gardner, J., Karmel, B., & Flory, M. (2003). Arousal modulation of neonatal visual attention: Implications for development. In S. Soraci & K. Murata-Soraci (Eds.), *Visual information processing* (pp. 125–153). Westport: Praeger.

Gerbasi, K. C. (2004). Gender and nonhuman animal cruelty convictions: Data from pet-abuse.com. *Society & Animals, 12*, 359–365.

Gleyzer, R., Felthous, A. R., & Holzer, C. E. (2002). Animal cruelty and psychiatric disorders. *Journal of the American Academy of Psychiatric Law, 30*, 257–265.

Gray, J. A. (1975). *Elements of a two-process theory of learning*. New York: Academic Press.

Gunnar, M. R., & Vasquez, D. M. (2001). Low cortisol and a flattening of expected daytime rhythm: Potential indices of risk in human development. *Development and Psychopathology, 13*, 515–538.

Hare, R. D. (1996). Psychopathy: A clinical construct whose time has come. *Criminal Justice and Behavior, 23*, 25–54.

Harlow, H. F., Harlow, M. K., & Suomi, S. J. (1971). From thought to therapy: Lessons from a primate laboratory. *American Scientist, 59*, 538–549.

Hazan, C., & Shaver, P. (1987). Romantic love conceptualized as an attachment process. *Journal of Personality and Social Psychology, 52*, 511–524.

Henderson, A. J. Z., Bartholomew, K., Trinke, S. J., & Kwong, M. J. (2005). When loving mean hurting: An exploration of attachment and intimate abuse in a community sample. *Journal of Family Violence, 20*, 219–232.

Henry, B. C. (2004). The relationship between animal cruelty, delinquency, and attitudes toward the treatment of animals. *Animals & Society, 12*, 185–207.

Hensley, C., & Tallichet, S. E. (2005). Learning to be cruel?: Exploring the onset and frequency of animal cruelty. *International Journal of Offender Therapy and Comparative Criminology, 49*, 37–47.

Herman, A. I., Philbeck, J. W., Vasilopoulos, N. L., & Depetrillo, P. B. (2003). Serotonin transporter promoter polymorphism and differences in alcohol consumption behavior in a college student population. *Alcohol and Alcoholism, 38*, 446–449.

Hershorn, M., & Rosenbaum, A. (1991). Over- versus undercontrolled hostility: Application of the construct to the classification of martially violent men. *Violence and Victims, 6*, 151–158.

Hoffman, M. J. (2000). *Empathy and moral development*. Cambridge, UK: Cambridge University Press.

Humane Society of the United States. (2006). Report of animal cruelty cases (2003). Retrieved June 26, 2006, from http://www.hsus.org/web-files/PDF/2003AnimalCrueltyRprt.pdf

Johnson, D. E., Miller, L.C., Iverson, S., Thomas, W., Franchino, B., Dole, K., et al., (1992). The health of children adopted from Romania. *Journal of the American Medical Association, 268*, 3446–3451.

Katcher, A. H., & Wilkins, G. G. (1994). The use of animal assisted therapy and education with attention-deficit hyperactive and conduct disorders. *Interactions 12*(4), 1–5.

Kempe, C. H., Silverman, F. N., Steele, B. F., Droegmue, W., & Silver, H. K. (1962). The battered-child syndrome. *Journal of the American Medical Association, 181*, 17–24.

Kreppner, J. M., O'Connor, T. G., Rutter, M., & English and Romanian Adoptees Study Team. (2001). Can inattention/overactivity be an institutional deprivation syndrome? *Journal of Abnormal Child Psychology, 29*, 513–528.

LeDoux, J. (1996). *The emotional brain: The mysterious underpinnings of emotional life*. New York: Simon & Schuster.

Lester, D. (1975). Firesetting. *Corrective and Social Psychiatry and Journal of Behavior Technology, Methods, and Therapy, 21*, 22–26.

Levine, D. S. (2002). Introduction to the special issue on brain development and caring behavior. *Brain and Mind, 3*, 1–7.

Lezak, M. D. (1983). *Neuropsychological assessment: Second Edition*. New York: Oxford Press.

Lezak, M. D. (1995). *Neuropsychological assessment*. New York: Oxford University Press.

Lipton, J. E., & Barash, D. P. (2005). Sociobiology. In B. Sadock & V. Sadoc (Eds.), *Comprehensive textbook of psychiatry, Volume 1* (pp. 634–644). Baltimore, MD: Williams & Wilkins.

Luria, A. R. (1966). *Higher cortical functions in man*. New York: Basic Books.

Luria, A. R. (1973). *The working brain*. New York: Basic Books.

Lynam, D. R. (1996). The early identification of chronic offenders: Who is the fledgling psychopath? *Psychological Bulletin, 120*, 209–234.

Macovei, O. (1986). *The medical and social problems of the handicapped in children's institutions in Iasi Bucharest, Romania*. Bucharest, Romania: Institutl de Igiena si Sanatate Publica.

Maiuro, R. D., & Avery, D. H. (1996). Psychopharmacological treatment of aggressive behavior: Implications for domestically violent men. *Violence and Victims, 11*, 239–261. Also in L. K. Hamberger & C. Renzetti (Eds.), *Partner Abuse*. New York: Springer.

Maiuro, R. D., Cahn, T. S., & Vitaliano, P. P. (1986). Assertiveness and hostility in domestically violent men. *Violence and Victims, 1*, 279–289.

Maiuro, R. D., Cahn, T. S., Vitaliano, P. P., Wagner, B. C., & Zegree, J. B. (1988). Anger, hostility, and depression in domestically violent versus generally assaultive men and nonviolent control subjects. *Journal of Consulting and Clinical Psychology, 56*, 17–23.

Maiuro, R. D., & Eberle, J. A. (in press). State standards for domestic violence perpetrator treatment: Current status, trends, and recommendations. *Violence and Victims*.

Maiuro, R. D., Townes, B. T., Vitaliano, P. P., & Trupin, E. W. (1984). Age norms for the Reitan-Indiana Neuropsychological Test Battery for Children Aged 5–8. In R. A. Glow (Ed.), *Advances in the behavioral measurement of children: A research annual* (pp. 159–173). Greenwich, CT: JAI Press.

Maiuro, R. D., Wachs, K., Tzovarras, T., Wu, A., & Vitaliano, P. P. (2003). *Correlates of pet abusing versus non-pet abusing men who commit domestic violence*. Paper presented at the 8th International Family Violence Research Conference, Durham, NH: Family Research Laboratory & Crimes Against Children Research Center.

Martin, J. A. (1981). A longitudinal study of the consequences of early mother infant interaction: A microanalytic approach. *Child Development, 46*(3 Serial No. 190).

McBurnett, K., Lahey, B. B., Rathouz, P. J., & Loeber, R. (2000). Low salivary cortisol and persistent aggression in boys referred for disruptive behavior. *Archives of General Psychiatry, 57*, 38–43.

Meloy, J. R. (1992). *Violent attachments*. Northvale, NJ: Jason Aronson.

Merz-Perez, L., Heide, K. M., & Silverman, I. J. (2001). Childhood cruelty to animals and subsequent violence against humans. *International Journal of Offender Therapy and Comparative Criminology, 45*, 556–573.

Nebbe, L. (1998). The human-animal bond's role with the abused child. Paper presented at the Delta Society 17th Annual Conference, Seattle, WA.

Patterson, G. R. (2002). The early development of coercive family process. In J. B. Reid, G. R. Patterson, & J. Synder (Eds.), *Antisocial behavior in children and adolescents: A developmental analysis and model for intervention* (pp. 25–44). Washington, DC: American Psychology Association.

Perry, B. D. (2002). Childhood experience and the expression of genetic potential: What childhood neglect tells us about nature and nurture. *Brain and Mind, 3*, 79–100.

Pollak, S., & Sinha, P. (2002). Effects of early experience on children's recognition of facial displays of emotion. *Developmental Psychology, 38*, 784–791.

Poresky, R. H. (1996). Companion animals and other factors affecting young children's development. *Anthrozoös, 9*, 159–168.

Prentky, R. A., & Carter, D. L. (1984). The predictive value of the triad for sex offenders. *Behavioral Sciences and the Law, 2*, 341–354.

Quinn, D. (1992). *Ishmael: An adventure of the mind and spirit* (p. 238). New York: Bantam Books.

Quinsey, V. L., Chaplin, T. C., & Upfold, D. (1989). Arsonists and sexual arousal to fire setting: Correlation unsupported. *Journal of Behavior Therapy and Experimental Psychiatry, 20*, 203–209.

Raine, A., Moffitt, T. E., Loeber, R., Stouthamer-Loeber, M., Caspi, A., & Lynam, D. (2005). Neurocognitive impairments in boys on the life-course persistent antisocial path. *Journal of Abnormal Psychology, 114*, 38–49.

Reitan, R. M., & Davison, L. A. (Eds.). (1974). *Clinical neuropsychology: Current status and applications*. Washington, DC: V. H. Winston & Sons.

Robbins, E., & Robbins, L. (1967). Arson: With special reference to pyromania. *New York State Journal of Medicine, 67*, 795–798.

Rosenbaum, A., & Hoge, S. K. (1989). Head injury and marital aggression. *American Journal of Psychiatry, 146*, 1048–1051.

Rosenbaum, A., Hoge, S. K., Adelman, S. A., Warnken, W. J., Fletcher, K. E., & Kane, R. L. (1994). Head injury in partner-abusive men. *Journal of Consulting and Clinical Psychology, 62*, 1187–1193.

Rosenbaum, A., & Maiuro, R. D. (1989). Eclectic approaches in working with men who batter. In P. L. Caesar & L. K. Hamberger (Eds.), *Therapeutic interventions with batterers: Theory, practice, and programs* (pp. 165–195). New York: Springer.

Rosenbaum, A., & Maiuro, R. D. (1990). Perpetrators of spouse abuse. In R. T. Ammerman & M. Hersen (Eds.), *Treatment of family violence: Sourcebook* (pp. 280–309). New York: John Wiley & Sons.

Rothstein, R. (1963). Explorations of ego structures of firesetting children. *Archives of General Psychiatry, 9*, 246–253.

Rourke, B. P., Bakker, D. J., Fisk, J. L., & Strang, J. D. (1983). *Child neuropsychology: An introduction to theory, research, and clinical practice*. New York: Guilford Press.

Sakheim, G. A., & Osborn, E. (1999). Severe versus nonsevere firesetters revisited. *Child Welfare, 78*, 411–434.

Sakheim, G. A., Osborn, E., & Abrams, D. (1991). Toward a clearer differentiation of high-risk from low-risk firesetters. *Child Welfare, 70*, 489–503.

Saltzman, K. M., Holden, G. W., & Holahan, C. J. (2005). The psychobiology of children exposed to marital violence. *Journal of Clinical Child & Adolescent Psychology, 34*, 129–139.

Saunders, E. B., & Awad, G. A. (1991). Adolescent female firesetters [Special issue: Child and adolescent psychiatry]. *Canadian Journal of Psychiatry, 36*, 401–404.

Serpell, J. A. (1999). Animals in children's lives. *Society & Animals, 7*, 1–8.

Serrano, J. M., Iglesias, J., & Loesches, A. (1992). Visual-discrimination and recognition of facial expressions of anger, fear, and surprise in 4-month-old to 6-month-old infants. *Developmental Psychobiology, 25*, 411–425.

Skeem, J. L., Mulvey, E. P., Appelbaum, P., Banks, S., Grisso, T., Silver, E., et al. (2004). Identifying subtypes of civil psychiatric patients at high risk for violence. *Criminal Justice and Behavior, 31*, 392–437.

Spitz, R. A. (1945). Hospitalism: An inquiry into the genesis of psychiatric conditions in early childhood. *Psychoanalytic Study of the Child, 1*, 53–74.

Teichner, G., Golden, C. J., Van Hasselt, V. B., & Peterson, A. (2001). Assessment of cognitive functioning in men who batter. *International Journal of Neuroscience, 111*, 241–253.

Thompson, K. L., & Gullone, E. (2003). The children's treatment of animals questionnaire (CTAQ): A psychometric investigation. *Society & Animals, 11*, 1–15.

Timmerman, I. G., & Emmelkamp, P. M. (2006). The relationship between attachment styles and Cluster B personality disorders in prisoners and forensic inpatients. *International Journal of Law in Psychiatry, 29*, 48–56.

Trauner, D. A., Nass, R., & Ballantyne, A. (2001). Behavioral profiles of children and adolescents after pre- or perinatal unilateral brain damage. *Brain, 124*, 995–1002.

Triebenbacher, S. L. (1998). Pets as transitional objects: Their role in children's emotional development. *Psychological Reports, 82*, 191–200.

Van den Boom, D. C. (1994). The influence of temperament and mothering on attachment and exploration: An experimental manipulation of sensitive responsiveness among lower-class mothers with irritable infants. *Child Development, 65*, 1457–1477.

Van den Boom, D. C. (1995). Do first-year intervention effects endure? Follow-up during toddlerhood of a sample of Dutch irritable infants. *Child Development, 66*, 1798–1816.

Van Voorhees, E., & Scarpa, A. (2004). The effects of child maltreatment on the hypothalamic-pituitary-adrenal axis. *Trauma, Violence, & Abuse, 5*, 333–352.

Ward, T., & Hudson, S. M. (1996). Attachment style in sex offenders: A preliminary report. *Journal of Sex Research, 3*, 17–26.

Wax, D. E., & Haddox, V. G. (1974). Enuresis, fire setting, and animal cruelty: A useful danger signal in predicting vulnerability of adolescent males to assaultive behavior. *Child Psychiatry and Human Development, 4*, 151–156.

Wechsler, D. (1974). *Manual for the Wechsler Intelligence Scale for Children—Revised (WISC-R)*. Cleveland: Psychological Corporation.

Wechsler, D. (1989). Manual for the Wechsler Pre-school and Primary Scale of Intelligence—Revised (WPPSI-R). Cleveland: Psychological Corporation.

Weinstock, M. (2001). Alternations induced by gestational stress in brain morphology and behavior of the offspring. *Progress in Neurobiology, 65,* 427–451.

Weisz A. N., Tolman, R. M., & Saunders, D. G. (2000). Assessing the risk of severe domestic violence: The importance of survivors "predictions." *Journal of Interpersonal Violence, 15,* 75–90.

Yarnell, H. (1940). Firesetting in children. *American Journal of Orthopsychiatry, 10,* 272–287.

A Sociological Analysis of Animal Abuse

Clifton P. Flynn
University of South Carolina Upstate

Until relatively recently, sociology had ignored human–animal interaction, including human violence against other animals (Arluke & Sanders, 1996). In 1979, Bryant admonished his fellow sociologists, calling them "singularly derelict" for overlooking our roles and relationships with animals. He went on to say that it may be in the area of crime, delinquency, and deviancy involving animals—"zoological crime"—that sociologists will "encounter the most fertile phenomenological fields to plow" for human–animal research in sociology (Bryant, 1979, p. 412).

Over a decade later, Bryant's call for including animals within sociology generally, and more particularly, deviance involving animals (including animal cruelty), had gone largely unheeded. In fact, Bryant and Snizek (1993, p. 32) emphatically stated that "no area of human–animal behavior is more neglected than animal-related crime and deviance."

Since this time, however, sociologists have begun to consider human interaction with other animals, including, as Rowan (1992) termed, the "dark side" of human–animal relationships. This chapter provides a sociological perspective for analyzing animal abuse. Historically, animal cruelty has been framed and analyzed from a psychological perspective, with social and cultural factors given little attention. After discussing the relevance and significance of a sociological approach to animal abuse, structural factors that help explain animal abuse will be examined. Then, specific sociological research on animal cruelty will be explored, along with relevant theoretical perspectives. Finally, I will look at future directions for sociological scholarship on animal abuse.

Psychological vs. Sociological Models of Violence and Abuse

In the early years of research on family violence in the 1960s and 1970s, the initial studies were undertaken employing primarily a psychiatric or psychological model. From this individualistic orientation, wife or child abusers were viewed as mentally ill or "sick." Social factors, such as gender, age, social position, and societal attitudes and norms regarding animals and their treatment, received little attention from researchers.

Yet as Gelles (1993, 1997) and Straus (1980) have pointed out, psychological explanations, while attractive, are inadequate for explaining family violence. Gelles argues that psychological models of family violence lead us to focus on the most extreme cases of abuse, causing perpetrators to be stereotyped as crazy, sadistic monsters, while ignoring others whose profiles and actions fail to match the pathological stereotype. Such a social construction of family violence enables us to "construct a problem that is perpetrated by 'people other than us'" (Gelles, 1993, p. 40). Gelles also argues that the notion that abusers are mentally ill amounts to little more than a circular argument. The abuse itself is both the behavior that is attempting to be explained, and simultaneously, the factor serving as the explanation. Further, clinicians have been unsuccessful in distinguishing abusers from non-abusers using psychological profiles alone. Straus (1980) estimates that only about 10% of abusive incidents can be explained by mental illness.

A similar pattern has occurred regarding animal cruelty (Arluke, 2002; Beirne, 1999; Flynn, 2000a, 2001). Much like the early research on family violence in the 1960s and 1970s, the initial studies on animal cruelty also applied a psychological model (see Rigdon & Tapia, 1977; Tapia, 1971). Early researchers, often clinicians, viewed perpetrators as having defective personalities.

A psychological approach continues to dominate research on animal abuse. According to Arluke (2002), "until recently, understanding violence toward animals remained the sole province of psychologists and animal welfare advocates. Their approach sees animal abuse as an impulsive act that reflects psychopathological problems in the offender" (p. 405). Thus, the social context of animal abuse has been largely overlooked.

Just as with family violence, individual-level explanations for animal abuse are insufficient. Animal abuse is undoubtedly a social phenomenon (Flynn, 2001). As will become clear, violence toward animals virtually always occurs in the context of human interaction and relationships. Whether animals are being threatened or abused by perpetrators of family violence to control wives or silence victims of sexual abuse; by victims of family violence to scapegoat less powerful animals; or by male adolescents who are trying to prove their manhood, impress their peers, or express their anger at social or personal rejection, animal cruelty also involves, and reveals much about, our relations with other humans. As we shall see in the next section, animal abuse cannot be fully understood by relying solely on the characteristics of individuals. Rather, social structural factors, including social institutions and norms, contribute significantly to our understanding of cruelty to animals.

Social Structure and Animal Abuse

Gender

Perhaps the most consistent factor related to animal abuse is gender. Regardless of the source of the data—official records (e.g., Arluke & Luke, 1997; Coston & Protz, 1998), college undergraduates (e.g., Flynn, 1999b), school-age children (e.g., Baldry, 2003), or clinical samples (e.g., Rigdon & Tapia, 1977; Tapia, 1971)—perpetrators are overwhelmingly male. This is true irrespective of age or nationality. The only exception involves hoarding, a passive form of cruelty whereby individuals keep excessive numbers of neglected animals in poor conditions leading to poor health, starvation, behavioral problems, and death. Patronek (1996) estimates that approximately three-fourths of all hoarders are

female (see *Animal Hoarding: A Third Dimension of Animal Abuse* by Patronek, this text).

Arluke and Luke (1997) examined all animal cruelty cases prosecuted in Massachusetts between 1975 and 1996. Approximately 97% of the perpetrators were male. This finding fits with other criminological studies showing that crimes in general, and particularly violent crimes, are significantly more likely to be committed by males. In addition, the majority of complainants in these cases were female.

In studies involving college undergraduates, again males are typically three to four times more likely than females to report having committed animal abuse in their childhood (Flynn, 1999a, 1999b; Miller & Knutson, 1997). Flynn (1999a, 1999b) found that not only were male students more likely to have perpetrated animal abuse, they were also more likely to have witnessed it. Two-thirds of males had either witnessed or committed animal cruelty, compared with 40% of females. Yet among females who had experienced animal abuse, three-fourths had only witnessed it; however, among the males, half had abused animals.

And in studies of children and adolescents, abuse by males predominates. Baldry (2003) surveyed 1,392 Italian youth ages 9 to 17, finding that boys committed two-thirds of the animal abuse. For all types of abuse assessed by Baldry (bothering, tormenting, harming, being cruel to, and hitting animals), boys were two to three times more likely to have engaged in abuse than girls.

What explains these gender differences in animal cruelty? Both male socialization and the dominant position of males in society are likely contributors to their abuse of animals. Masculine socialization includes lessons of dominance and aggression. Given a male socialization process that minimizes empathy and encourages aggression, and given a social structure in which men's dominant position in society leads them to both minimize empathy and to use violence as a way to maintain dominance, we should not be surprised at the high rate of male violence against animals (and humans).

Age

The limited data from official records suggests that, like other forms of criminal behavior, late adolescence and early adulthood are typical ages for the perpetration of animal cruelty. In the Massachusetts study cited above, the average age of all perpetrators was 30. Slightly over one-fourth of the offenders were teenagers, and over half—56%—were under 30 (Arluke & Luke, 1997).

Arluke and Luke (1997) also found that age was related to the kind of animal abused, as well as the method of cruelty used. Adults were more likely to hurt dogs and to do so by shooting. For adolescents, cats were the more likely victims, and beating was the most common method of abuse. Such variations probably are related to different age statuses. Adults not only have greater access to guns, but adult males may feel an obligation to protect their families and their property, and dogs may be seen as more serious threats than cats. Teens, especially males, are more likely to commit expressive, rather than instrumental, violence, whereby inflicting harm is the intended purpose of the abuse. Consequently, smaller animals, like cats, are preferable targets of abuse.

Age also appears to be relevant when looking at nonclinical samples of children. In the study of Italian school-age children, ages 9 to 17, older children were more likely to commit animal abuse than younger ones. In general, the rate of abuse increased as children moved from elementary school (10.4%–28.1%), to middle school (13.8%–36.9%), to high school (18.6%–42.3%). Of course, this may also indicate that, compared to younger children, older children have had more opportunity to abuse animals.

There is limited evidence that age may be related to different forms of animal abuse among children. Flynn (1999a, 1999b) found that although school-age children were more likely than teens to have hurt or tortured animals, adolescents were more likely to have killed stray animals.

Childhood Socialization

Consistent with research on other forms of violence, experiencing violence in one's family of origin, whether as a victim, a perpetrator, or witness, has been shown to be related to subsequent animal abuse. Clinical studies of troubled youth who have abused animals have revealed that many were also victims of violence themselves, often at the hands of their fathers (Rigdon & Tapia, 1977; Tapia, 1971). Kellert and Felthous (1985) examined the history of child abuse and childhood animal cruelty among a sample of aggressive criminals, nonaggressive criminals, and noncriminals. Aggressive criminals were more likely than the other two groups to have committed animal cruelty as children, and to have been abused as children.

In the first study to directly investigate the link between family violence and animal abuse, DeViney, Dickert, and Lockwood (1983) found that in 88% of New Jersey families that had been identified by authorities as being involved in physical child abuse, pet abuse had also occurred. Although fathers were the abusers in two-thirds of the cases, in the remaining cases, the children themselves were the abusers.

The study of Italian students conducted by Baldry (2003) shows the link between experiencing family violence and children's animal abuse. Students who had harmed animals were more likely than those who had not to have been exposed to some form of domestic violence, as well as animal abuse, by their parents. In particular, animal abusers were more likely to have witnessed physical violence and threats of violence between their parents (this was true for both father-to-mother violence and mother-to-father violence). In addition, youth who had abused animals were more likely to have fathers and mothers who had been violent toward animals.

Peers are also important agents of socialization regarding animal abuse. Baldry found that children who had witnessed a peer's violence against an animal were more likely to engage in animal abuse than those who had not. Overall, the strongest predictors of a child's abuse of animals were violence against animals by their mothers and their peers.

Boys may also engage in animal cruelty to prove their masculinity to, and thus gain approval from, their peers. In the Massachusetts study, juvenile offenders were much more likely than adult offenders to have committed animal abuse in the presence of others. Nearly half of minors (48%) abused animals in a group, while 7 of 8 adult offenders committed animal cruelty alone (Arluke & Luke, 1997).

Baldry (2003) also sought to determine whether the predictors of children's animal abuse differed depending on whether the children had been abused themselves by their parents and exposed to domestic violence (exposed-abused) or had just been exposed to domestic violence (exposed only). Interestingly, for both groups, gender (males), peer's animal abuse, and mother's animal abuse were the strongest predictors. For the exposed-abused group, father's animal abuse, age, and mother-to-father violence were also significant predictors; for the exposed-only group, only father's animal abuse reached significance. These results support social learning theory, suggesting the important role of modeling in children's socialization regarding animal abuse.

Cultural Attitudes and Norms

As has been noted by other observers, one of the most consistent features of our attitudes toward other animals is inconsistency. Much of the western world holds contradictory, conflicting, paradoxical attitudes about animals (Arluke & Sanders, 1996; Rowan, 1992). Survey studies have revealed that while a majority of Americans believe that animals should live free of suffering and deserve moral consideration similar to human beings (e.g., Agnew, 1998), a majority also believe in and support the practices that cause the most pain and suffering to other animals—eating animals for food and animal experimentation.

Historically, western philosophical and religious traditions have reinforced an instrumental view of other animals, constructing them as lesser objects to be exploited by "man" (Singer, 1990). Judeo-Christian tradition reinforces human superiority over animals, arguing that humans are superior to other animals and have "dominion" over them. This anthropocentric view helps to render other animals powerless, making them more vulnerable to exploitation and abuse. A study of Christian denominations in Australia found that less humane attitudes toward animals were held by members of more conservative denominations (Bowd & Bowd, 1989).

Western philosophical traditions, starting with the ancient Greeks and climaxing with Descartes, also emphasize animals' lower status and lack of moral standing. The Cartesian view holds that animals are simply machines that are incapable of feeling pain, and thus are not worthy of any moral consideration. The combined effect of the Judeo-Christian perspective and Cartesian dualism continues to influence the attitudes of contemporary individuals, making it easier not only to dismiss or ignore animal suffering, but perhaps also easier to inflict it.

As noted above, most of the practices that render the greatest amount of harm to the greatest number of animals—factory farming, animal experimentation, product testing, and hunting and trapping—are legal. These practices not only appear to have the support of most Americans, but equally importantly, are supported by such powerful social institutions of religion, science, and the government. The result of the extensive amount of socially acceptable violence against other animals may make unacceptable violence—animal abuse—more likely as well.

Finally, some animal abuse may result from cultural attitudes that are biased against particular species of animals. If certain animals are viewed more negatively than others, they may be at a greater risk for victimization. Cats, for example, are often a victim of cultural prejudice. One study of 16 aggressive criminals who had committed extensive and severe animal abuse as children found that cats were victimized more often and were subjected to a greater variety of abuses than any other type of animal (Felthous & Kellert, 1987).

Power and Inequality

In our anthropocentric society, humans enjoy absolute power over other animals. As with other forms of family violence, more powerful members of society, typically male, are more likely to use violence against less powerful others, often women, children, and other animals. Obviously, animal abusers are larger physically than their nonhuman victims. Most animal abusers tend to select victims that are smaller and physically weaker compared to themselves. Dogs, cats, and small animals (such as rabbits, birds, rodents, and reptiles) are the most common victims of animal cruelty (Arluke & Luke, 1997; Coston & Protz, 1998; Flynn, 1999b). Felthous and Kellert's (1987) study of adult men (mostly aggressive criminals) who had perpetrated animal cruelty in childhood found that typically their target animals were harmless vertebrates. Not only are these animals more accessible, they are also safer targets. Few reported abusing animals because the animals were dangerous or because the animal had attacked them.

Socially, as noted above, since animals are valued less than humans, they are not always seen as worthy of moral consideration. Legally, animals are considered as property, and this status makes them easy targets for abuse. Since humans determine the laws and norms regarding how animals are treated, which animals are worthy of legal protection, and when the maltreatment of animals is socially "acceptable" or "necessary," then humans' dominant status means that animal abuse is a low-risk act and abusers are not likely to be deterred from their harmful actions. Finally, animals are the only victims of systematic discrimination and exploitation who truly cannot speak on their own behalf. Thus the superior physical, legal, and social status of humans contributes to the abuse of other animals.

Social Institutions

Family. Years of family violence scholarship have revealed that the unique characteristics of families contribute to violence among family members (Gelles & Straus, 1988). In particular, high levels of interdependence, inequality, and privacy make it likely that assaults may occur within families, leading Gelles and Straus (1979) to refer to families as "violence-prone interaction settings."

In America, households are more likely to contain companion animals than children, and homes with children are even more likely to have pets. Studies reveal that a large majority who share their homes with other animals consider them to be members of the family (Albert & Bulcroft, 1988; Cain, 1983; Siegel, 1993). Unfortunately, because of their status as family members, pets may also be vulnerable to abuse. Stress experienced by families, including stress that might be caused by pets, may contribute to violence against other family members, including animals.

Veevers (1985) argued that companion animals may serve the function of human surrogates in families, including that of surrogate enemies. As such, the potential for pets to be victimized by other family members was evident. She suggested that pets might be victimized as "scapegoats" or that they might be threatened or harmed to control or emotionally abuse another family member. She also hypothesized that violence against companion animals might serve as a training ground for later interpersonal violence.

Criminal Justice System. Although all 50 states have anti-cruelty statutes, current laws may fail to protect animals and may have little deterrent effect (Arkow, 1999; Francione, 1996; Lacroix, 1999). They are ineffective because they were enacted not to protect animals, but to protect humans from other humans, and to do so while only minimally interfering with property rights. Since animals have always been, and still are, considered property, they have no legal standing.

Additionally, the legal profession has been reluctant to legislate and enforce animal cruelty laws for a number of reasons, including (a) society's ambivalent attitudes toward animals; (b) the difficulty in defining cruelty; (c) most violations are misdemeanors, and thus are not prosecuted aggressively; and (d) a lack of funding and personnel for enforcement, which has led states to delegate enforcement authority to humane organizations (Kruse, 2002; Lacroix, 1999).

In Massachusetts from 1975 to 1996, of the 268 cases of animal cruelty that were prosecuted, less than half resulted in a guilty verdict. Only a third of those prosecuted were fined, 21% had to pay restitution, 20% were given probation, 10% went to jail, 10% were required to undergo counseling, and 7% were ordered to do community service (Arluke & Luke, 1997). The minimal nature of these sentences is even more distressing when one considers that these cases, because they were taken to trial, are likely to represent the most serious offenses.

Similar results were found for recent animal cruelty complaints in a North Carolina jurisdiction (Coston & Protz, 1998). Of the 958 complaints received in Charlotte/Mecklenburg County, North Carolina in 1996, only 27% were unfounded. Of the remaining grounded complaints, 75% had received at least one prior complaint; 15% had two prior complaints, and 10% had three to nine complaints. Yet, only six cases resulted in an arrest—all involving animal fighting—and only one of those resulted in a trial where the defendant was found guilty and received prison time. The animal was impounded in only 5% of the cases, and rarely was a criminal summons issued. Most of the time, the police just made suggestions, tried to educate the owner, made follow-up visits, or issued a warning.

In short, when animal cruelty is only mildly sanctioned through weak laws, sporadic prosecution, and minimal sentences, then it should come as no surprise that it occurs. Furthermore, with the historical legacy in America of honoring and protecting both family privacy and property rights, as long as animals are legally considered property, then whatever rights they might have will always be outweighed by the rights of human property owners, who all too often are also their abusers.

There is evidence that attitudes are changing and that animal cruelty may be taken more seriously. In recent years there has been a shift to strengthen animal cruelty statutes, with many states elevating some acts of abuse from misdemeanors to felonies. As of 1995, fewer than 10 states had passed felony-level animal cruelty legislation. By 2000, the number had increased to 31 (Ascione & Lockwood, 2001). As of August 2004, 41 states had enacted legislation raising some forms of animal cruelty to felonies.

Sociological Studies on Animal Abuse: Empirical Data and Conceptual Issues

As noted earlier, most studies outside of sociology have approached animal abuse as an indicator of psychopathology. Cruelty to animals is now officially recognized as a diagnostic symptom of conduct disorder (see Chapter 6, by Dadds, this volume), and several studies have linked animal abuse with this condition (e.g., Guymer, Mellor, Luk, & Pearse, 2001; Luk, Staiger, Wong, & Mathai, 1999). In addition, animal abuse has also been associated with other psychiatric diagnoses, such as antisocial personality disorder (Gleyzer, Felthous, & Holzer, 2002). Yet psychological conceptualizations of animal abuse tend to overlook the social influences that may cause animal abuse, and significant numbers of abusers may not display symptoms of psychopathology. Most sociological research has tended to examine animal abuse from various perspectives as deviance—the violation of cultural norms. These studies have looked at animal abuse (a) and its relation to family violence; (b) as associated with, and as a predictor of, interpersonal violence; or (c) as a stigmatizing behavior that must be rationalized. More recently, animal abuse in childhood has been conceptualized and investigated as normative behavior, as seen in the "dirty play" of children (Arluke, 2002).

Animal Abuse and Family Violence

Evidence of the coexistence of animal abuse with family violence was present in many earlier domestic violence studies; however, it was often hidden and overlooked. Although mentioned in secondary and anecdotal fashion, examples of animal abuse can be found in studies of child abuse (DeViney et al., 1983), wife abuse (Browne, 1987; Dutton, 1992; Walker, 1979), sibling abuse (Wiehe, 1990), and lesbian battering (Renzetti, 1992). More recently, the relationship between animal abuse and domestic violence has become the focus of several social science researchers, including sociologists.

Animal Abuse and Battered Women. Several studies have examined animal abuse as a part of, and as a form of, domestic violence. The first study to look at pet abuse and battered women was undertaken by the psychologist Frank Ascione (1998). Using a sample of women from a Utah battered women's shelter, Ascione found that 71% of women with pets reported that their pets had been threatened, harmed, or killed by their batterers. One-fifth of the women had delayed seeking shelter out of concern for the safety of their companion animals.

To replicate and extend Ascione's findings, Flynn (2000b) examined pet abuse among a sample of clients from a battered women's shelter in South Carolina. For a six-month period in 1998, the shelter agreed to add several questions regarding pets and pet abuse to their intake questionnaire. Of the women with pets, nearly half—46.5%—reported

that their partner had either threatened or actually harmed their companion animal.

Pets were important sources of emotional support for the women in dealing with their abuse. This was particularly true for women whose pets had been abused, as well as for women without children. One could reasonably argue that male batterers may be targeting pets precisely because their partners are strongly attached to them. And for women without children, companion animals may take on an even greater meaning as surrogate children, as family members, which implies that the abuse they suffer is all the more hurtful to the woman. Battered women's relationships with their companion animals may be especially important, given the isolation that is known to frequently accompany abuse.

This could help explain why women are slow to leave abusive relationships. As in the Ascione (1998) study, one-fifth of the women delayed leaving due to their concern about the safety of their companion animals. But coming to the shelter meant leaving the companion animal behind, because few shelters allow women to bring their pets. In about half of the cases, the animal was still with the abusive partner or ex-partner. This created much anxiety and concern among the women, who were not only worried about their animals' well-being, but who were now also vulnerable to batterers' attempts to control them by threatening to harm their companion animals.

Taken together, these findings are significant because they demonstrate the interconnection between gender, power, and control in understanding the relationship between animal abuse and domestic violence. The abuse of companion animals by male batterers, the targeting of pets because of their close relationship with the women, women remaining in violent relationships because of their pets, and women worrying about pets that are still with their abusers after the women have left all illustrate how men employ violence against animals as a cruel, yet effective way to inflict emotional abuse upon, and thus to control, women.

In a subsequent qualitative study, Flynn (2000c) interviewed 10 battered women to gain more in-depth knowledge about their relationship with their companion animals, the use of pet abuse by the batterers to control the women, as well as how both the women and the pets were affected by the other's victimization.

Both women and children were powerfully affected by male violence toward their pets. This violence included both physical and psychological abuse. The women (and their children) interpreted men's pet abuse as a means to control and dominate them. Several women insightfully recognized the parallels between their partners' treatment of their pets and his treatment of the rest of the family.

Several women reported that their children had witnessed their companion animals' victimization and, like the women, the children were both angered and terrified. In many ways, the impact of children witnessing the violence toward their animal companions parallels the effects of wife abuse on children. Not only was a loved one, a valued member of the family, being harmed, but they were powerless to do anything about it at the time, and often prevented from comforting the animal immediately following the abuse. In general, the abuse contributed to a climate of control, intimidation, and terror for the children, women, and animals.

These findings clearly demonstrate that animal abuse was clearly another method of wife (and child) abuse. But it is also important to remember that the women and children strongly considered their companion animals as members of the family. Thus animal abuse should be conceptualized not just as a type of wife or child abuse, but also as a separate form of family violence in itself. Consequently, pets were also victimized when women were abused. When companion animals witnessed the woman being assaulted, they typically played either one of two roles: comforter, providing emotional support to women after a violent episode; or protector, sometimes risking their own physical safety. Either way, witnessing a woman's abuse was often very emotionally upsetting for her animal companion. Similar to symptoms of stress in humans, women reported several physical manifestations of stress in their pets when the animals witnessed her abuse, including shivering or shaking, cowering, hiding, and urinating.

These examples reveal the multidimensional nature of domestic violence involving companion animals. It is important to see that both women and animals are victimized by abuse of the other. A man's violence toward an animal also hurts his partner (and children), just as his violence toward her also hurts the animal.

Corporal Punishment and Animal Abuse. As cited previously, researchers have found that children who abuse animals often grew up in violent families. Yet recent research has also suggested that the violence does not have to be severe for lessons about violence to be learned, at least for boys. Flynn (1999b), using a sample of college undergraduates, explored the relationship between corporal punishment and childhood animal abuse. The results showed that the more frequently students had been spanked by their parents, the more likely they were to have abused an animal as children. Yet further analysis uncovered a more complex relationship. When the gender of the parent and the child was incorporated into the analysis, this relationship held only for boys spanked by their fathers. The more often boys were physically punished by their fathers, the more likely they had abused an animal. This was true even after controlling for other variables, including whether the child had been abused and father-to-mother violence. The relationship did not hold for boys spanked by their mothers, or for girls spanked by either parent. Still, this finding is consistent with other studies that have found a relationship between corporal punishment and problem behaviors (Straus, 1991, 1994).

Why might male-to-male physical punishment increase the likelihood of boys' abuse of animals? Research on male socialization, corporal punishment, and animal abuse provides possible answers. Boys generally are expected to be more aggressive, are spanked more frequently than girls, and fathers are more likely to hit sons than daughters (Day, Peterson, & McCracken, 1998; Wauchope & Straus, 1990). Yet fathers are generally less involved in childrearing than mothers. Finally, as we have seen, males are significantly more likely to commit animal abuse than females. Thus, the greater impact of fathers' spanking on sons may result because it is potentially harsher, inflicted by the less-involved parent, and models a behavior—aggression—that males are expected to imitate.

The correlational nature of this study makes it difficult to establish causality, as well as the direction of the relationship between corporal punishment and animal abuse. It could be that children who harm animals are more likely to be physically punished by their parents and not the other way around. Further, males are more likely to engage in deviant behavior, including cruelty to animals, and thus may be more apt to be spanked. Either way, the combination of committing animal abuse and being physically punished may not only increase the opportunity for learning to approve of and engage in violence, but may also compound the negative consequences associated with both experiences.

Animal Abuse and Attitudes Toward Family Violence. Childhood violence toward animals has also been shown to be related to favorable attitudes toward certain forms of family violence. In Flynn's (1999a) sample of university undergraduates, students who had abused animals in their youth were more likely to support the corporal punishment of children. This relationship held even after controlling for gender, race, frequency of childhood spanking, and biblical literalism. Further, respondents were also asked to indicate the degree to which they agreed or disagreed that they could "imagine a situation in which they would approve of a husband slapping his wife." Those who had perpetrated animal abuse as children were also three times more likely to approve of a husband slapping his wife—15.6% vs. 5.4%.

Animal Abuse and Its "Link" to Interpersonal Violence

Much of the scholarship on animal abuse in a variety of disciplines has been driven by its supposed connection to interpersonal violence toward humans (Ascione & Arkow, 1999; Lockwood & Ascione, 1998). Animal abuse has been linked to various forms of violence against humans among clinical samples of children (Rigdon & Tapia, 1977; Tapia, 1971), as well as among aggressive criminals (Felthous & Kellert, 1986; Kellert & Felthous, 1985), including sexual assault and child molestation (Tingle, Bernard, Robbins, Newman, & Hutchinson, 1986), school shootings (Verlinden, Hersen, & Thomas, 2001) and serial homicide (Ressler, Burgess, Hartman, Douglas, & McCormack, 1986; Wright & Hensley, 2003).

In an effort to examine the relationship between animal cruelty and other criminal behavior, Coston and Protz (1998) cross-referenced cases of individuals in Charlotte/Mecklenburg county, North Carolina, who had been investigated for animal cruelty in 1996 with 911 calls two years earlier and one year later. Of the 1,016 matches for crimes investigated two years before 1996, the resulting written reports were for sexual assaults (40%), mental health requests (23%), assaults (22%), animal cruelty (6%), missing person (5%), and domestic violence (4%). One-third had been arrested for criminal offenses other than animal cruelty during this earlier period.

There were 754 matches with 911 calls during the fiscal year 1996. The written reports were for creating a disturbance (32%), domestic violence (31%), assault (16%), missing person (6%), man with a gun (5%), animal cruelty (4%), mental health (2%), sexual assault (2%), and drugs (1%). Thirty percent were arrested, and 10% of those were convicted of assault, domestic violence, and drug possession. Clearly, then, as with family violence, animal abuse frequently has been found to coexist with other forms of violence against humans.

More specifically, however, many observers, often psychologists and animal welfare professionals, posit more than just the co-occurrence of animal abuse with interhuman violence. Rather, they suggest what Beirne (2004) calls a "progression thesis," or what Arluke, Levin, Luke, and Ascione (1999) refer to as the "graduation hypothesis"—namely, that individuals begin abusing animals, often as children, and then "progress" or "graduate" to committing violence against humans. Most of the evidence supporting "the link" (Beirne, 2004) comes from retrospective samples of criminals who were asked about acts of animal cruelty committed during their youth.

As a test of the graduation hypothesis, Merz-Perez, Heide, and Silverman (2001) interviewed 45 violent and 45 nonviolent incarcerated offenders regarding their abuse of animals in childhood. Violent criminals were nearly three times more likely than nonviolent criminals to have abused animals as children—56% versus 20%. Merz-Perez and her colleagues found that the relationship was particularly strong for pets, with violent offenders being nearly four times more likely than nonviolent offenders to report childhood abuse of their pets (26% vs. 7%).

Critically Assessing "the Link." However, other researchers caution against the total acceptance of "the link." Some suggest that the evidence for a progression or graduation hypothesis—that is, that violent perpetrators start with abusing animals and then progress or graduate to abusing humans, is not as empirically sound as animal welfare advocates might suggest (Arluke et al, 1999). Other observers have argued that the thesis is based on studies that are conceptually flawed and methodologically problematic. Piper (2003) and Beirne (2004) suggest that much of the evidence comes from studies where methodological problems—including samples comprised of extreme and nonrepresentative individuals such as convicted criminals, unclear definitions of abuse, flawed logic, and retrospective studies that "work backwards" from criminal to childhood animal cruelty—plague conclusions supporting the link.

In a study designed to test the graduation hypothesis, Arluke and his colleagues (Arluke et al., 1999) compared the criminal records of 153 animal abusers and 153 matched controls. The controls were matched on gender, age, socioeconomic status, and street or neighborhood. As expected, animal abuse was significantly related to criminal behavior, with abusers being 3.2 times more likely than non-abusers to have a criminal record—70% vs. 22%. There was a strong association with violent crime, with abusers being five times more likely to have a violent criminal record—37% vs. 7%.

However, animal abuse was as likely to follow violent offenses than to precede them. Only 16% of animal abusers "graduated" to committing violence against human victims. Beyond this, animal abuse was also related to a variety of nonviolent offenses—property crimes, drug-related offenses, and disorderly behavior. The authors argue that this evidence is more consistent with a "generalized deviance hypothesis" rather than a graduation hypothesis. "Rather than being a predictor or a distinct step in the development of increasingly criminal or violent behavior, animal abuse, as shown in these results, is one of many antisocial behaviors committed by individuals in society, ranging from property to personal crimes" (Arluke et al., 1999, p. 969).

Yet one must be cautious in reading too much into the findings of this study as well. First of all, the data came from official records, which, by definition, only contain reported crime. Thus, early animal cruelty offenses, crimes that are particularly unlikely to be detected, prosecuted, and to result in conviction, are not factored into this analysis. Further, the study focused only on individuals in late adolescence and adulthood. The pattern of committing animal abuse as a child and then graduating to violence against humans—the more typical version of this hypothesis—could not be tested in this study (see Beirne, 2004).

Neutralizing Deviance: Cockfighting and Dog Fighting

Two forms of animal cruelty that are illegal in almost every state—dog fighting and cockfighting—have received attention from sociologists (Darden & Worden, 1996; Forsythe & Evans, 1998; Hawley, 1993). Currently, dog fighting is banned in all 50 states, and cockfighting remains legal only in Louisiana and New Mexico. (However, at the time of these studies, cockfighting was still legal in Arizona, Missouri, and Oklahoma.) What is significant about these studies is that they are qualitative in nature, focusing on the participants' perceptions of their deviance. They examine the social construction of deviance,

the meanings of the actors, and reveal the efforts that individuals make to excuse or justify their deviance, in an attempt to protect their self-image.

Neutralization theory, introduced by Sykes and Matza (1957), holds that contrary to more traditional views of deviance as a rejection of prevailing norms, individuals who violate the law really accept the conventional moral order. However, they attempt to counter the stigma of their deviance by making exceptions or rationalizations called neutralization techniques. According to Sykes and Matza, individuals use five "techniques of neutralization" to rationalize their deviant behavior. The five major neutralization techniques are (a) denial of the victim (the harm was deserved, so, in reality, there is no victim), (b) denial of responsibility (the harm done was caused by an accident, mistake, or forces that were beyond the offender's control), (c) denial of injury (no one was really harmed, and thus, again, there is no real victim), (d) appeal to higher loyalties (attachment to smaller or more intimate groups takes precedence over attachment to society), and (e) condemnation of the condemners (those who denounce our behavior have engaged in acts that are equally bad or worse).

Forsythe and Evans (1998) applied neutralization theory (Sykes & Matza, 1957) to explore the rationalizations used by "dogmen"—men who breed and fight pit bulls. This field research, involving interviews with dogmen and observations of dogfights, took place in Louisiana, considered by many to be the center of dog fighting in the United States, and in Mississippi.

In their ethnographic study of dogfighters, Forsythe and Evans (1998) identified the use of three of these techniques—denial of injury, appeal to higher loyalties, and condemnation of the condemners. They also uncovered a fourth used by dogmen to neutralize their deviance, which they labeled "we are good people." According to the authors, this technique "defends dogmen as good people and maintains their dog fighting is expunged by their good characters and/or good deeds" (Forsythe & Evans, 1998, pp. 206–207).

Although not explicitly identified, studies of cockfighting illustrate similar endeavors at neutralization. Hawley (1993) spent 15 years doing ethnographic research on the culture of cockfighting in the southern and midwestern regions of the United States (including areas where cockfighting was still legal), as well as parts of Latin America and the circum-Caribbean area. Darden and Worden

(1996) examined cockfighting in a setting on the Oklahoma-Arkansas border. Both studies revealed that cockfighters, overwhelmingly male and rural, rationalized their criminal activity in a variety of ways, fitting with the main techniques identified by Forsythe and Evans (1998). They also raised pseudo-scientific arguments, stating that it was part of the bird's nature to fight, and that, because of the bird's simple central nervous system, no pain was experienced (denial of injury). Another rationalization argued that there was a strong historical precedent in favor of cockfighting, with individuals often affirming their own status by mentioning the names of famous men who were also cockfighters—for example, George Washington, Abraham Lincoln, Andrew Jackson, Henry VIII, and Robert E. Lee (appeal to higher loyalties). Other rationalizations suggested that opponents had a bias against a rural lifestyle, that government was overextending its reach into the private lives' of citizens and had no right to regulate this activity (condemnation of the condemners). Cockfighters justified their deviance by claiming that animals exist for human use, often citing biblically based arguments, and that cockfighting builds character ("we are good people"). Thus, like dogfighters, cockfighters attempt to minimize their deviance by redefining it, thereby maintaining their self-images.

Animal Abuse as Normative

Although most research on animal abuse proceeds from the assumption that such behavior is pathological and deviant, Arluke (2002) presents an alternative view. Drawing on a symbolic interactionist perspective, which argues that a full understanding of human behavior depends on knowing how the participants define their actions, Arluke suggests that it is also possible to frame animal abuse by children and adolescents as normative and instrumental. As Arluke states, "lumping together all instances of harming animals as impulsive and pathological does not allow for the possibility that abuse can be instrumental and normative, in the sense that abusers may gain things from their acts that the larger society supports and defines as essential" (p. 406).

To determine what young people gain from animal abuse, Arluke interviewed 25 college undergraduates about their past abuse of animals. His respondents were screened from two large introductory sociology classes at a large, urban, northeastern university. The sample, whose mean age was 19, was predominantly white and middle class, and the interviews lasted for 60–90 minutes. According to Arluke, animal abuse is a form of "dirty play" (see Fine, 1986), through which children attempt to appropriate adult identities and culture. By asserting their autonomy and control over not only their own lives, but also animals' lives, harming animals enabled adolescents to resist and challenge adult authority and the standards of the adult world. Through their abuse of animals, youths appropriate four kinds of adultlike powers: "keeping adultlike secrets, drawing adultlike boundaries, doing adultlike activities, and gathering and confirming adultlike knowledge" (Arluke, 2002, p. 413).

Arluke found that animal abuse was viewed as serious by respondents, in part because it was seen as risky and secretive, and thus, something they were "getting away with." Respondents abused animals not as an end in itself, but to experience the thrill of not getting caught, and this was empowering. Their shared secret of abuse allowed respondents to exercise their independence from, while at the same time incorporating essential aspects of, the adult culture.

A second developmental lesson of animal abuse concerns the drawing of boundaries. Through their abuse, children learn the significance of classifying others as "not us," which justifies differential, and sometimes, exploitative, treatment. As is true with human groups, Arluke's respondents justified their prior cruelty by distinguishing not only animals from humans, but also between different categories of animals, based on their status (e.g., domestic vs. wild). In a similar vein, many respondents abused animals with peers and playmates, indicating that the companionship was more important to them than the actual abuse. Beyond companionship, individuals were rewarded within peer groups with status by abusing animals. So, animal abuse enabled children to draw boundaries that marked not only who was excluded, but also who was included as part of the in-group.

Third, acting like adults was another way to assume adult statuses. Many respondents framed their animal abuse as similar to hunting. As such, it was exciting because it involved the use of weapons, it required planning, and it was seen as developing adultlike skills, such as marksmanship. Animal abuse was also viewed as constraining the behaviors of animals that had overstepped their boundaries, much like parents physically discipline children. Other respondents saw their abuse as a way to develop skills that would be required for success in the adult world of work, such as emotional detachment. As with the other types of appropriation, animal abuse was not an end in itself, but as a means to rehearse their future adult statuses.

Finally, Arluke suggests that animal abuse is a way for individuals to gather and confirm information from adults. In this way, the abuse enabled children to determine if adults had been truthful with them, and to obtain information that adults had kept from them. Thus, curiosity was often mentioned as an explanation for harming animals. Respondents often talked about their abuse as a form of experimentation, illustrating once again that their cruelty to animals was undertaken to acquire adultlike knowledge through adultlike methods, rather than an end in itself.

Interestingly, Arluke's respondents displayed two different responses to their past abusive behaviors. Some individuals felt badly about their behavior, with some remembering their guilt at the time, while others reported feeling guilty now because they didn't remember feeling guilty at the time they committed the abuse. Either way, this redefinition of their "dirty play" as behavior that is offensive rather than fun, enabled participants to present themselves as mature, moral young adults. Others, however, still referred to their abuse of animals as fun and exhibited little evidence of remorse. For these respondents, animal abuse was a normal part of childhood that they had simply outgrown, and for which they had forgiven themselves. Arluke argues that these two different forms of self-presentation reflect not maturational differences in the respondents, but rather the ambivalent and paradoxical attitudes about animals that exist in American society.

Arluke's symbolic interactionist analysis is important because it challenges a traditional psychopathological approach to children's cruelty to animals, reminding us that not all animal abuse has the same significance or trajectory for its perpetrators. Some acts of abuse may be neither impulsive nor pathological, and most children who harm animals do not grow up to be "psychopaths, cold-blooded killers, or sadists" (Arluke, 2002, p. 406). That is not to say that children's animal abuse should be ignored or dismissed by parents and other concerned adults (a point that Arluke readily acknowledges)—far from it. However, the abuse must be viewed from a wider social context that reveals our conflicted cultural notions about our relations with other animals.

Theoretical Approaches to Animal Abuse

Feminist Theories

Feminist perspectives, which have been extremely valuable in explaining domestic violence (e.g., Yllo, 1993), and violence toward women in general have also been successfully applied to the analysis of animal abuse. Adams (1994, 1995) argues that the abuse of animals is part of a larger dominance and exploitation by males of less powerful others—women, children, and animals. From this perspective, patriarchy has led dominant males to use violence as a means to control other less powerful individuals, including other animals. "A hierarchy in which men have power over women and humans have power over animals, is actually more appropriately understood as a hierarchy in which men have power over women, (feminized) men and (feminized) animals" (Adams, 1995, p. 80).

Adams (1994) draws on Spelman's (1982) notion that hostility to the body, which Spelman refers to as "somatophobia," is symptomatic of sexism, racism, classicism, as well as speciesism. Adams argues that the hostility to "despised and disenfranchised bodies, that is, those of animals, children, women, and nondominant men," is interconnected (Adams, 1994, p. 64). Adams identifies seven forms of exploitation, illustrating the ways in which women, children, and animals are harmed by sexually violent men. According to Adams, these interconnections can be found in battering, marital rape, pornography, child sexual abuse, ritual abuse, serial killing, and sexual harassment. "Clearly," Adams says, "women's oppression is interwoven with that of animals, so that women and animals are both trapped by the control exercised over their own *and* each other's bodies" (1994, p. 70, emphasis in the original).

A man's harming of animals as a part of battering reveals the intentionality of his efforts to control his partner. Adams (1995) has identified nine ways or strategies that men control women through pet abuse. By harming animals, batterers (a) demonstrate their power, (b) teach submission, (c) isolate women from supportive networks and relationships, (d) express their rage at women's independence, (e) perpetuate a climate of terror, (f) intimidate women to keep them from leaving, (g) punish women for leaving, (h) coerce women into observing or participating in the animals' abuse, and (i) confirm their power.

A growing number of empirical studies on pet abuse and woman-battering, both quantitative and qualitative, reveal the central role of gender, power, and control in male violence toward both women and animals (Ascione, 1998; Faver & Strand, 2003; Flynn, 2000b, 2000c; Loring & Bolden-Hines, 2004). Batterers control, intimidate, and silence their partners by threatening or actually harming and killing their companion animals. Some female victims are unwilling participants in their pets' abuse, coerced by their batterers to witness, or actually engage in, sexual acts with animals.

One recent study found that batterers have even threatened pet abuse in order to coerce their female victims into committing illegal behavior (Loring & Bolden-Hines, 2004). One hundred seven women who had been referred in 1999 to a family violence center in Atlanta, Georgia, specializing in legal issues participated in this study. The women were predominantly white (63%), with African-Americans and Hispanics accounting for 22% and 11% of the sample, respectively. Their ages ranged from 16–73, with an average of 31 years. Each of the women had committed at least one illegal act, which included such crimes as bank robbery, credit card theft or fraud, stock fraud, bank fraud, and/or drug trafficking. In addition, all women met the criteria for being diagnosed with Post-Traumatic Stress Disorder.

Of the 107 women, 62% owned pets currently or in the past year, and three-fourths of these women (54 of the 107) reported actual or threatened pet abuse. Within this latter group, 44% (24 out of 54) reported that they were coerced by means of threats and actual harm to their pets to commit illegal acts. All 24 women said that their criminal acts were undertaken in order to keep their pets from being abused. "They all reported a sense of desperation and anguish at having to violate their own value systems and become victim-perpetrators" (Loring & Bolden-Hines, 2004, p. 33).

Symbolic Interactionism

Another theory that has been employed in the analysis of animal abuse is symbolic interactionism (Blumer, 1969; Mead, 1962). From this perspective, through interactions with others, individuals give meaning to their experiences and actively construct reality. To interact symbolically, and to develop a sense of self, actors must be able to role-take—to imagine how others define the situation, including how the actors themselves are perceived by others.

Symbolic interactionist perspectives of animal abuse have typically focused on the meaning participants give to the concept of "abuse." As has been shown, this has led to two different lines of research. One approach has focused on how adult animal abusers account for their deviant behavior, redefining it to make it more acceptable (e.g., Forsythe & Evans, 1998). A second approach has been to ask late adolescents and young adults to define their childhood acts of "abuse," illustrating that, in some ways, the abuse may be normative (e.g., Arluke, 2002). Both strands point to the importance of not imposing the researcher's meaning on the behavior or interaction being studied, how respondents' definitions shape their behavior, and how perpetrators' social constructions of the abusive acts are central to preserving the sense of self.

A third approach, following the lead of Sanders (1993, 1999) and Alger and Alger (1997, 1999), has challenged traditional sociological thought that only humans are capable of symbolic interaction. Challenging Mead, this new perspective argues that animals are minded, social actors that have selves, can role-take, can create shared meanings with humans (and sometimes other animals) with whom they interact, and thus are also capable of interacting symbolically.

In Flynn's (2000c) study, many battered women saw their companion animals as being very upset upon witnessing the woman's battering, often trying to protect her during the attack or comfort her afterward. The women see these actions as evidence of their pets' mindedness—intentional, reciprocal, thoughtful behavior. Their pets were capable of expressing emotion and were attuned to the women's emotional states.

If other animals are capable of symbolic interaction, then empirical investigation of their abusive treatment by humans needs to expand to new and challenging levels. What does animal abuse mean to animals? How do animals and their human companions respond to victimization of the other? Animal abuse is no longer relevant merely as an indicator of human psychopathology or an instrument of male power and control over women, but as another form of violence against individuals who can experience terror and pain, and should receive attention for that reason alone.

Agnew's Social-Psychological Theory of Animal Abuse

To date, only one theory of animal abuse has been put forward. Agnew (1998) has presented a social-psychological theory, drawing heavily on leading criminological theories such as social learning theory, strain theory, and control theory to help explain why individuals abuse animals. Agnew argues that the causes of animal abuse should be examined not only because animal abuse is correlated with human interpersonal violence, but also because animals are worthy of moral consideration irrespective of their relationship to humans.

Agnew's theorizing is groundbreaking in another way—his definition of animal abuse. Departing from traditional definitions that have conceptualized abuse as being behavior that is socially unacceptable, intentional, and/or unnecessary, and that is committed by individuals or small groups, Agnew broadly defines animal abuse as "any act that contributes to the pain or death of an animal or that otherwise threatens the welfare of an animal" (p. 179). This definition, according to Agnew, has several advantages: It includes the actions that account for the vast majority of harm inflicted against animals (factory farming, animal experimentation, etc.); it is not linked to current beliefs that would be shaped by social actors with the most power; and it does not limit abuse only to illegal behaviors.

Agnew's theory begins with three individual factors that are directly related to increasing the likelihood that an individual will harm animals. Animal abuse is more likely to occur when individuals are either (a) ignorant of the abusive consequences of their actions, or (b) believe their abusive treatment is justified, and (c) when they perceive that the benefits of their actions outweigh the costs. These propositions are derived from the animal abuse literature, as well as from social learning theory and neutralization theory.

A second set of factors, whose effects are both direct and indirect, helps to explain the variation in the abuse caused by the first set of intervening variables. Included in this set of exogenous variables are (a) individual traits, such as empathy, impulsivity, or self-control; (b) socialization; (c) strain or stress; (d) level of social control; and (e) the nature of the animal.

Finally, Agnew recognizes that structural factors related to one's social position are related to animal abuse. These factors include gender, age, race, education, occupation, urban/rural residence, and region. Social position variables may directly affect the three immediate causes of animal abuse, but more often they indirectly influence these factors

via their effect on the second set of factors (individual traits, socialization, etc.).

Agnew cautions that this model is a general one, and that it is based on conclusions drawn from limited empirical research. Future studies might refine the categories of socially acceptable versus unacceptable animal abuse, and seek to determine the factors that are more likely to be predictors of each form. For example, ignorance about the consequences of abusing animals may be more helpful in explaining harm that is socially accepted and indirectly inflicted. On the other hand, socially unacceptable animal abuse, which is usually direct and intentional, may be better explained by strain, social control, and individual characteristics.

Further, Agnew acknowledges that the theory does not adequately address how variables within each set of factors are related to each other, or interaction effects. For instance, one possible hypothesis might be that the greater the benefits of the abuse for an individual, the more likely one may be to distance oneself from the abuse, using neutralization techniques to justify one's actions. Regarding interaction effects, it may be that harm resulting from strain "caused" by the animal is more likely when the abuse is seen as justified.

Moreover, the theory focuses primarily on the micro-level, without fully examining macro-level forces, such as the economic system or the western religious and philosophical tradition, that may cause animal abuse. Future research might examine how cultural norms regarding animals support their mistreatment. How do the structure and practices of social institutions (e.g., the government, economy, education, religion, and science) reinforce and perpetuate animal abuse?

Agnew's theory represents an impressive effort to systematically explain animal abuse. His significant work should serve to generate many hypotheses for future researchers, and it provides a solid theoretical foundation onto which scholars can continue to build.

Directions for Future Sociological Research

There is a multitude of topics waiting to be explored by researchers. More information is needed concerning the structural causes of animal abuse, as well its consequences for individuals, families, groups, and society. Very little, for example, is known about the role of race/ethnicity or social class in explaining animal abuse.

Knowledge about cultural and subcultural norms could help explain differences in the occurrence of animal abuse between different societies, or between social groups within societies. One area where data are lacking concerns the norms and attitudes of the public toward animal cruelty. In addition, what is the role of the media is influencing the public's knowledge of and response to animal cruelty?

Another fruitful area of research is the analysis of social policies addressing various aspects of animal cruelty. Possible research questions include: Has the increase in felony-level animal cruelty offenses resulted in increased prosecution and conviction rates? Have laws mandating the cross-reporting of animal abuse by human service professionals led to increased detection of animal abuse? Has mandatory counseling for juvenile offenders been effective?

Defining and Measuring Animal Abuse

Much like the early years of family violence research, studies on animal abuse have been plagued by definitional problems. Animal cruelty or abuse, as noted earlier (Agnew, 1998), generally has been conceptualized around three related issues: whether the action was intentional, whether it was necessary, and whether it was socially acceptable. Some definitions have included only intentional abuse, such as the one proposed by Kellert and Felthous (1985, p. 1113), who defined animal cruelty as the "willful infliction of harm, injury, and intended pain on a nonhuman animal." Yet this definition would eliminate neglect, which accounts for the vast majority of animal cruelty cases (Solot, 1997). In perhaps the most widely used definition, Ascione (1993, p. 28) defines animal cruelty as "socially unacceptable behavior that intentionally causes unnecessary pain, suffering, or distress to and/or death of an animal." Here, neglect would be included, but only if it were intentional. Yet socially acceptable behaviors that cause harm to animals, such as factory farming, hunting, or animal experimentation, would be excluded. Vermeulen and Odendaal (1993) developed a typology of companion animal abuse, which they defined as the "intentional, malicious, or irresponsible, as well as unintentional or ignorant, infliction of physiological and/or psychological pain, suffering, deprivation, and the death of a companion animal by humans." This broader definition encompasses behaviors regardless of the intent of the abuser, of the perceived necessity or acceptability of the action by the abuser and society. This definition, however, is limited to companion animals.

Future researchers must attempt to refine their conceptual definitions, addressing some of the following issues: What specific behaviors are included as abusive? Should psychological and emotional abuse be incorporated alongside physical violence? Should abuse be restricted only to behaviors that are intentional? Is animal abuse confined only to certain species? Only companion animals? Only vertebrates? Is abuse limited to actions committed only by individuals or small groups, or should systemic acts of institutional-level violence be included? And should definitions of abuse be restricted by current social norms, or should any harm to animals, regardless of its social acceptability, perceived legitimacy, or legality be considered?

As a result of this definitional confusion, operational definitions of animal abuse have also been problematic. Research that relies on official records of criminal animal cruelty to operationalize abuse limits abuse only to illegal behavior, and as we know from the domestic violence literature, there is much maltreatment that is not criminal (see *The Impact of Improved American Anti-Cruelty Laws* by Frasch, this text). In addition, there is considerable variability in the anti-cruelty statutes from state to state. Most importantly, official records tend to both distort and underestimate the actual incidence and nature of animal cruelty, as only the most horrific and visible cases are included, while multiple incidents and less extreme cases often go undetected (Beirne, 2004).

Instruments to reliably and validly measure animal abuse are much needed. Most studies relying on self-reports from individuals have employed a variety of different instruments, while other studies have operationalized abuse using only a single item. Standardized measures are needed not only to have reliable data on the incidence and prevalence of animal abuse, but also for meaningful comparisons to be made across empirical studies.

Better Data and Samples

There is a great need for national data, based on probability samples, comparable to research on family violence (Straus, Gelles, & Steinmetz, 1980; Gelles & Straus, 1988). Similarly, much of the data has come from clinical and criminal populations, with only limited information from more normal populations, typically college undergraduates. As Beirne notes, the government has not generated any data on the occurrence of animal abuse. "Indeed, no technologically advanced society has generated large-scale, police-based data on the incidence and prevalence of animal abuse. There are no large-scale self-report studies on animal abuse, no household victimization surveys" (Beirne, 2004, p. 41). Finally, all of the studies attempting to establish a connection between animal abuse to other types of violence, either as cause or effect, have been retrospective or cross-sectional in nature. No longitudinal studies have yet been conducted to address this question.

With regard to self-report surveys of animal abuse committed by children, researchers need to also be aware of who the respondent is. Lower rates of abuse are obtained when parents report on their children's violence toward animals than when children report on their own behavior, suggesting that parents may underestimate their children's cruelty (Ascione, 2001; Baldry, 2003).

Qualitative Research

Although the issues raised above regarding measurement, sampling, and research design focus on quantitative methods, it is vitally important that researchers also employ qualitative techniques. Arluke (1997) has published helpful interviewer guides for abusers, complainants, and battered women with abused companion animals. As several studies have shown, the meanings of the participants involved in animal abuse is essential in helping to understand and explain their behavior. This includes not only perpetrators, but others whose perspectives are relevant, such as parents and other family members of abusers, battered women with companion animals, law enforcement and animal control officers, as well as prosecutors and judges. And researchers should explore ways to include the perspective of the victims of animal abuse—the animals themselves.

Theory and Theory Development

Clearly, there is much overlap between animal abuse and other types of interpersonal violence, particularly family violence. Consequently, theoretical approaches from the domestic violence arena could have promise for investigations of animal abuse. Further, decades of family violence scholarship have shown that animal cruelty cannot be explained relying exclusively on psychological models. Theory development based on social and cultural factors will be essential.

The parallels with family violence also suggest that researchers need to investigate the effects of witnessing animal abuse. We know that observing interparental violence is associated with not only violent behavior (Straus et al., 1980), but also with more acceptable attitudes toward violence (Owens & Straus, 1975). Early studies on witnessing animal abuse show similar effects (Baldry, 2003; Flynn, 2000a). Beyond that, limited empirical evidence has revealed that students often are troubled about witnessing animal abuse long after its occurrence, and observing someone else abuse an animal in the past tends to still bother individuals more than their own past cruelty to animals (Flynn, 2000a). Thus theories need to be developed that explain not only animal abuse, but its effects on those who are exposed to it.

Beyond family violence paradigms, there are major sociological and criminological theories that should prove fruitful when applied to animal abuse. As already noted, symbolic interactionist and feminist perspectives have much to offer. Agnew's (1998) theory of animal abuse provides an excellent framework for theory development, and its proposed hypotheses offer an excellent opportunity for his theory to be refined through empirical research.

Other theories from related areas may have promise in the animal abuse arena as well. One possibility is Straus' (1991, 1994) "cultural spillover theory." According to Straus, high levels of culturally approved violence may lead to a spillover effect, into illegitimate violence. For example, states with the highest level of legitimate violence—that is, noncriminal, socially approved violence, as measured by such indicators as hunting licenses sold, circulation rates for magazines with violent content, execution rates, and laws permitting corporal punishment in schools—also have higher homicide rates (Baron & Straus, 1988). Additionally, children who were spanked more frequently by their parents—another form of legitimate violence—were more likely to engage in violent acts as adolescents and adults. A similar relationship may exist with regard to animal abuse. "The more we harm animals in ways that society deems acceptable, the more likely individuals may be to engage in animal cruelty and the less likely individuals and social institutions may be to seriously sanction it" (Flynn, 2001, p. 79).

Finally, as previously stated, the evidence for the thesis that individuals graduate or progress from abusing animals to committing violence against people may not be as strong as many think. That does not mean that the hypothesis is not true, only that stronger support is needed. Certainly, a compelling theoretical argument for the link can be made. Future researchers need to try to establish the link, preferably using longitudinal studies.

Yet it may be a mistake for researchers to focus exclusively on this relationship. Piper (2003) argues that the dominant discourse of "the link" closes off other ways of conceptualizing and theorizing about other causes and pathways of animal abuse. She claims that the explosion of research in recent years has been "predominately psychological in orientation and is largely uncritical, starting from the premise that animal abuse is indicative of something pathological and more sinister" (2003, p. 163). Piper goes on to say that an approach where this assumed connection is the dominant discourse limits our knowledge and understanding.

> In any case, it seems reasonable to suggest, regardless of any research findings, that some young people who harm animals have been hurt themselves, others will have observed violence and some will be going through a phase along with their friends. Others will conform to none of these categories, but their behaviour may perhaps be explained in a variety of other ways. Unless such a diverse account can be applied, animal abuse must be a unique social phenomenon, if it is largely dependent upon a single causal process. (p. 162)

Expanding the Sociological Imagination: An Inclusive Sociology of Animal Abuse

Increasingly, scholars are recognizing that research on animal abuse has been anthropocentric and speciesist. This is true in at least two significant and interrelated ways. First, research on animal abuse, unlike other forms of violence, has been motivated almost exclusively by its association with violence against humans, rather than being seen as worthy of academic investigation in its own right (Cazaux, 1998; Solot, 1997). As Beirne (1999, p. 140) has stated, "perhaps society will eventually reach the conclusion that animal abuse should be censured not because it is similar to the abuse of humans but because it is loathsome to animals themselves."

Second, research has focused on violence toward animals that is defined as socially unacceptable, unnecessary, and illegal actions committed by individuals. Such an approach excludes from consideration legal forms of violence committed both by individuals (e.g., hunting) and institutionalized violence (e.g., factory farming and animal experimentation) that account for the vast majority of the harm inflicted upon other animals (Agnew, 1998; Beirne, 1999, 2004). By linking the definition of animal abuse to prevailing beliefs about animals, beliefs that are social constructions that vary by time and place, "we let those political and social actors with the greatest power determine our definition of animal abuse" (Agnew, 1998, p. 180). To avoid this problem, Agnew advocates a significantly expanded definition of animal abuse, noted earlier in this chapter, which includes any act that causes pain or death to, or threatens the welfare of, an animal.

In a powerful critique that incorporates both of these issues, Beirne (2004) argues that "The field of human-animal studies has no scientific warrant to deploy societal definitions of acceptable and unacceptable behavior—these often are anthropocentric, arbitrary, and capricious. … The link between animal abuse and interhuman violence surely must be sought not only in the personal biographies of those individuals who abuse or neglect animals but also in those institutionalized social practices where animal abuse is routine, widespread, and often defined as socially acceptable" (p. 54).

Criminologists have led the way in studying animal abuse from a sociological perspective that reconceptualizes it a less anthropocentric way (Agnew, 1998; Beirne, 1997, 1999; Cazaux, 1998). Agnew's (1998) social-psychological theory of animal abuse is an excellent example. Additionally, Beirne (1999) has argued persuasively for a "nonspeciesist criminology," in which animal abuse is recognized as a legitimate subject for research, irrespective of its relationship to interhuman violence. As an example, Beirne (1997) applied a nonspeciesist approach to the analysis of bestiality. Human–animal sexual relations, he argued, share certain key features with sexual assaults against women and children: namely, they are coercive and painful (and sometimes deadly), and animals are unable to give their consent or report their abuse (see *Bestiality and Zoophilia* by Beetz, this text). Recognizing the parallels between the sexual assault of animals with that of women and children, Beirne proposes replacing the anthropocentric term "bestiality" with the term "interspecies sexual assault."

These innovative approaches point the way to a more inclusive sociology of animal abuse, where other animals are seen as worthy of moral consideration, and whose victimization, like that of other disadvantaged groups—women, racial/ethnic minorities, the poor—is seen as systemic and institutional, not just individual and pathological. Sociology, which has historically exposed and challenged oppression and inequality based on gender, race, and class, must once again widen its scope to include other animals in its sphere of study, and to include speciesism in its rightful place alongside other forms of oppression.

References

Adams, C. J. (1994). Bringing peace home: A feminist philosophical perspective on the abuse of women, children, and pet animals. *Hypatia, 9*, 63–84.

Adams, C. J. (1995). Woman-battering and harm to animals. In C. J. Adams & J. Donovan (Eds.), *Animals and women: Feminist theoretical explorations* (pp. 55–84). Durham, NC: Duke University Press.

Agnew, R. (1998). The causes of animal abuse: A social-psychological analysis. *Theoretical Criminology, 2*, 177–209.

Albert, A., & Bulcroft, K. (1988). Pets, families, and the life course. *Journal of Marriage and the Family, 50*, 543–552.

Alger, J. M., & Alger, S. F. (1997). Beyond Mead: Symbolic interaction between humans and felines. *Society & Animals, 5*, 65–81.

Alger, J. M., & Alger, S. F. (1999). Cat culture, human culture: An ethnographic study of a cat shelter. *Society & Animals, 7*, 199–218.

Arkow, P. (1999). The evolution of animal welfare as a human welfare concern. In F. R. Ascione & P. Arkow (Eds.), *Child abuse, domestic violence, and animal abuse: Linking the circles of compassion for prevention and intervention* (pp.19–37). West Lafayette, IN: Purdue University Press.

Arluke, A. (1997). Interviewer guides used in cruelty research. *Anthrozoös, 10*, 180–182.

Arluke, A. (2002). Animal abuse as dirty play. *Symbolic Interaction, 25*, 405–430.

Arluke, A., Levin, J., Luke, C., & Ascione, F. (1999). The relationship of animal abuse to violence and other forms of antisocial behavior. *Journal of Interpersonal Violence 14*, 963–975.

Arluke, A., & Luke, C. (1997). Physical cruelty toward animals in Massachusetts, 1975–1990. *Society & Animals, 5*, 195–204.

Arluke, A., & Sanders, C. R. (1996). *Regarding animals*. Philadelphia: Temple University Press.

Ascione, F. R. (1993). Children who are cruel to animals: A review of research and implications for developmental psychology. *Anthrozoös, 6*(4), 226–247.

Ascione, F. R. (1998). Battered women's reports of their partners' and their children's cruelty to animals. *Journal of Emotional Abuse, 1*, 119–133.

Ascione, F. R. (2001). Animal abuse and youth violence. *Juvenile Justice Bulletin*. Washington, DC: Office of Juvenile Justice.

Ascione, F. R., & Arkow, P. (1999). *Child abuse, domestic violence and animal abuse: Linking the circles of compassion for prevention and intervention*. West Lafayette, IN: Purdue University Press.

Ascione, F. R., & Lockwood, R. (2001). Cruelty to animals: Changing psychological, social, and legislative perspectives. In D. J. Salem & A. N. Rowan (Eds.), *State of the Animals 2000* (pp. 39–53). Washington, DC: Humane Society Press.

Baldry, A. C. (2003). Animal abuse and exposure to interparental violence in Italian youth. *Journal of Interpersonal Violence, 18*, 258–281.

Baron, L., & Straus, M. A. (1988). Cultural and economic sources of homicide in the United States. *Sociological Quarterly, 29*, 371–390.

Beirne, P. (1997). Rethinking bestiality: Towards a concept of interspecies sexual assault. *Theoretical Criminology, 1*, 317–340.

Beirne, P. (1999). For a nonspeciesist criminology: Animal abuse as an object of study. *Criminology, 37*, 117–147.

Beirne, P. (2004). From animal abuse to interhuman violence? A critical review of the progression thesis. *Society & Animals, 12*, 39–65.

Blumer, H. (1969). *Symbolic interactionism: Perspective and method*. Englewood Cliffs, NJ: Prentice-Hall.

Bowd, A. D., & Bowd, A. C. (1989). Attitudes toward the treatment of animals: A study of Christian groups in Australia. *Anthrozoös, 3*, 20–24.

Browne, A. (1987). *When battered women kill*. New York: Free Press.

Bryant, C. D. (1979). The zoological connection: Animal-related human behavior. *Social Forces, 58*, 399–421.

Bryant, C. D., & Snizek, W. E. (1993). On the trail of the centaur, *Society, 30*, 25–35.

Cain, A. (1983). A study of pets in the family system. In A. H. Katcher & A. M. Beck (Eds.), *New perspectives on our lives with companion animals* (pp. 72–81). Philadelphia: University of Pennsylvania Press.

Cazaux, G. (1998). Legitimating the entry of "the animals issue" into (critical) criminology. *Humanity and Society, 22*, 365–385.

Coston, C., & Protz, C. M. (1998). Kill your dog, beat your wife, screw your neighbor's kids, rob a bank? A cursory look at an individuals' vat of social chaos resulting from deviance. *Free Inquiry in Creative Sociology, 26*, 153–158.

Darden, D. K., & Worden, S. K. (1996). Marketing deviance: The selling of cockfighting. *Society & Animals, 4*, 211–231.

Day, R. D., Peterson, G. W., & McCracken, C. R. (1998). Predicting spanking of younger and older children by mothers and fathers. *Journal of Marriage and the Family, 60*, 79–94.

DeViney, E., Dickert, J., & Lockwood, R. (1983). The care of pets within child abusing families. *International Journal for the Study of Animal Problems, 4*, 321–329.

Dutton, M. A. (1992). *Empowering and healing the battered woman*. New York: Springer.

Faver, C. A., & Strand, E. B. (2003). To leave or to stay? Battered women's concern for vulnerable pets. *Journal of Interpersonal Violence, 18*, 1367–1377.

Felthous, A. R., & Kellert, S. R. (1986). Violence against animals and people: Is aggression against living creatures generalized? *Bulletin of the American Academy of Psychiatry Law, 14*(1), 55–69.

Felthous, A. R., & Kellert, S. R. (1987). Psychosocial aspects of selecting animal species for physical abuse. *Journal of Forensic Sciences, 32*, 1713–1723.

Fine, G. A. (1986). The dirty play of little boys. *Society, 24*, 63–67.

Flynn, C. P. (1999a). Animal abuse in childhood and later support for interpersonal violence in families. *Society & Animals, 7*, 161–172.

Flynn, C. P. (1999b). Exploring the link between corporal punishment and children's cruelty to animals. *Journal of Marriage and the Family, 61*, 971–981.

Flynn, C. P. (2000a). Why family professionals can no longer ignore violence toward animals. *Family Relations, 49*, 87–95.

Flynn, C. P. (2000b). Woman's best friend: Pet abuse and the role of companion animals in the lives of battered women. *Violence Against Women, 6*, 162–177.

Flynn, C. P. (2000c). Battered women and their animal companions: Symbolic interaction between human and nonhuman animals. *Society & Animals, 8*, 99–127.

Flynn, C. P. (2001). Acknowledging the "zoological connection": A sociological analysis of animal cruelty. *Society & Animals, 9*, 71–87.

Forsythe, C. J., & Evans, R. D. (1998). Dogmen: The rationalization of deviance. *Society & Animals, 6*, 203–218.

Francione, G. L. (1996). *Rain without thunder: The ideology of the animal rights movement*. Philadelphia: Temple University Press.

Gelles, R. J. (1993). Through a sociological lens: Social structure and family violence. In R. Gelles & D. Loseke (Eds.), *Current controversies on family violence* (pp. 31–46). Newbury Park, CA: Sage.

Gelles, R. J. (1997). *Intimate violence in families* (3rd ed.). Thousand Oaks, CA: Sage.

Gelles, R. J., & Straus, M. A. (1979). Determinants of violence in the family: Toward a theoretical integration. In W. R. Burr, R. Hill, F. I. Nye, & I. L. Reiss (Eds.), *Contemporary theories about the family* (Vol. 1, pp. 549–581). New York: Free Press.

Gelles, R. J, & Straus, M. A. (1988). *Intimate violence*. New York: Simon and Schuster.

Gleyzer, R., Felthous, A. R., & Holzer, C. E. (2002). Animal cruelty and psychiatric disorders. *Journal of the American Academy of Psychiatry and the Law, 30*, 257–265.

Guymer, E. C., Mellor, D., Luk, E. S. L., & Pearse, V. (2001). The development of a screening questionnaire for childhood cruelty to animals. *Journal of Child Psychology and Psychiatry, 42*, 1057–1063.

Hawley, F. (1993). The moral and conceptual universe of cockfighters: Symbolism and rationalization. *Society & Animals, 1*, 159–168.

Kellert, S. R., & Felthous, A. R. (1985). Childhood cruelty toward animals among criminals and noncriminals. *Human Relations, 38*, 1113–1129.

Kruse, C. R. (2002). Baby steps: Minnesota raises certain forms of animal cruelty to felony status. *William Mitchell Law Review, 28,* 1649–1680.

Lacroix, C. A. (1999). Another weapon for combating family violence: Prevention of animal abuse. In F. R. Ascione & P. Arkow (Eds.), *Child abuse, domestic violence and animal abuse: Linking the circles of compassion for prevention and intervention* (pp. 62–80). West Lafayette, IN: Purdue University Press.

Lockwood, R., & Ascione, F. R. (1998). *Cruelty to animals and interpersonal violence: Readings in research and application.* West Lafayette, IN: Purdue University Press.

Loring, M. T., & Bolden-Hines, T. A. (2004). Pet abuse by batterers as a means of coercing battered women into committing illegal behavior. *Journal of Emotional Abuse, 4,* 27–37.

Luk, E. S. L., Staiger, P. K., Wong, L., & Mathai, J. (1999). Children who are cruel to animals: A revisit. *Australian and New Zealand Journal of Psychiatry, 33,* 29–36.

Mead, G. H. (1962). *Mind, self, and society.* Chicago: University of Chicago Press.

Merz-Perez, L., Heide, K. M., & Silverman, I. J. (2001). Childhood cruelty to animals and subsequent violence against humans. *International Journal of Offender Therapy and Comparative Criminology, 25,* 556–573.

Miller, K. S., & Knutson, J. F. (1997). Reports of severe physical punishment and exposure to animal cruelty by inmates convicted of felonies and by university students. *Child Abuse and Neglect, 21*(1), 59–82.

Owens, D. J., & Straus, M. A. (1975). The social structure of violence in childhood and approval of violence as an adult. *Aggressive Behavior, 1,* 193–211.

Patronek, G. (1996). Hoarding of animals: An under recognized public health problem in a difficult to study population. *Public Health Reports, 114,* 82–87.

Piper, H. (2003). The linkage of animal abuse with interpersonal violence: A sheep in wolf's clothing? *Journal of Social Work, 3,* 161–177.

Renzetti, C. M. (1992). *Violent betrayal: Partner abuse in lesbian relationships.* Newbury Park, CA: Sage Publications.

Ressler, R. K., Burgess, A. W., Hartman, C. R., Douglas, J. E., & McCormack, A. (1986). Murderers who rape and mutilate. *Journal of Interpersonal Violence, 1,* 273–287.

Rigdon, J. D., & Tapia, F. (1977). Children who are cruel to animals—A follow-up study. *Journal of Operational Psychiatry, 8*(1), 27–36.

Rowan, A. (1992). The dark side of the "Force." *Anthrozoös, 5,* 4–5.

Sanders, C. R. (1993). Understanding dogs: Caretakers' attributions of mindedness in canine-human relationships. *Journal of Contemporary Ethnography, 22,* 205–226.

Sanders, C. R. (1999). *Understanding dogs: Living and working with canine companions.* Philadelphia: Temple University Press.

Siegel, J. M. (1993). Companion animals: In sickness and in health. *Journal of Social Issues, 49,* 157–167.

Singer, P. (1990). *Animal liberation.* New York: Avon Books.

Solot, D. (1997). Untangling the animal abuse web. *Society and Animals, 5,* 257–265.

Spelman, E. V. (1982). Woman as body: Ancient and contemporary views. *Feminist Studies, 8,* 109–131.

Straus, M. A. (1980). A sociological perspective on the causes of family violence. In M.R. Green (Ed.), *Violence and the family* (pp. 7–31). Boulder, CO: Westview.

Straus, M. A. (1991). Discipline and deviance: Physical punishment of children and violence and other crime in adulthood. *Social Problems, 38,* 133–154.

Straus, M. A. (1994). *Beating the devil out of them: Corporal punishment in American families.* New York: Lexington Books.

Straus, M. A., Gelles, R. J., & Steinmetz, S. K. (1980). *Behind closed doors.* New York: Doubleday/Anchor.

Sykes, G. M., & Matza, D. (1957). Techniques of neutralization: A theory of delinquency. *American Sociological Review, 22,* 664–670.

Tapia, F. (1971). Children who are cruel to animals. *Child Psychiatry and Human Development, 2*(2), 70–77.

Tingle, D., Barnard, G. W., Robbins, G., Newman, G., & Hutchinson, D. (1986). Childhood and adolescent characteristics of pedophiles and rapists. *International Journal of Law and Psychiatry, 9,* 103–116.

Veevers, J. E. (1985). The social meanings of pets: Alternative roles for companion animals. *Marriage and Family Review, 8,* 11–30.

Verlinden, S., Hersen, M., & Thomas, J. (2001). Risk factors in school shootings. *Clinical Psychology Review, 20*, 3–56.

Vermeulen, H., & Odendaal, J. S. J. (1993). Proposed typology of companion animal abuse. *Anthrozoös, 6*, 248–257.

Walker, L. E. (1979). *The battered woman*. New York: Harper and Row.

Wauchope, B., & Straus, M. A. (1990). Physical punishment and physical abuse of American children: Incidence rates by age, gender, and occupational class. In M. A. Straus & R. J. Gelles (Eds.), *Physical violence in American families: Risk factors and adaptations to violence in 8,145 families* (pp. 133–148). New Brunswick, NJ: Transaction Publishers.

Wiehe, V. R. (1990). *Sibling abuse*. New York: Lexington Books.

Wright, J., & Hensley, C. (2003). From animal cruelty to serial murder: Applying the graduation hypothesis. *International Journal of Offender Therapy and Comparative Criminology, 47*, 71–88.

Yllo, K. (1993). Through a feminist lens: Gender, power, and violence. In R. Gelles & D. Loseke (Eds.), *Current controversies on family violence* (pp. 47–62). Newbury Park, CA: Sage.

Unleashing Compassion: Social Work and Animal Abuse

Catherine A. Faver and Elizabeth B. Strand

Introduction

This chapter has three purposes: (1) to explain why animal abuse and the link between animal abuse and human violence merit the attention of social workers, (2) to provide a research-based overview of what social workers need to know about animal abuse and family violence, and (3) to offer strategies social workers can use to prevent and intervene more effectively in family violence through attention to the web of abuse.

Why Social Workers Should Care About Animal Abuse

Historically, social work's primary mission has focused on human welfare. Why should social workers extend their concern to animals? On the whole, the evidence suggests that in order to help people more effectively, social workers must attend to the plight of animals. This is true for several reasons.

First, animals are part of the natural environment and the home environments of people. A majority of families have pets, and many people regard their pets as family members. Because animals play significant roles in human environments, social workers must attend to the welfare of animals in order to foster the well-being of people. The ecological systems perspective, which social workers use to guide assessment and intervention, provides a theoretical basis for attending to the important roles that animals play in human life.

Second, research on the human–animal bond shows the importance of animals as sources of companionship and social support for people in diverse situations throughout the life course. Social workers have recognized the importance of the human–animal bond in particular contexts such

as grief after pet loss (Quackenbush & Glickman, 1984), animal-assisted therapy (Mason & Hagan, 1999; Valentine, Kiddoo, & LaFleur, 1993), and pets as support for elderly clients (Hoffman, 1991; Netting & Wilson, 1987). Yet, attention to the human–animal bond is incomplete without recognition of the relationship between animal abuse and interpersonal violence. The issue of animal abuse reflects the complexity of the human–animal bond, which social workers must understand in order to work effectively with people.

Third, a growing body of research (summarized in the next section of this paper) documents the coexistence of animal abuse and various forms of abuse and neglect of human family members. Family violence is best described as a "web of violence" in which there is often more than one victim and more than one perpetrator. To intervene effectively, social workers must be alert to the violence experienced by pets as well as people.

Fourth, attention to animal abuse is part of social work's historical legacy. In the late 19th century, the movement to protect abused children was closely associated with the animal welfare movement. Indeed, the connection between child welfare and animal welfare is often traced to the widely publicized case of Mary Ellen Wilson, a child who was severely abused by her foster mother in New York in the early 1870s (American Humane, 2005c; Ascione, 2005a; Watkins, 1990). Etta Wheeler, a church worker who discovered the child's plight, sought help from Henry Bergh, president of the New York Society for the Prevention of Cruelty to Animals (NYSPCA). Bergh and his lawyer, Elbridge Gerry, successfully petitioned the court to have Mary Ellen removed from the abusive home in 1874. It is important to note that Bergh acted as a concerned citizen, not in his role as president of the NYSPCA. Notably, Bergh had previously intervened on behalf of an abused child. The Mary Ellen Wilson case led to the formation of the New York Society for the Prevention of Cruelty to Children (NYSPCC), which became a model for child protection organizations in the United States during that period (Ascione, 2005a). Moreover, in 1877 a national organization, the American Humane Association (currently American Humane), was formed with a focus on protecting both children and animals (American Humane, 2005b).

The link between animal welfare and human welfare was also evident in the emergence of humane education in the late 19th century. Humane education groups for children called "Bands of Mercy," based on the book *Friends and Helpers* (1899) by Sarah Eddy, were sponsored in the United States by the Massachusetts Society for the Prevention of Cruelty to Animals (MSPCA) beginning in 1882. The purpose of such groups was to teach children to prevent animal cruelty, and Eddy believed that as children learned to respect animals, they would learn to respect the rights of other people as well. Moreover, during the 1880s the president of the MSPCA, George Angell, publicly presented his view that cruelty to animals is a warning of potential violence to people and, conversely, teaching kindness toward animals is a strategy to prevent interpersonal violence (Ascione, 2005a, pp. 10, 25). It is noteworthy, too, that during the early 20th century a humane society in Chattanooga, Tennessee, focused its humane education program on protecting women and children as well as animals (Ascione, 2005a, p. 11).

Yet despite this early connection between the child welfare and animal welfare movements, early in the 20th century separate organizational structures began to evolve for these two concerns (Arkow, 1999). Services for battered women and abused elders emerged much later in the 20th century. Now, after many years of fulfilling separate functions, human service and animal welfare organizations are discovering the value of joining efforts to prevent and end violence. It is time to return to the profession's early understanding that violence against animals and violence against people are integrally connected, and these forms of violence must be addressed in a holistic way.

There is a fifth reason to care about animal welfare. Ignoring the suffering of animals diminishes social workers' capacity for empathy and compassion for their human clients. Throughout the profession's history, social workers have participated in social movements to counter oppression and discrimination and to extend social justice to all people. Yet even as social workers have sought to eliminate arbitrary distinctions between groups of people and to create an inclusive society, we have maintained a species barrier. This contradiction hinders our professional development. When we ignore the suffering of any being, we diminish our capacity for compassion. Our professional values demand that we think critically about artificial distinctions among those who suffer. Our mission of social justice requires that we reach out to help all vulnerable populations, regardless of species. Mary Lou Randour (2000) summarized the demands of justice and compassion in this way:

> Love demands that we stretch ourselves beyond our usual way of thinking, often characterized by defining ourselves by our differences. Sometimes the difference is gender or race. Other times it is religion or nationality. As the human race has matured, we have begun to realize that organizing ourselves by these differences not only disenfranchises others but also diminishes us. But even as we find unity within the human race, we still go to great lengths to distinguish ourselves from other species. We need to extend our care and understanding to all species ... The goal of compassion is not to care because someone is like us but to care because they are themselves (pp. 30, 7).

The Web of Abuse: What Social Workers Should Know

This section will provide some definitions of animal abuse and an overview of what is known about the relationship between animal abuse and various forms of family and community violence. An in-depth literature review is beyond the scope of this chapter. Instead, our purpose is to summarize what social workers need to know about animal abuse and the link between animal abuse and family violence in light of the relevant research. The information in this section may be used to guide strategies for prevention and intervention.

Animal Abuse

What is animal abuse or animal cruelty? How we define animal abuse is important because our definition of a problem shapes our response to it. To illustrate the range of definitions and their implications, we will briefly examine three definitions of animal abuse.

First, Ascione (1993) defined animal abuse as "socially unacceptable behavior that intentionally causes unnecessary pain, suffering, or distress to and/or death of an animal" (p. 228). Note that this definition explicitly excludes socially acceptable forms of violence to animals, such as hunting as a sport and the maltreatment of animals used for food and clothing, a point we will return to shortly.

Second, Vermeulen and Odendaal (1993) developed a definition specifically for *companion* animal abuse: "the intentional, malicious, or irresponsible, as well as unintentional or ignorant, infliction of physiological and/or psychological pain, suffering, deprivation, and the death of a companion animal by humans" (p. 249). In short, abuse occurs whenever the animal's basic needs are not met, regardless of whether the abuse is inflicted intentionally or out of ignorance and regardless of whether the maltreatment violates social norms for the treatment of animals.

Finally, Agnew (1998) defines animal abuse more broadly as "any act that contributes to the pain or death of an animal or that otherwise threatens the welfare of an animal" (p. 179). Thus, Agnew's definition of abuse pertains to all animals and includes harm to animals that is normative in our culture, such as the use of animals for food, clothing, entertainment, and laboratory research.

In sum, these three definitions of animal abuse illustrate a range of behaviors that may be considered as animal abuse: intentional, socially unacceptable harm such as kicking, throwing, torturing, or maliciously killing an animal; neglect or failure to provide adequate food, water, shelter, and veterinary care; and "socially acceptable" forms of harm to animals such as hunting, use of animals for food, clothing, and other products, and use of animals for entertainment and in research. Agnew (1998) argues that "socially acceptable" harm to animals increases society's tolerance of violence and contributes to an environment in which other forms of violence are more likely to occur.

Agnew's point about the dangers of "socially acceptable" violence to animals is worth pondering. How ARE people affected by socially acceptable forms of animal maltreatment? In factory farms, research laboratories, circuses, rodeos, and steel-jaw traps, millions of animals suffer intensely in the production of food, clothing, medicine, personal care and household products, and entertainment for

human consumption. For the most part, our society trains us to be unaware of much of this suffering (e.g., most schools do not teach children where their food comes from) or we learn to be unconcerned about it.

Weil (2003) described one witness's account of how a father taught his child not to care about animals who suffered for human "sport." For many years an annual "pigeon shoot" was held in a small town in Pennsylvania. As thousands of caged birds were released, shooters killed the birds as they attempted to fly away. One year a protester at the event witnessed the following interaction between a father and son, which is recounted by Weil:

> The young boy … started to cry when he saw what was happening to the birds. He turned his back to the shooting field and held his father's pants, burying his head against his father's body. His father did not comfort him. Instead, he grabbed him by the shoulders, jerked him around to face the field and told him to watch. The boy began to cry harder and turned his back again, but this time his father swung him around, held him in place, and said, "You *will* watch!" (p. 100)

Reflecting on this incident, Weil (2003) continued: "I have often thought about the young boy whose compassion was punished. Presumably, he is a teenager now. Are his heart and soul intact? Does he allow himself to love, to care, to empathize, and to be vulnerable, or was his kind spirit and reverence for animals crushed that day on the shooting field?"(p. 100)

In Tribe of Heart's documentary *Peaceable Kingdom* (2004), three adults explain the high personal and social costs of squelching compassion:

- Environmental activist Jim Mason, who was raised on a hog farm, vividly described the trauma he experienced as a young child when he first witnessed a hog slaughter.
- Influenced by university courses in modern agriculture, former cattle rancher Howard Lyman turned his ranch into a cattle-producing factory farm. The consequences were devastating for the soil, the water, the animals, and Lyman's own mind and spirit.
- As a young farm child, Harold Brown learned that it was all right to feel sad when animals were killed, but those feelings

should never be shown. As he grew older, Harold himself slaughtered animals and learned the "emotional discipline" of killing without feeling. As a result, compassion became something that he could turn on and off like a light switch.

Fortunately, compassion that is punished or extinguished can be re-ignited. All three of the adults described above are now actively demonstrating the power of compassion that is not limited by species barriers. As social workers, we must ask ourselves: Can we afford to limit our compassion to humans only? Can we afford to draw arbitrary lines between beings that merit our concern and those who do not?

Consider the following connection between "socially acceptable" maltreatment of animals and harm to humans: Most meat is produced on factory farms where animals are unnaturally confined, mistreated, and denied fulfillment of their behavioral needs. These factory farms are responsible for the deaths of billions of animals and the pollution of rivers, soil, and groundwater through output of waste and manure. Because the process of slaughtering cattle has accelerated to kill more animals in less time, many animals are still alive when their throats are slit. During meatpacking, injuries to workers such as lost limbs or fingers, back injuries, repetitive motion syndrome, and deep wounds are common, making slaughterhouse work one of the most dangerous types of work in the United States (Coats, 1991; Mason, 1988; U.S. Department of Labor, 1999, 2003; U.S. Senate Committee on Agriculture, 1997; Warrick, 2001; Weil, 2003). In light of these connections, what are the consequences of turning compassion on and off like a light switch? Do we have an obligation to help our profession "unleash compassion" and distribute it widely to all?

Some individuals and organizations that do not oppose human consumption of animal products are nevertheless attempting to reduce the suffering of animals in food production. Two examples will illustrate this work.

First, American Humane (AH), which is a national nonprofit organization working on behalf of both child and animal welfare, has been concerned with the treatment of farm animals since its inception in 1877 (American Humane, 2005b). Currently American Humane is trying to improve farm practices through its Free Farmed program, which began in 2000 (American Humane, 2005a). Through this initiative, American Humane provides independent verification that farms certified by the program are meeting American Humane's own animal welfare standards for the care and handling of livestock and poultry. The standards require that animals be given sufficient food, water, shelter, medical care, space for movement, protection from weather hazards, an environment that allows the animals to express their own nature, and freedom from "unnecessary" fear and distress. In addition, the program requires that farm managers and staff must be thoroughly trained and competent in their work.

Second, Dr. Temple Grandin, Associate Professor of Animal Science at Colorado State University, is a researcher and author on livestock behavior. Her work focuses specifically on designing facilities for livestock that will reduce stress and "improve animal welfare at slaughter plants" (Grandin, 1996, 2005). She created a scoring system to assess the handling of cattle and pigs at slaughterhouses. She also identified five basic causes of animal welfare problems in slaughter plants and made recommendations for correcting these problems (Grandin, 1996). The purpose of her web page (http://www.grandin.com) is "to educate people about modern methods of livestock handling to improve animal welfare and *productivity*" (emphasis added). In other words, an underlying assumption is that by better handling of animals, productivity (in terms of quantity and quality of animal products) will improve. Thus, the focus on animal welfare is at least in part a means to an end, not simply an end in itself.

Despite efforts such as these, most animals used as food are produced in the inhumane conditions of factory farms (Mason, 1988; Coats, 1991). Moreover, investigations indicate that vast numbers (probably most) of these animals suffer horrific deaths (Eisnitz, 1997; Grandin, 1999; Warrick, 2001). The bottom line is that as long as animals are used for human profit, animal exploitation and immense suffering will persist. Just as social workers are committed to preventing and ending the maltreatment of children, women, and dependent adults, so also we should not rest while animals continue to suffer.

We have seen that billions of animals are killed for purposes that many regard as "socially acceptable." What types of abuse are considered socially unacceptable and thus prohibited by law? How common are these forms of abuse? These are not simple questions. All 50 states have legal statutes regarding animal abuse, but the prohibitions in these statutes vary. Animal abuse is at least a misdemeanor offense in most states and 41 states now define particular types of animal abuse as felony offenses (Arkow, 2003). Animal abuse is not monitored in a systematic, standardized way across states and localities, and no statistics on animal abuse are gathered as part of national crime statistics (Ascione, 2005b). Moreover, it is likely that much animal abuse is unreported to law enforcement agencies even at the local level. Thus, we lack sufficient data on the incidences of animal abuse.

The question "how prevalent is animal abuse?" can be answered in several ways. One approach is to determine the percentage of people (of different ages and genders) who abuse animals. Thus, some researchers estimate prevalence by using data from assessment instruments that address child behavior problems, including children's abuse of animals. These instruments rely on self-reports or caregiver reports of children's harm to animals and are limited in several ways. The instruments do not define animal abuse for the respondents, who may vary greatly in their own definitions of animal abuse. In addition, animal abuse is often a covert activity, and there is evidence that caregivers underestimate the amount of animal abuse that actually occurs. For a review of the available data from these instruments and an assessment of their limitations, see Ascione (2005b).

Another approach to assessing the prevalence of animal abuse is to ask how many animals of various species are abused and what types of abuse they experience. Given the lack of a national monitoring and tracking system for animal abuse, the Humane Society of the United States (HSUS) has been compiling information on "high-profile" cases of animal abuse each year since 2000 (HSUS, 2004; see *Counting Cruelty* by Lockwood, this text). The sources of their information include media reports and local humane societies and animal welfare organizations. The HSUS 2003 report is based on 1,373 animal cruelty cases in which there were at least 1,682 perpetrators. The incidents in the report include cases of intentional cruelty, animal fighting, neglect, and animal hoarding. Table 1 defines the types of animal cruelty included in the report, and Table 2 provides a percentage distribution of the cases of intentional animal cruelty. As Table 2 shows, the five most common forms of violent offenses against animals were shooting, animal fighting, torturing, beating, and mutilation. The overall report indicated that males were the perpetrators in 92% of the cases of intentional cruelty and in 93% of the cases of animal fighting, but in only 54% of the neglect cases and 34% of the animal hoarding cases.

In sum, as this overview demonstrates, there are a number of ways to define and assess the extent of animal abuse. At this juncture, it is important to emphasize that the lack of a commonly accepted definition of animal abuse should not inhibit social workers' efforts to improve the welfare of animals. Indeed, social workers have confronted similar definitional issues in dealing with abuse of humans. For example, as previously noted, cruelty to children was recognized as a social problem in the United States in the late 19th century, prompting

Table 1   HSUS 2003 Report of Animal Cruelty Cases: Types and Definitions

Intentional cruelty or abuse: A person knowingly deprives an animal of food, water, shelter, socialization, or veterinary care or maliciously tortures, maims, mutilates, or kills an animal. People who are intentionally cruel to animals take satisfaction in causing harm.

Neglect: A person fails to provide an animal with proper shelter, food, water, attention, grooming, or veterinary care. Cases of neglect are acts of omission rather than commission and do not give satisfaction to the person whose animals are neglected.

Cockfighting: Two or more specially bred birds, known as gamecocks, are placed in an enclosure to fight, for the primary purposes of gambling and entertainment. A cockfight usually results in the death of one of the birds; sometimes it ends in the death of both.

Dog fighting: Two dogs—specifically bred, conditioned, and trained to fight—are placed in a pit (generally a small arena enclosed by plywood walls) to fight each other, for the spectators' gambling and entertainment.

Animal hoarding: Refers to the accumulation of a large number of animals, where the caregiver provides minimal standards of nutrition, sanitation, and veterinary care; and fails to act on the deteriorating condition of the animals and/or the environment.

Source: HSUS First Strike Campaign 2003 Report of Animal Cruelty Cases (http://www.hsus.org/firststrike)

Table 2 HSUS 2003 Report of Animal
Cruelty: Intentional Animal Cruelty (Percentage
Distribution)

Type of Offense	%
Shooting	17
Animal Fighting	17
Torturing	11
Beating	11
Mutilation	10
Throwing	7
Burning	6
Poisoning	4
Stabbing	3
Kicking	3
Dragging	3
Suffocating	1
Drowning	1
Animal Sexual Abuse	1
Hanging	1
Run Over with Vehicle	1

Source: HSUS First Strike Campaign 2003 Report of
Animal Cruelty Cases (http://www.hsus.org/firststrike)

the development of the child welfare movement.
Yet a national "standard" by which to identify child
maltreatment was not clearly defined until the federal child abuse legislation of the early 1970s. Even
today, in dealing with child maltreatment social
workers recognize that care of children can be
assessed on a continuum. Some caregiver behaviors
are totally unacceptable and are defined as abuse
or neglect. Quite often, social workers confront
childcare practices that do not fall to the level of
maltreatment but are less than ideal. In these situations, social workers are always aiming to help
caregivers improve the level of care to ensure an
environment in which children can flourish. In
short, even if caregivers' current practices are not
defined as "maltreatment," the aim is to achieve the
highest standard of care possible. The same is true
of animal abuse. While some practices may not be
legally defined as abuse, animal welfare advocates
strive to help caregivers and the general public to
achieve a standard of care that enables animals to
be healthy and to flourish in accordance with the
unique characteristics of each species.

The Link Between Animal Abuse
and Family Violence

A *web of violence* rather than a single one-
directional relationship between an abuser and a
victim is often characteristic of families in which
there is violence (DeViney, Dickert, & Lockwood,
1983; McKibben, DeVos, & Newberger, 1989; Solot,
1997). For example, a man who batters his wife may
also hurt the family pet. A child who witnesses his
father hurt his mother may become abusive toward
the pet. In short, there may be more than one victim
and more than one perpetrator of violence in one
family. Because various forms of violence (e.g.,
child maltreatment, intimate partner battering, and
animal abuse) may occur in the same family, it is
important to view family violence holistically. The
purpose of this section is to summarize basic information about the link between animal abuse and
interpersonal violence that can help social workers
prevent and intervene more effectively in family and
community violence.

Beginning with *community violence*, research
indicates that animal abuse is more likely to be found
in the developmental histories of violent criminal
offenders than in the histories of nonviolent criminal offenders and non-offenders (see, e.g., Kellert
& Felthous, 1985; Langevin, 2003; Miller & Knutson, 1997; Schiff, Louw, & Ascione, 1999). After
reviewing the relevant research, Ascione (2005b)
concluded that animal abuse is likely to be in the
developmental histories of between 25% and almost
67% of violent criminal offenders. Based on their
research on abuse of animals among adult criminals and noncriminals, Kellert and Felthous (1985)
compiled a list of motivations for cruelty to animals,
which are listed in Table 3. If social workers become
aware of these motivations, they will be more alert
to animal abuse in the developmental histories of
violent offenders and can ask appropriate questions
in psychosocial assessments.

Research also indicates that pets are often abused
in families in which there is *child maltreatment*. For
example, pet abuse or neglect was found in 60% of
a sample of 53 New Jersey families in which child
abuse or neglect had been substantiated (DeViney,
Dickert, & Lockwood, 1983). Moreover, the rate of
pet abuse was 88% among the 21 families in which
there had been child physical abuse (as opposed to
sexual abuse or neglect).

Children's abuse of animals is an indicator
that the child perpetrator may have been the target of abuse and may be at risk of perpetrating

Table 3   Motivations for Adults' Cruelty to Animals

To control an animal

To retaliate against an animal

To satisfy a prejudice against a species or breed

To express aggression through an animal

To enhance one's own aggressiveness

To shock people for amusement

To retaliate against another person

Displacement of hostility from a person to an animal

Nonspecific sadism

Source: Kellert, S. R., & Felthous, A. R. (1985). Childhood cruelty toward animals among criminals and noncriminals. *Human Relations, 38,* 1113–1129. (Motivations listed on pages 1122–1124.)

interpersonal violence. Abuse of animals is listed as one of 15 symptoms of Conduct Disorder in the fourth edition of the *Diagnostic and Statistical Manual of Mental Disorders* (American Psychiatric Association, 1994). Conduct Disorder is a behavior pattern that reflects persistent disregard for the feelings and rights of others. There is evidence that animal abuse is often the first symptom of Conduct Disorder to emerge in a child. Factors associated with children's abuse of animals include corporal punishment, child maltreatment (physical or sexual abuse), and witnessing domestic violence. We will briefly consider each of these factors.

In a study of 267 undergraduate students, Flynn (1999) found that 34.5% of the males and 9.3% of the females reported having perpetrated animal abuse during childhood. Male students who had experienced corporal punishment inflicted by their fathers were more likely to perpetrate animal abuse. Moreover, male students who had perpetrated animal abuse were more likely to approve of a husband slapping his wife.

Children who are abused or who witness abuse may imitate the abuse by hurting animals. In the study by DeViney et al. (1983) cited above, the researchers found that one or both adults in the family were responsible for most of the pet abuse that involved either inflicting pain on the animal or causing an inhumane death. However, in 14% of such cases children were the sole pet abusers.

Additional evidence regarding child maltreatment as a factor in children's abuse of animals emerges from a study by Friedrich (unpublished study, cited

in Ascione, 1993), which examined incidences of pet abuse in sexually abused and non-abused children ages 2–12. The findings indicated that 34.8% of 89 sexually abused boys, compared to 4.9% of 453 non-abused boys, had abused animals. Similarly, 27.5% of 182 sexually abused females, compared to 3.3% of 426 non-abused females, had abused animals.

Children's abuse of animals has also been associated with the experience of witnessing domestic violence. Studies of women in domestic violence programs and shelters indicate not only that the women's partners threatened or harmed their pets, but also that their children witnessed the abuse and in some cases imitated the abuse by harming a pet (Ascione, 1998; Quinlisk, 1999). For example, in Ascione's (1998) survey of 38 women in a domestic violence shelter in Utah, 71% of 28 pet owners reported that their batterer had threatened to harm their pet, 57% reported that their batterer had actually harmed their pet, and 32% of the 22 pet-owning mothers in the study reported that one of their children had hurt or killed a pet.

In sum, children who experience or witness violence may imitate the abuse they have seen or express the abuse they have felt by harming a pet. Ascione, Thompson, and Black (1997) have identified a number of developmentally relevant motivations for children's abuse of animals, which are listed in Table 4. For a thorough review of research on abuse of animals among children and adolescents, see Ascione (2005b).

There are many contexts in which social workers interact with children who have abused animals and with adults who perpetrated or witnessed animal abuse during childhood. During counseling sessions at community mental health centers, schools, in-patient hospitals, and private practices, as well as during interactions in home visits or assessments at juvenile court, social workers are in contact with troubled children and families in which animal abuse has occurred. Often social workers miss an opportunity to gather important information about the nature and frequency of violence in the home by not asking about violence toward animals. Yet attention to animals can serve as a social lubricant, increasing people's comfort in conversing with others. This effect can carry over into discussions about family violence, providing aid in starting difficult discussions about such painful topics.

For example, a child may not want to tell a social worker that she was sexually abused by her

Table 4 Developmentally Related Motivations for Cruelty to Animals Among Children and Youth

Curiosity or exploration

Peer reinforcement

Mood enhancement

Sexual gratification

Forced abuse

Attachment to an animal

Animal phobias

Identification with the child's abuser

Imitation

Posttraumatic play

Self-injury

Rehearsal for interpersonal violence

Vehicle for emotional abuse

Source: Ascione, F. R., Thompson, T. M., & Black, T. (1997). Childhood cruelty to animals: Assessing cruelty dimensions and motivations. *Anthrozoös, 10,* 170–177.

stepfather, but when asked about her kittens, the child may be able to say that her stepfather hurt them. Equipped with information about human motivations for animal abuse, the social worker may be able to explore this disclosure gently to determine the child's perception of why her stepfather hurt the kittens. When the social worker shows compassion and care for the plight of the kittens, the child learns something about the social worker: "She cares and understands!" In turn, the child gains trust in the social worker and may be more willing to share what happened to her, anticipating that the social worker will show the same care and compassion toward her. Thus, asking about animals opens conversation in a way that the question "Has anyone ever harmed you?" cannot.

Treatment models for intervening with children who have abused animals are also available. Ani-Care Child, a treatment approach developed by the Society & Animals Forum (see Appendix A), assesses the reasons a child may have abused an animal and provides treatment methods depending on the degree of abuse. The model also prepares social workers to facilitate the development of skills such as accountability and empathy in a child who has abused an animal.

Social workers also have opportunities to work therapeutically with adults who have been convicted of animal abuse and with incarcerated and non-incarcerated violent offenders who have animal abuse in their developmental histories. The AniCare Model of Treatment for Animal Abuse (see Appendix A), developed by the Society & Animals Forum for use with adult animal abusers, is designed to confront and therapeutically address lack of empathy and poor impulse control so often found in people who resort to violence against animals and people. Social workers employed in the criminal justice system are likely to supervise convicted animal abusers during probation or parole. In such cases, it is imperative that social workers have extensive knowledge of motivations for animal abuse and treatment methods in order to rehabilitate the offender, ensure appropriate placement after incarceration, prevent recidivism, and protect animals and people in the community.

Animal abuse often occurs in the context of *domestic violence.* The significance of companion animals in the lives of battered women became apparent in early investigations of violence against women (Walker, 1979). The research on battered women to date suggests that (1) many battered women consider their pets an important source of emotional support (Faver & Strand, 2003b; Flynn, 2000a, 2000c), (2) batterers often threaten or harm their partner's pet (Ascione, 1998; Ascione, Weber, & Wood, 1997; Faver & Strand, 2003b; Flynn, 2000b, 2000c; Weber, 1998), (3) battered women worry about the safety of their pets both within abusive relationships (Ascione, 1998; Flynn, 2000b) and after coming into domestic violence shelters (Flynn, 2000a, 2000c), and (4) concern for the safety of companion animals affects women's decision making about staying with or leaving an abusive partner (Ascione, 1998; Ascione, Weber, & Wood, 1997; Faver & Strand, 2003b; Flynn, 2000b, 2000c; Weber, 1998). In sum, male batterers often threaten or harm a pet in order to intimidate, control, or coerce their female partner. Social workers need to be aware that a battered woman's attachment to and concern for her pet may be a factor in her decision about leaving or staying with an abusive partner. Moreover, the lack of adequate "safe havens" for pets in the network of domestic violence services may be a significant barrier hindering battered women from entering a shelter.

The social worker's role in domestic violence is to provide counseling and advocacy services to victims. These services include helping a victim to file an order of protection, obtain housing or a job, reunite with children who were in protective custody due to perceived danger, and increase the victim's self-esteem and life mastery skills. From the human–animal bond perspective, a domestic violence social worker should ask whether there are animals in the home, and if so, whether the animals have been abused and whether their safety is affecting the victim's decision about leaving or staying with the abuser. Domestic violence social workers should also develop methods of providing a safe haven for the victim's animals, thus eliminating that barrier to seeking safety.

Animal abuse is also linked to *elder abuse and neglect*. An elder's neglect of a companion animal may indicate that the elder is no longer able to care for herself or her pet. Moreover, an elder's adult children or other family members may threaten to harm or remove a pet in order to coerce the elder to comply with the abuser's wishes (Loar, 1999). In 2001, the Humane Society of the United States (HSUS) and the National Center on Elder Abuse surveyed almost 200 Adult Protective Service supervisors and caseworkers in 40 states (cited in Arkow, 2003). Over 92% of the respondents reported that they knew of cases in which a client's self-neglect coexisted with animal neglect; over 35% stated that clients had reported that their pets had been threatened, injured, killed, or denied care; over 45% reported that they had seen intentional animal abuse or neglect while visiting clients; and 75% reported that decisions about interventions in clients' lives were affected by the clients' concern for their pets' welfare.

In working with the elderly, social workers must always be alert to the presence of animals and ask questions about the elder's relationship with animals in the home. As noted above, neglect of the pet may be a signal that the elder can no longer care for himself or herself. In all cases in which animals are abused or neglected, social workers must assess who is perpetrating the maltreatment and why. In addition, social workers must develop programs to provide safe havens for the animals of elders. When elders anticipate leaving their homes to enter residential care, they may fear losing their bond with their pets. At such a time, elders may neglect themselves and pour all their resources into caring for their animals. Thus, programs that make it possible for elders to visit with their pets even after entering residential care can ease this important life transition and make an important contribution to elders' health and well-being.

Animal hoarding is a form of animal abuse (see *Animal Hoarding* by Patronek, this text). An animal hoarder has been defined as someone who "accumulates a large number of animals; fails to provide minimal standards of nutrition, sanitation, and veterinary care; fails to act on the deteriorating condition of the animals (including disease, starvation, and even death), or the environment (severely overcrowded and unsanitary conditions); fails to act on or recognize the negative impact of the collection on their own health and well-being" (Nathanson & HARC, 2002).

Hoarders are more likely to be female, and most are over 60 years old. Some hoarders have a mental illness or other psychological problem, but others seem to have a sincere desire to rescue animals without realizing the challenges and difficulties of such an enormous task. Hoarders are usually socially isolated, and self-neglect often occurs in conjunction with hoarding. There are varied opinions about the best way to address the problem of hoarding and how to help hoarders. Prosecution of hoarders has been recommended only if there is criminal or fraudulent intent involved. Yet education and counseling are unlikely to be adequate to help hoarders whose hoarding stems from persistent psychological or emotional problems and needs. A collaborative effort of veterinarians, animal welfare organizations, animal control officers, and social service agencies has been recommended to help hoarders (Patronek, 1999; Patronek & HARC, 2001; HSUS & WI Dept. of Health and Family Services, 2003; see *Animal Hoarding* by Patronek, this text).

A social worker's role in animal hoarding cases may include psychosocial assessment, social support, treatment, and assistance in achieving compliance with a court mandate. During assessment, the social worker must be alert to signs of self-neglect by the hoarder and to environmental hazards for any children present. Collaboration with Adult Protective Services or Child Protective Services will be needed if self-neglect or child neglect or abuse is discovered. The social worker's role in achieving compliance with court orders is important because animal hoarding has an extremely high recidivism rate. A social worker may be assigned to make home visits to ensure that an animal hoarder who has been mandated to have no more than one or two animals is complying with this mandate. Such visits afford an opportunity for the social worker to assess needs regularly, make referrals to community resources, provide social support, and facilitate the individual's ability to comply with the court order.

The Web of Abuse: Social Work Strategies to Help People and Animals

Social workers can use many strategies to prevent and combat violence against people and animals. In the following list, strategies 1–4 can be implemented by individual social workers practicing in a variety of contexts. Given the nature and extent of abuse within families and communities, however, the most effective way to stop violence is through coalitions of human services providers and animal welfare workers. Thus, strategy 5 focuses on the process of building a community coalition against violence, and strategies 6–12 focus on actions that can be implemented by such coalitions.

Many of the strategies listed below are addressed in-depth elsewhere. For such strategies, we provide only a brief explanation and direct the reader to other resources for further information. We provide more in-depth coverage of four topics that have been a primary focus of our own work: humane education (strategy 1), assessing animal abuse in the context of family violence (strategy 2), building community coalitions (strategy 5), and gathering data on "the link" in local communities (strategy 12).

Before describing the specific strategies, we must emphasize the importance of grounding all social work interventions in the profession's ethics and values. As in all areas of social work practice, addressing the link between animal abuse and interpersonal violence requires cultural sensitivity and cultural competence. Beliefs about the role of animals in society vary widely both across and within cultural groups. Considering companion animals, for example, some people perceive dogs as pets to be pampered, while others regard dogs as "guards" for property, serving (with little or no veterinary care) as a relatively inexpensive residential security system. In our discussion of definitions of animal abuse, above, we noted that many forms of harm to animals are currently "socially acceptable" in the United States. Thus, social workers must know and understand the varied belief systems of community members in order to advocate firmly for the welfare of both people and animals while respecting the dignity and worth of every being.

A useful social work principle to guide our efforts in a culturally competent way is "start where the client is." Listening, reflecting feelings, and asking open questions provides an opportunity for an individual, family, or group to explore their own beliefs about the role of animals in their lives and communities. Social workers can then facilitate people's ability to clarify their values, consider alternative beliefs and behaviors, and make informed decisions about future actions. The analogy we used previously comparing social workers' role in animal welfare work with their role in child welfare work is relevant to cultural competence also. Specifically, we noted that childcare practices vary on a broad continuum. Some of these behaviors may not be conducive to children's well-being, but they are not currently defined as "maltreatment." In order to help clients improve their child care practices, a social worker must first understand the clients' own perspective on childrearing. This is "starting where the client is," which is an essential aspect of cultural competence. Analogously, to facilitate a process in which people learn to regard and treat animals more humanely, social workers must understand the clients' beliefs about animals, the cultural and social factors that formed these beliefs, and how central these beliefs are in the clients' worldview. The first strategy listed below, which focuses on humane education, highlights a method social workers can use to foster humane living through a respectful, culturally sensitive process.

1. Promote humane education and practice humane living. Scholars have suggested that two social causes of animal abuse and interpersonal violence are patriarchy (male power over women, children, and animals) and the socialization of children (especially males) toward aggression (see Flynn, 2000b; Adams, 1995). Clearly, nothing short of social transformation is required to dismantle patriarchy and counter aggression in all its forms. Broadly defined, humane education fosters such a transformation by preparing people to make intentional choices that are kind and compassionate to the earth, to all animals, and to all people both near and distant, known and unknown (Weil, 2003; International Institute for Humane Education [IIHEd], 2005). Thus, humane education is a fundamental antidote to violence.

In *Above All, Be Kind: Raising a Humane Child in Challenging Times*, humane educator Zoe Weil (2003) explains how adults can model humane living and help children grow into humane adults. Humane education begins by defining the qualities that we wish to foster in ourselves and others. Such qualities include, for example, kindness, compassion, honesty, integrity, and willingness to choose and change. Note that "kindness," according to Weil, means to choose the action that does the most good and causes the least harm.

Weil's (2003) model of humane education includes four elements. The first is to "enhance reverence, respect and responsibility for the earth, animals, and all people" (IIHEd, 2005). According to Weil, reverence is an emotion of awe and wonder directed toward the natural world, animals, and people. Respect is the attitude that follows from a sense of awe and wonder, and responsibility involves taking action that is consistent with our respect for people, animals, and the earth.

The second element is to seek out (for ourselves) and to provide (for others) accurate information about the impact of our choices as consumers and citizens on the earth, animals, and people everywhere. Often such information is not readily available. As noted earlier, schools typically may not teach children how food and clothing are produced. Moreover, the information that is available may reflect biases and distortions that hide suffering and promote a particular set of interests. Thus, we need to seek alternative perspectives.

The third element is to encourage critical thinking. As children's cognitive skills develop, they must learn to assess information with curiosity and a healthy degree of skepticism. Critical thinking enables people to detect the biases of advertising and media messages and to discover the truth about human and animal suffering.

The fourth element is to provide positive behavioral choices to respond to suffering. As people discover the breadth of suffering of people and animals, they also need to learn what they can do to stop the suffering and build a safe, humane world.

Finally, the value of integrity requires us to practice humane living ourselves if we wish to foster kindness and compassion in others. Weil (2003) cites an incident in which Gandhi was asked by a journalist, "What is your message?" and Gandhi replied, "My life is my message." Regardless of what we say, people will see what we actually do. Note that humane qualities such as kindness, compassion, honesty, and willingness to change are also the personal characteristics needed to be competent social workers (see, e.g., Segal, Gerdes, & Steiner, 2005). As we consistently apply the four elements

of humane education in our own lives, we will also become better social workers.

Social workers can introduce the purpose and process of humane education in many contexts, including professional presentations, in-service trainings, workshops, and consultations with parents, teachers, counselors, clergy, and community groups. Weil (2003) offers numerous suggestions for teaching and applying the four elements of humane education in age-appropriate ways. Other useful resources are listed in Appendix A. These resources include guides for parents and lesson plans which teachers can use to foster humane values in the process of teaching core skills in language arts and science. Yet many parents and teachers may not discover these resources on their own. Social workers must be familiar with humane education resources in order to guide parents and teachers to age-appropriate materials that match their parenting or curricular needs.

2. Include questions about animals and animal abuse in assessment interviews in all social work settings. These settings include, for example, child protective services, adult protective services, schools, mental health clinics, medical clinics and hospitals, domestic violence shelters and crisis hotlines, and juvenile justice centers. Assessing animal abuse is important not only to combat the web of violence, but also to contribute to the knowledge of the incidence and prevalence of animal abuse (Arluke & Lockwood, 1997). As noted previously, currently there are no federal requirements for mandated reporting of animal cruelty (Ascione, 2005b). Thus, collecting data at the local level in multiple sites across the country can contribute to the knowledge base of the incidence and prevalence of animal abuse in family violence situations.

As in all assessments, the clarity and specificity of the questions will determine the quality of the data gathered. This section will briefly review some of the questions used previously to assess animal abuse in the context of family violence. A subsequent section (strategy 12) will address how and where data about animal abuse can be collected by social workers at the local level and how data can be aggregated and used to support policy and program development.

In a program evaluation of a domestic violence program, Jorgenson and Maloney (1999) initially asked domestic violence victims whether animal abuse had ever occurred during their abusive relationships. Women frequently answered "no," only to report later that indeed their partners had hit and kicked their pets. As a result, the researchers changed the question to "Has an animal you care about ever been hurt?" This question elicited more reports of animal abuse from battered women. The researchers also added a question about the batterers' threats to animals because anecdotal stories of battered women indicated that batterers used threats to animals as a way to gain power and control (Jorgenson & Maloney, 1999). These changes illustrate the importance of conducting both qualitative and case study research in assessment of animal abuse. Indeed, coalitions often emerge from "case studies" of battered women which point to ways to improve community services (Boatfield & Vallongo, 1999).

Assessment of the impact of animal abuse on battered women's decision making has also evolved. For example, The Battered Partner Shelter Survey (BPSS)—Pet Maltreatment Assessment (Ascione, 1998), which was administered to battered women residing in a shelter, included the following question: "Did concern over your pet's welfare keep you from coming to this shelter sooner than now?" A subsequent instrument, the Domestic Violence Pet Abuse Survey (Ascione, 2000a), asked: "Does concern over your pet affect your decision making about staying with or leaving your partner?" The latter form of the question takes into account that while some women may delay leaving their abuser because of concern for their pet, other women may be prompted to leave their batterer because of his threats or abuse to the pet, as anecdotal evidence suggests (Strand, 2003). Moreover, some anecdotal evidence now suggests that the impact of concern for pets on battered women's decision making may be different for childless women than for mothers (Strand, 2003)

Questionnaires also vary in their degree of specificity in assessing types of animal abuse. For example, some studies combine hurting and killing pets into one category (Ascione, 1998; Faver & Strand, 2003b; Quinlisk, 1999) and some use three categories for threats to pets, hurting pets, and killing pets (Flynn, 2000c).

Measurement efforts have been developed in assessing children's experiences with animals and animal abuse as well. Measurement tools such as the Boat Inventory of Animal-Related Experiences (BIARE) (Boat, 1999; see also *Collaborating to Assess, Intervene, and Prosecute Animal Abuse* by Boat, Loar, & Phillips, this text), the Children and

Animals Assessment Instrument (CAAI) (Ascione, 1993; Ascione, Thompson, & Black, 1997), and the Childhood Trust Events Survey (Boat, Baker, & Abrahamson, 1996) assess animal loss, social support by animals, and animal abuse. Moreover, questions about children's experiences with animal abuse have been included on instruments such as the Battered Partner Shelter Survey (BPSS) (Ascione, 1998) and Children's Observation and Experience with their Pets (COEP) (Ascione & Weber, 1995). The Child Behavior Checklist (CBCL) (Achenbach, 1991, 1992) also includes a question about animal abuse that is used in assessing conduct disorder in children. Table 5 includes examples of questions used on several instruments mentioned in this discussion.

The human–animal bond is also assessed on some surveys addressing animal abuse in the context of family violence. For example, in a survey administered to women who had been battered, Flynn (2000c) asked: "How important was your pet as a source of emotional support in dealing with the abuse?" A more complete assessment of the level and type of bond people have with their animals is essential to understand how people make decisions about the care of their animals and themselves in violent situations. Many measures that assess the human–animal bond allow greater variance in the level of the bond as well as more precision in assessing what factors contribute most to the bond (Bryant, 1990; Poresky, 1997; Poresky, Hendrix, Mosier, & Samuelson, 1987; Zasloff, 1996). For example, there is some evidence that commitment to pets is different from attachment to pets. Commitment refers to the willingness of an owner to continue caring for a pet even when the pet has problems or the owner's life situation makes keeping the pet difficult. Such commitment is illustrated by children who attempt to protect their pets in family violence situations (see Ascione, 1998). Attachment, on the other hand, usually reflects the emotional bond people report having with their pets. People can be high on commitment, but low on attachment, or vice versa (Voith, 1985).

3. Educate other professionals about the link between animal abuse and interpersonal violence. Social workers should be active in educating domestic violence professionals, teachers, law enforcement officials, child and adult protective service practitioners, animal control and humane society workers, attorneys, and veterinarians about the link between family violence and animal cruelty.

Table 5 Overview of Animal Abuse Assessment Questions

Assessment Questions	Population	Authors
• Have you ever had pets in this relationship? • Do you currently have pets? • In dealing with the abuse, how important has your pet been as a source of emotional support? (very important, somewhat important, not at all important?) • Has your partner ever threatened to harm your pet, actually harmed your pet, or killed your pet? • Has your child ever threatened to harm your pet, actually harmed your pet, or killed your pet? • Where is your pet now? (with a family member, with a friend/neighbor, with my partner/ex-partner, no longer alive, took animal to the shelter, gave pet away) • Do you worry about your pet's safety? • Did concern about your pet's safety keep you from seeking shelter sooner? • If yes, how long did you delay seeking shelter due to your concern for your pet's safety? (Less than a week, 1–2 weeks, 3–4 weeks, 5–8 weeks, more than 8 weeks)	Domestic Violence Victims	Flynn (2000c)
Qualitative Semi-structured Interview • What was the nature of the companion animal abuse? • How was the animal cruelty used by the batterer to control, hurt, or intimidate you? • What was the relationship like between you and your companion animal? • What role did your companion animals play in the family? • Has your companion animal helped your cope with abuse by your batterer? How? • How was your companion animal affected by abuse toward you from the batterer?	Domestic Violence Victims	Flynn (2000a) Symbolic Interaction
• Has an animal you care about ever been hurt?	Domestic Violence Victims	Jorgenson and Maloney (1999)
• Have you had a pet animal or animals in the past 12 months? • How many pets have you had in the last 5 years? • Has your partner (or child) helped care for your pets? • How did you feel after the pet was threatened (or harmed or killed): Numb, I was extremely upset but felt nothing; Terrible, I felt very upset; Mildly upset; It didn't bother me at all. • How close were you to the pet that was abused or threatened? • Does concern over your pet affect your decision making about staying with or leaving your partner? • Have you noticed any change in your partner's willingness to threaten or abuse your pet?: No, he has NEVER threatened to hurt our pet(s); No, he always threatened or hurt our pet(s); Yes, he has become LESS threatening and abusive toward pets; Yes, he has become MORE threatening and abusive toward pets.	Domestic Violence Victims (including children)	Domestic Violence Pet Abuse Survey [DVPAS] (Ascione, 2000a).

(Continued)

Table 5 *(Continued)*

Assessment Questions	Population	Authors
Qualitative	Domestic Violence Workers	Strand (2003)
• Did you notice any differences in the types of relationships battered women had with pets based on whether women had children or not?		
• Have there ever been difficult or stressful times when a pet or animal was a source of comfort for you, even if you did not own the animal?	Children	Boat Inventory on Animal Related Experiences (Boat, 1999)
• Are there times that it has been easier to talk with animals than to people?		
• Have you ever lost an animal you really cared about?		
• If your pet died, was the death: (a) natural (old age, illness, euthanasia, (b) accidental (hit by a car), (c) deliberate (strangled or drowned), (d) cruel or violent (pet was tortured)?		
• Was the death or loss used to punish you or make you do something?		
• Did you ever see anyone deliberately hurting, torturing, or killing a pet or animal in a cruel way?		
• Have you ever seen others do sex acts or sexual touching with animals?		
• Have you ever done sex acts or sexual touching with animals?		
• Does seeing movies or TV shows where animals are hurt or mistreated bother you?		

Without knowledge about the link, human service and animal welfare workers may miss important opportunities to prevent or interrupt family violence. For example, domestic violence workers who are uninformed about the link may not recognize battered women's attachment to their pets as a barrier to leaving an abusive partner. Teachers who are unaware of the link may perceive children's abuse of animals as an indicator of emotional problems but may not be alert to the possibility of family violence within the child's household. Child and adult protective service workers who lack information about the link may not inquire about animal cruelty and thus miss an opportunity to learn about the extent and nature of violence in a household. Similarly, animal control and humane society workers who are unaware of the link may not recognize signs of interpersonal violence in households where they are investigating animal cruelty. If uninformed about the link, prosecutors may miss an opportunity to create stronger legal cases against batterers, and veterinarians who suspect animal abuse in a patient may not recognize that the pet owner is also abused.

In order for social workers to serve as educators to other professionals, they must be well-informed

themselves. Thus, social work education must include information about the link in the curriculum in both the baccalaureate and graduate programs. Regarding the link between animal abuse and domestic violence, specifically, Faver and Strand (2003a, 2004) have identified the type of information that is needed in the curriculum and where in the curriculum this information should be integrated. Information about the human–animal bond is a foundation for knowledge about the link and must be included in foundation courses such as human behavior and the social environment. In general, curriculum content on families, communities, and interpersonal violence should always include animals as a dimension of these topics. Just as other topics are mandated in the curriculum by social work's accrediting organization (Council on Social Work Education), so too should content on the human–animal bond and animal abuse be integrated into the social work curriculum.

The Humane Society of the United States (HSUS) began a campaign in 1997 called "First Strike: Animal Cruelty and Human Violence" with the purpose of educating professionals and lay people about the connection between violence against animals and violence against people (HSUS,

2005a). The HSUS First Strike website (http://www. hsus.org/hsus_field/first_strike_the_connection_ between_animal_cruelty_and_human_violence/) has extensive materials on the link that can be downloaded, including fact sheets targeted at specific professionals and "concerned citizens." Appendix A lists numerous video, print, and web resources that social workers can use to educate people about the link and to train professionals to use their knowledge of the link to prevent and intervene more effectively in family and community violence.

4. Build relationships with animal welfare organizations. Social workers need to establish active relationships with animal welfare agencies such as humane societies, animal control departments, and veterinary clinics. These organizations are often the first to be informed of animal cruelty. By cultivating close relationships with these agencies, social workers are more likely to be alerted to animal cruelty cases in which other forms of family violence may also be occurring. In addition, these contacts can be useful in finding care for the pets of battered women who need to seek shelter.

5. Establish a community coalition or create an animal abuse task force within an existing community coalition working to prevent and combat family violence. Such coalitions typically include representatives of all human services and animal welfare organizations and agencies whose work addresses animal abuse or family violence. Professional social work training in grassroots organizing and community development prepares social workers to be instrumental in establishing these coalitions, which are vital in preventing and combating all forms of family violence.

Several useful resources are already available to assist practitioners in building coalitions of animal welfare and human service providers to address the link. For example, Arkow (2003) describes several types of collaborative relationships (including coalitions) and provides guidelines for building a coalition. In addition, the HSUS has a guide to coalition building entitled "What Communities Can Do to Prevent Violence" (HSUS, 2005b). Each of these guides provides useful ideas and further resources about the process of building a coalition and about specific tasks and activities a coalition can undertake to address the link. In addition, members of several community antiviolence coalitions have documented their own process of initiating and developing their coalitions (see Arkow, 2003; and Ascione & Arkow, 1999).

Developing strong relationships within coalitions is essential. Thus, throughout the coalition-building process, social workers must attend to building and maintaining healthy relationships between human and animal welfare organizations. Ideological conflicts between human and animal welfare organizations can impede cooperation. For example, a domestic violence worker may believe it is important to support a woman's decision to return to her abusive partner, taking her beloved dog with her back to the home, because the domestic violence worker views the woman's leaving as a process that may involve several exits from the home. The domestic violence worker does not want the woman to be re-victimized by having her dog, who may be her only source of emotional and social support, taken from her when she chooses to return to her batterer. On the other hand, the animal welfare professional's main focus is keeping animals out of homes where animal abuse may occur. Some animal welfare organizations willing to provide "safe havens" for the pets of women entering domestic violence shelters require women to relinquish their rights to their pets so that they can retrieve their pets only if they are not returning to the abusive partner. This stipulation would prevent a woman from taking her beloved pet home if she returns to her abuser. If the woman obtains another pet, she will remember that when she tried to leave her abuser the previous time she lost her companion animal and therefore she may not come into the shelter again.

Developing and maintaining healthy relationships in the coalition-building process may also be negatively affected by high levels of compassion fatigue in both human services and animal welfare professions. Compassion fatigue and burnout can lead to irritability, apathy, and resentment (Boatfield & Vallongo, 1999). The grim reality of the high numbers of children and women that are abused and the high number of homeless animals who are killed by euthanasia may contribute to compassion fatigue among both human services providers and animal welfare workers. Compassion fatigue in turn may affect coalition members' ability to deal with tension and ideological conflict in order to engage in the cooperative communication needed for the work of the coalition. Maddie's Fund, a granting agency whose purpose is to fund the creation of no-kill animal shelters, recognizes that in-fighting among organizations is an enormous barrier to coalition building and thus it supports conflict management processes within communities (see http://www.maddiesfund.org).

In sum, apparent conflicts of interest between animal and human welfare organizations and the stress inherent in attempts to protect and save lives (human or animal) can make it very difficult to create and maintain interdisciplinary coalitions. Yet such coalitions are absolutely essential to combat violence and can work beautifully with the proper nurturance. Often it is each organization's habit of tenaciously holding onto its own stance that stalls efforts to work collaboratively. Therefore, a social worker's role in these situations is to work toward building consensus among the various stakeholders. Social work training at both the micro and macro levels prepares social workers for this type of work. Skills used in grassroots organizing and skills used in clinical social work practice, especially the skills of empathy and validation, are the very tools that are needed to invite creative solutions to ideological conflicts between various stakeholders attempting to combat family violence. In addition, utilizing communication strategies and approaches outlined in resources such as Rosenberg's (2003) "Nonviolent Communication" and Rivers' (2004) "The Seven Challenges: A Workbook and Reader about Communicating More Cooperatively" may enhance communication among coalition members and elicit compassion and cooperation instead of resentment and conflict. Social workers' ability to introduce these resources and model these skills in the coalition-building process is extremely important in building strong, well-functioning working groups.

6. Anti-violence community coalitions can assess the animal cruelty laws at the state and local level and advocate for enforcement of these laws and prosecution of animal abusers. Animal cruelty laws vary widely across states and localities, but most state anti-cruelty laws include the following components: "1) the types of animals protected, 2) the types of acts prohibited or duties imposed, 3) the mental culpability required to impose liability, 4) the defense to liabilities, 5) certain activities exempted from the law, and 6) the penalty for each offense" (Lacroix & Wilson, 1998).

Coalitions can assess the legal definitions of animal cruelty in their state laws and local ordinances, the penalties assigned, and the frequency and outcomes of prosecutions within their state and local area. Some questions to consider include:

How is animal cruelty defined in our state statutes? What types of offenses are felonies? What types of offenses are misdemeanors? What are the local ordinances regarding animal cruelty?

What types of animals are included in the legal definition of animal cruelty? In addition to "owned" animals (that is, pets), are stray animals and wild animals included?

What are the penalties for various forms of animal cruelty? Is treatment mandated for abusers?

How often, and under what circumstances, is animal cruelty prosecuted?

What happens to animals while cases are being prosecuted? Are the animals released to humane societies for adoption or held indefinitely as "evidence" of the crime?

Based on their analysis of current policies and outcomes of implementing policies, coalitions can advocate for policies that adequately define and actively intervene in cases of animal abuse. Coalitions can also support court-ordered psychological evaluations for perpetrators of animal cruelty, which will help to identify individuals who are also abusing their partners or children. Social workers can take an active role by seeking training in methods of assessing and treating animal abuse such as the AniCare and AniCare Child models (see Appendix A). Social workers can also inform their local judges and court systems that they have been trained and are available to work with convicted animal abusers. When attorneys and judges are aware of the local resources available for assessing and treating animal abuse, they may be more likely to apply laws that allow mandatory assessment and counseling of convicted animal abusers. In short, coalitions can seek changes that afford greater protection for both animals and their human companions.

7. Coalitions can seek to establish cross-training and cross-reporting procedures between animal welfare organizations (e.g., animal control offices, humane societies) and human services organizations (e.g., child and adult protective services, law enforcement units) in their local community. Cross-training means that animal welfare professionals learn to recognize signs of child or adult abuse, and human services professionals learn to recognize signs of animal cruelty. Cross-reporting means that if human services professionals observe signs of animal cruelty, they will report it to the appropriate animal welfare agency (humane society or animal control agency). Similarly, if animal welfare professionals observe signs of human abuse, they will report it to the appropriate agency (Arkow, 2003). For example, an animal cruelty investigator who observes

signs of child abuse would make a report to child protective services. The agency to which the report is made has the responsibility to investigate and decide whether action is needed. To date, relatively few states have enacted laws mandating cross-reporting, and the existing statutes require animal welfare officers to report child or dependent adult abuse. Human services workers are not yet mandated to report suspected animal cruelty. Even without mandated reporting, however, coalitions can establish cooperative agreements between animal welfare and human services organizations for voluntary cross-reporting.

8. Coalitions can establish "safe pet" programs to address the needs of battered women who are concerned about the safety of their companion animals. By providing shelter for these pets, such programs seek to ensure that women's concern for their companion animals does not interfere with their ability and willingness to seek shelter (Ascione, 2000b) Guidelines for safe pet programs and relevant forms that can be adapted for specific organizations are provided in the document "Starting a Safe Havens for Animals Program," which is available on the website of the Humane Society of the United States (http://www.hsus.org/hsus_field/first_strike_the_connection_between_animal_cruelty_and_human_violence/) and in *Safe Havens for Pets: Guidelines for Programs Sheltering Pets for Women Who Are Battered* (Ascione, 2000b).

9. Coalitions can initiate or support humane education programs in schools. In the first strategy we described the principles of humane education and how individual social work practitioners can promote humane education. Coalitions can work with school districts and individual schools to encourage the systematic incorporation of humane education into the curriculum to prevent violence by instilling respect, kindness, and compassion toward all humans and animals (see Ascione, 1997). To convince school administrators of the importance of humane education, coalitions can cite research such as a study by Ascione and Weber (1996), which showed the effectiveness of a humane education curriculum in a sample of 4th grade children and indicated that humane attitudes toward animals generalized to empathy for humans.

10. Coalitions can develop a persistent public education campaign about the link between animal abuse and interpersonal violence. Media campaigns can highlight different aspects of the link in posters, brochures, and public service announcements (PSAs). For example, one media message may focus on the link between animal cruelty and woman battering, and another may suggest that a child's abuse of animals is a sign that the child may be a victim of abuse and may be at risk of becoming a perpetrator of interpersonal violence. Launching a persistent media campaign can increase the possibility that the public will take animal abuse seriously and report their observations of animal or human abuse to the appropriate agencies. A media campaign may also alert adults or children who are risk of being abused to the significance of animal abuse and prompt them to seek help before violence escalates.

11. Coalitions can work with animal welfare specialists and specially trained social workers and counselors to establish animal-facilitated programs designed to prevent violence and to interrupt the cycle of violence. In recent years animal-facilitated therapy programs have been established for humans with a variety of special physical, social, and emotional needs. Some animal-facilitated programs are designed specifically for people who have witnessed or have been the targets of violence, for those who have perpetrated violence, and for those at risk of becoming perpetrators of violence. These programs are based on the assumption that at the core of violence is a lack of empathy. Through animal-facilitated programs, people can learn nurturance, empathy, kindness, and compassion as they develop appropriate relationships with animals in supervised settings (Duel, 2004). There are a wide variety of animal-facilitated therapy programs. For a description of specific programs, see the resources listed under "Animal-Facilitated Therapy" in Appendix A.

12. Coalitions can gather data in their local community on the incidence and prevalence of animal cruelty in the context of family violence. There are four critical steps in the process of gathering and using such data.

The first step is to educate stakeholders (human services and animal welfare workers) about the need to obtain accurate estimates of the occurrence of animal abuse. Local data are needed to inform local governmental officials about the link. With clear evidence of the problem, government officials are more likely to allocate resources to support programs to address the link at the local level. Obtaining data on animal cruelty in the context of family violence is also essential in order to obtain grant support for these programs.

The second step is to target data collection sites. Certainly all domestic violence services (shelters, crisis hotlines, and court advocacy programs) must include questions about animals and animal abuse in their psychosocial assessment intake forms. In addition, including questions about the presence of animals and animal abuse on orders of protection not only alerts court domestic violence advocates to the human–animal bond and possible animal abuse, but also alerts the local judicial system to the existence and significance of animal abuse. The intake systems of child and adult protective services must also collect data on the presence and abuse of animals in the families they serve. Law enforcement agencies, including police and sheriff's departments as well as city and county animal control offices, must also maintain records on animal abuse cases that involve family violence. As noted previously, animal abuse is not generally tracked by law enforcement agencies. Community anti-violence coalitions must advocate for record-keeping regarding animal abuse. Poorly funded and poorly supported animal control offices typically do not have the resources needed to utilize informational management systems that would allow simple tracking of animal abuse cases in which interpersonal violence is also present. Nevertheless, tracking the number of "link" cases investigated by animal control officers is essential in demonstrating the need for resources to be allocated to animal abuse investigations in the interests of both human and animal welfare.

The third step is to develop lists of animal abuse assessment questions appropriate for different contexts and to provide these lists to the appropriate agencies and organizations. Some questions used in previous research are shown in Table 5, and questions recommended for several settings are shown in Appendix B. Developing appropriate questions and providing them to the organizations that are being asked to collect data reduces one barrier to collection and aggregation of data on the link. For example, directors of child protective services agencies may agree that animal abuse is important, but they may be too overwhelmed with their own mandated responsibilities to devote time or resources to assessing animal abuse. By providing local and regional CPS directors with appropriate animal abuse questions for assessment, an anti-violence coalition will increase the likelihood that CPS agencies will cooperate in collecting animal

abuse data. This is true in multiple human services settings. Anti-violence coalition members should meet with agency directors and provide them with appropriate questions for assessing animal abuse in their particular human services context. Because time for psychosocial intake interviews is limited, the animal abuse questions must be limited to the most critical, such as whether animals were present, whether they were harmed, who harmed them, and whether the animals are currently in need or danger.

The fourth step is to establish regular intervals to retrieve the data collected from agencies and organizations. The community coalition can retrieve the data from the human and animal welfare organizations on a monthly or quarterly basis and summarize the findings in a report. Ideally, representatives from the various human and animal welfare organizations will be members of the coalition and can report the data from their own organizations. The data can then be aggregated and analyzed to portray the prevalence and nature of animal abuse in the context of family violence within the local community, and anti-violence programs can be built on the basis of this knowledge.

Conclusion

Concern for animals is well within the mission, scope, and value system of the social work profession. Moreover, professional social work education provides training in interpersonal and organizational skills needed to facilitate the development of humane education programs and effective anti-violence coalitions. As noted earlier, the women and men who sought to protect animals and children in the late 19th century perceived the connection between cruelty to animals and violence to people. Today, in a return to this early insight, we are witnessing a growing number of collaborative efforts between animal welfare and human services professionals. These efforts include community anti-violence coalitions, animal-assisted therapy programs, and humane education projects. As social workers initiate, support, and join these collaborative efforts, we will return to our historical roots in the inextricable link between the welfare of people and animals.

Appendix A
Resources

Connection Between Animal Abuse and Family Violence

Videos

The Humane Society of the United States. (1998). *First strike campaign video* [8 minutes, 30 seconds]. Available from First Strike Campaign, The Humane Society of the United States, 2100 L Street, Washington, DC 20037. http://www.hsus.org/hsus_field/first_strike_the_connection_between_animal_cruelty_and_human_violence/

Society & Animals Forum (formerly: PSYETA). (1999). *Beyond violence: The human-animal connection* [13 minutes, includes Discussion Guide. Available in English or Spanish]. Available from Society & Animals Forum, P.O. Box 1297, Washington Grove, MD 20880-1297. Phone/Fax: 301.963.4751, E-mail: kshapiro@societyandanimalsforum.org or malauffer@societyandanimalsforum.org. Web: http://www.societyandanimalsforum.org/

The Latham Foundation. (2004). *Breaking the cycles of violence*. [26 minutes, video and cross-training manual]. Available from The Latham Foundation, Latham Plaza Blvd., 1826 Clement Avenue, Alameda, CA 95401. Phone: 510.521.0920. Fax: 510.521.9861. E-mail: orders@latham.org. Web: http://www.latham.org/

Websites

American Humane
http://www.americanhumane.org/

Humane Society of the United States
http://www.hsus.org/hsus_field/first_strike_the_connection_between_animal_cruelty_and_human_violence/

The Latham Foundation
http://www.latham.org/

Society & Animals Forum
http://www.societyandanimalsforum.org/

Intervention Models

The AniCare Model of Treatment for Animal Abuse. Society & Animals Forum and the Doris Day Animal Foundation. Available from Society & Animals Forum, P.O. Box 1297, Washington Grove, MD 20880-1297 or http://www.societyandanimalsforum.org/.

AniCare Child: An Assessment and Treatment Approach for Childhood Animal Abuse. Society & Animals Forum and the Doris Day Animal Foundation. Available from Society & Animals Forum, P.O. Box 1297, Washington Grove, MD 20880-1297 or http://www.societyandanimalsforum.org/.

Humane Education

Books

American Humane. (1996). *Growing up humane in a violent world: A parent's guide*. Denver, CO: American Humane. http://www.americanhumane.org/

Raphael, P., Colman, L., & Loar, L. (1999). *Teaching compassion: A guide for humane educators, teachers, and parents*. Alameda, CA: The Latham Foundation. http://www.latham.org/

Selby, D. (1995). *EarthKind: A teachers handbook on humane education*. Trentham Books.

Weil, Z. (2003). *Above all, be kind: Raising a humane child in challenging times*. Gabriola Island, BC, Canada: New Society Publishers.

Weil, Z. (1990). *Animals in society: Facts and perspectives on our treatment of animals*. Animalearn. Available from the International Institute for Humane Education, http://www.IIHEd.org/

Weil, Z. (1994). *So, you love animals: An action-packed, fun-filled book to help kids help animals*. Animalearn. Available from the International Institute for Humane Education, http://www.IIHEd.org/

Websites

International Institute for Humane Education
http://www.IIHEd.org/

Teachkind
http://www.teachkind.org/

Farm Sanctuary
http://www.farmsanctuary.org/

Doris Day Animal Foundation
www.ddaf.org/

The Fund for Animals
http://www.fund.org/

National Association for Humane and Environmental Education
http://www.nahee.org/

Latham Foundation
http://www.latham.org/

Humane Society of the United States
http://www.hsus.org/

American Humane
http://www.americanhumane.org/

American Society for the Prevention of Cruelty to Animals
http://www.aspca.org/

The Center for Nonviolent Communication
http://www.cnvc.org/

Animal-Facilitated Programs

Arkow, P. (2003). *Breaking the cycles of violence: A guide to multi-disciplinary interventions for child protection, domestic violence and animal protection agencies* (2nd ed.). Alameda, CA: Latham Foundation. http://www.latham.org/

Duel, D. K. (2004). *Violence prevention and intervention: A directory of animal-related programs*. Washington, DC: Humane Society of the United States. http://www.hsus.org/hsus_field/first_strike_the_connection_between_animal_cruelty_and_human_violence/

Loar, L., & Colman, L. (2004). *Teaching empathy: Animal-assisted therapy programs for children and families exposed to violence*. Alameda, CA: Latham Foundation. http://www.latham.org/

The Delta Society
http://www.delta.org/

Appendix B:
Screening and Assessment Questions

For Domestic Violence Shelters Psychosocial Intakes

1) Do you have pets currently, or have you had pets in the last 12 months?
   ☐ Yes
   ☐ No
2) Have these pets been threatened with harm or actually harmed *(check all that apply)*?
   ☐ Threatened
   ☐ Harmed or Killed
   ☐ Neglected
3) The person who threatened or harmed the pets was *(check all that apply)*:
   ☐ My abuser
   ☐ My child
   ☐ Me
4) How many pets have you owned in the past 5 years? ——
5) Please describe what happened? *(optional)*

For Department of Children Services Psychosocial Intakes

1) Are there pet(s) currently in the home (or within the last 12 months)?
   ☐ Yes
   ☐ No

2) Have these pet(s) have been threatened with harm or actually harmed? *(check all that apply)*
   ☐ Threatened
   ☐ Harmed or Killed

3) The person who threatened or harmed these pet(s) was *(check all that apply)*:
   ☐ The person who was abusive to me, my child, or an elderly person in my home.
   ☐ My child
   ☐ Me

4) Please describe what happened? *(optional)*

For Orders of Protection

There *are* ☐, *are not* ☐, pets in the household (now or in the last 12 months)
These pets *have* ☐, *have not* ☐, been threatened with harm, or injured by the Respondent's abuser.
Name of pets:_____. Describe what happened
_____   _____
_____   _____.

These pets *have* ☐, *have not* ☐, been threatened with harm, or injured by the Respondent's child.
Name of pets: _____.
Describe what happened _____.

References

Achenbach, T. M. (1991). *Manual for the child behavior checklist/4–18 and 1991 profile.* Burlington, VT: University of Vermont Department of Psychiatry.

Achenbach, T. M. (1992). *Manual for the child behavior checklist/2–3 and 1992 profile.* Burlington, VT: University of Vermont Department of Psychiatry.

Adams, C. J. (1995). Woman-battering and harm to animals. In C. J. Adams & J. Donovan (Eds.), *Animals and women: Feminist theoretical explorations* (pp. 55–84). Durham, NC: Duke University Press.

Agnew, R. (1998). The causes of animal abuse: A social-psychological analysis. *Theoretical Criminology, 2,* 177–209.

American Humane. (2005a). Farm animals. Retrieved April 6, 2005 from http://www.americanhumane.org/

American Humane. (2005b). How American Humane began. Retrieved April 6, 2005 from http://www.americanhumane.org/

American Humane. (2005c). The real story of Mary Ellen Wilson. Retrieved April 6, 2005 from http://www.americanhumane.org/

American Psychiatric Association. (1994). *Diagnostic and statistical manual of mental disorders* (4th ed.). Washington, DC: Author.

Arkow, P. (1999). The evolution of animal welfare as a human concern. In F. R. Ascione & P. Arkow (Eds.), *Child abuse, domestic violence, and animal abuse* (pp. 62–79). West Lafayette, IN: Purdue University Press.

Arkow, P. (2003). *Breaking the cycles of violence: A guide to multi-disciplinary interventions for child protection, domestic violence and animal protection agencies.* Alameda, CA: The Latham Foundation.

Arluke, A., & Lockwood, R. (1997). Guest editors' introduction: Understanding cruelty to animals. *Society and Animals, 5*(3), 183–193.

Ascione, F. R. (1993). Children who are cruel to animals: A review of research and implications for developmental psychopathology. *Anthrozoös, 6,* 226–247.

Ascione, F. R. (1997). Humane education research? Evaluating efforts to encourage children's kindness and caring toward animals. *Genetic, Social,*

and General Psychology Monographs, 123(1), 57–77.

Ascione, F. R. (1998). Battered women's reports of their partners and their children's cruelty to animals. *Journal of Emotional Abuse, 1*(1), 119–133.

Ascione, F. R. (2000a). *Domestic violence pet abuse survey.* Logan, UT: Author.

Ascione, F. R. (2000b). *Safe havens for pets: Guidelines for programs sheltering pets for women who are battered.* Logan, UT: Author.

Ascione, F. R. (2005a). *Children & animals: Exploring the roots of kindness & cruelty.* West Lafayette, IN: Purdue University Press.

Ascione, F. R. (2005b). Children, animal abuse, and family violence—The multiple intersections of animal abuse, child victimization, and domestic violence. In K. A. Kendall-Tackett & S. M. Giacomoni (Eds.), *Child victimization: Maltreatment; bullying and dating violence; prevention and intervention* (pp. 3-1–3-36). Kingston, NJ: Civic Research Institute, Inc.

Ascione, F. R., & Arkow, P. (Eds.). (1999). *Child abuse, domestic violence, and animal abuse.* West Lafayette, IN: Purdue University Press.

Ascione, F. R., Thompson, T. M., & Black, T. (1997). Childhood cruelty to animals: Assessing cruelty dimensions and motivations. *Anthrozoös, 10,* 170–177.

Ascione, F. R., & Weber, C. V. (1995). *Children's observation and experience with their pets (COEP).* Logan, UT: Authors.

Ascione, F. R., & Weber, C. V. (1996). Children's attitudes about the humane treatment of animals: One-year follow-up of a school-based curriculum. *Anthrozoös, 9*(4), 188–195.

Ascione, F. R., Weber, C. V., & Wood, D. S. (1997). The abuse of animals and domestic violence: A national survey of shelters for women who are battered. *Society and Animals, 5*(3), 205–218.

Boat, B. W. (1999). Abuse of children and animals: Using the link to inform child assessment and protection. In F. R. Ascione & P. Arkow (Eds.), *Child abuse, domestic violence, and animal abuse* (pp. 83–100). West Lafayette, IN: Purdue University Press.

Boat, B. W., Baker, D., & Abrahamson, S. (1996). *The childhood trust events survey.* Department of Psychiatry, University of Cincinnati, Cincinnati, OH.

Boatfield, M. P., & Vallongo, S. (1999). How to build a successful community coalition. In F. R. Ascione & P. Arkow (Eds.), *Child Abuse, Domestic Violence, and Animal Abuse* (pp. 351–360). West Lafayette, IN: Purdue University Press.

Bryant, B. K. (1990). The richness of the child-pet relationship: A consideration of both benefits and costs of pets to children. *Anthrozoös, 3*(4), 253–261.

Coats, C. D. (1991). *Old MacDonald's factory farm: The myth of the traditional farm and the shocking truth about animal suffering in today's agribusiness.* New York: Crossroad Publishing Co.

DeViney, E., Dickert, J., & Lockwood, R. (1983). The care of pets within child abusing families. *The International Journal for the Study of Animal Related Problems, 4*, 321–329.

Duel, D. K. (2004). *Violence prevention and intervention: A directory of animal-related programs.* Washington, DC: Humane Society of the United States.

Eddy, S. (1899). *Friends and helpers.* Boston: Ginn and Company.

Eisnitz G. A.(1997). *Slaughterhouse: The shocking story of greed, neglect, and inhumane treatment inside the U.S. meat industry.* Amherst, NY: Prometheus Books.

Faver, C. A., & Strand, E. B. (2003a). Domestic violence and animal cruelty: Untangling the web of abuse. *Journal of Social Work Education, 39*, 237–253.

Faver, C. A., & Strand, E. B. (2003b). To leave or to stay? Battered women's concern for vulnerable pets. *Journal of Interpersonal Violence, 18*, 1367–1377.

Faver, C. A., & Strand, E. B. (2004). Domestic violence and animal cruelty: The web of abuse. In F. Danis & L. L. Lockhart (Eds.), *Breaking the silence in social work education: Domestic violence modules for foundation courses* (pp. 93–98). Alexandria, VA: Council on Social Work Education.

Flynn, C. P. (1999). Animal abuse in childhood and later support for interpersonal violence in families. *Society and Animals, 7*, 161–171.

Flynn, C. P. (2000a). Battered women and their animal companions: Symbolic interaction between human and nonhuman animals. *Society & Animals, 8*(2), 99–127.

Flynn, C. P. (2000b). Why family professionals can no longer ignore violence toward animals. *Family Relations, 49*(1), 87–95.

Flynn, C. P. (2000c). Woman's best friend: Pet abuse and the role of companion animals in the lives of battered women. *Violence Against Women, 6*(2), 162–177.

Grandin, T. (1996). Animal welfare in slaughter plants. *Proceedings of the 29th Annual Conference of American Association of Bovine Practitioners, 22–26.*

Grandin, T. (1999). *Improvements in handling and stunning of beef cattle in slaughter for 1999.* Fort Collins, CO: Grandin Livestock Handling Systems, Inc. (updated October 2004)

Grandin, T. (2005). Who is Dr. Temple Grandin? Retrieved April 6, 2005 from http://www.grandin.com/temple.html/

Hoffman, R. G. (1991). Companion animals: A therapeutic measure for elderly patients. *Journal of Gerontological Social Work, 18*(1–2), 195–205.

Humane Society of the United States (HSUS). (2004). 2003 report of animal cruelty cases. Retrieved September 22, 2004, from http://www.hsus.org/firststrike/

Humane Society of the United States (HSUS). (2005a). Making the connection: A campaign against violence. First strike: Animal cruelty/human violence. Retrieved April 5, 2005 from http://www.hsus.org/firststrike/

Humane Society of the United States (HSUS) (2005b). The role of the community in reducing violence. Retrieved April 5, 2005 from http://www.hsus.org/firststrike/

Humane Society of the United States (HSUS) & Wisconsin Department of Health and Family Services. (2003). *Creating safer communities for older adults and companion animals.* Washington, DC and Madison, WI: HSUS and Wisconsin Department of Health and Family Services. (Publication No. PDE-3181).

International Institute for Humane Education (IIHEd). (2005). Definition of humane education. Retrieved April 5, 2005 from http://www.IIHEd.org/

Jorgenson, S., & Maloney, L. (1999). Animal abuse and the victims of domestic violence. In F. R. Ascione & P. Arkow (Eds.), *Child Abuse, Domestic Violence, and Animal Abuse* (pp. 143–158). West Lafayette, IN: Purdue University Press.

Kellert, S. R., & Felthous, A. R. (1985). Childhood cruelty toward animals among criminals and noncriminals. *Human Relations, 38*, 1113–1129.

LaCroix, C., & Wilson, J. (1998). State animal anti-cruelty laws. In P. Olson (Ed.), *Recognizing and reporting animal abuse: A veterinarian's guide.* Englewood, CO: American Humane Association.

Langevin, R. (2003). A study of the psychosexual characteristics of sex killers: Can we identify them before it is too late? *International Journal of Offender Therapy and Comparative Criminology, 47*, 366–382.

Loar, L. (1999). "I'll only help if you have two legs," or why human service professionals should pay attention to cases involving cruelty to animals. In F. R. Ascione & P. Arkow, *Child abuse, domestic violence, and animal abuse* (pp. 120–136). West Lafayette, IN: Purdue University Press.

Mason, J. (1988). *Animal factories.* Santa Clarita, CA: Crown Publishing Co.

Mason, M. S., & Hagan, C. B. (1999). Pet-assisted psychotherapy. *Psychological Reports, 84*(3), 1235–1245.

McKibben, L., DeVos, E., & Newberger, E. H. (1989). Victimization of mothers of abused children: A controlled study. *Pediatrics, 48*(3), 531–535.

Miller, K. S., & Knutson, J. F. (1997). Reports of severe physical punishment and exposure to animal cruelty by inmates convicted of felonies and by university students. *Child Abuse and Neglect, 21*, 59–82.

Nathanson, J. N., & the Hoarding of Animals Research Consortium (HARC). (2002). Animal hoarding: Recommendations for intervention by family and friends. North Grafton, MA: Tufts University Center for Animals and Public Policy.

Netting, F. E., & Wilson, C. C. (1987). Restrictive leasing: Issues confronting the elderly and their companion animals. *Journal of Gerontological Social Work, 11*(3–4), 181–189.

Patronek, G. J. (1999, January/February). Hoarding of animals: An under-recognized public health problem in a difficult-to-study population. *Public Health Reports*, 81–87.

Patronek, G. J., & the Hoarding of Animals Research Consortium (HARC). (2001, May/June). The problem of animal hoarding. *Municipal Lawyer Magazine.* Retrieved April 7, 2005 from http://www.tufts.edu/vet/cfa/hoarding/pubs/municipalawyer.pdf/

Poresky, R. H. (1997). The companion animal bonding scale: Internal consistency and factor structure when administered by telephone. *Psychological Reports, 80*, 937–939.

Poresky, R. H., Hendrix, C., Mosier, J. E., & Samuelson, M. L. (1987). The companion animal bonding scale: Internal reliability and construct validity. *Psychological Reports, 60*, 743–746.

Quackenbush, J. E., & Glickman, L. (1984). Helping people adjust to the death of a pet. *Health and Social Work, 9*, 42–48.

Quinlisk, J. A. (1999). Animal abuse and family violence. In F. R. Ascione & P. Arkow (Eds.), *Child abuse, domestic violence, and animal abuse* (pp. 169–175). West Lafayette, IN: Purdue University Press.

Randour, M. L. (2000). *Animal grace: Entering a spiritual relationship with animals.* Novato, CA: New World Library.

Rivers, D. (2004). *The seven challenges: A workbook and reader about communicating more cooperatively* (3rd ed.). Retrieved April 7, 2005 from http://www.newconversations.net/workbook.htm/

Rosenberg, M. (2003). *Nonviolent communication: A language for life* (2nd ed.). Encinitas, CA: Puddle Dancer Press.

Schiff, K., Louw, D., & Ascione, F. R. (1999). Animal relations in childhood and later violent behavior against humans. *Acta Criminologica, 12*, 77–86.

Segal, E. A., Gerdes, K. E., & Steiner, S. (2005). *Social work: An introduction to the profession.* Belmont, CA: Brooks/Cole—Thomson Learning.

Solot, D. (1997). Untangling the animal abuse web. *Society and Animals, 5*(3), 257–265.

Strand, E. B. (2003). Battered women's experiences with pet abuse: A survey of women in two domestic violence shelters. (Doctoral dissertation, The University of Tennessee, 2003). *Dissertation Abstracts International, 65*, (01A), 290.

Tribe of Heart. (2004). *Peaceable kingdom.* (Video). Boston, MA: Tribe of Heart.

U.S. Department of Labor, Bureau of Labor Statistics. (2003). Census of fatal occupational injuries, 2003 data: Information on deadly work hazards. Retrieved April 8, 2005 from http://www.bls.gov/iif/oshwe/cfoi/cfch0002.pdf/

U.S. Department of Labor, Bureau of Labor Statistics. (1999). Meat-packing plants have the highest rate of repeated-trauma disorders. Retrieved April 8, 2005 from http://www.bls.gov/opub/ted/1999/aug/wk1/art04.htm/

U.S. Senate Committee on Agriculture, Nutrition, & Forestry. (1997, December). Animal waste pollution in America: An emerging national problem. Washington, DC: Report compiled by the minority staff for Senator Tom Harkin.

Valentine, D. P., Kiddoo, M., & LaFleur, B. (1993). Psychosocial implications of service dog ownership for people who have mobility or hearing impairments. *Social Work in Health Care, 19*(1), 109–125.

Vermeulen, H., & Odendaal, J. S. J. (1993). Proposed typology of companion animal abuse. *Anthrozoös, 6,* 248–257.

Voith, V. L. (1985). Attachment between people and their pets: Behavior problems of pets that arise from the relationship between pets and people.

Veterinary Clinics of North America: Small Animal Practice, 15(2), 289–295.

Walker, L. (1979). *The battered woman.* New York: Harper Perennial.

Warrick, J. (2001, April 10). "They die piece by piece": In overtaxed plants, humane treatment of cattle is often a battle lost. *The Washington Post.*

Watkins, S. A. (1990). The Mary Ellen myth: Correcting child welfare history. *Social Work, 35*(6), 500–503.

Weber, C. V. (1998). A descriptive study of the relation between domestic violence and pet abuse. *Dissertation Abstracts International, 59,* (08B), 4492.

Weil, Z. (2003). *Above all, be kind: Raising a humane child in challenging times.* Gabriola Island, BC, Canada: New Society Publishers.

Zasloff, L. R. (1996). Measuring attachment to companion animals: A dog is not a cat is not a bird. *Applied Animal Behavior Science, 47*(1–2), 43–48.

Bestiality and Zoophilia: A Discussion of Sexual Contact With Animals

Andrea M. Beetz

Introduction

Sexual contact with animals is a phenomenon that has gained growing attention during the last few years. Recent research from the fields of psychology, psychiatry, criminology, and sociology provided a large amount of information and added some new insights to the rather scarce knowledge existing until then. Also organizations for animal protection, veterinary medicine, and law have begun to address sexual contacts of humans with animals, and even in public discussion, this last taboo in a world where nearly any other kind of sexual activity is discussed openly—at least in Western societies—has been broken. Two terms are widely used to describe sexual acts with animals. The first, "bestiality," usually refers to any kind of sexual contact with animals, while the second, "zoophilia," is more widespread among clinicians and can imply a clinically relevant sexual preference for animals or an emotional involvement with the animal in addition to the sexual activity.

The focus of discussions of bestiality varies in accordance with the field—psychology, sociology, and psychiatry seek to understand underlying reasons, motives, and links to developmental history or mental disorders and fields like criminology and law that emphasize the criminal relevance of this behavior take a mainly anthropocentric approach. Animal protection and veterinary medicine are obviously interested in the welfare of the animal that is involved in a sexual encounter with a human and address it mostly in the context of animal abuse. For the layperson, bestiality is usually mentioned in jokes and with disgust or ridicule, and rarely discussed with a genuine interest. Independent from the field, however, in most cases the subject of bestiality evokes very strong emotional reactions and thus complicates serious investigation and discussion

of bestiality and zoophilia. This contribution tries to provide an overview of the existing knowledge about bestiality and zoophilia with a focus on the relevance of these phenomena in regard to animal abuse and connections to interpersonal violence, and thus to aid future research and discussions of sexual animal contacts. Therefore, the following points will be addressed, even though it needs to be kept in mind that only a rough and incomplete account of all available information can be provided here.

In the next section, more exact definitions of bestiality and zoophilia and related phenomena are given, followed by a short introduction to the different forms of sexual involvement with animals. This is followed by reports on the history of sexual contacts with animals reaching from prehistoric times, Ancient Greece, and Ancient Rome to current developments in society. The variety of species involved in bestiality and sexual practices with animals are described next. Then, data on the prevalence of bestiality in the normal population as well as special populations are presented. An important base for the discussion of bestiality, especially in criminology, are the findings from research that focuses on connections between the practice of bestiality and interpersonal violence, in particular sexual offending, and these are introduced. A short introduction to the laws on bestiality in different countries and states, leads directly to the question of consent that, if not necessarily influencing the laws, nonetheless, should be regarded as relevant from the view of animal welfare as well as for comparisons to acts of interpersonal violence and abuse. The few available data and statements from the field of veterinary medicine are presented, as well as the findings of some studies that focused exclusively on the practice of bestiality and zoophilia, especially the more recent works of Beetz (2002), Miletski (2002), and Williams and

Weinberg (2003). Based on the presented information, the connection between bestiality and zoophilia and interpersonal violence as well as the relevance of sexual contacts to animals for animal protection are discussed.

Definitions of Bestiality, Zoophilia, and Zoosexuality

A term that has been widely used in former times to describe bestiality as well as other forms of "deviant" sexual behavior, like anal intercourse or homosexual contact, was "sodomy" (Stayton, 1994). Later, this term was replaced, at least in the clinical field, by the term "zoophilia." Many persons who practice sex with animals prefer to call themselves "zoophiles" or "zoos" instead of employing the term "bestiality." In 1894, the well-known psychiatrist Krafft-Ebing described cases of sexual contacts with animals in his well-known work *Psychopathia Sexualis* (Schmidt, 1969). He defined all non-pathological sexual acts with animals as "bestiality," while he referred to cases that were comparable to an animal fetishism as "zoophilia erotica"—thus he became one of the first to use the term "zoophilia"—and to pathological cases as "zooerasty." Masters (1962), however, had defined zooerasty as sexual contact with animals that lack an emotional involvement of the human and therefore could be compared to masturbation. Later, Karpman (1954) employed the term "zoophilia" only when referring to "sexual excitement experiences with stroking or fondling of animals" (p. 15), while he addressed any sexual contact between humans and animals as "bestiality" or "zooerasty." According to Masters (1966), several other authors named an exclusive or predominant desire for sexual contacts with animals as "zoophilia." Money (1986) defined zoophilia as "a paraphilia of the stigmatic/eligibilic type, in which sexuoerotic arousal and facilitation or attainment of orgasm are responsive to and dependent upon engaging in cross-species sexual activities" (p. 273). Besides the just mentioned interpretation of the terms "bestiality" and "zoophilia," it needs to be known that sometimes a general love of animals, without any sexual interest or activity, was also named "zoophilia."

In the field of mental health, zoophilia is regarded as a paraphilia, and the third edition of the *Diagnostic and Statistical Manual of Mental Diseases* (DSM-III, American Psychiatric Association [APA],

1980) defines it as: "The act or fantasy of engaging in sexual activity with animals is repeatedly preferred or the exclusive method of achieving sexual excitement" (p. 270). The following, more exact criteria for a paraphilia were named in the fourth edition of the DSM (DSM-IV, APA, 1994): "recurrent, intense sexually arousing fantasies, sexual urges, or behaviors generally involving 1) nonhuman objects, 2) the suffering or humiliation of oneself or one's partner, or 3) children or other nonconsenting persons, that occur over a period of at least 6 months (Criterion A). …The behavior, sexual urges, or fantasies cause clinically significant distress or impairment in social, occupational, or other important areas of functioning (Criterion B)" (p. 523). Since legal consequences can be interpreted as a clinically significant impairment, this criterion is usually applicable in states that have criminalized bestiality. Thus, a person who may not suffer from any other distress or impairment than legal consequences because of sexual acts with animals nevertheless should receive a diagnosis, while this criterion may not apply and thus this diagnosis may not be appropriate in a state without laws against bestiality. Obviously, this could lead to a somewhat artificial application of the diagnosis of zoophilia, and thus mental health would be directly linked to legislation. This is especially evident in the United States where only about half of the states have a law prohibiting sexual contact with animals and thus crossing a state border could "officially" change the criminal status as well as a diagnosis of a mental disorder from one minute to another.

More recently, a new definition of zoophilia was put forward by Miletski (2002) and Kurrelggyre (1995, cited in Miletski 2002, 2005b). According to Miletski, the main characteristic of "zoophilia" is an emotional attachment to animals that leads to a preference for animals as sexual partners or includes a sexual attraction. Today, "bestiality" is mainly used to refer to any sexual contact of humans with animals or any physical contact with animals that causes sexual excitement and pleasure for the involved human. Sometimes, authors or legislation define bestiality exclusively as an act of penetration involving a human and an animal. Miletski (2002) pointed out that bestiality and zoophilia cannot be understood as distinct categories, since these phenomena may occur in combination or flow into each other on the spectrum of human–animal relations. These definitions of bestiality, describing all sexual animal contacts, and zoophilia are also used by most persons who practice sex with animals. Another term, "zoosexuality," was introduced by Miletski (2002). Miletski conducted a study with a sample of 82 male and 11 female volunteers who reported that they had sexual contact with an animal at least once in their life. Most of them learned about the study via the Internet (advertisement, and messages from online friends). Using a detailed questionnaire, Miletski obtained—among other information (presented later in this chapter)—data on the sexual activity and preferences with humans and animals, sexual fantasies, and affectional orientation toward humans and animals. Her main research question regarded the existence of a sexual orientation toward animals. Therefore, Miletski adapted the definition of "sexual orientation" from Francouer (1991, cited in Miletski, 2002). Francouer defined three interrelated aspects that form a sexual orientation: affectional orientation—what or who people bond with emotionally; sexual fantasy orientation; and erotic orientation—with what or whom people prefer to have sex. From Miletski's sample, 87% of the men and 91% of the women indicated an emotional/psychological attraction to animals, and 74% of the men and 67% of the women reported that they have sex with animals because they want to express love or affection to the animal. Also in regard to fantasies, the majority of the men (76%) and 45% of the women related that they primarily or always fantasized about sex with animals. Ninety-one percent of the men and all of the women reported that they had sexual contact with animals because they were sexually attracted to them. More than half of the male participants (58%) and three (27%) women reported being sexually inclined more toward animals than humans, and 15% and 27%, respectively, stated they were equally sexually inclined to animals and humans. In reference to her data, Miletski (2002) proposed that in some, but not all cases, the criteria for a sexual orientation as defined by Francoeur (1991, cited in Miletski, 2002) that could be named "zoosexuality" were met. "Zoosexuals" would have both an emotional and a sexual attraction and relationship to animals (Miletski, 2002). As with other sexual orientations, it would be difficult to distinguish this sexual orientation strictly from another sexual orientation like homosexuality or bisexuality, since fantasy life and desire are not always acted out in reality. Several studies (e.g., Beetz, 2002; Miletski, 2002; Williams & Weinberg, 2003) showed that the majority of persons practicing bestiality also have sexual experiences with human partners and that some prefer to have sex with animals as well as humans. The diagnosis of an exclu-

sive zoosexual orientation might apply only for persons who have a predominant or exclusive attraction to animals and who do not or rarely engage in sexual activity with humans. Nothing can be said about the prevalence of real "zoosexuals" among the whole group of people who practice sex with animals. In the study by Miletski (2002) as well as in the studies of Beetz (2002) and Williams and Weinberg (2003), very likely the group of zoosexuals is greatly overrepresented due to the voluntary participation. It can be assumed that persons for whom sexual activity with animals is very important and who define themselves at least partly via their zoosexual orientation are more likely to take the time and risk to participate in such research. A further limitation of all three studies is the sample acquisition process via the Internet, which leaves out all possible participants that do not or only rarely use the Internet and do not visit zoophilia/bestiality-related websites where the advertisements for the studies were placed.

Forms of Sexual Involvement With Animals

Degrees and forms of sexual interest in animals vary widely. Some authors claim (see Massen, 1994) that a latent sexual interest in or arousal by animals, for example, by watching them mate, can be found in many persons. The other end of the continuum would be represented by an exclusive sexual orientation toward animals (Miletski, 2002). A distinction of nine basic forms of "zoophilia/bestiality," which may occur in combination, was proposed by Massen (1994, p. 57):

1. incidental experience and latent zoophilia
2. zoophile voyeurism (also called mixoscopic zoophilia)
3. frottage (Massen described this as physical contact as source of pleasure)
4. the animal as a tool for masturbatory activities
5. the animal as a surrogate object for a behavioral fetishism (like sadomasochistic practices, sexual murder, etc.)
6. the animal as fetish (fixation on one specific kind, breed, or individual)
7. physical contact and affection
8. the animal as a surrogate for a human sex partner
9. the animal as deliberately and voluntarily chosen sex partner

This list is not exhaustive in its description of forms and motivations, and zoophilia and zoosexuality especially need to be named as further forms. Another very special form of sexual contact with animals is "zoosadism." Zoosadism describes the deriving of sexual pleasure when killing or torturing animals, sometimes in combination with more or less obvious sexual practices, similar to "sadism" as the experience of sexual pleasure from inflicting pain and killing in an interpersonal sexual context. A variety of cases in this area is known, involving different kinds of animals and types of injury, but in particular the sexual abuse of poultry and rabbits falls into this category. The combination of penetrating and strangling the animal or breaking its neck is sexually stimulating to the zoosadist, psychologically as well as mechanically due to the spasms of the dying animal (Beetz, 2002; Miletski, 2002).

Bestiality Throughout History and Different Cultures

Accounts of bestiality can be found throughout history—from prehistoric time up until today—and in different cultures. Only a short introduction into the history of bestiality can be given here [for a more detailed account see Dekkers (1994) or Miletski (2002, 2005a)].

Prehistoric Accounts of Bestiality

It is likely that the practice of bestiality reaches as far back as the Fourth Glacial Age, between 40,000 and 25,000 years ago (Rosenberger, 1968). Cave paintings of the Iron Age (Italy) (Gregersen, 1983; Taylor, 1996) and of the Bronze Age (Sweden) (Dekkers 1994; Liliequist, 1988, cited in Miletski, 2002) have been found that show the penile penetration of a large animal by a man. According to Salisbury (1994), it is likely that sexual contact with animals was also one expression of human sexuality from the time on when humans lived closely together with animals. Another example represents an engraved bone rod from the later Ice Ages (around 25,000 years ago) found in France that, according to Taylor (1996), depicts a lioness licking the opening of either a human vulva or penis. And a cave painting from the Iron Age (7th century B.C.) supposedly shows a man penetrating the vagina or anus of a donkey (Gregersen, 1983; Taylor, 1996). Waine (1968) stated that such depictions as cave drawings and carvings leave no doubt that prehistoric humans had frequent and pleasurable sexual contact with animals, or that it was, at least, a desired act.

Bestiality in Ancient Greece, Ancient Rome, and Other Cultures

Religious or cultic rites that included sexual contact with animals were widespread in Ancient Greece. Male goats were used for copulation during the worship rites for the god Mendes who was symbolized by these animals (Davis, 1954; Love, 1992; Masters, 1962; Rosenfeld, 1967), while sexual acts with snakes were performed by priestesses in the worship of the god Aesculapius (Dekkers, 1994) and the god Bacchus (Dyonisus). Many accounts of sexual contact with animals can be found in art from Ancient Greece (Dekkers, 1994), and it was also a main theme in Greek mythology (Kinsey, Pomeroy, Martin, & Gebhart, 1953; Masters, 1962; Rosenfeld, 1967). Well-known examples are the story of Leda and Zeus in the shape of a swan, and the sexual encounter of Zeus in the shape of a white bull with Europa. Further, the mating of the half-goddess Pasiphae, who was the wife of King Minos of Crete, with a white bull can be named. The offspring of the latter alliance was the Minotaurus, a creature half bull, half human. Furthermore, Greek mythology tells of satyrs, creatures half man, half goat, who were a symbol of virility and lust (Dekkers, 1994). The play "The Golden Ass" by Apuleius was also very popular. It describes the, sometimes intimate adventures of a man, in the shape of an ass, with humans. Supposedly, in Ancient Greece, bestiality was even performed on stage.

The same was true for Roman performances on stage as well as Roman mythology (Kinsey et al., 1953). In Ancient Rome, some brothels were named according to the animals they offered for sexual purposes. According to Schmidt (1969), goats were provided in the "caprarii," dogs in the "belluarii," and birds in the "ansenarii." Furthermore, animals had been specifically trained for sexual interactions with women for the games at the Coliseum and Circus Maximus, namely raping women and men as a public spectacle and for public amusement (Dekkers, 1994; Masters, 1962). Bestiality was also said to have been widespread among shepherds (Masters, 1962).

In Ancient Egypt, gods were worshiped in their animal shapes, and depictions of sexual contacts between humans and animals were sometimes found on the tombs (Bullough, 1976). Several queens and kings were known to engage in bestiality

(Rosenberger, 1968; Rosenfeld, 1967), among them Cleopatra, who supposedly used a box filled with bees for sexual stimulation by holding it to her genitalia (Love, 1992). It is also suspected that, in Ancient Egypt, the worship of the Apis-bull had some sexual components (Miletski, 2002) and reports from old India refer to a fertility ritual during which a stallion was sacrificed and coitus with the dead animal was attempted by the wife of the man who brought the sacrifice (Hentig, 1962).

Bestiality in Ancient Religious and Legal Codes

In the old legal code of the Hittites (around 13th century B.C.), punishments for bestiality differed according to the kind of the animal involved (Gregersen, 1983; Kinsey, Pomeroy, & Martin, 1948). Sexual contact of a man with a pig, dog, or cow was punished by death, while sexual relations with a horse or mule were not punished except that the man was not allowed to approach the king and to become a priest. Also, the book Leviticus in the Old Testament and the Talmud prohibited sexual contact with animals, and the act was to be punished by death. The Bible, in particular, influenced the handling of detected cases of bestiality in Christian countries, and still today opinions about sex with animals in Western societies are strongly ruled by its statements and religious beliefs in general. In the Middle Ages, the witchcraft trials often included accusation of bestiality and usually ended with the death penalty (Greenland, 1983). The underlying assumption was that bestiality represented intercourse with a demon or the devil in the shape of an animal. In countries under the strong influence of the Roman Catholic Church, the death penalty was not only applied to the person but also to the animal. Severe penalties up to life imprisonment prevailed until the middle of the 19th century. Bestiality was prohibited because the act was repulsive to the public and out of religious concerns. Further, the common opinion was that such relations resulted in hybrids, creatures with human and animal features. Overall, it can be deducted from the explicit mentioning of bestiality in these legal and moral codes that this practice must have occurred with a non-negligible frequency.

Bestiality During the Last Century and Today

During the last century up until today, bestiality has been practiced all over the world. Sex with animals was offered in the brothels of Paris, and Mexico was known for its availability of animals for sexual purposes and its live shows (Miletski, 2002), where sex with animals such as dogs and donkeys was performed for certain circles. Furthermore, accounts of bestiality via court reports can be found in states that prosecuted this practice, and in some states, such as Hungary, magazines depicting sex with animals were and still are traded quite openly. Pornographic videos with animals were and still are produced and distributed, even though in many Western countries the ownership or/and the trade of such material is illegal. Animals most often depicted in such videos are dogs and horses, mainly performing with women, but farm animals or exotic animals are also sometimes used in these productions. It seems likely that even though the majority of pictures and videos feature women engaging in sexual contact with animals this does not mirror the reality of enacted bestiality. Bestiality is probably much more often practiced by men, and the pornography is rather intended for a male audience that just likes to see something unusual instead of having a strong interest in attempting sexual contact with animals themselves.

Laws on bestiality changed during the last century. While some states such as Germany abolished their laws on bestiality, sometimes due to lack of use, and handle cases according to the animal protection laws, others, like Great Britain, kept their (possible) penalties on a very high level up to life imprisonment until recently. Other states recently introduced or reintroduced laws prohibiting bestiality, especially penetrative acts, as, for example, in the United States.

Even though its influence on public opinion about bestiality may be doubted, the studies of Kinsey and colleagues (1948, 1953) provided the first information about the prevalence of bestiality, while before, criminological studies based on court reports could only inform about specific cases. This research, for the first time, gave scientists and practitioners in the field of mental health and criminology an idea about the overall frequency of occurrence of bestiality, and showed that sexual contacts with animals happen not as infrequently as thought before. These studies probably opened the way for other scientists to investigate bestiality and zoophilia in more detail.

Another recent development in regard to sexual animal contacts also emerged. More zoophiles now dare to talk openly about their sexual interest and activities with animals, and thus increase the awareness of the existence of bestiality and zoophilia. One example is Mark Matthews' (1994) autobiography,

The Horseman, which tells about his life and problems as a zoophile. Furthermore, the Internet presented zoophiles and others interested in bestiality a platform for the exchange of information and connecting to other like-minded people. Even though many of the websites focus on the trade of pornographic material, websites also exist that help zoophiles to talk about their interest, sometimes for the first time (Beetz, 2002, 2005b; Miletski, 2002). Sites answering "Frequently Asked Questions" (FAQs) not only provide "tips" and "to-do" and "not to-do" information about animal sex, but also inform about zoonoses, diseases that can be transferred from animals to humans, and risks when approaching certain animals. Frequent discussions further address the differentiation between zoophilia and bestiality and related issues, like the question of consent and a "code of ethics" for zoophiles (Beetz, 2002, 2005b).

The general public rarely becomes aware of the subject of bestiality, but when it does, people often react with disgust, ridicule, or fast dismissal since its occurrence is regarded as too infrequent and unimportant. Only in the fields of criminology, sociology, mental health, psychology, and in particular animal protection and animal ethics have sexual acts with animals been discussed more frequently. The level of acceptance of bestiality in the general public remains unknown, and even in states where bestiality is legal, only rarely do people actually convey their opinions about bestiality. A strong influence of old moral and religious codes and values condemning sexual contact with animals still seems to prevail, and any mentioning of bestiality evokes strong emotional reactions rather than objective discussion. Even with publications about bestiality or zoophilia in a scientific context, authors are sometimes faced with severe criticism. The recent example of Peter Singer, well known for his work *Animal Liberation* (1975), showed that any statement about bestiality needs to be made with the outmost precaution and worked out thoroughly. He was heavily criticized for his review of Dekkers' book on bestiality, *Dearest Pet* (1994). His review was not intended for a scientific community but rather to provoke discussion of bestiality. Nonetheless, his critics accused him of promoting an "attitude of liberal tolerance toward bestiality" (Beime, 2001, p. 44). Singer probably had never imagined the problems he would experience because of his short review.

More surprising are the overall more positive reactions to a new contribution on zoophilia among the public in comparison to the scientific community. Edward Albee's play "The Goat" portrays the private conflicts of a man who fell in love with a goat. The play even received an award and was performed on Broadway as well as internationally.

Overall, there is a certain trend today that information on bestiality is becoming more visible and accessible and is noticed by the public as well as science.

Spec ies Involved in Bestiality and Sexual Practices

It seems to be commonly assumed that animals involved in bestiality are mainly farm animals. This may be based on the old stereotype that bestiality is practiced only in rural areas where there is better access to livestock such as donkeys, cows, calves, bulls, sheep, goats, and horses. Also, sexual acts with chicken or rodents are mentioned in the literature and usually included violent practices and may lead to severe injuries and death of the animal. Further animals approached for sexual purposes are male and female pigs, and supposedly even penetration of the human by male animals occurs (Beetz, 2002). However, equines like horses, donkeys, and mules but also sheep or goats are more frequently involved. Even reports of sexual acts with bulls—including masturbation and penetration of men and women by the animal—exist (Masters, 1966; Rosenfeld, 1967). Recent research (Beetz, 2002, 2005b; Miletski, 2002; Williams & Weinberg, 2003) suggests that today dogs, mostly female but also male animals of large breeds, as well as male and female horses are frequently involved in sexual contacts with humans.

Furthermore, infrequent reports of sexual contact with more unusual mammals, such as deer, tapirs, antelopes, camels, or other species, were found (Massen, 1994). In Ancient Egypt, crocodile hunters supposedly even practiced intercourse with female crocodiles before killing them (Massen, 1994). Fish and snakes are sexually abused by inserting them into the vagina of the human (Dekkers, 1994; Massen, 1994), and cats can be used for sexual stimulation by letting the animal eat food from the penis or vagina or lick the human genitalia (Miletski, 2002). Sometimes, male and female cats are masturbated for sexual excitement. Chideckel (1935) and Rosenfeld (1967) reported intercourse between women and monkeys, and even sexual contact with dolphins or at least a sexual interest in them can be found (Beetz, 2002).

Sexual contact with animals can take as many forms as sexuality between human partners. Masturbation of male and female animals or rubbing against the body of the animal as well as oral–genital contact or mouth-to-mouth "kissing" are common practices (Beetz, 2002, 2005b; Miletski, 2002). Also, the penetration of men and women by male animals and anal and vaginal penetration of the animal by men occur (Beetz, 2002; Miletski, 2002; Williams & Weinberg, 2003). In regard to many practices, the size and anatomy of the involved animal are of importance and directly related to possible infliction of pain or injuries to the animal, especially due to penetration. Masturbation and oral contact usually do not result in pain or injuries for the animal. In some cases, however, perpetrators do not care if their acts stress or harm the animal, and in zoosadistic cases, death or suffering of the animal are intended and serve as the main source of sexual arousal.

The Prevalence of Bestiality

Only a few studies provide information about the occurrence of sexual contact with animals among the normal population. Most important in this regard are the studies of Kinsey et al. (1948, 1953) and Hunt (1974), and their central findings are reported in the next sections.

The Studies of Kinsey and Colleagues (1948, 1953)

In studies on the sexual behavior of the American male (Kinsey et al., 1948) and the American female (Kinsey et al., 1953), which were later known as the Kinsey report, data on sexual contacts with animals were also obtained. Interviews about sexual experiences and preferences were conducted with about 5,300 adult white men and 5,800 adult white women. Even though there was criticism of the objectivity of the methods used, new and important insights into human sexuality were gained. Nevertheless, with such a sensitive subject as bestiality it seems likely that behaviors were rather under- than over-reported. According to Kinsey and his colleagues (1948, 1953), about 40%–50% of the boys in rural areas at that time had at least one sexual encounter with an animal. Seventeen percent of the men had even achieved orgasm as a result of sexual contact with an animal at one time during adolescence. Later, Ammons and Ammons (1987, cited in Holmes, 1991) also found that 17% of men in rural areas had reached orgasm via sexual contact with an animal. However, the prevalence of sexual animal contacts among the average American male population was much lower, at 8% (Kinsey et al., 1948). About 3% of the female population indicated that they had sexual contact with an animal at least once in their lifetime (Kinsey et al., 1953). The frequency of the animal contacts varied between just once and several times a year or even several times per week. In a few cases, animals were sexually approached over a period of several years or even a whole lifetime with a varying frequency. Oral practices as well as masturbation through rubbing against the body of the animal and vaginal or anal penetration were reported.

The Study of Hunt (1974)

About 20 years later, in 1974, Hunt conducted the only other study that allowed insights into the prevalence of bestiality. Hunt investigated sexual behaviors, including bestiality, among a sample of 982 American men and 1,044 American women. Results showed that the prevalence rates were lower than the ones found by Kinsey et al. (1948, 1953), but still about 2% of the women and about 5% of the men had sexual contact with an animal at least once. According to Hunt (1974), this decline in prevalence rates could be explained by urbanization—people moving to the cities where they had less access to animals. Also the majority of Hunt's participants, 67% of the women and 75% of the men with sexual animal experiences, had approached animals in a sexual manner on only a few occasions, mostly during adolescence and young adulthood.

The Study of Alvarez and Freinhar (1991)

Alvarez and Freinhar (1991) investigated sexual fantasies and activities with animals among a special sample consisting of 20 psychiatric inpatients, 20 medical inpatients, and 20 psychiatric staff members. Fifty-five percent of the psychiatric inpatients, but also 10% of the medical inpatients as well as 15% of the psychiatric staff members, fantasized about bestiality or had at least one sexual contact with an animal. Even though Alvarez and Freinhar did not distinguish between fantasy and actual contact, they concluded that questions regarding bestiality should be included in every psychiatric assessment.

Bestiality in the Context of Interpersonal Violence

There are only a few studies that focused exclusively on bestiality. However, several studies collected data about sexual contacts with animals, mostly among groups with a history of sexual or nonsexual offending, sexual abuse, or other clinically relevant problems.

In a recent study, Ascione, Friedrich, Heath, and Hayashi (2003) investigated the prevalence of animal cruelty and "touching an animal's sex parts" among 1,433 6- to 12-year-old children. Data were obtained from a norm group of 540 children, a group of 412 psychiatric outpatients, and a group of 481 sexually abused children. Cruel acts toward animals were reported by the maternal caregivers for 3.1% of the norm group, 15.6% of the psychiatric outpatients, and 17.9% of the sexually abused children. The touching of an animal's sex parts was indicated much less frequently. Only 0.37% of the norm group and 0.9% of the psychiatric outpatients had touched animals' sex parts, but 6.3% of the sexually abused children. Furthermore, touching an animal's sex parts was significantly related to animal cruelty ($r=0.12$) and cruelty to others ($r=0.12$) among the whole sample, but when differentiated by groups, these correlations were only found among the sexually abused children were reported to have done so. According to Ascione et al. (2003), "sexualized forms of cruelty may be more specifically related to a history of sexual abuse" (p. 206).

A comparison of animal-related experiences, including those of a sexual nature, among a group of 100 violent criminals and a normal matched control group (N=75), was undertaken by ten Bensel, Ward, Kruttschnitt, Quickley, and Anderson (1984). According to the authors, the participants reacted quite emotionally and rejecting to the question about bestiality, and no violent offender admitted to sexual contact with animals. However, 3.9% of the control group reported sexual animal experiences. Sexual acts with animals were also assessed in a sample of 314 inmates by Miller and Knutson (1997). Twenty-two participants (7%) had seen others engaging in bestiality and 16 participants (5.1%) had touched animals sexually. Sexual intercourse with animals was reported by nine inmates (2.9%). Overall, about 11% of the criminal sample had observed or practiced bestiality.

Several studies on sexual offending addressed, among others, the subject of bestiality. In a study of connections between sexual abuse in childhood or adolescence and sexual activities, interests, and deviations, Ressler, Burgess, Hartmann, Douglas, and McCormack (1986) also assessed an interest in sex with animals. Twenty-three percent of their

sample of 36 sex murderers admitted to such an interest in bestiality.

Gebhard et al. (1965) conducted an important early study in this field. They assessed the prevalence of sexual animal contacts among a sample of over 1,000 white male convicted sex offenders in comparison to a sample of 881 men convicted of felonies or misdemeanors, but never sex offenses (prison group), and a sample of 471 white males who had never been convicted of any serious offenses (control group). The authors only counted sexual animal contacts that occurred after the onset of puberty and included penile penetration of the animal. The control group as well as the sex offenders who had abused adults of the opposite sex showed the lowest incidence rate for bestiality of 8.3%, a number that is comparable to the results of Kinsey et al. (1948) for the overall male population. The highest incidence rate of 33.3% was found among the sex offenders who had abused female minors (non-incestuous). Between 12.5% and 24% of the other offender subgroups had engaged in sexual animal contacts.

Similarly high rates of 37% for bestiality were reported by Frazier (1997, cited in Ascione, 1999) who had investigated a group of 30 sexually violent juvenile offenders. In a study of 27 juvenile sex offenders, Beetz (2002) found that only two (7.4%) juvenile sex offenders admitted to having seen others engage in sex with animals, while another two (7.4%) had engaged in bestiality themselves. Sexual fantasies involving animals were denied by 59.3% of the juveniles, while the rest of the group refused to answer this question at all. In particular with such a delicate subject as sexual contact with animals, it seems very likely that numbers underreport the true prevalence rates, since there is a strong refusal to answer questions on this subject honestly.

To obtain more accurate numbers in regard to sexual animal contacts, especially from criminal samples, probably another approach is necessary. English, Jones, Patrick, and Pasini-Hill (2003) used a post-conviction polygraph approach when investigating experiences of bestiality among 180 convicted sex offenders. While prior to the polygraph investigation only 4.4% had admitted to bestiality, afterwards 36% reported to have engaged in bestiality.

Fleming, Jory, and Burton (2002) studied bestiality among 381 institutionalized male juvenile offenders. While only 6% of the juveniles admitted to sexual acts with one or several animals without having been forced to do so, 42% indicated that they had sexually abused another person. Twenty-three of the 24 juveniles with sexual animal experiences had also sexually offended humans, while only 12 of them had been adjudicated for sex offenses. This shows that a high number of cases remain undetected, and the data further suggest a strong link between sexual offenses toward humans and bestiality. While 14 of the 24 juvenile offenders had used the animal for masturbation, 10 juveniles reported intercourse with the animal. Four juveniles had orally manipulated the animal's genitals, two juveniles had inserted an object, and six juveniles a finger into the animal. According to Fleming et al. (2002), such acts could have been motivated by curiosity, expected sexual gratification, sexual sadism, or a combination of these motives.

Masochistic as well as sadistic practices may include sexual contact with animals. Miletski (2002) investigated a voluntary sample of 93 men who engaged in bestiality and found that only 4% of the men fantasized "always" or "primarily" about sadomasochistic sex and that 9% admitted to having "forced someone to do something sexually that person did not want to do" (Miletski, 2002, p. 118). Another sample of 113 men who had engaged in sexual contact with animals was studied by Beetz (2002). Experiences with sadistic sex were reported by 1.8%, while 1.8% had forced another person in a sexual context, and 4.4% had practiced masochistic sex. The use of physical force in connection with sexual animal contacts was indicated by 9.7% of the men (Beetz, 2002).

In a study of sadistic and masochistic practices with consenting partners by Sandnabba, Santtila, Beetz, Nordling, and Alison (2002), 7.4% of the sample had sexual experiences with animals, and this subgroup also engaged in further unusual sexual practices and was, overall, more experimental. The data could not affirm a general link between sadomasochistic practices and bestiality, since very few participants had experiences with bestiality and sadomasochistic sex (Sandnabba et al., 2002). It would have been interesting to know if bestiality was directly combined with masochistic or sadistic sexual practices, but unfortunately, this information had not been obtained.

In contrast to the just described parallel practice of bestiality and sadomasochistic sex with the consent of the partner, bestiality also occurs in cases of domestic violence. Women are known to have been forced by their partners to perform sexual acts with animals (Dutton, 1992; Walker, 1979, cited in Ascione, 1993). And another extreme form of

sexually connoted animal contacts exists. The torture or killing of an animal may be used for practice or as surrogate for the murder of a human victim. Nonsexual acts may involve a sexual connotation, but direct sexual acts or harming the animal in the genital or anal area for sexual arousal have also been found as, for example, in some of the "horse-ripper" cases (Doninger, 1993; Schedel-Stupperich, 2002).

Laws on Bestiality

Laws on bestiality have changed dramatically over time, in particular during the last century, and, today vary widely among different countries and states.

As mentioned before, throughout history in today's Western societies Christian beliefs, in particular, had a strong influence on opinions and prosecution of bestiality. Sexual acts with animals had been considered heresy and a crime against God and nature. In particular during the witchcraft trials bestiality was a severe accusation, since during the Middle Ages it was a widely accepted truth that the devil or demons change into the shape of animals to have intercourse with humans (Dekkers, 1994).

Changes in the attitudes toward the prosecution of bestiality occurred during the end of the 18th century. A separation of law and morals was favored then, and some states, like France and Italy in 1791, and later, Spain, Portugal, Belgium, Rumania, and the Netherlands, deleted the offense of bestiality from the national law (Bolliger & Goetschel, 2005) and have not reintroduced it until now. According to Bolliger and Goetschel, Japan, Turkey, Russia, and the South American states also lack a law on bestiality or have abolished it. Even though at the beginning of the last century bestiality was not seen as a sin against God anymore, states like Germany, Austria, the majority of Swiss Cantons, and the states of Scandinavia and Northern America still outlawed sexuality with animals (Bolliger & Goetschel, 2005). Punishment, however, changed from execution and life-long imprisonment to milder sentences. Today, the Scandinavian countries, Germany, most Swiss Cantons, and Austria have no specific laws on bestiality. Sexual acts that cause severe distress, suffering, or death of the animal are prosecuted on the basis of animal cruelty laws. The legislation on pornographic material depicting sexual contact with animals varies from country to country. In former times, one argument for criminalizing bestiality was that sexual acts with animals supposedly humiliate the human in a way that disgraces all humankind.

However, when Germany abolished its bestiality law in 1969 with the reformation of its penal code, the decision was influenced by the opinion that morals, which are very changeable over time, cannot serve as the basis of penal law (Hanack, 1968). The committee responsible for the change argued that only persons who cannot be held fully responsible for their actions, such as the mentally impaired, juveniles, "primitive" persons, and persons with abnormal sex drives engage in bestiality (Hentig, 1962). Furthermore, persons engaging in sex with animals would only humiliate themselves, not mankind in general. About 200 persons had been convicted of sexual conduct with animals per year before 1969. Today, in Germany, such persons may be charged according to animal protection laws if cruelty is involved, or may be found guilty of, for example, damage to property, trespassing, and offensive sexual acts in public.

Even though all except two U.S. states (Illinois, New Hampshire) had once outlawed bestiality, today only about half still do so and classify it as a felony or misdemeanor. Masters had remarked in 1966 that many of the proposed penalties in the United States, ranging from one year of imprisonment to a life sentence, were too harsh. Masters (1966) further criticized law enforcement for not further investigating the circumstances of the bestiality cases like the motivation or the use of violence during the act. In some states like California, Delaware, or Utah, bestiality is explicitly named in the legislation, while other states subsume it under "crimes against nature." Sentences range from fines to several years (up to 20 years) of imprisonment, and throughout the United States, even in states without bestiality laws, sexual acts with animals represent a valid cause for divorce by civil law (Bolliger & Goetschel, 2005). A new development, however, shows itself in the considerations of some U.S. states to create or re-introduce specific bestiality laws, probably influenced, among others, by pressures from the field of animal protection.

Canada generally has sanctions against bestiality, and sentences of up to 10 years imprisonment are possible. Also, Great Britain did and still does outlaw genital sexual contact between humans and animals, even though just recently, in 2003 (Home Office, Great Britain, 2003), the maximum penalty was reduced from a possible life sentence to a maximum of 2 years imprisonment. In 2000, the Home Office of Great Britain proposed a reformation of the British sex law, including the law on bestiality.

After a discussion of decriminalizing bestiality overall and prosecuting it according to animal protection laws, the review committee came to the conclusion that bestiality constitutes a criminal behavior in itself. Bestiality was defined as follows: "to sexually penetrate or to be sexually penetrated by an animal" (Home Office, Great Britain, 2000, p. 145). It was argued that bestiality is against the dignity of humans and animals and represents a "profoundly disturbed behavior," that animals cannot give free consent, and that there exists a link between animal abuse and other forms of sexual offending like the abuse of children. Furthermore, the committee felt that "society has a profound abhorrence for this behavior" (Home Office, Great Britain, 2000, p. 126).

The Question of Consent

Even if sexual contacts with animals do not necessarily involve obvious force, and in some cases the animals seem to react with indifference or boredom, to be willing participants, to enjoy the sexual attention to a certain extent (Beetz, 2002; Beirne, 2000), or to even initiate it (Dekkers, 1994), an issue repeatedly raised is the question of consent. The opinion prevails that any form of sexual contact with animals and especially penetrative acts are per se abusive, since it is not possible—as with children or the mentally impaired—to obtain consent to such an act from the animal (Ascione, 1993; Beirne, 2000). Beirne (2000) provided a thorough and informative discussion of this question of consent and argued for a definition of any kind of sexual contact with animals as *interspecies sexual assault* instead of bestiality with its varying definitions. However, this term poses some problems. The author agrees with Munro and Thrusfield (2001) that it is not precise, since it also addresses sexual activities between two animal species, and more clearly implies sexual abuse of one species by another. Even if such sexual contacts are probably rare, accounts of sexual interactions between different species exist. Jane Goodall reported that sometimes chimpanzees and pavians copulate (male chimpanzees with female pavians and vice versa) (cited in Miersch, 1999), and according to Miersch (1999) young male elephants in South Africa sometimes try to copulate with female rhinos (however, anatomically the copulation is not possible). Furthermore, Dekkers (1994) as well as Beetz (2002) provided accounts of sexual contact between a dolphin and sea lion in captivity. Nevertheless, with exception of the female rhinos, no clear conclusion about which species assaulted the other can be drawn. Furthermore, as mentioned before, the term "interspecies sexual assault" was introduced by Beirne (2000) to relate to sexual contact between a human and an animal, to identify any kind of bestiality, and thus fails to provide an exact definition.

Beirne (2000) stated that, independent from the kind of force used and the reactions of the animals, all sexual acts between humans and animals are wrong. One argument he proposed is the potential for coercion that prevails in almost every situation between humans and animals (Adams, 1995, cited by Beirne, 2000). Livestock as well as domestic pets rely on humans for shelter, food, and affection. This also applies to wild animals, since humans have the capacity to capture them and to subject them to their will. This potential for coercion applies also to sexual activities with animals. Physical, psychological, economic, or emotional coercion is almost always involved in sexual approaches to animals (Adams, 1995, cited by Beirne, 2000), as in the sexual assault of children or women, and therefore consent cannot be given, and the sexual activity is forced (Beirne, 2000). The decisive criterion, according to Beirne (2000), is not the imbalance of power, but rather that one of the involved parties cannot consent or communicate such consent to sexual acts. Both involved parties must be conscious, fully informed, and positive in their desires in order to be able to give genuine consent. Given that animals are sentient beings, Beirne (2000) demanded that these criteria should also apply to humans' sexual advances to animals, not only to human–human sexual relations. He further stated that humans cannot understand animals and therefore consent could not be communicated, and that animals cannot resist humans effectively, even though they scratch, bite, or display other nonverbal signs of resistance. Where the line between nonsexual touch and sexual acts is to be drawn poses a difficult question that was left unanswered by Beirne (2000). While, according to Beirne milking cows, for example, is a clearly nonsexual act, it is more difficult to judge acts like artificial insemination or electrically induced ejaculation in breeding. These acts obviously intrude on the genital area of the animal, they are penetrative acts, but the main underlying motivation is clearly not sexual, but rather frequently economic. Furthermore, Beirne (2000) proposed a typology of interspecies sexual assault that distinguishes between sexual fixation, commodification, adolescent sexual experimentation,

and aggravated cruelty. Sexual fixation, according to Beirne, regards cases where animals are the preferred (and/or exclusive) sexual partners of humans. Commodification is the main element in cases of sexual contacts between humans and animals that are "packaged as commodities for sale in the market" (Beirne, 2000, p. 325), be it in the form of life shows or the production of videos or pictures. Adolescent sexual experimentation refers to the fact that, particularly in rural areas (Kinsey et al., 1948), young men with easy access to animals experiment with sexual intercourse with animals. As aggravated cruelty Beirne (2000) defines cases in which the animals suffer physical, emotional, or psychological pain due to sexual intercourse, penetration with objects, or injuries to their genitalia. Also the use of sex with animals as a humiliation of a partner in an abusive relationship falls into this category.

Adams (1995) stated that many persons who suffer from such a sexual fixation as zoophilia—like child sexual abusers and rapists—describe the sex as consensual and pleasurable for the sexual partners as well as themselves. Results from recent studies support Adam's claim (Beetz, 2002; Miletski, 2002), even though these authors do not favor a comparison of zoophilia to child molestation and rape. Their data document the existence of a group of persons engaging in sex with animals who emphasize their emotional involvement in a sexual relation to an animal.

Beirne's (2000) discussion of bestiality as interspecies sexual assault is important since his approach focuses on the rights and welfare of the animal. More often a quite anthropocentric view prevails where bestiality is condemned because of societal, religious, or moral concerns. In many countries, reactions to the mention of bestiality were or still are "moral, judicial and aesthetic outrage" (Beirne, 2000, p. 314), bewilderment, or disgust rather than an intellectual inquiry.

From religion and criminal law, societal control of bestiality passed to the medical profession of psychiatry, and it seems that, to a certain degree, dismissal if not tolerance for zoophilia can be found among certain groups. According to Beirne (2001) this is a "pseudoliberal" tolerance. Also, the philosopher Peter Singer (2001), known for his work *Animal Liberation* (1975), was heavily criticized by Beirne (2001) and others for his review of Dekkers' book *Dearest Pet* (1994), one of the few informative books on sexual human–animal relations. The reason that there still exists such a strong taboo against bestiality, Singer (2001) claimed, is the wish of humans to differentiate themselves from animals, in regard to sexuality and other areas. In his comment Singer wanted to raise the question about whether bestiality should be condemned at all, if it does not involve cruelty.

Another question that needs to be raised concerns the relevance of consent in sexual acts with animals in comparison to other procedures carried out on animals. In what other area is the—very valid—argument of consent of such an importance? There is a general agreement that if an animal is deliberately hurt or killed by someone for personal pleasure this constitutes animal abuse. Procedures for the purpose of breeding that do not necessarily involve pain are widely accepted by society, even though they involve a severe intrusion into the sexual liberty of the animal and its reproductive organs. However, even hurting or killing is not condemned if it is carried out for the gain of society, as in food production or medical research. In regard to these actions, the issue of consent is rarely stressed. It needs to be considered if the underlying intention, sexual or nonsexual, makes a difference from the view of the animal. Still, such questions are often approached from an anthropocentric point of view, and it seems that as soon as the gain of sexual pleasure is involved, reactions of society turn more emotional and moralistic.

As proposed by Bolliger and Goetschel (2005), it might be more useful to focus on the "dignity" of animals that should not be violated in this discussion of sexual contact between humans and animals. Bolliger and Goetschel suggested that instead of focusing on the interests of society this "dignity of the animal"—which is protected in Switzerland since 1992 by the Swiss Constitution as an aspect of "dignity of creature"—should be the focus of attention when discussing sexual acts between man and animal. The basis for this legislation and concept is the ethical view that an animal is an emotional creature that deserves respect and protection of its physical and mental integrity in its own right. This integrity includes protection from excessive exploitation, humiliation, interference with an animal's appearance, as well as sexual integrity. Thus, even in cases where no objective suffering, physically or emotionally, can be detected, the violation of the dignity of the animal and its right to a free sexual development justify viewing such an act as harmful to the animal.

The Relevance of Bestiality for Veterinary Sciences

The issue of bestiality will probably only come to the attention of veterinary practitioners if infections or injuries to the animal resulted and if the owner takes it for an examination. As in other areas of research, this subject is addressed only reluctantly, and only a few studies have investigated the relevance of bestiality for the field of veterinary medicine.

In a study by Weidner (1972), veterinarians in Germany reported on cases of sexual and sadistic animal abuse that they had encountered in their practice. Thirty-six percent of the 294 veterinarians who replied (out of 400 contacted) had seen animals that had been involved in bestiality. Cows and calves were the most frequently sexually or sadistically abused animals, but cases also involved horses, pigs, sheep, fowl, and goats. Horses were most often involved, if the number of cases was put into relation to the number of animals of a certain species in Germany at that time. Only a few cases involving dogs were reported and, therefore, Weidner concluded that dogs were only rarely sexually approached even though they had become more popular as pets. The recent studies by Beetz (2002), Miletski (2002), and Williams and Weinberg (2003) showed that this was a misconception. Sexual contacts with dogs, even penetration, do not always lead to an injury and thus, even if the animal is taken to regular examinations, are not likely to be noticed by the veterinarian (Beetz, 2002). However, if intended or unintended injuries resulted, a veterinarian will often not be contacted because of shame or fear of the owner who probably has caused them (Beetz, 2002). A review of information (literature, court reports, research) on sadistic and sexual acts with animals led Weidner (1972) to the conclusion that about 29% of the cases reported in the literature that she reviewed had a mainly sexual background or motive and 56% of the cases a sadistic background. In 15% of the cases a combination of sadism and bestiality prevailed. According to Weidner, only sadistic acts had caused perforations in the vaginal or rectal tissue, which almost always resulted in death, while mere coital activities usually only led to irritations and minor injuries. Furthermore, other negative reactions to sexual contact with a human included diminished food intake and nervousness in some cases.

Another study on animal abuse by Munro and Thrusfield (2001) also collected data on injuries that point to sexual abuse of the animal. Of the cases reported by 404 veterinarians in the United Kingdom, 6% were classified as sexual abuse due to the injuries in the genital and anal area and reproductive organs and surrounding tissue that in some cases were caused by insertion of foreign bodies. Twenty-one dogs and three cats showed injuries pointing to a sexual motive for the abuse. Munro and Thrusfield concluded that the sexual abuse of animals represents a relevant problem for veterinary practice.

Stettner (1990) discussed bestiality as a problem for animal protection in Germany. Since the German law on bestiality was abolished in 1969, sexual acts with animals are only considered animal abuse if serious or longer-lasting pain, suffering, or injuries are inflicted upon the animal. According to Stettner, however, practices like masturbation, frottage, or oral–genital contact engaged in by the animal or by the human do not constitute a problem for animal protection. Penetration of the animals may be considered relevant abuse if injuries or pain result, but this again depends on the degree of force used and the size of the animal. Sadistic acts, insertion of larger objects, or any other actions that cause pain or injuries to the animal constitute abuse and need to be prosecuted according to the animal protection laws.

Recent Research on Bestiality and Zoophilia

A special characteristic of the studies described next is that they all investigated exclusively participants who admitted to engaging in sex with animals. While the research of Beetz (2002), Miletski (2002), and Williams and Weinberg (2003) was conducted quite recently, Peretti and Rowan had studied the phenomenon of chronic zoophilia and factors related to its sustained practice already in 1983.

Peretti and Rowan (1983) investigated a sample of 27 men and 24 women, aged 17 to 28, who had practiced sexual contact with animals at least twice a month for a minimum of 2 years. Participants had been referred by their physicians and volunteered to being interviewed face-to-face about their sustained practice of bestiality. All participants reported that they also had satisfactory human sexual relations. For the majority of men (93%) *sexual expressiveness* was a factor for engaging in sexual contact with animals over this long period of time. *Sexual fantasies* were named by 81%, *no need for negotiation* by 74%, no *human social involvements necessary* by 63%, *economical reasons* by 59%, and *emotional involvement* by 26% of the men. The most important factors for the women were *emotional involvement* (88%), *no human social involvements necessary* (75%), *no negotiation* (58%), *sexual expressiveness* (46%), *sexual fantasy* (38%), and *economical reasons* (21%). Those participants who named *sexual expressiveness* as the reason for engaging in zoophilia considered this practice "as only one form of possible sexual behavior" (Peretti & Rowan, 1983, p. 129) that allows them more freedom than sexual activities with humans that involve "entangling cares and civilized pretense" (p. 129) and more variation of erotic techniques such as oral stimulation of or by the animal or anal intercourse.

The studies of Beetz (2002), Miletski (2002), and Williams and Weinberg (2003) all used a similar approach and since results are often corresponding they are presented together here.

Miletski (2002) employed conventional sources like advertisements as well as the Internet to find participants who had sexual experiences with animals and volunteered to answer her 350-item questionnaire asking for personal data and information on childhood history, sexual history, and current sexual behaviors and preferences with humans and animals. Questionnaires were exchanged via postal mail after a personal phone contact and, overall, data from 82 men and 11 women who had engaged in sexual contact with animals were obtained. Due to the small number of female participants, only the data for men will be reported from her study as well from the studies of Beetz (2002) and Williams and Weinberg (2003). Thirty-six percent of the men were between 19 and 29 years old, 27 percent between 30 and 39, and 36 percent between 40 and 49. More than 90 percent had a Caucasian background, and about half of the sample were college graduates or had an even higher education. Eighty-seven percent of the participants were from the United States. Twenty-six percent had never been married or never lived in an intimate relationship with another person for a month or more.

At around the same time as Miletski (2002), Williams and Weinberg (2003) used a specialized website to contact persons who engaged in bestiality and collected data from 114 volunteering men (and five women and one transgendered individual) via a self-designed questionnaire. Questions addressed "shared identity"—how participants label themselves with respect to their sexual interest in animals and how they relate to others with the same interest, the nature of the sexual interest in animals, sexual contact with animals, human sexual desires and contacts, and the relation of sexual desires for animals and humans (Williams & Weinberg, 2003, p. 526). All men were white, and 91% lived in the United States. Their ages ranged from 18 to 70. Eighty-three percent of the men had at least some college education or had completed college. Sixty-four percent were single and had never been married. Thirty-four percent of the men were from a rural area and 36% from a large city or its suburbs.

In 2000, Beetz (2002) obtained data from 113 volunteering men (and three women) who practiced sexual contact with animals. Here, also, participants were contacted via the Internet and a self-designed questionnaire asked about personal data, animal ownership, sexual experiences with humans and animals, preferences in regard to sex with animals and humans, and mental problems. In addition to that, several standardized instruments were used to allow a personality assessment and comparison with the normal population. All questionnaires, except one, were available in English and German, and thus, different from the other studies, a larger group of only German speaking interested men could be included in the assessment. The personality measures represented an important part of this study, since never before had such information been obtained from a large sample. Characteristics like aggression, interpersonal problems, sociability, or psychopathy were of special interest. In addition to the questionnaires, detailed interviews were conducted with 36 men, 22 of them in a face-to-face situation. Only 35% of Beetz's (2002) male participants were from the United States, but 56% were from Europe with 32% from Germany. On the average, participants were 30 years old and about 70% had at least some college education or a higher level of education. Only 21% of the men lived in a steady relationship at the time of data collection.

Miletski (2002), as well as Williams and Weinberg (2003) and Beetz (2002), also had personal contact (face-to-face) with participants, either at group meetings and/or during their data collection. In addition to questionnaire data alone, such contact probably aids a more comprehensive impression and understanding.

Species and Sex of Animals Involved in Sexual Contact with Humans

The species most often involved in sexual contact with humans seems to be the dog. About 70% of Beetz's (2002) sample and 63% of Williams and Weinberg's (2003) sample had sex with dogs, and in Miletski's (2002) study 90% reported that they had sex with a male dog and 72% with a female dog. Percentages from Beetz's (2002) sample were lower, but sex with male dogs was also reported more frequently (60%) than sex with female dogs (46%). While Williams and Weinberg (2003) found that 37% of their male sample had sexual experiences with horses, about half of the men investigated by Beetz (2002) did, more often with female horses (41%) than male horses (35%). Miletski (2002) reported for both sexes of horse a rate of somewhat more than 50%. Surprisingly, many more participants, 40% of the men in Miletski's (2002) study in comparison to 6% of the male participants in Beetz's study (2002), reported sex with cows. Even sexual contact with bulls was named by 18% of Miletski's male sample and 4% of the men investigated by Beetz. These results are surprising since it is commonly assumed that mainly female (farm) animals are approached. However, among the investigated samples clearly male dogs were most often involved in sexual relations with the men. Additional species named in Miletski's (2002) study were female sheep (21%); female felines (20%); male felines (17%); female swine (16%); female goats (13%); and male swine, male goats, and female fowl (10% each). A few reports also involved llamas/camels, donkeys, deer, tapirs, rabbits, rhesus macaques, wolfs, large cats like lions and tigers, and a rhinoceros. Even though this list includes rather unusual species and it might perhaps seem that fantasies instead of actual experiences were related, sexual contact with such species is possible and the records are believable. Access to such species is often gained in zoos or animal parks (e.g., tapirs, large cats, rhinos, dolphins) or private animal farms (deer). Access to wolves is also not that unlikely, particularly in the United States, where there once was a trend to keep wolves and wolf-hybrids as pets. Also, in Beetz's sample (2002), two participants had sexual experiences with large cats (in a zoo and at a private place that kept large cats that were former circus animals) and two men with dolphins, one of them in the wilderness. These men consented to a detailed interview and convincingly described these experiences to the author (Beetz, 2002). Miletski (2002) further reported that men had sex with several animals of one species. On average 22 dogs had been sexually approached by one man (Miletski, 2002), while the men investigated by Williams and Weinberg (2003) reported an average number of 8 animals.

Sexual Practices Involving Animals

Masturbation of dogs was a practice reported quite frequently (96%, Beetz, 2002), but horses were also masturbated by a large number of men (88%, Beetz, 2002). For obvious reasons, this practice was concentrated on male animals (Miletski, 2002). A substantial number of men had at least once received oral stimulation from a dog (78%, Beetz, 2002; 44%, Williams & Weinberg, 2003) and far fewer men from a horse (30%, Beetz, 2002; 14%, Williams & Weinberg, 2003). That they had orally stimulated the animal was reported by 80% of the men for dogs and by 66% for horses (Beetz, 2002). All of the men in William's and Weinberg's (2003) sample who had sexual relations with a horse had practiced vaginal intercourse, but only 70% of Beetz's (2002) sample reported this practice. The corresponding numbers for dogs were 74% (Williams & Weinberg, 2003) and 50% (Beetz, 2002). Of the men who had sexual experiences with horses, 50% (Williams & Weinberg, 2003) and 40% (Beetz, 2002) had practiced anal intercourse. Much less frequently, anal intercourse was practiced with dogs (Beetz, 2002: 14%; Williams & Weinberg, 2003: 24%). However, receiving anal intercourse from a dog was practiced by approximately 63%–64% of the men (Beetz, 2002; Williams & Weinberg, 2003); and 18% (Beetz, 2002) and 32% (Williams & Weinberg, 2003) reported that they received anal intercourse from a horse/pony/donkey. About 53% of the men active with dogs investigated by Beetz (2002) engaged in sexual contact with this species several times a week, and 18.6% about once a month. With horses, only 21.4% of the men practiced bestiality several times a week, while the majority had sexual animal contact with this species between once a month and once a year. Among Miletski's (2002) sample, the average frequency of sexual animal contact in regard to all species was about three times per week. About half of the men in Miletski's (2002) male sample, and 10% in Beetz's (2002) sample, admitted to having forced an animal into sex at least once. Six men (5.3%) assessed by Beetz (2002) reported that they had harmed/injured an animal in connection with sexual activity, although three of them stated that this happened unintentionally. Among Miletski's (2002) sample, three men indicated that they had at least once been forced by others to engage in sex with animals.

Sexual Activities With Human Partners

In all three studies, the majority of men reported sexual experiences with human partners. Miletski (2002) found that 83% had had heterosexual intercourse and about two-thirds had homosexual contacts. Also, sexual experiences with both sexes were reported quite frequently (43%, Beetz, 2002). However, 24% of Beetz's (2002) sample and 17% of Williams and Weinberg's (2003) sample did not have any sexual experiences with human partners and 25% (Beetz, 2002) and 13% (Williams & Weinberg, 2003) stated that they were not sexually interested in human partners at all. Questioned about other sexual interests or activities, about 7% indicated an interest in sex with minors/children (Beetz, 2002; Miletski, 2002), use of faeces/urine (11.5%), exhibitionism (9.7%), bondage (8.8%), masochistic sex (4.4%), and sadistic sex (1.8%) (Beetz, 2002).

The majority of participants, more than two-thirds in Williams and Weinberg's (2003) study and 57% in Beetz's (2002) sample, stated that sex with animals was more important or preferred than sex with humans. That sex with humans and animals is equally important for them was indicated by about a quarter of each sample, and for 14% (Beetz, 2002), sex with humans was more important. A lack of sexual experiences with humans seemed to be linked to placing more importance on the practice of bestiality (Beetz, 2002; Williams & Weinberg, 2003). About a quarter of the men (Beetz, 2002) rarely engaged in sex with animals, while for 58%, sexual contact to animals was the predominant or only sexual activity besides masturbation.

The Personality of Zoophile Men

A comparison of the male sample investigated by Beetz (2002) with normative data showed that the zoophile men described themselves as more uneasy in social situations, shy, and more detached and self-sufficient than the general population. Norms were derived either from the published test manuals or from other published research that had used the instrument with a larger sample of the normal population. Scales showed further that they did not like the investment of time and effort necessary for social relations, even though they liked company. The zoophile men described themselves as more self-centered and distrusting. Overall, information from several scales suggested that, on average, these men have more difficulties in interpersonal relationships than the norm (Beetz, 2002). In a self-report, the majority of zoophile men indicated they had friends and were of average sociability (Miletski, 2002). However, many of them primarily socialize with other zoophiles (51.3%, Beetz, 2002). Data did not support the assumption that the zoophile men have a higher need for control and dominance than the average population (Beetz, 2002). Obviously, these results cannot be generalized to the whole group of persons who practice sex with animals, since the time and effort necessary for participation in this study very likely led to a self-selection of men with more favorable characteristics.

Mental Health Problems

Half of Miletski's (2002) and 38% of Beetz's (2002) male sample had at least once been in psychotherapeutic treatment. The most frequently named specific cause was depression (12%, Beetz, 2002), but few men received treatment because of their sexual interest in animals (7%, Beetz, 2002). Other causes for seeking professional help were social problems (5%, Beetz, 2002), attention deficit hyperactivity syndrome, compulsions, antisocial personality disorder, phobias, family problems, nervous breakdowns, and paraphilic behaviors. Half of the men (Miletski, 2002) in psychotherapeutic treatment told the therapist about their sexual activity with animals. Reactions from the therapist were quite negative in half of the cases, ranging from disbelief, ridicule, a lack of knowledge about the existence of bestiality, to the threat to report the client to the police (Miletski, 2002).

Emotional Involvement With the Animal

As mentioned before, the existence of an emotional involvement with the animal accompanying the sexual contact represents the main difference between bestiality and zoophilia (as defined by Miletski, 2002; Beetz, 2002). Only a few men, about 4% of Beetz's sample (2002), reported no emotional attachment to the animal, and about 20% stated that the strength of the attachment was the same as to a normal pet. However, the majority, 76%, reported a very strong emotional attachment to the involved animals that they compared to the love of a human partner. Also, of the men investigated by Miletski (2002), 74% indicated that one reason for sexually approaching a certain animal was the *wish to express love and affection to the animal.*

Further Findings

Not unexpected, but very intriguing, was the finding that about one out of three of the investigated zoophile men (Beetz, 2002) reported an active involvement in animal protection. However, less than 10% (Beetz, 2002; Miletski, 2002) had general contact with animals in their workplace (e.g., animal caretaker in a zoo or shelter, veterinarian, farmer). Beetz (2002) and Miletski (2002) both found that most of the men interested in sex with animals rated the information available on the Internet (FAQs, chatrooms) as very important. Even more, they value exchanges with others having the same interest via the Internet, since there, for the first time, they can openly talk about their sexual activity and obtain information about bestiality and zoophilia.

Discussion

Based on the presented information on bestiality and zoophilia, two points in particular will be discussed here in more detail: the existence of a connection between the practice of bestiality and interpersonal violence, especially sexual offending; and the relevance of sexual contacts with animals as animal abuse for the field of animal protection (see also Beetz, 2005a).

When comparing the prevalence rates for the practice of bestiality or an interest in it among the general population with the rates found among samples of violent offenders and sex offenders, it becomes obvious that bestiality is much more frequently found among the latter groups. While "only" 5%–8% of men (Hunt, 1974; Kinsey et al., 1948) among the general population report having sexual experiences with animals, up to 36%–37% (English et al., 2003; Frazier, 1997, cited in Ascione, 1999) of sex offenders do. Comparing sex offenders to violent offenders who show no signs of sexual offending besides their nonsexual violent offenses against others, rates of sexual contact with animals are probably lower than among sex offenders, even though only few data on this relation are available (Miller & Knutson, 1997; ten Bensel et al., 1984). Also, within the group of sex offenders the occurrence of bestiality seems to vary, as the data from Gebhard et al. (1965) suggest. Overall, it is difficult to obtain reliable data on the prevalence of bestiality among criminal samples, since the proneness to lie about such a delicate subject is very high if there are no ways to assess honesty (English et al., 2003).

Sexual experiences with animals are likely underreported to a great extent. This, however, may be also true for the normal population. The general prevalence data of Kinsey et al. (1948, 1953) and Hunt (1974) were obtained decades ago, and can probably only give a rough approximation of the current prevalence of bestiality in the normal population. Nonetheless, sexual contacts with animals or sexual forms of animal cruelty seem to be clearly connected to interpersonal forms of sexualized violence and abuse. Connections to nonsexual interpersonal violence seem to be much less strong, and thus, the use of sexuality as a way to hurt or control seems to be the common underlying factor. However, as reported above, not all sexual practices with animals necessarily involve force or violence, unlike Adam's (1995, cited in Beirne, 2000) conceptualization that defines force as imminent in all human–animal sexual interactions. Touching an animal's genitals out of curiosity with sexual excitement, masturbation of the animal, frottage, or oral–genital contact performed by the animal do not necessarily need physical force, even though, obviously, those acts represent an unusual sexual activity. But other contacts like penetration can also be carried out without the use of violence, and practices like penetration by male animals, an act that puts the human in the more submitting position, may rather require sexual excitement of the animal instead of force from the side of the human. It becomes clear that it would be helpful for further conclusions and more exact interpretations of results if the sexual contact with the animal would be assessed in more detail (Beetz, 2004). Even though some studies distinguished between penetrative and non-penetrative acts of bestiality, no data on the use of force and violence, injuries to the animal, the underlying motivation, and circumstances were collected. To establish a clear link between bestiality and interpersonal violence and sexual offending, more detailed data are needed. Furthermore, it cannot be dismissed that there is probably a large group of persons who engage in sexual contacts with animals who do not display signs of interpersonal violence or sexual offending or were at least never convicted of such offenses. The studies of Beetz (2002), Miletski (2002), and Williams and Weinberg (2003) and also other authors (e.g., Peretti & Rowan, 1983; Wilson, 1987) suggest the existence of such a group. Therefore, it cannot be easily assumed that every person who has sexual contact with an animal also displays violent behavior or sexually offends. The same is true for psychiatric diagnosis. Even

though the practice of bestiality seems to be more frequent among psychiatric inpatients (Alvarez & Freinhar, 1991), the probability that persons engaging in bestiality suffer from a severe mental disorder is not necessarily higher than among the general population. Overall, it would be useful for a better comprehension of bestiality and zoophilia and more meaningful research, if the fact that sexual contact with animals can occur in many different forms would be considered and accepted (Beetz, 2005a).

The same applies for a discussion of bestiality as animal abuse and thus as an issue for animal protection. Again, the question of consent, the dignity of the animal, and imminence of violence in all human–animal interactions will be left aside for further discussion, and only obvious use of force and violence are addressed. Even though very few of the known animal protection organizations provides a public statement on their stance on the issue of sexual animal contacts, the author has the impression that most condemn any sexual approach to animals that would result in the personal sexual pleasure of the human or is intended for the sexual excitement of third parties, as in live shows or the production of animal pornography. As an example, the Humane Society of the United States (HSUS; 2003) supported the move to add bestiality to the definition of criminal animal cruelty in the state of Maine in 2001. This implies that the HSUS has a clear stance against the toleration of any such sexual contact with animals. Very quickly, it seems, all sexual human–animal interactions are judged as severe animal abuse, probably due to the related emotions of disgust and abhorrence. A more differentiated approach, however, needs to be taken, since a person sexually abusing an animal, causing injuries, severe distress, or even death, should not be judged the same as a person who does not inflict stress or injuries. Also, the intention of the offender, if injuries result, needs to be taken into consideration, since hurting an animal intentionally or unintentionally makes an important difference, not necessarily for the animal but for the prospect of further sexual animal abuse or even interpersonal violence committed by this person. Single, nonviolent acts of curious touching of an animal's genitalia, of attempts to masturbate the animal, or oral–genital contacts may not carry much relevance for animal protection, if they do not point to a further graduation to chronic bestiality and more violent practices. A study by Ascione et al. (2003) investigating connections between sexual abuse, cruel behavior toward animals and others, and touching an animal's sex parts among children, showed only for the group of sexually abused children a significant correlation between touching an animal's sex parts and both forms of cruelty. For less than 1% of the comparison groups, a psychiatric and a normal sample, touching an animal's sex part was reported by the maternal caregiver, while 6.3% of the sexually abused children showed this behavior. The authors concluded that "sexualized forms of cruelty may be more specifically related to a history of sexual abuse" (Ascione et al., 2003, p. 206). Simple acts of touching an animal's sex parts were rare and not significantly related to cruelty toward animals or others.

However, with the repeated practice of penetrative forms of bestiality it cannot be readily assumed that the animal suffers relevant physical or psychological stress and injuries, even though this may be true for many cases that come to the attention of animal protection. Another problem is exactly this selection of only those cases that result in severe negative consequences for the animal—probably the majority of the bestiality cases are not detected by any third party, as the high prevalence rates for sexual animal experiences even among the general population suggest. Sexual contacts between humans and animals occur very frequently if projected on the whole population of a state or country and are relevant enough to deserve more attention from different fields such as mental health, animal protection, veterinary sciences, criminology, and law.

Our knowledge about sexual contacts with animals is far from complete, but the recent development of serious discussion of bestiality in science as well as its increased visibility among the public opened the way for a more thorough investigation of this phenomenon. Interdisciplinary research from psychology, psychiatry, criminology, sociology, veterinary medicine, and ethology is needed to compile data not only on the human side of this interaction but also on the behavior and stress for the involved animal. Today, there are several possible ways to obtain information, but it seems as if scientists or other interested professionals still have to be prepared to experience serious criticism from colleagues and others when they touch such a taboo subject as sexual contact with animals.

References

Adams, C. J. (1995). Woman-battering and harm to animals. In C. Adams & J. Donovan (Eds.), *Animals and women: Feminist theoretical explorations* (pp. 55–84). Durham, NC: Duke University Press.

Alvarez, W.A., & Freinhar, J. P. (1991). A prevalence study of bestiality (zoophilia) in psychiatric in-patients, medical in-patients, and psychiatric staff. *International Journal of Psychosomatics*, 38(1–4), 45–47.

American Psychiatric Association. (1980). *Diagnostic and statistical manual of mental disorders* (3rd ed.). Washington, DC: Author.

American Psychiatric Association. (1994). *Diagnostic and statistical manual of mental disorders* (4th ed.). Washington, DC: Author.

Ascione, F. R. (1993). Children who are cruel to animals: A review of research and implications for developmental psychopathology. *Anthrozoös, 6* (4): 226–247.

Ascione, F. R. (1999). The abuse of animals and human interpersonal violence. In F. R. Ascione & P. Arkow (Eds.), *Child abuse, domestic violence, and animal abuse*. West Lafayette, IN: Purdue University Press.

Ascione, F. R., Friedrich, W. N., Heath, J., & Hayashi, K. (2003). Cruelty to animals in normative, sexually abused, and outpatient psychiatric samples of 6- to 12-year-old children: relations to maltreatment and exposure to domestic violence. *Anthrozoös, 16*(3), 194–212.

Beetz, A. (2002). *Love, violence, and sexuality in relationships between humans and animals*. Aachen, Germany: Shaker Verlag.

Beetz, A. (2004). Bestiality/zoophilia: A scarcely investigated phenomenon between crime, paraphilia and love. *Journal of Forensic Psychology Practice, 4*(2), 1–36.

Beetz, A. M. (2005a). Bestiality and zoophilia: Associations with violence and sex offending. In A. M. Beetz & A. L. Podberscek (Eds.), *Anthrozoös, special issue: Bestiality and zoophilia: Sexual relations with animals* (pp. 46–70). West Lafayette, IN: Purdue University Press.

Beetz, A. M. (2005b). New insights into bestiality and zoophilia. In A. M. Beetz & A. L. Podberscek (Eds.), *Anthrozoös, special issue: Bestiality and zoophilia: Sexual relations with animals* (pp. 98–119). West Lafayette, IN: Purdue University Press.

Beirne, P. (2000). Rethinking bestiality: Toward a concept of interspecies sexual assault. In

A. L. Podberscek, E. S. Paul, & J. A. Serpell (Eds.), *Companion animals and us* (pp. 313–331). Cambridge: Cambridge University Press.

Beirne, P. (2001). Peter Singer's "Heavy Petting" and the politics of animal sexual assault. *Critical Criminology, 10*, 43–55.

Bolliger, G., & Goetschel, A. F. (2005). Sexual relations with animals (zoophilia)—an unrecognized problem in animal welfare legislation. In A. M. Beetz & A. L. Podberscek (Eds.), *Anthrozoös, special issue: Bestiality and zoophilia: Sexual relations with animals* (pp. 23–45). West Lafayette, IN: Purdue University Press.

Bullough, V. L. (1976). *Sexual variance in society and history*. Chicago, IL: The University of Chicago Press.

Chideckel, M. (1935). *Female sex perversions*. New York: Eugenics Publishing Company.

Davis, P. (1954). *Sex perversion and the law* (Vols. 1 & 2). New York: Mental Health Press.

Dekkers, M. (1994). *Dearest pet: on bestiality*. New York: Verso.

Doninger, W. (1993). Diary. *London Review of Books*. 23 September: 25. Cited in C. J. Adams. (1994). Bringing peace home: A feminist philosophical perspective on the abuse of women, children, and pet animals. *Hypatia: A Journal of Feminist Philosophy, 9*, 63–84. Reprinted in R. Lockwood & F. R. Ascione (Eds.). (1998). *Cruelty to animals and interpersonal violence*. West Lafayette, IN: Purdue University Press.

Dutton, M. A. (1992). *Empowering and healing the battered woman*. New York: Springer.

English, K., Jones, L., Patrick, D., & Pasini-Hill, D. (2003). Sexual offender containment use of the postconfiction polygraph. *Annals of the New York Academy of Sciences*. 989: 411–427.

Fleming, W. M., Jory, B., & Burton, D. L. (2002). Characteristics of juvenile offenders admitting to sexual activity with nonhuman animals. *Society and Animals, 10*, 1.

Gebhard, P. H., Gagnon, J. H., Pomeroy, W. B., & Christenson, C. V. (1965). *Sex offenders: An analysis of Types*. New York: Harper and Row Publishers, and Paul B. Hoeber, Inc. Medical Books.

Greenland, C. (1983). Sex law reform in an international perspective: England and Wales and Canada. *Bulletin of the American Academy of Psychiatry and the Law, 11*(4), 309–330.

Gregersen, E. (1983). *Sexual practices: The story of human sexuality*. New York: Franklin Watts.

Hanack, E. W. (1968). *Empfiehlt es sich, die Grenzen des Sexualstrafrechts neu zu bestimmen?* Band 1, Gutachten A zum 47. Deutschen Juristentag. München: Beck.

Hentig, H. V. (1962). Soziologie der zoophilen Neigung. *Beiträge zur Sexualforschung, Bd.25*. Stuttgart: Ferdinand Enke.

Holmes, R. M. (1991). *Sex crimes*. Newbury Park: Sage Publications.

Home Office, Great Britain. (2000). *Setting the boundaries. Reforming the law on sex offences* (Vol. 1). London: Home Office. Building a safe, just and tolerant society.

Home Office, Great Britain. (2003). *Protecting the Public. Strengthening protection against sex offenders and reforming the law of sexual offences*. Norwich: HMSO.

Humane Society of the United States. (June 18, 2003). *The HSUS Adds to Reward Fund in University of Maine Animal Cruelty Case*. Retrieved July 2005 from http://www.hsus.org/press_and_publications/press_releases/the_hsus_adds_to_reward_fund_in_university_of_maine_animal_cruelty_case.html

Hunt, M. (1974). *Sexual behavior in the 1970s*. Chicago, IL: Playboy Press.

Karpman, B. (1954). *The sexual offender and his offenses*. Washington, DC: Julian Press.

Kinsey, A. C., Pomeroy, W. B., & Martin, C. E. (1948). *Sexual behavior in the human male*. Philadelphia: Saunders.

Kinsey, A. C., Pomeroy, W. B., Martin, C. E., & Gebhart, P. H. (1953). *Sexual behavior in the human female*. Philadelphia: Saunders.

Krafft-Ebing, R. v. 1894, (1924). *Psychopathia sexualis* (9th ed.). Stuttgart: Enke.

Love, B. (1992). *Encyclopedia of unusual sex practices*. Fort Lee, NJ: Barricade Books.

Massen, J. (1994). *Zoophilie. Die sexuelle Liebe zu Tieren*. Köln: Pinto Press.

Masters, R. E. L. (1962). *Forbidden sexual behavior and morality*. New York: Julian Publishers.

Masters, R. E. L. (1966). *Sex-driven people*. Los Angeles, CA: Sherbourne Press, Inc.

Matthews, M. (1994). *The horseman—obsessions of a zoophile*. Amherst, NY: Prometheus Books.

Miersch, M. (1999). Das bizarre Sexualleben der Tiere. Frankfurt/Main: Eichborn.

Miletski, H. (2002). *Understanding bestiality and zoophilia*. Bethesda, MD: Author.

Miletski, H. (2005a). A history of bestiality. In A. M. Beetz & A. L. Podberscek (Eds.), *Anthrozoös, special issue: Bestiality and zoophilia: Sexual relations with animals* (pp. 1–22). West Lafayette, IN: Purdue University Press.

Miletski, H. (2005b). Is zoophilia a sexual orientation? A study. In A. M. Beetz & A. L. Podberscek (Eds.), *Anthrozoös, special issue: Bestiality and zoophilia: Sexual relations with animals* (pp. 82–97). West Lafayette, Indiana: Purdue University Press.

Miller, K. S., & Knutson, J. F. (1997). Reports of severe physical punishment and exposure to animal cruelty by inmates convicted of felonies and by university students. *Child Abuse and Neglect*, Vol. 21 (1), 59–82.

Money, J. (1986). *Lovemaps*. New York: Irvington Publishers, Inc.

Munro, H. M. C., & Thrusfield, M. V. (2001). "Battered Pets": sexual abuse. *Journal of Small Animal Practice, 42*, 333–337.

Peretti, P. O., & Rowan, M. (1983). Zoophilia: factors related to its sustained practice. *Panminerva Medica, 25*, 127–131.

Ressler, R. K., Burgess, A. W., Hartmann, C. R., Douglas J. E., & McCormack, A. (1986). Murderers who rape and mutilate. *Journal of Interpersonal Violence*, 1, 273–287.

Rosenberger, J. R. (1968). *Bestiality*. Los Angeles, CA: Medco Books.

Rosenfeld, J. R. (1967). *The Animal Lovers*. Atlanta, GA: Pendulum.

Salisbury, J. (1994). *The Beast Within: Animals in the Middle Ages*. New York: Routledge.

Sandnabba, N. K., Santtila, P., Beetz, A. M., Nordling, N., & Alison, L. (2002). Characteristics of a sample of sadomasochistically-oriented males with recent experience of sexual contact with animals. *Deviant Behavior, 23*(6), 511–530.

Schedel-Stupperich, A. (2002). *Schwere Gewaltdelikte and Pferden. Phänomenologie, psychosoziales Konstrukt und die Ableitung von präventiven Verhaltensmaßnahmen*. Warendorf: FN-Verlag.

Schmidt, W. (1969). *Neurosenpsychologische Aspekte der Sodomie*. Dissertation. Universität München.

Singer, P. (1975). *Animal Liberation*. New York: Avon.

Singer, P. (2001, March/April). Heavy petting. *Nerve*. Retrieved July 2005 from http://www.nerve.com/Opinions/Singer/heavyPetting

Stayton, W. R. (1994). Sodomy. In V. L. Bullough and B. Bullough (Eds.), *Human sexuality: An encyclopedia*. New York: Garland Publishing.

Stettner, M. (1990). Unzucht mit tieren—ein tierschutzproblem. *Deutsche Tierärztliche Wochenschrift, 97*, 137–192.

Taylor, T. (1996). *The prehistory of sex*. New York: Bantam Books.

ten Bensel, R. W., Ward, D. A., Kruttschnitt, C., Quigley, J., & Anderson, R. K. (1984). Attitudes of violent criminals toward animals. In R. K. Anderson, B. L. Hart, & L. Hart (Eds.), *The pet connection: Its influence on our health and quality of life*. Minneapolis: Censhare, University of Minnesota.

Waine, W. W. (1968). *Canine sexualis*. San Diego, CA: Publisher's Export, Inc.

Weidner, E. (1972). *Sodomie und sadismus als tierschutzproblem*. Doctoral dissertation, University of Giessen, Germany.

Williams, J. W., & Weinberg M. S. (2003). Zoophilia in men: A study of sexual interest in animals. *Archives of Sexual Behavior, 32*(6), 523–535.

Wilson, G. D. (1987). An ethological approach to sexual deviation: In G. D. Wilson (Ed.), *Variant sexuality: Research and theory*. London/Sidney: Croom Helm.

Animal Hoarding: A Third Dimension of Animal Abuse

Gary Patronek

Abstract

Animal hoarding is a poorly understood aspect of human–animal interaction of uncertain etiology that results in substantial animal suffering and death. In some cases, animal hoarding may begin with the pretext of providing care or preventing euthanasia, but inevitably progresses into an obsessive desire to acquire and control animals. The onset of cruelty begins when the hoarder simultaneously becomes unable to provide even minimal standards of care and fails to recognize and correct this deficiency. Eventually, animal hoarding degenerates into protracted animal suffering and death, potentially encompassing human victims who are either financially or emotionally dependent upon the hoarder.

Animal hoarding is characterized by contradictory features that preclude incorporating it within two well-recognized categories of animal cruelty (i.e., deliberate animal abuse and neglect from indifference). In deliberate animal abuse, the perpetrator acts intentionally, with full knowledge of his or her actions, and derives some enjoyment from the suffering. By comparison, in neglect, the perpetrator has no particular affinity for animals, is indifferent to their suffering, derives no pleasure from it, and is often oblivious to the conditions, even though a willful component can be ascribed to the failure to act. Both of these forms of animal cruelty occur with little, if any, obvious detriment to the welfare of the perpetrator. Paradoxically, in animal hoarding, considerable physical and psychological animal suffering occurs without professed intent to harm, in conjunction with a strong human–animal bond, often with considerable compromising of the welfare of the perpetrator, and with lack of insight as to the true nature of the situation. Denial frequently colors public discourse on the topic, and the lack of intent, coupled with professed good intentions,

often mitigates the seriousness of these crimes in the eyes of the law. Unlike deliberate animal cruelty or neglect, which tend to be socially censured, animal hoarding is often facilitated by a broad network of active or passive enablers.

The true scope of the pathology underlying animal hoarding is only beginning to be appreciated. Our direct experience with animal hoarders indicates that animal hoarding appears to be frequently complicated by a variety of serious co-morbid psychological conditions, which confound prevention, intervention, and treatment. This is consistent with other research. Brown and Katcher (2001) have demonstrated that dissociation, which may serve in buffering people from an external trauma, is the only personality variable that consistently correlates with pet attachment. Rynearson (1978) has noted how, for children in dysfunctional families, the consistently receptive pet may be used as a means of escape, and as a substitute for human relationships. Given these findings, it is not surprising that the Hoarding of Animals Research Consortium (HARC) (2002) has found indications that animal hoarding may be traced to childhood when the pet relationship becomes a compensatory attachment and bonding experience for children faced with abusive or absent parents.

These characteristics suggest that animal hoarding is a deviant expression of the human–animal bond that represents a third dimension of animal abuse. The lack of fit with current models of animal abuse and human–animal relationships identifies a gap in the empirical research in this field. The challenges in advancing knowledge in this area are further compounded by our limited understanding of the psychological underpinnings of hoarding behavior in general. The available evidence suggests animal hoarding is a distinct variant in the phenomenology of animal abuse, and underscores the need to develop a new theoretical basis upon which to build understanding of this phenomenon.

Introduction

Hoarding vs. Collecting

Until very recently, animal hoarding was colloquially referred to within the animal sheltering community as "animal collecting." This terminology is inappropriate and inaccurate, and has compromised recognition of this behavior as a distinct, severe, and novel form of animal abuse. Collecting, defined as *"an orderly process in which the collector accumulates the objects of desire and arranges them into an orderly pattern,"* denotes a hobby or pastime that is perceived to be generally harmless, even virtuous (Halperin & Glick, 2003).

By comparison, the definition that has been offered for the hoarding of inanimate objects is *"The acquisition and failure to discard large numbers of possessions which appear to be useless or of limited value"* (Frost, Hartl, Christian, & Williams, 1995). Hoarding has been described as a less organized pursuit in which the hoarder is preoccupied with the scale and quantity of hoarding (Halperin & Glick, 2003). Even a superficial comparison of the features of collecting vs. hoarding indicates that animal hoarding has much more in common with the latter than the former. Furthermore, numerous published reports of the symptomology of hoarding indicate the presence of a significant pathological component to that behavior (discussed in a later section).

The first formal definition of animal hoarding, put forth in 1999 (Patronek, 1999), was phenomenological in nature, and described an animal hoarder as someone who:

- Accumulates a large number of animals;
- Fails to provide minimal standards of nutrition, sanitation, and veterinary care; and
- Fails to act on the deteriorating condition of the animals and the environment, or the negative effect of the collection on his or her own health and well-being or that of other family members.

This definition was incorporated largely intact in the 2001 revision of the Illinois Animal Cruelty Statute—the first in the country to specifically define animal hoarding in the context of a criminal act (Public Act 92–0454).

Description of Animal Hoarding

The aforementioned clinical definition of animal hoarding does not begin to convey the true nature of a case. Words, and even pictures, are insufficient to describe the extent of squalor and suffering endured by animal victims of hoarding. Although animal hoarding does exist on a spectrum, by the time most cases are discovered and investigated, conditions have often deteriorated beyond belief. Characteristics that can be present include:

Severe squalor and dysfunctional households

- Extensive accumulations of feces and urine throughout the dwelling, sometimes many inches deep, resulting in structural damage so extensive that demolition is necessary.
- Air so toxic due to extensive ammonia accumulation and lack of any ventilation that non-acclimated persons are not able to tolerate the environment without protective breathing apparatus.
- Stench so pervasive that exposed clothing cannot be adequately washed and must be discarded.
- Lack of running water in the home precluding normal sanitary activities
- Dead animals left where they died, or systematically stored in some fashion (e.g., by color, species, time of death).
- Rooms so cluttered normal use is precluded.

Lack of sufficient food and/or potable water

- Water absent or contaminated with dirt or feces.
- Food absent, spoiled, contaminated, of poor nutritional quality, or simply not fed to the animals; animals unable to reach or access food
- Chronic malnutrition, with death from starvation not uncommon.
- Live animals cannibalizing the dead.

Untreated disease or injuries present

- Animals with severe chronic disease (e.g., end-stage skin or ear infections, respiratory disease; heart disease; cancer).

- Animals with untreated injuries (e.g., broken limbs, injured eyes, wounds, visible tumors).
- Extensive infestation with internal and external parasites.
- Infectious diseases such as parvovirus, panleukopenia, feline leukemia

Psychological stress

- Lack of exercise or freedom of movement.
- Being confined to small cages, which limit ability to engage in normal species-specific behaviors.
- Lack of socialization to humans and possibly other animals of the same species.
- Exposure to hostile or aggressive animals or natural predators.
- Having to compete or even fight for food or water.

It is important to add that, even in the early stages of the typical animal hoarding case, husbandry conditions fall far short of acceptable care for companion animals in institutional settings, such as legitimate shelters or laboratory animal facilities. Unfortunately, this degree of lapse in care may still be above the threshold that would allow the person to be successfully prosecuted for cruelty under most existing state statutes.

Frequency of Animal Hoarding

The frequency of animal hoarding is difficult to estimate, but has been calculated using several different approaches. In one study, using self-reported data from animal shelters, the frequency was estimated based on extrapolating to the animal intakes of the shelters per year and the human population served. This resulted in an estimated incidence of roughly 700–2,000 cases annually across the United States, depending on whether median or mean values were used in the calculation (Patronek, 1999).

The above was a very rough calculation, given the difficulty in obtaining accurate data about reported cases, and probably was an underestimate. Passive surveillance of newspaper reports by the author over the past 6–7 years have yielded, on average, at least 3 cases a day, which suggests that the previous figure would be substantially higher with complete reporting.

In another survey, health officers in Massachusetts were queried about reported cases of all types of hoarding over a 5-year period; the 5-year prevalence rate was estimated as 5.3 cases per 100,000 population per year (Frost, Steketee, & Williams, 2000). This study had advantages over the shelter-based study because health departments are more likely to receive and record information in a retrievable fashion than animal shelters. Animals were hoarded in roughly a third of these cases, which suggests an incidence of about 1.75 cases of animal hoarding per 100,000 population per year. The authors of that study also indicated that methodological problems likely resulted in an underreporting during the first 3 years of the study, suggesting this was a minimum estimate. By comparison, the only other study that examined frequency was conducted in New York City nearly 25 years ago, and suggested an incidence of 0.40 cases per 100,000 (Worth & Beck, 1981).

The current Massachusetts estimate (1.75 cases/100,000), if extrapolated to the entire U.S. population of about 291 million people (U.S. Census Bureau, 2003), would indicate a minimum of 5,092 reported animal hoarding cases per year. To the extent that the data are representative of the entire United States, and using a median of either 39 or 47 animals per case (HARC, 2002; Patronek, 1999), it would not be unreasonable to suggest that up to a quarter million animals are subjected to this form of abuse each year.

Demographics of Animal Hoarding and Household Characteristics

The basic descriptive characteristics of animal hoarding and animal hoarders were investigated in two case series, comprising 56 (Patronek, 1999) and 71 cases (HARC, 2002). The data were obtained via solicitation of a convenience sample of shelters and other investigative agencies with knowledge of hoarding cases, using a standardized report form (see the appendix). Results of both case series were similar, as shown in Table 1. The total number of animals was not normally distributed—it ranged from as few as 10 in the cases studied to as many as 918, and numbers of ≥100 were not uncommon.

Although the data from these two case series supported the stereotype of animal hoarders as female, single, living alone, and not working outside the home, it should also be emphasized that animal hoarding can be seen in both genders, all ages, in married couples, and among persons having "white

Table 1 Characteristics of animal hoarders from two case series
Study 1 (Patronek, 1999); Study 2 (HARC, 2002)

	Study 1, n=56	Study 2, n=71
Gender	76% female	83.1% female
Age	37%>60 yrs	Median age: 55 yrs women 53 yrs men
Marital status	72.2% single, widowed, divorced	71.8% single, widowed, divorced
Living situation	55.6% lived alone	46.5% lived alone
Employment	Not well documented	54.9% unemployed, retired, or disabled
Number of animals	Median=39	Median=47 (men), 50 (women)

collar," professional jobs. There have even been cases documented among health care workers (e.g., physicians, nurses, veterinarians) who were able to successfully lead a double life, with their colleagues unaware of the conditions in their homes.

Utilities and major appliances were commonly reported to be out of order, (e.g., shower or tub, stove, toilets, and sinks). Activities considered basic to maintaining a functional and sanitary household (for example, using bath or shower, sleeping in a bed, or preparing food) were rated as very much impaired in from one-half to three-quarters of cases, and greater impairment in these activities was reported for single-person compared with multiple-person households (HARC, 2002). Therefore, it is not surprising that the majority of cases also satisfied criteria for adult self-neglect. More worrisome was that dependent elderly people, children, or disabled individuals were sometimes present and could be considered co-victims in these cases. About 17% of homes were ultimately condemned or deemed unfit for human habitation, and hoarders eventually were placed in some type of permanent or temporary protective care in one-quarter of the cases. These findings suggest, that like other forms of animal abuse, animal hoarding may be a sentinel for a range of medical, mental health, social, and economic problems.

Animal Hoarding Does Not Fit Into Current Models for Community-based Animal Abuse

Over the past 15 years, a large body of empirical research has firmly established the link between deliberate animal abuse and other forms of antisocial behavior, including domestic violence and child abuse. Much of this work is discussed in other chapters in this volume and will not be reviewed here. Sociologically, with the exception of some forms of abuse institutionalized as sport, such as dog fighting, cockfighting, pigeon shoots, and bull fighting, for example, which linger due to acceptance within existing, albeit increasingly archaic, cultural or subcultural norms, causing deliberate harm to animals without any justifiable human benefit is generally met with swift and widespread condemnation. This attitudinal shift has occurred in parallel with a veritable explosion of research on the beneficial aspects of the human–animal bond. Today, deep attachment to animals has become viewed as a positive, desirable trait.

This broad cultural phenomenon has contributed to support for the revision of animal cruelty statutes, which have established stronger penalties for deliberate acts of cruelty. Furthermore, as of October 2004, 24 states had provision for either recommended or mandatory psychological counseling or anger management for certain crimes—particular felonies or multiple acts, or when juveniles are involved (see *The Impact of Improved American Anti-Cruelty Laws* by Frasch, this text). Although the details of the statutory modifications vary, they reflect a growing understanding that deliberate mistreatment of animals has important societal implications, and that remediation should include punitive, therapeutic, and preventive components.

Current Models of Abuse

From a pragmatic perspective, community-based animal cruelty involving companion animals and encountered by humane officers employed by animal shelters has traditionally been distilled into two general types—cruelty arising from neglect that is unintentional (passive), lacks a deliberate component, and represents sins of omission; and cruelty that is both deliberate and intentional, involving commission of specific acts.

Cases of neglect that are unintentional are typically dealt with as relatively minor offenses, often via education of the caregiver and/or removal of the animals if the person is unable to provide proper care. These comprise the vast majority of reports of animal cruelty investigated by humane law enforcement agencies, and in many situations, such an approach probably is justifiable, particularly for first offenses. From the standpoint of protecting animals as well as society this approach makes intuitive sense, because the danger to animals is at least roughly coupled to the degree of intent.

Existing Typology

In the 1990s, Vermeulen used several victimological typologies as a guideline for construction of the first typology of animal abuse (Vermeulen & Odendaal, 1993). The typology of child abuse was particularly influential in his work because the three major categories (as described at the time) of physical abuse (active maltreatment, passive neglect, and commercial exploitation) as well as the two major categories of mental abuse (active and passive) seemed applicable

to animals. In terms of human behavior, he envisioned a continuum from negative interaction to no interaction to positive interaction with animals (Table 2).

Motivations Associated With Animal Abuse

In the previous typology, animal neglect is ascribed to indifference to animal suffering and failure to act; animals and their condition are generally ignored and the abuser takes no pleasure in the suffering that may result. By contrast, in deliberate abuse, there is great focus on the animal; the abuser intends to cause pain and distress, and likely derives some pleasure from his or her actions. Motivations for deliberate abuse of animals have been described in some detail (Ascione 2001; Kellert & Felthous, 1985). They include:

- To control an animal.
- To retaliate against an animal.
- To satisfy a prejudice against a species or breed (e.g., hatred of cats).
- To express aggression through an animal.
- To enhance one's own aggressiveness.
- To shock people for amusement.
- To retaliate against other people.
- To displace hostility from a person to an animal.

Table 2 Summary of typology of companion animal abuse as proposed by Vermeulen & Odendaal, 1993

Type of Abuse	Characteristics	Examples
Physical abuse		
Intentional	Active maltreatment	Assault, burning, poisoning, shooting, mutilation, abandonment
	Commercial exploitation	Labor, fights, sport, experimentation, indiscriminate breeding
Non-intentional	Passive neglect or ignorance	Lack of food, water, shelter, sanitation, veterinary care, general neglect
Mental abuse		
Intentional	Active maltreatment	Instillation of fear, anguish, anxiety
Non-intentional	Passive neglect	Deprivation of love and affection
		Lack of recreational stimuli

- To experience nonspecific sadism.
- Curiosity or exploration.
- Peer pressure.
- Mood enhancement (e.g., to relieve boredom or depression).
- Sexual gratification (i.e., bestiality).
- Forced abuse.
- Attachment to an animal (e.g., the child kills an animal to prevent its torture by another individual).
- Animal phobias (that cause a preemptive attack on a feared animal).
- A victim's attempt to regain a sense of power by victimizing a more vulnerable animal.
- Reenacting violent episodes with an animal victim.
- Imitation of a parent's or other adult's abusive actions.
- Using an animal to inflict injuries on the child's own body.
- Rehearsal (i.e., "practicing" violence on stray animals or pets before engaging in violent acts against other people).
- Vehicle for emotional abuse (e.g., injuring someone else's pet).

There is no evidence whatsoever that any of these apply to animal hoarding, with the possible exception of the need to control, suggesting that the underlying reasons driving animal hoarding are fundamentally different from other forms of abuse with a deliberate component.

A Third Dimension of Animal Abuse

Animal hoarding cases do not fit into the prevailing models of animal abuse because the cruelty from failure to provide care is inflicted passively, and paradoxically occurs in conjunction with a strong and positive human–animal bond. This suggests a previously unrecognized dimension of animal cruelty in which animal suffering has been uncoupled from the intent and bond of the human actor, and is represented schematically in Figure 1. As illustrated in the figure, the ideal relationship occurs in the context of a strong bond in which both animals and people benefit (ideal caretakers). Neglect, by contrast, occurs in the presence of a weak human–animal bond in which neither the animal nor the person benefits. (Note that under this schema, a negative bond is not necessarily bad if it means that the person avoids pet ownership or contact with companion animals.) When a person with a negative affinity toward animals actively seeks contact with animals, deliberate abuse is likely to occur. Hoarding is unique because animal suffering

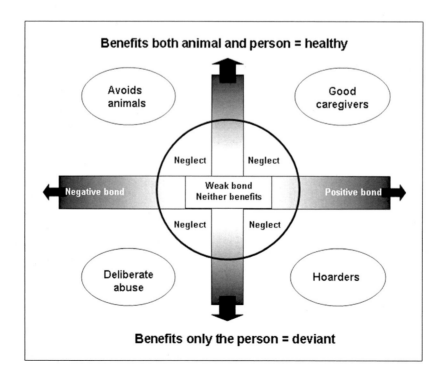

Table 3   Revised typology of animal abuse

Defining Characteristics	Animal Neglect	Animal Abuse	Animal Hoarding
Intent	To ignore	To harm	To acquire and control
Actions causing abuse	Disregard has a willful component, intent to harm does not	Deliberate	Acquisition has a deliberate component, intent to harm does not
Human–animal bond	Weak or neutral	Strong and negative	Strong and positive
Number of animals involved	Low	Low	Moderate to high
Likelihood of repetition	Low to moderate	Moderate to high	Almost inevitable

occurs in the presence of a strong positive bond, which has somehow become warped so that human but not animal needs are met. The accompanying revised typology of animal abusers is presented in Table 3.

This new dimension of animal cruelty highlights the deficiency of the current theoretical approach to human–animal relationships, because a strong bond and (stated) good intentions do not preclude substantial animal suffering. Therefore, existing interventions and preventions, which are based on the premise that animal suffering occurs when there is a negative or absent human–animal bond, are woefully inadequate. This weakness extends to statutory remedies, because the punitive and deterrent abilities of existing animal cruelty laws are largely tied to intent to harm. This will be discussed under the role of prosecution.

Current Theories About Hoarding Behavior

Despite the evidence that hoarding of inanimate objects is both common and potentially detrimental to all involved, there is surprisingly little empirical research into the psychological underpinnings of this behavior, leaving many questions about pathogenesis and treatment unanswered (Damecour & Charron, 1998). Research indicates that hoarding of inanimate objects is driven by a number of distorted fears and obsessional beliefs (Damecour & Charron, 1998; Frost & Gross, 1993; Stein, Seedat, & Potocnik, 1999). These include:

- Fear of losing important items
- Distorted beliefs about the importance of possessions
- Excessive emotional attachment to possessions

- Fear of making the wrong decision about discarding items

Stein has suggested that the phenomenology of hoarding may vary with the underlying disorder, for example, delusions in psychotic patients may result in hoarding bizarre items, or as occurs in dementia, hoarding may be a consequence of cognitive impairment, which limits ability to discriminate about what to discard (Stein, Seedat, & Potocnik, 1999).

Frost et al. have developed a cognitive behavioral model of hoarding (Frost, Krause, & Steketee, 1996) that the Hoarding of Animals Research Consortium (HARC) has, in a preliminary form, applied to animal hoarders. In this model, hoarding is a multifaceted problem that results from a series of behavioral deficits. The avoidance of these problems eventually leads to the chaotic behavior seen in hoarding. These problems include:

- Information-processing deficits
- Emotional attachment to possessions
- Lack of insight into their behavior
- Need for control over possessions

As HARC has pointed out, there are striking parallels between the observed behavior of animal hoarders and this cognitive behavioral model (Frost & HARC, 2000). These conclusions have been derived following a series of structured interviews conducted with dozens of hoarders, onsite interventions and personal counseling, as well as review of hundreds of cases and media reports by HARC members.

The information-processing deficits seen in hoarding include problems with decision making, memory, and concentration, which contribute to difficulties in weighing relevant information and with the process of categorization. The inability of animal hoarders to maintain a fully functional home and provide for the basic husbandry needs of animals is certainly consistent with this component of the model. Even with assistance in closely supervised interventions by trained counselors, hoarders have shown great difficulty in maintaining the routine necessary to ensure adequate animal care.

The excessive sentimentality to inanimate objects with little or no intrinsic value seen in conventional hoarding appears to be magnified in animal hoarding. The reasons for this are uncertain, but it is likely that the interactive component present with animals vs. inanimate objects is an important factor. Cases of almost instantaneous attachment to new animals and inability to discriminate between long-beloved pets vs. new additions are not uncommon. This excessive sentimentality may account for some of the resistance to downsizing a collection, as well as intense suspicion about the motivation of outsiders.

The third behavioral deficit outlined by Frost et al. (erroneous beliefs about the nature of possessions) is closely aligned with the previous one (Frost et al. 1995). Hoarders of inanimate objects frequently express great concern about waste and missing lost opportunities if an item is discarded. HARC has found that animal hoarders often believe they have a special gift for empathizing with animals, and that care for animals is their life's mission. Interviews conducted with animal hoarders indicate that animals are major components of hoarders' identities, providing feelings of security and safety. With this in mind, it is easy to appreciate the intense feelings of loss when an animal must be given up, and the effort that hoarders will expend to deflect perceived threats to maintaining their accumulation.

Hoarders often cope with these behavioral deficits by avoiding them as much as possible. As Frost and Gross have hypothesized, saving avoids the discomfort associated with making a decision about what to do with an object, and the distress that accompanies discarding a cherished possession (Frost & Gross, 1993). Inability to turn away an animal is a feature of many animal hoarding cases. It is not uncommon to find the bodies of dead animals systematically preserved or stored in some fashion, or at other times simply ignored in the accumulated detritus of the home; such behavior would be consistent with denying the death and/or acknowledging their own neglectful care, which was the precipitating factor.

Phenomenologically, the behaviors seen in animal hoarding include the following:

- Passive and active accumulation of animals
- Attempts to maintain control of the collection
- Indifference to varying degrees of squalor
- Resistance to downsizing
- Suspicion and reclusiveness
- Denial of the true conditions
- Reluctance to seek or accept help

Conceptualizing Hoarding as a Symptom Rather Than a Syndrome

Hoarding likely has a variety of neurobiological and psychosocial determinants, thus it has been argued that it should be best understood as a symptom rather than a syndrome (Damecour & Charron, 1998). This is probably true for animal hoarding as well. Hoarding behavior spans a continuum, which in its extreme manifests as pathological self-neglect and can be associated with a wide variety of clinical disorders, including psychoses, organic mental disease, obsessive-compulsive personality disorder (OCPD) and OCD (Damecour & Charron, 1998). In a non-clinical population, hoarding was associated with higher levels of general psychopathology (Frost, Krause, & Steketee, 1996). Characteristics of hoarders include the following (Damecour & Charron, 1998; Frost, Steketee, & Williams, 2000; Greenberg, 1987; Greenberg, Witztum, & Levy, 1990):

- Lack of insight
- Avoidance
- Pathological doubting
- A greater number of symptoms as well as greater severity of OCD
- Denial of hoarding
- Minimizing/rationalizing the behavior
- No resistance to the hoarding
- Preoccupation with hoarding to the detriment of their personal lives
- Lack of interest in behavioral psychotherapy
- Failure to limit their behavior in the absence of external pressure
- Possible exacerbation after stressful life events
- Feeling of persecution
- Reluctance to cooperate with officials

The Role of Co-morbid Psychological Disorders

The potential for co-morbid conditions such as attention deficit hyperactivity disorder or personality disorder to complicate the treatment of hoarding of inanimate objects has been described, and it is likely these conditions may account for some of the resistance of hoarders to seek therapy (Kaplan & Hollander, 2004). To date, we do not know what the range of potential diagnoses might be in animal hoarding. However, the characteristics listed above are entirely consistent with what HARC has observed in 7 years of research and interest in this topic. Futhermore, it has been suggested that co-morbid conditions (e.g., schizoaffective/schizophrenia; depression, attention deficit disorder, anxiety, post-traumatic stress, generalized social phobia, and major depressive disorder) can contribute substantially to the pathogenesis of animal hoarding and that disorders associated with lack of essential early childhood attachment and bonding with parents or primary caregivers— that is, the personality disorders (i.e., borderline, narcissistic, anti-social) and paranoia—may not only be common but also unusual in their severity in animal hoarding (Patronek, Loar, & Nathanson, 2005). Although nothing is known about the utility of pharmacotherapy in animal hoarding, treatment of known co-morbid conditions is something which can be attempted using accepted psychotherapeutic and pharmacotherapeutic modalities.

The Zoonosis Hypothesis.   For completeness under the topic of co-morbid conditions, it is worth mentioning that a hypothesis has been put forward that cats may be vectors for viral and parasitic agents that could cause schizophrenia if transmitted to people under the right genetic, environmental, and temporal background (Mihm, 2001; Torrey & Yolken, 1995; Torrey & Yolken, 2003). Toxoplasma in particular has been implicated because cats are the definitive host for this parasite and it has a known affinity for tissues of the central nervous system. Furthermore, serologic evidence of exposure to toxoplasma has been epidemiologically linked with schizophrenia and bipolar disorder, and patients with serologic evidence of toxoplasma infection have shown alterations in behavior (Torrey & Yolken, 2003). Schizophrenia is an important mental illness that causes significant morbidity, however, to my knowledge, there has been no indication that this disorder has ever been documented in animal hoarders, and the viral zoonosis theory has been challenged on empirical grounds (Waltrip, 1995). The etiologic role of toxoplasmosis in schizophrenia remains speculative at present. Furthermore, this hypothesis does not explain the occurrence of animal hoarding in species other than cats. Nevertheless, the possibility that a zoonotic agent could contribute to the etiopathogenesis of some cases of animal hoarding is sufficiently plausible to merit consideration in future research.

The OCD Connection

In the medical literature, hoarding behavior is dealt with primarily, although not exclusively, under the context of obsessive-compulsive disorder (OCD). OCD is a common psychological disorder in the United States, affecting from 1%–2% of the adult population (Steketee & Frost, 2003). Although standard diagnostic classifications consider OCD to be a single entity, recent works indicates that OCD is multi-dimensional and etiologically heterogeneous (Saxena et al, 2004). A distinct subset of OCD patients (18%–31%) can be identified who have hoarding, saving, and collecting symptoms (Frost, Krause & Steketee, 1996; Rasmussen & Eisen, 1992). It is not known what portion of these cases might involve animals, but, as previously discussed, there are many reasons why animal hoarders may be underrepresented in clinical populations.

In OCD, hoarding symptoms appear stable over time and have different patterns of inheritance (i.e., recessive), co-morbidity, and response to treatment than other expressions of that syndrome (Saxena et al, 2004). Among OCD patients, subjects with hoarding behavior have been found to have clinically significant differences compared to non-hoarding OCD patients. OCD hoarding patients scored higher on depression, anxiety, and family and social disability, and had a greater frequency of dependent and schizotypal personality disorder symptoms than non-hoarding OCD patients (Frost, Steketee, Williams, & Warrens, 2000). They also have been reported as having less insight into their symptoms (Greenberg, 1987), which makes them less likely to seek treatment (Saxena et al, 2004). When treatment is sought, they tend to respond poorly to pharmacotherapy with selective serotonin reuptake inhibitors or to cognitive behavioral therapy (Saxena et al, 2004).

Several attempts have been made to identify neuroanatomical or neurophysiological determinants of hoarding behavior. In a recent study, PET scans were performed on the brains of 45 adult subjects who met the criteria for OCD, 12 of whom had hoarding as their primary symptom (Saxena et al, 2004). Subjects with hoarding compulsions had a different pattern of cerebral glucose metabolism than either non-hoarding OCD patients or non-OCD controls, suggesting a neurobiological component to the behavior. However, at present, the etiology remains speculative.

The Self-Neglect Component: Diogenes Syndrome

The term "Diogenes syndrome" was coined in 1975 and generally describes patients, particularly the elderly, exhibiting extreme self-neglect, living in squalor, being reclusive, and stubbornly resisting all attempts to help (Reyes-Ortiz, 2001). Women and men tend to be equally affected. These individuals tend to have average or above-average intelligence, be single, live alone and be socially isolated; the condition can be seen in all socioeconomic groups (Reyes-Ortiz, 2001).

Diogenes syndrome is classified as primary if it occurs in the absence of mental illness, and as secondary if there is an underlying psychiatric disorder. It has been postulated that these individuals suffer from a life-long personality disorder that gradually turns into gross self-neglect and isolation (Reyes-Ortiz, 2001). Personality traits associated with Diogenes syndrome include unfriendliness, obstinacy, aloofness, aggressiveness, independence, detachedness, stubbornness, secretiveness, quarrelsomeness, and eccentricity (Cooney & Hamid, 1995; Reyes-Ortiz, 2001). Despite the well-recognized clinical syndrome, research into this behavior is lacking. It has been suggested that the social breakdown may be triggered by a stressful life event (Reyes-Ortiz, 2001). Intervention in these cases is difficult and often not successful.

Surprisingly, animal hoarding has never been formally described as a feature of Diogenes syndrome, although it has been alluded to (Reifler, 1996), despite its many shared traits. This may reflect the relatively small body of literature, an even greater reclusiveness on the part of animal hoarders than others with Diogenes syndrome, or a tendency on the part of social service and adult protective services workers to attribute the conditions to the accumulation of animals instead of as a sign of underlying tendency to adult self-neglect compatible with Diogenes syndrome. There are some inconsistencies as well between animal hoarding and Diogenes syndrome; many animal hoarders are not elderly and not all animal hoarders neglect personal hygiene and appearance, even though they may still live in squalor. This is further evidence of the heterogeneity of animal hoarding.

Consistency With the OCD Hoarding Model

The OCD model was a logical and intuitive approach in our initial efforts to understand animal hoarding. However, it should also be noted that at that time, animal hoarding per se had never been clinically linked with OCD. The essentially complete absence of any discussion of animal hoarding in OCD research studies is likely due, in part, to selection bias in the patient population represented in most academic studies of hoarding behavior, for example, people voluntarily seeking treatment at OCD clinics and participating in clinical research. These individuals are likely to be quite different from those encountered by social workers in the field: isolated, community-dwelling hoarders who are in denial and extremely resistant to treatment, and unlikely to be represented in clinical research. It is also possible that when animal hoarding is encountered in clinical studies, the unique role of the animals is unrecognized, with the symptom (i.e., unlivable premises and self-neglect due to large numbers of animals) being mistaken for the problem by human health professionals (Patronek et al., 2006).

Despite superficial similarities, animal hoarding shows inconsistencies with, and is not adequately explained by, the conventional OCD model. In particular, the less common psychological symptoms and disorders seem to be over-represented in animal hoarding. The OCD model also fails to adequately explain the caregiving aspect of animal hoarding, or the frequently mentioned history of childhood neglect, abuse, or trauma described in our clinical interviews. This may not be surprising in light of the fact that the classification of hoarding behavior as a symptom of OCD is being questioned (Wu & Watson, 2005). Furthermore, as our clinical work has progressed, our insight has been shaped by in-depth clinical assessments of people exhibiting a much more serious expression of animal hoarding. This experience has suggested that many clues lie in early childhood trauma and attachment disorder, and how this experience may lead to compulsive caregiving and a controlling pattern of relationships in adulthood. An excellent description of how attachment disorder can lead to addictive behavior and compulsive caregiving has recently been published by Flores (2004).

Role of Childhood Experiences, Attachment, and Dissociation

Despite a voluminous literature on how early childhood experiences can result in a variety of maladaptive or deviant behavior in adults, comparatively little has been written about the role of childhood experiences with pets and problematic behaviors in adults. It could be argued that the existing literature on the role of animals in child development has predominantly emphasized the positive contributions companion-animals-as-family-members can have for children, for example, as confidants or sibling substitutes, to learn nurturing and caregiving skills (Beck & Katcher, 1996; Melson, 2001) and on the therapeutic benefits animals can have for children and adults suffering from a wide variety of physical, medical, and mental disabilities (Fine, 1999). A noteworthy exception to this generally positive portrayal of pets in families is the work of Ascione and Lockwood, who have explored the sentinel value of deliberate animal abuse in children as a sentinel for either child abuse or as a predictor for future violent behavior (Ascione & Arkow, 1998; Lockwood & Ascione, 1997).

However, emerging research is providing provocative hints that certain forms of deviant human–animal bond during adulthood, such as animal hoarding, may be traced to experience with pets during childhood, particularly when the pet relationship has been the primary attachment and bonding experience for the child. Jane N. Nathanson, a social worker and member of HARC who has extensive experience counseling animal hoarders and reviewing hoarding cases, has begun to more deeply explore the role of attachment issues and personality disorders in the genesis of animal hoarding. As Nathanson has commented about the work of Brown and Katcher (2001):

They have written about pet attachment and dissociative disorders, as occurring with children who have been victimized by abuse, neglect, or other traumatizing events. They have further noted that:

"Dissociation may be the only personality variable, to date, that has been shown to correlate consistently with pet attachment. … Dissociation may be an important personality factor influencing the degree of pet attachment for a subset of people … it appears possible that having high levels of dissociation could predispose an individual to becoming strongly attached to pets. This could be true for several reasons. One possible explanation is that high levels of dissociation usually correlate with childhood abuse. A history of abuse by people could predispose a person to

mistrust humans. Relationships with companion animals could serve as a safe substitute for relationships with people or as a bridge to begin relating to others." (Brown & Katcher, 2001).

Brown and Katcher make reference to Judith Herman, MD, who, in her text *Trauma and Recovery* has stated that:

People with high levels of dissociation or trauma tend to be more socially isolated and in more emotional distress. (Herman, 1997).

In cases of animal hoarding, we are seeing behaviors that would be considered antisocial, often fraught with conflict and crisis, and dysfunctional with regard to their own as well as their dependent animals' quality of life. Nevertheless, there is this subset of animal hoarders who assert defensiveness, denial, and dissociation with the conditions of squalor that are considered violations of both animal welfare and public health regulations. There are numerous medical and psychiatric conditions, as well as other contributing factors that we are currently delineating with regard to the incidence of animal hoarding—a behavior that may well have its origins in an early childhood that was devoid of consistent human nurturance on the part of primary human caregivers." (Jane N. Nathanson, personal communication, January 27, 2005)

In her research, Nathanson has also noted consistency with the work of Rynearson (1978):

As Rynearson suggests, children in dysfunctional families may use the pet, which is consistently receptive as an object of love and care as a means of escape, and as a substitute for human relationships, particularly when parents are absent or rejecting. This may become an over-generalized distrust of people, which degenerates into anxious attachment or compulsive care-giving." (Jane N. Nathanson, personal communication, January 27, 2005)

The possibility that what appears to be conventional pet ownership can have such a dark side has generally been ignored by researchers, policy makers, and funders. A full understanding of the contribution of childhood experiences to animal hoarding will require a more nuanced approached to the study of human–animal relationships in general, and one that encompasses a wider range of possibilities than a simple dichotomy of "good pet owner vs. animal abuser" allows. This will also force us to challenge the assumption that the relationship between animal welfare and the strength of the human–animal bond is always positive and linear.

A Sociological Perspective: Excuses and Justifications Shed Light on the Worldview of Animal Hoarders

One of the most exasperating parts of working with animal hoarders can be the wide range of excuses that are offered in response to inquiries and accusations concerning their behavior and the condition of the animals and environment. However, from a research perspective, in no other form of animal abuse is such a rich dialogue present. Sociologist Arnie Arluke (Vaca-Guzman & Arluke, 2005) has emphasized the importance of examining the world view of animal hoarders if we are to understand the roots and role of this behavior:

> Any attempt to understand individuals such as hoarders, who engage in deviant behavior, must try to discover why they think and behave as they do, because without understanding their voice, hoarders, or for that matter any other person identified solely via their deviant behavior, become one dimensional figures whose actions are solely explained by the biases of researchers and others who presume to understand them.

Hoarders have provided a wealth of information about their worldview in the guise of excuses used to justify their behavior. The sociological role of excuses has been described in a seminal paper by Snyder (1985), brought to our attention by Arluke and also examined in depth by Arluke and Vaca-Guzman (2005) Snyder's underlying assumption is that excuses are driven by a person's attempts to maintain a positive self-image and self-esteem in the face of criticism. These actions are important, and perhaps even essential, to enable a person to continue certain types of behaviors and avoid certain consequences. Snyder (1985) has described four factors contributing to the perceived negativity of a person's actions.

Clarity of standard—As the standards for a particular activity become increasingly clear, the negative repercussions of failure to meet that standard also increase.

Importance of activity—Activities that pertain to important identity dimensions for a person will tend to generate more negative repercussions if they are not successful.

Intentionality—If a person intends to act in a negative fashion deliberately, the behavior will be judged more severely than if intention was not present.

Power of the critic—The intensity of the threat of feedback from an external source may be related to the expertise, status, and general power or perceived power of the critic.

Minimum standards for caring for common domestic pets (dogs, cats, rabbits, birds, etc.) are not ambiguous from a common-sense perspective, although as has been discussed, legally they may be more ambiguous. Most people would accept that fresh water, adequate food, fresh air, exercise, and a sanitary environment are obvious and basic needs of companion animals. Hoarders go to great lengths to minimize the true nature of the conditions. In my experience, they are often quite successful in this in their interactions with the media and the courts; their stated [noble] intentions are a surprisingly persuasive device.

Animal care or rescue is often central to a hoarder's identity; therefore, failure in this important domain could have severe psychological repercussions. Hoarders rarely, if ever, admit to failing to provide proper care, and also fail to acknowledge their own intentional actions and decisions that may have contributed to the situation (e.g., continued acquisition in the face of deteriorating conditions). It is possible that conscious and even obsessive attempts to acquire more animals as the situation around them deteriorates may be an identity-preserving device in the face of clear failure in this area, whereas the more logical strategy of downsizing to better care for existing animals would be an admission of failure.

The hoarder may feel particularly threatened by animal control officers or family members who may have the power to enter the home or exert some other type of control over the hoarder, therefore, avoiding official paraphernalia such as police badges and uniforms when contacting hoarders may mitigate their defensive response. Hoarders frequently claim that they have some type of professional or quasi-professional credentials as a breeder, a sanctuary, a no-kill shelter, a rescuer, etc. There is ample evidence in case reports that this device successfully works to elevate some hoarders to the level of their critics.

A threatened self-image depends on both a negative performance and a sense of responsibility for that performance. Animal hoarders are often quite adept at simultaneously denying the extent of their bad actions and attributing responsibility for the situation to factors outside of their control. Snyder (1985) indicates that three kinds of information (consensus, consistency, and distinctiveness) help to determine if a particular bad behavior should be attributed to the person or to situational factors outside of the person.

Consensus—This reflects the extent to which other people have behaved similarly in the same situation. A person is held more responsible for his or her behavior when others have not behaved that way under similar circumstances.

Consistency—Consistency represents the extent to which a person has acted in the same situation over time. A person is held to greater responsibility when he or she repeatedly acts in the same manner.

Distinctiveness—Distinctiveness taps the degree to which a person acts in one situation relative to another situation. A person is held more responsible when his or her behavior is the same regardless of the situation.

Low consensus, high consistency, and low distinctiveness in behaviors may all contribute to a heightened sense of personal responsibility for a bad performance. The greater the negativity of the performance and responsibility, the greater will be the threat to a person's self-image and the more exaggerated the effort to protect themselves via a complex network of excuses.

The Strategy of DIRTEing. A common thread to all of these excuse strategies has been termed "*DIRTEing*" (Directing of Internal Responsibilities To External sources) by Snyder (1985), an acronym that has particular irony in hoarding situations. DIRTEing involves various attempts to move the responsibility from the person to outside factors by a variety of different methods. Vaca-Guzman and Arluke (2005) have identified many of these in their recent analysis of animal hoarding cases, several of which are described below.

Lessening apparent responsibility—these types of excuses attempt to cut the link between the person and the bad performance in some way. These take the form of

proclaiming innocence or blaming someone or something else (e.g., a temporary caretaker let them down, a sudden illness forced them to travel unexpectedly and neglect the animals).

Reframing the bad performance—these excuses share the common theme of diminishing the negativity of the performance. This includes "*See no evil*" excuses such as "Its really not so bad," "I didn't notice the animals were sick," "It just happened yesterday." There may also be attempts to manipulate the standards so that the observed behavior does not seem to fall so far from the mark. One way to do this is to question the clarity of the standards, or to claim that there is no way to judge the situation. Hoarders frequently assert that because they are doing a public service, the standards should be shifted to account for their volunteer efforts. Another strategy is to embed the bad act into another, more virtuous one. In hoarding situations, this frequently involves claiming that they were caring for animals no one else would help or trying to save the animals from death, either on the street or from euthanasia in a shelter. A final method of reframing is discrediting sources of negative feedback. Hoarders frequently claim that humane societies, animal control officers, other officials, others involved in animal rescue networks, and even family members have vendettas against them.

For animal hoarders, because animals may be an important identity-building device, perceptions of their [good] care may be critical for the hoarder's self-esteem. The role of animals as an identity device has been described in previous work by HARC (Frost & HARC, 2000). Given the extent of the lapses in care seen in hoarding situations and the degree to which self-esteem is tied to the animals and their care, the threat to self-esteem that would occur if the hoarder were to accept the reality of the situation could be overwhelming. This may explain the great effort expended to explain away the situation. Snyder (1985) points out that the excuse maker, particularly in a chronic situation, may not be aware that they are making excuses and perform them out of habit. As Vaca-Guzman and Arluke (2005) have emphasized, as excuses become more extreme and encompass more of a person's life, they may become self-defeating and gradually shift from being adaptive and normal to pathological.

Typology of Animal Hoarding

At a recent expert workshop to develop guidelines and resources for interdisciplinary interventions (Patronek et al., 2006), participants recognized that animal hoarding is a heterogeneous syndrome, and that different types of animal hoarding likely exist, having shared characteristics, albeit with the potential for considerable overlap, which might suggest different etiological influences and lend themselves to different kinds of interventions. Three preliminary working classifications have been proposed:

- Exploiter hoarder
- Rescuer hoarder
- Overwhelmed caregiver hoarder

The characteristics of these three types are still being refined; however, from an intervention perspective, they may suggest differences in approach and the importance of utilizing a palette of solutions when dealing with animal hoarders. For example, the overwhelmed caregiver hoarder is likelier to respond to offers of help and a therapeutic or counseling approach, whereas the exploiter hoarder is likely to harbor true sociopathic tendencies and require aggressive prosecution to inhibit the behavior.

Treatment and Intervention Models

Treatment and intervention in animal hoarding cases poses substantial challenges for a variety of reasons. These include:

- Prosecution for cruelty to animals addresses only a portion of the problem.
- Current treatment models are heavily based on self-selected populations of hoarders seeking treatment at OCD clinics, whereas animal hoarding likely involves populations that may be clinically more heterogeneous with a variety of serious psychological co-morbidities.
- There are no accepted interventions or counseling protocols published specifically for animal hoarding.
- The strong, albeit warped, human–animal bond present in these cases is a barrier to recognizing a deviant situation is present.
- Denial, lack of insight, and the presence of enablers can undermine intervention efforts.

- Misperceptions on the part of law enforcement, the media, and the public impedes recognition that serious psychological disorder may be driving this behavior.

Prosecution: Role and Limitations in Animal Hoarding

Prosecution under cruelty to animals statutes is one of the most widely used tools for intervention in animal hoarding cases. There is no doubt that such an approach is essential and invaluable in some, and perhaps many, cases of animal hoarding. However, it is also clear that cruelty statutes were not developed with animal hoarding cases in mind, and that the limitations of current statutes can hinder effective prosecution and resolution of animal hoarding cases. Many of these issues were highlighted in a recent study of 56 cases of animal hoarding which were followed up retrospectively (Berry, Patronek, & Lockwood, 2005).

Intent. In recent years, efforts on the part of animal protection groups to increase awareness of "the link" between cruelty to animals and human violence have resulted in much stronger penalties for deliberate acts of cruelty. However, some state cruelty statutes require intent, at least for stronger penalties to apply. Paradoxically, the degree of death and suffering may be much greater in magnitude and frequency in some hoarding cases. This can work against prosecution of animal hoarding cases, because, by definition, intent is absent, leaving investigators with the unsatisfactory option of filing lesser charges.

The intent issue often spills over into public perception of animal hoarding. Statements attributed to investigators in media reports often imply, if not state directly, that the hoarder "meant to do the right thing, but got overwhelmed" or "loved animals too much." This may occur because such statements are taken out of context by reporters, or because humane investigators can empathize with a professed intent to help animals and/or fail to understand or communicate that the hoarders' need to acquire and control animals took precedence over their ability to provide proper care. There is little appreciation that the intent to hoard animals, even if the intent to harm is absent. Furthermore, some hoarders appear to have begun as at least quasi-legitimate animal sheltering or rescue operations, thus, their claims of good intentions can appear to be supportable. In fact, what is likely to have occurred in many of these cases is that people with an underlying psychopathology were initially drawn to animal rescuing activities for self-serving reasons of which they may not have been consciously aware. It is only after becoming immersed in these animal rescue activities that their underlying tendencies are able to develop into full-blown animal hoarding.

Responsibility. Hand-in-hand with the lack of intent goes the refusal to accept personal responsibility for the situation. Unlike other forms of animal abuse, hoarding is unique in that courts, the public, and the media are all too willing to accept the premise that the hoarder had no, or very limited, responsibility for the situation as it developed. Blame of others and of society in general is a well-accepted excuse, even to the extent that the hoarder is portrayed and understood as a victim instead of a perpetrator.

Suffering and Quality of Life. The link between poor quality of life, which occurs when there is collective, chronic neglect of a large number of animals, is not well appreciated nor is it well addressed under current statutory language. Media portrayals of animal hoarding can exacerbate this problem because they often fail to link the extreme conditions of the environment with equally severe descriptions of the impact on animals. When relatively benign-sounding conditions that are common to the experience of many pet owners, such as fleas, skin infections, or being underweight are described, this may leave the public with the impression that the neglect was minor and compatible with good intentions (Arluke et al., 2002).

There is little agreement on how to establish and quantify the extent of suffering due to poor quality of life from long-term crowding and intensive confinement, lack of exercise, and lack of socialization for companion animals, particularly if the basics of food and water are more or less present and the medical conditions are not dire. Neither the veterinary literature nor the behavioral literature adequately addresses this problem. Consequently, courts have little appreciation of the cumulative nature of this type of chronic deprivation and how it corresponds to a lack of care and concern for the animals' welfare. This lack of awareness of how suffering can occur from chronic neglect, crowding, squalor, and lack of socialization essentially removes the strongest cumulative evidence in court—that is, that the whole can be much greater than the sum of its parts—leaving prosecutors and expert veterinary witnesses to establish cruelty on the basis of reductionist criteria such as whether a particular disease or condition was present in an individual animal, or a particular animal had not been fed for a certain length of time, etc. Forcing prosecution in such a manner, particularly when large numbers of animals are involved, creates a huge loophole that allows defendants and their attorneys to attack and trivialize each minor point, thereby avoiding any meaningful evaluation of the situation as a whole.

In many hoarding situations, the animals are suffering in part precisely because of their extensive extended confinement. This poses a terrible choice for humane investigators who may feel that if they do prosecute and the case goes to trial, that the animals will be victimized a second time by another protracted incarceration in the shelter, albeit under better conditions. The result may be to "strike a bargain with the devil" to get immediate custody of the animals so they may be adopted, in return for waiving requirements (e.g., limiting the number of animals owned or monitoring of the situation) that might limit recidivism (Berry et al., 2005).

No Recognition of Pattern. Present statutory language forces investigators and prosecutors to approach hoarding cases like multiples of routine, single-animal neglect cases. This fails to capture the pattern present, ignores the psychopathology that may be contributing to the behavior, and facilitates acceptance of clever excuses and claims of good intentions. In some cases, defense attorneys have successfully challenged prosecution by shedding doubt on the ability of the prosecution to accurately identify individual animals. Allowing this type of defense fails to recognize the collective nature of the neglect.

One study indicated that investigators often feel like they are between a rock and a hard place—it may anger some magistrates or judges to get dozens or even hundreds of citations that individually appear trivial (failure to provide proper food or sanitation, failure to license) (Berry et al., 2005). However, if the number of charges is reduced, there is a mismatch between the number of offenses actually prosecuted and the severity of the situation. District attorneys may adopt the strategy of focusing on just a handful of the worst animals in a case, essentially dropping charges for the rest of the involved animals, because of concern over the "clog" factor and less confidence that taken one by one, they could prove individual charges of cruelty using currently accepted criteria.

Vagueness of Statutory Language About Care. Many state cruelty statutes include language about providing "proper shelter, food, a sanitary environment, and necessary veterinary care." When the stakes are not so high, as in run-of-the-mill single animal neglect, this language may suffice and actually be advantageous, as it allows investigators considerable latitude in determining how best to proceed to achieve proper care. However, hoarding cases may be more likely to be challenged by defendants than cases of simple neglect, because the hoarder has a much more vested interest in retaining control and maintaining the behavior. Furthermore, there may be support from enablers who see their own interests threatened by any attempts to prevent the hoarder/rescuer from engaging in this behavior, particularly if this involves attempts to impose regulatory authority over animal rescue efforts. Thus, any imprecision or vagueness in statutory language can be quite detrimental to successful intervention when the situation becomes adversarial.

Shelters or rescue operations are generally unregulated entities from an animal care perspective. The Federal Animal Welfare Act, which would apply to dealers, does not apply in these circumstances. There are also no other widely recognized standards for husbandry of companion animals in these particular types of institutional settings, leaving another large loophole for a variety of clever defenses aimed at disputing minor points of individual charges. The American Veterinary Medical Association (AVMA) recently issued guidelines for companion animal care in shelters and animal rescue operations, which could help educate the court about proper care (AVMA guidelines, 2003).

Failure to Deal With Mental Health Issues and Recidivism. Anecdotal reports and many years of personal experience with these cases suggest that recidivism in the typical animal hoarding case approaches 100%. One of the major limitations of current cruelty statutes is that they fail to adequately deal with the mental health components of animal hoarding, and therefore are largely ineffective in preventing recidivism.

As of October 2003, 24 states had some provision that dealt with psychological counseling and/or anger management counseling for persons convicted of certain violations in their cruelty statutes. These provisions, however, typically fall short of addressing the unique situations involving animal hoarding. Such counseling is mandatory in less than half

$(n = 11)$ of these statutes. Of those 11, the mandatory counseling provisions are often restricted to juveniles or persons convicted of deliberate acts of torture, neither of which is likely to apply to cases of animal hoarding. Furthermore, in the event such counseling is ordered, there is no model for therapists to use or guidance on how to select an appropriate professional.

It was suggested at an expert workshop on animal hoarding that the typical consultation with a psychologist or psychiatrist attempting to fit these individuals into a standard DSM-IV classification during an office visit would be unproductive for several reasons (Patronek et al., 2005). First, it was thought that the shock of being forced into a clinical diagnostic environment might be sufficient to alter and perhaps normalize the behavior of many of these individuals. Also, an in-office consultation would remove the person from the influence of the home environment, which would affect both behavior as well as the ability of a therapist to obtain a complete picture of the circumstances. Although there are currently no data on which to base the recommendation, it was the opinion of the working group that a professional accustomed to conducting in-home evaluations and counseling would be preferable to the standard in-office assessment.

Recognizing Animal Cruelty as a Serious Offense. Animal protection groups have worked long and hard to increase judicial awareness of the seriousness of crimes against animals, and have largely been successful in obtaining stronger penalties for crimes involving deliberate abuse. This is as it should be. The situation in animal hoarding often runs at odds with the intent of these statutory changes, because, while the hoarder does in fact often cause substantial animal suffering and can engage in both deliberate and passive actions that facilitate and exacerbate the abuse, there is rarely if ever intent to cause harm.

Sentinel Value of Animal Hoarding for Human Neglect and Abuse

As indicated earlier, it is well accepted that deliberate animal abuse can be a valuable indicator of current violent behavior, or the potential for future violent behavior, toward people. Consequently, in recent years there have been a plethora of grassroots programs designed to foster awareness among domestic violence resource groups, child protection agencies, and to some extent adult protective services groups about the importance of recognizing deliberate animal abuse as a warning sign. The First Strike campaign of the Humane Society of the United States, pioneered by psychologist Dr. Randy Lockwood, can be credited with substantially increasing awareness of these interconnections and encouraging greater cooperation among stakeholders. There has been much less empirical research linking the neglect of animals to neglectful care of humans. It should come as no surprise that, similar to child or spousal abuse which often is associated with deliberate cruelty to animals, in animal hoarding cases the human victims share the same neglectful care as the animals, living in unsanitary conditions, having poor nutrition, and being unable to maintain personal hygiene.

In one retrospective study of animal hoarding cases, other people were present in over half (53.5%) of the households (Frost & HARC, 2000). In these cases, vulnerable dependent elders, disabled individuals or minor children were as much a victim of the hoarding behavior as the animals. I estimate that dependent children were specifically mentioned in about 10%–15% of animal hoarding cases. More disturbing in these reports was a recurrent theme that educators or other mandated reporters did not recognize, or delayed recognition of, obvious warning signs of neglect (e.g., strong odor of children's clothing, repeated respiratory infections, lack of personal hygiene).

Considerations for Intervention

The optimal strategy for intervention in animal hoarding remains to be determined and will likely require a palette of solutions, tailored to each individual case (Patronek et al., 2006) Concerning the hoarding of inanimate objects, Hogstel (1993) has emphasized that it is important to determine the underlying need fulfilled by the hoarding behavior before selecting an intervention for a particular individual, which should take into account the following principles:

- Transfer hoarding behaviors to safer objects
- Rewarding behaviors that reduce hoarding
- Establishing contracts which limit further accumulation
- Avoid confronting or arguing
- Avoid removing objects without consent

These general principles all have application in animal hoarding. In the future, as the underlying etiology of animal hoarding, the precipitating factors, the role of co-morbid psychological conditions, and the various typologies present become better understood, it may be possible to tailor interventions to the features of individual cases in a much more sophisticated fashion.

Future Research and Policy Needs

Our understanding of animal hoarding is in its infancy. What is unambiguous is that it affects hundreds of thousands of animals each year, causes extreme suffering, puts people and communities at risk, is poorly understood, and is not well-addressed by existing statutory remedies. In order to begin to rectify this problem, a number of research and policy needs are clear. Some of these are quite pragmatic in scope and can be readily addressed, whereas others require a more long-term investment in empirical work. These needs include the following:

- Psychological evaluations of animal hoarders are essential to improve understanding of the underlying characteristics and scope of co-morbid disorders to guide treatment strategies.
- Longitudinal studies of animal hoarders are needed to elucidate developmental aspects of animal hoarding, including identifying psychological, social, or environmental triggers for the behavior.
- More sophisticated understanding of the types of animal hoarding behavior, and the interventions best suited to each variant.
- Additional legally sound avenues for intervention that do not depend entirely on meeting the evidentiary requirements for a cruelty-to-animals conviction, or that offer the potential for more effective resolution when a conviction is obtained.
- More comprehensive and creative sentencing guidelines for judges, which will limit recidivism and address the mental health component often present.
- Boilerplate templates for strong negotiated agreements that will provide for more effective prevention, with long-term monitoring of all premises or other situations in which a hoarder could maintain his or her behavior.
- Improved evidence-gathering protocols appropriate to the uniqueness of hoarding situations, and that will stand up under vigorous cross-examination in court.

- Improved tactics for establishing the extent of suffering arising from chronic confinement and lack of socialization for companion animals.
- Better strategies for defusing the efforts of enablers who come to the assistance of hoarders when they are found and prosecuted; this includes improved education of the media, prosecutors, and judges.
- More sophisticated communications strategies for shelters when dealing with the media to better educate all stakeholders. Hoarders are very effective at getting the moral high ground with their "saving from euthanasia" claims and managing the dialogue along those lines.

Finally, from the larger perspective of understanding the full scope of our relationship with non-human animals and how it can degenerate into this form of abuse, there is an urgent need for more complex and nuanced empirical studies of the human–animal bond, particularly as it develops throughout life and how it is influenced by attachment, dissociation, and other experiences during childhood.

Acknowledgments

This chapter draws extensively on the work of my colleagues in HARC, the Hoarding of Animals Research Consortium, and reflects their individual and collective intellectual contributions to this emerging field of inquiry over the past nine years. This interdisciplinary research group was established in 1997 to increase awareness of this troubling behavior, to investigate etiology, and pioneer solutions. Their formal collaboration concluded in 2006. I am indebted to these individuals for their support, their insight, and their commitment to improve the lives of human and non-human animals who are victims of this poorly understood behavior that leads to so much avoidable suffering. HARC members include:

Arnold Arluke, PhD, Northeastern University, Boston, MA; Randy Frost, PhD, Smith College, Northampton, MA; Carter Luke, Massachusetts Society for the Prevention of Cruelty to Animals, Boston, MA; Edward Messner, M.D., [deceased] Massachusetts General Hospital, Boston, MA; Jane Nathanson, LCSW, LRC, CRC, Boston, MA; Michelle Papazian, MS, formerly of Children's Hospital, Boston, MA; and Gail Steketee, PhD, Boston University, Boston, MA.

The work of HARC was largely volunteer; however, we have received support for research and program expenses from the Edith Goode Trust and the Kenneth Scott Charitable Trust. The Massachusetts Society for the Prevention of Cruelty to Animals (MSPCA) has provided invaluable in-kind institutional support for hosting meetings and logistical arrangements for HARC. The MSPCA is also supporting the gathering of new insights into intervention and treatment via piloting counseling and other therapeutic strategies in selected cases within their own law enforcement division. Finally, I wish to acknowledge inspiration from Dr. Alan Beck, a valued friend and mentor, who had the foresight to author the first paper in the medical literature (Worth & Beck, 1981) documenting this dark side of the human–animal bond.

References

Arluke, A., Frost, R., Steketee, G., Patronek, G. J., Luke, C., Messner, E., et al. (2002). Press reports of animal hoarding. *Society & Animals 10*, 113–135.

Ascione, F. R. (2001). Animal abuse and youth violence. OJJDP Juvenile Justice Bulletin. Retrieved January 15, 2005 from http://www.ncjrs.org/html/ojjdp/jjbul2001_9_2/contents.html.

Ascione, F. R. and Arkow, P. (Eds.). (1999). *Child abuse, domestic violence, and animal abuse: linking the circles of compassion for prevention and intervention*. West Lafayette, IN: Purdue University Press.

AVMA Companion Animal Care Guidelines. (2003). Retrieved January 15, 2005 from http://www.avma.org/issues/policy/companion_animal_care.asp

Beck, A. M., & Katcher, A. (1996). *Between pets and people: The importance of animal companionship*. West Lafayette, IN: Purdue University Press.

Berry, C., Patronek, G.J., & Lockwood, R. (2005). Animal hoarding: A study of 56 case outcomes. *Animal Law*, 11, 167–194.

Brown, S.-E., & Katcher, A. H. (2001). Pet attachment and dissociation. *Society and Animals, 9*, 25–41.

Cooney, C., & Hamid W. (1995). Review: Diogenes Syndrome. *Age and Ageing, 24*, 451–453.

Damecour, C. L., & Charron, M. (1998). Hoarding: A symptom, not a syndrome. *Journal of Clinical Psychiatry, 59*, 267–272.

Fine, A. H. (Ed.). (2000). *Handbook on Animal-Assisted Therapy: Theoretical Foundations and Guidelines for Practice.* San Diego, CA: Academic.

Flores, P. J. (2001). Addiction as attachment disorder. Lanham, MD: Jason Aronson.

Frost, R. O., & Gross, R. C. (1993). The hoarding of possessions. *Behavior Research and Therapy, 31,* 367–381.

Frost, R. O., Hartl, T. L., Christian, R., & Williams, N. (1995). The value of possessions in compulsive hoarding: Patterns of use and attachment. *Behavior Research and Therapy, 33,* 897–902.

Frost, R., & the Hoarding of Animals Research Consortium (HARC). (2000). People who hoard animals. *Psychiatric Times, 17,* 25–29.

Frost, R. O., Kim, H-J., Morris, C., Bloss, C., Murray-Close, M., & Steketee, G. (1998). Hoarding, compulsive buying, and reasons for saving. *Behavior Research and Therapy, 36,* 657–664.

Frost, R. O., Krause, M. S., & Steketee, G. (1996) Hoarding and obsessive-compulsive symptoms. *Behavior Modification and Therapy, 20,* 116–132.

Frost, R. O., Steketee, G., & Williams, L. (2000). Hoarding: a community health problem, *Health and Social Care in the Community. 8,* 229–234.

Frost, R. O., Steketee, G., Williams, L. F., & Warrens, R. (2000). Mood, personality disorder symptoms and disability in obsessive compulsive hoarders: A comparison with clinical and non-clinical controls. *Behavior Research and Therapy, 38,* 1071–1081.

Frost, R. O., Steketee, G., Youngren, V. R., & Mallya, G. K. (1999). The threat of the housing inspector: A case of hoarding. *Harvard Review of Psychiatry, 6,* 270–278.

Greeenberg, D. (1987). Compulsive hoarding. *American Journal of Psychotherapy, 41,* 409–416.

Greenberg, D, Witztum, E., & Levy, A. (1990). Hoarding as a psychiatric symptom. *Journal of Clinical Psychiatry, 51,* 417–421.

Halperin, D. A., & Glick, J. (2003). Collectors, accumulators, hoarders, and hoarding perspectives. *Addictive Disorders & Their Treatment, 2,* 47–51.

Hartl, T. L., & Frost, R. O. (1996). A cognitive-behavioral model of compulsive hoarding. *Behavior Research and Therapy, 34,* 341–350.

Herman, J. (1997). *Trauma and Recovery.* New York: Basic Books.

Hoarding of Animals Research Consortium (HARC). (2002). Health implications of animal hoarding. *Health & Social Work, 27,* 125–136.

Hogstel, M. O. (1993). Understanding hoarding behavior in the elderly. *American Journal of Nursing, 93,* 42–45.

Kaplan, A., & Hollander, E. (2004). Comorbidity in compulsive hoarding: A case report. *CNS Spectrums, 9,* 71–73.

Kellert, S. R., & Felthous, A. R. (1985). Childhood cruelty toward animals among criminals and noncriminals. *Human Relations, 18,* 1113–1129.

Lockwood, L., & Ascione, F. R. (Eds.). (1997). *Cruelty to Animals and Interpersonal Violence: Readings in Research and Application.* West Lafayette, IN: Purdue University Press.

Melson, G. F. (2001). *Why the wild things are: Animals in the lives of children.* Cambridge, MA: Harvard University Press.

Mihm, S. (2001). Pet Theory. Do Cats Cause Schizophrenia? *Linguafranca 10,* 32–40. Retrieved January 15, 2005 from http://www.stanleylab.org/Document/cat%20press%20release.htm.

Patronek, G. J. (1999). Hoarding of animals: An under-recognized public health problem in a difficult-to-study population. *Public Health Reports, 114,* 81–87.

Patronek, G. J., Loar, L., & Nathanson, J. N. (Eds.). (2006). Animal hoarding: Structuring interdisciplinary responses to help people, animals, and communities at risk. A report of an expert workshop, April 3, 2004, Boston, MA. http://www.tufts.edu/vet/cfa/hoarding/pubs/AngellReport.pdf.

Rasmussen, S.A., Eisen, J.L. (1992) The epidemiology and clinical features of obsessive compulsive disorder. *Psychiatric Clinics of North America 15:*743–758.

Reifler, B. V. (1996) Diogenes syndrome: of omelettes and souffles. *Journal of the American Geriatrics Society* 1484–1485.

Reyes-Ortiz, C. A. (2001). Diogenes syndrome: The self-neglect elderly. *Comprehensive Therapy 27,* 117–121.

Rosenthal, M., Stelian, J., Wagner, J., & Berkman, P. (1999). Diogenes syndrome and hoarding in the elderly: Case reports. *The Israel Journal of Psychiatry and Related Sciences, 36,* 29–34.

Rynearson, E. K. (1978). Humans and pets and attachment. *The British Journal of Psychiatry, 133,* 550–555.

Saxena, S., Brody, A. L., Maidment, K. M., Smith, E. C., Zohrabi, N., Katz, E., et al. (2004). Cerebral glucose metabolism in obsessive-compulsive hoarding. *The American Journal of Psychiatry, 161,* 1038–1048.

Snyder, C. R. (1985) The Excuse: an amazing grace? In B. Schlenker (Ed.), *The self and social life.* New York: McGraw-Hill.

Stein, D. J., Seedat, S., & Potocnik, F. (1999). Hoarding: A review. *The Israel Journal of Psychiatry and Related Sciences, 36,* 35–46.

Steketee, G., & Frost, R. O. (2003). Compulsive hoarding: Current status of the research. *Clinical Psychology Reviews, 23,* 905–927.

Torrey, E. F., & Yolken, R. H. (1995). Could schizophrenia be a viral zoonosis transmitted from house cats? *Schizophrenia Bulletin 21,* 167–171.

Torrey, E. F., & Yolken, R. H. (2003). Toxoplasma gondii and schizophrenia. *Emerging Infectious Diseases 11,* 1375–1380.

U.S. Census Bureau. (2003). Retrieved January 15, 2005 from http://eire.census.gov/popest/data/states/NST-EST2003-ann_est.php

Vaca-Guzman, M., & Arluke, A. (2005). Normalizing passive cruelty: The excuses and justifications of animals hoarders. *Anthrozoös, 18,* 338–357.

Vermeulen, H., & Odendaal, J. S. J. (1993). Proposed typology of companion animal abuse. *Anthrozoös, 6,* 248–257.

Waltrip, R. W. (1995). Evaluation of Torrey and Yolken's feline viral zoonosis theory of schizophrenia. *Schizophrenia Bulletin 21,* 173–178.

Winsberg, M. E., Cassic, K. S., & Koran, L. M. (1999). Hoarding in obsessive-compulsive disorder: A report of 20 cases. *Clinical Psychiatry, 60,* 591–597.

Worth, D., & Beck, A. M. (1981). Multiple ownership of animals in New York City. *Transactions & Studies of the College of Physicians of Philadelphia, 3,* 280–300.

Wu, K.D. & Watson, D. (2005). Hoarding and its relation to obsessive-compulsive disorder. Behaviour Research and Therapy, 43, 897–921.

Appendix

Case Report Form Used in Two Case Series by the Hoarding of Animals Research Consortium

Animal Hoarding Monitoring Project Case Report Form

For purposes of this project, only submit cases consistent with the following definition of an animal hoarder:

Someone who has accumulated a large number of animals and who fails to provide minimal standards of nutrition, sanitation, and veterinary care; and fails to act on the deteriorating condition of the animals (including disease, starvation, or death) and the environment (severe overcrowding, extremely unsanitary conditions) or the negative effect of the collection on their own health and well being and on that of other family members.

1. What was the origin of the complaint? Circle all that apply:

1. Stranger	2. Friend or acquaintance	3. Relative not living there
4. Family member or roommate	5. Social service agency	6. Service person visiting home
7. Landlord / tenant / neighbor	8. Fire or Police Dept.	9. Veterinarian
10. Anonymous	11. Other:	

2. Please list the people living in the house, their age, sex, and relationship to the person in question:

Person	Age (yrs)	Sex	Relationship to hoarder (circle correct choice)
1. Hoarder		M F	n/a
2. Person 2		M F	parent, child, sibling, grandparent, other relative, partner, roommate
3. Person 3		M F	parent, child, sibling, grandparent, other relative, partner, roommate
4. Person 4		M F	parent, child, sibling, grandparent, other relative, partner, roommate
5. Person 5		M F	parent, child, sibling, grandparent, other relative, partner, roommate

3. Please circle the marital status of the hoarder:

Single	Married	Divorced	Widowed	Partner / sig. other	Unknown

4. Please circle the type of residence:

Single family home	Apartment/Condo	Trailer	Other (describe):

Source: This form is Copyright 2002, National Association of Social Workers, Inc., *Health & Social Work*. Reprinted with permission.

5. Please indicate the occupation of the hoarder: _____

6. Please indicate what other agencies are involved in the case:

Mental Health	Yes	No	Unknown
Fire Department	Yes	No	Unknown
Police Department	Yes	No	Unknown
Department of Aging	Yes	No	Unknown
Child Welfare	Yes	No	Unknown
Court	Yes	No	Unknown

7. Please indicate what areas of the house were cluttered and the degree of clutter present:

Cluttered Areas	Extent of Clutter (circle best choice)				
Bedroom	None	Moderate	Substantial	Severe	Unknown
Bathroom	None	Moderate	Substantial	Severe	Unknown
Living room	None	Moderate	Substantial	Severe	Unknown
Kitchen	None	Moderate	Substantial	Severe	Unknown
Dining room	None	Moderate	Substantial	Severe	Unknown
Stairwell	None	Moderate	Substantial	Severe	Unknown
Hallway	None	Moderate	Substantial	Severe	Unknown
Basement	None	Moderate	Substantial	Severe	Unknown
Attic	None	Moderate	Substantial	Severe	Unknown
Outside	None	Moderate	Substantial	Severe	Unknown

8. Please indicate whether the following appliances/utilities were in working order:

Stove/Oven	Yes	No	Unknown
Kitchen sink	Yes	No	Unknown
Washer/Dryer	Yes	No	Unknown
Electricity	Yes	No	Unknown
Furnace/Heat	Yes	No	Unknown

Fridge/Freezer	Yes	No	Unknown
Bathroom sink	Yes	No	Unknown
Toilet	Yes	No	Unknown
Water heater	Yes	No	Unknown
Shower/Tub	Yes	No	Unknown

9. Please indicate the extent to which each of these activities is impaired or affected by the hoarding:

Due to clutter, does this person have difficulty:

	Not Applicable	Not at All	Somewhat	Very Much
a. preparing food	N/A	1	2	3
b. using the kitchen table?	N/A	1	2	3
c. using chairs in the kitchen?	N/A	1	2	3
d. using the sink in the kitchen?	N/A	1	2	3
e. moving around in the kitchen?	N/A	1	2	3
f. using the toilet?	N/A	1	2	3
g. using the bath or shower?	N/A	1	2	3
h. using the bathroom sink?	N/A	1	2	3
i. sitting in the living room?	N/A	1	2	3
j. moving around in the living room?	N/A	1	2	3
k. using the dining room table?	N/A	1	2	3
l. moving around in the dining room?	N/A	1	2	3
m. exiting the house quickly?	N/A	1	2	3
n. sleeping in the bed?	N/A	1	2	3
o. moving around in the bedroom?	N/A	1	2	3
p. going up and down the stairs?	N/A	1	2	3
q. finding important papers / objects when needed?	N/A	1	2	3
r. maintaining basic hygiene?	N/A	1	2	3
Are there places in the home that are fire hazards due to clutter near furnaces or heaters?	N/A	1	2	3
Is the person in danger of falling and getting hurt due to the clutter present?	N/A	1	2	3
How unsanitary is the residence?	N/A	Reasonably Sanitary 1	Somewhat Unsanitary 2	Very Unsanitary 3

10. Was there any danger in addition to that noted above for the hoarder or other family members from the clutter or hoarding? If so, please describe:

_____
_____
_____
_____

11. Please indicate the extent to which each of the following types of items were hoarded:

Hoarded Objects	Extent of Hoarding (circle best answer)				
Newspapers or magazines	None	Moderate	Substantial	Severe	Unknown
Books	None	Moderate	Substantial	Severe	Unknown
Other paper	None	Moderate	Substantial	Severe	Unknown

Clothing	None	Moderate	Substantial	Severe	Unknown
Containers (plastic, paper, bottles, glasses)	None	Moderate	Substantial	Severe	Unknown
Food or food garbage	None	Moderate	Substantial	Severe	Unknown
Animals	None	Moderate	Substantial	Severe	Unknown
Clutter outdoors	None	Moderate	Substantial	Severe	Unknown
Other (describe):	None	Moderate	Substantial	Severe	Unknown

12. List number, type, and vital status of all animals in the collection (note: if estimated rather than an actual count of the animals, please note using "≈"symbol):

Type of animal	Number in good or adequate health	Number alive but in poor condition; not in immediate risk of death	Number alive but severely injured, diseased or extremely malnourished	Number dead	Total
Dogs					
Puppies (<1 yr old)					
Cats					
Kittens (<1 yr old)					
Birds					
Reptiles					
Small mammals					
Horses					
Cattle / sheep / goats					
Other: _____					

13. How long has this individual been monitored or investigated for animal hoarding related problems?

<1 year	1–3 years	4–5 years	>5 years

14. Please describe how the majority of animals were acquired. Rate the most common method as 1, the next as 2, etc. Use each ranking only once.

	Animals bred deliberately in hoarder's home
	Animals bred accidentally in hoarder's home
	People brought animals to the hoarder
	Hoarder purchased or adopted new animals
	Hoarder actively solicited new animals by advertisement, picking up strays
	Other (describe) _____

15. What were the reason(s) stated by the hoarder for having the animals? Check all that apply:

	Saving them
	Love animals
	Animals are like children
	No one else would care for them
	Animals are their only friends or companions
	Other (describe):

16. Circle how many of the individual animals the hoarder was able to identify by name:

ALL	MOST	SOME	FEW	NONE	UNKNOWN

17. Did the hoarder attempt to conceal the presence of the animals in any of the following ways?

YES	NO	Unknown	Covered windows (shades drawn, blackened, etc)
YES	NO	Unknown	Solid fences or other similar external barriers
YES	NO	Unknown	Overgrown vegetation – bushes, trees, hedges, etc.
YES	NO	Unknown	External debris sufficient to block view or access
YES	NO	Unknown	Deny investigator or other persons access to residence

18. What was the resolution of the case investigation? Circle all that apply:
   1) All animals were removed from hoarder
   2) Some animals were removed from the hoarder
   3) Hoarder prohibited from owning animals for a period
   4) Hoarder agreed to ongoing monitoring
   5) Hoarder ordered to undergo psychiatric evaluation
   6) Hoarder was institutionalized or placed under protective care
   7) Hoarder penalized by fine or jail term————
      describe: _____

Please briefly summarize the status of the case and the animals. Please describe any unusual features of the case, including interaction with the mental health system. Continue on reverse if needed.

_____
_____
_____
_____

19. Please indicate if there was media coverage:

Newspaper	Yes	No	Unknown
Radio	Yes	No	Unknown
Television	Yes	No	Unknown

Name and title of person completing case report form: _____

Agency: _____

Street: _____

City/State / ZIP _____ Phone _____

20. Did you <u>personally</u> investigate and view this case?   YES   NO

Animal Abuse Experiences Described by Italian School-Aged Children

Camilla Pagani, Francesco Robustelli, and Frank R. Ascione

In this chapter, we present the first comprehensive examination of children's concepts and experiences related to both socially acceptable and socially unacceptable forms of animal maltreatment. The responses of a large sample (N = 800) of Italian school children, 9 to 18 years of age, to a questionnaire designed specifically for this study are described and used as the basis for discussing future research directions in the study of animal abuse in the lives of children and adolescents and more general issues of violence in society.

Introduction

In order to accomplish an appropriate analysis of children's animal abuse[1] experiences, it is important to begin by examining the concept of violence in general as well as the significance of children's relationships with animals.

Most people think that human violence is innate, instinctive, and, thus, unavoidable (Goldstein, 1994). It can be expressed in one way or another but it cannot be eliminated. Obviously, such a concept does not predispose individuals to try to attain a better, less violent world. For this reason in 1986, on the occasion of the United Nations–sponsored International Peace Year, an international team of specialists (biologists, psychologists, psychiatrists, ethologists, anthropologists, and sociologists) met at the University of Seville and drew up a scientific document, called the *Seville Statement on Violence* (Adams, 1991). In it they maintain that human violence is fundamentally produced by sociocultural, and not biological, factors (Groebel & Hinde, 1991; Ramirez, 1994; Ramirez, Hinde, & Groebel, 1987). Hence, it can be effectively countervailed and prevented, especially through specific educational action (Pagani, 2000a; Robustelli, 2003; Robustelli & Pagani, 1996). The *Seville Statement on*

Violence was adopted by Unesco and was endorsed by the American Psychological Association, the American Orthopsychiatric Association, the American Anthropological Association, the American Sociological Association, and the International Society for Research on Aggression—Commission on Violence.

Presumably children's relationships with animals constitute an optimal situation through which children can concretely experience the meaning of diversity. As a matter of fact, it often happens that, at an early phase, children are unaware of animals' diversity and, hence, tend to anthropomorphize them. With adults' help, children can move beyond this phase and understand diversity, since children and animals are certainly very different. The knowledge of this diversity can provoke a mobilization of children's empathic abilities so that children are capable of identifying those characteristics they share with animals, for instance, animals' capacity for suffering. Though an empathic relationship is all the more likely when the other is perceived as similar, it is also possible that a great diversity, like the diversity between children and animals, can, as it were, shake children's *self*, strengthen their process of cognitive and affective decentering, and mobilize their empathic abilities. Identifying similarities in what is diverse can be very stimulating. It is like understanding pieces of a mystery. This way children's relationships with animals can become a useful exercise to establish positive relationships with human beings as well. Sometimes, however, similarities in what is diverse are not identified. Empathic abilities are not activated and are not strengthened. In such cases children's relationships with animals are often characterized by violence, since apparently these children have already developed an aggressive personality. Therefore, it is necessary to understand children's perceptions of animals in all their aspects and to challenge these perceptions in order to modify them, if needed, and to orient them in the direction of empathy.

Putting it in Piagetian terms, we can regard children's disturbed relationships with animals as a situation of *disequilibrium* in children's psychological development (Piaget, 1928, 1965). If we penetrate this disequilibrium and if we also help children understand it and address it, hopefully they will attain a new and higher *equilibrium*, considered as a more mature form of thinking as well as of behavior. Obviously, as Piaget also pointed out, children's ideas of mutual respect cannot be imposed from without. On the contrary, children actively construct them in the context of their relations with others.

What is more, the experience of violence encompasses not only perpetrating violence but also witnessing it. Obviously, the effects of witnessed violence have to be evaluated both at the level of the emotional impact and at the level of values, namely of transmitted patterns of behavior.

At this point another problem has to be addressed. Both the general concept of violence and the significance of children's relationships with animals are clearly related to cultural context. It is a fact that psychological phenomena are sometimes strongly conditioned by culture (Robustelli & Pagani, 2005). Here, it is sufficient to mention the concept of *basic personality* (Kardiner, 1939), according to which a specific cultural context tends to foster the development of a specific type of personality. For example, a culture characterized by a contradictory value system may foster the development of insecure personalities. Similarly, a culture that enforces men's supremacy may foster the development of women's dependent personalities. Obviously, the relation between culture and personality is far from being absolute. Culture produces tendencies. However, as Kardiner points out, individuals may react in different ways to the same cultural influences. Brislin (1994) justly observed that in psychology a special section on cross-cultural studies should not exist, since the whole of psychology should be cross-cultural.

Most research on children's animal abuse experiences has so far been conducted in English-speaking countries. Hence, we considered it useful to carry out research in this area in Italy, since Italian culture, though it belongs to western culture, is rather different from the cultures of English-speaking countries. In particular, the interest in nature, including animals, is no doubt traditionally weaker in Italy. If, as we said above, violence is mainly caused by sociocultural factors, it follows that different sociocultural factors can differ-

ently condition violence both at the qualitative and the quantitative level. In the same way, different sociocultural factors can differently condition children's relationships with animals in general.

We also have to bear in mind that a cultural context is not only characterized by specific geographical and social features but that it includes, as an intrinsic part of its nature, temporal aspects as well. We can illustrate this point with an example, drawn from a very short sequence of an Italian film, *The Window Looking on to the Fairground*, which was directed in 1956 by Luigi Comencini. A young boy of about 7 is worried that he has to tell his parents he has failed at school. He is walking out of the school on his way home with a classmate through the fields of a drab suburb in Rome with ugly high-rise buildings in the background. His friend would like to help him. Suddenly he stops as he has noticed a stick insect in the grass among the stones (the scene is extremely vivid and natural). The two friends crouch down and look at it. Holding a stone in his hand the friend asks him: "Shall we kill it?" The child disconsolately shakes his head. The friend looks at him with sad eyes. They continue on their way home, the friend keeping his hand on the young boy's shoulder. The sequence is not more than 60 seconds long. All the various elements in the scene converge into inducing the spectator to interpret the friend's proposal to kill the insect in the same way as if he had suggested having an ice cream or playing football together, only aiming at consoling the child who has not done well at school. In sum, this is a typical example of prosocial behavior. The children's awareness of the cruelty of the act is practically nonexistent. The two young boys are unquestioningly presented as good-hearted and gentle children. The film director is here portraying Italy's poor conditions in the years following World War II. At that time, issues such as the preservation of the environment, respect for animals, and the results of ethological research on animal behavior had not yet become a matter for discussion in schools and in the media and, accordingly, were not part of Italian mainstream culture.

Moreover, the concept of temporal context is not only related to historical aspects in the evolution of a country or a group (as in the example cited above) but also to developmental changes in an individual's life (Smith, Cowie, Olafsson, & Liefooghe, 2002). We will consider this point in more detail when discussing animal cruelty research and addressing the issue of the definition of "animal cruelty" and of methodological problems related to it.

Animal Welfare Issues in Contemporary Italian Society

We will now present a brief survey of themes, such as childhood animal abuse, animal welfare, and educational interventions, as they have been debated in Italian society in the last few years.[2] This will help us to better understand the results of our research on Italian pupils' animal abuse experiences, as we will be able to analyze them within the context of present Italian culture.

Unquestionably, childhood animal abuse is considered a minor issue by Italian media. Cruel acts perpetrated by young people (as well as by adults) are most often covered only by local radio and TV channels and local newspapers. National newspapers may sometimes report on such acts, but they generally give them very small space, either describing the facts in not more than 10 lines or relegating them to the local news. The following are some of the cruel acts that have been reported in the last few years: setting a hen on fire, shooting birds and cats with an air gun, playing football with a kitten used as a ball, and torturing and killing cats and dogs in various ways, some of the most common being inserting a firecracker into the animals' anus, crucifying them, burning them, stoning, punching and kicking them to death, and blinding them with pointed objects. These acts have been perpetrated most often in groups and by males. Moreover, animal abuse seems to occur in all parts of Italy. Interestingly, a few of these acts have been committed near a school or in an unguarded schoolyard. In most cases, the young perpetrators get away with their violent behavior. In one case, the three boys who played football with a kitten used as a ball and thus caused its death (incidentally, they lived in a small town a few miles from Rome where one of the schools involved in our research is located) were judged by a juvenile court which decided that an animal welfare organization, LAV (Antivivisection League), should educate them to respect animals and take care of them.

In addition, the relation between animal abuse, disordered development, and domestic violence is almost never mentioned by the media, though since 1997 one of the authors of this chapter (Pagani) has presented the results of psychological and sociological research in this field both in academic circles and to the general public in Italy. For instance, on the occasion of a suicide committed in jail in January 2004 by a 30-year-old man who had just been charged with murder and had previously spent 8 years in prison for other crimes, the media described him as a violent man, who in the past had also attacked two disabled people and tortured a cat. However, the media did not explicitly mention the significance of the association between violence to people and violence to animals, nor did they underline the fact that disabled people and most animals are both weak creatures, occupying the lowest rungs in the social ladder, over whom violent individuals may easily exercise their power (Pagani, 2000b; Robustelli & Pagani, 1994, 1996).

In one case, in 1997, national as well as local newspapers gave ample space to the denunciation of a courageous teacher in Palermo regarding a number of atrocities perpetrated against animals. Her 9-year-old pupils had informed her about these atrocities and had described what they had found in an abandoned and decaying nursery school, later called "the horror nursery school," located close to their school: cats and dogs strangled with iron wires or run through with needles or syringes, heads of pigeons and owls pinned on twigs, and, on the floors, graffiti written with the blood of animals. At first she had refused to believe her pupils' stories and had personally wanted to verify their truthfulness. The children also showed her some marbles made with the dogs' eyes, which had been desiccated and colored, and pendants made with the pigeons' heads and the dogs' paws. Some adult dogs and puppies were also found in the abandoned nursery school. After reporting what she had seen to the police, the teacher was under their protection for one month. The perpetrators of these atrocities were boys between the ages of 10 and 14. In the neighborhood where the two schools are located, unemployment is very high and drug abuse, as well as drug pushing, are quite common. Child sexual abuse and dog fighting also seem to occur. It is important to point out that the children had informed their teacher about the atrocities in the abandoned nursery school when she had spoken in class about animals' rights and their capacity for suffering. Surprisingly, since then nothing has changed. None of the perpetrators has been identified and the nursery school is still abandoned and visited mostly by drug addicts. From their school, pupils can easily see what is going on in there.

In Italy, a number of welfare animal organizations are present and their influence on public opinion is getting stronger. Some are more involved in education, in improving legislation, and in supporting the police in their struggle against the connection between organized crime, the mafia, and the exploitation of animals; others are more frequently involved in campaigns against furs, animal experimentation, and in support of vegetarianism.

A major change in animal legislation occurred in Italy in the last few years. According to a new bill, which was passed in July 2004, animal maltreatment is no longer a misdemeanor but a felony. Penalties have become more serious (a jail sentence from 3 months to 1 year or a fine from 3,000 to 15,000 euros [3,829 to 19,148 USD at the time of this writing] for animal maltreatment; a jail sentence from 1 to 3 years and a fine from 50,000 to 160,000 euros for those who organize dog fighting; a jail sentence for up to 1 year or a fine from 1,000 to 10,000 euros for those who abandon a domestic animal). In addition, cats and dogs can no longer be used to produce skins and furs. These rules do not apply to hunting, fishing, farming, slaughtering, animal transportation, zoos, animal experimentation, circuses, and folk festivals where animals are abused. The new bill also provides for the possibility to integrate school traditional curricula with special programs aimed to improve students' knowledge of animals' ethological characteristics and to foster their respect for animals. A protocol of understanding was drawn up in October 1999 between the Ministry of Education and LAV (Antivivisection League), which establishes a concrete cooperation between the two parties. In collaboration with the Ministry of Defense, LAV has also recently set up a telephone service for reporting cases of animal abuse.

Other important legislative changes are taking place. In October 2004, the Chamber of Deputies proposed to amend article 9 of the Italian constitution by inserting the clause "the Republic protects biodiversity and promotes the respect for animals." Hopefully, the amendment will soon be discussed by the new Parliament. Further, the European constitution, which was signed in Rome on October 29, 2004, states that animal welfare will be taken into serious consideration, as animals are "sentient beings."

In conclusion, it seems that in the last few years, at least a part of the Italian population has become more interested in animal welfare. In fact, the number of pets has increased (44% of families have one or more pets) (Cirm, 2003), as well as the number of vegetarians (Francone & Cattelan, 2004) and the number of people who prefer to buy cruelty-free products (Bartocci, 2004). The number of hunters decreased by half in the last 12 years (Vukovic, 2003), animal rights campaigns are more frequent and effective, and the media are showing greater interest in animal-related issues. However, negative attitudes and behaviors toward animals are still common. For example, every year 150,000 dogs and 200,000 cats are abandoned (Cavallieri, 2004), and private animal shelters, which are often run by people related to criminal gangs and where animals are kept in dreadful conditions, have proliferated (Troiano, 2002a). People rarely choose to adopt an abandoned or injured animal and pets are sometimes still regarded as "objects." Some folk festivals where animals are abused still survive (Bottigelli, 2004) and ritualistic sacrifices where animals are involved are increasing (Lugli, 2004). Dog fighting, mostly controlled by criminal gangs and associated with clandestine gambling, has become more frequent (Troiano, 2004). Circus performances, where animals are used, are often shown on both private and public TV channels, whilst the number of spectators at live performances has reduced (Guadagna, 2004). Knowledge of animal psychology remains scarce among common people, in the media, and at governmental and judicial levels. One of its consequences is that the aggressive behavior of some breeds of dogs is considered innate and scant attention is paid to incorrect training methods of aggressive dog owners (Troiano, 2002b).

We will conclude this introductory section with two notations, one regarding youths' attitudes and the other the opinion of a part of the Catholic Church on animals' rights. A recent survey on Italians' donations (Adnkronos, 2004) revealed that young people give more donations for animal welfare than the rest of the population (8.5% versus 5.8%). Another recent survey (Eurispes, 2004) on Italian youth demonstrated that 85% of adolescents condemn animal maltreatment.

Some years ago *La Civiltà Cattolica*, the Jesuits' official journal, published an editorial (La Civiltà Cattolica, 1999) that provoked animal-rights supporters' harsh criticism (Pocar, 1999; Politi, 1999). In the article, it is peremptorily claimed that animals have no rights. Amazingly, the author seems to have no knowledge of animal psychology, namely of the data scientific research has gathered on animals' cognitive and emotional abilities as well as on the continuity of biological evolution. In the editorial, it is stated that "The difference between animals and humans … is not a question of 'degree' but is 'intrinsic', since, unlike animals, humans can 'reason'" (p. 325). It is also claimed that only normal adult humans "are aware of their present suffering and can foresee their future suffering" (p. 321). All these considerations are definitely based on a pathological conception of what a human being is, "the only being endowed with intelligence and, thus, capable of understanding reality in all its vastness and complexity, as there is nothing they are not able to comprehend" (p. 330). Obviously, according to the editorial, the difference between humans and animals is based on the fact that humans have a spirit. Although in the Catholic Church there is also a tradition of deep love and respect for animals, the position embraced by *La Civiltà Cattolica* certainly reflects and partly conditions many Catholics' attitudes and beliefs regarding animals. As a matter of fact, the role some religions play in supporting the exploitation of animals has been clearly indicated (Bowd & Bowd, 1989; Flynn, 2001; Singer, 1990). We also agree with Flynn's hypothesis (2001) that the high level of socially accepted violence toward animals contributes to unacceptable violence.

Italian School Children's Conceptual Understanding, Attitudes, and Experiences Related to the Maltreatment of Animals

Our research on Italian pupils' animal abuse experiences was carried out within a broader research program[3] that aimed to investigate different aspects of child–animal relations, such as pet ownership, pet loss, worries about pet, animal abuse (as a witness), animal abuse (as a perpetrator), fear of animals, animals as a source of comfort, feelings toward road kill, attitudes toward hunting, the use of furs and leather clothes, feelings toward zoos, and the use of animals in circuses (Pagani, Robustelli, & Ascione, 2007). The analysis of the results of our study will now be limited to the animal abuse issue, though some references will be made to the relationship between animal abuse and other aspects of child–animal interaction.

Methods

Our research involved 12 schools: 3 primary schools, 5 middle schools, and 4 high schools. The schools were located in central Italy: 10 in Rome, 1 in a small town in the province of Rome, and 1 in a small town in the province of Florence. The schools in Rome are situated in different areas of the city, which are characterized by different socioeconomic conditions. In 9 schools, all the classes (starting from grade 4 in primary schools) participated in the research, while in the remaining 3, only some classes participated, due to the schools' organizational difficulties. All the pupils of the involved classes participated in the research. Therefore, in contrast to other studies in this field (e.g., Ascione, Thompson, & Black, 1997; Dadds, Whiting, Bunn, Fraser, Charlson, & Pirola-Merlo,

2004; Flynn, 1999a, 1999b; Guymer, Mellor, Luk, & Pearse, 2001; Thompson & Gullone, 2003), participation in the study was total and not limited to volunteering subjects. Pupils ranged in age between 9 to 18 years. We developed a six-page self-administered questionnaire based on the "Children and Animals Assessment Instrument" (CAAI) (Ascione et al., 1997) and on the "Boat Inventory on Animal-Related Experiences" (BIARE) (Boat, 1999) (see *Collaborating to Assess, Intervene, and Prosecute Animal Abuse* by Boat, Loar, and Phillips, this text) in three forms, according to participants' age range: 9–10, 11–12, and 13–18. The questionnaire is anonymous. Participants only had to indicate their gender. Their age could only be inferred with a good approximation from the grades they were attending (questionnaires were collected separately in each class). Pupils were assured that their teachers would not have access to the questionnaires. From the total number of questionnaires we obtained, we randomly selected 800 questionnaires (403 females and 397 males), which represent each school and participants' different ages. In our questionnaire, most of the dimensions of animal cruelty indicated in the CAAI (namely, *severity, frequency, recency, diversity across and within categories, animal sentience level, isolate, empathy*) were considered. Through this instrument, we aimed to obtain qualitative, as well as quantitative, data. (See the Appendix for a copy of the questionnaires.)

The forms for those aged 11–12 and 13–18 are practically identical, apart from some slight linguistic differences in the wording of the instructions and of a couple of questions. More differences are present between these forms and the form for those aged 9–10. We will mention only those specifically related to the animal cruelty items and sub-items. In the 9–10 years form, in the two items regarding animal abuse experiences (both as witnesses and as perpetrators) we did not provide (as we actually did in the two forms for older pupils) any examples of animal abuse. We decided to do so out of consideration for particularly sensitive young children and also because we wanted them to elaborate and express their own personal concept of animal abuse with minimal influence on our part. In addition, multiple-choice questions regarding participants' feelings related both to witnessed and perpetrated animal abuse were changed into open-ended questions, as we realized young children had some difficulties in discriminating between different specific alternatives, such as, for example, "a lot," "somewhat," "a little," or "not at all." Obviously, the evaluation and interpretation of open-ended answers required special attention. It is a fact that the interpretation of children's, and especially young children's, written productions is sometimes more difficult as compared to adults'. Apart from spelling, grammar, syntactic, or lexical mistakes that may be more frequent, one has to bear in mind that some young children express their views and experiences in a very personal and imaginative style. Hence, in these cases, a correct interpretation is not always easy, as we cannot consult the children themselves.

Defining "Cruelty"

A challenging issue to be addressed in a study of animal cruelty regards the definition of animal cruelty itself (e.g., Ascione, 1993; Beirne, 1999; Caputo, Brodsky, & Kemp, 2000; Flynn, 1999b; Guymer et al., 2001; Miller & Knutson, 1997; Piper, Johnson, Myers, & Pritchard, 2003; Rowan, 1999). As Piper et al. (2003) noted, this issue has been ignored in numerous studies. The issue is all the more relevant if we want to carry out correct national and cross-national comparisons of research findings. To better illustrate this point, we will refer to research on bullying and will try to understand how the issue of definition has been addressed by researchers in this field.

A clear and precise definition of bullying has been elaborated by the scientific community and has become the basis for any kind of research in this area (e.g., Baldry, 1998; Fonzi, 1997; Olweus, 1993; Pellegrini, 1998; Smith, 1991). Defining bullying is probably a less controversial task than defining animal cruelty (Piper et al., 2003). For our present purposes, we will follow Ascione (1993), who defines animal cruelty as "socially unacceptable behavior that intentionally causes unnecessary pain, suffering, or distress to and/or death of an animal" (p. 28). The term "unacceptable" is here clearly related to societal norms and, thus, its meaning largely depends on sociocultural factors, which, as we said above, can change in the course of time and from one social group to another (Agnew, 1998; Merz-Perez, Heide, & Silverman, 2001; Piper et al., 2003). Accordingly, social scientists belonging to different countries and different cultures have to bear in mind that, even if they agree on a particular definition of "animal cruelty" as a whole, the specific meanings they attach to this phenomenon do not always perfectly coincide.

A second problem we have to face, when carrying out research on animal cruelty, is the concrete possibility that researchers' definition of "animal cruelty"

and the personal definitions of research participants do not always coincide. As a matter of fact, these two problems have been brilliantly addressed by cross-cultural studies on bullying (e.g., Smith et al., 2002; Smorti, 2003). Some of the main points put forward by a group of researchers on bullying (Smith et al., 2002), which can be useful to us, are (a) the difficulty of the comparability of terminology related to bullying in national and cross-national comparisons; (b) the terms related to bullying "may be understood differently by persons answering questionnaires" since "respondents … may well refer to their personal definition of this term rather than that given early on by the researcher" (p. 1121); (c) there is evidence for developmental changes in the ways in which pupils construe bullying; (d) there might be gender differences in perceptions of bullying; and (e) researchers on bullying have to be aware that, like the rest of the population, they are involved "in the process of constructing its meaning in a social and historical context" (pp. 1131–1132). On introducing our discussion about the problem of Italian pupils' animal cruelty experiences, we have already addressed point (e). We will now discuss some of the results of our study with reference to point (b), namely to the possible imperfect correspondence between scientific and popular definitions of "animal cruelty." In fact, a significant result in our research is related to the analysis and interpretation of participants' concept of animal cruelty. Their ideas on animal cruelty sometimes only partly correspond to the concept of animal cruelty most researchers have agreed upon. This regards both perpetrated and witnessed cruelty.

As we said above, in the 9–10 years form of our questionnaire, in the two items concerning animal cruelty experiences ("*Did you ever hurt an animal?*" and "*Did you ever see anyone hurt an animal?*"), we did not provide any examples of animal maltreatment. Instead, in the 11–12 and 13–18 years forms, we suggested some examples, namely *teasing, torturing, wounding*, and *killing*. However, in all cases, participants had the possibility of autonomously elaborating their own concept of animal cruelty and of answering accordingly. Hence, their responses implicitly allowed us to infer the fundamental idea of animal cruelty of each pupil. This way we obtained a broad concept of violence toward animals, which encompassed both socially unacceptable behavior (in line with Ascione's definition) and socially acceptable behavior resulting in injury or harm to an animal (e.g., unintentionally running over a cat with a car).

As regards animal cruelty experiences as per-petrators, 11% of our pupils mentioned socially acceptable behavior resulting in injury or harm to an animal. Such behavior included:

- Killing invertebrates, such as ants, flies, mosquitoes, and gnats, either by accident or because they are a source of bother
- Causing minor injury to vertebrates, such as birds, cats, and dogs, either inadvertently or by accident
- Justly reproaching an animal by causing them very little annoyance
- Killing an animal for food
- Euthanasia

The cruelest socially acceptable perpetrated act was killing a pig for food committed by a male pupil of 15. Interestingly, two male pupils of 11 also per-ceived fishing as a form of animal cruelty.

As regards animal cruelty experiences as wit-nesses, 4% of our pupils mentioned:

- Socially acceptable behavior resulting in injury to or the death of an animal (namely killing an animal for food, and hunting)
- Socially acceptable behavior causing acci-dental injury to an animal (namely unin-tentionally running over a cat or a dog with a car[4])
- Hunting
- Killing bothersome insects

The most frequently mentioned socially accept-able witnessed cruel act was killing an animal for food (pig, hen, rabbit, lamb, duck, goose, and pigeon). This is consistent with Italian social reality, as even children and adolescents who live in urban areas sometimes still retain a link with the country-side especially if their grandparents, uncles, aunts, and other relatives live there. In some cases, either a grandfather or an uncle, and in one case a father, are mentioned by our pupils as the perpetrator of the killing. This may produce an inner conflict in some children. Our pupils sometimes describe the killing of an animal for food in very realistic and dramatic terms and write about how they were very concerned about the animal's suffering. The reported words of a mother to her daughter of 12, who witnessed the killing of a hen by her uncle, sounded particularly cynical: "Don't worry, since hens are born to be eaten." Also, the data about animals run over by cars is consistent with Italian social reality, given the presence of stray animals in the streets and the

almost general difficult situation as far as traffic is concerned (incidentally, one of the most frequent causes of worry for participants with a pet was that their pet might be run over by a vehicle). As to hunt-ing, though, as we said above, the number of hunters has diminished in the last few years, it is still popular in some Italian regions, like Tuscany or Lombardy.

This broad concept of animal cruelty has prac-tically never been fully considered in previous research on children's animal cruelty experiences, except by Piper et al. (2003). The fact that some participants in our study also mention socially acceptable behavior resulting in injury to an ani-mal may be related to cultural factors. It is possible that only children belonging to specific cultures include both socially acceptable hostile behav-ior and socially unacceptable hostile behavior in their personal definition of animal cruelty. In other words, it is possible that in some cultures (which may refer not only to a nation, but also to a region, city, town, or neighborhood) socially unacceptable violence toward animals is particularly common and worrying so that hostile socially acceptable behavior, such as squashing a mosquito or killing a hen for food, are not even taken into consideration by those who belong to these cultures. Interest-ingly, it seems that the concept of animal cruelty expressed by some of our pupils corresponds to the concept of animal abuse expressed by Beirne (1999), who defines animal abuse as "any act that contributes to the pain, suffering, or death of an animal or that otherwise threatens its welfare" (p. 121). Beirne also states that "Animal abuse … may involve active maltreatment or passive neglect or omission; and may be direct or indirect, inten-tional or unintentional" (p. 121).

Reports of Animal Cruelty—Socially Unacceptable Acts

We will now analyze only those cruel acts toward animals, either perpetrated or witnessed, that are encompassed by the scientific community's defi-nition (in particular, by Ascione's [1993] defini-tion), that is on animal cruelty in its strict sense, as "socially unacceptable behavior."

We divided the kinds of abused animals into three categories, on the basis of the animal's level of sen-tience (Ascione et al., 1997): warm-blooded verte-brates, cold-blooded vertebrates, and invertebrates. Another obvious distinction we made was between pets and non-pets.

Perpetrating Abuse

We will now focus on animal cruelty experienced by our pupils as perpetrators. It goes without saying that in the analysis of data the inevitable limits of the methodology we used should be taken into account. For instance, in our society, aggression is traditionally considered a positive aspect of males' personality. Consequently, a number of male participants may report being more cruel toward animals than they actually are. On the other hand, since in the last few years animal cruelty has been more frequently criticized and condemned, some male participants may report being less cruel than they actually are. In both cases, male participants' motivation, namely social desirability, is identical, though it is expressed in opposite directions, according to the value system they refer to. Hence, in both cases, in spite of the anonymity of questionnaires, respondents may not be always completely sincere. We will address this issue again when we discuss the differences in empathic attitudes toward animals between females and males.

Overall, 18% of participants (n = 136) reported perpetrating some kind of animal abuse. Males were three times more likely than females to commit animal cruelty (27% of males versus 9% of females) (χ^2 = 43.30, df = 1, p = 0.0000). The cat was the most frequent target of animal abuse, followed by the dog. As far as cold-blooded vertebrates are concerned, the lizard was the most frequent target, consistent with Italian tradition.[5] Finally, in more than one-fifth of the cases (22%), the target was a pet.

We classified cruel acts according to their severity: from level 1 (very low) to level 4 (very high). These are some examples for each level:

- Treading on an insect/bothering a mammal (level 1)
- Killing a lizard/cutting its tail (level 2)
- Throwing stones against a cat from a distance, without killing the animal (level 3)
- Killing a warm-blooded vertebrate/torturing a cold-blooded or a warm-blooded vertebrate (level 4)

Level 3 acts are the most frequent (35%), followed by level 2 (33%), level 1 (24%), and level 4 (8%). A level 4 act against a pet was reported by two pupils. Interestingly, the more severe acts (level 3 and 4 acts) were more often committed with other people, compared with the less severe acts (χ^2 = 10.53, df = 1, p = 0.0012). In almost two-thirds of cases animal cruelty was committed with other people, usually with peers.

Participants were also asked to describe their acts. The most common acts (in order of decreasing frequency) were:

- Killing (mostly insects, but also lizards, spiders, a cat, and a dog)
- Causing harm in various and sometimes elaborate ways (e.g.: tossing up, hurting with a firecracker, throwing against a wall; mostly cats and dogs)
- Bothering (the target being often a pet)
- Throwing dangerous objects, like stones, arrows, marbles, and shoes (the target often being a cat)

Other less frequent acts were "torturing" (insects, lizards, frogs, fishes, and cats), "kicking" (dogs and cats), "beating" (dogs, cats, and hamsters), clubbing (cats, dogs, and other animals), "frightening" (birds), and "throwing non-dangerous objects (like eggs)" (against cats and dogs).

We also analyzed our pupils' reported motivations for their behavior. The most common motivations (in order of decreasing frequency) were:

- For fun
- Aversion or indifference
- I wanted to play (we kept this motivation distinct from "for fun," as this latter motivation may more easily involve a sadistic pleasure, compared with "I wanted to play")
- I wanted to punish the animal
- Curiosity
- I wanted to discipline the animal
- I was afraid
- I wanted to imitate my friends

It is interesting to point out that the motivation "curiosity" seldom occurred (only seven cases), though some educators and even some social scientists erroneously attach a great importance to it in order to explain and justify childhood animal cruelty. Furthermore, Lewchanin and Zimmerman (2000) clearly state that "Contrary to what some people may think, it is not normal for children to go through a developmental phase where they hurt animals" (p. 9).

Obviously, we have to bear in mind that, as a matter of fact, these may not be respondents' real motivations but simply their *statements regarding their possible motivations*.

Pupils aged 13–14 more often reported being cruel to animals (28% of pupils in this age range), followed by pupils aged 15–18 (20%), 11–12 (16%), and 9–10 (9%). We expected older participants, namely those between the ages of 15 and 18, to report committing animal cruelty more often, considering the results of a study conducted in Italy by Baldry (2003) and the very simple fact that older pupils had more time to perpetrate animal abuse, compared with younger pupils, as questions concerned all abusive acts committed by pupils during their lifetime. Three reasons might explain this contradiction. A number of pupils between the ages of 15 and 18 may have been less sincere than younger respondents when answering this question; a number of them may have forgotten about their hostile acts, especially if they were negligible and committed during their early childhood; and, finally, some of them, while completing their questionnaires, may have been less interested and less involved in the task than younger pupils. It is a fact that, compared with pupils from elementary and middle schools, some pupils from high schools seemed to be somewhat less keen to participate in the study and to collaborate with the researchers. This is almost certainly due to the difficult relations that sometimes occur in Italy between students, mainly those attending high schools, on one hand and school staff, public institutions, and adults in general on the other. Besides, the item regarding the experience of animal cruelty as a perpetrator is followed by 15 sub-items aiming to obtain information about several aspects of this experience. Thus, if the answer to the item is affirmative, participants also have to respond to the entire sequence of sub-items. Less interested and less involved high school pupils may have preferred either to provide a negative answer or not to answer at all in order to avoid answering the 15 sub-items.

We also requested that participants describe their feelings while perpetrating animal abuse. The two most frequent answers were "nothing" and "pleasure" (this was an open-ended question). However, the interpretation of these data is difficult. For instance, in a few cases, lack of feelings seems to be connected with respondents' young age at the time of their behavior and, consequently, with their being partly unaware of the animal's suffering. Seventeen percent of pupils who abused animals stated they had felt sad or distressed while committing the abuse. Three pupils reported feeling happy and sad at the same time.

As to their feelings at the present time regarding animal abuse committed in the past, 35% reported being "very sorry." We can see this percentage is more than double with respect to similar feelings in the past (as we said above, only 17% stated they had felt sad or distressed). Flynn's study (2000) also indicates that some perpetrators appear to be affected more later in their lives by their abuse than at the time they committed it. Thirty-one percent reported feeling "nothing."

More than half (55%) of pupils (with no difference between males and females) who were cruel to animals spoke to someone about their behavior: about one-half (53%) spoke to peers, more than one-third (38%) to one or both parents (to mothers almost three times more frequently than to fathers), 8% to other adult relatives, and 1% to teachers. Pupils were often reproached (55% of cases), especially by parents (73% of parents), and less often by peers (47% of peers). As a matter of fact, in more than half of the cases peers approved or did not criticize pupils' behavior. Mothers, compared with fathers, seemed to be more concerned about their educational role, as they often tried to explain to their children why such behavior was to be avoided. In a few cases, cruel behavior was approved, especially by peers, or it was not disapproved.

We did not find any significant differences between pupils who abused animals and pupils who did not with regard to the following experiences: witnessing animal cruelty, being comforted by an animal in times of stress, having or having had a pet, and being worried about one's pet. On the contrary, our results indicate that participants who have never abused animals more frequently feel a deep affection for their pet; more frequently feel "very sorry" when they see road kill; are more frequently against hunting, the use of furs and leather clothes, the use of animals in circuses and zoos; and less frequently fear animals.

Exposure to Cruelty

We now present the data regarding witnessed animal cruelty. Only socially unacceptable forms of animal cruelty will be considered. Obviously, being a witness and being a perpetrator are distinct and very different experiences, though at times they may probably be related (as we said, in our study we did not find any relation between them).

Being a witness of animal abuse was quite a common experience among Italian children and adolescents of both sexes (we did not find any significant gender difference). Of our pupils, 65% reported witnessing some form of animal cruelty. In contrast, gender differences were striking when we consider the perpetrators of witnessed animal cruelty, as males were reported being the perpetrators in almost all cases (94%). In fact, though participants had not been asked to indicate the perpetrator's gender, the perpetrator is usually defined as "he." Incidentally, practically the same figures (93% male adults, 6% female adults, and 1% children) were provided in a 2004 survey conducted by LAV (Antivivisection League), which, as we said above, set up a telephone service for all citizens who want to report animal maltreatment (Troiano, 2005). This difference related to perpetrators' gender is all the more impressive if we compare these data with the data regarding gender differences in the experience of animal cruelty committed by participants themselves. In the case of witnessed animal cruelty, males are 15.5 times more likely to commit animal abuse than females and, in the case of perpetrated animal cruelty, males are 3 times more likely to commit animal abuse than females.

A few hypotheses can be put forward in order to try to explain this difference. For instance, male pupils may have been more sincere when relating their animal abuse experience as witnesses than as perpetrators. Compared with females, males' self-esteem is generally higher and, consequently, males are sometimes inclined to ignore their misbehaviors. As stated above, in our present society, contradictory cultural patterns coexist, such as considering aggression as a positive aspect of males' personality on one hand and considering aggression as a negative aspect of human behavior on the other. This situation may induce some young males to behave aggressively and, at the same time, to be reluctant to admit it. Furthermore, when comparing committed and witnessed animal cruelty, we have to bear in mind that the characteristics of perpetrators in the two cases are partly different, thus rendering the comparison more difficult. Pupils who were cruel to animals are obviously young (the oldest are about 18), while witnessed perpetrators can be of all ages. Though we did not ask pupils to specify the witnessed perpetrators' ages, we were able to infer from their answers with acceptable certainty whether perpetrators were young people (up to 18 years) or adults. In 51% of cases they were adults. Some conjectures can be made. For example, the older generation of perpetrators may be more numerous and with a more substantial presence of males due to adherence to more traditional cultural patterns related to masculinity. As we will see later, animal welfarists' campaigns and educational interventions in schools aiming to foster children's respect for animals have certainly improved children's attitudes toward animals in the last decade.

Another difference was found between perpetrated and witnessed animal cruelty, namely in the degree of severity of the two kinds of cruelty. Witnessed acts

were usually much more severe than perpetrated acts. Eighty-three percent were level 3 and level 4 acts (62% and 21%, respectively), compared with 43% of perpetrated acts. Also, this difference may be partly due to the same reasons we have hypothesized when we tried to explain gender differences in perpetrators in witnessed animal cruelty and in animal cruelty committed by pupils themselves.

The most frequent targets of witnessed cruelty were dogs, followed by cats, and, much less often, by other animals, like lizards, birds, and frogs. The data seem to be consistent with the witnessed perpetrators' inferred age, compared with the age of pupils who abused animals. It is generally easier for children and adolescents to be cruel to a cat (the most frequent target of our pupils' cruelty) than to a dog, while for adults, compared with children, it can be generally easier to be cruel to a dog. The fact that adults are more likely to abuse dogs and that children are more likely to abuse cats is confirmed by other researchers (Arluke & Luke, 1997; Flynn, 2001).

In only 5% (n = 26) of cases of witnessed animal cruelty were the targets the pupils' pets. In eight of these cases the perpetrator was a relative or a member of the family (namely, father, parents, brother, mother's ex-partner, aunt, cousin). In the remaining cases pupils generically refer to peers (e.g., "a friend," "a boy," "some boys") or, more often, to adults (e.g., "a man," "a person," "some grown-ups"). It is possible that in some of these remaining cases respondents may have preferred not to reveal that the perpetrators were members of their families. We will shortly return to this point. In the eight cases where the perpetrator was a relative or a member of the family three acts were level 3 and five were level 2.

We thoroughly examined the questionnaires of these eight cases, in all their parts (that is, including items regarding, for instance, pet ownership, pet loss, worries about pet, fear of animals, animals as a source of comfort, attitudes toward zoos, hunting, etc.), as we tried to understand whether they yielded a particularly negative image, as far as these pupils' and their families' general relationships with animals were concerned. However, only in three cases were we able to hypothesize that some kind of disturbed relationship between one or more members of the family and animals might exist. For example, in the case of a girl of 16, who saw her father "a few times" clubbing her cat and kicking a neighbor's cat and who was cruel to lizards, scorpions, spiders, and ants, could we deduce that some of her pets may have been neglected (cat was lost, dog was run over by a vehicle, other pets were given away). A boy of 13, whose brother kicked the pet dog because the dog had bitten his foot, stated that he also had teased the same pet and that, as a consequence, the pet had bitten his nose. It goes without saying that when a pet harms its caretaker this may easily indicate the existence of a disturbed relationship between them. Besides, this participant, who lost a pet (another dog) a few years ago, wrote that he "does not suffer at all" about it. He is in favor of hunting and the use of animals in circuses. A boy of 12, whose brother teased and hurt the pet cat, wrote he had often fired rubber bullets against his pet dog. The language he used to describe his acts, which he perpetrated alone, is slightly vulgar. He is in favor of hunting and zoos (his opinion about the use of animals in circuses is not clear). In contrast, a little girl of 9, who reported in a sad and dramatic language that her father sometimes beats their pet dog, seems to be deeply attached to her pets (whose names she mentioned) and to feel very angry with her dad. She is against furs and leather clothes and against animals in circuses (the question about hunting was not present in the 9–10 years form and her answer about zoos was "I do not know"). This last case seems to be an exemplar of a child who opposes a violent parental model and is capable of developing positive attitudes toward and concern for animals.

We also analyzed the relationship between respondents and the perpetrators of witnessed animal (pet and non-pet) abuse. This relationship was inferred from participants' responses, as we had not specifically asked them to indicate it. In the majority of cases (84%), the perpetrators were "strangers" (i.e., unfamiliar adults or peers). Peers, who were also respondents' friends or acquaintances, comprised about 11%, family members, including members of the enlarged family, 4%, and adult acquaintances, 1%. The two most surprising findings relate to the high number of "strangers" and the very low number of family members. Other findings in our study, besides the very small number of pets that are the target of witnessed animal abuse and the very small number of family members as perpetrators, may help us understand this point more clearly. For example, when we examined our pupils' worries regarding their pets, we found out that their worries, which are very frequent indeed (76% of pupils with pets are worried), were not only related to "natural" causes (natural death and

illness being the most common) but were also, and more often, related to causes where human beings were involved and which were therefore potentially avoidable (e.g., the pet might be run over by a car; escape; fall from a balcony; or be killed, injured, or stolen). In this latter case, parents or other members of the family were almost never held accountable. The source of threat for the pet's welfare was seldom mentioned. Participants seemed to think their pets were in danger because of a threatening environment, which is usually vaguely defined, but which presumably often coincides with the dangerousness of their neighborhood. In sum, danger seems to come from outside, rather than from inside, the home. We do not know whether Italian families are really safe havens or, more probably, whether some participants avoided uncovering disreputable behaviors occurring in their homes. We might conclude that, at least for a number of Italian pupils, family is an almost untouchable institution, a unique point of reference, which must be defended at all costs.

Some of the most frequently reported cruel acts witnessed by respondents are (in order of decreasing frequency):

- Kicking (mostly dogs and cats)
- Throwing stones or other dangerous objects (especially against dogs and cats)
- Beating (mostly dogs)
- Clubbing (mostly dogs and cats)
- Torturing (lizards, frogs, dogs, cats, and birds)
- Killing (mostly insects, lizards, frogs, dogs and cats)
- Bothering (dogs and cats)
- Providing scarce food, water, and space/keeping on a chain all the time/abandoning (dogs)/not taking to the vet
- Tossing up (cats and small dogs)
- Frightening (dogs, cats, and birds)
- Punching (dogs)
- Deliberately running over with a vehicle (cats and dogs)

Bestiality (with a dog) was mentioned only twice. We may add some sinister color to this picture by mentioning that "throwing stones" was once called by a male respondent of 18 "playing intifada" (the act being perpetrated in this specific case by some boys against a cat).

As far as we can infer from our pupils' answers, we can state that cruelty was frequently committed by animals' owners against their own pets, mostly with the aim to discipline them, and that some of these cases can be labeled as "ordinary maltreatment."

However, our pupils sometimes did not report a single violent act, but a sequence of violent acts. The following are only a few of the numerous examples of such sequences: a peasant fastens a dog to a tree and slays it with a hoe; peers kick and throw stones and firecrackers against cats and dogs; a man ties a dog's feet, violently shakes it, clubs it, and sets it on fire. Children's cruelty can sometimes be very refined and can be carried out with great precision. For instance, some children fasten frogs to a catapult and hurl them or cut short lizards' tails and put them into their friends' drinks. Young men, however, are not inferior to children. Some male youngsters, aged 20, injected denatured alcohol into kittens with a syringe to see the effect it would have on the animals. This form of cruelty has been described in a study by Buchta (1988).

It is interesting to analyze the motivations for witnessed cruel acts, according to our pupils' opinions. Apart from a large number of respondents who declared they did not know why the cruelty they witnessed was committed, the following were among the most often reported motivations (in order of decreasing frequency):

- Perpetrators did it for fun (the most frequently reported motivation also for animal cruelty perpetrated by respondents themselves)
- They are wicked/they feel no affection and have no sense of responsibility toward the animal/they don't like animals
- They wanted to discipline the animal
- They are "bastards," "stupid," "brainless," and "ignorant" people, or people "who have nothing better to do" (we labeled it as "generic motivation")
- They are psychologically disturbed
- They wanted to punish the animal
- They wanted to show off
- They wanted to improve their self-esteem
- They were very young and were not completely aware they were causing suffering to the animal

One of the most worrisome reported motivations (which we related to psychological disturbances) referred to some boys who took some newborn kittens, placed them on a flat reed, and drowned them in the waters of a river. The respondent, a girl of 11, stated they did it because they enjoyed seeing how animals die.

When the motivation was "they wanted to show off" or "they wanted to improve their self-esteem," perpetrators were generally adolescents. When animal cruelty was committed "for fun," perpetrators were mostly children or adolescents. Perpetrators were almost always adults when cruelty was committed to discipline or punish the animal, or because the animal was hated or was not loved and taken care of.

As was the case with animal cruelty perpetrated by pupils, as far as witnessed animal cruelty is concerned, the frequency of this experience is positively related to participants' age, but only up to the age of 14 (62% of pupils aged 9–10, 70% of pupils aged 11–12, 72% of those aged 13–14, and 55% of those aged 15–18). As we can see, pupils aged 15–18 report witnessing animal cruelty even less frequently than the youngest pupils, aged 9–10. One of the hypotheses we put forward to explain this contradiction when addressing the issue of cruelty perpetrated by respondents themselves may also be valid in this case. If the answer to the item regarding witnessed animal cruelty is affirmative, participants also have to respond to a long sequence of sub-items (13 in this case), which aim to obtain information about several aspects of this experience. Hence, we can presume that a number of older, high-school pupils, less motivated in completing the questionnaires and less interested in school activities in general, may have preferred either to provide a negative answer or not to answer at all in order to avoid answering the 13 sub-items.

About two-thirds (65%) of all respondents reported feeling "very sorry" at the time they witnessed animal cruelty. Among them the most numerous were the youngest pupils (aged 9–10; 94% of pupils of this age range) and the least numerous were those between 13 and 14 years (49%). Females more frequently reported feeling "very sorry" than males at the time of the experience (78% versus 51%; $\chi^2 = 32.84$, df = 1, p = 0.0000). This picture is partly confirmed as regards respondents' current emotions related to their past experiences as animal cruelty witnesses. About one-half (51%) reported still feeling "very sorry." Among them the most numerous were again the youngest pupils (aged 9–10; 81%), while the least numerous were those between 15 and 18 years (33%). Also in this case, females more frequently reported feeling "very sorry" than males (65% versus 36%; $\chi^2 = 36.55$, df = 1, p = 0.0000). All these findings regarding participants' emotions related to witnessed abuse (both at the time and currently) indicate that they are generally more affected compared with those participants who actually committed the abuse. This fact is consistent with Flynn's results (2000).

More than half of participants (55%) who witnessed animal abuse spoke to someone about their experience. Females more often spoke than males (59% of females versus 52% of males), though the difference does not reach significance ($\chi^2 = 2.08$, df = 1, p = 0.15). Notably, almost all of those who did not speak to anyone witnessed level 3 and level 4 cruel acts. Pupils generally spoke (in order of decreasing frequency) to one or both parents (the mother being the parent with whom they shared this experience four times more frequently than the father), to peers, and to other adult relatives. In only four cases were teachers involved. The people participants spoke to often showed a critical attitude toward the abuse, though their disapproval was very often rather generic. Only in 14% of cases did they think that something should be done to stop or prevent the abuse and suggested various possibilities. In ten cases these people (in order of decreasing frequency, parents, young relatives, and friends) directly intervened as soon as they learned about the facts. If we consider that many of the people pupils spoke to are adults, we can easily understand how adults often still play a very poor educational role in our society. It is also interesting to point out that, fortunately in only a few cases, some adults, though disapproving of the abuse, showed a fatalistic and resigned attitude, as is indicated in these words: "It happens, most of times we can't do anything," and "All the harm the woman has caused to the dog should fall upon her." In the former case, the witnessed acts were particularly cruel: A male pupil of 12, who admitted to killing some cats, reported seeing some people bothering, kicking, and throwing pointed arrows against dogs and cats. Interestingly, this pupil's school is located in the small town where three boys played football with a kitten used as a ball and thus caused its death (an episode we have already mentioned and which was covered by the media). Finally, as regards this specific episode, it was reportedly witnessed by two female pupils from our sample. Neither of them spoke to anyone about it. One of the two, a girl of 11, wrote she "did not have the courage to speak to anyone about it." The other, a girl of 14, stated she had not spoken to anyone because she "would not think of that dramatic event any longer."

Research Comparisons and Discussion

The evaluation of the prevalence of child animal abuse experiences is a major problem. As we said above, the problem becomes even more serious if we want to carry out appropriate national and cross-national comparisons of the phenomenon. Definitions of animal abuse,[6] methodologies, type of participants, and cultural and temporal contexts are very often different. Again, however, an important distinction should be clearly made, namely between perpetrated and witnessed abuse.

As to perpetrated abuse occurring mainly during childhood and adolescence in normative community samples the following are some of the percentages yielded by different studies, all of which used self-reports:

- 10% (Offord, Boyle, & Racine, 1991)
- 20.5% (Miller & Knutson, 1997)
- 17.6% (Flynn, 1999a, 1999b, 2000)
- 50.8% (Baldry, 2003)
- 30.6 % (Dadds et al., 2004)
- 21% (Henry, 2006)

As we said, in our study, 18% of pupils reported committing some form of animal abuse. Of the six studies mentioned above the only one we might possibly consider if we want to compare its results and the results of our study is Baldry's, who aimed to assess the effects of exposure to domestic violence on childhood animal abuse. There are some similarities between the two studies: The geographical context is practically the same (schools in central Italy), the age of participants is almost identical, and in both studies all pupils of the classes involved participated in the research. The number of participants is somewhat different, but in both studies it is high (1,396 in Baldry's study and 800 in ours). Though the ratio between males and females in respondents who committed animal abuse is quite similar (2 to 1 in Baldry's study and 3 to 1 in our study), her results are different from ours as regards the greater frequency both of perpetrated animal abuse reported by participants in general (almost three times higher in Baldry's study) and of perpetrated animal abuse reported by older boys, compared with younger boys, in her study (we have already discussed in the present chapter the problem related to the lower prevalence in our survey of committed animal abuse reported by pupils between 15 and 18 years of age compared with those between 9 and 14 years of age). Perhaps the difference in the prevalence of per-petrated animal abuse in the two studies is partly due to the different instruments used (Baldry used the P.E.T.—Physical and Emotional Tormenting Against Animals—Scale) and to the fact that Baldry presum-ably did not distinguish between socially acceptable and socially unacceptable animal cruelty.

With regard to witnessed abuse reported by children and adolescents in the normative commu-nity, the following are some of the prevalence rates obtained from the research literature:

- 57% of participants (Miller & Knutson, 1997)
- 45% of participants (Flynn, 1999a, 1999b, 2000)
- More than 50% of participants (Piper et al., 2003) (actually in this study the percentage refers to children and adolescents who "had some knowledge" of another person harm-ing an animal)

In our study, 65% of respondents witnessed ani-mal abuse. Some of the findings obtained by Piper et al. (2003) are similar to ours. For example, when their participants, aged 10–17, spoke about animal cruelty that had been committed by other people, not by themselves, they often referred to the perpetrator as "someone I know" and this someone was often described as "he." As noted, in our study, though we also did not ask the perpetrator's gender and the perpetrator's relationship with participants in the questions regarding witnessed animal abuse, almost always participants described the perpetrator as "he" and as a "stranger." In any case, it seems that both British and Italian young people prefer to respect the anonymity of animal cruelty perpetrators.

Piper et al. (2003) were also particularly inter-ested in identifying how young people define animal abuse. Their findings indicate that their participants, like the participants in our study, expressed a broad concept of animal abuse (socially acceptable as well as socially unacceptable cruelty) and that they were generally aware of the contradictions in everyday life in people's attitudes to animal welfare. Some slight differences between males and females' perceptions of animal abuse were also found in their research.

"For fun" is a frequently reported motivation by animal abuse perpetrators (Hensley & Tallichet, 2005a; Merz-Perez et al., 2001; Schiff, Louw, & Ascione, 1999). In our study, "for fun" was the most frequently reported motivation. In particular, Merz-Perez et al. demonstrated that this motivation is more

common among violent offenders than among non-violent offenders. This fact also supports the choice we made, in analyzing motivations, in distinguish-ing between "for fun" (which may include sadistic pleasure) and "I wanted to play." "For fun" was also the most frequently reported motivation by a group of male aggressive and nonaggressive criminals (Schiff et al., 1999) and the second most frequently reported motivation by a group of inmates in Hensley and Tallichet's study (2005a). Finally, "for fun" is a motivation children and adolescents frequently offer to explain young people's animal cruelty (Piper et al., 2003), as our study also indicates, where "for fun" is the most frequently reported motivation to explain witnessed animal abuse.

As mentioned above, the percentages of pupils in our study who spoke to someone about their ani-mal abuse experiences was 55%, both among those who admitted to animal abuse and among those who observed animal abuse. The issue of communication on animal abuse, either perpetrated or observed, between youths and significant others is very impor-tant, especially from an educational point of view (Flynn, 1999a). We have seen that our data suggest that the quality and quantity of this communication are rather scarce. It is interesting to note that two participants, a female pupil of 13 and a male pupil of 11, when responding about their animal abuse experiences as witnesses (level 3 acts in both cases), reported they had spoken about it "to you" and "only to you," respectively ("you" being referred to the researchers).

As other studies have also indicated (Driscoll, 1992; Kellert, 1985), our research demonstrates that age can sometimes play a significant role in attitudes toward animals and that there is, in some cases, a positive relation between young age and empathy toward animals. Our younger pupils, for example, besides feeling more frequently "very sorry" as regards witnessed animal abuse both at the time of the abuse and at the present time, were also more frequently against zoos and the use of animals in cir-cuses, and were less frequently afraid of animals in general. This fact can be partly related, as Driscoll also suggests, to young people being more exposed in the last few years, especially in schools, to issues such as the conservation of the environment and ani-mal welfare (Pagani, 1999).

We also found that committing animal abuse is negatively correlated with some positive attitudes toward and experiences with animals (pupils who perpetrated animal abuse, compared with pupils who did not, were more frequently afraid of animals; were less frequently against hunting, the use of furs and leather clothes, zoos, and the use of animals in circuses; were less frequently "very sorry" when they saw road kill; and less frequently felt a deep attachment for their pet). The few empirical data on a possible relation between animal abuse and fear of animals (Hensley & Tallichet, 2005a; Schiff et al., 1999) and anecdotal data seem to suggest that, at least in some cases, fear of animals, often related to a limited knowledge of animals, may be one of the causes of a cruel act against an animal.

Our pupils often (in almost two-thirds of cases) reported abusing animals with other people, usually with peers. This is supported by previous research (e.g., Arluke & Luke, 1997; Baldry, 2003; Boat, 1995; Flynn, 2001). Besides, they more frequently commit cruelty with someone when their acts are particularly severe and when they do it "for fun." Peer group influence on children and adolescents' behavior is well known (e.g., Baldry, 2003; Flynn, 2001). Five participants, all males, explicitly reported being cruel to imitate their companions. One of these is the 12-year-old pupil, whom we have already mentioned, whose school is located in the small town where, as we said above, three boys played football with a kitten used as a ball. This boy admitted killing some cats with his friends "for fun and because other people did it."

Moreover, though our respondents more often abused animals with someone when their acts were particularly severe, solitary perpetration of severe acts (levels 3 and 4) of animal abuse is not so infrequent (25% of all acts perpetrated alone). The fact that solitary perpetration of animal cruelty may indicate more significant pathology (Hensley & Tallichet, 2005b) makes this percentage of special concern.

The research literature has so far always underlined the major role played by males, compared with females, in animal abuse (e.g., Flynn, 2000, 2001). As regards normative community samples, ratios may vary from one study to another; for example, almost 4 to 1 in Flynn's study (1999a, 1999b), almost 2 to 1 in the Dadds et al.'s study (2004), 2 to 1 in Baldry's study (2003), and 5 to 1 in Henry's study (2006). In our study, we found that females were not only much less involved in animal cruelty experiences as perpetrators (the ratio being 3 to 1) but that also in other significant aspects of their interaction with animals (for instance, emotions related to witnessing animal abuse, kind of relation with their pets,

feelings toward road kill, and attitudes toward hunting, zoos, the use of furs and leather clothes, and the use of animals in circuses) they were generally more empathic than males. Our findings are supported by research on human–animal interactions and on empathy in general (e.g., Flynn, 2000; Henry, 2006; Hoffman & Levine, 1976; Thompson & Gullone, 2003; Wells & Hepper, 1995). However, as far as our questionnaires are concerned, we have to consider that, except in one specific case where participants' personal involvement is absent—namely gender differences in perpetrators of witnessed animal abuse—females may sometimes have been inclined to appear more empathic than they actually are, as they might be desirous to comply with prevailing cultural patterns, according to which females are expected to behave and to feel more empathically than males. Similar considerations can also be found in Piper et al. (2003).

Understanding motivations for animal cruelty and comparing different motivations as they are reported in a few studies is a very hard task. Methodologies and the characteristics of participants involved can vary. We will refer to Kellert and Felthous' nine motivations[7] (Kellert & Felthous, 1985), derived from interviews with a group of criminals and a group of noncriminals, to the motivations suggested by Ascione et al. (1997), to those presented by Piper et al. (2003), and to those considered by Hensley and Tallichet (2005a) in their study conducted on a group of inmates. As regards animal abuse perpetrated by participants themselves, the motivations "I wanted to discipline" and "I wanted to punish the animal" reported by our pupils are presumably close to Kellert and Felthous' two motivations "To control an animal" and "To retaliate against an animal," while their motivation "To satisfy a prejudice against a species or breed" can partly correspond to some forms of aversion expressed by our participants, especially against cats, spiders, insects, and snakes. Incidentally, hatred of cats was also found in Piper et al.'s study (2003). None of the participants in our study mentioned "To shock people for amusement." Instead, on reporting witnessed animal abuse, some respondents suggested that perpetrators were cruel to animals because "they wanted to show off" or because "they wanted to improve their self-esteem." As to the remaining motivations listed by Kellert and Felthous only one, "Nonspecific sadism," can be similar to one of our pupils' motivations, namely "for fun." Ascione et al. (1997), who also used interviews in assessing animal cruelty, suggested a number of developmentally related motivations. Of these only "Curiosity or exploration," "Peer reinforcement," "Animal phobias," and "Imitation" are close to our pupils' reported motivations as regards both perpetrated and witnessed animal abuse. Some of Hensley and Tallichet's (2005a) motivations, namely "for fun," "dislike for the animal," "fear of animal," "to control the animal," and "imitation" are identical or very close to most of the reported motivations we identified for animal cruelty committed by participants themselves. The motivations presented by Piper et al. (2003) (i.e., retaliate, fun, lack of empathy, carelessness/ignorance/immaturity, wickedness, mental illness) are also very similar to those we derived from our data both for perpetrated and witnessed animal abuse. Quotations from their participants' (aged 7–17 years) responses such as "probably for fun," "to make themselves look good," and "the animal might be tearing your best shirts and socks" echo, even in their style, some of the responses provided by our pupils to explain witnessed animal abuse.

Our research findings also indicate that animal cruelty is often related to incorrect methods of training. Of cases of witnessed animal cruelty reported by our pupils, 23.5% refer to animals being maltreated by their caretakers (notably, in four cases the animal was abandoned), often with the aim to discipline them. Raupp (1999) maintains the importance to further investigate what she defines as "societally tolerated maltreatment" of pets and its influence on children's affective and cognitive development. In particular, like the exposure to other forms of violence, it can interfere with the development of empathy (Ascione, 1992, 1993).

Cruelty to animals is a complex phenomenon. As Merz-Perez et al. (2001) state, "each and every act [of cruelty to animals] should be investigated as a specific act committed by a specific individual against a specific animal" (p. 571). As we said above, our research findings indicate that perpetrating animal abuse is negatively correlated with some empathic attitudes toward animals. However, we should also point out that we did not find any significant relation between engaging in animal abuse on one side and being comforted by an animal and being worried about one's pet on the other. This fact confirms the complexity of the phenomenon of animal cruelty and the necessity to deepen its analysis at the individual level and to integrate this analysis at the social and cultural level.

In any case we can assert that any form of violence, including violence to animals, is mainly the expression of an ideology based on power relationships. It goes without saying that this ideology, which unfortunately often characterizes human relationships as well as humans' relationships with the other living beings, is irrational and destructive (Robustelli & Pagani, 1996).

Notes

1. In this chapter we will use "animal abuse," "animal maltreatment," and "violence to animals" as synonyms.
2. On this issue see also Pagani (2007).
3. The research programe was partly funded by the Municipality of Rome, Department for Animals' Rights.
4. However, it is useful to point out that in Italy car accidents where animals are involved are obviously more frequent when vehicles exceed the speed limit and, consequently, when socially *unacceptable* behavior occurs.
5. Traditionally, one of Italian male children's playing activities is the so-called lizard hunting.
6. As we said, there are broad definitions, like in our study, and strict definitions, like in Henry's study (2006), where the concept of animal abuse includes only killing a pet, killing a stray animal (except in case of hunting, euthanasia, and killing for food), torturing an animal, and controlling someone by threatening or harming an animal.
7. (1) To control an animal, (2) to retaliate against an animal, (3) to satisfy a prejudice against a species or breed, (4) to express aggression through an animal, (5) to enhance one's own aggressiveness, (6) to shock people for amusement, (7) to retaliate against another person, (8) displacement of hostility from a person to an animal, (9) nonspecific sadism.

References

Adams, D. (Ed.). (1991). *The Seville Statement on Violence*. Paris: Unesco.

Adnkronos. (2004, October 20). *Le donazioni degli italiani*. Press release, Milano.

Agnew, R. (1998). The causes of animal abuse: A social-psychological analysis. *Theoretical Criminology, 2*, 177–209.

Arluke, A., & Luke, C. (1997). Physical cruelty toward animals in Massachusetts, 1975–1990. *Society and Animals, 5*, 195–204.

Ascione, F. R. (1992). Enhancing children's attitudes about the humane treatment of animals: Generalization to human-directed empathy. *Anthrozoös, 5*, 176–191.

Ascione, F. R. (1993). Children who are cruel to animals: A review of research and implications for developmental psychopathology. *Anthrozoös, 6*, 226–247.

Ascione, F. R., Thompson, T. M., & Black T. (1997). Childhood cruelty to animals: Assessing Cruelty dimensions and motivations. *Anthrozoös, 10*, 170–177.

Baldry, A. C. (1998). Bullying among Italian middle school students. *School Psychology International, 19*, 361–374.

Baldry, A. C. (2003). Animal abuse and exposure to interparental violence in Italian youth. *Journal of Interpersonal Violence, 18*, 258–281.

Bartocci, R. (2004). Test cosmetici. In M. Falvo (Ed.), Gli animali e gli italiani. Rapporto LAV 2004 – IV Edizione. *Impronte, 8*, 56.

Beirne, P. (1999). For a nonspeciesist criminology: Animal abuse as an object of study. *Criminology, 37*, 117–147.

Boat, B. W. (1995). The relationship between violence to children and violence to animals. *Journal of Interpersonal Violence, 10*, 228–235.

Boat, B. W. (1999). Abuse of children and abuse of animals. In F. R. Ascione & P. Arkow (Eds.), *Child Abuse, Domestic Violence and Animal Abuse: Linking the Circles of Compassion for Prevention and Intervention* (pp. 83–100). West Lafayette, IN: Purdue University Press.

Bottigelli, M. (2004). Palii e feste con animali. In M. Falvo (Ed.), Gli animali e gli italiani. Rapporto LAV 2004 – IV Edizione. *Impronte, 8*, 30–33.

Bowd, A. D., & Bowd, A. C. (1989). Attitudes toward the treatment of animals: A study of Christian groups in Australia. *Anthrozoös, 3*, 20–24.

Brislin, R. W. (1994). Cross-cultural psychology. In R. J. Corsini (Ed.), *Encyclopedia of psychology* (2nd ed., Vol.1) (pp. 352–361). New York: John Wiley & Sons.

Buchta, R. (1988). Deliberate intoxication of young children and pets with drugs: A survey of an adolescent population in a private practice. *American Journal of the Diseases of Children, 142*, 701–702.

Caputo, A. A., Brodsky, S. L., & Kemp, S. (2000). Understandings and experiences of cruelty: An exploratory report. *The Journal of Social Psychology, 140*, 649–660.

Cavallieri, M. (2004, July 9). In carcere chi abbandona gli animali. OK a norme che proteggono cani e gatti. *La Repubblica*.

Cirm. (2003). Ha mai avuto un animale domestico? *Quark, 31*, 106.

Dadds, M. R., Whiting, C., Bunn, P., Fraser, J. A., Charlson, J. H., & Pirola-Merlo, A. (2004). Measurement of cruelty in children: The cruelty to animals inventory. *Journal of Abnormal Child Psychology, 32*, 321–334.

Driscoll, J. W. (1992). Attitudes toward animal use. *Anthrozoös, 5*, 32–39.

Eurispes. (2004, November 19). *Giovani 2004*. ANSA. Press release.

Flynn, C. P. (1999a). Animal abuse in childhood and later support for interpersonal violence in families. *Society and Animals, 7*, 161–172.

Flynn, C. P. (1999b). Exploring the link between corporal punishment and children's cruelty to animals. *Journal of Marriage and the Family, 61*, 971–981.

Flynn, C. P. (2000). Why family professionals can no longer ignore violence toward animals. *Family Relations, 49*, 87–95.

Flynn, C. P. (2001). Acknowledging the "zoological connection": A sociological analysis of animal cruelty. *Society and Animals, 9*, 71–87.

Fonzi, A. (1997). *Il bullismo in Italia*. Firenze: Giunti.

Francone, M., & Cattelan, A. (2004). Carnivori o vegetariani? In M. Falvo (Ed.), Gli animali e gli italiani. Rapporto LAV 2004 – IV Edizione. *Impronte, 8*, 12–13.

Goldstein, A. P. (1994). Aggression. In R. J. Corsini (Ed.), *Encyclopedia of psychology* (2nd ed., Vol.1) (pp. 39–43). New York: John Wiley & Sons.

Groebel, J., & Hinde, R. A. (Eds.). (1991). *Aggression and War*. Cambridge, UK: Cambridge University Press.

Guadagna, G. (2004). Circhi con animali. In M. Falvo (Ed.), Gli animali e gli italiani. Rapporto LAV 2004 – IV Edizione. *Impronte, 8*, 12–13.

Guymer, E. C., Mellor, D., Luk, E. S. L., & Pearse, V. (2001). The development of a screening questionnaire for childhood cruelty to animals. *Journal of Child Psychology and Psychiatry, 42*, 1057–1063.

Henry, B. C. (2006). Empathy, home environment, and attitudes toward animals in relation to animal abuse. *Anthrozoös, 19*, 17–34.

Hensley, C., & Tallichet, S. E. (2005a). Animal cruelty motivations: Assessing demographic and situational influences. *Journal of Interpersonal Violence, 20*, 1429–1443.

Hensley, C., & Tallichet, S. E. (2005b). Learning to be cruel?: Exploring the onset and frequency of animal cruelty. *International Journal of Offender Therapy and Comparative Criminology, 49*, 37–47.

Hoffman, M. L., & Levine, L. E. (1976). Early sex differences in empathy. *Developmental Psychology, 12*, 557–558.

Kardiner, A. (1939). *The Individual and His Society.* New York: Columbia University Press.

Kellert, S. R. (1985). Attitudes toward animals: Age-related development among children. *Journal of Environmental Education, 16*, 29–39.

Kellert, S. R., & Felthous, A. R. (1985). Childhood cruelty toward animals among criminals and noncriminals. *Human Relations, 38*, 1113–1129.

La Civiltà Cattolica. (1999). Gli animali hanno "diritti"? *La Civiltà Cattolica, 1*, 319–331.

LAV-Lega Anti Vivisezione. (2004, November 11). *Animali. SOS maltrattamenti.* Press release.

Lewchanin, S., & Zimmerman, E. (2000). *Clinical Assessment of Juvenile Animal Cruelty.* Brunswick, ME: Biddle Publishing Company and Audenreed Press.

Lugli, M. (2004, July 15). Notte al Verano, caccia ai satanisti. *La Repubblica.*

Merz-Perez, L., Heide, K. M., & Silverman, I. J. (2001). Childhood cruelty to animals and subsequent violence against humans. *International Journal of Offender Therapy and Comparative Criminology, 45*, 556–573.

Miller, K. S., & Knutson, J. F. (1997). Reports of severe physical punishment and exposure to animal cruelty by inmates convicted of felonies and by university students. *Child Abuse and Neglect, 21*, 59–82.

Offord, D. R., Boyle, M. H., & Racine, Y. A. (1991). The epidemiology of antisocial behavior in childhood and adolescence. In D. J. Pepler & K. H. Rubin (Eds.), *The development and treatment of childhood aggression* (pp. 31–54). Hillsdale, NJ: Lawrence Erlbaum Associates.

Olweus, D. (1993). *Bullying at School. What We Know and What We Can Do.* Oxford, UK: Blackwell.

Pagani, C. (1999). Bambini che maltrattano gli animali. *Psicologia Contemporanea. 153*, 30–37.

Pagani, C. (2000a). Education and the problem of violence. In V. Scalera (Ed.), *Investigations in and for Teaching. In-service Teacher Training and Quality of Education* (pp. 271–274). Milano: Franco Angeli.

Pagani, C. (2000b). Perception of a common fate in human-animal relations and its relevance to our concern for animals. *Anthrozoös, 13*, 66–73.

Pagani, C. (2007). Foreword to the Italian edition of Ascione, F. R. *Children and Animals: Exploring the Roots of Kindness and Cruelty (Bambini e animali: le radici dell'affetto e della crudeltà).* Torino: Edizioni Cosmopolis.

Pagani, C., Robustelli, F., & Ascione, F. R. (2007). Italian Youths' Attitudes Toward, and Concern for Animals. *Anthrozoös, 20*, 275–293.

Pellegrini, A. D. (1998). Bullies and victims in school: A Review and Call for Research. *Journal of Applied Developmental Psychology, 2*, 165–176.

Piaget, J. (1928). *Judgment and Reasoning in the Child.* London: Routledge & Kegan Paul. (Original work published 1924.)

Piaget, J. (1965). The Moral Judgment of the Child. New York: Free Press. (Original work published 1932.)

Piper, H., Johnson, M., Myers, S., & Pritchard, J. (2003). Children and young people harming animals: Intervention through PSHE? *Research Papers in Education, 18*, 197–213.

Pocar, V. (1999). La civiltà cattolica e gli animali. *Bioetica, 2*, 316–321.

Politi, M. (1999, February 19). Lite gesuiti-animalisti sui diritti delle bestie. *La Repubblica.*

Ramirez, J. M. (Ed.). (1994). *Violence—Some Alternatives.* Madrid: Centreur.

Ramirez, J. M., Hinde, R. A., & Groebel, J. (Eds.). (1987). *Essays on Violence.* Seville: University of Seville Press.

Raupp, C. D. (1999). Treasuring, trashing or terrorizing: adult outcomes of childhood socialization about companion animals. *Society and Animals, 7*, 141–159.

Robustelli, F. (2003). Violence, rationality, education. In M. S. Dajani & A. Nadler (Eds.), *Social and Psychological Factors in Conflict and its Resolution: The Mid-Eastern and European*

Experience (pp. 123–124). Brussels: European Commission.

Robustelli, F., & Pagani, C. (1994). Bambini e animali. *Bambini, 5*, 10–17.

Robustelli, F., & Pagani, C. (1996). L'educazione contro la violenza. *Psicologia contemporanea, 136*, 4–10.

Robustelli, F., & Pagani, C. (2005). Le variabili della violenza umana. *Psicologia contemporanea, 187*, 60–63.

Rowan, A. N. (1999). Cruelty and abuse to animals: A typology. In F. R. Ascione & P. Arkow (Eds.), *Child Abuse, Domestic Violence, and Animal Abuse* (pp. 328–334). West Lafayette, IN: Purdue University Press.

Schiff, K-G., Louw, D. A., & Ascione, F. R. (1999). Animals relations in childhood and later violent behavior against humans. *Acta Criminologica, 12*, 77–86.

Singer, P. (1990). *Animal Liberation*. New York: Avon Books.

Smith, P. K. (1991). The Silent nightmare: Bullying and victimization in school peer groups. *The Psychologist, 4*, 243–248.

Smith, P. K., Cowie, H., Olafsson, R. F., & Liefooghe, A. P. D. (2002). Definitions of bullying: A comparison of terms used, and age and gender differences, in a fourteen-country international comparison. *Child Development, 73*, 1119–1133.

Smorti, A. (a cura di). (2003). Nucleo monotematico. Bullying e prepotenze: ricerche sul significato. *Età evolutiva, 74*, 47–91.

Thompson, L. L., & Gullone, E. (2003). The children's treatment of animals questionnaire (CTAQ): A psychometric investigation. *Society and Animals, 11*, 1–15.

Troiano, C. (2002a). Il business dei canili e il traffico di cani. In C. Troiano, Rapporto zoomafia 2002. *Impronte, 3*, 14–15.

Troiano, C. (2002b). Nessun cane nasce killer. *Impronte, 9*, 21.

Troiano, C. (2004). Zoomafia. In M. Falvo (Ed.), Gli animali e gli italiani. Rapporto LAV 2004 – IV Edizione. *Impronte, 8*, 59–63.

Troiano, C. (2005). L'Italia che maltratta. *Impronte 5*, 11.

Vukovic, E. C. (2003, December 20). Dalla parte dei pettirossi. *D di Repubblica*.

Wells, D. L., & Hepper, P. G. (1995). Attitudes to animal use in children. *Anthrozoös, 8*, 159–170.

Appendix
Questionnaire (11–12 Year Form)
A Survey on Children's Relationships with Animals

We would like to understand children's relationships with animals better. Can you help us? Answer the following questions clearly and frankly. The questionnaire is **anonymous**. This means that nobody will know who answered the various questions. You have only to write **F**, if you are a girl, or **M**, if you are a boy, in the top left-hand square. Depending on the case, you can answer either by placing a cross inside the square you have chosen or by using your own words. If you want to answer in greater detail and the space is not enough, you can ask for one or more sheets of paper. On these sheets you will write the number of the question you are going to answer (or the number and the letter of the question). Your questionnaire will not be graded. Do not care about misspellings or grammatical errors. Do not worry if you have to express ideas and feelings that might be different from ours. Furthermore, do not worry if you have to write something we might not like. You have **2 hours** to complete your work.

1) **Do you have a pet (or pets)?** YES ☐ NO ☐
   If YES:
1a) What kind of pet? (If you have more than one pet, mention all of them)
1b) How old were you when it/they began living in your home?
1c) How long has it/have they lived in your home?
1d) What do you feel for it/them?
   I am very fond of it/them ☐   I am somewhat fond of it/them ☐
   I am a little fond of it/them ☐   I feel indifferent toward it/them ☐
   I feel hostile toward it/them ☐

2) **Did you have a pet (or pets) in the past?** YES ☐ NO ☐
   If YES:
2a) What kind of pet? (If you had more than one pet, mention all of them)
2b) How old were you when it/they began living in your home?
2c) How long did it/did they live in your home?
2d) What did you feel for it/them?
   I was very fond of it/them ☐   I was somewhat fond of it/them ☐
   I was a little fond of it/them ☐   I felt indifferent toward it/them ☐
   I felt hostile toward it/them ☐

3) **Have you ever lost a pet (for example, the animal died, was given away to another family, you could no longer find it, etc.)?** YES ☐ NO ☐
   If YES:
3a) How did you lose it? (Write what happened. Also write what your family said or did on that occasion)
3b) How did you feel when you lost it?
   I suffered a lot ☐   I suffered somewhat ☐
   I suffered a little ☐   I did not suffer at all ☐
   other (describe) ☐

3c) How do you feel now when you think of your lost pet?
    I suffer a lot ☐   I suffer somewhat ☐
    I suffer a little ☐   I do not suffer at all ☐
    other (describe) ☐

4) **Answer this question only <u>if you have or if you had</u> a pet:**
4a) Have you ever worried about bad things happening to your pet?   YES ☐   NO ☐
    If YES:
4b) Explain what your worries are/were.

5) **Answer these questions only <u>if you have never had</u> a pet:**
5a) Why have you never had a pet?
5b) Would you have liked to have a pet?   YES ☐   NO ☐

6) **Did you ever see anyone hurt an animal (for example, by teasing, torturing, wounding, or killing it)?**   YES ☐   NO ☐
    If YES:
6a) Was it your pet?   YES ☐   NO ☐
6b) What kind of animal was it?
6c) Who was hurting it?
6d) Write what this person/these persons did to the animal.
6e) What was the animal doing while it was being hurt?
6f) How many times did you see this person/these persons hurt an animal?
6g) How old were you when you saw someone hurt an animal?
6h) How did you feel about it?
    I suffered a lot ☐   I suffered somewhat ☐
    I suffered a little ☐   I felt indifferent ☐
    other (describe) ☐
6i) How do you feel about it now?
    I suffer a lot ☐   I suffer somewhat ☐
    I suffer a little ☐   I feel indifferent ☐
    other (describe) ☐
6j) Why was/were this person/these persons hurting an animal?
6k) Did you speak to anyone about what you saw?   YES ☐   NO ☐
    If YES:
6l) Who did you speak to about it?
6m) What were you told?

7) **Did you ever hurt an animal (for example, by teasing, torturing, wounding or killing it)?**   YES ☐   NO ☐
    If YES:
7a) Was it your pet?   YES ☐   NO ☐
7b) What kind of animal was it?
7c) Were you alone?   YES ☐   NO ☐
7d) If you were not alone, who was with you?
7e) What did you do to the animal?
7f) On that occasion did you think the animal was suffering?   YES ☐   NO ☐
7g) What was the animal doing while you were hurting it?
7h) How many times did you hurt an animal?
7i) How old were you when you hurt an animal?
7j) Try to explain why you hurt an animal.

7k) Write about your feelings while you were hurting an animal.

7l) How do you feel now if you think about that?

I feel very sorry ☐   I feel somewhat sorry ☐

I feel a little sorry ☐   I feel indifferent ☐

other (describe) ☐

7m) Did you speak to anyone about what you did?   YES ☐   NO ☐

If YES:

7n) Who did you speak to?

7o) What were you told?

8) Are you afraid of <u>animals in general?</u>   YES ☐   NO ☐

If YES:

8a) Why are you afraid of them?

9) Are you afraid of <u>some animals?</u>   YES ☐   NO ☐

If YES:

9a) What kind/s of animals are you afraid of?

9b) Why are you afraid of them?

10) Has an animal ever been a source of comfort for you in difficult times?   YES ☐ NO ☐

If YES:

10a) What kind/s of animal/s was/were a source of comfort for you?

11) How do you feel when you see road kill?

I feel very sorry ☐   I feel somewhat sorry ☐

I feel a little sorry ☐   I feel indifferent ☐

other (describe) ☐

12) Are you in favor of hunting?   YES ☐   NO ☐

13) Are you in favor of the use of furs and leather clothes?   YES ☐   NO ☐

14) Are you in favor of the use of animals in circuses?   YES ☐   NO ☐

15) Are you in favor of zoos?   YES ☐   NO ☐

Animal Abuse: An Evolving Issue in Japanese Society

Mika Maruyama
Portland State University

Frank R. Ascione[1]
Utah State University

Introduction

Japan was once called "one of the safest countries in the world." Living in a collectivistic culture, people were very caring and helped each other naturally. Children played outside with many friends until it got dark, and they developed problem-solving and interpersonal skills through their play. When children misbehaved, there were always adults who gave children a scolding even if they were strangers to the children, and children always respected adults' advice. It was the nature of the society that all adults raise any children in a community. Living in such a society, children naturally felt protection from adults and a fear of crime was rarely an issue both for children and adults.

However, today's children do not know that Japan was once a safe country. Today, a significant number of Japanese, including children, become both victims and offenders of crimes and abuses, and every child faces the fear of crime in his or her daily life. News of juvenile delinquencies, child abuse, and domestic violence is reported daily, and significant numbers of people lose their lives due to these social issues. Of course, abuses and crimes did exist decades ago, however, they were not reported by media as frequently as today.

When Japan was regarded as the safest country in early 1970s, the Ministry of Justice (1977) discussed reasons why Japan had such a lower rate of crimes. It pointed out that (1) Japan was a racially homogeneous nation; (2) Japan had a centralization of administrative government; (3) Japan had a uniform culture; (4) people did not differ significantly in their economic status;

(5) most people were well educated; (6) economics and family lifestyle were stable; (7) traditionally, people unofficially controlled safety in their own society; and (8) officially, criminal administration of justice was effectively operated. However, Japanese society has dramatically changed in the last 30 years, becoming racially and culturally diverse, and the collapse of the "bubble" economy in early 1990s has brought about the present economic recession, which may be affecting family structure and many other social values negatively. Many crimes and abuses may be a product of the competitive and stressful society into which Japan has evolved. The fact that the backgrounds of criminals are significantly different from decades ago is also one of the reasons people have started paying attention to violence in society. Today, people who are supposed to have high moral standards are committing crimes. For instance, six students who organized a club, called "The Rabbit Hunters," ran over rabbits with their cars, conducted autopsies on the rabbits, and put photographs of these autopsies on their website, which was advertised at their school ("Miyazakidai" 2005). Ironically, these six students are medical school students who are going to be doctors presumably dedicated to saving humans' lives. Such examples make people unwilling to trust others, even their own family members.

In addition, each social issue that Japan faces today is closely linked with other social issues. Ascione and Arkow (1999) reported that social issues, such as domestic violence, child abuse, and animal maltreatment, are closely linked to one another. Specifically, they noted that the cycle of violence often started with violence toward animals, and such violence against animals may consequently be linked to child maltreatment and domestic violence. Empirical research has also consistently found high correlations between criminal activity and histories of animal abuse (Arkow, 1998; Lockwood & Ascione, 1998).

The purposes of this chapter are to identify the background of these social problems in Japan and to explain possible mechanisms that have produced more criminals and abusers under the Japanese social system. Although we discuss each social problem separately, we focus on how each social issue is linked to others. After discussing Japanese social background, we address violence against animals and how that relates to children. Abusing animals is often an early symptom of later interpersonal violence (Ascione, 1999), and animal abuse by young children has been gaining attention in Japan. Specifically, the number of brutal crimes committed by young children has dramatically increased, and these young perpetrators often have histories of animal abuses. Thus, it is important to understand the social context that leads young children to cruel behaviors toward animals and its spillover to other types of violence. Throughout the chapter, we discuss how children face these social issues, and how the legal system functions to help people, specifically young children in Japan. Moreover, we discuss possible mechanisms contributing to cases where Japanese society and individuals become dysfunctional. We believe understanding the lives of children as abuse victims or as offenders is important, and that it will help to develop prevention and intervention efforts and a better society.

Cultural and Societal Background of Japan

Japan has been well protected from outside invasions and maintained its isolated culture and societal values for over 2,000 years (Sugihara & Katsurada, 2002). Historically, Japanese culture includes very strong norms relating to gender-appropriate behaviors. Men were taught to be strong and encouraged to exert control and dominance over women while women were encouraged to be reserved, subservient, and to obey men (Sugihara & Katsurada, 1999). Despite shifts toward egalitarianism in gender role ideology, traditional gender roles are still highly valued and strongly encouraged by the majority of people in Japan (Sugihara & Katsurada, 1999).

However, Japan has begun to change demographically and has advanced socioeconomically over the past 30 years (Hashizume, 2000). Specifically, westernization in Japan began after World War II, and Japanese economic power gained its stable status in the world, changes that encouraged the society to become more international. Facing westernization, Japanese culture and values have been blended with western cultures. Many people, especially young people or feminists, have come to feel that the social status assigned to various groups based on their gender and seniority within the traditional, hierarchical society is unfair. Although a hierarchically based social status system is less intensive today as a result of educational changes after WWII and the feminist movements of the 1960s (Sugihara & Katsurada, 2000), traditional social values still remain strong.

Confucianism has had a tremendous influence on Japanese people and society (Ornatowski, 1996; Sugihara & Katsurada, 1999). Confucianism focuses on the collective, and values a harmonious society with a hierarchical social structure. Structures within economic, political, educational, and family systems have been greatly influenced by Confucian values (Ornatowski, 1996). It teaches the values of loyalty, piety, sacrifice for the common welfare, and respect for superiors and authorities as well as emphasizing internal strengths such as integrity, righteousness, and warm heartedness. It also teaches people to obey their superiors and men to dominate women and children. By envisioning a strict hierarchical society and forcing a strong moral pressure to conform to their socially expected roles (e.g., husband–wife, father–son, employer–employee, etc.), Confucianism aimed to create social harmony (Winfield, Mizuno, & Beaudoin, 2000). Confucianism became a system of social ethics rather than a religion (Winfield et al., 2000).

However, some values of Confucianism may also be affecting people negatively. For instance, some teachers of Confucianism may be unconsciously discouraging victims or other vulnerable individuals to seek help because many people believe that to stand pain without complaining and to remain silent are the correct ways to show the internal strength that Confucianism values so highly. In addition, such values traditionally have discouraged people from "burdening" others with their problems, and taught people to highly value "perseverance" (Knight et al., 2002). Consequently, some people may maintain the mistaken belief that violence from men or authorities is unavoidable as part of their hierarchical cultural values. Moreover, people deeply fear being stigmatized by being unique (e.g., claiming victimization and seeking help) and disturbing social harmony (e.g., social misperception that Japan is the safest country), because such a disturbance is likely to result in complete social isolation (e.g., "the nail that stands out gets pounded down"). Consequently, this social value may be causing significant problems and seriously affecting Japanese people's psychological health today. In the following sections, we discuss serious social problems that Japanese society faces. Further, we explore how to begin to address these problems and suggest some changes that might support building a psychologically healthier society in the future.

Juvenile Crimes and Delinquencies

Crisis of Japanese Society: Significant Increases in Violent Juvenile Crimes

Crime rates, especially serious violent crimes committed by juveniles, have risen sharply in the last three decades. This includes extremely serious crimes such as the brutal murder of a family member or teacher, attacking homeless people, and serial killings committed by young children. The National Police Agency (2005b) reported that the number of juveniles (aged 14 to 19) who committed penal code offenses (i.e., felonious crimes, violent crimes, theft, intellectual offenses, and sexual crimes) in 2004 was 134,852 (see Table 1). This figure (16.8 per 1,000) was 6.7 times higher than the rates of crimes committed by adults (i.e., 2.5 per 1,000), and the number of penal code offenders per 1,000 juveniles (aged younger than 20) has significantly increased from the post-war period compared with the number of adult offenders (see Table 2).

Although the current law does not apply to young criminals who are younger than 14, the increasing rates of children who committed crimes but were not punished for their behaviors because they were younger than 14 cannot be ignored. Even though the number of violent criminal offenses (i.e., murder, injury, arson, and rape) committed by individuals between the ages of 14 and 19 in 2004 was relatively small (1,588; National Police Agency, 2005b), the brutality of the crimes being committed by young children is very disturbing.

What Made Japan a Competitive Society?

Dolly (1993) pointed out that the level of stress Japanese children experience due to the expectations

Table 1 Trend in Numbers of Juvenile Penal Code Offenders (Aged 14–19) in Japan (Adopted from the National Police Agency, 2005b)

Year	1995	2004
Number of offenders	126,249	134,852
Number per 1,000	12.5	16.8
Felonious crimes[1]	1,291	1,588
Violent crimes[2]	15,449	11,435
Robbery	81,060	76,636
Intellectual offenses[3]	505	1,241
Sexual crimes	492	344
Other penal codes	27,452	43,608
Number of juvenile offenders per whole penal code offenders	43.1%	34.7%

[1] Felonious crimes include murder, rape, arson, and robbery.
[2] Violent crimes include bodily injury and threat of violence.
[3] Intellectual offenses include fraud, embezzlement, forgery, and malfeasance.

and demands placed on them by their schools and by society have increased considerably. The highly competitive society places great value on academic achievement (called "cramming and examination hell"), and the educational system is extremely demanding. Because Japan was devastated in World War II and had to reconstruct its society in the aftermath of the war, all aspects of Japanese society, including its educational system, became very competitive. This competitiveness continues unabated today.

Most schools stress success in examinations and encourage students to achieve high grades. In Japan, school diplomas are strongly emphasized and many students spend their time at *juku* (cram school) in order to pass. Dolly (1993) commented that *juku* plays a major role in ensuring the success of Japanese students on national and international tests. It is reported that more than two million secondary students are enrolled in *juku*, which specialize in intensive courses that go beyond the standard curricula (Hitchcock, 2000). Children as young as 2 are now experiencing examinations in order to enter elite kindergartens, and most preschoolers master how to read and write, and can even do simple computations (Dolly, 1993). Typically, students spend 7 hours at their schools, and additional hours to study at home or in *juku*. Most parents believe that the regular school curriculum fails to provide

Table 2 Trend in Numbers in Penal Code Offenders in Japan (Adopted from "White Paper on Crimes" The Ministry of Justice, 2005)

Year	1946	1950	1960	1970	1980	1990	2000	2003
Juvenile offenders*	111,790	158,426	196,682	224,943	269,769	244,122	193,260	203,684
Number per 1,000	6.7	9.2	9.7	13.3	15.7	13.2	13.8	15.5
Adults offenders	333,694	458,297	413,565	883,254	653,958	683,688	987,359	1087,640
Number per 1,000	8.4	10.1	7.4	12.6	8.1	7.5	9.8	10.5

* Juvenile offenders are younger than 20 years old.

sufficient preparation for the examinations. It is evident that this extreme pressure causes considerable suffering for many children. Jobs that are secure and well-paid can be attained only by attending elite universities, which only students with the highest marks from top high schools are able to attend. Many people have the illusion that their future will be successful if one goes to a good school. This idea may be a product of Japanese competitive society, which often measures people only by status or achievement. Additionally, students are facing considerable uncertainty regarding their future careers due to a prolonged economic recession and rising unemployment. The employment rate for university graduates was 65.6 percent in 1998 (Hitchcock, 2000). In response, many parents have intensified the already high levels of pressure they exert on their children to achieve academic success in order to obtain a solid job in the future.

Though it cannot be denied that achieving academic success itself is a benefit to children, and learning at the *juku* will certainly help to make a superior scholar, what *juku* teaches students is how to solve exam questions effectively within a short time. Students memorize many equations that help to save time. Because there are always correct answers in examinations, Machizawa (2000b) pointed out that children lack the creativity and autonomy that are needed to develop in their life due to the lack of experiences outside of *juku*. In addition, because many children spend most of their time either at the school or at *juku*, they don't have much time to interact with friends, and these children lack the opportunity to develop their social skills. Their classmates may be seen more as rivals than as friends. In this highly competitive society, many children are continually under stress because they are always afraid of falling behind others in class.

The financial costs borne by families are also significant. Machizawa (2001) reported that approximately 40% of a family budget is used for children's education. Because compulsory education ends at the junior high school, parents are obliged to pay for children's schooling fees during high school in addition to the cost of *juku*. In many cases, both parents are required to work outside the home in order to pay for the children's education. Oftentimes, parents are forced to work in different locations on different schedules in order to meet the cost of their children's academic training. Further, because children spend so much time at school or *juku*, there is little time left for family life. Lack of family bonding and parents' (specifically fathers) under-involvement in children's activities due to conflicting schedules may be affecting the psychological development of children.

Acknowledging the effect of the competitive educational system on students, the Ministry of Science and Education reduced school attendance from 6 days to 5 days a week in 2002. Facing the shortened schedule, most elementary schools cut extra programs, such as moral education, in order to accommodate the shortened hours. However, students are going to *juku* on weekends (Dolly, 1993). Ironically, changes in school hours designed to prevent unreasonably high demands did not reduce their stress. Enomoto (1996) pointed out that one of the significant reasons for student suicide was school-related, and he summarized the reasons that caused suicide from 1984 to 1993 from the report of the Metropolitan Police (see Table 3).

In the most updated statistical report (Ministry of Health, Labor, and Welfare, 2005a), suicide is one of the leading causes of death for people between 15 and 19 (see Table 4). Suicide has been consistently ranked the first or second highest cause of death across the years, and this trend applies to those between 10 and 64 years old (Ministry of Health, Labor, and Welfare, 2005a). Moreover, it is reported that the number of people who attempted suicide is 10 times higher than the number who committed a suicide (Takahashi, 1997). Though Japan recovered from the loss from WWII and became a

Table 3 The Reasons for Suicide Attempted by Students Between 1984 and 1993 (*"Library Seishunki-no Kokoro no SOS 9," Enomoto, 1996*)

	Male		Female	
1	Matter related to school	27.1%	Matter related to school	21.3%
2	Mental disorder	14.1%	Mental disorder	18.1%
3	Matter related to family	11.5%	Matter related to relationships	15.8%
4	Sickness	9.2%	Sickness	13.8%
5	Matter related to relationships	8.8%	Matter related to family	12.0%

Matter Related to School	Male	Female
Slump in education	362	143
Trouble with friends	109	100
Suffering/pain for entrance examination	167	36
Failure on entrance examination	88	25
Others	241	117
	967	421
	(27.1%)	(21.3%)

materially wealthy country, many Japanese may feel loneliness or stress, which may link to suicide.

When Mothers' and Children's Relationships Become Distorted

In addition to pressure from society, the structure and roles within families influence children's mental health. For instance, Spinrad and Losaya (1999) explored how parents' affective responses influence children's personality development and encouraged (or discouraged) the development of empathy-related responding and moral behavior. In their studies,

Table 4 The Causes of Death of People Aged Between 15 and 19 (Adopted from the data from Ministry of Health, Labor, and Welfare, 2005a)

	1958		2003	
	Male	**Female**	**Male**	**Female**
1	Accident (25.7%)	Suicide (29.6%)	Accident (43.5%)	Suicide (28.1%)
2	Suicide (25.2%)	Tuberculosis (10.1%)	Suicide (21.5%)	Accident (25.6%)

parents' positive affect and encouragement were associated with children's sympathetic responses. They found that a parent's warm support for the child's own decisions was necessary for his or her well-being. In contrast, many children suffer as they face tremendous pressure for academic achievement from their parents. Cultural beliefs emphasizing that greater effort will inevitably lead to better performance lead many mothers to push their children to engage in ever-increasing academically oriented efforts during their school years. Many children may study hard, not for themselves, but to live up to their parents' expectations.

Japanese culture still emphasizes that the father should work outside the home and the mother should stay home and take care of children. Thus, many fathers typically leave parenting responsibility to mothers. Culturally, people may place more weight on work than the value of family life, and many fathers stay at work even on holidays. This may reflect the lifetime employment system and cultural value of loyalty to work. However, at the same time this is also correlated with a high rate of suicide for males younger than 65 years old (Ministry of Health, Labor, and Welfare, 2005a).

Mothers who are responsible for raising their children and spend significant time at home (though many mothers have started to work part-time today) tend to believe their children are their life and put all their priority on making their children's lives better. Such mothers may expect reciprocal rewards because they contribute a significant portion of the family budget, and children's statuses (e.g., which school they attend, what scores they receive on tests) become parents' achievements. It is common that many mothers introduce themselves by announcing the names of their husband's company or children's school names. This unique "child-centered family structure" may create situations where "everything is for children" and children are treated as kings or queens.

Machizawa (2001) noted that there are no other countries with parents who so overprotect their children. This overprotection may contribute to some children have excessively high self-esteem, and sometimes these children commit crimes. Children with such high self-esteem are also more likely to refuse to go to school, and later this may be linked to *hikikomori. Hikikomori* are defined as people who never leave their bedrooms for more than 5 months and avoid interacting with others in a society (Machizawa, 2003). For instance, 60% of children who refuse to go to school reasoned that school bullying is the reason (Machizawa, 2001). Because these children have such high self-esteem, they may take trivial sarcasm as bullying, and too easily experience stress. As is common with juvenile crime offenders, they try to fill up their lack of communication ability by achieving academic success to keep their high self-esteem (Machizawa, 2003). When they experience a breakdown, some may try to gain attention by committing a crime. In fact, many juvenile crimes (e.g., incident in Kobe, bus hijacking in Saga, etc., to be discussed below) are committed by such children.

In addition to increases of serious juvenile crimes, family style may also be linked to the current increase of domestic violence in Japan. Generally, "domestic violence" indicates violence between partners, such as husband to wife or husband to children. However, the numbers of domestic violence incidents by children against parents are significant in Japan, and this tendency is seen only in Japan (Machizawa, 2003). As possible reasons, Machizawa (2001) explained that overprotection from parents and high expectations for academic success can be a form of emotionally abusing children.

For instance, once a common goal of mother and the child (e.g., passing the high school entrance examination, achieving certain grades in school) does not come true, many mothers are more likely to be more disappointed with the results than their children. Faced with their mothers' disappointment, some children start to use violence against them and blame their failure on their parents. In addition, many children are treated like kings or queens so that they can concentrate on studies, and the children treat their parents, especially mothers, like slaves. This historical background may spur children's oppressive behaviors toward mothers. This is one unique fact that may explain why the rates of domestic violence by children against parents, specifically to mothers, are so high in Japan.

Another example of the results Japan's unique family style may create is a relatively high rate of incest between mother and son compared with the rates in other countries (e.g., the United States). It is often reported that sexual abuse is more often perpetrated by a child's father than mother in the United States. However, Minami (1984) reported that more Japanese mothers approach their sons for sexual intercourse. Mishima (2005) pointed out this unique characteristic by referring to a report from the tele-

phone hotline service regarding contraception in 1979. It was reported that they received 521 calls from 1977 to 1978. Among these calls, 110 reports were about incest between mother and son while only 12 reports were about incest between father and daughter (Arakawa, 1979).

Minami (1984) listed three key points that may prompt incest between mother and son: competitive academic environment, lack of communication between father and mother, and lack of communication between father and son. Wives do not communicate with their busy husbands, but husbands expect their wives to manage all housework and to take care of their children. Lonely Japanese mothers may start diverting all their love to their sons and may start to see their sons as if they were their partners. Because their sons study all day in their rooms for examinations, mothers may want to get rid of their sons' frustration or stress through sexual intercourse. Some mothers worry that their sons might sleep with prostitutes to relieve their stress, and noted they would rather sleep with their sons than worry that their sons would receive sexually transmitted diseases by sleeping with strangers.

Machizawa (2003) reported that while 80% to 90% of patients who have borderline personality disorder in the United States are victims of domestic violence (40% are victims of sexual abuses), 62.7% of Japanese patients are from a family with parental overprotection. Additionally, Someya et al. (2000) found that more panic disorder patients rated their parents as both more rejecting and overprotective than did the control subjects. In sum, the high levels of stress most children experience and unique family structure may be factors driving them to engage in violent behavior or to develop other forms of psychopathology. One of the unique characteristics of serious juvenile crimes is they are often committed by highly educated children. According to Schreiber (1997), about half of Japanese juvenile offenders were from poor or dysfunctional families during the 1950s. However, by 1995, more than 90% of young offenders were from well-educated, upper or middle class, dual-parent families.

Not all serious crimes are committed by highly intelligent children, but the fact that many children suffer from high academic pressure for scholastic achievement in education cannot be denied. Also, such social factors strongly affect Japanese family styles, which are producing children who do not acquire the ability to be patient, solve conflict with others, and develop communication abilities because of lack of experience and being spoiled by their parents. Many children who grow up in such a society do not know "what is morally wrong to do" (Maeda, 2002). Moreover, it cannot be denied that many animals are prone to be the target of those children's stress. Cases such as the murder of an 11-year-old boy in Kobe, Japan, provide shocking examples.

Case in Kobe and Other Significant Cases

Boy A: Case in Kobe [Detail is retrieved from "Shounen A: 14 saino shouzou" (Takayama, 1998), and "Jigokuno kisetu: Sakakibara Seito ga itabasho" (Takayama, 2001)]. According to Takayama (1998, 2001), an 11-year-old boy was reported missing in May 1997. Three days later, police found his head on the gate to a junior high school. A memo was placed in his mouth, which indicated that this savage act had been perpetrated as, "revenge against the compulsory educational system and the society that created it." Two months before the severed head was deposited on the gate, two girls had been stabbed, one of them fatally. Many animals' horribly abused carcasses had been left on the school's gate or were found in the same community. The murderer even sent a provocative letter to the police and the newspapers. Finally, 32 days after the severed head incident, the murderer was arrested. Shockingly, this brutal crime had been committed by a 14-year-old boy (referred to as "Boy A").

Boy A was born in a traditional family. His friends from elementary school described him as bright and popular. However, as he entered junior high school, where academic pressure increases significantly, he became withdrawn and uncommunicative. He was bullied at school and later became a bully himself. When he was a fifth grader, his grandmother passed away and he became fascinated with death. He began by killing frogs or slugs to understand more about death and he performed many necropsies. Soon, his targets changed to larger animals, such as cats and pigeons, and by the age of 13, Boy A had repeatedly abused and killed several different types of animals. In a macabre foreshadowing of events to come, he confessed to his teacher that his hobby was to kill insects, but he was afraid these insects would be turned into humans. By the age of 14, he had attacked three girls, killing one of his victims without a sense of guilt. By this time, many people had seen him kill animals. On May 24, Boy A met an 11-year-old male friend and choked him to death.

The next day, he returned to the place where he hid the body to sever the boy's neck. Later, he confessed that he was aroused and ejaculated while mutilating the body. After he cut off the head, he drank some of the blood and took more of it home. Amazingly, Boy A calmly answered all of the questions posed to him by police during multiple interrogation sessions. Although he was not diagnosed with any mental disorders, the court decided to put him into medical reformatory school because the law applied only for criminals older than 16 at this time. Thus, there was no law to hold this young offender liable or punish him for his crime.

Two aspects of Boy A's pathology deserve close attention: (1) Boy A's disturbing imaginary friend (which he called "invisible me"), and (2) the connections between brutality and his sexuality. From the entries in his diary, it is clear that he adored his imaginary friend, *Bamoidooki*, as he shares details of his attacks on his young victims. He records his appreciation of the success of the attacks (which he refers to as "sacred experiments) to this imaginary friend (see Appendix).

From his memoirs, it is obvious that he did not have any close relationships with other people. His parents also commented that he spent most of his time alone. From this statement, we can assume that this imaginary friend was created from Boy A's fantasies. Although Boy A wrote his diary as if they were discussing their experiments, Boy A and his imaginary friend were unlikely to have different opinions or conflicting ideas, especially because Boy A was not diagnosed with any mental disorder likely to support such conflict, such as dissociative identity disorder or schizophrenia. Together, his diary and comments of the people around him suggest that Boy A lacked the ability to communicate with other human beings possessing different opinions or thinking processes.

Subsequently, his lack of communication ability probably contributed to his twisted sexuality. Boy A confessed that he ejaculated while he mutilated the dead body. Generally, boys at his age start to show an interest in the opposite sex. His inability to communicate effectively with others may have led him to express his frustration in unhealthy behaviors. For instance, most young boys start masturbating during puberty. While this behavior is not in itself unhealthy, it is important to note that during this stage, the boys' sexual behaviors are solitary, which means they do not have to care about anyone else and do not communicate with anyone else. When boys move to the next stage, sexual intercourse with a partner, they are required to communicate with their partners because this behavior is usually the product of an agreement between two people. At this time, most boys learn how to communicate with their partners and move from masturbation to sexual intercourse as a part of normal human development. However, Boy A sought brutality and violence instead of developing relationships with others.

Subsequently, Boy A devoted himself to watching horror movies, which usually contain scenes of brutal violence. These brutal visions might have influenced this lonely young boy's perceptions of society. Without any interaction with others, the distorted ideas Boy A gathered from these media were not corrected. Although multiple reports on his animal abuse history from the community led to his arrest, it is unfortunate that people in his community did not report their observations much sooner, which might have saved both Boy A and his victims. Additional issues on relationships between sexuality and animal abuses will be discussed in the next section.

Other Notable Incidents. After the shocking news of Boy A's brutality, the Japanese Juveniles Acts changed its applied age from "at least 16 years old" to "at least 14 years old" in 2001. However, this change has not impacted the rate of juvenile crimes. For example, in 1998, a 13-year-old student stabbed his school teacher in the classroom. In 2000, a 17-year-old boy killed a 64-year-old woman who was a complete stranger just because he wanted to have the experience of killing someone (Fujii, 2001). Two days after this incident, a 17-year-old boy hijacked a bus and killed one passenger (Machizawa, 2000a). In 2003, a 12-year-old boy kidnapped and sexually molested a 4-year-old boy. When the 4-year-old screamed in pain and cried out for help after his tormentor cut his penis, the 14-year-old decided to drop the screaming child from the top of the parking structure to kill him ("Shocking news," 2003).

All of these young criminals were top students at high ranking schools. Even after they committed these crimes, their teachers or neighbors described them as very intelligent, well-behaved, and quiet children ("Shocking news," 2003). The 17-year-old boy who hijacked a bus later said that he was extremely offended by his parents' insistence that he go to *juku* despite his already outstanding perfor-

mance in school. So, he decided to hijack a bus to cause trouble for his parents.

In 2001, Mamoru Takuma, 40, rampaged through Ikeda elementary school, killing 8 students and severely hurting 13 other students as well as 2 teachers. He chose Ikeda because he had failed the entrance examination there. He felt that subsequent failures in his life stemmed from being unable to pass Ikeda's stringent entrance examination. He was executed by hanging in 2004, but apologies or regret for his conduct were hardly heard from him.

In 2004, 62 children (57 aged 14 to 19 years and 5 aged under 13 years) took another's life (National Police Agency, 2005b) and 784 students took their own lives (National Police Agency, 2005a). Compared with the previous year (96 children committed murder in 2003), the murder rate has declined. However, the rate of penal code offenses committed by children younger than 13 has been consistently over 20,000 since 1950, and the rate of penal code offenses committed by children aged 14 to 19 has also been consistently high. Further, although statistics from the National Police Agency (2005b) indicate that boys are indicted significantly more often for serious violent offenses than girls (75.5% versus 24.5%), brutal murders are still committed by young girls. For instance, in 2004, an 11-year-old girl savagely slashed the neck of her classmate and left her to bleed to death in the classroom.

Issues of School Violence and Bullying

Along with the issues of serious crime committed by youths, the issue of school violence and violence against teachers cannot be ignored. For instance, 4,416 incidents of violence against other students and 1,966 incidents of violence against teachers by students were reported in 2003 (Ministry of Science and Education, 2004). (See Table 5.) According to the Ministry of Science and Education, 2.7% of elementary schools (620 cases), 33.3% of junior high schools (3,446 cases), and 44.2% of high schools (1,819 cases) reported school violence incidents in 2003. Additionally, 11.9% of elementary schools (2,787 schools), 38% of junior high schools (3,934 schools), and 26.6% of high schools (1,094 schools) reported school bullying. Among these cases, it is not rare that junior high school students set fire to their schools, broke school windows at night, or killed school pets.

It is assumed that junior high school students may be spending significant time preparing for high school entrance examination, and they may suffer

Table 5 Rates of School Violence and Violence Against Teachers (National Police Agency, 2005b)

		School Violence		Violence Against Teachers	
		1995	2004	1995	2004
Total	Incidents	464	828	258	456
	Offenders	1,005	1,161	328	504
	Victims	624	924	317	525
Elementary school students	Incidents	–	14	–	2
	Offenders	–	25	–	2
	Victims	–	15	–	2
Junior high school students	Incidents	434	754	251	446
	Offenders	917	1,022	319	495
	Victims	582	840	310	515
High school students	Incidents	30	60	7	8
	Offenders	88	114	9	7
	Victims	42	69	7	8

from high pressure for academic achievement. This may be one of reasons why the rate of school violence or bullying among junior high school students is so high. The seriousness of school bullying and its effects on victims are significant. For instance, 94% of people who have dissociative identity disorder are victims of domestic violence (specifically, 40% were victims of sexual abuse) in the United States (Machizawa, 2000b). However, not only sexual abuse but also school bullying have become associated with dissociative identity disorder in Japan today. It is unclear whether the situation of school bullying is more serious (e.g., brutal physical attacks) or whether today's children are more easily hurt emotionally. However, the fact that many children suffer from mental illness due to school bullying cannot be ignored.

Facing this high rate of school violence, in 2004, the number of school teachers who took a leave of absence from teaching due to mental disorder (e.g., stress, depression) reached its highest rate ("The number of teachers," 2005). According to the report from the Ministry of Education, Culture, Sports, Science, and Technology (2004), among all teachers in Japan (921,600 teachers), 6,308 teachers were absent from school due to sickness in 2003. Among them, 56.4% claimed some kind of mental disorder, such as depression, and this was three times higher than the rate 10 years ago.

Generally, there are 40 students in each class, and one teacher has to take care of all students. Thus, it is naturally assumed that teachers do not have enough time and mental capacity to pay attention to all students. In addition, faced with fewer numbers of children due to the low birth rate in Japan, fewer young teachers are likely to be employed today. This may increase the generation gap between students and teachers, and this consequently makes teachers less likely to notice any behavioral or psychological changes in students and intervene early due to lack of communication.

The Effects of a Wealthy Society on Children

Living in a materially wealthy society, people can obtain almost everything very easily. Moreover, as technology advances, more new products are developed (e.g., Walkman, cellular phone, and video games), and often these products reduce contact with humans. Machizawa (2000a) commented that we can obtain whatever we want without effort, but this will also make people lose motivations in life. Such people are more likely to suffer from a sense of emptiness, and they are eager to have excitement and pleasure in their lives. Sometimes this leads to abuses or crimes, with brutality always getting worse because humans always look for more excitement.

People who cannot find a way to find their values or pleasures in life may also commit suicide. The rate of suicide in Japan (24.0 per 100,000; World Health Organization, 2005) is high; it is the third highest country in male suicide and the second highest in female suicide in the world (Ministry of Health, Labor, and Welfare, 2005a). Also, Machizawa (2000a) reported that people who have a desire to commit a suicide sometimes commit a murder as well. It may sound contradictory that as people become richer materially, the more they feel emptiness in Japan. However, other materially rich countries, such as the United States and Great Britain, have lower suicide rates (e.g., United States = 10.7; Britain = 7.0, per 100,000; World Health Organization, 2005). What is the difference between the United States and Japan, and why does it seem like the high rates of crimes and suicide are negative outcomes for the materially rich society in Japan today? There is no simple answer for this question. Yet Japanese collectivistic society should value each individual's differences instead of excluding each individual's unique characteristics from the society. For instance, while Americans regard lack of self-control as deviant, Japanese regard disrupting social harmony as deviant (Crystal & Stevenson, 1995). Though it is important to value their traditional cultural beliefs, people should learn the different cultural values and social norms of other countries through acculturation, and accept them accordingly. Further, it is most important that people who are in a position to directly change politics understand why the number of people who suffer from stress is increasing in Japan before these people commit a crime or suicide. Then, we hope they will actively adopt any positive intervention strategies (e.g., cognitive behavioral treatment, introducing more medication for patients with mental disorders) from other countries. This may help to reduce the number of people who feel emptiness in their lives, and this may help to reduce the overall crime and suicide rates in Japan.

As long as it is socially acceptable to judge children only by their academic achievement, children will continue to experience a lack of freedom with potentially devastating effects on the development of empathy and a corresponding numbing to the value of life.

Issues of Legal and Medical Supports for Juvenile Crime Offenders

It is often discussed that legal supports toward criminal juveniles need to be developed in Japan. For instance, the mother of the 17-year-old bus hijacker sought urgent help from many organizations when she found out her son was beating his family and also kept various kinds of knives, stun guns, a hammer, pepper spray, a suicide note, and a statement of criminal intent, which indicated his attempt to attack the junior high school he graduated from. Though his mother contacted a psychiatry department many times to have her son hospitalized, the hospital rejected her request every time and told her to go to the police, who also turned down her request and told her to go to the health center (Machizawa, 2000a).

Although the 17-year-old boy would be hospitalized in the end, the psychiatrist, with a simple psychological test and 10-minute interview, diagnosed him as having only a slight neurosis due to a psychogenetic reaction and did not prescribe any medication. Because the psychiatrist was not aware this boy was suffering from schizophrenic auditory hallucinations or the boy's background, including bullying experiences, the doctor permitted the boy to stay out of the hospital overnight despite his mother's

great concern. The bus hijacking happened while he was visiting his home (Machizawa, 2000a).

Though parents are often criticized and blamed when their children commit a crime, many worried parents in our society may face dilemmas like the parents of the young bus hijacker. In his case, we should note that the psychiatrist did not diagnose him correctly, did not give him medication, ignored his mother's reports regarding his son's crime plan, and let him visit home overnight without providing any treatment. Connections among the police, hospitals, and schools need to be well developed and need to be supported legally. In addition, there is a need for more education for psychiatrists in Japan. For instance, the number of mental clinics or counselors is still small in Japan; this may be because Japanese people are historically less likely to discuss their own personal concerns with a stranger. Thus, people who have psychological problems visit psychiatrists who are generally working in a general hospital. This makes people less likely to visit professionals because meeting with psychiatrists at the hospital might give people the impression that only people who have serious mental issues, such as some mental disorder that needs medication, will visit the hospital.

However, facing the increasing number of people who suffer from stress, the necessity for counselors has often been raised. From 1995, the government set the regulation that each public school introduce part-time counselors (twice a day, 8 hours), and this regulation has been applied from 2001 to all public schools in Japan. Though the government invested a great amount of money in order to spread this system to all schools, only 2,250 schools out of more than 40,000 schools in Japan implemented this new regulation by 2000 (Niregi, 2002).

Though the numbers of school counselors are still few, these counselors should make well-developed connections with psychiatrists for more professional help, such as medication. Also, it is important to educate these counselors that cruel behaviors toward animals may be linked to violence against humans because they may be able to detect children's cruel behaviors toward animals in early stages and prevent other antisocial behavior. This may be directly linked to a potential decrease in the rate of crimes and suicide.

Although the government modified the Juvenile Act to lower the age that applies to juvenile crime, this change itself will not help to reduce the number of juvenile crimes because many of these young criminals do not think about the consequences of their behaviors. As we listen to their motivations for crimes, they kill people because they want to show their existence, they want to experience killing others, or they want to watch the process of death. Thus, it is hard to believe that modifying the law is the solution to prevent further juvenile crimes because children who commit a crime may not care about consequences. Furthermore, the medication needs of children who suffer from some mental disorder, such as borderline disorder, should be addressed. Machizawa (2000b) pointed out that some medications that are often used to lower male hormones (i.e., anti-androgen) are not used in Japan. This is mainly because people's understanding of mental health is still less developed when compared with the United States. This issue will be further discussed in the next section. Instead of revising the law to prevent further juvenile crimes, what we have to do is to understand why juvenile crimes are happening.

Animal Abuse and Maltreatment

Animal Abuse in Japan and Its Risk Factors

As previously discussed, the increase in violent crimes committed by young children is one of the most serious social problems in Japan today. Consequently, animal abuse committed by young children has gained attention in Japan as many of these young offenders have a history of abusing or killing animals before they commit crimes against people. Because many children spend a significant amount of their time studying from a very young age, they have fewer opportunities to interact with diverse people in different settings or to learn how to consider the feelings of others. This lack of exposure may leave children unprepared to deal with their feelings of anger or sadness when they face an unexpected situation. Also, the competitive nature of contemporary Japanese society may leave children with few options for releasing stress as they strive to cope with high levels of pressure for academic achievement from their parents and competitive pressure from classmates. Media outlets frequently report that quiet children often lose their tempers suddenly and have difficulty controlling their emotions. This may be an indication that these children are suppressing their emotions to act like a "good child, good student" in their daily lives. In such cases, taking their aggression or stress out on smaller animals may be easy for

them. Now, they control another's life and they can feel superior when wielding their power.

Ascione (1993) defined cruelty to animals as "socially unacceptable behavior that intentionally causes unnecessary pain, suffering, or distress to and/or death of animals" (p. 2). Yet young children often show unintentional cruelty in their behavior toward animals. For example, many children have killed at least one small insect out of simple curiosity. By watching the process of death, they learn what causes death, the process of death, and how easy it is to take life. Most children soon experience a sense of guilt and regret taking an innocent life and never repeat the action. However, others develop brutal rituals that involve torturing or killing animals. Over time, these behaviors may often escalate to greater and greater atrocities as they seek more excitement.

Although there have been no empirical studies investigating the relationship between having a history of cruelty toward animals and later violence toward humans in Japan, this topic has recently gained significant attention. A number of studies, mainly conducted in the United States, show a relationship between displaying cruelty toward animals during childhood and subsequent violence against people and have been reviewed in other chapters in this volume.

As previously discussed, Japanese society has become a materialistic culture where many children are given anything they request from their parents without exerting effort in order to obtain what they want as a result of hard work or as a reward. In such cases, children are less likely to appreciate the value of the gifts they receive and do not learn how to control their desires because they are not expected to. Springing from the success of Japan's economy, the pet industry has grown significantly in last two decades. This trend may result in a society that allows people to treat pets as a product rather than a living organism. If a pet dies, people can easily replace them by buying a new pet. Thus, some children treat animals as a product and may be killing them as though they were destroying a toy. Because such children treat animals as objects, they may not feel guilty killing animals, and new pets will be soon given to children as replacements. Children who were given everything and were not expected to control their desires feel emptiness inside because they often do not have goals in their lives (Machizawa, 2000b). This may relate to killing animals for excitement.

As we previously discussed, the 14-year-old boy from Kobe and Mamoru Takuma repeatedly abused and killed animals in brutal ways before they killed children, and these behaviors were often witnessed by neighbors. By the time the 14-year-old boy was arrested, neighbors reported that all wandering cats disappeared; they later discovered these disappearances were a direct result of the boy killing them (Takayama, 1998). It is surprising that these neighbors did not immediately report what they witnessed. Sadly, many adults tend to be intimidated by juveniles today in Japan. As a traditional hierarchical society, seniors have had power and status in Japan, and younger people are expected to respect seniors. Until recently, adults were expected to raise their children to be respectful and adhere to this hierarchical model. However, it is less likely that adults call attention to unfamiliar juveniles when they witness juvenile's misconduct. This may be because many of today's children are more likely to lose their temper suddenly. There are many news stories where young children pick a fight with adults that end in murder. Thus, Japan may no longer be a society where adults can easily stop children's misconduct, such as animal abuse. However, information concerning where adults can report children's animal abuse needs to be distributed more widely. Preventing such behaviors in children's early years may help to prevent further cruel behaviors toward both animals and humans given the documented relation between animal cruelty history and later violence toward humans.

In the first author's Master's thesis (Maruyama, 2005), it was found that 19.7% of Japanese students (fourth and fifth graders) had abused socially valued animals (e.g., dogs, cats), and 41.1% of students reported their own abusive experiences toward less socially valued animals (e.g., fish, insects) in the past 6 months. Because research from outside Japan found correlations between abusive behaviors toward animals and violent behaviors toward humans, Maruyama's study with a survey method may indicate a possible link to those students' future violent behaviors toward humans. It is important to conduct further studies to investigate Japanese students' abusive behaviors toward animals, and develop both prevention and intervention programs for them.

Law Enforcement for Animal Abuse and Maltreatment

Incidents of savage animal abuse have been reported by the media and occasionally catch people's attention in Japan today. Subsequently, these media reports often lead to copycat crimes or even greater atrocities in order to gain media attention. Oftentimes, school pets become victims as well. Yet arresting these abusers and punishing them under the law has been unsuccessful and these brutal incidents are usually forgotten as time goes by.

However, in 1997, the news that a 14-year-old young animal abuser had brutally slain an innocent 11-year-old boy in Kobe, Japan, deeply shocked many people and brought the issue of animal abuse as a serious problem to the forefront of public attention for the first time. Further, in acknowledgment that this 14-year-old criminal and other young criminals had been frequently reported as having a history of animal abuse, the movement to revise animal protection laws began among animal rights protection activists.

Although the law has protected animals in Japan since 1973, this law was made only to reduce pressure and appease critics from other countries who argued that Japan did not have laws developed to protect animals. The law consisted of only 13 articles, and the content was very poor. Even though this law specified that animal abusers can be penalized by fines up to 30,000 yen ($360), regulations applying other forms of punishment (e.g., probation) were vague. Therefore, hardly anyone was prosecuted for animal maltreatment (Aoki, 2004).

However, after the crime in Kobe occurred and the boy's history of animal abuse was made public, several nonprofit organizations for the protection of animal rights were organized, and they started collecting citizens' signatures in order to submit a petition to the government to revise the animal protection laws. Finally, the issues regarding the laws protecting animals and punishing animal abusers were reviewed at the National Diet, and the law was revised in December 1999.

The previous law recognized only "humans" and "property." Animals were put into the latter category. Now, "animal" has been added as a third category. This represents a significant change in public recognition of the value of animals' lives. Moreover, the title of the law was revised to "The law on animal control and protection." This was a big step for the Japanese government as it clearly indicates that animals are seen as valuable living creatures and not property under the law. In 2000, this title was again revised to "The law on animal kind treatment and protection" in recognition of the movement to treat animals as valuable creatures, like humans.

The revised law consists of 31 articles, and the punishment is much more strict than before with specific and detailed guidelines. While the previous law levied a fine of less than 30,000 yen ($360) if people abuse or kill animals, they now face fines of up to 1,000,000 yen ($12,000) or one year of imprisonment. If pet owners abandon their pets, a fine of less than 300,000 yen ($3,600) will be levied.

In addition, the types of animals that are protected by the law have been expanded. For instance, the previous law applied only to cows, horses, pigs, sheep, goats, dogs, cats, domestic rabbits, domestic fowls, domestic pigeons, and ducks. The revised law applies to "any animals that are any mammals, birds, or reptiles people own." Moreover, specific behaviors that are punishable under the law and the responsibilities of animal owners are clearly defined. In addition to prescribing that animal owners must claim their ownership, breeding that exceeds the owner's capability of keeping is restricted, and operations that limit breeding are encouraged. Further, each prefectural governor has the authority to advise animal owners who are disturbing their neighborhoods due to their animals to address the problem, and the governor can punish them with a fine of no more than 200,000 yen ($2,400) if necessary.

Although animal laws have been modified for the increased protection of animals recently, there is still a concern that awareness of the need to take action when people initially witness animal abuse remains low in Japan. Yokoyama (2006) conducted a survey study to investigate veterinarians' exposure to animals with non-accidental injuries caused by their owners or other family members. Among these veterinarians (n=86), 81% believed non-accidental injuries caused by owners or family members can occur, and 64% reported that they were exposed to animals with non-accidental injuries. Among veterinarians who were exposed to abused animals (n=64), 88% of these abused animals were dogs (vs. 15% cats), and 76% of owners brought their pets to animal hospitals. Veterinarians reported that 80% of owners or family members who cause animal injuries were male. Surprisingly, only 35% of these veterinarians "clearly" confronted pet owners about animals' injuries (13% of them "somewhat," 11% of them "a little bit," and 39% of them "not at all"). In addition, only 42% of veterinarians "clearly" warned pet owners about the possible non-accidental injuries of their pets (6% of them "somewhat," 21% of them "a little bit," and 26% of them "not at all"). Further, 90% of the veterinarians who treated abused animals did not report these animal abuse cases to humane societies, police, or other related offices.

Not only modifying the law, but also encouraging veterinarians to report animal abuse cases is necessary because veterinarians are often the first people who can detect animal abuse and take legal actions to protect animals. One possible reason why reporting rates for suspected animal abuse from veterinarians are so low in Japan may be because, culturally, Japanese people believe they should let each household solve their own family problems and that outsiders should not get involved. Traditionally, fathers have the role of solving family problems and decision making for families. Therefore, some people still believe that not interfering or getting involved with others' family problems is respectful, although this norm has been changing. Yet there may be a need for the law to mandate veterinarians to report animal abuse cases if veterinarians' cultural values interfere with their decision to report. Also, it is important to develop cross-reporting systems between agencies (e.g., veterinarians, police, humane societies) to share information about animal abuse cases.

Rather than only educating veterinarians, educating people in a community about how to take action against animal abuse is also necessary. For instance, the study of the Cabinet office also found that most people cannot describe the law for animals, and 46.8% answered they didn't even know of this law's existence (Prime-Minister Cabinet Office, 2003). In addition to encouraging people to report any animal maltreatment activities they witness, organizations (e.g., health centers) need to educate people about the laws that apply to animal protection and where they can report animal abuse cases they have witnessed.

People's Attitude Toward Animals

In 2003, the Prime Minister's Cabinet office conducted a public poll on animal protection in order to gather information about people's opinions regarding animal protection and their attitudes toward pets to develop better protection policy. They randomly selected 3,000 people who were at least 20 years of age, and among them, 2,202 were individually interviewed. The majority of participants (65.5%) reported that they would like to have a pet. When asked about pet ownership, 36.6% answered that they currently had at least one pet. Among them, 62.4% answered they had a dog and 29.2% had a cat as a pet. When asked why they owned a pet, 60.5%

stated that they had a pet because their family likes animals and 47.9% answered that having a pet helps them to relax.

As we can see from these findings, many Japanese people own pets and treat them as important family members. Ishida et al.'s (2004) survey study (n=249) found that more Japanese people regarded their pets as family members and more people believed having pets would enhance their quality of life as compared to 10 years ago. Specifically, more pet dog and cat owners believed "pets could fulfill their lives" compared with non-pet owners, and 53% of pet owners strongly agreed with "treating pet as a family member" whereas only 10% agreed with this 10 years ago. This may indicate that more people have started owning pets and they are likely to treat pets as family members. Additionally, it was found that more people are interested in ecology compared to 10 years ago, and more females showed positive naturalistic attitudes, regardless of age, whereas more males showed this attitude compared with females 10 years ago. For humanistic attitudes, people showed strongly negative attitudes toward animal experiments where pain was involved; this rate remained the same from 10 years ago.

It was also found that the younger generation has started to believe in the potential unexplainable and mysterious powers of nature and animals. Animism is the belief that animals and nature are sacred. High rates of animism have been consistently reported for the last 10 years. Conversely, overall rates of dominonistic attitudes were low. Additionally, many people believe pets are valuable to humans' life.

Though most people showed strong negative attitudes toward mixed breeds, it was also found that many people own pets that are mixed breeds. Ishida et al. (2004) commented that this characteristic is uniquely Japanese. They showed negative attitudes toward the idea of mixed breeds; however, they will enjoy the results of mixed breeding that is done by someone else. For example, respondents in Ishida et al.'s survey reported negative feelings toward purposively created mixed breeds. However, participants also reported that they would own mixed breeds, despite these negative attitudes.

In sum, Ishida et al. (2004) concluded that Japanese people's attitude toward animals has not dramatically changed in the last 10 years. People still revere animals as sacred creatures and strongly hesitate to manipulate animals' lives due to humans' wills. At the same time, positive atti-

tudes toward pets have grown stronger in the last 10 years. More people regard pets as family members, and pets have gained status in society. Specifically, people reported more females treated pets as a family member, disagreed with painful animal experiments, and prefer having animals' pictures displayed in the home. Males, however, agreed more with the idea of mixed breeds, the use of elephant tusks for practical matters (e.g., stamps), eating whales, putting a priority on regional development, disinterest in reading animal magazines, and disinterest in birds. On the other hand, males were more interested in collecting insects and were more likely to encourage the idea of euthanizing pets. Additionally, they found that people in their 50s showed different attitudes toward animals compared with people between the ages of 20 and 50. Ishida et al. discussed that people in their 50s showed traditional views on beauty and the fear of nature that is beyond humans' control. They were also more likely to make dogs obey them and disagree with using elephant tusks, both of which were regarded as socially acceptable until recently. Although the younger generation has displayed more positive attitudes toward animals, some young people, regardless of their attitudes toward animals, abuse them. This abuse often manifests itself in conduct disorder.

Conduct Disorder and Animal Abuse

Children's cruelties toward other people are also a diagnostic sign of antisocial and conduct disorders. Ascione (1993) pointed out that children's cruelty to animals has been added to diagnostic criteria for Conduct Disorder in children and adolescents (DSM-III-R, American Psychiatric Association, 1987). Although not all children diagnosed with conduct disorder show cruel behaviors toward animals, Ascione has commented that certain issues addressed by research on conduct disorder and, more specifically, on interpersonal aggression in children and adolescents, may have relevance for animal cruelty.

According to AERA ("Teinenreikasuru," 2000), approximately 1.5% to 2.5% of children under 18 in Japan are diagnosed with conduct disorder under DSM-IV criteria, while prevalence rates of 6% to 8% are reported in the United States ("Teinenreikasuru," 2000). The term "conduct disorder" gained significant attention when the boy in Kobe was diagnosed as conduct disordered after murdering an 11-year-old boy. However, the details of this disorder are not widely known in Japanese society. Because of the intense media attention focused on a single aspect of this disorder, many people may still assume that children suffering from conduct disorder are always likely to be violent and perhaps even murderous. These perceptions, combined with the emphasis on social harmony that is so prevalent within the culture, create considerable difficulties for families with a child diagnosed with this condition. Despite the increased prevalence rate of conduct disorder noted in recent years, parents' fear of the social stigma attached to this diagnosis may keep them from seeking assistance for children. Sometimes, the consequences are tragic. Although medical insurance is available to cover treatment, and specialists have achieved significant results in treating this disorder with early interventions, parents are often understandably reluctant to seek treatment for their children. A dearth of mental health practitioners specializing in the area compounds the problem. Ascione (1999) stated that animal abuse is significant because it is one of the earliest emerging symptoms of conduct disorder in children. Thus, it could serve as an early warning sign or red flag for a child in need of mental health attention.

Young Sexual Sadists and Animal Abuses

We are using the example of a boy in Kobe (Boy A) throughout the chapter, and it is assumed that sexual sadism may have been the key motivation in his crime (Machizawa, 2000b). Sexual sadists are defined as those who feel sexual excitement by killing or torturing animals and people. When Boy A was a fifth grader, his grandmother passed away. Faced with the death of his grandmother, he became interested in death and started to kill animals to understand the process of the death. However, he noticed that he ejaculated when watching dying animals having a convulsive fit. When he was watching horror movies with his friends, he had the same reaction. He was not, however, sexually aroused by pornographic movies he watched with his friends. At that time, Boy A knew he should stop abusing and killing animals to feel sexual satisfaction, and he later confessed his struggle with his dilemma (Takayama, 1998).

Generally, it is reported (Machizawa, 2000b) that sexual sadists repeat crimes, and often their brutality gets worse. In fact, Boy A killed his 11-year-old victim by choking him, which allowed him to watch the process of torturing and dying for a prolonged period of time. Though sexual sadists are uncommon across the world, Machizawa (2000b) commented that more sexual sadists exist in developed countries than in developing countries. Among such countries, the United States is one of the countries that has the highest rate of crimes committed by sexual sadists (Machizawa, 2000b). It may be that people in developed countries have time to spare and live materially rich lives. Thus, they seek some excitement in their lives, and abusing animals may be one way to fulfill their desires. Oftentimes, such people can be treated by medication, such as anti-androgen. However, Machizawa reported that there was no anti-androgen treatment in Japan. Understanding the treatment for aggression based on sexual energy has not been understood in Japan, specifically by the government, thus there are few doctors who can diagnose such disorders accurately and prescribe effective medication.

Of course, we are not blaming medical doctors who diagnosed Boy A and other juvenile crime offenders. Yet we have to point out the fact that all juveniles we used in this chapter as examples were diagnosed simply as neurotic or misdiagnosed, and appropriate treatment (i.e., medication) was not provided. Learning from the past and preventing such misdiagnoses will be essential in this troubled society.

Hikikomori and Animal Abuse

Although people's understandings of psychosis in children and other disorders, such as conduct disorder, need to be improved, a new psychological health symptom of youth, *hikikomori*, has also gained attention in recent years. *Hikikomori* are normally defined as people who avoid going to school or work, and never leave their bedrooms for more than 5 months and cannot interact with people outside of the home (Machizawa, 2003). It is discussed that *hikikomori* react with social withdrawal because they feel overwhelmed by societal pressure, and feel unable to fulfill their expected social roles.

There may be one million *hikikomori* in Japan and approximately 80% are boys (Machizawa, 2003). It is also said that 1 out of 10 boys are *hikikomori*. The number of male *hikikomori* is much higher than the number of females, and this may be because males experience much more pressure regarding their academic or career achievement than do girls. Many *hikikomori* suffer from fear of social pressure and the frustration stemming from the belief that they cannot change their situations, and sometimes, they take their frustrations out on their family members by attacking them (Machizawa, 2003).

Typically, *hikikomori* spend most of their time talking online or playing video games. These games are often violent, bringing excitement and stimulation to their small imaginary worlds. This focus on violence as their only source of stimulation may link with their possible real-world behaviors of killing animals or attacking people. The lack of social interactions accelerates the decline of social skills and retards the development of a moral code that is in keeping with the norms of society. Further, some *hikikomori* may have difficulty distinguishing between what is real and what is imaginary.

In recent years, the media have been making spurious connections between *hikikomori* and aggressive behavior. One of the reasons for this bias was that a 17-year-old boy who hijacked a bus and killed one passenger was a *hikikomori*. Experts argue that most *hikikomori* are too socially withdrawn and timid to venture outside of their rooms to attack someone, but it is also frequently reported that *hikikomori* attack their family members instead (Machizawa, 2003). Also, the incident of a 28-year-old male *hikikomori* who placed a 9-year-old girl under "house arrest" over 9 years cannot be ignored ("Niigata," 2006). Although there was no investigation into their family pets' victimization, there is no doubt that family pets could be targets of these attacks. Regardless of the name of psychological disorders that children are diagnosed with, it is crucial that Japanese society comes to realize the need for understanding each disorder and determining what society can do to prevent or diminish these children's psychological symptoms and to promote children's well-being.

Issues on Increasing Numbers of Abandoned Pets

In addition to incidents of animal abuse, pet abandonment is also a significant issue in Japan. Ishida et al. (2004) found that Japanese attitudes toward animals have not been changed; Japanese traditionally stand in awe of animals and regard them as a mysterious existence from the ancient period. Contrary to these attitudes, the number of abandoned animals is

significant. The present law provides that each prefectural administration must take charge of animals that are brought by their owners. This provision was made because of the growing number of incidences involving stray animals (e.g., dogs) attacking people since the previous law was developed. In addition, administrative offices collected all stray animals for the purpose of protecting the public from rabies and other infections. Administrative offices have a legal responsibility to maintain the safety and public health in their prefecture. That is why each regional health center is still taking charge of both abandoned and stray animals, and they encourage people to report stray animals in their neighborhood and receive stray animals or pets without a complicated procedure.

The numbers of animals that are received at the health centers or other related institutions are extensive (see Figure 1). According to the report of the nonprofit organization All Life in a Viable Environment (ALIVE) (2005) developed for animal protection in Japan, 95,717 dogs and 264,102 cats were received from owners and 103,691 dogs were protected by health centers as wandering animals in 2003. Among them, 173,032 dogs and 267,214 cats were euthanized. Only a small number of pets were given to others; this includes institutions that need animals for experiments. Though the number of pets that are euthanized at the health centers has been declining, a large number of innocent animals are killed because of humans' selfish reasons every day.

To date, there are more than 100 health centers, which are run by the government, that deal with protecting animals. Sadly, most protected animals are euthanized, and only a small number of animals are adopted by new owners. Also, the environment of the places where protected animals live is often very unsanitary, and infectious diseases spread easily (Nogami, 2005). It is often reported that these places do not have windows or sunlight, and protected animals do not go out for walks and sometimes go without food over the weekend. Even though there are some people who want to adopt animals from the health center, sometimes adoption is not allowed because these animals are likely to have some infectious disease. Such situations may make the health center less likely to encourage people to adopt their protected animals. Nogami pointed out that this may mean protecting animals is our duty in order to maintain public hygiene rather than for the purpose of enhancing animal welfare in a community.

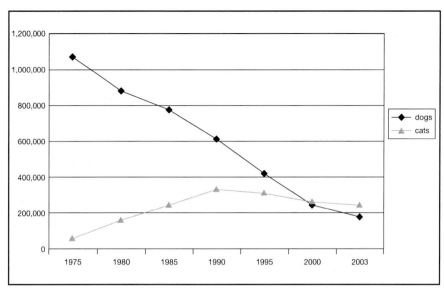

Figure 1   The Number of Animals That Were Killed at the Health Centers in Japan (ALIVE, 2005)

Subsequently, because the number of protected animals was so large, many protected animals were sent to laboratories as subjects of experiments. Because such organizations could obtain many animals on which to experiment for free, it often resulted in cruel treatment of the animals (Nogami, 2005). However, as attention toward animal experiments grew larger in the 1990s, the movement to abolish animal experimentation was successful in 2005, and animals are no longer used for experiments that result in death.

Yet the fact remains that a large number of animals are euthanized daily. Though those numbers have been declining each year, especially for dogs, large numbers of animals are affecting how euthanasia is paid for. Although taxes are used to perform euthanasia, budgets for those animals are very limited. Thus, some health centers had to kill many animals at once (e.g., putting many in a small room and introducing gas) rather than considering how those animals could die without pain. For instance, gas poisoning has been used; however, the machines are often very old and take time to fill the room with gas and render the animals unconscious (Nogami, 2005). Thus those animals have to experience significant pain for a prolonged amount of time. Today, most developed counties except Japan use anesthesia for euthanizing animals. Japan needs to reconsider how the health centers should conduct euthanasia. Most importantly, promoting people's morality toward the treatment of abandoned animals is an urgent need in Japan's society.

Of course, not all people who bring their pets to animal protection centers are leaving their pets because of selfish reasons. They may be people who have to move to another country for work, elderly people who have to be hospitalized for a long time, or those with a new family member who has an allergy to animals. Additionally, the issue of aging pets may spur the number of pets abandoned. As the quality of pet food and medication increases, so does the life span of pets. Some pets live longer than their owners and are consequently abandoned. It also occurs that older pets often have chronic diseases that require significant money to treat; those older pets are occasionally abandoned because of owners' financial stresses. Unfortunately there are very few shelters or related organizations that keep these pets for owners in Japan. There are some nonprofit organizations to protect abandoned pets in Japan. However, these organizations are small and less likely to have the capability of keeping protected animals like shelters in the United States or other European countries. Also, some of them only accept animals from the health centers, not from individuals. Thus, owners who cannot keep their pets must bring their pets to the administrative organizations that will later euthanize their pets if they cannot find a new owner.

However, there are some activities addressing the large number of abandoned pets. For instance, an animal photojournalist, Kodama, opened a photo exhibition in 2005 ("Matsuede," 2005). He exhibited 60 pictures of animals waiting for euthanasia at animal protection centers. These pictures were a powerful appeal to people about what innocent animals are facing due to humans' selfish reasons. Also, issues of animal rescue have been gaining the attention of people through experiencing a series of earthquakes and a volcanic eruption in recent years. Though there are no legal regulations to save animals from natural disasters in Japan, animal protection activists, veterinarians, and other related activists have been stressing this need and submitting requests to the government. When Mount Miyake erupted in 2000, a veterinary association in Tokyo helped create a shelter for animals. Many animals were saved and returned to their owners.

Recently, nonprofit organizations of activists for animal protection have approached the government to let them convert schools that are no longer being used into animal shelters. Due to declining birth rates, more schools are closing. Though this request is still in the process of approval, such movements are gaining more people's attention, and it is desirable that Japan can own more animal shelters that have enough capacity and budget to care for abandoned pets until they find new owners or live out their lives.

Additionally, the request to modify the law to extend the number of days for sheltering protected animals before euthanasia was submitted to the government and the police by some animal protection activists in 2005 (ALIVE, 2005). Under the current law, protected animals at the health center, including stray animals and lost pets, were kept only 3 days. The health center made information public about found animals for 2 days (mainly on the information board at their organization), but they euthanize those protected animals (e.g., dogs and cats) if their owners are not found after 2 days. Other animals are kept for a month. Thus, there are many cases where pet owners find their pets after their pets have been euthanized. Under current law, inanimate lost properties (e.g., umbrella, wallet) must be kept for 6 months at police stations or related organizations. Currently, the lives of animals appear to be valued less than those of inanimate objects.

Japan must consider revising the law to protect animals again. Aoki (2004) advised that the health centers should ask pet owners to prove that they cannot keep their pets any longer, set larger fees when they get pets, and make owners attend their pets' euthanasia. Although this may make some pet owners abandon pets in remote areas (e.g., mountainsides) so they do not have to pay the fine, this policy may prompt more pet owners to bring their pets to the health center without putting an effort into finding another owner for their pets. Also, by charging a fee or levying a fine on pet owners who bring their pets to the health center, the government can use this money to keep protected animals longer and to find their owners, which may link to a reduced need for euthanasia.

In addition, pet shops should require the registration of their pets (e.g., putting microchips in the animals), and encourage (or legally mandate) owners who do not plan to have more pets to have their pets sterilized. If the law requires registration of pets, the law should add heavier taxes for pet owners who do not conduct sterilization on their pets. Some other countries have already implemented this system (e.g., the United States, Australia). Also, the health center should conduct some investigation as to why owners cannot keep their pets and consult how they can find a new owner by themselves when owners bring their pets to the health center.

Subsequently, it is urgent that many facilities (i.e., health centers) need to make their places more open to the public (especially for children), which may lead to higher adoption rates of protected animals. Because of their unsanitary environments, they are less likely to have visitors. By gaining more visitors, they can open educational programs (e.g., animal care, etc.) for the community, and they can also recruit volunteers to make animals' lives better. Although the idea of obtaining a pet from a shelter or the health center instead of pet shops has not been common in Japan, more new pet owners may obtain pets from such organizations in the future.

Though support from the government is necessary in order to reduce the number of abandoned pets, some conflicts exist. For instance, if the government makes shelters for animals in order to keep pets, this may be directly linked to a reduced number of pets that are euthanized. However, the number of pet owners who bring their pets to these shelters may increase if they find that their pets will not be euthanized after they are abandoned.

Lastly, we still believe that shelters that keep abandoned animals for a longer period of time (e.g., a few months) are needed in addition to the shelters for animals that are in a violent family situation in Japan. More people regard pets as their family members today (Ishida et al., 2004). Those pets need to be protected by the law like human victims are. This problem will be discussed in the next section.

Domestic Violence

Historical and Cultural Context of Domestic Violence in Japan

In the 1980s and early 1990s, people in Japan understood the term "domestic violence" as "children's violent behavior toward their parents at home"

(Koyake, 2003). However, attention to domestic violence (DV) increased during the 1990s and the term domestic violence is now recognized as violence between married couples or romantic partners rather than as violence from children to parents. Prior to the late 1990s, DV was treated as a "trivial quarrel between couples," and most members of the Japanese collectivist culture, which values social harmony, pretended not to see. In fact, until recently, there was no Japanese word for an incident that would be described as "domestic violence" in English (Davey, 1995). Even with the increased awareness of DV, most members of Japanese society are reluctant to openly acknowledge incidents of DV. For instance, a survey conducted by the prime-minister imperial office in 2002 found that only 21.8% of respondents indicated they would report DV if they witnessed it. Most of those who said they would not report DV (68.9%) believed they should not do so out of respect for the private lives of others.

In the highly patriarchal society, corporal punishment has been tacitly approved and violence from husband to wife was hardly considered surprising news. This aspect of Japanese culture has fostered a maladaptive approach to responding to DV. The acceptance of violence within the household as normal and easily justifiable has prevented many from reporting instances of DV they have witnessed or experienced. However, preventing violence against women was raised as one of the significant concerns internationally at the World Conference on Women in 1995. The government is taking this issue very seriously and has responded by creating the new Gender Equality Bureau in the Cabinet office. Although the rate of DV remains unchanged, increased attention through books and the media has raised public awareness of this social problem. For instance, Kobayashi, Tatsumi, and Fukuju (2005) reported a significant increase in domestic violence report rates in 1998 (i.e., 48 reports) whereas only 2 reports were received in 1997. People's attitudes toward DV contributed to actions against DV, and a law against DV was finally enacted in 2001. This law clearly states that violence against spouses is a crime, and represents a significant acknowledgment for Japanese society.

Current Incidence of Domestic Violence

DV is the second most common reason Japanese women decide to divorce their husbands (Davey, 1995). The National Police Agency (2005b) reported receiving 14,410 letters of complaint from victims in 2004, a 14.7% increase over the previous year. Among those 14,410 reports, 81.4% of victims were married and 99.0 % were female.

Recently, the investigation of DV both academically and scientifically has increased in Japan. For example, the Gender Equality Bureau, Cabinet Office (2003) conducted a large survey of randomly selected individuals over the age of 20. From the survey (n = 3,322), they found that approximately one 1 of 5 (19.1%) females (n = 1,802) were victims of DV (physical abuse:15.5%; threat without physical abuse: 5.6%; sexual abuse: 9.0%). Among women who had experienced domestic violence, 22.9% felt their lives were threatened. Among victims with children, 40.2% of females who had experienced abuse reported that their children witnessed incidents. Sadly, 21% of those children were also victims. Further, they found that most victims did not report incidents to public organizations (e.g., police, shelter, programs for DV). Forty-two percent of female victims and 68.7% of male victims reported that they did not disclose their victimization to anyone. When survey respondents were asked if they had perpetrated domestic violence, approximately 1 out of 3 males (35.1%) reported engaging in violence against their partners, whereas 19.5% of females reported taking violent action violence against their partners.

Empirical studies (e.g., Ascione, 2000) found that many animals are also victimized at homes that are experiencing DV. Although it is reported that batterers abuse pets to hurt other family members' feelings (Ascione, 2000), it is also anticipated that some victims may abuse their pets to relieve their stress. In order to intervene in further abuses, possibly toward humans, it is important to investigate whether perpetrators of animal abuse are abusers or victims of abuses, such as children living with domestic violence. In addition to a better prevention and intervention system for DV, investigations need to be conducted in order to develop a better treatment system for DV victims, both humans and animals.

Law Enforcement Against DV Batterers and Protection for Victims

Although the Constitution of Japan explicitly states equality between the sexes, violence against women was not clearly discussed in the law until 2001. The law indicates that each prefecture should establish an office for DV victims (e.g., shelter, phone service). Originally, DV was defined as "violence that threatens the life or results in actual injury." In 2004, the definition was modified to "violence that harms or affects physical or emotional health." Restraining orders now apply to divorced spouses and the duration was extended from 2 weeks to 2 months. In addition, the law now applies to cases in which violence continues after divorce. In the most updated law for the prevention of spousal violence and the protection of victims (spousal violence law) in 2004, victims have access to counseling and support services through the Spousal Violence Counseling and Support Centers (120 locations nationwide) or the police. In addition, there are 51 shelters (23 public and 28 private shelters) in Japan today (Gender Equality Bureau, Cabinet Office, 2005). Each prefecture (n=51) has guidance clinics for battered women in Japan. These shelters received 35,943 reports in 2003 and 43,225 reports in 2004, which is a 25.5% increase from 2001.

Although a legal system to protect victims has been developed in Japan, there are no statutes relating to the treatment of batterers. For instance, there are no court-mandated intervention programs for arrested batterers to participate in or to follow up after the batterers have completed their term of imprisonment. Moreover, there is no law specifically designed to punish batterers in Japan. It is doubtful that batterers will change their violent behavior problems without treatment, and so the cycle of violence is often perpetuated. (See Maruyama, Mankowski, & Hara, 2005). The need for a legal system to intervene and rehabilitate batterers after they are arrested is especially critical. For instance, while 95.7% of the injuries were caused by males, 38.1% of murders between spouses were committed by wives in 2003 (Gender Equality Bureau, Cabinet Office, 2004). This may indicate that female victims are more likely to feel that they have no choice but to kill abusive partners to protect themselves. The comparatively high murder rate of abusive Japanese husbands by their wives may be partially due to the absence of a well-developed, systematic response to guard against DV or to protect the victims after abuse has occurred. Further, victims may be reluctant to report their spouses or partners until they feel their lives are threatened or unless reporting the abuse is likely to result in a prison sentence, rather than treatment. Rather, they may choose to suffer in silence to avoid bringing shame and adversity upon the family. Conversely, if the court can order batterers into DV intervention programs (treatment), it may encourage more victims to report the abuse before it is too late.

Domestic Violence and the Future

Although the number of perpetrators has not dramatically changed in the past few years, more DV perpetrators have been arrested by the police recently (Suzuki & Ishikawa, 1999). This may be an indication of changing attitudes toward DV, with more people reporting that they have witnessed DV or been a victim under the new law. Though the law was enacted relatively recently, DV and its legal significance are gaining attention as a serious social issue.

Although there has not yet been a study of animal abuse and DV conducted with Japanese samples, it is certain that many pets are victims of DV domestic violence in Japan. For instance, Ascione, Weber, and Wood (1997) reported that 85% of DV professionals questioned in a survey indicated that women fleeing domestic violence expressed that there had been pet abuse at home. However, there is no shelter for animals to be rescued from DV homes in Japan. The animal protection office in Kagawa reported that more than 10,000 dogs and cats are removed from their homes due to abuse or neglect each year (Nishi, Furuta, & Yamashita, 1998). There is an urgent need to investigate the current situation of pets in DV homes in order to develop a new intervention system to help those helpless pets immediately. Additionally, as Ascione (2000) commented, some victims choose not to go to shelters, but to stay at violent homes because they cannot leave their pet behind. Accepting pets in shelters as victims may also encourage more human victims to seek help from organizations (e.g., shelters).

Child Abuse and Neglect
Current Rates and Characteristics of Abuse

News on children's deaths as a result of abuse by their parents is reported daily. Sadly, these reports are not too surprising for Japanese people today. As the public's interest in and understanding of child abuse has increased, the media has taken up this issue as one of the most serious social problems Japanese society faces. Reports of child abuse have increased dramatically in recent years (Figure 2). According to the Ministry of Health, Labor, and Welfare (2005b), 26,569 incidents were reported in 2003 while only 1,101 incidents were reported in 1990. Yet this is not necessarily an indication that the numbers of child abuse incidents have increased dramatically; rather, people have started reporting incidents, and there are more organizations in place to receive these reports.

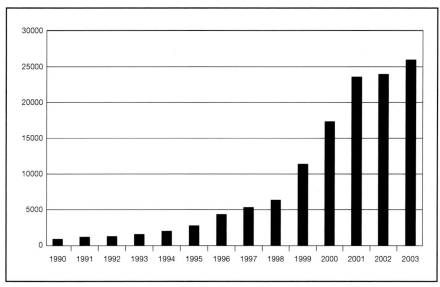

Figure 2   The Number of Reported Cases of Child Abuse and Neglect (Ministry of Health, Labor, and Welfare, 2005b)

However, questions concerning the accuracy of these reports remain when investigating sensitive issues such as child abuse. It is nearly impossible to obtain accurate information about the prevalence of child abuse incidents because the abuse often takes place at home or in a private institution where it is less likely to be witnessed by third parties. Moreover, victims are often reluctant to file reports accusing family members. Second, abused children often have not acquired the ability to report abuse; many are too young or are afraid of their abusers. Last, it sometimes happens that institutions that interact with children (e.g., hospitals, schools) do not have accurate information regarding how to report possible child abuse cases. As a result, reported rates of child abuse, which only reflect the cases that are reported to police or domestic child guidance clinics, are much lower than the actual rates of abuse.

According to a report from the National Police Agency (2005b), 253 abusers were arrested and 51 children were killed as a result of child abuse and neglect in 2004. They also reported that the number of arrests has been increasing dramatically annually. Turning to types of abuse detected, 193 abusers were arrested for physical abuse, 29 abusers were arrested for sexual abuse, 24 abusers for neglect, and there were no arrests for emotional abuse.

The Bureau of Social Welfare and Public Health (2001) investigated 1,940 cases received by the 11 different child guidance clinics in Tokyo in 2000. While only 217 cases were reported to the child

guidance clinics in Tokyo in 1994, the number of cases doubled in 1995. Similarly, after 1995, the numbers of cases have consistently increased annually, with 714 reported incidents in 1998 and 1,315 reported incidents in 1999, over 16 times the rate reported 5 years previously. According to the report, 1,242 children were abused (51.2% boys and 48% girls), and 60% of them were between the ages of 2 and 8. Physical abuse was the most frequently cited type of abuse (50.5%; Neglect = 32.7%; Sexual abuse = 4.3%; Emotional abuse = 11.3%). Among the sexually abused children, almost 60% of victims were between the ages of 2 and 8, and 43% of these children had been abused for more than one year.

Subsequently, when characteristics of abused children were examined to aid in identifying the causes of parental abuse, it was found that children's distinctive characteristics are less likely to be a cause or reason for parental abuse. On the other hand, when abused children protected by child guidance clinics met with psychologists, approximately 70% showed some psychological disturbance, such as depression and emotional disturbances.

Legal Protection and Laws Against Child Abuse and Neglect

When we talk about the legal movement to address child abuse, many people often talk about the story of Mary Ellen Wilson. A 9-year-old Mary Ellen had been brutally abused by her stepmother, however, there was no legal enforcement to protect abused children in the 1800s if the abuse occurred "behind closed doors." However, legal enforcement for animal abusers already had been enacted in the United States at that time. Mary Ellen was protected in 1874 by the involvement of an animal welfare agency. Federal law enforcement for child maltreatment was enacted in 1974 in the United States. Surprisingly, the draft of this law to protect abused children was made by the American Humane Association, which was an organization protecting children as well as animals. Interestingly, the movement to legally protect animals had started before the movement to protect abused children in Japan, too. The first organization for animal protection in Japan was established in 1902.

In 1947, the Child Welfare Law was enacted to protect children from abuse and maltreatment. Subsequently, the Maternal and Child Heath Law enacted in 1965 strengthened the child health care delivery system, which promoted health check ups for infants and young children, home visits to newborns, and provided psychological support to mothers and children. This system for child survival and development has enjoyed considerable success (Nakamura, 2002). However, although the health of Japanese children has improved since these laws have been enforced, the welfare system for child protection was not well developed. To address this weakness, laws for punishing acts related to Child Prostitution and Child Pornography and for Protection of Children were enacted in 1999. In the next year, the Child Abuse Prevention Law was finally enacted in Japan.

This law, which was designed to protect children from abuse or neglect, clearly states that no person can maltreat any children (aged under 18) under any circumstances. Child abuse is defined here as (1) physical abuse, (2) sexual abuse, (3) neglect, and (4) emotional abuse. Additionally, the law encourages early detection of and early response to these incidents to prevent further maltreatment. It states that schools, child welfare offices, hospitals, and other relevant offices and organizations have a duty to report possible incidents of child abuse to guidance clinics and exempts those who report such incidents from charges relating to violation of confidentiality rights. As child guidance clinics receive reports of incidents, they are obligated to investigate the safety of the children and to protect them immediately, calling in police assistance if necessary.

Though many positive changes have been made to protect abused children, those child welfare offices that help abused children should also make connections with animal protection offices. Research has shown a high correlation between the occurrence of child abuse and animal abuse in the same households. It is important that child welfare offices and animal protection offices develop cross-reporting systems and work together to help more child and animal victims.

Child Maltreatment and the Future

Stepfathers or stepmothers are often characterized as evil in children's fairy tales, and there is a myth that most child abuse or neglect is perpetrated by these "evil" stepparents. However, most reported abuse incidents were perpetrated by biological parents (53.8% by biological mothers and 18.2% by biological fathers; Ministry of Health, Labor, and Welfare, 2004). Although physical injuries caused by parental abuse will usually heal as time goes by, healing children's psychological disturbances may be more difficult. According to a study conducted by Yamamoto et al. (1999), some associations between specific categories of child maltreatment and the lifetime prevalence of different types of DSM-III-R psychopathology (e.g., anxiety disorder, depression) have been found. A psychiatrist, Machizawa (2001), also reported that one-fourth of females with dissociative identity disorder were victims of sexual abuse at the hands of their biological fathers.

Although it is necessary to develop more accessible medical and psychological care by professionals for those children, it is even more important that members of the community develop an understanding of these children's needs and support them as a community. Support for people who demonstrate abusive behavioral problems is also crucial. Community classes to learn about parenting, stressing the difference between discipline and abuse, at community centers where everyone can easily access them could be very effective.

Most importantly, communication with neighbors and extended family may be the most effective way to prevent further abusive behaviors. According to the Bureau of Social Welfare and Public Health (2001), more cases were reported to child guidance clinics by neighbors (28.2%) in Tokyo compared with other cities. It is assumed that because many people in a big city like Tokyo live close each other, such as in apartments, closer proximity may influence interactions with neighboring families, thereby increasing the likelihood of hearing familial confrontations. At the same time, most people don't associate with neighbors in a big city; they would be likely to report witnessed incidents to organizations rather than talking to their neighbors. In fact, more than 40% of reported cases were regarded as not meeting the criteria of abuse (Bureau of Social Welfare and Public Health, 2001).

It is important to develop community networks for reporting child abuse, such as schools, child guidance clinics, and hospitals, because identifying the early stages of abuse will prevent escalating severity of further abuse. It is equally important to develop more organizations in each prefecture to create better accessibility for members of the community when it is necessary to report abuse. Inter-agency communication networks need to be established to enable the efficient exchange of critical information and educational systems need to be developed so that so that anyone can learn basic information about child abuse and what communities can do.

Today, most people don't even know their neighbors' names and hardly ever communicate with them in their busy daily lives. However, if they have opportunities to discuss their problems and the stresses they are confronting with family or friends, they can seek advice and support in handling their behavior problems. This may be the best way to prevent increases of child abuse rates in Japan today.

Elder Abuse
The Effects of Changing Societal Values and Family Structure

When we discuss the links of violence between animals and humans, the issue of elder abuse cannot be ignored. For instance, Rosen (1995) discussed that elder abuse and animal abuse are often happening at the same households, and detecting one abuse case (e.g., animal abuse) frequently leads the investigators to find other abuse cases (e.g., elder abuse).

Although little attention is currently given to elder abuse in Japan, this is not an indication that elder abuse does not occur. Today, there are approximately 128 million Japanese people who live in the country (Prime-Minister Cabinet Office, 2005). Among them, 19.5% are older than 65 (cf. less than 5% in 1950), and this ratio has rapidly increased each year (Prime-Minister Cabinet Office, 2005). The Cabinet Office even estimated that elderly people (individuals aged 65 or older) will soon account for 35.7% of the population by 2050, and the number of elderly people is expected to keep increasing (while the number of children decreases). The birthrate has

declined from 4.32 in 1949 to 1.29 in 2004, and the life span of the people has been extended (78.36 for males and 85.33 for females in 2004 vs. 59.57 for males and 62.97 for females in 1950; Prime-Minister Cabinet Office, 2005). These changes are causing many social problems today.

For instance, the issue of nursing elderly people has become a serious challenge. According to the Gender Equality Bureau, Cabinet Office (2005), 28.6% of elderly people between 80 to 84 years old and 65.7% of elderly people who are older than 90 are designated as requiring nursing, and 70% of them are females. However, when elderly people need some assistance, it is often difficult for them to obtain immediate help from their adult children because both their children and their children's spouses are likely to have jobs. To make matters worse, most Japanese workers work in a different city from where they live. In such cases, elderly people often need to enter nursing homes or other institutions that offer medical assistance.

However, there is now a serious shortage of such institutions in Japan because the number of elderly people has significantly increased in recent years, even as the number of younger people, specifically taxpayers (whose taxes are needed to support such institutions) are decreasing. Moreover, not all elderly people enter a nursing home by their own decisions. Sometimes there is no choice for them except entering nursing homes because their family members are unable to care for them. Such behavior can best be described as neglect or emotional abuse if they are forcing elderly parents to enter the nursing homes and do not take time to visit them because of their busy lives. Occasional news coverage reporting elder abuse perpetrated by staff members at nursing homes or related institutions provides testimony that more sinister consequences can also occur. Within the hierarchical structure of Japanese society and culture elderly people are highly valued, and in the past they were shown great respect and deference. The situation elderly people are facing today is in conflict with Japan's cultural values and thus requires immediate attention.

Elder Abuse in Japan and Legal Issues

Given that academic studies on elder abuse began in 1994 (Yamada, 2004), it is surprising that nationwide investigation of elderly abuse was not conducted sooner (Kobayashi, 2004). Faced with a series of news stories on elder abuse, the Ministry of Health, Labor, and Welfare finally conducted the first nationwide research study on elder abuse in 2003. Surveys were sent to 16,802 organizations providing elder care, including nursing homes, hospitals, and all other related institutions in Japan, and 39.9% returned the survey (n = 1,991). The average age of victims was 81.6, and approximately 76.2% of them were females. Among them and their families, 66% reported that they do not have financial difficulties. More than a half of them are diagnosed as needing assistance, and more than 80% of the victims suffered from senile dementia.

Surprisingly, 32.1% of abusers were blood-related sons, and they were less likely to be the caregivers of the victims (victims' partners and the daughters-in-law accounted for another 20.3% of the perpetrators). In 88.6% of the cases, the victim and the abuser lived in the same household, and 51.5% reported that they spent most of their time together. More than 60% of abusers were the primary caregivers for their elderly victims.

Emotional abuse was the most frequently reported type of abuse (63.6%) followed by neglect (52.4%), physical abuse (50%), and economic abuse (22.4%). Although 10.9% of victims were experiencing life-threatening living conditions and 51.4% of them suffered serious emotional and physical health problems, more than a half of them answered that they did not regard their situation as abuse, while others tried to hide the facts. Further, 76.3% of abusers were not aware that their behaviors were abusive.

Surprisingly, it was found that only 71 (3%) out of approximately 3,000 cities in Japan have offices that can respond to the abuses found in this study. It is impossible for such a small number of offices to adequately cope with the abuses occurring every day. Moreover, these offices do not specialize in elder abuse cases and not all staff have specific training for addressing this type of abuse. Further, most staff members assigned to take care of these matters also hold additional posts with many other responsibilities. Kobayashi (2004) pointed out that because there is no governmental organization that is specifically responsible for coping with elder abuse, it is impossible to gather accurate statistics showing prevalence rates and severity or to adequately investigate the background of these cases. While there are a few nonprofit organizations working on prevention and intervention in cases of elder abuse (Kobayashi, 2004), their services are very limited (e.g., phone counseling for 3 days a week) due to small budgets and limited staffing resources.

Most surprisingly, there is no law to intervene in elder abuse cases in Japan. Though there is the Social Welfare regulation that prohibits some abusive behavior in nursing homes, there is no law that clearly states, "no one can maltreat elderly people" like the law for child abuse protection (Kobayashi, 2004). The small number of offices dedicated to coping with instances of elder abuse and the lack of training available to the staff compounds the problem. Consequently, it is hardly surprising that few (if any) elder abuse cases are effectively treated.[2]

Japan enacted a law for child abuse in 2000 and a law for domestic violence in 2001. Increases in the number of elder abuse cases and lack of legal protection has led to the demand for enactment of elder abuse laws and this has been raised even in the National Diet. Study meetings focusing on legal protection and other support systems for victims of elder abuse implemented in the United States have been conducted by the assembly from 2002. In 2003, a research team investigating elder abuse was inaugurated by 24 members of the assembly. They are examining the situation confronted by the few offices trying to cope with elder abuse to improve protection and services.

Elder Abuse and the Future

Since ancient times, Japanese people have respected and valued the older members of their society. However, abuse of elders, children, and partners are now among the most significant social issues confronting Japanese society. Despite the seriousness of the situation, there is no prevention policy or legal support system for elderly Japanese people. Even when cases of elder abuse case are discovered, there are neither legal standards to protect victims, nor offices that can cope with the matter. Thus, as things currently stand, there is no solution for the increasing prevalence of elder abuse. There is an urgent need for help from the government for this matter. For instance, governmental support for insurance fees for elderly people who need assistance may allow more elderly people to use facilities such as nursing homes when they are needed. This may significantly reduce the number of cases of abuse caused by caregivers' stress. As we previously cited, many abuses were perpetrated by family members. Because there is no well-developed support system for nursing elderly people in the society, these families are forced to take care of elderly family members, regardless of their ability and willingness (or lack of it) to provide adequate care. Although it is certainly not our intention to blame everything on the government, we cannot help thinking that more support from the government for elderly people in need of assistance would help to reduce the number of elderly people who are abused by family members. Yet the reality is that the government is also lacking the budgetary means to support people or organizations in need of financial support (e.g., the number of taxpayers is falling while the number of elderly people continues to increase). Thus the government is facing a financial crisis and may not be able to provide adequate funding for elder abuse prevention. This is particularly likely to occur if government officials fail to fully understand the situation and take an optimistic view.

Though more private nursing homes are being built today as a result of successful marketing, the price of those institutions is always high because they advertise better amenities than their competitors. Even so, elderly people who want to enter such nursing homes must win a lottery to obtain a bed. Of course, most regular nursing homes are short on space. In fact, there are many nursing homes where elderly people can stay only a short time, regardless of the amount of time they were forced to wait to get in, because there are always more elderly people who need the care they provide. It is obvious that there is a need fore more nursing homes and that a fixed price for these facilities should be set. In addition to nursing homes, other government-sponsored organizations catering to elderly people with limited financial resources may also be needed.

Second, there is a need for offices with specific expertise in coping with the elder abuse cases within each city's governmental office. Further, it is important to educate and train staff members working in such offices by developing connections with medical doctors, social workers, and other professionals who work with elderly people. Creating consulting windows or shelters for elderly abuse cases in each prefecture or city may help to identify cases of elder abuse in earlier stages, thus preventing many tragic deaths. Making a 24-hour hotline available for both elderly people and caregivers may also help to reduce stress and address the issues often encountered when nursing elderly people. Because there is no office designated for elder abuse thus far, there is no place for family, friends, and other members of the community to report abuses or potentially abusive situations when they are discovered. Like the child abuse support system, a system making the reporting of possible elder abuse

a legal duty is needed. Moreover, each office needs to create a network of connections with other elder abuse offices as well as other governmental offices, including the police and the health centers. As we previously discussed, elder abuse often takes place at the home where animal abuse is also taking place. Exchanging information and working together with the health centers, which work to rescue abused animals, may find more abused elderly people and protect them before abuse escalates. Such connections between various organizations need to be clearly described in manuals.

Finally, there is a need for elderly abuse checklists. Victims of elder abuse are less likely to be identified than victims of child abuse. This may be because victims did not view themselves as abused, or because victims may be reluctant to report abuse by family members. Even the staff who work at the nursing home or other offices who work with elderly people often do not have enough knowledge about elder abuse. Therefore, developing manuals and checklists may be helpful as a first step in educating staff members. Using a checklist to identify possible abuses and developing manuals detailing how to respond to abuse may help in discovering hidden abuse victims (e.g., pet animals, children) and in taking appropriate actions to protect victims.

Most importantly, all members of society need to obtain accurate information about the situation of elderly abuse and how they should react when they suspect that abuse might be occurring. Thanks to the help of the media and many other organizations, most Japanese people now know that they have a duty to report possible instances of child abuse to the police. This level of awareness is an important achievement because 10 years ago this belief was not prevalent. However, awareness of elder abuse is still very low, and the word "elder abuse" is rarely heard. Kobayashi (2004) has noted that 1 out of 4 Japanese will be older than 65 by 2015. Faced with an aging society, the issue of elder abuse must be highlighted as significant, and we hope that more research will be conducted to increase our understanding.

Elder Adults and Animals

In this section, we will discuss how we can promote elderly people's well-being and how animals may play a role for elderly people. As the population of elderly people increases, there is growing interest in promoting healthy aging and the independence of elderly people. Strategies to improve the quality of life for elderly people would not only benefit people in later life, but also have the potential to reduce the costs of health care services.

Loneliness is often cited as the worst aspect of aging (Perettie, 1990). Today, more Japanese elderly people live longer, and more of them have started to live alone (14.1% of males and 50.6% of females; Gender Equality Bureau, the Cabinet Office, 2005). As people get older, longtime friends die or move away. With the loss of relatives, friends, and associates, elderly people gradually withdraw from active participation in human interactions. This decrease in opportunities for communicating and interacting with family and others has resulted in increasing elderly people's stress, depression, and loneliness. These changes have led to serious challenges to the overall health and well-being of elderly people (Bustad, 1996).

The conflict between a large number of elderly people who need assistance and the lack of nursing homes may lead to some elder abuse at home. Even if elderly people can enter a nursing home, many of them are often forced into a restricted life because of lack of space and staff at the nursing homes. Thus, these elderly people are also more likely to suffer from depression or loneliness (Iwamoto & Fukui, 2002).

Bustad (1996) pointed out that humans' changes of lifestyle necessitate animal companionship. For many elderly people, pets can become a constant source of satisfaction when interaction with others is severely restricted (Fogle, 1981). According to the report from the Prime-Minister Cabinet Office (2003), 34.5% people aged between 60 and 69 (n=435), and 28.2% of people aged older than 70 (n=316) own pets compared to 32.9% of people aged between 20 and 29 (n=237), and 31.7% of people aged between 30 and 39 (n=375) who own pets. Even though the number of elderly people who own pets is smaller than for younger people, many elderly people own pets in Japan. There are no data on nursing homes that employ animals for therapeutic purposes (i.e., animal-assisted therapy). Additionally, Iwamoto and Fukui (2002) discussed volunteer activities that call for pet owners to visit nursing homes with their pets, programs that are very popular in Japan today. However, there are only a few welfare facilities, such as nursing homes, that allow elderly people to have a pet at their institutions, while the United States, England, France, and other countries allow patients to have pets at their nursing homes because the staff regards animals as healers (Iwamoto & Fukui, 2002).

One of the reasons why owning pets at nursing homes is prohibited in Japan is because many people (i.e., staff) do not believe animals can affect humans' health due to the lack of studies in this area. In addition, there is the lack of connection between organizations that provide animals' visits and organizations that seek such programs. Though it is important to be considerate of other elderly people's preference in the same nursing homes, more elderly people might be both physiologically and psychologically healthier if they could own their pets at the nursing homes. This might also encourage more elderly people to go to nursing homes if they do not want to leave their house because of their pets. It is necessary to conduct scientific studies to investigate how interacting with animals will affect elderly peoples' well-being in Japan, and optimistically, people's perception toward animals will be changed in positive way (e.g., animals as a healer). Hopefully, regulations of nursing homes and related institutions will be modified so that more elderly people can interact with animals in their daily lives, which may consequently promote their well-being.

The effects on psychological and physiological well-being through interacting with animals will be further discussed in the next section.

Treatment

Interaction with Animals as Prevention of and Intervention for Juvenile Crimes

We discussed how issues of violence against animals may link to violence against humans (i.e., domestic violence, child abuse, elder abuse) throughout the chapter, and in earlier sections, how children's aggression toward animals may link to violence against humans. Though violence against animals may be an early indication of violence that may escalate to humans, Ascione and Arkow (1999) pointed out that animal-based interventions can provide individuals a healing environment and give them opportunities to express nurturance and empathy. Past studies have found that children's aggressive behavior can be learned (Bandura, Ross, & Ross, 1963). Therefore, there is reason to think that if physical aggression can be induced, then it can also be prevented by teaching children strategies to deflect aggressive behavior, such as skills promoting empathic attitudes and behavior (Belloso-Curiel, 2002; Eisenberg, 1992). In this section, we will discuss school-based prevention and intervention programs for children's aggression and maltreatment of animals, which may prevent further violence against humans.

Today, violence intervention programs employing animals have started to gain attention, and some jails and detention centers in the United States have started intervention programs with animals and successes of those programs are often reported. One such program is Project Pooch (Positive Opportunities Obvious Changes with Hounds), which was implemented at the MacLaren Youth Correctional facility in Oregon in 1993. The program has juvenile offenders train abandoned dogs, which might otherwise be euthanized, to prepare them for adoption as family pets. Through training dogs, juvenile offenders learned how to manage their own behaviors and developed responsibility, patience, and the ability to work with others. To date, a zero recidivism rate among offenders who were in this program is reported (Project Pooch, 2005).

Preventing youth violence is one of the most significant issues in Japan, and the competitive style of the educational system has been proven to cause stress, which may be correlated with increased crimes perpetrated by students. Yet there are few prevention and intervention programs for this issue in Japan. As empirical research from outside of Japan has shown (e.g., Ascione, 1992, 1993, 1997), one program that might serve as prevention and intervention strategies for delinquency and criminal behaviors of children is implementing humane education at school settings. It has been reported that guiding children to be mindful of animals' needs and to treat animals with sympathy may affect children's future behavior toward other humans (Ascione, 1992, 1993, 1997). Numerous studies have shown that children who spend time with, care for, and interact with animals are more likely to show empathic behaviors toward humans in the future (e.g., Ascione, 1992, 1993, 1997; Cameron, 1983). Unfortunately, today's Japanese children have more challenges to be sensitive to nature and their surroundings because they are educated from when they are very young, which offers them fewer opportunities to learn how to interact with diverse people in different settings. This lack of experience may leave children unprepared to deal with their anger or sadness when they face an unexpected situation. However, by interacting with and caring for animals, children learn to interpret nonverbal signals based on behaviors and contexts. Thus, it is expected that introducing animals to children not only increases their current understanding

of nonverbal behaviors, it may also increase their future empathy toward humans.

Further, literature from several researchers (Arkow, 1998; George, 1998; Levinson, 1969b) indicates that the introduction of animals into the lives of children may be particularly effective in developing morality, empathic behaviors, self-esteem, and responsibility. Though the effectiveness of humane educational programs has been reported across studies in the United States, there is a lack of humane education programs and research on this topic in Japan. Although many public elementary schools in Japan have school pets (e.g., rabbits), schools tend to keep pets outside of classrooms (e.g., in a corner of the school yard). The survey study conducted by Hatogai (2004) found that 88% of public elementary schools have pets, yet 95.4% keep them outside the classrooms, and only 1.4% keep pets inside the classrooms. Unfortunately, the combination of the location and a lack of time or encouragement from others (i.e., teachers, peers, or guardians) make it unlikely that students will interact with these school pets.

Finch (1989) suggested that researchers and educators begin to link humane education to current social problems such as child abuse and delinquency. Further, Finch commented, "Humane education has the potential of being one of the most effective ways of teaching empathy toward animals and people" (p. 68). Introducing children to humane education and prompting them to care for animals may reduce their aggression and maltreatment of animals and possibly humans.

The Effects of Classroom Pets on Japanese Children's Empathy

Although preventing children's violence has gained attention as Japan faces an increased rate of juvenile crimes, effective prevention or intervention programs for juvenile delinquencies or crimes have not been implemented or well studied in Japan. In order to investigate whether humane education, specifically interaction with animals, will promote children's empathy toward humans, we conducted an experimental study in Japan from 2003 to 2004 (Maruyama, Ascione, & Nakagawa, 2005).

In the study, we investigated the influence of intensified daily interactions with living animals in the classroom on the development of empathy among Japanese children. Specifically, we examined (a) the effect of introducing animals into the classroom on children's empathic behaviors and attitudes, and

(b) the generalization of this animal-directed empathy to humans.

Eight hundred and fifty-three students (in grades two through five) from nine elementary schools in Japan either engaged in intensive, guided interactions with two to three guinea pigs per class (the experimental or E group) or did not interact with guinea pigs or otherwise receive special curricula (the control or C group). Throughout the study, the E group occasionally received traditional humane education with veterinarians, learning how to care for animals and about animal life. Students were further divided into two groups by grade: younger students (second and third graders) and older students (fourth and fifth graders). Students in the E group cared for the guinea pigs throughout the academic year. All students completed surveys designed to measure children's empathic attitudes toward animals and humans (i.e., Primary Attitude Scales (PAS) and Intermediate Attitude Scales (IAS), Ascione, 1988a, 1988b; Index of Empathy, Bryant, 1982) at the beginning of the academic year and again 11 months later, at the end of the year.

We did not find any significant difference between the groups (E group vs. C group) on the younger students' scores on empathic attitudes toward animals (PAS) across the study (pre-test vs. post-test). However, for the older students, we found that the E group students (classroom with pets) showed significantly greater gains in mean empathy scores (IAS) from the pre-test to the post-test than C group students who did not have any pets in the classroom. (See more statistical detail in Maruyama, 2005.)

Subsequently, we investigated whether children's empathy toward animals would generalize to human-directed empathy. A Pearson product-moment correlation coefficient analysis was performed to evaluate whether children's humane attitudes toward animals (PAS and IAS scores) were related to empathic skills toward humans (Index of Empathy score). For both the younger and older students, we found a significant correlation between humane attitudes toward animals (PAS/IAS) and empathy toward humans (Index of Empathy), $r = .19$, $p < .001$, $r = .50$, $p < .001$, respectively. Also, male students' correlation between empathy toward animals and humans was higher than that of female students.

Though the study has several limitations (e.g., lower accuracy of measuring children's empathy using a survey method, teachers' effect on children's empathy) that suggest future research to approach a remedy, the findings of the study supported the research hypotheses and indicated that having animals in the classroom may promote older children's empathy toward animals. Qualitative teachers' reports suggest that these results may be generalized to empathy toward peers. (See more detail in Maruyama, 2005.) Specifically, we found the program was more effective for the older children (fourth and fifth graders) than the younger children (second and third graders). Significant correlations between empathy scores toward animals and empathy scores toward humans indicated that students' empathy toward classroom pets might generalize to humans.

Since the Japanese Ministry of Education, Culture, Sports, Science, and Technology changed the school system from 6 days a week to 5 days a week in order to reduce intensity of academic pressure on children and to give students more free time, the rate of serious crimes committed by young children has remained the same. What children need most are daily learning experiences regarding the value of life, instead of cramming for examinations. If children have more opportunities to interact with animals in their daily lives, naturally they may have more occasions to take the perspective of animals. This experience may help their perspective taking abilities and these abilities are expected to apply when they interact with humans. Teaching children to be kind to animals may be the most effective way to raise our children to be healthy adults. We believe that school should be a place to teach children not only formal study but also how to be a better human who can fit in a society. Humane education may be one way to achieve that goal.

Background of Animal Therapy in Japan

Animals have long been perceived as beneficial to humans' well-being, and it has long been assumed that humans naturally form psychological bonds with animals. Research and clinical observations from outside of Japan have shown that bonding with animals can have a positive effect on human health. Across the world, and not only for children, animals have been employed to promote psychological and physiological well-being of people with different backgrounds (Allen, Blascovich, Tomako, & Kelsey, 1991; Friedmann, Katcher, Thomas, Lynch, & Messent, 1983; Katcher, 1988; Katcher, Segal, & Beck, 1984; Serpell, 1991; Wilson, 1991).

More recently, attention to animals as companions has been focused on healing humans psychologically, and the term "animal therapy" has been often used in the media and in Japanese society today. Though many activities employing animals (e.g., interacting with animals at nursing homes) have increased recently, the use of animals for medical treatment purposes are still very few (Iwamoto & Fukui, 2002). This is because Japanese people have different ideas toward animals compared with people in western society, and Yokoyama (1996) discussed that Japanese people would hesitate to be active in promoting employing animals in medical settings. Though there are a few studies regarding the effectiveness of animal therapy on humans' health in Japan, Iwamoto and Fukui (2002) commented that there is no theory behind many of these studies and their findings and conclusions are often difficult to interpret. This is because there is no standard or scientific or academic handbook on animal therapy in Japan, and such guidelines are needed to promote more scientific or academic research on this topic, which may promote more animal-assisted therapy in Japan.

As we discussed previously, employing animals for the purpose of promoting humans' well-being is a fairly recent practice in Japan. For instance, it was in 1978 that the Japanese Animal Hospital Association (JAHA), which is the first organization for promoting animal therapy, developed in Japan compared with the time when other countries organized (cf. from 1792 in England, from 1867 in Germany, 1944 in the United States; JAHA, 2006). However, more and more Japanese organizations have started to consider the effectiveness of introducing animals to people who may need what animals can offer. Though the effectiveness of such programs has not been academically or scientifically reported, both positive physiological effects (e.g., improvement of body balance, strengthening of body muscle) and positive psychological effects (e.g., promote motivation on activities, promote self-esteem) can be anticipated. Further studies are needed to investigate how animals can promote Japanese people's well-being within Japanese cultural and societal backgrounds.

Discussion

Links Between Animal Abuse, Domestic Violence, Child Abuse, and Elder Abuse: A Cross-Cultural Perspective

Today, Japanese culture and society have been westernized as globalization advances. We see a more internationalized culture than traditional Japanese culture in daily lives, and this interna-

tionalization also greatly affects people's value systems within society. For instance, learning English is required for all children in elementary schools. Inevitably, some of the positive elements relating to the events and social movements occurring in other countries will have an impact upon Japanese society. However, these movements are still a recent phenomenon. For instance, compared with U.S. society, where extensive research has been conducted on juvenile crimes, animal abuse, domestic violence, child abuse, and elder abuse, only a handful of studies have been conducted in Japan. Thus, there are limited data available on these topics, and movements for change on these social issues are very slow to develop and not yet fully supported by the government or the people in Japanese society.

Large numbers of studies on the issue of violence against humans have been conducted in the United States, which consequently made people in the United States much more aware of the issues than people in Japan where few studies are conducted. As a result, well-organized support systems and law enforcement systems have been established in the United States. For instance, the law provides for strict punishment of child abusers, domestic batterers, and animal abusers, and the rate of crimes (e.g., felonious offenses committed by both adults and juveniles) and intimate partner violence in the United States has been dramatically dropping in last decade. This may be due to the effects of extensive research, community-based programs (e.g., prevention/intervention), and the support from the government. In contrast to the United States, Japan's crime rates are increasing (Larimer, 2000). Although the rate of violence is still much lower than the rate in the United States, the crime rate reached its highest level in the past three decades and more than half of those offenses are accounted by violent crime committed by juveniles (Larimer, 2000). As the U.S. rates of violence declined through numerous investigations and active political movements (e.g., strict punishment under the law), now is the time that Japan has to learn from the United States success and consider implementing such programs or movements to prevent further increases in the rate of violence.

As psychologists working in Japan, we frequently obtain information from other countries and learn from their empirical data. However, we cannot always apply their findings or solutions to Japanese cases because of different cultural values. For instance, Japanese communications are not straightforward and an important message often is delivered indirectly (Iwasaki, 2005). Further, Japanese people traditionally tend to "read others' mind" whereas people in the western culture tend to "say what's on your mind" (Markus & Kitayama, 1991). While we can learn from empirical studies and statistical data relating to intervention programs from other countries, it is still necessary to modify many of these solutions to reflect traditional values within Japanese culture if these solutions are to be successful in Japan.

Although throughout this chapter we have discussed the serious social problems in Japan, often focusing on the contribution of societal values that sometimes prevent people from seeking help, the aim of this chapter is not to compromise the harmony of Japanese society or to change the collectivistic culture to an individualistic westernized culture. Rather, our suggestions point out the current lack of empirical studies and general knowledge of the legal system on social problems in Japan. In preliminary research, we found that few of the resources relating to topics discussed in these chapters had been translated into English or other languages. Exchanging information and learning from the data produced in other countries can provide critical assistance in designing and completing more studies in Japan, which will in turn promote the well-being of the Japanese people.

Moreover, even though we discussed each social problem separately (i.e., juvenile delinquency, animal abuse, domestic violence, child abuse, and elder abuse), each issue seems closely linked to the others, and factors that cause each issue may be similar. Thus, it is anticipated that more integrated and collaborative approaches may be appropriate in order to investigate and intervene in these social issues as Ascione and Arkow (1999) suggested.

The collective harmony and social sensitivity of the Japanese culture remain strengths we can be proud of. The people now living in this unique society face the task of figuring out how to promote optimal adaptation skills among individuals without giving up the strength of our traditional cultural and societal values. To achieve this goal, we first need to obtain accurate information about the true prevalence rates of problems and face the reality that Japan is no longer the world's safest country. This will allow us to generate constructive ideas about which actions we should take as a next step.

Second, governmental supports are necessary. As we pointed out, the number of shelters for violence victims, whether they are for humans or animals, is significantly lacking in Japan. Due to limited funding from the government, those victims often have to return to violent places without the situation being improved. Significant improvements have been made in recent years as laws on animal abuse, domestic violence, and child maltreatment have been enacted in Japan, and more prefectural offices to support violence victims have been created. Yet far more offices are needed, and the connections between these offices and the community as well as between each office and the government need to be made much stronger. Subsequently, these offices need to educate people in the community by sharing their information and encouraging people to visit them by providing an environment that is accessible and provides a welcoming environment. Only through educational efforts and making these offices a basic part of the community will it be possible to break down social prejudice toward these offices and the people who need their help.

The people and culture of today's Japan have changed dramatically in the last 50 years, mainly through economic development and internationalization. The hierarchical, male-dominated society is now changing to become more egalitarian, partly due to the influence of westernized cultural values. These new values have promoted positive changes in Japanese culture, but now it seems like many people, especially younger generations, have started to forget essential aspects of traditional Japanese culture, which values social harmony. For instance, many of the incidents listed as examples in the previous sections could easily have been prevented if these individuals had possessed the ability to communicate with other people. Today many people do not know their neighbors, and they now have fewer opportunities to communicate with others. Even within the family structure, there is often little communication as people move through their incredibly busy lives. As we write this chapter, we cannot help thinking that communication and adequate treatment are the keys to preventing further increases in violent crimes. Now is the time for Japanese people to rethink norms of isolating people in service to the value of "social harmony" and to focus more on the importance of communication. We hope this will once again make Japan "the safest country" in the international community.

Notes

1. The co-author is not of Japanese heritage. When observations and evaluations of Japanese society and culture are presented in this chapter, they represent the opinions of the first author (Maruyama). The authors express deep appreciation to Dr. Akimitsu Yokoyama of Teikyo Kagaku University for his generous advice on this paper.

2. Since the completion of this chapter, Japan enacted elder abuse legislation in 2006.

References

Allen, K., Blascovich, J., Tomako, J., & Kelsey, R. M. (1991). Presence of human friends and pet dogs as moderators of autonomic response to stress in women. *Journal of Personal and Social Psychology, 61,* 582–589.

All Life In a Viable Environment (ALIVE). (2005, December 1). *Alive news.* Retrieved January 5, 2006, from http://www.alive-net.net/law/kanren/isitubutuhou.html

American Psychiatric Association. (1987). *Diagnostic and statistical manual of mental disorders* (3rd ed., Revised). Washington, DC: Author.

Aoki, H. (2004). *Hou to doubutsu.* [The law and animals]. Tokyo, Japan: Akashi-Shoten.

Arakawa, K. (1979). *Denwasoudan ni miru "Nihon no sei no jittai houkokusho"* [Reports on sexual activity of Japanese from the report of telephone hotline service]. Japan: Daiyaru hinin Soudansitu-Onna no Karada Soudansitsu Press.

Arkow, P. (1998). *Pet therapy: A study and resource guide to the use of companion animals in selected therapies* (8th ed.). Stratfort, NJ: Author.

Ascione, F. R. (1988a). *Primary attitude scale: Assessment of kindergarten through second graders' attitudes toward the treatment of animals.* Logan, UT: Wasatch Institute for Research and Evaluation.

Ascione, F. R. (1988b). *Intermediate attitude scale: Assessment of third through sixth graders' attitudes toward the treatment of animals.* Logan, UT: Wasatch Institute for Research and Evaluation.

Ascione, F. R. (1992). Enhancing children's attitudes about the humane treatment of animals: Generalization to human-directed empathy. Anthrozoös, *5,* 176–191.

Ascione, F. R. (1993). Children who are cruel to animals: A review of research and implications for developmental psychology. *Anthrozoös, 6*(4), 226–247.

Ascione, F. R. (1997). Humane education research: Evaluating efforts to encourage children's kindness and caring toward animals. *Genetic, Social, and General Psychology Monographs, 123*(1), 57–77.

Ascione, F. R. (1999). The abuse of animals and human interpersonal violence: Making the connection. In F. R. Ascione & P. Arkow (Eds.), *Child abuse, domestic violence, and animal abuse.* West Lafayette, IN: Purdue University Press.

Ascione, F. R. (2000). *Safe havens for pets: Guidelines for programs sheltering pets for women who are battered.* Logan, UT: Author.

Ascione, F. R., & Arkow, P. (Eds.). (1999). *Child abuse, domestic violence, and animal abuse: Linking the circles of compassion for prevention and intervention.* West Lafayette, IN: Purdue University Press.

Ascione, F. R., Weber, C. V., & Wood, D. S. (1997). The abuse of animals and domestic violence: A national survey of shelters for women who are battered. *Society and Animals, 5*(3), 205–218.

Bandura, A., Ross, D., & Ross, S. (1963). A comparative test of the status envy, social power, and secondary reinforcement theories of identificatory learning. *Journal of Abnormal and Social Psychology, 67,* 527–534.

Belloso-Curiel. J. (2002). Humane education as an intervention for the development of empathic skills in children. *Berkeley McNair Research Journal, 8.*

Bryant, B. K. (1982). An index of empathy for children and adolescents. *Child Development, 53,* 413–425.

Bureau of Social Welfare and Public Health. (2001). *Jidou gyakutai no jittai.* [Investigation on the issue of child abuse]. Retrieved July 21, 2005, from http://www.fukushihoen.metro.tokyo.jp_press_reles/2001/pr1005.htm

Bustad, L.K. (1996). Recent discoveries about our relationships with the natural world. In *Compassion: Our Last Great Hope-Selected Speeches of Leo K. Bustad, DVM, Ph.D.* Delta society, Renton, WA.

Cameron, R. K. K. (1983). *The effects of two instructional treatments on eight-grade students' attitudes toward animal life.* Unpublished doctoral dissertation, Purdue University, West Lafayette, Indiana

Crystal, D. S., & Stevenson, H. W. (1995). What is a bad kid? Answers of adolescents and their mothers in three cultures. *Journal of Research on Adolescence, 5*(1), 71–91.

Davey, D. (1995). Survey on abuse rallies Japanese women. *Herizons, 9*(1), 31–33.

Dolly, J. (1993). The impact of *juku* on Japanese students. *Journal of Instructional Psychology, 20*(4), 277–286.

Eisenberg, N. (1992). *The caring child.* Cambridge, MA: Harvard University Press.

Enomoto, H. (1996). *Jisatsu: Ikiru chikarawo takameru tameni, Shishunkino kokorono SOS, Library 9.* [Suicide: To promote the ability to live. Library 9 SOS from adolescents with troubled heart]. Tokyo, Japan: Science Company.

Finch, P. (1989). Learning from the past. In D. Paterson & M. Palmer (Eds.), *The status of animals: Ethics, education and welfare.* Oxon, England: C.A.B International.

Fogle, B. (1981). *Interrelations between people and pets.* Springfield, IL: Charles C. Thomas.

Friedmann, E. Katcher, A. H., Thomas, S. A., Lynch, J. J., & Messent, P. R. (1983). Social interaction and blood pressure: Influence of animal companions. *Journal of Nervous and Mental Disease, 171*, 461–465.

Fujii, S. (2001). *Hitowo Koroshite mitakatta: Aichiken Toyokawashi shufu satsujin jiken.* [I wanted to experience murdering people: The case of murder in Toyokowa city in Aichi prefecture]. Tokyo, Japan: Futaba Press.

Gender Equality Bureau, Cabinet Office. (2003). *Haigushanadokarano bouryokunikansuru chousa.* [Investigation of violence from spouses]. Retrieved June 1, 2005, from http://www.gender.go.jp

Gender Equality Bureau, Cabinet Office. (2004). *Stop the violence: For individuals tormented by spousal violence.* Retrieved June 1, 2005, from http://www.gender.go.jp

Gender Equality Bureau, Cabinet Office. (2005). *Danjokyoudousanga hakusho.* [White paper of the Gender Equality Bureau]. Japan: Author.

George, M. H. (1998). Children and animals: A new way for an old relationship. In C. Schaefer (Ed.), *Innovative interventions in child and adolescent therapy.* New York: Wiley-Interscience.

Hashizume, Y. (2000). *Gender issues and Japanese family-centered caregiving for frail elderly parents or parents-in-law in modern Japan: From the sociocultural and historical perspec-* *tives.* Retrieved March 22, 2006, from http://drw.addr.com/x_courses/1017/1017.htm

Hatogai, T. (2004). *Seimeisonchou no taidoikuseinikakawaru seibutsukyouzai no kousei to hyoukanikannsuru chousakenkyu* [Research on humane education materials and program evaluation]. Tokyo, Japan: Kokuritukyouikuseisaku Laboratory.

Hitchcock, A. (2000). Violent juvenile crimes in Japan point to a deeper social crisis. *World Socialist Web Site.* Retrieved July 25, 2005, from http://www.wsws.org/articles/2000/act2000/japo18_prn.shtml

Ishida, O., Yokoyama, A., Kamijo, M., Akami, T., Akami, R., & Wako, K. (2004). *Nihonjinno doubutukan: Kono 10nenkanno suii.* [The change of Japanese thinking of animals, in this decade]. *Doubutukenkyu, 8*, 17–32.

Iwamoto, T., & Fukui, I. (2002). *Animal therapy no riron to jissai.* [Theory and practice in animal therapy]. Tokyo, Japan: Baifu-kan.

Iwasaki, M. (2005). Mental health and counseling in Japan: A path toward societal transformation. *Journal of Mental Health Counseling, 27*(2), 129–141.

Japan Animal Hospital Association (JAHA). (2006). *Homepage.* Retrieved January 30, 2006, from http://www.jaha.or.jp/

Katcher, A. H. (1988). The evolution of human affection: The significance of the living environment in the modern world. *Abstracts of presentations: People, animals and the environment: Exploring our interdependence.* Delta Society 7th Annual Conference, Orlando, FL, September 29–October 1.

Katcher, A. H., Segal, H., & Beck, A. H. (1984). Comparison of contemplation and hypnosis for the reduction of anxiety and discomfort during dental surgery. *American Journal of Clinical Hypnosis, 27*, 14–21.

Knight, B.G., Robinson, G. S., Flynn, C. V., Chun, L. M., Nakano, K., & Kim, J.H. (2002). Cross cultural issues in caregiving for persons with dementia: Do familism values reduce burden and distress? *Ageing International, 27*(3), 71–97.

Kobayashi, A. (2004). *Koureisha gyakutai: Jittaito boushisaku.* [Elderly abuse: The situation and the intervention]. Tokyo, Japan: Chuo-Kouron Shinsha Publications.

Kobayashi, H., Tastumi, E., & Fukuju, C. (2005). *Domestic violence: Otto, koibitokarano bouryoku.* [Domestic violence: Violence from husband and romantic partner]. Retrieved July 1, 2005, from http://syass.kwansei.ac.jp/tatsuki/sotsuron4/

Koyake, R. (2003). DV no jittaito kongono kadai. [Facts of DV and future assignment]. *Kyoiku Shinbun, 2392.* Retrieved May 31, 2005, from http://www.arsvi.com/2000/030731kr.htm

Larimer, T. (2000, August 28). Natural-born killers? *Time, 156*(9). Retrieved May 2, 2006, from http://web106.epnet.com/citation.asp?tb=1

Levinson, B. M. (1969b). *Pet orientated child psychotherapy.* Springfield, IL: Charles C. Thomas.

Lockwood, R., & Ascione, F. (Eds.). (1998). *Cruelty to animals and interpersonal violence: Readings in research and application.* West Lafayette, IN: Purdue University Press.

Machizawa, S. (2000a). *Abunai shounen.* [Juveniles at risk]. Tokyo, Japan: Koudansha Press.

Machizawa, S. (2000b). *Kodomoga ichibanha yamenasai.* [Stop putting all priorities to your child]. Tokyo, Japan: Kairyu Press.

Machizawa, S. (2001). *Jibunwo keshitai konokunino kodomotachi: "Kizuzukiyasui jisonshin" no seishinbunseki.* [The children that tend to erase their existence: Psychoanalyses of the "self-esteem that are easy to be destroyed"]. Tokyo, Japan: PHP Press.

Machizawa, S. (2003). *Hikikomoru wakamonotachi: "Hikikomori" no jittai to shohousen.* [Juveniles who are *hikikomori*: The actual situation and an intervention]. Tokyo, Japan: Yamato Shobou.

Maeda, M. (2002). *Saikinno hanzaino zoukani tuite.* [Reports on the recent increase of juvenile crimes rate]. Naikakufu Seishounen no Ikuseini Kansuru Yuushikisha Kondankai [Discussion on raising juveniles, The Prime-Minister Office], October, 18, 2002. Retrieved April 28, 2006, from http://www8.cao.go.jp/youth/suisin/ikuseikondan021018/08shiryou/08shiryou1.pdf

Markus, H. R., & Kitayama, S. (1991). Culture and the self: Implications for cognition, emotion, and motivation. *Psychological Review, 98,* 224–253.

Maruyama. M. (2005). *Humane education: The effects of animals in the classroom on children's empathy in Japanese elementary schools.* Unpublished master's thesis, Portland State University, Oregon.

Maruyama, M., Ascione, F. R., & Nakagawa, M. (2005). The effects of animals in the classroom on children's empathy in Japanese elementary schools. 55th *Annual Meeting of the Society for the Study of Social Problems*, Philadelphia, PA, August 11–14.

Maruyama, M., Mankowski, E. S., & Hara, K. (2005). Japanese batterer intervention: Program and participant characteristics. *9th International Family Violence Research Conference*, Portsmouth, NH, July 10–13.

Matsuede inochino toutosawo tutaeru shobun inuneko shashinten. [Picture exhibition of sheltered animals before they were euthanized in Matsue-city]. (2005, September 22). *Saninchuou Shinpou.* Retrieved January 10, 2006, from http://www.sanin-chuo.co.jp/news/modules/news/105917004.html

Minami, H. (1984). *Kateinai seiai.* [Incest]. Tokyo, Japan: Asahi Publications.

Ministry of Health, Labor, and Welfare. (2004). Jidougyakutai siboujirei no kenshouto kongono gyakutaiboushitaisaku nit suite. [Analysis of death cases of child abuse and prevention and intervention of child abuse]. Retrieved April 23, 2006, from http://www.mhlw.go.jp/bunya/kodomo/dv-01.html

Ministry of Health, Labor, and Welfare. (2005a). *Jisatsu Shibou Toukei 5th* [Suicide rates 5th]. Tokyo, Japan: Kousei Toukei Kyoukai.

Ministry of Health, Labor, and Welfare. (2005b). Kouseiroudou hakusho. [White paper of Ministry of Health, Labor, and Welfare]. Retrieved December 20, 2005, from http://wwwhakusyo.mhlw.go.jp/wp/index.htm

Ministry of Justice. (1977). *Hanzai hakusho.* [White paper of crimes]. Retrieved May 1, 2006, from http://www.moj.go.jp/HOUSO/hakusho2.html

Ministry of Justice (2005). *Hanzai hakusho* [White paper of crimes]. Retrieved March 6, 2006, from http://www.moj.go.jp/

Ministry of Education, Culture, Sports, Science, and Technology. (2004). *Seitosidoujou no shomondaino genjounituite.* [Reports of issues on guiding students]. Retrieved August 6, 2005, from http://www.mext.go.jp/b_menu/houdou/16/08/04082302.htm

Mishima, A. (2005). *Jidou gyakugai to doubutsu gyakutai.* [Child abuse and animal abuse]. Tokyo, Japan: Seikyusha Library Press.

Nakamura, Y. (2002). Child abuse and neglect in Japan. *Pediatrics International, 44,* 580–581.

National Police Agency. (2005a). *Heisei 16nenni okeru jisatsuno gaiyou siryou.* [Reports on the rate of suicide in 2004]. Tokyo, Japan: Author.

National Police Agency. (2005b). *Shounen hikou-nadono gaiyou* [The summary of juvenile crimes and its prevention]. Tokyo, Japan: Author.

Niigata shoujo kankin jiken [The case of imprisonment of the girl in Niigata]. (2006, April). *Wikipedia.* Retrieved May 1, 2006, from http://ja.wikipedia.org/wiki

Niregi, M. (2002). *School counseling no kisochishiki.* [Basic knowledge of school counseling]. Tokyo, Japan: Shinshokan.

Nishi, M., Furuta, T., & Yamashita, J. (1998). Aitsugu doubutsu gyakutai [Animal abuse one after another]. *Shikoku Shinbun.* Retrieved March 13, 2005, from http://www.shikoku-np.co.jp/feature/tuiseki/085

Nogami, F. (2005, September 3). Inunekono shobunsuuno genshouni mukete. [For the decrease of the number of dogs and cats that are euthanized]. *Alive News.* Retrieved December 22, 2005, from http://www.alive-net.net/companion-animal/hikihotori/syobun-genshou.html

The number of teachers who suffer from psychological illness reached the highest. (2005, December 15). *Yomiuri Newspaper,* p. 38.

Ornatowski, G. K. (1996). Confucian ethics and economic development: A study of the adaptation of Confucian values to modern Japanese economic ideology and institutions. *Journal of Socio-Economics, 25*(5), 571–591.

Peretti, P. O. (1990). Elderly-animal friendship bonds. *Social Behavior and Personality, 18*(1), 151–156.

The Prime-Minister Cabinet Office. (2003). *Public-opinion poll on animal protection.* Tokyo, Japan: Author.

The Prime-Minister Cabinet Office. (2005). *Koureishakai hakusho.* [White paper on aging society]. Tokyo, Japan: Author.

Project Pooch. (2005). Homepage. Retrieved December 23, 2005, from http://www.pooch.org/

Ran over rabbits with cars, conducted autopsies on the rabbits, and put pictures on the blog. (2005, December 13) *Yomiuri Newspaper,* p. 39.

Rosen, B. (1995). Watch for pet abuse: It might save your client's life. In R. Lockwood & F. R. Ascione (Eds.), *Cruelty to Animals and Interper-sonal Violence.* pp. 340–347. West Lafayette, IN: Purdue University Press.

Schreiber, M. (1997). Juvenile crime in the 1990s. *Japan Quarterly, 3,* 79–88.

Serpell, J. A. (1991). Beneficial effects of pet ownership on some aspects of human health and behaviour. *Journal of the Royal Society of Medicine, 84,* 717–720.

Shocking news for the society. (2003, July 10). *Online Nagasaki Newspaper.* Retrieved January 10, 2006, from http://www.nagasaki-np.co.jp/press/yuusatu/07/37.html

Someya, T., Kitamura, H., Uehara, T., Sakado, K., Kaiya, H., Tang, S.W., (2000). Panic disorder and perceived parental rearing behavior investigated by the Japanese version of the EMBU scale. *Depression and Anxiety, 11,* 158–162.

Spinrad, T., & Losaya, S. (1999). The relations of parental affect and encouragement to children's moral emotions and behavior. *Journal of Moral Education, 28,* 323–327.

Sugihara, Y., & Katsurada, E. (1999). Masculinity and femininity in Japanese culture: A pilot study. *Sex Roles, 40,* 635–646.

Sugihara, Y., & Katsurada, E. (2000). Gender-role personality traits in Japanese culture. *Psychology of Women Quarterly, 24,* 309–318.

Sugihara, Y., & Katsurada, E. (2002). Gender role development in Japanese culture: Diminishing gender role differences in a contemporary society. *Sex Roles, 47,* 443–452.

Suzuki, T., & Ishikawa, Y. (1999). *Darenimoienai ottono bouyoku.* [Violence from husband that you cannot tell anyone]. Japan: Honnojiyuusha.

Takahashi, Y. (1997). *Jisatsu no shinrigaku.* [Psychology of suicide]. Tokyo, Japan: Koudansha.

Takayama, F. (1998). *Shounen A: 14 saino shouzou.* [Boy A: The portrait of 14-year-old]. Tokyo, Japan: Shinchosha.

Takayama, F. (2001). *Jigokuno kisetsu: Sakakibara Seito ga itabasho.* [Season of the hell: A place where Sakakibara Seito was]. Tokyo, Japan: Shincho Bunko Publisher.

Teinenreikasuru kouishougaiheno mukiaikata. [How to face with conduct disorder that starts with younger ages]. (2000, November 13). *AERA.* Tokyo, Japan: Asahi Newspaper Publisher.

Wilson, C. C. (1991). The pet as an anxiolytic intervention. *Journal of Nervous and Mental Disease, 179*, 482–489.

Winfield, B. H., Mizuno, T., & Beaudoin, C. E. (2000). Confucianism, collectivism, and constitutions: Press systems in China and Japan. *Communication Law & Policy, 5*(3), 323–347.

World Health Organization. (2005). *Suicide rate per 100,000 by country, year, and sex.* Retrieved January 31, 2006, from http://www.who.int/mental_health/prevention/suicide_rates/en/index.html

Yamada, Y. (2004). *Kazokukaigoto koureisha gyakutai.* [Family nursing and elderly abuse].

Ichigase, Y. (Ed.), Tokyo, Japan: Hitotsubashi Publication.

Yamamoto, M., Iwata, N., Tomoda, A., Tanaka, S., Fujimaki, K., & Kitamura, T. (1999). Child emotional and physical maltreatment and adolescent psychopathology: A community study in Japan. *Journal of Community Psychology, 27*(4), 377–391.

Yokoyama, A. (1996). *Animal therapy tohananika.* [What is animal therapy]. Tokyo, Japan: Japan broadcast publication.

Yokoyama, A. (2006, May 26). Report on non-accidental injury at animal hospitals. *Japan Animal Hospital Association Symposium.* Tokyo, Japan.

Appendix

From *Season of the hell: A place where Sakakibara Seito was.* Takayama, F. (2001).

March 16, 1997

Dear "God Bamoidooki"

Today, I conducted a "secret experiment" to study how easily human's life could be destroyed. I asked a young girl who was playing alone in a park where I could wash my hand. Because she suggested to go to a school, I asked her to show me how to get there. I could not decide whether I should use a hammer or a knife. Yet in the end, I decided to use a hammer this time and would use a knife the next time. I asked her to look at me so that I could thank her, and I brought down the hammer as soon as she looked back. I hit her with the hammer a few times, but I could not remember clearly because I was too excited. On the way home, I found a little boy, but I soon lost him. So I was back on the way to home for lack of an alternative, but soon I found another little girl. So I forestalled her and I stabbed her with a knife when we passed each other. On the way home, it was very noisy with sounds of siren of the police cars and ambulance. Because I was too tired, I decided to go to bed that night. I appreciate the God Bamoidooki on my success of sacred experiment.

March 17, 1997

Dear "the God Bamoidooki"

When I opened the newspaper this morning, I was surprised at seeing the news about our "sacred experiment." It said that two girls did not die. I did not know whether humans were easily destroyed or not before the experiment, I now know that humans are much tougher than I expected.

Animal Abuse, Cruelty, and Welfare: An Australian Perspective

Eleonora Gullone and John P. Clarke

Introduction

Our major aim in writing this chapter is to provide a current review of the Australian environment in relation to animal cruelty and welfare attitudes, beliefs, and legislation. We begin with a general historical and current description of the Australian continent, followed by a historical account of the formation of Australia's Society for the Prevention of Cruelty to Animals. Several important issues need to be considered in order to provide a comprehensive account that enables the Australian situation to be examined within the context of important research in the area emanating mostly from the United States and Canada, and to a lesser extent from Great Britain. These issues include consideration of animal cruelty laws and their administration. We also review research relating to mandatory reporting of animal abuse. This is followed by a discussion of the important benefits of mandatory reporting of animal abuse, as well as welfare issues that arise, largely as a consequence of companion animal ownership. One of the major welfare issues for humans related to companion animal ownership is the dog bite issue. This is one particular area where Australia has led the way. Another important area of research concerns the co-occurrence of abuse, violence, and criminality. As with research in other countries, Australian research has provided clear support for the documented links between animal abuse, family violence, and criminal behavior. This Australian research will be reviewed within the context of past research from other countries. While it is acknowledged that animal farming also has significant welfare issues, discussion of this latter area is beyond the scope of this chapter.

The Continent of Australia

Australia was once known as New Holland. This land is one of the world's most ancient land masses, containing rocks that are over 4.5 million years old. The continent has a history of human occupation extending back at least 60,000 years. This history reveals a highly specialized people. It was not until 1788 that Europeans settled in Australia. In 1993, Australia's population was 18 million people, of whom only 265,000 could claim Australoid descent (i.e., have indigenous ancestry). It is predicted that by 2060, the population of Australia will have risen to 30 million, the vast majority of whom will live in cities of around 6 million people (Flannery, 1994).

Australia is a very large continent, a federation comprising six sovereign states and two self-governing territories. Several of its states are considered to be wholly dependent on agriculture, including the Northern Territory, Queensland, and Western Australia. Australia's vast size can be elucidated by the fact that it takes 6 hours to fly from east to west or north to south (RSCPA, 2000).

The Australian Royal Society for the Prevention of Cruelty to Animals

Australia's first Society for the Prevention of Cruelty to Animals was formed in 1871 in Victoria. People's concern regarding the welfare of horses was the main impetus driving its formation. By 1892, there were societies for the prevention of cruelty to animals in Tasmania, New South Wales, Queensland, and Western Australia. The establishment of societies in the Australian Capital Territory and in the Northern Territory occurred much later—in 1955 and 1965, respectively. The societies received the Royal Warrant in 1956 and formed a national organization in 1980. The two major stated objectives of the Royal Society for the Prevention of Cruelty to Animals are firstly to give the movement a national presence and secondly to promote a commonality of purpose and unity among the state and territory societies (RSCPA, 2000).

Australia's Animal Abuse and Cruelty Legislation

Each of the six states and two territories has jurisdiction over animal welfare through its own Prevention of Cruelty to Animals Act (POCTAA). With the exception of New South Wales (NSW) these acts control all aspects of animal use including experimentation. In NSW animal experimentation is controlled through a separate act.

Definition of "Animal"

Most of the acts define "animal" as a live member of the vertebrate species, which includes amphibians, reptiles, birds, and mammals. The Queensland, Western Australian, and Victorian acts include fish and crustaceans in their definition of "animal" but the remaining states and territories do not. Some definitions also include varied categories of animals depending on their use. For example, the Victorian POCTAA (1986) includes domesticated farm animals, animals used for recreational purposes, and animals used in research and educational institutions, in its definition of "animal."

Definition of Animal Cruelty

Animal cruelty is described through a list of acts of omission or commission rather than through a specific definition of cruelty (RSCPA, 2000). For example, the South Australian POCTAA (1985) defines cruelty as:

- deliberately or unreasonably causes the animal unnecessary pain;
- fails to provide it appropriate and adequate, food, water, shelter, or exercise;
- fails to take reasonable steps to alleviate any pain suffered by the animal;
- abandons the animal;
- neglects the animal so as to cause it pain;
- releases the animal from captivity for the purpose of it then being hunted or killed by another animal;
- causes the animal to be killed or injured by another animal;
- organizes, participates in, or is present at an event at which the animal is encouraged to fight with another animal;
- having injured the animal, fails to take reasonable steps to alleviate any pain suffered by the animal;

- kills the animal in a manner that causes the animal unnecessary pain;
- unless the animal is unconscious, kills the animal by a method that does not cause death to occur as rapidly as possible.

Enforcement of the Acts

The responsibility for the administration of the POCTAAs rests with the ministers for Agriculture in all states and territories with the exceptions of South Australia and Western Australia (WA POCTAA, 2002). Full-time officers of RSPCA, members of the police force, and designated officers of the Department of Agriculture have been vested with the legal authority to enforce the acts (RSPCA, 2000). In Western Australia, general inspectors have been appointed from the RSPCA, local governments, the Department of Agriculture, and the Conservation and Land Management Department. In South Australia, the Minister may appoint a person nominated by the South Australian branch of the RSPCA to be an inspector.

Penalties

Penalties that can be imposed under the POCTAAs vary quite substantially. For example, in South Australia, the maximum penalty is $10,000 (at the current Australian dollar exchange rate of .76, this would equal 7,600.00 USD) or imprisonment for 1 year. In NSW (POCTAA, 1979), the maximum penalty is $11,000 (8,360.00 USD) or up to 2 years imprisonment, and in Western Australia, which has the most recently revised act, there is a higher maximum penalty of $50,000 (38,000 USD) or up to 5 years imprisonment. However, maximum penalties under the law are rarely enforced.

Sharman (2002) has raised concern about the leniency with which anti-cruelty statutes are applied. In illustrating her position, Sharman gives examples of two particular cases of aggravated cruelty. The first occurred in October 2001 when Luke Park appeared in a New South Wales court for "allegedly putting his sister's kitten in a freezer for 40 minutes, attempting to set fire to its whiskers, spraying it with an aerosol can and throwing steak knives at it before stoning it to death" (p. 333). The second case described by Sharman is that of Trevor Duffy who was charged with beating his dog to death with an iron bar. Sharman describes "Duffy allegedly attacked his dog, 'Tess,' after he found her carrying a kitten in her mouth. Tess' skull was cracked with the force of the initial blow from the iron bar and her eye was knocked out of its socket but the beating continued until she died from massive head injuries" (p. 333). Although both Park and Duffy pleaded guilty to the charges, both men were released on good behavior bonds. Even if the maximum possible penalty had been imposed under the NSW POCTAA, as previously noted, this would only have amounted to $11,000 Australian dollars or 2 years imprisonment.

Such lenient sentencing is not unusual. Between January 1996 and December 2000, prison terms were handed down to only 3% of offenders who committed acts of animal cruelty. Further, for as many as 80% of these offenders, the prison terms were for 4 months or less. A total of 75% of offenders were fined, most (98%) $1,000 or less. A further 20% were dismissed and a further 2% received community service orders. Moreover, the differences in the harshness of sentencing did not adequately reflect the crime, with the bulk of aggravated cruelty cases being handed down a fine of $1,000 or less or a bond (Sharman, 2002).

Sharman concludes by arguing that the maximum penalty must be imposed for the most serious cases if the anti-cruelty legislation is not to be rendered futile. However, she also acknowledges that imprisonment is not the only way forward in ending animal cruelty. In particular, Sharman calls for the introduction of cross-reporting requirements in legislation. Acknowledging the documented links between human violence, criminal behavior, and animal abuse, Sharman argues that such cross-reporting would require such law enforcers as child protection agencies, firefighters, police officers, and animal cruelty inspectors, as well as ambulance officers, to report cases of suspected animal cruelty to relevant authority bodies. Such a position is consistent with that taken by many others (e.g., Green & Gullone, 2005; Gullone, Johnson, & Volant, 2004; Lawrie, 2001). Also of relevance is the inconsistency of legislative requirements whereby, for example, professionals, including general practitioners and teachers, are required to report cases of child abuse but veterinarians are not legally required to report cases of animal abuse.

Animal Welfare and Mandatory Reporting

In his review, Lawrie (2002) has called for greater awareness of animal abuse by veterinarians and the general public. Lawrie argues that veterinarians are well placed to both identify and deal with animal abuse. One of the primary rationales provided by

Lawrie to support such a stance is the increasing evidence that there is a link between animal abuse and human violence. Thus, he argues that mandatory reporting of animal abuse has the potential to prevent both human and animal suffering and to save lives. Moreover, Lawrie has argued that veterinarians are seen as role models of humane treatment of animals. As such, they are in an ideal position to set standards of behavior that the general public will be in a position to emulate.

In a recently completed Australian study, Green and Gullone (2005) investigated Australian veterinarians' exposure to animal abuse and human violence, as well as their beliefs about the link between the two, in addition to their perceived role in relation to both. A total of 185 veterinarians (with a response rate of 29%) participated in the study by completing a questionnaire that was either mailed out or hand delivered. The majority of respondents were male (58.8%) and there were about twice as many small animal veterinarians (66.3%) compared to mixed practice veterinarians (30.4%), with only a few (3.3%) large animal practitioners. The age of respondents ranged between 20 and 65 years with the majority of respondents being aged between 30 and 50 years.

As many as 86% of respondents believed animal abuse to involve physical maltreatment and 58% believed that passive neglect also constitutes abuse. However, questionnaire responses were based upon a definition of abuse provided by the authors, which was based on previous studies, and was as follows: "deliberate, physical maltreatment or neglect resulting in symptoms requiring veterinary treatment."

The results revealed that 0.12 cases of animal abuse were seen per veterinarian per 100 patients seen. The majority of veterinarians (76%) reported diagnosing animal abuse infrequently (i.e., less than one case per year) or occasionally (i.e., one to three cases per year). Fifteen percent reported diagnosing cases of animal abuse regularly (between 4 and 11 cases per year) or frequently (i.e., more than 12 cases per year). Only 8.3% of respondents reported that they had not diagnosed animal abuse. With regard to species, dogs (89.8%) were by far the most commonly reported species where abuse was seen, followed by cats (65.9%), horses (29.3%), and birds (25.1%). The remainder related mostly to cattle.

Providing support for the co-occurrence between human abuse and animal violence, as many as 24% reported known (6%) or suspected (18%) human abuse occurring in cases of animal abuse. As many as 62% believed that co-morbidity between child abuse and animal abuse exists and 57% believed that such co-morbidity exists with spouse abuse. The level of perceived co-morbidity between animal and human abuse in the Australian study was found to be lower than that reported in Sharpe and Wittum's (1999) U.S. study (86% agreement for child abuse and 77% for spouse abuse). The reason for this discrepancy may be the level of exposure of the two groups to the literature on the subject. Most of the data to date on the link between animal and human abuse have come from the United States, and both the U.S. and the Canadian Veterinary Medical Associations have held seminars and released position papers on the subject (Green & Gullone, 2005). In contrast, at the time that the Australian study was conducted, the only reference in the veterinary literature in Australia concerning the link between animal and human abuse was one article in one of the state Veterinary Board newsletters (Lawrie, 2002).

On the whole, the Australian data provide support for previous investigations with British and U.S. veterinarians. However, several differences were also found. In particular, Green and Gullone's finding that 91.7% of respondents reported diagnosing animal abuse is a much higher percentage than the 48.3% reported by Munro and Thrusfield (2001) in their survey of British veterinarians. This difference may be explained by the fact that the British data did not include neglect. Also, the actual reported incidence of animal abuse of 0.12% estimated in the Australian study was lower than that reported in Sharp and Wittum's (1999) U.S. study of 0.56%. Collectively, these findings refute comments made by some Australian as well as British (Munro & Thrusfield, 2001) veterinary respondents that abused animals are unlikely to be taken to veterinarians.

Regarding their believed moral responsibility to act in cases of suspected abuse, as many as 96% of respondents reported that they should intervene in cases of suspected animal abuse compared to 44.7% who believed they had such responsibility in relation to suspected family violence. Importantly, veterinarians' volunteered reasons for not reporting animal abuse included concerns about confidentiality, fear of loss of business, and distrust of the relevant authorities to handle the cases effectively. Also of interest was the finding that female veterinarians were more likely to recognize the co-morbidity of animal and human abuse and, along with younger

respondents, felt less well equipped to deal with abuse if confronted with it in practice.

These findings have implications for the training of Australian veterinarians with regard to increasing awareness of co-occurrence of human violence and animal cruelty. They also indicate that veterinarians need to be trained in relation to appropriate avenues of responding to suspected or known animal abuse.

Given the findings of Green and Gullone's study, it is somewhat reassuring that in March 2004, the Australian Veterinary Association (AVA), as part of its annual conference, assigned a full day to papers discussing the co-occurrence of animal abuse and human violence as well as holding an afternoon forum to discuss mandatory reporting. This is reflective of the marked shift in veterinarians' attitudes to animal welfare in Australia over the past 3 years. Such a shift can be further seen in the AVA's strong proactive role in campaigning taken against tail docking in dogs for cosmetic reasons (Bennett & Perini, 2003).

Bennett and Perini (2003) have provided a comprehensive review of the arguments for and against canine tail docking. At around the same time of the publication of this paper, which clearly detailed the animal welfare implications of tail docking, the Primary Industries Ministerial Council of Australia agreed to implement a nationally coordinated ban on routine tail docking for purely cosmetic reasons. The ban came into force nationally in April 2004. In addition to reflecting the stronger stance taken in relation to animal welfare by veterinarians, such legislation reflects a stronger acceptance by the wider population to changes in previously unquestioned attitudes.

Such changes in beliefs and behaviors are reassuring given predicted increased rates of pet ownership in the 21st century, which will undoubtedly coincide with increased potential for animal cruelty (Wirth, 2000). Given such movements in thinking, the present seems to be an optimal time to call for mandatory reporting of animal abuse by veterinarians. Further, legislating for mandatory reporting would bring Australia in line with several states in the United States and with Canada.

Companion Animal Ownership in Australia

As with other countries in the western world, the prevalence of pet or companion animal ownership in Australia is high. This is particularly true in relation to cats and dogs. A national survey involving 1,011 people aged 16 years and above (McHarg, Baldock, Headey, & Robinson, 1995) found that 68% of Australian households cared for one or more dogs, 45% of Australian households cared for one or more cats, and 25% owned birds. The survey also found that pets were part of the family during childhood for more than four out of five Australians. The main reasons identified for not owning pets included living in accommodations that were not suited to owning a pet (e.g., rental accommodation with no provision for pets) and the absence of someone at home who could care for the pet (McHarg et al., 1995). It was also found that more families than non-partnered individuals owned dogs and that about one in three dog owners also owned a cat. The survey results revealed that cat ownership was evenly spread across families and non-partnered individuals.

Reflecting increased consideration of pet welfare amongst pet owners, a total of 61% of dogs were reported to be de-sexed, with a lower percentage in lower income households. In relation to cats, it was found that 90% were de-sexed.

In a study examining attitudes toward cat and dog ownership, Mackay (1992) concluded that the emerging pattern in the Australian community was one favoring increased pet ownership and a stronger commitment to the care of pets. According to Mackay, this trend can be explained by changes in lifestyle over the last 20 or so years including increased rates of divorce and family breakups as well as a trend toward smaller households, with 50% of Australian households now containing only one or two people. Also, Australia's population is aging and the aged comprise a large portion of Australian adults living alone. With this increasing trend toward individuals rather than families becoming the most prevalent social unit, there is a growing sense of isolation and loneliness. Under such conditions, pet ownership is increasingly becoming recognized as a positive strategy to alleviate the pain of loneliness (Siegel, 1990).

Dog Attacks and Dog Bites

In addition to the documented positive aspects of pet ownership for both adults and children (Fawcett & Gullone, 2001), there are potential risks. This is particularly true with regard to dog attacks and dog bites, which constitute a major cause of injury, particularly for children (Chapman, Cornwall, Righetti, & Sung, 2000; Thompson, 1997). Ashby (2003) reported that, in Australia, up to 2 deaths and approximately 1,400

hospital admissions per year are recorded for dog bites. Children are more than twice as likely to be admitted to hospital for dog bite injuries compared to adults. Approximately 50% of dog bites to children are to the head and/or face, whereas for adults around 50% are to the upper limbs. A steady frequency of 0.004 per 100,000 cases or between 0 and 2 deaths from dog bite has been documented. This compares to a Canadian reported rate of 0.03 per 100,000 cases and a higher rate in the United States of 0.069 per 100,000 cases (Sacks, Sattin, & Bonzo, 1989).

Ashby (2003) has reported that a detailed examination of the distribution of dog bites by age clearly indicates that there is a marked peak in the 1–4 year age group, which decreases to a relatively level distribution by 15 to 19 years. The data reported by Thompson (1997) for Adelaide in South Australia support the finding that children in the 0–4 year age range are at greatest risk and that the injuries sustained by children were more likely to require hospitalization compared to those sustained by adults. Of note, Thompson also reported that males of all ages were more at risk of dog bite compared to females. Furthermore, over 50% of dog bites occur at a residential location as opposed to public places (Ashby, 2003).

In an innovative attempt to address this significant problem, Chapman et al. (2000) conducted a randomized controlled trial to evaluate the efficacy of an educational intervention program designed to teach people how to avoid being attacked by a dog. Their program was particularly targeted at children. A total of 346 children aged between 7 and 8 years from eight primary schools in metropolitan Sydney were cluster randomized into intervention schools and non-intervention control schools. The "Dog Safe" intervention consisted of one 30-minute lesson and was conducted by an accredited dog handler. The lesson involved the demonstration of a variety of interactions, classified as either do's or don'ts, with dogs. For example, children were told how to approach owners and their dogs when they wanted to pat a dog. Children were also given the opportunity to practice the instructed interactions. For example, in patting a dog, children were instructed to ask permission, approach slowly, extend their hand palm down, and to pat the dog under the chin and on the chest while avoiding eye contact, and then to walk away slowly and quietly. Children were also instructed in the recognition of friendly, angry, or frightened dogs. In addition to the 30-minute lesson, a resource kit, including activities to be undertaken before and after the demonstration, was provided for teachers.

Evaluation of the program took place between 7 and 10 days post-intervention. A docile Labrador dog was tethered 5 meters away from its owner in the school yard and the intervention group children were let out to play without any supervision. The owner was disguised as a tradesperson and the children were not told that they were being videotaped. This procedure was also implemented for children in the control group. The results, which involved a comparison of the numbers of children who breached the proscribed behaviors across groups, clearly showed that the children who had received the intervention displayed significantly fewer breaches. The majority of the children in the control group patted the dog without hesitation, whereas the majority of the children in the intervention group did so only after a period of careful assessment. While the authors recommended a follow-up study to determine the long-term efficacy of the intervention, the findings of this study are encouraging in addressing what perhaps constitutes the most serious human well-being problem related to companion animal ownership. Given Wirth's (2000) prediction of increased companion animal ownership in the future, the need to educate people about companion animal ownership and interactions will only become more pressing.

Wirth (2000) has also argued that, given a predicted acceleration in the pace of change associated with modern living, the keeping of companion animals as an antidote to loneliness will undoubtedly become more popular in the 21st century. Increased rates of pet ownership are likely to result in many people new to pet ownership acquiring pets. Given the increased prevalence of single adult households, generally longer working hours, and living space restrictions, what will the impact on animal welfare be?

At present, community attitudes and beliefs are that pet ownership is a right that individuals are entitled to exercise with very little accountability. However, according to Wirth (2000), in order to prevent possible increases in animal cruelty and suffering that are likely to coincide with increased rates of pet ownership in the future, animal welfare movements must demand restrictions on the breeding of animals so that only sufficient numbers and species are bred to meet community requirements. Wirth has also argued that control laws need to address all of the principles of responsible pet ownership and that rehousing programs should be given maximum priority for dealing with relinquished or abandoned pets to minimize euthanasia rates.

Australian Animal Abandonment, Relinquishment, and Abuse Statistics

In the period covering 2001 to 2002, the RSPCA received a total of 132,702 animals across Australia. This included 61,692 dogs and 49,754 cats. Among the other animals received were horses and livestock as well as wildlife including bandicoots, echidnas, blue-tongue lizards, sea lions, ferrets, and a large variety of native birds. In addition to the animals received by the RSPCA, there are a large number of welfare shelters in Australia that receive animals, including dog pounds, wildlife shelters, and cat shelters. Numbers of animals are therefore significantly greater than those reported by the RSPCA alone. As an example of the numbers received by a large dog shelter, for the 2003 calendar year the Lost Dog's Home received a total of 10,708 dogs and 8,876 cats in Victoria alone. A total of 4,648 (43.4%) dogs were reclaimed and 1,299 (12%) were re-homed. In relation to cats, 329 (3.7%) were reclaimed and 407 (4.6%) were re-homed.

In contrast to the Lost Dog's Home figures (Lost Dog's Home Newsletter, 2004), the RSPCA percentage for dogs reclaimed is substantially lower but that for cats is comparable (see Table 1,

Table 1 Total animals received by the RSPCA Australia-wide during 2001 to 2002, by outcome

Animal Species	Received		Reclaimed		Re-homed		Euthanized	
	No.	%	No.	%	No.	%	No.	%
Dogs	61,692	46.5	15,019	24.0	20,696	34.0	23,608	38.0
Cats	49,754	7.7	1,423	3.0	15,413	31.0	31,009	62.0
Other Species	20,608	6.0						

Notes: 1. The percent of animals received is a proportion of the total number. For all other categories, the percentage is calculated from the total for the particular animal species.

2. No statistics regarding outcomes are provided by the RSPCA for species other than cats and dogs.

which provides a breakdown of the numbers and percentages of dogs and cats received, reclaimed, re-homed, and euthanized during the 2001 to 2002 period) (RSPCA, 2004). The re-homing rates for the Lost Dog's Home, for both cats and dogs, are substantially lower than those reported by the RSPCA.

When compared to RSPCA statistics provided for the previous 5 years, the statistics reported in Table 1 indicate that there has been a small but steady decrease in the numbers of animals received from 160,128 in the 1997–1998 period to 132,054 in the 2001–2002 period. While reclaiming and re-homing rates appear to have fluctuated somewhat over the 5-year period, most particularly for dogs, the euthanasia rates have shown a steady trend downwards for both cats (from 43,375 in 1997–1998 to 31,009 in 2001–2002) and dogs (from 36,037 in 1997–1998 to 23,608 in 2001–2002).

Given that other organizations apart from the RSPCA receive and re-home animals, the RSPCA statistics are limited with regard to comprehensiveness. Nevertheless, they provide a relatively good indication of the scope of the problem. This is particularly true regarding the number of successful prosecutions relative to the number of cruelty complaints.

During the 2001 to 2002 period, the RSPCA received a total of 51,216 cruelty complaints, of which 51,205 were investigated. A total of 925 charges were laid (1.81% of all complaints) and a total of 339 prosecutions were instigated (36.7% of charges laid), eventuating in 290 successful convictions (85.5% of prosecutions) (RSPCA, 2004).

The greatest number of complaints related to dogs (49%), followed by livestock (15%), horses or donkeys (11%), and cats (10%). The remainder of complaints related to birds, wildlife, or animals not otherwise specified (RSPCA, 2004).

The number of recorded prosecutions compared to the number of charges laid is disappointingly low (36.7%). This low prosecution rate is largely due to RSPCA's reluctance to follow through with cases unless there is a very high degree of certainty that the charges laid will be upheld. Given that the RSPCA is primarily funded as a charity organization, the prudence shown in this regard is defensible. However, this remains a cause of serious concern, particularly given the increased evidence for a link between animal abuse, human violence, and criminal behavior as will be discussed in the following section.

Co-occurrence of Human Violence, Criminal Behavior, and Animal Abuse

Over the last decade professionals have become increasingly aware of a link between violence toward humans and animal cruelty (e.g., Ascione, 1998; Flynn, 2000a, 2000b). Although existent data do not constitute empirical evidence that animal abuse *leads to or causes* interpersonal violence (Beirne, 2004), there is sufficient evidence to suggest that the two types of violence are strongly associated.

That the presence of one type of violence may predict the increased likelihood of another type is supported by Pelcovitz, Kaplan, DeRosa, Mandel, and Salzinger (2000), who have noted that as the frequency of marital violence in the family increases, the likelihood that child abuse will also be present increases dramatically. The statistics they provide indicate that one incident of marital violence predicts a 5% probability of child abuse while 50 or more such incidents predict almost certainly that child abuse will occur.

Given the co-morbidity across different types of violence, it may be that identification of the presence of animal abuse and determination of its severity may play a role in making predictions about other types of violent behavior. There have been several proposals put forth in an attempt to better explain and understand the link. In particular, an effort has been made to better understand the factors that underlie the abuse of animals.

Proposed Explanatory Factors for the Abuse of Animals

A significant amount of anecdotal and some empirical data show that animals are killed or harmed in an effort to intimidate, frighten, or control others including battered women or abused children (Arkow, 1996; Ascione, 2001a; Ascione & Arkow, 1999; Boat, 1995). As reported by battered women themselves, in an effort to assert their control or continue their campaign of terror, perpetrators have stabbed, shot, hanged, and otherwise mutilated the family pets. In some cases, the animals disappear or die mysteriously.

It has also been proposed that a central common explanatory factor for animal abuse may be an underdeveloped or compromised level of empathy. As argued by Ascione (1999), abusing animals may represent the perpetrator's reduced capacity to empathize with a potential victim (human or animal). Such a claim is supported by the demonstrated inverse relationship between *callousness* and empathy, with high callousness and low empathy revealing low levels of concern for others (Lahey, Waldman, & McBurnett, 1999).

Family Violence and Animal Abuse

A particular focus on research examining the co-occurrence of animal abuse and human-directed violence has been in the area of family violence. Indeed, over the past decade there has been an increase in the number of studies that have demonstrated a co-occurrence of animal abuse and family violence. One of the earliest was a study conducted by Arkow (1994) in which 24% of 122 women seeking refuge from domestic violence and 11% of 1,175 women seeking restraining orders or support services reported observing animal cruelty by the perpetrator. In 1997, Ascione, Weber, and Wood (1997) published a study reporting the findings of a U.S. national survey of shelters. One shelter from nearly every U.S. state was selected for participation. All shelter staff were surveyed about the coexistence of animal abuse and domestic violence and children's cruelty toward animals. The results showed that as many as 85% of staff who were interviewed reported that they were aware of incidents of pet abuse. A total of 63% of the staff also reported hearing children talk about animal abuse. Eighty-three percent of workers answered "yes" to the question "have you observed the coexistence of domestic violence and pet abuse?"

In a subsequent study, 38 women who sought shelter for domestic violence were directly interviewed (Ascione, 1998). The author reported that 74% (68% owned more than one pet) owned a pet. Of these women, 71% reported that threats of harming, actual harming, or killing of pets by the perpetrators had occurred. Also, approximately 30% of children exposed to violence were themselves reported to be abusive toward animals. Ascione also found that a significant proportion (18%) of women delayed seeking shelter for themselves and their children for fear of their companion animal being harmed.

Quinlisk (1999) reported the findings of another survey conducted as part of the Domestic Violence Intervention Project. The study involved 72 female victims of domestic violence of whom 58 had pets. Of these women, 68% reported violence directed toward their companion animals. In other cases, women reported experiencing threats to kill or to give away their pets. In 88% of cases the abuse was committed in their presence and in 76% of cases, children had been witness to the abuse. The study found that 54% of child witnesses copied the behaviors they had observed. Of particular note is the fact that Quinlisk (1999) reported almost identical results for an additional survey involving 32 women.

In another similar investigation, Daniell (2001) reported the findings of a survey conducted by the Ontario Society for the Prevention of Cruelty to Animals (Ontario SPCA). More than 100 women's shelters throughout Ontario were contacted and a total of 21 agreed to participate. This resulted in 130 women being surveyed, 80 of whom owned pets at the time of entering the women's refuge and a further 31 had owned a pet some time in the past 12 months. The results were largely consistent with past studies. Of the 111 women owning pets, 44% stated that their partner had previously abused or killed one or more of their pets and 42% stated that their partner had threatened to hurt or kill one of their pets. Finally, as many as 43% of respondents indicated that concern over their pet's welfare had caused them not to leave their abusive situation sooner.

Flynn's (2000b) study attempted to replicate and also extend upon previous research examining the human–animal violence link. Specifically, four questions were asked. These related to the nature and extent of pet abuse suffered by physically abused women, the importance of the pets as sources of emotional support for the women, whether they worried about their pet's welfare after seeking shelter, and whether their concern for the pet's welfare delayed their seeking refuge. One hundred and seven women from a South Carolina shelter were involved in the study, of whom 43 had pets. Of the pet owners, 47% reported that they had experienced threat of harm or actual harm to their pet(s) by the perpetrator of the domestic violence. In contrast to previous research, only two instances of pet abuse by children were reported. Regarding emotional importance, almost half (46%) of the women reported their pet to be a very important source of emotional support. Not surprisingly, almost as many (40%) reported being worried about their pet's safety and 19% of the women reported delaying seeking shelter.

In a more recently reported investigation, Ascione etal. (2005) included a comparison community sample. The study involved a convenience sample of 101 women recruited through five different domestic violence programs. The community sample included 120 women who were recruited through newspaper advertisements and flyers in local businesses. A recruitment requirement of the comparison sample included the criterion that the women did not self-report experiencing intimate partner abuse. All women currently owned pets or had owned pets in the past year. This study constitutes one of very few incorporating a comparison community sample of women. The findings included that shelter women were more likely to report that their partners had threatened to hurt or kill their pets (52.5%) and that their partners had actually hurt or killed their pet (54%). This compared with 12.5% and 5%, respectively, in the community sample of women.

The shelter women's reports included multiple incidents of killing or hurting pets. This contrasts with the reports of community sample for whom incidents were typically isolated and were more likely to occur within the context of disciplining the animal for bad behavior (e.g., biting). The most horrific incidents of animal abuse were reported by the shelter women who reported, among other acts of violence, nailing a pet to the woman's bedroom door, drowning a pet, and poisoning a pet.

Overall, 22.8% of the shelter women reported that concern for the welfare of their pet had kept them from seeking refuge sooner. This percentage was markedly higher for those women whose pets had already been hurt (34.3%). There was also a difference between women who delayed leaving and had children (19.5%) and those without children (33.3%).

Ascione et al. (2005) also assessed the experiences and behaviors of children and found that over 61.5% of the shelter women reported that their children had witnessed pet abuse. This contrasted with only 2.9% for the community sample. A total of 38 shelter group children were also directly interviewed. Nearly two-thirds of these children (61.5%) reported that they had witnessed pet abuse incidents as perpetrated by their father, stepfather, or women's boyfriend. As many as 51% of the children said that they had protected one of their pets to save it from being hurt.

In the only Australian investigation carried out to date to determine the extent of co-occurrence between animal abuse and human-directed violence, Gullone et al. (2004) surveyed 102 women recruited through family violence refuge or outreach services and a comparison community sample of 102 women from neighborhood houses and community centers. The inclusion criterion for participating women was that they owned at least one pet during their current or most recent relationship. For the community

sample, an additional criterion required that there be no current or past experience of family violence. The findings were highly comparable to those of past similar studies as reported above. Specifically, it was found that 46% of women in the family violence sample reported that their partner had threatened to hurt or kill their pet compared with 6% of women in the community sample. Similarly, a markedly larger percentage of family violence group women (53%) reported that their partner had hurt or killed their pet compared to 0% of women in the community sample. Out of the 102 family violence cases, 17.3% reported that their pet(s) had been killed.

A total of 33 women in the family violence sample were living in a refuge, crisis accommodation, or transitional housing (as opposed to outreach services). Of these 33 women, a total of 33% reported that they had delayed leaving: 3% reported that they delayed leaving for one week, 3% delayed leaving for between 3 and 4 weeks, 21% delayed leaving for 8 weeks, and a further 6% were unable to quantify their period of delayed leaving.

Also, consistent with past similar studies, Gullone et al. (2004) asked the women in the family violence sample about their children's experiences. The comparison sample percentages are given in parentheses. In 29% (1%) of cases, children were reported to witness threats of abuse and 29% (0%) were reported to witness actual abuse. A total of 19% (1%) of the women reported that their child had abused their pet. Further, a total of 5% (1%) of the children were reported to have threatened to hurt or kill their pet(s). The differences were all found to be statistically significant.

The outcomes of the research reviewed above leave little room for doubt that a relationship between human violence and animal cruelty exists. At the very least, this research suggests that the detection of animal abuse should be of significant concern to professionals and researchers. The research outcomes also suggest that when children are found to be abusing animals, there is a significant probability that they have witnessed and/or experienced abuse. Ideally, children's abuse of animals should be taken very seriously as it may well be a marker of other sinister crimes. Also of importance are research outcomes suggesting that animal abuse is predictive of other types of criminal behaviors.

Criminal Behavior and Animal Abuse

Arluke, Levin, Luke, and Ascione (1999) conducted an investigation into the relationship between animal abuse and other forms of anti-social behavior including violence. To overcome many of the limitations of past research (e.g., retrospective reports, potentially biased self-reports from incarcerated adults), they obtained their data from official records of criminality rather than through self-disclosure of criminals. They also included a comparison group. Specifically, they identified people who had been prosecuted for at least one form of animal cruelty from the records of the Massachusetts Society for the Prevention of Cruelty to Animals (MSPCA) between 1975 and 1986.

They operationalized cruelty as cases "where an animal has been intentionally harmed physically (e.g., beaten, stabbed, shot, hanged, drowned, stoned, burned, strangled, driven over, or thrown)" (Arluke et al., 1999, p. 966). This resulted in a group of 153 participants of whom 146 were male. The sample had a mean age of 31 years, 58% of whom were aged younger than 21. The largest proportion of abused animals was dogs (69%) compared with cats (22%) and the remaining were birds, wildlife, horses, or farm animals. The control group was constituted from individuals matched to the abuse group on gender, socioeconomic status, age, and street of residence in the same year as the cruelty incident. The assumption for including this last variable was that people who reside in the same neighbourhood tend to form homogenous groups on variables such as socioeconomic status and related characteristics. The control group details were obtained from municipal voting lists.

Following this, computerized criminal records were used to track criminal cases from the state's criminal justice records system. This was done for both the control and abuse group. Criminal offenses were classified into five groups as violent, property-related, drug-related, public disorder, and other.

The study results indicated that animal abusers were significantly more likely than control participants to be involved in some form of criminal behavior, including violent offenses. Specifically, 70% of those who abused animals also committed at least one other offense compared with 22% of the control group participants. The differences ranged from 11% for the control group and 44% for the abusive group on property-related crimes to 12% for the control group and 37% for the abusive group on public disorder–related crimes. For violent crimes, the two groups differed substantially (7% and 37% for the control and abusive groups, respectively).

Based on their findings, the authors concluded that animal abuse appears to be one of many antisocial

behaviors displayed by individuals in society ranging from property to personal crimes. Of significance is the fact that Arluke et al.'s (1999) research included a non-institutionalized sample of people who were cruel to animals. Thus, their finding that a single known act of animal abuse was significantly predictive of increased participation in other criminal offenses when compared to a matched sample of adults who did not abuse animals is particularly compelling. This is further reinforced by the fact that, in many cases, the animal abuse identified was far less torturous and sadistic than has been the case in past related studies (e.g., Kellert & Felthous, 1985).

Providing strong support for Arluke et al.'s conclusion that animal abuse may provide an important marker for antisocial behaviors are the findings of a recent investigation carried out by Gleyzer, Felthous, and Holzer (2002) in which 48 criminal defendants with a history of substantial animal cruelty were matched with a sample of defendants who did not have a history of animal cruelty in order to investigate whether a history of animal abuse was associated with a diagnosis of Antisocial Personality Disorder (APD) in adulthood. Support for the proposal was found with a statistically significant correlation between a history of cruelty to animals in childhood and a diagnosis of APD in adulthood. Specifically, a diagnosis of APD and also antisocial personality traits were significantly more frequent in the animal cruelty group.

The aforementioned research findings indicate that animal cruelty can constitute an important marker of antisocial or criminal behavior. Therefore, it appears that the same underlying factors that predict or increase the likelihood an individual engaging in animal abuse may also increase the likelihood that the same individual will engage in other types of criminal behavior. Providing further support for this proposition are Australian Victoria Police data. These data are considered next.

Criminal Offenses and Animal Abuse Offenses: Victorian Data

Data were obtained from the Statistical Services Division of Victoria Police for all recorded offenses in Victoria, Australia, for the years 1994 to 2001 (inclusive). Out of four categories of offense (see Tables 2 and 3) for all alleged offenders, the data clearly show that the largest proportion of offenses was consistently that against property, ranging between 79.52% (number = 344,905) of total

Table 2 Numbers of offenses recorded per year, 1994 to 2001

	1994	1 995	1996	1997	1998	1999	2000	2001	All years 1994–2001
Offenses against the person	30,251	31,449	30,667	32,871	34,181	32,151	31,389	36,271	259,230
Offenses against property	309,447	313,790	328,246	332,003	344,905	354,785	364,976	369,355	2,717,507
Drug offenses	16,105	16,220	15,048	16,153	18,354	17,487	15,946	12,838	128,151
Other offenses	27,927	32,666	30,932	31,716	36,303	34,372	31,028	34,246	259,190
Total	383,730	394,125	404,893	412,743	433,743	438,795	443,339	452,710	3,364,078

Note: Animal abuse offenses are not counted in this table.

offenses in 1998 and 80.85% (number=354,785) in 1999. As shown in Tables 2 and 3, over the 8-year period offenses against property constituted 80.8% of the total 3,364,078 crimes committed in Victoria. Drug offenses consistently constituted the smallest proportion and ranged between 2.84% (n=12,838) in 2001 and 4.23% (n=18,354) of total offenses in 1998. Of note, offenses against the person also constituted a relatively small proportion of the total number of crimes at an average of 7.71% of all crimes over the 8-year period with the lowest percentage of 7.98 recorded in 2000 and the highest percentage of 8.01 recorded in 2001.

The equivalent statistics relating to criminal offenses, classified in the same way as depicted in Tables 2 and 3, for alleged animal abuse offenders only are shown in Tables 4 and 5. What is immediately apparent upon examination of Table 5 is that, for animal abuse offenders, the average percentage of offenses committed against the person is substantially higher compared to the percentage for all alleged offenders (25% compared to 8%). The category of offenses against

the person included such crimes as homicide, rape, assault, abduction/kidnap, and harassment. Importantly, these statistics are remarkably similar to those reported by Arluke et al. (1999) as previously described.

The other marked difference found was that for offenses against property, which were found, on average, to be substantially lower for animal abuse offenders compared to all alleged offenders (48.5% compared to 80.8%). Offenses against property included such crimes as robbery, arson, property damage, and theft from motor vehicle. Thus, there appears to be a greater likelihood that people alleged to have abused animals will engage in offenses against the person, including violent crimes, when compared to all alleged offenders.

A breakdown into age categories by sex for each of the classifications provided in Tables 2 and 3 is provided in Tables 6 (number of offenses) and 7 (percentage of offenses). These data show that alleged offenders (all alleged offenders, not only animal abuse offenders), across crime categories, are characteristically male across all categories of offense,

Table 3 Offense as percentage of all offenses recorded per year, 1994 to 2001

	1994	1995	1996	1997	1998	1999	2000	2001	All years 1994–2001
Offenses against the person	7.88	7.98	7.57	7.96	7.88	7.33	7.08	8.01	7.71
Offenses against property	80.64	79.62	81.07	80.44	79.52	80.85	82.32	81.59	80.76
Drug offenses	4.20	4.12	3.72	3.91	4.23	3.99	3.59	2.84	3.82
Other offenses	7.28	8.29	7.64	7.68	8.37	7.83	6.99	7.56	7.71
Total	100.00	100.00	100.00	100.00	100.00	100.00	100.00	100.00	100.00

Table 4 Numbers of offenses recorded per year between 1994 to 2001 for alleged animal offenders only

	1994	1995	1996	1997	1998	1999	2000	2001	All years 1994–2001
Offenses against the person	176	214	251	611	320	358	203	353	2,486
Offenses against property	423	434	549	610	627	686	758	556	4,643
Drug offenses	57	60	94	87	103	100	93	46	640
Other offenses	113	165	216	317	321	342	272	226	1,972
Total	769	873	1,110	1,625	1,371	1,486	1,326	1,181	9,741

Note: Animal abuse offenses are not counted in this table.

Table 5 Offense as percentage of all offenses recorded per year between 1994 to 2001 for alleged animal abuse offenders only

	1994	1995	1996	1997	1998	1999	2000	2001	All years 1994–2001
Offenses against the person	22.89	24.51	22.61	37.60	23.34	24.09	15.31	29.89	25.03
Offenses against property	55.01	49.71	49.46	37.54	45.73	46.16	57.16	47.08	48.48
Drug offenses	7.41	6.87	8.47	5.35	7.51	6.73	7.01	3.90	6.66
Other offenses	14.69	18.90	19.46	19.51	23.41	23.01	20.51	19.14	19.83
Total	100.00	100.00	100.00	100.00	100.00	100.00	100.00	100.00	100.00

Note: Animal abuse offenses are not counted in this table.

with an average percentage difference across age categories of 7.55% in favor of males. From years 26 to 35 onward, there is a steady decrease in the overrepresentation of males compared to females so that by 66 years and over, the male to female ratio is almost 2 to 1. In general, for the Victorian population, the prevalence of alleged offenses appears to be highest between the ages of 12 and 35 years for both males and females but particularly for males, with a peak for both males and females between the ages of 18 and 25 years.

When examining age and sex trends for alleged animal abuse offenders and animal abuse offenses only (see Tables 8 and 9), there again appears to be a peak in frequency between the ages of 18 and 25 years for both males and females. There are also comparatively high frequencies of alleged offenses for age groups 12 to 17 years, 26 to 35 years, and to less extent for age categories 36 to 45 years and 46 to 55 years. Again, males are overrep-

resented across all age categories. Of the various categories of animal abuse, by far the most frequently occurring offense type is "inflict physical pain/suffering."

Thus, as depicted in Tables 7 and 9, males are overrepresented for both general alleged offenses and alleged animal abuse offenses. Males are also overrepresented across all age categories for both general alleged offenses and for specifically animal abuse offenses, with very few exceptions. Further, there appears to be a peak of offending between the ages of 18 to 25 years that decreases steadily beyond these years.

The particular importance of these statistics lies in their indication that there are clear sex differences in the frequency of criminal behaviors and that there are identifiable age trends. Thus, it appears that people most at risk of offending are male and aged between the ages of 12 and 35, but particularly between 18 and 25 years. Ideally,

Table 6 Number of offenses recorded by offender age and sex for all offenses recorded per year between 1994 to 2001

	1–11 years		12–17 years		18–25 years		26–35 years		36–45 years		46–55 years		56–65 years		66+ years	
	Female	Male	Female	Male	Female	Male	Female	Male	Female	Male	Female	Male	Female	Male	Female	Male
Offenses against the person	87	750	7,290	26,628	20,650	76,389	18,046	68,600	8,109	33,069	2,240	13,710	515	4,094	130	1,654
Offenses against property	1,184	6,760	36,971	158,668	35,617	172,018	26,798	87,897	12,613	30,859	5,498	9,780	2,818	3,884	2,372	3,119
Drug offenses	4	31	2,315	12,017	8,010	45,342	6,161	27,783	2,366	10,056	504	2,680	90	641	14	109
Other offenses	70	557	6,381	33,119	9,323	54,509	7,773	37,673	3,413	17,251	1,096	7,316	217	2,252	81	818
Total	1,345	8,098	52,957	230,432	73,600	348,258	58,778	221,953	26,501	91,235	9,338	33,486	3,640	10,871	2,597	5,700

Note: Animal abuse offenses are not counted in this table.

Table 7 Percentages of offenses by offender age and sex for all offenses recorded per year, 1994 to 2001

	1–11 years		12–17 years		18–25 years		26–35 years		36–45 years		46–55 years		56–65 years		66+ years	
	Female	Male	Female	Male	Female	Male	Female	Male	Female	Male	Female	Male	Female	Male	Female	Male
Offenses against the person	0.03	0.26	2.55	9.31	7.22	26.70	6.31	23.98	2.83	11.56	0.78	4.79	0.18	1.43	0.05	0.58
Offenses against property	0.20	1.12	6.12	26.26	5.89	28.47	4.43	14.55	2.09	5.11	0.91	1.62	0.47	0.64	0.39	0.52
Drug offenses	0.00	0.03	1.93	10.03	6.68	37.84	5.14	23.19	1.97	8.39	0.42	2.24	0.08	0.53	0.01	0.09
Other offenses	0.04	0.30	3.46	17.93	5.05	29.52	4.21	20.40	1.85	9.34	0.59	3.96	0.12	1.22	0.04	0.44
Total	0.27	1.71	14.06	63.53	24.84	122.53	20.09	82.12	8.74	34.40	2.70	12.61	0.85	3.82	0.49	1.63

Table 8 Numbers of alleged animal abuse offenders by age, sex, and category of animal abuse offense, 1994 to 2001

	1–11 years		12–17 years		18–25 years		26–35 years		36–45 years		46–55 years		56–65 years		66+ years	
	Fem	Male	Fem	Male	Fem	Male	Fem	Male	Fem	Male	Fem	Male	Fem	Male	Fem	Male
Inflict physical pain/suffering	0	3	4	104	13	128	7	78	10	64	5	47	1	14	3	18
Neglect (Failure to provide food and water)	0	0	0	1	2	1	0	1	0	1	0	3	0	0	0	1
Abandon animal kept for domestic purpose	0	0	0	0	1	2	0	0	0	0	0	0	0	0	0	0
Fail to provide necessary medical care	0	0	0	0	0	0	1	1	1	0	0	0	0	0	0	0
Poison animal/lay bait	0	0	0	0	0	0	0	0	0	0	0	0	0	1	0	0
Worry/Terrify/Abuse/Torment	0	1	1	3	0	2	0	4	1	2	0	1	0	0	0	1
Total	0	4	5	108	16	133	8	84	12	67	5	51	1	15	3	20

Table 9 Percentages of alleged animal abuse offenders by age, sex, and category of animal abuse offense, 1994 to 2001

| | 1–11 years | | 12–17 years | | 18–25 years | | 26–35 years | | 36–45 years | | 46–55 years | | 56–65 years | | 66+ years | |
	Fem	Male	Fem	Male	Fem	Male	Fem	Male	Fem	Male	Fem	Male	Fem	Male	Fem	Male
Inflict physical pain/suffering	0.00	0.59	0.78	20.35	2.54	25.05	1.37	15.26	1.96	12.52	0.98	9.20	0.20	2.74	0.59	3.52
Neglect (Failure to provide food and water)	0.00	0.00	0.00	9.09	18.18	9.09	0.00	9.09	0.00	9.09	0.00	27.27	0.00	0.00	0.00	9.09
Abandon animal kept for domestic purpose	0.00	0.00	0.00	0.00	33.33	66.67	0.00	0.00	0.00	0.00	0.00	0.00	0.00	0.00	0.00	0.00
Fail to provide necessary medical care	0.00	0.00	0.00	0.00	0.00	0.00	25.00	25.00	25.00	0.00	0.00	0.00	0.00	0.00	0.00	0.00
Poison animal/lay bait	0.00	0.00	0.00	0.00	0.00	0.00	0.00	0.00	0.00	0.00	0.00	0.00	0.00	50.00	0.00	0.00
Worry/Terrify/Abuse/Torment	0.00	5.88	5.88	17.65	0.00	11.76	0.00	23.53	5.88	11.76	0.00	5.88	0.00	0.00	0.00	5.88
Total	0.00	6.47	6.66	47.09	54.05	112.57	26.37	72.88	32.84	33.37	0.98	42.35	0.20	52.74	0.59	18.49

prevention and interventions efforts should focus on individuals that meet these criteria. Also of particular importance are the data suggesting that people who abuse animals are more likely than alleged offenders who do not abuse animals to engage in offenses classified as being those against the person. That this category of offenses includes violent crimes such as homicide and rape further supports the claim made by other researchers that animal abuse is an important marker of violent criminal behavior (Arluke et al., 1999; Dadds, Turner, & McAloon, 2002; Felthous & Kellert, 1986; 1987).

Criminal Offenses and Animal Abuse: New South Wales Data

In 2002 the New South Wales Police Service Forensic Services Group commissioned research to investigate the links between animal cruelty and other criminal offenses in an Australian context (Clarke, 2002). While the research did investigate links between animal cruelty and other criminal behaviors, it differed from previous studies because some aims were directly related to how effectively law enforcement agencies can use animal cruelty information in the investigation of crime.

More specifically, the research had three main aims: (1) to investigate whether the link reported between animal cruelty and other criminal behaviors by international researchers would be observed in an Australian context, (2) to investigate whether incidents of animal cruelty investigated by bodies such as the Australian RSPCA and Australian Animal Welfare League were recorded on the NSW Police Computerized Operational Policing System (COPS), and (3) to identify any benefits to investigations looking at major serial and violent crime that could result from the NSW police capturing and/or taking action on information relating to animal cruelty incidents.

The methodology used in the following three studies, comprising the NSW Police Service Animal Cruelty Research Project, involved both qualitative case study and quantitative techniques. Study 1 reported five cases of animal cruelty that demonstrated different motivations underlying a variety of animal cruelty offenses. Study 2 examined frequency and type of criminal behaviors performed by 200 persons convicted of animal cruelty in New South Wales. Participants in study two were randomly selected from a total of 947 cases recorded

on the COPS database. Study 3 examined links between animal cruelty offenses (both convictions for and self-reported animal cruelty) in a randomly selected sample of homicide and sexual homicide offenders.

Study 1: Case Study Analyses. Five case studies were reported in Study 1. Each case study was reviewed with the aim of identifying different motivations underlying acts of animal cruelty. The case studies were also used to explore potential links between animal cruelty and other types of criminal behaviors for the subsequent quantitative studies. These are reported below.

Case Study 1: The victim Ms. X and the defendant Mr. Y met in 2000 and commenced a domestic relationship. They have lived together for the past month with the victim's 15-year-old daughter. About 7.00 PM on Thursday the victim and defendant went to a local club with friends. While at the club all parties consumed full-strength beer with the defendant consuming almost double that of the victim. The victim and defendant returned home by taxi when the club closed. They both resumed drinking full-strength beer in the lounge room of the home, then started to argue about a Doberman dog that the victim was minding for her friend only known as Ms. Z. The defendant stood up and walked out of the lounge only to return a short time later. He sat near the victim and said, "The dog's dead, I cut its throat. It's fuckin dead." The victim ran outside to the rear yard where she found the dog in the shed. The dog was lying on its side gasping for air. The victim tried to stop the bleeding coming from the dog's neck. Realizing the dog was dead she returned to the house where an argument escalated between the victim and the defendant.

The victim attempted to make a phone call, when the defendant grabbed the phone and threw the victim against the wall. The victim landed on a chair nearby. The defendant then started to punch the wall, causing his fist to smash through the gyprock lining. The victim ran out of the house to alert a neighbor who contacted the police. Police arrived a short time later and spoke with the victim. The victim was concerned for her safety and that of her daughter who had run off for help when the incident started. The victim returned to the premises while police accompanied her. She started to cry as she discovered the amount of damage that had occurred whilst she was at her neighbors asking for help. The lounge room had been completely overturned with a smashed coffee table in the middle of the room. Broken glass could be seen all over the floor of the lounge room. The kitchen had holes in the gyprock-lined walls and the telephone was on the floor. A 30-cm knife was discovered sticking into the architrave of the kitchen window.

Case Study 1 represents a "typical" description of animal cruelty in the context of domestic violence as recorded on the NSW Police COPS database. The offender described in the event had an extensive list of prior criminal charges, including resisting arrest (7 times), assault (12 times), breach of apprehended violence order (14 times), malicious damaging (4 times), placing child/young person at risk (6 times), animal cruelty (3 times); assaulting a police officer (2x), street offenses (2x), breach of bail (7 times), stalking (1 time), sexual assault (domestic violence related) (1 time), and stealing (4 times).

It is also of interest that the female victim was more upset about the property damage caused by the defendant than the suffering and death of the animal described in the event. It is plausible that the victim, a repeat victim of domestic violence, had become habituated to acts of animal cruelty as a result of other incidents recorded in the defendant's criminal record history.

Case Study 2: Mr. A repeatedly shot a dog for no reason other than that it was "annoying him." When police searched his premises (after being notified by the RSPCA) he was found to be in possession of a number of illegal firearms (in NSW it is illegal to possess any firearm unless a firearms licence is held), in addition to drug-growing equipment and a large amount of marijuana. This individual expressed no remorse for his behavior and was a known marijuana dealer with a prior criminal history for drug dealing, possessing/cultivating prohibited plants, assault, domestic violence, motor vehicle theft, theft from motor vehicle, and armed robbery. The offender was also known to associate with violent criminal gangs.

Case Study 2 illustrates that drug, firearm, robbery, and other violent and property offenses may also be present in the criminal histories of individuals who perform acts of animal cruelty. Previous research has largely focused upon the link between violent behaviors and animal cruelty. Case Study 2 suggests it may be valid to examine the extent to which individuals who are cruel to animals also display nonviolent criminal behaviors.

Moreover, anecdotal evidence provided by RSPCA inspectors and NSW police investigators suggests that individuals who are involved in organized animal cruelty (e.g., dog fighting, cock fighting rings) may be involved in large-scale fraud offenses, firearms trafficking, and drug manufacture. Anecdotal evidence also suggests that offenders who are involved with organized animal cruelty are not infrequently members of organized criminal gangs.

Case Study 3: An offender who was convicted of two sexual homicides reported that as a child he was exposed to animal cruelty by parental figures. The offender reported that he was given kittens by his grandmother when he visited and both he and his grandmother would torture and mutilate the animals until they died. This mutilation involved dismembering the animals.

It is of note that the offender in Case Study 3 dismembered one of his two victims, and the forensic pathologist commented that the cuts were of a very precise, skillful nature. The offender also admitted that he was cruel to a variety of native animals including water-dragon lizards, and also to cats and dogs. This animal cruelty took place in the same location as one of his sexual homicide offenses. The offender had also been charged with drug offenses and stealing prior to his conviction for the sexual homicides. Of particular interest to the NSW police and law enforcement investigators, in terms of investigation strategy in serial sexual homicide investigations, was the offender's verified self-report that he was cruel to animals in childhood, adolescence, and adulthood. Implications are that if animal cruelty offenses and offenders are reported to police, investigators could focus on these offenders as part of the suspect pool in the investigation of serious violent crimes. At present animal cruelty is not given priority in the investigation of serious violent crime by other Australian or international law enforcement agencies because too few animal cruelty cases are recorded on law enforcement databases (Clarke, 2003).

Case Study 4: This case study represents an unsolved series of animal cruelty incidents. It appears an unknown offender is nailing cats to crucifixes in the inner western suburbs of Sydney, New South Wales. The crucified animal is then displayed in a prominent position to be found by the cat's owner. No further information is available about the offender at the time of writing as the series remains unsolved.

The offender's display of the crucified animals is argued to be important for a number of reasons. First, the fact that the offender wants to distress individuals who find their pet dead may indicate a deviant or abnormal psychological need on the part of the offender. Second, the perpetrator's indifference to (or perhaps even enjoyment of) the obvious suffering caused to the animal during crucifixion suggests he/she is desensitized to the pain of a living organism. It is plausible that an individual who displays these types of characteristics may not stop at inflicting suffering on animals. Habituation to the emotional gratification experienced from killing or torturing animals may occur, in which case novel stimuli upon which to target the violence are needed by the offender. Research is needed to address whether this need is generalized to humans, and if so, in what ways this psychological need manifests itself behaviorally.

Case Study 4 also has important implications for the investigation of incidents involving violent behavior directed toward humans. In particular, sexual assault, domestic violence, and homicide have been identified by previous researchers as relevant (Flynn, 2000a; Giannopolous, 1994; Hazelwood & Burgess, 1995). If individuals who had performed the types of animal cruelty observed in Case Study 4 were recorded on a database, these records could facilitate the prioritization of suspects in investigations of violent and serial crime.

Case Study 5: This case study involves a neighborhood dispute in which the offender beheaded his neighbor's dog and left the animal's head on the victim's barbeque as a symbolic message. There is very little information available about this case from the RSPCA, and no data were recorded on the COPS system.

Perhaps the most important aspect of Case Study 5 concerns not the circumstances surrounding the case, but the fact that they could not be found on the COPS database. It seems that the suspect, with an extensive criminal history for other matters, has not come under police notice in relation to this animal cruelty incident. Case Study 5 is included to illustrate that serious matters of animal cruelty are not necessarily being recorded on a law enforcement database. Perhaps a more centralized repository of animal cruelty incidents could go some way to solving this problem.

Study 2: Animal Cruelty as a Predictor of Criminal Behavior. As previously noted, animal cruelty has been highlighted in the literature as a potential indicator of subsequent or simultaneous violent criminal behavior. The possibility of such a link in Australia has been supported by anecdotal evidence of notorious violent adult offenders. For example, mass murderer Martin Bryant was known to RSPCA officers in Tasmania in relation to animal cruelty offenses. Similarly, serial killer Ivan Milat was known for being cruel to animals prior to murdering seven victims in New South Wales. Concern has also been increasingly focused on the pain and suffering experienced by animal victims of abuse. Study 2 attempted to elucidate first the descriptive characteristics of persons who perform animal cruelty, and second, what if any other types of criminal behaviors are performed by animal cruelty offenders.

Instances of animal cruelty are increasingly being seen as grounds for investigation into the welfare of children and their families, and more generally, as a sign of concurrent or impending violence toward humans (Dadds et al., 2002). A number of researchers have attempted to clarify the behavior of animal cruelty in childhood and its possible contribution to the development of aggressive or violent tendencies into adulthood. Research focusing on family dynamics, as discussed earlier in this chapter, suggests that animal cruelty may be a symptom of something in a child's life that requires clinical intervention.

Ascione and Arkow (1999) have suggested a possible association between witnessing a parent being cruel toward animals and childhood animal cruelty. This has obvious implications in terms of social learning theory. Giannopolous (1994) has stated that the child may be desensitized toward animal suffering, in addition to imitating animal cruelty exhibited by the parent. It is plausible that the adverse vicarious learning situation may lead to increased levels of both adult interpersonal and animal abuse. As noted earlier, childhood animal cruelty, independent of context, may interfere with the development of empathy in children, a process that could affect attitudes along with vulnerabilities toward violence in adulthood (Clarke & Shea, 2003). This absence of empathy concurs with findings reported by Ressler, Burgess, and Douglas (1988), who have suggested that childhood animal cruelty is a "powerful indicator of violence elsewhere in a sexual homicide offender's life" (p. 40).

In light of existing research, the NSW Police Service Forensic Service Group considered it would be valuable to investigate the types of criminal behaviors that are observed in the backgrounds of individuals who had been recorded on the COPS database as having a record of animal cruelty offenses. It should be noted that the research was approached from a law enforcement rather than psychological or criminological standpoint. Therefore it primarily focused on the implications of animal cruelty for law enforcement agencies (Clarke, 2002).

A total of 200 participants in Study 2 were randomly selected from a database containing 947 persons involved in animal cruelty incidents in which police were involved. The definition of animal cruelty used was consistent with that outlined earlier in the chapter (RSPCA, 2000). The sample included 38 female ($M=32.8$ years, $SD=12.6$ years) and 162 male ($M=28.4$ years, $SD=8.7$ years) participants. Of the male offenders, 62.9% (n = 102) resided in urban areas, whereas 73.7% (n = 28) of the female offenders lived in urban areas.

Participants in Study 2 were located using the NSW Police Service COPS data collection system. This data system allowed for searches to be conducted across all animal cruelty offenders who have come to police attention since 1994. Records for all individuals convicted of animal cruelty between 1994 and 2002 were downloaded from the COPS database using a variety of criterion search models to ensure that a maximum number of offenders was identified from this database. Upon examination of the records of the 200 offenders, it was decided that each individual was suitable for the study based upon their being involved in the animal cruelty incidents recorded. The records of each offender, including all criminal charges and events noted on the system, were then examined individually, and a cumulative total of historical criminal events was compiled.

As is clear from Figure 1, the results indicated that offenders who reported incidents of cruelty to animals had also committed a number of additional

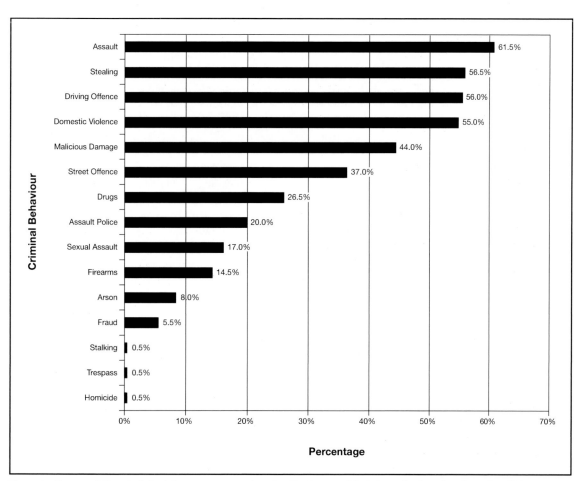

Figure 1   Representation of criminal charge as a percentage for offenders convicted of an animal cruelty offense from highest to lowest frequency

offenses. These offenses were characterized by assaults, stealing, and driving offenses. While normal comparative data were not available (for NSW police operational reasons), it is plausible that out of a sample of 200 participants who had performed animal abuse, the fact that 61.5% had also committed an assault could be considered higher than what would be observed in a non-animal cruelty comparison sample.

Also, more than half of the individuals who had a history of animal abuse also had convictions for driving offenses, domestic violence, and stealing (see Figure 1). Other offenses observed included drug and firearms offenses, sexual assaults, malicious damage, assaulting police, and street offenses. It is noteworthy that 17% of offenders who had performed animal cruelty had also performed sexual abuse. Importantly, animal abuse was a better predictor of sexual assault than previous convictions for homicide, arson, or firearms offenses. Finally, individuals with a conviction for animal cruelty displayed low frequencies for homicide, stalking, and trespassing convictions (see Figure 1), although it can be argued that such crimes are of lower incidence anyway.

Correlational analyses, performed within the animal cruelty offender group, revealed that offenders who had a history of animal cruelty were also more likely to perform assaults, sexual assault, stealing, and street offenses. Domestic violence offenses also featured prominently in their criminal histories.

Among those individuals who had performed animal cruelty, a number of more specific associations were observed. First, animal cruelty offenders who had a record for domestic violence were also more likely to engage in stealing, drug offenses, assaults, and sexual assaults. Animal cruelty offenders who had a conviction for sexual assault were more likely to have been convicted for drug offenses, whereas animal cruelty offenders who had convictions for assault were more likely to also have convictions for stealing.

In relation to the total number of criminal offense categories that offenders with a record of animal abuse could be classified into, the average was 4.03 (SD = 2.64). The total number of actual offenses committed by offenders would undoubtedly be significantly higher than this figure. Importantly, the 4.03 figure indicates that individuals with a record for animal cruelty are likely to commit a variety of other crimes. Overall,

the number of criminal offense categories that the crimes performed by animal cruelty offenders could be classified into ranged from 0 to 10. Only 1% (n = 2) of animal cruelty offenders exclusively had conviction for animal cruelty.

Overall, the results revealed support for the prediction that animal cruelty offenders would also have convictions for other types of criminal offenses, though unexpected findings were observed for stalking and homicide convictions. Perhaps the most salient finding was that individuals with a history of animal cruelty were highly likely to be involved in other types of criminal behaviors including, but not limited to, assault, domestic violence, and stealing. The range of criminal behaviors performed by individuals with a history of animal cruelty was also quite large, averaging four different types of criminal offense. This finding is important because it suggests that not only do individuals with a record of animal cruelty perform violent offenses (e.g., sexual assault, domestic violence, and assault), they also appear to perform nonviolent offenses such as drink driving, stealing, malicious damage, fraud, and drug offenses. This generalization across different types of criminal activity has not been observed in previous research.

Animal abusers were highly unlikely to have a conviction for homicide. This was contradictory to both previous research findings and expectations. This result may have occurred for two reasons. First, it may be that animal cruelty offenders generally do not engage in homicide. It is more likely, however, that homicide offenders are not detected by police for animal cruelty offenses. This issue was addressed in Study 3, which specifically examined homicide offenders and animal cruelty.

Similarly, low rates of stalking convictions were observed for offenders convicted of animal cruelty. In the absence of other research, no definitive conclusions can be made about this finding, other than to emphasize the need for more in-depth research to be conducted in a stalker population using structured interviews specifically asking about animal cruelty. This may clarify whether animal cruelty is not being performed by stalkers versus the more likely explanation that animal cruelty is not being detected by police.

Sexual assault, domestic violence, and firearms offenses all featured relatively prominently in the animal cruelty offenders' criminal histories. Arson convictions were recorded for 8% of animal cruelty offenders. These conviction rates may be comparatively high when compared with the rest of the offender population, which has been documented to be between 1% and 3% (Clarke, 2002). Further research comparing animal cruelty with non-animal cruelty offenders is required before the research findings can be applied to investigative frameworks and decision process models used by police.

In light of the observed associations between animal abuse and subsequent criminal behavior, a number of implications are apparent for law enforcement. The results of Study 2 could aid law enforcement agencies in three main ways.

1. In terms of criminal investigations, knowledge of previous criminal behaviors that are statistically infrequent (such as deliberate animal cruelty) could narrow lists of persons of interest in suspect prioritization plans for serious violent crime.

2. Risk assessment frameworks could be established based upon known information about animal cruelty. This could take the form of a matrix in which all known information is entered relating to criminal offenses, and a mathematical calculation (based upon regression analyses) could estimate a predicted level of future dangerousness taking into account the presence or absence of previous animal cruelty. The present research suggests that individuals with a history of animal cruelty are more likely to engage in criminal behaviors, and therefore should be monitored by law enforcement and other relevant agencies. This is particularly relevant for assault, domestic violence, fraud, and sexual assault.

3. Law enforcement agencies should work with other government agencies to identify and address individuals abusing animals as children prior to their potentially committing more serious violent offenses against people. This long-term "proactive strategy" may lead to a reduction in serious violent crime. Also, the judiciary could be provided with the research findings to ensure proper consideration of animal cruelty is taken into account in sentencing and bail determination hearings.

It should be noted that Study 2 was not designed to examine the psychological factors underlying animal cruelty or abuse, therefore these factors were not examined in detail. Nevertheless, the findings of Study 2 identified animal cruelty as one factor that may be useful in terms of both investigation of specific types of crime, as well as an area that may identify early offenders with a view to clinical intervention before any potential cycle of violence commences.

Study 3: Animal Cruelty and Homicide in New South Wales. A multiplicity of reasons underlie the act of killing another human being. These range from greed to revenge, jealousy to pleasure, and a diverse array of factors in between. There is an abundance of anecdotal evidence to suggest that the developmental histories of many homicide offenders are characterized by behaviors and cognitions directed against society. In particular, cruelty to animals has been identified as one behavior that may be present in offender developmental histories (Britton, 1997; MacDonald, 1963; Prentky & Carter, 1984; Ressler et al., 1988; Skrapec, 1996).

However, there is a relative paucity of systematic empirical studies that examine the developmental characteristics of homicide offenders (Clarke & Shea, 2003). In particular, there is a notable absence of research examining animal cruelty as a factor specifically in the histories of homicide offenders. Instead, studies have focused on more broad issues of adult violence, including domestic violence, assault, aggressive behavior, and child abuse. Until credible, scientifically sound research begins to examine whether such a link between animal cruelty and homicide exists, policy and decision makers have no way of knowing the significance of existing anecdotal accounts of such links.

Moreover, for research to be of value in providing information about a phenomenon, there must be a context by which to make an evaluation about the meaning of specific results. The context in psychological research is usually obtained by using normative data, in particular a comparison group, from which observations can be made about deviations observed in a group of interest. To date, this has not occurred in research investigating the phenomenon of animal cruelty in the developmental history of homicide offenders. To give a contextual framework to the second part of Study 3, it is necessary to review behavioral indicators associated with a specific form of homicide, namely sexual homicide.

A range of behavioral indicators may be important in identifying and clarifying the difference between sexual homicide offenders and non-offenders. Patterns of antisocial behavior in childhood and adolescence have been identified among sexual homicide offenders (Arrigo & Purcell, 2001; Canter, 1994; Dietz, Hazelwood & Warren, 1990; Folino, 2000; Giannopolous, 1994; Hickey, 1997; Keppel & Walter, 1999; Skrapec, 1996). These behaviors have been argued by the aforementioned researchers to indicate future sexual homicide behavior. A summary of these behavioral indicators is presented in Table 10.

It is evident from Table 10 that such factors as cruelty to animals and children, enuresis, compulsive masturbation, frequent daydreaming, chronic lying, rebelliousness, and fire setting feature with a large degree of prominence in the behavioral repertoire of sexual homicide offenders in childhood, adolescence, and adulthood. In the literature on sexual homicide, behavioral indicators are important for three reasons. First, they show that the socialization experiences of offenders are translated into negative behavioral expressions (Arrigo & Purcell, 2001; Giannopolous, 1994; Ressler et al., 1988). Second, these behavioral indicators are inextricably linked with the development of violent sexual fantasies (Hazelwood & Burgess, 1995;

Hickey, 1997; Skrapec, 1996). Third, they provide a potential means by which to predict future sexual homicide behavior using objective, observable measures (Canter, 1994; Dietz et al., 1990; Folino, 2000; Keppel & Walter, 1999).

Study 3, therefore, had two main aims. First, to examine to what extent sexual and nonsexual homicide offenders displayed a history of animal cruelty as either children or adults. Second, to establish whether a history of animal cruelty was unique to a subset of the homicide sample who had performed sexual homicides in comparison to a matched non-offender comparison group. Implications for law enforcement in the area of homicide investigation are also discussed.

Study 3 was made up of two parts. Part 1 examined criminal histories of sexual and nonsexual homicide offenders. Part 2 was designed as a comparison between two participant groups: a sexual homicide offender group and a control group.

Part 1 of the present study comprised a group of 49 randomly selected homicide offenders from the COPS law enforcement database. Types of homicide offense included, but were not limited to, domestic homicide, homicide for profit, sexual homicide, group cause homicide, and excitement homicide.

Table 10 Frequency of reported behavioral indicators in childhood, adolescence, and adulthood for sexual homicide offenders as reported in the Ressler et al. (1988) study

| | Frequency | | | | | |
| Behavior | Childhood | | Adolescence | | Adulthood | |
	n	%	n	%	n	%
Daydreaming	28	82	27	82	27	81
Compulsive masturbation	28	82	28	82	27	81
Isolation	28	71	26	77	26	73
Chronic lying	28	71	28	75	28	68
Enuresis	22	68	20	60	20	15
Rebelliousness	27	67	25.5	84	25	72
Nightmares	24	67	22	68	21	52
Destroying property	26	58	26	62	23	35
Fire setting	25	56	25	52	25	28
Cruelty to children	28	54	28	64	27	44
Running away	28	36	26	46	26	11
** Cruelty to animals **	28	36	26	46	25	36
Destroying possessions	25	28	23	35	23	35
Self-mutilation	26	19	24	21	25	32

Two of the participants were female and 47 were male. Part 2 of the study examined two groups: (1) 20 incarcerated adult male sexual homicide offenders, and (2) 20 adult male students enrolled in an introductory Psychology course for adult education students at The University of Sydney. The students were matched with the offenders for gender, age, and ethnicity. This was to control for both differential experience levels and variation in cultural factors hypothesized to influence developmental characteristics of sexual homicide offenders (Canter; 1994; Keppel & Walter, 1999; Ressler et al., 1988).

Participants were found using the New South Wales Police Service COPS data collection system. This data system allowed for searches to be conducted across all records of offenders who have come to police attention since 1994. Participants' criminal records were examined and coded in Part 1 of Study 3.

With regard to Part 2 of Study 3, the sexual homicide offender and non-offender comparison groups indicated on a structured interview questionnaire the degree to which they had performed animal cruelty as a child, adolescent, and adult. Responses were coded on a Likert-type scale, and included never, rarely, sometimes, often, and always. Three separate questions were asked for childhood, adolescence, and/or adulthood. The question specifically asked "Did you ever deliberately injure or kill an animal?" (Note—animals do not include insects, fish, or reptiles)." Participation in Part 2 of Study 3 was voluntary for participants in each group.

Records for all individuals convicted of a homicide between 1994 and 2002 were downloaded from the COPS database using a variety of criterion search models to ensure that a maximum number of offenders were identified. From this pool of offenders, 49 were randomly selected for inclusion in the present study. Upon examination of the records of all 49 offenders, it was decided that each individual was suitable for inclusion in the study based upon their being tried and convicted for the homicides described in the database. The records of each offender, including all criminal charges and events noted on the system, were then examined individually, and a cumulative total of historical criminal events were compiled.

With regard to Part 2 of the study, the sexual homicide offender and non-offender comparison groups were asked three separate questions as described in the methods section for Study 3 above.

Homicide Offender Group (n = 49). Only one of the participants examined with a record for homicide also had a record for animal cruelty. Analysis of criminal behaviors present in the homicide offenders' criminal records indicated a high prevalence of stealing and assault among this participant group. Driving and drug offenses also featured prominently, as did firearms offenses. The lowest frequency of criminal convictions recorded for homicide offenders was for animal cruelty offenses. All criminal history percentages for the homicide offender participant group are presented in Figure 2.

Comparison Between Sexual Homicide Offenders and Control Group. Of the sexual homicide offender group, none of the 20 offenders reported *never* being cruel to an animal as a child, only one reported never being cruel to an animal as an adolescent, and three reported never being cruel to an animal as an adult. None of the sexual homicide offender sample reported never being cruel to animals in childhood, adolescence, and adulthood. In other words, all 20 sexual homicide offenders reported being cruel to animals at some stage in their life.

The reported amount of animal cruelty at each developmental stage was compared between sexual homicide offenders and non-offenders. The sexual homicide offender sample reported significantly higher frequencies of cruelty to animals than the control group as measured on a five point Likert Type scale where a score of 1 equalled 'never' cruel to animals and a score of five indicated 'always' cruel to animals. ($M=3.05$, $SD=0.94$) were more likely to be cruel to animals than non-offenders ($M=1.40$, $SD=0.82$) ($t_{38}=-5.897$, $p<0.001$). A similar result was observed for sexual homicide offenders ($M=3.45$, $SD=1.31$) when compared with non-offenders ($M=1.65$, $SD=1.13$) during adolescence ($t_{38}=-4.627$, $p<0.001$). In adulthood sexual homicide offenders ($M=4.15$, $SD=1.22$) were also more likely to report being cruel to animals when compared with controls ($M=2.05$, $SD=1.43$) ($t_{38}=-4.983$, $p<0.001$).

These findings were congruent with previous research findings examining an American sample of sexual homicide offenders (Ressler et al., 1988) (see Table 10). Importantly, only one of the 20 sexual homicide offenders who reported being cruel to animals had any conviction on the law enforcement database for animal cruelty offenses.

Thus, the results of Study 3 revealed only partial support for each of the predictions put forth. In

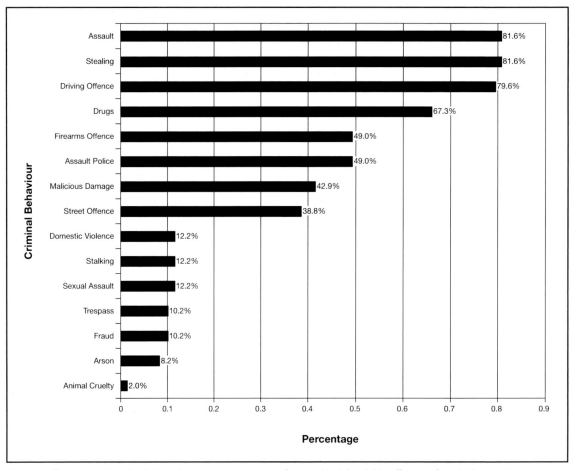

Figure 2   Representation of criminal charge as a percentage for convicted homicide offenders from highest to lowest frequency

relation to the first aim, the criminal behaviors of homicide offenders obtained from the criminal records database did not lend support to any link between animal cruelty and homicide. This finding is significant because, at first glance, it suggests that findings of a link between homicide and animal cruelty observed by previous researchers may not represent the situation in an Australian homicide offender sample.

A number of explanations are possible for the low rate of animal cruelty convictions in the homicide offender sample. First, the fact that research examined all types of homicide, rather than a specific form such as sexual homicide, may have obscured the relevance of animal cruelty as an associated factor. It is possible that animal cruelty is only observed in the developmental histories of specific types of homicide offenders. Second, similar to Study 2, it is plausible that any animal cruelty performed by homicide

offenders has not been detected by or reported to police.

The important issue raised by these observations is whether a method of analysis based upon routine and systematic comparison of criminal history records for homicide offenders could reveal the extent to which animal cruelty was a regular feature in the developmental histories of such offenders. This potential inadequacy in the record system, or indeed low rates of detection of animal cruelty offenses, was addressed by examining self-reported animal cruelty in a sample of sexual homicide offenders in greater detail through the use of a structured interview questionnaire. This led to Part 2 of Study 3, which attempted to establish whether a history of animal cruelty would be reported by a subset of homicide offenders who had performed sexual homicides. It was observed that not only were the sexual homicide offenders in Part 2 of this study more likely to abuse animals as both children, adolescents, and adults, but they also reported abusing animals more frequently than a matched non-offender comparison group. The high incidence of animal cruelty in sexual homicide offenders, which is congruent with the observations of previous researchers (e.g., Giannopolous, 1994; Keppel & Walter, 1999; Ressler et al., 1988), suggests that, at least for sexual homicide offenders, there may be a link between animal cruelty and subsequent homicide behavior. Equally important, the animal cruelty reported by offenders was not recorded on a law enforcement database in 95% of cases. This suggests that rather than no link being present between homicide and animal cruelty as observed in Part 1 of Study 3, it is more likely that homicide offenders are not being identified by law enforcement agencies for performing animal cruelty offenses (Clarke, 2002, 2003).

Interestingly, this research demonstrated that homicide offenders had criminal records for a diverse array of offenses. Upon more detailed examination, these offenses can be grouped according to a number of common themes. The most common offenses display a lack of long-term planning and a willingness to profit at other individuals' expense. Stealing, assault, and driving offenses all indicate spontaneous types of criminal behavior, as do drug offenses, which may have been linked to the commission of a number of the homicides. It also seems that these individuals were not hesitant to assault police, or to illegally use firearms. It could be argued that these high-frequency offenses are indicative of a more general trend toward impulsive behaviors, in which poor behavioral controls are displayed. These characteristics have been associated with a lack of responsibility and early behavioral problems (such as animal abuse) by Hare (1991). These findings further highlight the surprising lack of documented animal cruelty in the offenders' criminal histories, suggesting that this is an element of these individuals' behaviors that goes unnoticed by law enforcement.

The implications of these research findings are potentially far reaching for law enforcement agencies. First, in light of the discrepant findings between Parts 1 and 2 of Study 3, it would appear that detection and/or prosecution of animal cruelty instances when homicide offenders are children, adolescents, and adults is not occurring. This is supported by the observation that only one sexual homicide offender had a record of animal cruelty, yet all sexual homicide offenders, when surveyed, reported being cruel to animals. This suggests that detection procedures used at present in relation to animal cruelty are inadequate.

Implications of the Present Findings for the Investigation of Violent Crime. The NSW Police Animal Cruelty Research Project has a number of implications for both the prevention and investigation of both serial and violent crime. Specifically, offender profiling of such offenses as homicide, sexual assault, arson, stalking, and child abuse, to name but a few, would benefit a great deal from law enforcement agencies having more information about animal cruelty.

Offender profiling involves inferring personality characteristics from crime scene behaviors. Given the research findings that people who are cruel to animals are also more likely to be involved in a variety of serious and serial violent crimes, a database of animal cruelty offenders would be highly useful.

One aim of offender profiling is to prioritize a large number of suspects identified by police as potentially being responsible for a particular crime. Prioritization of suspects ensures that the actual offender is identified as quickly as possible from the list of possible suspects identified by criminal intelligence and other law enforcement techniques. Given that animal cruelty is statistically infrequent in most populations when compared with violent offender populations, it provides a useful marker to identify high-priority suspects in violent crime investigations.

Offender profiling research (e.g., Clarke, 2003; Clarke & Shea, 2003; Keppel & Walter, 1999) also suggests that individuals who perform sexual homicide and sexual assault crimes, for example, are also likely to display convictions for trespassing, peeping, fetishistic burglary, telecommunications offenses (telephone scatologia), and other sexual paraphilia–related convictions. These sexual paraphilia–related convictions are not statistically infrequent in offender populations. However, individuals with a combination of animal cruelty and these sexual paraphilia–related convictions are statistically infrequent. Therefore, these individuals may be identified by an offender profiler as high-priority suspects in the investigation of sexual assault and sexual homicide crimes, for example (see *Bestiality and Zoophilia* by Beetz, this text).

Unfortunately the operational usefulness of this offender profile characteristic is reduced because it is often the case that very few or no animal cruelty convictions are recorded on the law enforcement database being used. Certainly the NSW Police Research Project suggests that animal cruelty convictions recorded on one law enforcement database do not represent the true rate of animal cruelty in one group of sexual homicide offenders. While further research is necessary to establish whether similar underreporting is occurring for other types of crime (which one suspects is highly likely given clinical research findings discussed in this and other chapters), law enforcement databases need to capture all instances where people display cruelty to animals for use in subsequent investigation of crime. An example of an investigation where the recording of an animal cruelty conviction aided in the timely identification and arrest of a serial rapist is provided below.

Offender Profiling Case Study. In 2001 a violent sexual assault took place in Sydney, New South Wales. An offender profile was developed, and the profile stated that the offender was an anger-hostility type offender who would most likely display animal cruelty, and have convictions for domestic violence, assault, drunk and disorderly, as well as minor sex offense convictions. Investigators prioritized all identified suspects based on the profile information, and a very small number of suspects emerged at the top of the suspect list with convictions for animal cruelty offenses and sexual paraphilia–related offenses, in addition to convictions for assault and domestic violence. After extensive investigation of each "high priority" suspect, DNA evidence indicated that one of the high-priority suspects may be responsible for the sexual assault. What is important from the point of view of animal cruelty is that the few offenders identified as "high priority" were differentiated from the remainder of the suspects based on their history of animal cruelty. It could arguably be said that it was good fortune rather than good management that the identified offender had a recorded conviction for animal cruelty. The fact that he did resulted in him being identified, arrested, and charged much more quickly than would otherwise have been the case. Ultimately the swift arrest of the offender may have prevented another victim from being sexually assaulted, in addition to providing some closure for his victim when he was convicted for the offense.

As a result of both the offender profiling experience and the issues identified in the NSW Police Animal Cruelty Research Project, a number of recommendations were made. First, it was recommended that a national database be established to record all animal cruelty incidents. Contributors to this database should be veterinarians, the Department of Agriculture, RSPCA, Health Department, Child Welfare agencies, Department of Community Services (government child welfare protection agency in NSW), National Parks and Wildlife Service, the Department of Education, and other relevant agencies. This database would ensure the maximum possible number of animal cruelty incidents are recorded and therefore available to investigators.

Second, the research identified that effective liaison systems could be implemented to allow better communication between various departments who deal with animal cruelty so that no information is lost between "bureaucratic cracks."

Third, it was recommended the judiciary be informed about links between animal cruelty and other forms of criminal behavior. This was to ensure that any bail hearings, sentencing hearings, etc., adequately reflect the potential dangerousness of offenders.

Fourth, it was recommended that all police officers be educated about the links between animal cruelty and other forms of criminal behavior during their initial training. This recommendation was based on anecdotal evidence that some police officers see animal cruelty as a "minor" crime that is more a matter for the RSPCA than the police.

Fifth, it was recommended that a decision process model be developed for police officers who may encounter different types of animal cruelty. Officers could use the decision process model to categorize the type of animal cruelty, and then evaluate offender dangerousness level both for officer risk assessments (given the high rate of resisting arrest and assaults on police officers performed by animal cruelty offenders) as well as other potential crimes (domestic violence, firearms, drugs, sexual assault, homicide). It is important that future research investigate whether different types of animal cruelty are associated with different types of crimes.

Finally, in the interests of early intervention, it was recommended that joint teams be set up between police, Departments of Health, Departments of Community Services, and animal welfare organizations to evaluate the cognitions of children and adolescents who have been identified as animal cruelty offenders. This evaluation could involve detailed, structured interviews investigating such facets as children's escape mechanisms from reality (i.e., fantasy and play patterns), and symptomatology of such psychopathologies as conduct disorder and oppositional defiant disorder. A risk assessment matrix could identify children for whom early intervention may be valuable in possibly preventing subsequent violent or antisocial behavior.

Summary and Conclusions

In this chapter, we have reviewed a breadth of research relating to animal welfare and cruelty issues as they relate to the Australian context. In recent years, several trends have been apparent. First, it is increasingly being recognized by proponents of animal welfare that animal cruelty is not given the recognition that it deserves by legislators or the judiciary. This has brought about a call for more serious sentencing of animal abuse crimes and for mandatory reporting of animal abuse by veterinarians. It appears, however, that there is still some way to go before mandatory reporting is accepted by Australian veterinarians. Certainly, incorporation into the Australian veterinary training curriculum of specific information regarding the diagnosis of cruelty and appropriate responses to its identification is essential if mandatory reporting is to be perceived as a viable requirement. We have also reviewed Australian research that provides additional empirical support for the proposed link between animal abuse and human violence and criminal behavior. The Australian data demonstrating a high degree of co-occurrence between family violence and animal abuse are concordant with data from international studies. More importantly, however, we have reported data derived from police records in two Australian states (namely Victoria and New South Wales). These data demonstrate that animal abuse is predictive of other criminal behaviors including violent crimes. On the basis of the reported outcomes of the Australian research reviewed, we echo the calls made by others (e.g., Arkow, 2001; Arluke et al., 1999; Ascione, 2001b; Flynn, 2000a) for a coordinated response to identified animal cruelty. There also needs to be increased attention given to developing profiles of animal abusers across developmental stages. More thorough understanding of the role played by animal abuse within families is also needed. In line with the general emphasis, in recent times, on the promotion of mental health through primary prevention, developing a comprehensive knowledge of important screening variables is essential to any successful prevention effort.

References

Arkow, P. (1994). Animal abuse and domestic violence: Intake statistics tell a sad story. *Latham Letter, XV*(2), 17.

Arkow, P. (1996). The relationships between animal abuse and other forms of family violence. *Family Violence and Sexual Assault Bulletin, 12,* 29–34.

Arkow, P. (2001, Spring). Putting the "link" all together: Ontario SPCA's violence prevention initiative. *The Latham Letter, 15.*

Arluke, A., Levin, J., Luke, C., & Ascione, F. (1999). The relationship of animal abuse to violence and other forms of antisocial behavior. *Journal of Interpersonal Violence, 14,* 963–975.

Arrigo, B. A., & Purcell, C. E. (2001). Explaining paraphilias and lust murder: Toward an integrated model. *International Journal of Offender Therapy and Comparative Criminology, 45*(1), 6–31.

Ascione, F. R. (1998). Battered women's reports of their partners' and their children's cruelty to animals. *Journal of Emotional Abuse, 1,* 119–133.

Ascione, F. R. (1999). The abuse of animals and human interpersonal violence: Making the connection. In F. R. Ascione & P. Arkow (Eds.), (1999). *Child abuse, domestic violence, and animal abuse: Linking the circles of compassion for prevention and intervention* (pp. 50–61), West Lafayette, IN: Purdue University Press.

Ascione, F. R. (2001a, September). Animal abuse and youth violence. *Juvenile Justice Bulletin.*

Ascione, F. R. (2001b). *What veterinarians need to know about the link between animal abuse and interpersonal violence.* Paper presented at the 127th AVMA meeting, Salt Lake City, UT.

Ascione, F. R., & Arkow, P. (1999). Preface in F.R. Ascione & P. Arkow (Eds)., *Child abuse, domestic violence, and animal abuse* (pp. xv–xx). West Lafayette, IN: Purdue University Press.

Ascione, F. R., Weber, C. V., Thompson, T. M., Heath, J., Maruyama, M., & Hayashi, K. (2005). *Battered pets and domestic violence: Animal abuse reported by women experiencing intimate violence and by non-abused women.* Paper submitted for publication.

Ascione, F. R., Weber, C. V., & Wood, D. S. (1997). The abuse of animals and domestic violence: A national survey of shelters for women who are battered. *Society and Animals, 5*, 205–218.

Ashby, K. (2003). Dog bite injury. *Selected short reports—Victorian Injury Surveillance and Applied Research System.* Retrieved September 6, 2004, from http://www.general.monash.edu.au/muarc/visar/srdog.htm

Beirne, P. (2004). From animal abuse to interhuman violence? A critical review of the progression thesis, *Society & Animals, 12*, 39–66.

Bennett, P. C., & Perini, E. (2003). Tail docking in dogs: A review of the issues. *Australian Veterinary Journal, 81*, 208–218.

Boat, B. W. (1995). The relationship between violence to children and violence to animals: An ignored link? *Journal of Interpersonal Violence, 10*, 228–235.

Britton, P. (1997). *The Jigsaw Man*. London: Bantam Press.

Canter, D. (1994). *Criminal shadows: Inside the mind of a serial killer.* London: Harper Collins.

Chapman, S., Cornwall, J., Righetti, J., & Sung, L. (2000). Preventing dog bites in children: Randomised controlled trial of an educational intervention. *British Medical Journal, 320*, 1512–1513.

Clarke, J. P. (2002). *New South Wales police animal cruelty research project.* Unpublished report, New South Wales Police Service, Sydney, Australia.

Clarke, J. P. (2003). *International review of offender profiling: Investigative considerations.* Unpublished report, New South Wales Police Service, Sydney, Australia.

Clarke, J. P., & Shea, A. (2003). *Psychopaths*. London: John Blake.

Dadds, M. R., Turner, C., & McAloon, J. (2002). Developmental links between cruelty to animals and human violence. *Australian and New Zealand Journal of Criminology, 35*, 363–382.

Daniell, C. (2001, Spring). Ontario SPCA's women's shelter survey shows staggering results. *The Latham Letter*, 16–17.

Dietz, P. E., Hazelwood, R. R., & Warren, J. (1990). The sexually sadistic criminal and his offenses. *Bulletin of the American Academy of Psychiatry and Law, 18*(2), 163–178.

Fawcett, N. R., & Gullone, E. (2001). Cute and cuddly and whole lot more? A call for empirical investigation into the therapeutic benefits of human-animal interactions for children. *Behavior Change, 18*, 124–133.

Felthous, A. R., & Kellert, S. R. (1986). Violence against animals and people: Is aggression against living creatures generalized? *Bulletin of the American Academy of Psychiatry and Law, 14*, 55–69.

Flannery, T. (1994). *The future eaters*. Adelaide: Griffin Press.

Flynn, C. P. (2000a). Why family professionals can no longer ignore violence toward animals. *Family Relations: Interdisciplinary Journal of Applied Family Studies, 49*, 87–95.

Flynn, C. P. (2000b). Women's best friend: Pet abuse and the role of companion animals in the lives of battered women. *Violence Against Women, 6*, 162–177.

Folino, J. O. (2000). Sexual homicides and their classification according to motivation: A report from Argentina. *International Journal of Offender Therapy and Comparative Criminology, 44*(6), 740–750.

Giannopolous, S. (1994). *Psychopathology and serial murder*. Boca Raton, FL: CRC Press.

Gleyzer, R., Felthous, A. R., & Holzer, C. E. (2002). Animal cruelty and psychiatric disorders. *Journal of the American Academy of Psychiatry and Law, 30*, 257–265.

Green, P. C., & Gullone, E. (2005). Knowledge and attitudes of Australian veterinarians to animal abuse and human interpersonal violence. *Australian Veterinary Journal, 83*, 17–23.

Gullone, E., Johnson, J., & Volant, A. (2004). The link between animal abuse and family violence: A Victoria-wide study. *Australian Veterinary Association, Welfare Conference.* Canberra.

Hare, R. D. (1991). *The Hare Psychopathy Checklist—Revised*. Toronto: Multi-Health Systems.

Hazelwood, R., & Burgess, A. (Eds.), (1995). *Practical aspects of rape investigation: A multidisciplinary approach* (2nd ed.). Boca Raton, FL: CRC Press.

Hickey, E. (1997). *The serial murderer and his victims* (2nd ed.), Belmont, CA: Wadsworth.

Johnson, B. R., & Becker, J. V. (1997). Natural born killers?: The development of the sexually sadistic serial killer. *Journal of the American Academy of Psychiatry and Law, 25,* 335–348.

Kellert, S. R., & Felthous, A. R. (1985). Childhood cruelty toward animals among criminals and non-criminals. *Human Relations, 38,* 1113–1129.

Keppel, R. D., & Walter, R. (1999). Profiling killers: A revised classification model for understanding sexual murder. *International Journal of Offender Therapy and Comparative Criminology, 43*(4), 417–437.

Lahey, B. B., Waldman, I. D., & McBurnett, K. (1999). Annotation: The development of anti-social behavior: An integrative causal model. *Journal of Child Psychology and Psychiatry, 40,* 669–682.

Lawrie, M. (2001). There should be a law. *Animals, 42,* 14.

Lawrie, M. (2002). The mandatory reporting of animal abuse. *Veterinary Surgeons Board of Western Australia: Current Issues.* Retrieved August 14, 2004, from http://www.vetsurgeonsboardwa.au.com/0302_02Abuse.htm

Lost Dog's Home Newsletter (2004). Retrieved August 18, 2004, from http://www.dogshome.com/newsletter

MacDonald, J. (1963). The threat to kill. *American Journal of Psychiatry, 120,* 125–130.

Mackay, H. (1992). *What Australians feel about their pets: A study of our attitudes to cat and dog ownership.* Retrieved October 31, 2001, from http://www.petnet.com.au/mccallum/index.html

McHarg, M., Baldock, C., Headey, B., & Robinson, A. (1995). *National people and pets survey.* Retrieved October 31, 2004, from http://www.petnet.com.au/People_and_Pets/52UAMR.HTML

Munro, H. M. C., & Thrusfield, M. V. (2001). Battered pets': Features that raise suspicion of non-accidental injury. *Journal of Small Animal Practice, 42,* 218–226.

Myers, W. C., Reccoppa, L., Burton, K., & McElroy, R. (1993). Malignant sex and aggression: An overview of serial sexual homicide. *Bulletin of the American Academy of Psychiatry and Law, 21*(4), 435–451.

Pelcovitz, D., Kaplan, S. J., DeRosa, R. R., Mandel, F. S., & Salzinger, S. (2000). Psychiatric disorders in adolescents exposed to domestic violence and physical abuse. *American Journal of Orthopsychiatry, 70,* 360–369.

Prentky, R. A., and Carter, D. L. (1984). The predictive value of the triad for sex offenders. *Behavioral Sciences and Law, 2*(3), 341–354.

Prevention of Cruelty to Animals Act (POCTAA) (1979). New South Wales. Retrieved August 14, 2004, from http://www.austlii.edu.au/legis/nsw/consol_act/poctaa19793601.

Prevention of Cruelty to Animals Act (POCTAA) (1985). South Australia. Retrieved August 14, 2004, from http://www.austlii.edu.au/legis/sa/consol_act/poctaa1979360index.html

Prevention of Cruelty to Animals Act (POCTAA) (1986). Department of Natural Resources and the Environment, Melbourne, Victoria, Australia.

Prevention of Cruelty to Animals Act (POCTAA) (2002). Department of Local Government and Regional Development, Government of Western Australia, West Perth, Australia.

Quinslick, J. A. (1999). Animal abuse and family violence. In F. R. Ascione & P. Arkow (Eds.), *Child abuse, domestic violence, and animal abuse: Linking the circles of compassion for prevention and intervention* (pp. 168–175). West Lafeyette, IN: Purdue University Press.

Ressler, R. K, Burgess, A. W, & Douglas, J. E. (1988). *Sexual Homicide: Patterns and Motives.* New York: Lexington Books.

RSPCA (2000). *Animal welfare in Australia.* Retrieved June 10, 2004, from http://www.rspca.org.au/news_info/article.htm

RSPCA (2004). *RSPCA National Statistics.* Retrieved June 10, 2004, from http://www.rspca.org.au/news_info/stats_2001_2002.htm

Sacks, J. J., Sattin, R. W., & Bonzo, S. E. (1989). Dog bite-related fatalities from 1979 through 1988. *Journal of the American Medical Association, 262,* 1489–1492.

Sharman, K. (2002). Sentencing under our anti-cruelty statutes: Why our leniency will come back to bit us. *Journal of the Institute of Criminology, 13,* 333–338.

Sharpe, M. S., & Wittum, T. E. (1999). Veterinarian involvement in the prevention and intervention of human violence and animal abuse: A survey of small animal practitioners. *Anthrozoös, 12,* 97–104.

Siegel, J. M. (1990). Stressful life events and use of physician services among the elderly: The moderating role of pet ownership. *Journal of Personality and Social Psychology, 58,* 1081–1086.

Skrapec, C. A. (1996). The sexual component of serial murder. In T. O'Reilly-Fleming (Ed.), *Serial and mass murder: Theory, research and policy.* Toronto: Canadian Scholar's Press.

Thompson, P. G. (1997). The public health impact of dog attacks in a major Australian city. *Medical Journal of Australia, 167,* 129–132.

Wirth, H. (2000). The future of companion animals in the 21st century. Retrieved June 10, 2004, from http://www.rspca.org.au/news_info/articles_pets_21.htm

Attachment and Animal Abuse

Dr. Ken Magid

Introduction—Divergent Pathways

"They Can Feel Pain Just Like Us": Attachment and Animal Abuse

Aaron, age 12, liked to walk at a brisk pace. I kept up with him as we walked around the block and we talked about his desire to play baseball rather than do homework. His high achieving parents had brought him in to see me because they believed he needed some help in school.

All of a sudden Aaron stopped and said, "Watch out. You're gonna step on those ants, and they are carrying something." Aaron dropped to his knees to get a better look as he continued to inform me about ant habits. I wondered to myself if this was how young E. O. Wilson (the eminent myrmecologist or ant expert) saw the world at 12. "They can feel pain just like us," said Aaron in an empathetic tone. I later learned that he had several pets at home and he took special pride in taking good care of them. I supported Aaron for his awareness and segued into how *cool* it was that he cared for living things.

Many years ago I remember treating another 12-year-old boy I'll refer to as Derek who had been in a highly abusive home for the first two years of his life. He was repeatedly spanked, inconsistently fed, and left alone for long periods of time by his single, drug-addicted mother. Social services removed the child, and for several years, Derek moved from one foster home to another, largely because of behavioral problems. At age 6 he was adopted into a supportive family. His young parents were never informed about all of the behavior problems he had, and they wanted a child so much that they largely brushed aside anything negative in his file. They simply believed in the Beatle's anthem, "All You Need is Love."

But Derek distanced himself emotionally from his new parents as well as from his own inner pain, and he certainly never empathized with the pain of others, especially that of animals which he constantly teased and secretly tortured. In one home, he had repeatedly dropped his pet hamster from the top of the stairs until it died. Other pets also suffered premature deaths at his hand, but these violent acts were not outlined in information given to his adoptive parents. In one foster home he threatened another child with a pair of scissors. No foster home wanted him for long. He had no friends, and children and pets alike gave him a wide berth.

When he was 10 years old, he expressed his rage at his adoptive mother by secretly poisoning his own pet cat. The family, who had several pets, assumed that the animal died by natural causes. Derek feigned personal grief to get sympathy and made a point of telling everyone how upset he was at the loss. Derek's mother had a favorite pet cat that also suddenly died one month later. Derek had killed his own cat first and feigned great sorrow so that no one would suspect him of killing his mother's favorite animal later. It was all part of his original predatory plan.

Later that same year, Derek was caught setting homes on fire in the neighborhood. At first he was seen as a hero, because he would frequently engage a stranger nearby and innocently query, "Do you smell smoke?" and then urge someone to call the fire department. He was finally caught when his parents searched his room and found fuel accelerant and matches. "It was after the second cat died that we got real suspicious," his mother said. Derek had previously taken pleasure in abusing animals, and now he had escalated to setting homes on fire. Fortunately he was caught before anyone died. "I just don't understand why he does such terrible things," his mother said.

A Story Retold

The first child, Aaron, loves to protect and nurture animals while Derek loves to torture and kill them. One embodies empathy while the other has a deficit in empathy and expresses hostility. Each child pursues a radically different path. What motivates them? How did each boy get this way? One child's behavior is healthy while the other child's profile is pathological. The Derek in this case example was born in the 1980s, yet he shares a great deal in common with another child named Derek who was born in England in 1930.

Although time and distance separated these two children's lives, their negative behaviors and patterns of thinking are almost interchangeable. One child could jump into a time machine and replace the other without missing a beat. In short, they lie, they steal, they hurt others, and they have no remorse for their acts, only excuses. As a caregiver, you could try to reason with them, talk to them sternly, or even administer spankings, but none of this would have much effect. We know more today about how the American-born Derek got that way, in great part because of one man who scientifically studied the similar-thinking, English-born Derek over 60 years ago.

John Bowlby was a psychiatrist who published a paper entitled, "Forty-Four Juvenile Thieves: Their Characters and Home Life" (1944). The paper carefully examined 44 different children, ages 6 to 16, who chronically displayed delinquent behaviors. His work was unique in psychiatry because he chose to look at family dynamics instead of just the individual psyche, and he used statistical tests to make his points. Bowlby's first case involved a 6-year-old child named Derek, who at 18 months of age caught diphtheria and had to be hospitalized for 9 months. Hospital policy at the time didn't allow parents to visit, so little Derek was separated from his mother and family members for the entire time. When he finally returned home, his mother reported that he had drastically changed. He now seemed distant and detached, and Dr. Bowlby commented about Derek's lack of empathy or affectionless character. After studying 43 other children who demonstrated similar types of delinquent behavior, Bowlby could discern a distinct pattern.

These children had all suffered varying degrees of maternal deprivation and separation early in their lives, and there was no one there to consistently nurture or support them in the mother's absence. Shifts of well-meaning doctors and nurses just couldn't provide the continuity of psychological nurturing necessary to replace an attentive mom. Of course, it should be noted that many moms and dads in Bowlby's study, especially those who had *affectionless* children, were troubled themselves and were not extremely attuned parents in the first place (Bretherton, 1995).

This certainly compounded the risk factors for the child, but Bowlby knew that many children in the community with less than ideal parents still turned out better than Derek, so he decided to focus initially on the early separations from the primary caregiver. His colleague, John Robertson, observed the separation reactions of the children in the hospital and he identified three patterned responses as protest, despair, and detachment (Bowlby, 1988; Bretherton, 1995; Karen, 1994). Each phase illustrated the baby's attempt to adapt to the loss of a primary caregiver. It was from this focus on early maternal infant separations that Bowlby launched his research platform for understanding the etiology of troubled children like Derek (Bowlby, 1969/1982). It's children like these who more often abuse animals and it's their earliest childhood experiences that help launch them into that violent trajectory.

Overview and Discussion

As the director of America's first child guidance clinic in Chicago, William Healy wanted to know why children became juvenile delinquents. After studying many cases, he came to the conclusion that there was no single one cause for delinquency but instead a complex *web of causative factors* that corresponded to each individual child (Silk, Nath, Siegel, & Kendall, 2000). Furthermore, Healy found that most juvenile delinquents were not psychopaths but instead normal children who were just experiencing serious problems in many different areas of their lives (Silk et al., 2000). The year was 1915, and Healy's observations and comments were amazingly farsighted.

Causality regarding children's behaviors is always complex, because one must consider the heterogeneity of the disorders and how the many risk and protective factors constantly interact within a multidimensional developmental process (Cicchetti & Sroufe, 2000). For example, a highly controlling parent might be a protective factor for one high-risk child while the same strategy might become a liability factor for a low-risk child. The context and the individual child's reactions are important considerations, and risk categories end up being more probabilistic than simple cause–effect explanations

(Cicchetti & Sroufe, 2000). It is rare that a single risk factor acts in a linear manner by itself to push a child into committing chronic psychopathological acts (Cicchetti & Sroufe, 2000). Similarly, in the medical field, we find that cardiovascular disease has many diverse possible causes including smoking, high cholesterol, laziness, obesity, ongoing stress, sex hormone problems, genetic vulnerability, and other risk factors that interact and increase one's probabilities of developing the disease (Rutter & Sroufe, 2000). Nature and nurture are constantly interacting.

The term *aggression* is equally nonspecific, and it does not represent a unitary concept since it has too many different interpretations and applications (Cairns & Cairns, 2000). One could be using the term to describe the actions of a toddler (who acts impulsively) pulling the tail of a pet cat, or an adolescent (who acts impulsively) shooting a cat. Besides not clarifying developmental status and age, the term *aggression* does not specify the biological or social etiology or contextual influences, which could include brain chemistry abnormalities, gender differences, peer group pressure, motivation, intention, substance abuse, attachment status, and much more (Cairns & Cairns, 2000). Aggression could be considered defensive and functionally adaptive (for survival or protection) or unprovoked, unwarranted, and pathological. Therefore, definitions and evaluative criteria and necessary caveats always need to be clarified.

We should establish at the outset that while attachment features can act as influential risk or protective factors concerning why children help or harm animals, we should also be clear that attachment processes operate within a lengthy causal chain and do not account for everything that happens in a relationship (Rutter & Sroufe, 2000), whether it be with humans or animals. As we will soon see, Bowlby took pains to clarify that other *systems* operate in children's lives and that attachment is but one link in the causal chain that explains why we do the things we do.

After concentrating primarily on pathological child development, Bowlby soon realized that he needed to compare it to a standard of normal development, and with his colleague Mary Ainsworth he observed how children grow up healthy (Ainsworth, 1990; Marvin & Britner, 1999). It is important that the normal development of a child be thoroughly understood before one attempts to understand what's not normal. Of course the devil is in the details and

there will always be questions surrounding the exact boundaries of normal and abnormal (Cicchetti, 2003; Silk et al., 2000). (This topic will be the subject of a forthcoming book by this author, entitled *Good Weird, Bad Weird*.) The point is that both sides of the coin must be addressed to better comprehend either particular side.

Therefore, this chapter will look at how children with secure attachment patterns are more likely to engage in healthy integrated brain functioning and empathetic care of animals while those with insecure attachments are more at risk of maladaptive behaviors. There are many motivations children have for harming animals, including preemptive attacks, gang initiation, identification with an aggressor, impulsivity, reenactment, and more (Ascione, 2005). I will look at how different attachment patterns might inhibit or promote maladaptive behaviors and the etiology of the internal working models children use to control their emotions and guide their actions. I will also integrate how pets interface with child development and attachment theory. I will discuss how pets serve children as models and caregivers, as objects of attachment, and as peers to increase both the exploratory and the sociability systems of attachment. I will review how attachment is related to compulsive hoarding of animals and discuss what roles insecure attachment plays in those who breed animals for fighting. I will address how pets can act as buffers to protect children from traumatic early experiences and how children can better identify with similarities between themselves and animals to increase empathy.

Part One will lay out the fundamentals of attachment theory including how children develop a relationship compass and how differences in attachment patterns are formed contingent upon the caregiver–child interactions. It's important to understand the basic attachment model. Part Two will address the problems, pathways, and probabilities of attachment profiles as risk factors for clinical problem behaviors as well as their descriptive limitations. Part Three will take a psychosociobiological look at why children with secure attachments are more likely to treat animals with empathy while insecure children who have experienced suboptimal parenting and maltreatment are more likely to objectify animals and harm them. Part Four will wrap up the chapter with some concluding remarks about our evolutionary connections with animals and the challenges we all have to educate future generations to be better stewards of all the animals in the world.

Part One—The Fundamentals of Attachment Theory

Attachment Theory Evolves

Perhaps the first attachment theorist was Charles Darwin, since he made scientific observations on the social nature of animals and how parental instincts for the early protection of offspring enhanced the survival and reproductive advantages of a species (Simpson, 1999). He also surmised that this same strong directional selection pressure for establishing social interactions and early protection for the young operated for humans as well (Simpson, 1999). We are all still deeply indebted to Darwin's groundbreaking work, and it's from his established platform that scientists launched modern evolutionary theory.

The study of animals played a big part in Bowlby's theory of attachment. Bowlby found that Darwin and other observers of animal behavior such as ethologists Lorenz, Tinbergen, and Hinde could provide a biological basis for his theory of attachment in humans (Bowlby, 1988; Bretherton, 1995). In 1937, Lorenz discovered a way to never be lonely. He simply became the first moving object that newborn ducklings saw during their time-sensitive period of attachment as they *wired in* his form as their parent. They followed him everywhere and even courted him sexually after they matured. This imprinting behavior was genetically motivated learning that was contingent upon a moving stimulus experience that could be generalized to several stimuli (Bowlby, 1969/1982; Bowlby, 1988; Starr & Taggart, 1992).

Bowlby proposed that a less critical or rigid time-sensitive developmental process operated in humans and that social bond formation did not have to be tied to feeding, as Freud had proposed (Bowlby, 1969/1982; Bretherton,1995). And not unlike our waddling friends, we all came into this world with an agenda prescribed by evolutionary pressures.

Your First Resume … Attachment Behaviors

Your very first job in life was to capture a parent and according to Bowlby you were born with a repertoire of innate talents to engage your caregivers and to ensure protection, nurturance, and basic survival (Marvin & Britner, 1999). Any activity that has the predictable outcome of getting a child closer to the attachment figure (which is usually the parent) can be termed an attachment behavior (Cassidy, 1999). This means that all five senses (auditory, kinesthetic, olfactory, gustatory, and visual) are employed in the engagement process. They jointly serve a dual purpose in binding the child to the attachment figure and binding the attachment figure to the child. Children with sensory integration deficits often experience difficulty attuning to others, which can compromise their adaptive functioning (Fisher, Murray, & Bundy, 1991)

Our prehensile grasp allows us to cling tightly to our caregiver and receive kinesthetic skin-to-skin comfort promoting nerve growth stimulation, while our sucking rooting behavior gives us kinesthetic comfort, nurturance, and stress reduction. The caregiver has an opportunity early on to regulate the infant's physiological systems by offering warmth, nutrition, olfactory, and kinesthetic stimulation. These have been termed *hidden regulators* (Polan & Hofer, 1999). Natural selection has also favored those infant behaviors that reward the mother, such as reduction in mammary gland pressure while nursing and the release of the feel good neurohormone oxytocin (Janov, 2000). Some innate behaviors are used for signaling, such as cooing or smiling, which act as another trigger or releaser for the parent to smile back, which can then start a positive feedback loop of engagement (Simpson, 1999). Remember the last time a baby smiled at you and how you responded? Without thinking you smiled back, because mother nature prewired your brain to do that with specialized feature detector cells that gave you a preference for human faces (Perrett & Puce, 2003). Mother Nature equipped the youngest humans with a kid attachment system that is designed to couple up with an adult caregiving system.

A newborn just 8 weeks old already has the neural networks laid down for smiling. All that is needed is an environmental stimulus or releaser such as a human face, or, for that matter, anything resembling a human face such as a flat round object with two dots for eyes. Leave one dot off the round object and you'll get no smile. The baby is preprogrammed for two eyes to elicit the response (Johnson & Morton, 1991; Kraemer, 1992). Interestingly, at birth, a baby's eyes are proportionately quite large for its small head and this can be compelling, especially as those big beautiful eyes follow you and draw you closer like a powerful magnet. Perhaps without knowing why, Walt Disney capitalized on this attachment behavior and made all his cartoon characters with overly enlarged appealing eyes. As an aside, Disney also introduced many generations of children to animal characters that were approachable and sentient, which may have had the effect of increasing viewers' empathetic responses to the animals. Freud had earlier stated that children identify strongly with animals (Ascione, 2005).

Another innate attachment behavior is crying, which tends to motivate the sensitive caregiver to stop the aversive noise and to meet the infant's needs (Bretherton, 1995). There are many types of cry signals that attuned parents can soon distinguish in their offspring. Some signify hunger while others signal fear or pain. It is also believed that evolutionary forces favored each baby's unique human cry to communicate across long distances and, like many animals, each infant's individual cry is a distinct vocal signature (Solter, 1984). A baby's cry usually elicits an alarm reaction to engage the mother's caregiving response (Marvin & Britner, 1999). With later maturation, babies use active physical approaches such as crawling, climbing, and walking. These attachment behaviors are designed to not only achieve and maintain closeness to a caregiver but also to restore it when it has been impaired. The predisposition of infants to gain proximity to caregivers is referred to as the biological function of attachment behavior (Cassidy, 1999). With time, the baby forms a repertoire of attachment behaviors to achieve predictable proximity to attachment figures.

A Systems Approach

Bowlby proposed that the internal organization of many different attachment behaviors comprised an attachment behavioral system that evolved to assist the relatively helpless human baby survive despite its immature abilities for self-defense, warmth, feeding, and locomotion (Bowlby, 1969/1982; Cassidy, 1999). The child's desired proximity to the parent and the chosen attachment behaviors will vary depending on the specific situation and the biological or environmental trigger that elicited it.

Bowlby described three different causes or triggers to elicit the attachment system. One was the condition of the child, which means that if the child is tired, hungry, cold, sick, or in any pain the attachment processes were more likely to be activated (Bowlby, 1969/1982; Marvin & Britner, 1999). Another trigger concerns the location and behavior of the primary caregiver, whether he or she is leaving, rejecting, or absent. And finally, there are other environmental conditions. Is the environment threatening in some way, via siblings, other adults, noises, animals, or other noxious stimuli? Sometimes only one trigger is sufficient to activate an attachment response in a child, while at other times

several triggers are combined. Proximity and nurturance by the primary caregiver usually reestablishes the homeostatic equilibrium despite the perceived environmental threat (Marvin & Britner, 1999).

There was a time in early human evolution (long before weaponry was invented) that predatory animals found us vulnerable humans quite delicious. The smallest humans, the children, were especially at risk if they did not have a healthy wariness of unfamiliar and unpredictable creatures that were larger and faster than them. Even today, a baby's innate fear and wariness of a pet dog that is growling or loudly barking serves as a protective measure against getting too close and getting bitten. But as I shall later discuss, the fear wariness system can also promote preemptive strikes against non-threatening animals by older fearful children who have disordered attachments and who unreasonably assume that all animals are threatening.

Interestingly, in the normal course of development, as the baby passes the half year mark, unfamiliar *human faces* can elicit the fear wariness system into action as much as or more than unfamiliar objects (Bretherton & Ainsworth, 1974). This makes sense in evolutionary terms. Unfamiliar humans can also pose danger, so the infant is very sensitive to strange unfamiliar faces for about 24 months (Bowlby 1969/1982). Fortunately, babies are usually around familiar faces that offer enough security and protection to deactivate or reduce the fearful responses, allowing another strong inborn system called the exploratory behavioral system to emerge.

Bowlby (1969/1982) suggested that the attachment control system operates somewhat like a thermostat. As the temperature drops, the thermostat turns on the heater and turns it off after the room warms up. Children feel comfortable exploring or affiliating with others until a threatening trigger (i.e., coldness) causes the attachment thermostat to activate and the child once again seeks proximity and closeness (i.e., emotional warmth). Bowlby later clarified that the attachment thermostat was never fully off, but rather always in a state of increased or decreased activation (Cassidy, 1999). The attachment behavioral system is now viewed along a continuum throughout the lifespan and is evident in one's thoughts and behaviors concerning proximity seeking in times of stress or need (Mikulincer & Shaver, 2004).

The attachment behavioral system interacts with other internally motivating biobehavioral control systems that also help us survive and thrive. According to Bowlby, the fear wariness system biologically predisposes children to be on guard when certain potentially dangerous stimuli occur, such as sudden movements, loud noises, extreme darkness, or being left alone. Then it interfaces with the attachment system to help the child seek proximity to a protective caregiver and ultimately, after safe passage into adulthood, to pass on his genes (Bowlby, 1969/1982; Cassidy, 1999; Marvin & Britner, 1999).

Bowlby (1969/1982) said that the exploratory behavioral system ties in with our natural curiosity and motivates the baby to learn about the environment so he can better adapt to it. This motivation to explore and seek autonomy supports all early forays into the unknown and later skill building proficiencies in a variety of survival essentials such as tool use, shelter construction, food acquisition, and other necessary activities (Bowlby 1969/1982; Cassidy, 1999; Marvin & Britner, 1999). The exploratory and the attachment systems generally act in a complementary balanced fashion. The child usually needs to feel protected and somewhat secure before he is willing to leave his caregiver and go off exploring the surrounding environment. Bowlby's colleague Mary Ainsworth said the child uses the attachment figure as a *secure base* to explore the world (Bowlby, 1988). It's not difficult to see how learning new skills might be more challenging for a fearful child who is being continually intimidated by environmental stimuli.

When the exploratory behavioral system is in effect and the child feels secure, he can see animals as intriguing objects worthy of investigating. This attraction increases as the toddler gains more awareness, locomotion, object permanence, and the desire for more autonomy. But animals, despite their physical animation, are largely treated like all other objects by young children since the concept of "aliveness" or even empathy cannot be adequately comprehended by an infant (Piaget, 1972; Ascione, 2005). Therefore, unintentional but significant harm can come to animals under the care of young children who have not been properly shown how to care for pets in the home. Although increased age usually brings increased ability to understand how animals can be hurt, age alone does not guarantee proper care of animals, especially in scenarios where low supervision, poor modeling, or disrupted attachments are prevalent (Ascione, 2005).

Another biobehavioral motivator is the sociable or affiliative system that predisposes the baby to interact

with other people, such as peers, and this adds to his growing understanding of social dynamics and hence his overall survival chances (Cassidy, 1999). Studies on isolated monkeys by Harry Harlow confirmed the importance of affiliation for normal primate development (Harlow, & Zimmerman, 1959; Kraemer, 1992). As I will later discuss, extreme and prolonged isolation of infants can result in later maladaptation, including violent externalizing behaviors (Cairns & Cairns, 2000; Kraemer, 1992). The sociable system also interfaces with the attachment process in a complementary balancing way so that when one system is activated the other one usually is not (Marvin & Britner, 1999).

Even before modern civilization arose, mankind wisely enlisted the support of animal allies to aid him in a variety of ways, including protection, hunting, herding, modeling and companionship (Bierer, 2000). With modern mechanization came more personal alienation and an increased need for reliable companionship and nonjudgmental love that many animals provide for their human caretakers. The companion animal connection (while not as complex as Bowlby's attachment concept) is nevertheless a bond worthy of intense affection, as behaviorally demonstrated by millions of pet owners. In one study, 87% of the adult pet owners surveyed stated that their pets were considered members of their family (Cain, 1983). It's also not uncommon for young children to consider their pets as peers, since they ascribe more similarities (such as small size, high energy, dependency, and so on) between themselves and animals than they do between themselves and adults (Ascione, 2005). For kids, companion animals can become good playmates that offer kinesthetic reciprocal interactions and unconditional love.

Helpless human infants also survive because of a strong biologically based motivation for caregiving from others. One of the principal behaviors exhibited within the caregiving system is providing comfort and protection for the infant. Specific behaviors may include searching, calling, grasping, restraining, and retrieving an infant facing danger (Cassidy, 1999). Comfort behaviors vary within cultures but can include stroking, rocking, and soft vocalizations (Cassidy, 1999). This same caregiving impetus can be expanded toward helping other people in need as well as protecting and nurturing animals. A basic premise of this chapter is that the attachment behavioral system can positively or negatively influence the expression of the caregiving behavioral system and, thus, influence how children think about and treat animals.

The Relationship Compass Inside All of Us

It's a misconception that we instantly *bond* with our primary caregiver as if super glue is applied at birth. Bowlby suggested that the attachment behavioral system unfolded through four experiential phases rather than through distinct inflexible stages (Bowlby 1969/1982; Marvin & Britner, 1999). The first phase, which occurs from birth to the first 2 or 3 months, is marked by the baby's orientation to social stimuli from almost everyone with only a limited ability to differentiate his primary caregiver. Virtually everyone is special for the newly minted infant. Bowlby believed that this was part of a preattachment process. The second phase (which happens with a biological maturation shift that occurs after 2 months) then allows the infant to regulate himself more so he can discriminate a bit better and direct his attachment behaviors (smiling, cooing, visual following) to those people who are more familiar (Bowlby, 1969/1982; Marvin & Britner, 1999). Bowlby described this as an attachment in the making process (Bowlby, 1969/1982; Marvin & Britner, 1999).

Another biobehavioral maturation shift occurs around 7 months and this is when Bowlby's third phase starts (Bowlby, 1969/1982; Marvin & Britner, 1999). The now crawling infant has a wide repertoire of attachment behavioral responses to capture his preferred caregiver(s). He can approach and follow her and use her as a secure base from which to explore the environment. His attachment preferences are now more clearly established and he will actively seek out familiar faces while expressing caution over strange ones. Choices are now regularly being acted upon, and for Bowlby, this third phase is when the child is clearly *attached*. He admits that attachment may happen a bit earlier, but it is not a clear-cut demarcation.

The last phase starts around the third year and involves what Bowlby referred to as a goal-corrected partnership (Bowlby, 1969/1982; Cassidy, 1999). Here the rapidly maturing child has developed the capacity to use language and gain some understanding not only about his mother's actions but also about her motives and emotions. He can use this information when planning his behaviors, correcting his goals along the way according to her responses in order to negotiate mutual outcomes.

Bowlby suggested that this process was not unlike a heat-seeking missile that can utilize new information about changes in the target's location and consequently change its trajectory to obtain its goal (Cassidy, 1999). Birds and bats do this routinely while pursuing an insect in flight. This differentiation of himself from his caregiver, coupled with his improved communication ability, allows both him and his caregiver an opportunity to form a lifetime partnership. Such a complex interactive union is built upon an internalized model about how all existing and future relationships can work.

How the Relationship Compass Was Built, Memories and Language

The infant's earliest mental representations are holistic in scope. He does not distinguish himself as being separate from *others*. With some maturity comes the discovery that he is different, which is the start of a profound new mental representation of *self* and *other* (Stern, 1985). So, the infant's first task in life is to make a secure and reliable attachment connection with his caregiver, and the second task is to develop a differentiated self that can increasingly act in autonomous ways (Cicchetti, Toth, & Maughan, 2000). As the differentiation process continues forward, new challenges are presented to the infant, such as figuring out how things work, including his own actions on the environment. But all learning and successful use of past experiences depends upon one's memory.

There are many ways of storing knowledge and knowing something in the world. In the beginning we simply experience life and develop certain skills through repeated efforts that are beyond our conscious awareness. These early skills, which are correlated with Piaget's sensorimotor period, are called procedural or *implicit* memory knowledge bits, and they involve both minute perceptions and motor actions that can last for a lifetime (and originate during the first three biobehavioral shifts of infant development) (Pipp-Siegel & Pressman, 1996). For example, a mother of a 5-month-old could blow bubbles with her mouth to engage her infant in a reciprocal game and not be able to describe the exact microsecond timing between turns or the number of bubbles in each turn (Pipp-Siegel & Pressman, 1996). Yet once the baby practices the motions, they can stay with him for a lifetime.

We learned how to do certain things without thinking about the specific processes involved (such as turning the pages of this chapter or how to walk).

Still, each task is routinely accomplished with our procedural knowledge. Robots must be extensively programmed to execute such simple human actions. Procedural knowledge memory influences our future expectations (including fear-based items) and helps regulate our daily behavior. It does not embody symbols but simply refers to the act of *doing* without describing or analyzing. By repeated actions, we form memories of how the world works and how to follow norms. It is a somatosensory experience, and each experiential procedure forms a building block for later cognitive organization (McCrone, Egeland, Kalkoske, & Carlson, 1994). A child can have a positively embedded procedural memory of engaging a purring cat or a negative experience of being bitten by a cat, and then encode an unconscious predisposition for or against cats that is long lasting.

As the baby grows and acquires a language, new options for memory develop. These other ways of storing knowledge and knowing something require the use of semantic and episodic memory systems that are often referred to as declarative knowledge (Pipp-Siegel & Pressman, 1996). These learned behaviors are usually represented by symbols or strong sensory images and events that can be called forth with conscious effort as the child develops language skills. With this memory a child can identify his or her gender and name and consciously structure communication patterns. So, declarative knowledge allows symbolic descriptions of oneself and others and helps frame up one's evolving personality. I will address self–other issues and how they get distorted later, but suffice it to say now that both procedural and declarative memories guide the child with critical information about how to sequence behaviors, negotiate relationships, develop verbal generalizations, and adaptively form a sense of self as he relates to others (Crittenden, 1997).

The young baby's sensory systems and brain are continually taking in new information about everything that is going on around him. As interactive experiences with attachment figures are repeated, the maturing baby codifies these patterns into both affective and cognitive components and then processes them through his memory circuits for future use (both procedural and later declarative) (Pipp-Siegel & Pressman, 1996). These memories help the baby to become aware of who the attachment figure is, to know when she leaves, and to recognize when she returns. The caregiver is now represented in the brain as a special relationship that can later be generalized to other interactive situations. With this

significant representation clearly in mind the child can better turn on and turn off the attachment system as needed (Berman & Sperling, 1994; Diamond & Blatt, 1994).

Sometime during the latter part of the first year the baby starts to utilize these memory traces for self-comfort by bringing up the caregiver's mental image when the caregiver is not physically present (West & Sheldon-Keller, 1994). Interestingly, the great hypnotist Dr. Milton Erickson would utilize this same concept to continue his hypnotic inductions long after the client had left his office by simply saying, "My voice will go with you" (M. Erickson, personal communication, October 30, 1979). Children internalize the voice, the smell, the image, and the other sensory characteristics of their primary caregivers to achieve the desired mental proximity even when apart.

Active mental images can also be problematic when there is a death in the family and the child has to cope with the now increasing absence of a loved one. But frequently, the child has already been exposed to a grieving and mourning process because one of the family pets has died, and the child has transitioned successfully through it by learning some valuable lessons about life and death. With parental support, such role training can teach children that death events occasionally happen in families and that sadness is appropriate as everyone grieves together. Yet, in time, family members move through it to new beginnings (Robin & ten Bensel, 1998). Although even young children can experience some transitional pain after such a loss, it's the older children and adolescents who recognize the finality of death and suffer the most grief, especially if they witnessed their beloved pet die in some tragic manner, or if they themselves had been abused, and thus possessed limited resources for sharing their emotional burdens (Robin & ten Bensel, 1998). Securely attached children can be less vulnerable to pathological grief reactions, since they trust that their caregivers will provide a secure base and comfort them in times of need.

An Individualized Mental Compass

The internal working model (IWM), or personalized mental representational process, is the core of the attachment behavioral system (Bowlby, 1969/1982). These internal compasses are the guidance systems that organize relationships, and they are a reflection of the good and not so good transactions that have occurred between the baby and the primary caregiver(s). We should note that a child can form multiple attachments (and different adaptive styles) such as that with a mother and a father and other primary caregivers (Patrick, Hobson, Castle, Howard, & Maughan, 1994; Thompson, 2000). From these earliest ongoing interactions the baby learns to anticipate events and to develop expectations about the behaviors of the caregiver. With these predictions the baby can better regulate his own behavior and achieve some sense of stability and comfort. The brain of the baby creates and registers these models about past experiences and then generalizes about how certain new experiences might work and how he can structure his own behavior to alter events and to achieve his goals.

If pets are in the home, children often identify with them and form close emotional bonds to selected animals that they favor. From a Darwinian standpoint we evolved from animals and still manifest some similar biological structures as well as some continuities of emotional expression (Darwin, 2002; Wynne, 2004). Human babies are born with biologically based emotional behaviors, such as crying and smiling, and they are quickly able to experience and express nonverbally those sensations that are painful or pleasurable. Just like humans, some animals can also engage in coordinated state matching and express sympathy when another of their kind is experiencing pain (de Waal, 1996). It has been suggested that cross species expressions of sympathy and other emotional communications can also occur, even between babies and their pets (Ascione, 2005).

I will address more about cross species empathy later in this chapter when I talk about the newly discovered mirror neurons in both animals and humans, but suffice it to say that human babies are great observers, and they possess specialized cells for discerning facial characteristics that allow them to affectively attune with their mothers and socially reference them for guidance (Goldman, 2005). It is highly likely that young children can also observe nonverbal animal emotions and cognitively register an empathetic expression for how the animal is feeling, as well as use the trusted pet as a substitute social reference guide for how they should feel when a human caregiver is not present. We can also assume that the emotional prerequisites for human empathy and compassion came well before our species evolved. Therefore, the continuity of emotional expression for higher life forms is ongoing, and we still have a strong relationship with our mutual

affective links (Davidson, 2002). When young children correctly interpret the emotional signals of pets and act in pro-social ways toward them, parents need to reaffirm their behavior, as well as give them guidance when there is a need to correct misunderstandings (Ascione, 2005).

Thus, the internal working model is an organizing construct for the self, the other person, and the mutual interaction between them. Goal-corrected behavior requires an individual to engage in increasingly complex, dynamic, internal mental representations about one's behaviors, the environment, and the thing or person toward whom the behavior is directed (Bowlby 1969/1982; Marvin & Britner, 1999). Use of an IWM allows a child to more efficiently understand and predict his relations with his environment and to create useful strategies for achieving goals (Bowlby 1969/1982; Marvin & Britner, 1999).

As children mature, the IWMs of themselves and others normally become more sophisticated and accurate as they incorporate implicit and explicit norms for social behavior and interaction (Marvin & Britner, 1999). Of course accurate IWMs require accurate reflections of reality and necessary updates of the model when contextual situations require new adaptations (Cassidy, 1999). Accurate IWMs increase one's ability to predict future events, but Bowlby warns of potential pathological outcomes when one's model is out of date, incomplete, or otherwise not in synch with reality (Bowlby 1969/1982; Patrick, Hobson, Castle, Howard, & Maughan, 1994). Although powerful, early internal working models are not cast in stone, but rather become a work in progress, they can change with experiential and cognitive developments (Thompson, 2000).

Individual Differences in Attachment

Mary Ainsworth, who was a colleague of Bowlby's, observed mother–infant interaction patterns, in both the home and in a laboratory setting. Ainsworth's Strange Situation lab experiment procedure was simple in design but robust in its scientific benefits (Ainsworth & Wittig, 1969; Ainsworth, Blehar, Waters, & Wail, 1978; Bretherton, 1995). In it, the child (12 to 18 months) is encouraged to explore new toys in a room with only his mother present. Then, an unfamiliar female face enters the room and tries to engage the child in play. Next, the mother slips out of the room leaving the child and stranger together. After that, the mother comes back and the stranger leaves the room. The biggest stressor occurs when the mother again leaves the room, and the child is now by himself. The stranger then comes in and attempts to comfort the child. In the last episode, the mother returns to the room. Meanwhile, researchers observe and code the patterns of interaction during each episode through a one-way mirror (Ainsworth et al., 1978; Greenspan & Lieberman, 1988; Bretherton, 1995).

After many documented observations of children Ainsworth noted that they expressed three fundamental patterns of attachment (Ainsworth et al., 1978; Bretherton, 1995). The first, which included two-thirds of all children observed, was identified as type B, *secure*. The next most frequently observed attachment pattern, with approximately 20% of children, was identified as type A, *avoidant*. The remaining 10% of children observed demonstrated an *anxious* or *ambivalent* attachment profile called type C (Ainsworth et al., 1978; Bretherton, 1995).

Ainsworth reported that the securely attached children differed from the ones coded as insecure. As the name implies, the securely attached children eagerly explored the toys using their mother as a rechargeable secure base. Many were upset by the experimental changes or the stranger's face, but as attachment theory predicted, they actively sought their mothers out for comfort as needed. Once recharged, they returned to play and explore (Ainsworth et al., 1978; Bretherton, 1995). When their mothers returned from a separation, they unhesitatingly greeted her with familiar approach behaviors to receive comfort, and they were easily calmed, ready for more exploration. They soon resumed other activities (Ainsworth et al., 1978; Bretherton, 1995). It's like they felt they had a safety net. They all seemed to have a more harmonious relationship with their more sensitive caregiving mothers (Bretherton, 1995).

No one likes rejection, and everyone develops strategies to deal with it, including babies and small children. Infants can experience stress when their primary caregiver is not reliably available to provide them with security by responsively and sensitively attending to their needs. Natural selection has provided infants with several adaptive attachment strategies for increasing proximity contingent upon the parents' dominant behavior patterns. As noted earlier, Ainsworth refers to these two attachment patterns as insecure avoidant and insecure ambivalent. The parents of the avoidant type A children appear to be consistently distant, cold, and not prone to physical closeness with their babies (Ainsworth et al., 1978; Simpson, 1999). They have a low tolerance

for affective displays. Perhaps physical closeness reminds them of their own painful pasts, which they want to forget. In type A patterns, the babies' natural affective approach efforts and experiences in the past did not elicit the nurturing responsiveness from a significant primary caregiver that would enable them to reduce their anxiety or meet their needs.

For example, signaling behaviors like crying or even approaching the parent may result in rebuffs or cause the caregiver to leave. Therefore, the only way the baby can maintain proximity to these wounded parents is to mask his inner emotions and neediness from others (including himself) and cognitively focus on external stimuli in the hope that the caregiver will not abandon him. The baby acts like he doesn't have a problem because problems drive the caregiver away. In evolutionary terms this makes good sense, and it's perhaps the best way to remain reasonably close to an overwhelmed or highly volatile caregiver.

If the avoidant child continues to utilize this strategy into adulthood, he may fear that all neediness is a sign of weakness and become *compulsively self-sufficient* with an *I don't need anyone* type of attitude (West & Sheldon-Keller, 1994). In many social situations this defensive posture is maladaptive since such an attitude tends to push people away and increase loneliness. He may also avoid being vulnerable by becoming a *compulsive caregiver* who can stay in control by helping others, or an extremely compliant person (Crittenden, 1997; West & Sheldon-Keller, 1994). He can maintain proximity and control by having others indebted to him although he may have great difficulty receiving from others. In some cases, the avoidant attachment strategy is one of self-imposed isolation from others (Crittenden, 1997).

Early experiences of rejection and isolation from largely inconsistent and distant parents may prompt avoidant children to grow up expecting hostility from others and their hostile attribution motivates them to prematurely aggress against others in an effort to prevent more hurt to themselves (Dodge, 1991). The behavior of those diagnosed with antisocial personality disorders often includes such negative attributional styles accompanied with a non-integrated and highly distorted internal working model (Crittenden, 1997).

One does not need to be diagnosed with a hostile, non-caring, antisocial personality disorder to harm animals. Some caring individuals have obsessive desires to rescue animals and often compulsively collect and hoard more animals than they can adequately care for and thus create significant problems (see *Animal Hoarding* by Patronek, this text). Not only are the animals themselves inadequately fed and housed, but due to overcrowding and excremental waste buildup, the levels of toxic ammonia can put all living creatures in the residence, including the overwhelmed owner, at risk of lung and neurological damage (Arluke et al., 2002).

One pattern that repeatedly arises when animal hoarders are interviewed is that many of them were exposed to disruptive and unstable home environments with substandard parenting. Also noted in the interviews was that their exposure to pets in the home played important emotional roles in their lives (Frost, 2000). A child who is not developing a secure attachment with his human caregivers may adaptively seek out the kinesthetic nonjudgmental bonding that can come from close interaction with a beloved pet. In one study, Robert Bierer found that fifth grade children who exhibited strong bonding behaviors with their dogs had higher self-esteem and empathy scores than did those children who did not own pets (2000). With hoarders, it's possible that the intensity of the early bonding experience with animals (while simultaneously living within an emotionally impoverished environment) not only increases the subsequent levels of generalized empathy for animals, but in certain instances results in obsessive desires to reenact early comforting feelings and to repay or rescue animals for past services rendered.

It's hypothesized that this reenact and repay cycle can take two different trajectories. One, which at its motivational center incorporates good intentions, involves the misguided empathy of hoarders that includes significant denial of one's ability to properly care for multiple animals and oneself. This denial and lack of insight is dimensional with extreme cases (approximately 26%) requiring institutionalization or supervised guidance while the majority are simply sanctioned or given remedial assistance (Patronek, 1999). The other trajectory, which also involves insecure attachment histories, also distorts reality. It too seeks to reenact and repay, but its motivational center is fueled by rage and revenge at earlier victimization where animals become easily accessible targets of displaced anger. This displacement may have been modeled by significant adults, other children, or even the media (Bandura, 1959; Dodge, 1991). Some of the children in Bowlby's (1944) early studies exemplified this type of inner anger and lack of empathy. Of course it must be kept in

mind that children can be motivated by many different co-morbid factors when they abuse animals (Ascione, 2005).

In the Strange Situation experiment the avoidant baby may actively protest his caregiver's departure, but he expresses disinterest or even irritation upon her return. His inhibition and avoidance of seeking physical closeness with his mother is simply a defensive strategy to lure her back and to avoid potential abandonment and the pain of rejection. The insecure avoidant child may appear to an untrained eye as independent and autonomous as he plays by himself, but he seldom smiles or expresses joy in seeing his mother, whether she is coming or going. He treats her much like he does a stranger and he doesn't utilize her as a secure base. He is defending himself from loss through a largely cognitive, inhibited presentation. It should be noted again that all babies of one code do not respond the same way to all situations or to all caregivers, so there are multiple attachment possibilities and subtypes of each pattern that may result in a mixture of responses (Crittenden, 1997). A baby can have a varied repertoire because to adapt is to survive.

Parents of insecure ambivalent children (sometimes referred to as anxious or resistant type C attachment) display inconsistent or erratic sensitivity to their baby's signals of need (Ainsworth et al., 1978). Sometimes they seem connected and other times they appear neglectful. They often display inattentive care and appear under-involved as parents (Simpson, 1999). From the infant's perspective, the best strategy is to become a squeaky hinge, protesting loudly and often to gain proximity and support. Unlike the avoidant babies, the ambivalent children don't hesitate to express themselves emotionally. They seem upset and anxious when they are away from their mother and angry, fussy, and resistant when they are with her. They cry when she leaves and actively approach her when she comes back, but they can't seem to be comforted from her holding. They push and squirm to get away and take some time before they return to exploration and play.

Such ambivalent babies remind one of thirsty sailors who drink salty sea water to quench their thirst, but it only makes them thirstier. The babies want a secure base and closeness but feel anxious or untrusting that this caregiver can provide it, therefore, they feel caught in the middle. This attachment strategy can be accelerated into multiple other patterns of extroverted coercion, aggression, and seduction (Crittenden, 1997). Although lack of caregiver sensitivity can strongly influence the quality of the child's attachment, the parents' mental status and internal working model is perhaps the most salient factor in determining ongoing interactive processes and outcomes (Atkinson, 1997). This is especially evident when the caregivers exhibit severe clinical symptomatology themselves, such as depression and bi-polar or borderline personality disorder.

Having No Compass At All ... Our Disorganized and Disoriented Children

It was truly puzzling. Former Ainsworth student Mary Main and her colleague, Judith Solomon, were observing some unusual behaviors in some babies and described their actions (Main & Solomon, 1990). One baby in the Strange Situation moved his hand toward his mother and, before reaching her, suddenly withdrew it as if he might be touching a hot stove. Another baby was crying and distressed, yet without apparent cause abruptly stopped all of his affect and quickly moved away from the parent. And equally puzzling was a child who pushed and struck at his mother all in slow motion as if he was *underwater*. Later he froze his body in odd shapes for 30 seconds or more (Main, 1995; Main & Solomon, 1990). What attachment strategy was this? Since it did not share ongoing consistencies with types A, B, or C, infants with stranger than strange behavior in the Strange Situation were reluctantly marked *unclassifiable* (Main & Solomon, 1990).

With admirable patience, Main and Solomon meticulously reviewed over 200 videotapes of children displaying odd behaviors in the Strange Situation experiment. These children all shared a common characteristic of being disorganized or disoriented about how to obtain felt security. Their behavior didn't seem to make sense, and there was no apparent goal or adaptive plan to deal with their stressful circumstances. At times their behaviors vacillated between mixtures of avoidant and anxious strategies, but nothing appeared to represent a stable strategy. Main and Solomon (1990) categorized these odd behaviors under seven thematic headings such as *mistuned movements* and *contradictory behavior patterns* to form a new attachment classification.

For these babies, ages 12 to 18 months, an additional attachment classification type besides A (avoidant), B (secure), and C (anxious or resistant) was now available. It would be called type D or *disorganized/ disoriented* attachment, and it was meant to describe babies who had no coherent or consistent strategy or organized means to deal with the stress of separations or reunions with their mother. It was like these children were trying to negotiate their life journey without a compass. Main discovered that troubled parents of type D infants frequently have their own unresolved histories of early traumas, such as being sexual molested, witnessing parental violence, losing an attachment figure, or experiencing chronic maltreatment. These unresolved parental issues are passed on and act as an intergenerational transmission of insecurity for the child (i.e., the *ghost in the nursery* concept) (Fraiberg, Adelson, & Shapiro, 1975). These parents may also be active alcoholics, or have a bipolar disorder or have a history of maltreating their children (Main, 1995; Main & Solomon, 1990; Zeanah, Mammen, & Lieberman, 1993).

When a distressed parent frightens a child, there is often nowhere for the child to turn since the evolutionary source of the primary attachment comfort is also the source of the fear. It is a no-win paradoxical situation for the child because none of the usual strategies of approaching, diverting attention, or fleeing the angry parent will bring security or comfort. Consequently, the child may vacillate between strategies, becoming immobilized, disorganized, or disoriented (Main & Solomon, 1990). Few things are more difficult to contemplate than a child experiencing a strategic meltdown with nowhere to run and nowhere to hide. Interestingly, in subsequent testing of these children (when they were 6 years old), Main found that many had tried to resolve their immobilizing no-win situation by trading in their overt disorganized behaviors for other strategies. When a pet is in the home, even very young children may assume a parenting role with the animal (Robin & ten Bensel, 1998). Additional strategies include role reversal and controlling or placating behaviors with parents to assume some sense of autonomy (Main, 1995; Main & Solomon, 1990).

As an individual attempts to achieve some control over his disorganized environment, he may want a powerful ally that will not only protect him but also be available as a weapon to bolster his own limited power (Ascione, 1998). In this case the more frightening his animal ally is to others, the more status and fear-based respect he may receive. Therefore, he may train the dog or cock rooster to fight on his command. The power of having a proxy fighter may bring a certain amount of hedonic pleasure as well as financial remuneration, but at the great expense and suffering of the animal. As an example, in a *Wall Street Journal* article on roosters bred for fighting, it was disclosed by the reporter that some of the birds were injected with testosterone and methamphetamines to make them more aggressive (Efrati, 2005).

Type D classification might also stand for *danger*, especially if the conditions that helped bring it about in the child's life continue unabated. We will look more closely at this pattern when we discuss maltreatment of children. Suffice it to say that in one study approximately 80% of maltreated infants had D attachments with their troubled parents and this style is a high-risk precursor to violence (Zeanah, Mammen, & Lieberman, 1993). And a child with no inhibition for committing violence toward humans would be more likely to hurt animals as well. Therefore, any animal under the care or exposure of a child with a type D attachment profile is at a higher risk for abuse. Type D attachment spells danger for animals.

Part Two—Problems, Pathways, and Probabilities

Attachment Complexities and Caveats

Attachment theory is all about relationships, but relationships, whether they are good or bad, are about more than just attachment. We are who we are in relationships because of the complex interactions between nature and nurture. Our brain development influences our behavior and our experiences impact our brain development. In other words, our genetic expression, our brain architecture, including our neuronal and synaptic connections, and our brain functioning are all influenced in a multidimensional, transactional way with our social and psychological experiences so that each has pathways to impact the other (Cicchetti & Sroufe, 2000). And while the environment may impact the child, it's also the active child who selects and influences the environment in a dynamic way (Cicchetti & Sroufe, 2000).

Nothing happens developmentally within a vacuum. A respected developmental theorist put it succinctly when he said that there is no such thing as a baby, meaning that one cannot understand a child without the supportive context of a caregiver, a system of support, and many other factors (Winnicott, 1965). The most common factors of interaction include genetic, neuronal, behavioral, and environmental (which includes cultural, social, and the physical aspects of an organism's environment) (Gottlieb & Tucker Halpern, 2002). Sociologists have long maintained that human development

must incorporate a larger social context since many factors interact with and influence the mother–child dyad. When looking at what impacts the quality of attachment, one needs to consider all of the support or stress factors operating simultaneously within the caregiver and infant's relational world (marriage, neighborhood, work setting, and immediate and extended family members). The temperament, belief systems, and ecologies of both the caregiver and the infant can impact the attachment outcomes. Brofenbrenner (1979) suggested that human development be viewed with this wider angle lens via a larger ecological perspective.

So, development is complex with a very low probability of most pathological disorders, including those involving abuse to animals, having a single main cause. Most likely, whatever are seen as main effects are, in actuality, interactions (Brofenbrenner, 1979). And while attachment is a powerful developmental factor, it should not be seen as the Holy Grail of psychopathology but rather as a significant potential influencer among many transactional factors (Greenberg, 1999). It must be noted that children who are coded as securely attached also are represented in clinical populations, although in far less numbers than for those coded insecurely attached (Greenberg, 1999).

Perhaps the most integrative framework from which to view developmental adaptations and maltreatment is the ecological-transactional model (Cicchetti et al., 2000; Manly, Cicchetti, & Barnett, 1994). We must also consider the diversity in process and outcome regarding pathology, or put another way, the multiple pathways to and from a disorder. Different combinations of risk factors, or a diversity of separate paths, may lead to the same disorder (i.e., equifinality) (Curtis & Cicchetti, 2003; Greenberg, 1999). For example, we wouldn't expect that *all* people who abuse animals arrive at that outcome traveling along the same pathway or process. Conversely, *different* outcomes may result from the same original starting point and be influenced by a risk factor's timing and interaction with other risk elements (i.e. multifinality) (Curtis & Cicchetti, 2003; Greenberg, 1999).

The relationship between risk factors and end results is never static and seldom linear, so it must include all risk elements that can be associated with maladaptive outcomes. A partial list of risks and host factors include pre- and postnatal abnormalities, parental psychopathology and family violence, neighborhood violence and peer group deviance, child abuse, head injuries, extreme poverty, and much more (Greenberg, 1999). As risk factors interact, it's easy to see how complicated things can get, which then begs the question of whether environmental risk and internal mechanisms can ever be considered separate causal agents (Beauchaine, 2003). In light of all the interacting risk factors, the effects of insecure attachments cannot be isolated and overly accentuated, since they must be counterbalanced with a child's protective factors, including multidimensional buffering effects (genetics, mentors, opportunities, and so on) (Mrazek, 1993; Cicchetti et al., 2000). As previously mentioned, this can be challenging since an infant can have multiple attachments and be classified as securely attached to one caregiver while simultaneously classified as insecurely attached to the other caregiver (Zeanah et al., 1993). This multiplicity confounds predictability for future negative acts depending upon the contextual relationship the child finds himself in, which must also be commingled with the balance of other risk/protective factors (Mzarek, 1993; Zeanah et al., 1993).

It should be noted that Ainsworth's individual patterns of attachment (ABC) were research constructs and never intended to be used for diagnoses of children in clinical settings (Rutter, 1997). Attachment researchers have long warned of reifying the Strange Situation dyadic relationship as the most important future predictor of development without considering other social systems (Cicchetti, Cummings, Greenberg, & Marvin, 1990; Emde, 1990; Rutter, 1997). Attachment as a descriptor varies since it has been used in several ways. With babies and young children it's used to indicate an attribute of the child's relationship with a specific person; however, from adolescence through adulthood it's more commonly used to describe the individuals themselves as either *secure* or *insecure* (Thompson, 2000). This social practice buttresses the assumption that early attachment patterns are important to later personality development, since from adolescence on we become identified by the quality and security that we experienced within those earliest relationships, although attachment patterns can and do change contingent upon influential experiences (Thompson & Raikes, 2003).

Dysfunctional families do not automatically produce insecure children. If a child living within a dysfunctional family is genetically predisposed to acquire metacognitive skills that reduce stress or has a supportive friend or an influential teacher who

promotes empathy and metacognitive exchanges, then the odds are improved for that child to thrive despite the challenges. Pets can serve as both support systems for children as well as buffers to help reduce psychosocial stressors. As stated earlier, they can bolster the exploratory and sociable system by offering security (protection and a secure base) and companionship, especially when human nurturing is not available. Animals can act as familiar and comforting kinesthetic transitional objects for children, and since they are animated and reciprocal, the effect is more powerful than with an inanimate object like a favorite blanket (Ascione, 1998). Pets are great nonjudgmental listeners that can elicit maternal feelings and empathy within the normal caregiving process (Ascione, 1998). Such nurturing, other-directed perspective taking, and nonverbal cue reading can build mastery skills and offer these children pleasure as they build personal responsibility and self-confidence (Ascione, 2005).

By both design and fortune, misattunements with caregivers can be reattuned and corrective emotional experiences can help a child recover (Kohut, 1977). As an adult, this child could become effectively categorized as *earned secure* (Main, 1999; Roisman, Padron, Sroufe, & Egeland, 2002; Werner & Smith, 1986). In her extensive, longitudinal study, Emmy Werner found that a child's constitutional variables, such as high activity and sociability levels, plus low excitability and anxiety traits, can act as protective mechanisms for the child (Werner & Smith, 1986). Waddington (1957) had also addressed how genetic predispositions can act as a buffer to insulate children against environmental insults and keep them on normal developmental pathways (developmental canalization). Neural plasticity, or the ability of the brain to positively reorganize itself after traumatic experiences, is an important healing factor that can impact brain development at multiple levels including molecular, cellular, neuro-chemical, and anatomical (Curtis & Cicchetti, 2003).

Kraemer (1992) reminds us, however, that genetic resilience doesn't act alone, but expresses itself within the ongoing social attachment process. And Werner suggests in her longitudinal study that those children who had the most positive outcomes combined their genetic resilience with a close bond of support given by at least one positive caretaker in the first years of life (Werner & Smith, 1986). Beyond this, clarification is still needed concerning how children integrate multiple attachments and what criteria children utilize when prioritizing significant others throughout their different developmental milestones (Thompson & Raikes, 2003). Despite the tendency to see attachment descriptors as categorical or rigidly bound, it's more realistic to see them as continuous and dimensional with boundaries that are more fluid than clearly demarked (Mikulincer & Shaver, 2004).

Some qualifiers are important to keep in mind. Avoidant attachment, type A, and ambivalent attachment, type C, in and of themselves should not be seen as pathological strategies, just as insecure attachment per se should not be equated with a diagnosable childhood disorder (Greenberg, 1999; Greenberg, DeKlyen, Speltz, & Endriga, 1997). And while there is a high probability that children with attachment disorders will exhibit insecure attachments, it's also likely that very few children simply classified as insecurely attached will be deemed to be pathological or attachment disordered (Greenberg et al., 1997). The different attachment patterns are simply strategies to adapt and evolution favors certain behavioral strategies to survive and reproduce contingent upon the environmental challenges. As previously mentioned, children can change their attachment patterns over time due to variable life experiences, and in one study less than 50% maintained the same classification from infancy to 4 years of age (Goldberg, 1999) so it is not static.

Attachment originally arose out of what Bowlby referred to as an Environment of Evolutionary Adaptedness (EEA) where our ancestors had to be creative in how they solved problems within their particular physical and social environment (Bowlby, 1969/1982; Simpson, 1999). So, it's hypothesized that attachment survival strategies differed depending upon available resources, and that a cooperative secure attachment strategy was the most frequently favored pattern (Belsky, Steinberg, & Draper, 1991). But insecure patterns of attachment also have survived throughout human history and thus were likely selected within some developmental situations. These patterns were perhaps more adaptive under extremely harsh conditions involving interacting factors such as low paternal investment, maternal mood disorders, family stress, and few resources, where infant mortality might have been very high (Simpson, 1999). And today, children who live in these types of environments, including the Romanian orphanages where competition for everything is high and resources are low, tend to exhibit an ambivalent attachment pattern (O'Connor et al., 2003). Parents who have ambivalently attached

children are more inconsistent, insensitive, unpredictable, and otherwise dysfunctional and are often desperately trying to make ends meet in a world that has limited resources. They have to deal with stressors such as marital discord, economic or occupational problems, and non-supportive social networks (Simpson, 1999).

The grind of daily life can elevate physiological systems (including the HPA axis, which I will discuss shortly) and result in a high allostatic load (overall wear and tear on a person) (McEwen & Seeman, 1999). This allostatic load addresses not only stressful life experiences but genetic vulnerability and a person's individual adaptive responses, such as exercise regimens, diet, substance abuse, and developmental histories, which all together can prescribe life-long behavioral habits and bio-psychological reactivity patterns (McEwen & Seeman, 1999).

Conversely, when children are raised in less hostile environments, with parents who have less allostatic load and within ecologies where there are more supportive resources available, it's more likely that those children will experience more sensitive parents who model the adaptive benefits of cooperation, trust in others, and secure attachment patterns (Simpson, 1999). So, in evolutionary terms, while there is no *best mothering or attachment style* since different environmental challenges may require different adaptations (Simpson, 1999), there still are significant advantages to being classified as securely attached, as I will soon discuss. Furthermore, while insecure attachments may not by themselves be the sole cause of a disorder, they can increase its probability, especially when there is severe and ongoing maltreatment (Greenberg, 1999).

As previously discussed, there are obvious risk factors associated with the ambivalent and the avoidant attachment strategies. Like a quarterback with only one good play, each of these adaptive strategies is best suited for one particular type of compromised caregiving situation, and when the environmental situations change, then a rigid or insecure specialized strategy is far less effective. This means that type As and type Cs would be least well suited for adaptation in the other's environment (Crittenden, 1997). This is easy to see, since one (type A) favors a cognitive and inhibitive compliant focus, while the other (type C) tends to exhibit a more uninhibited affective focus with coercive ambivalent action (Crittenden, 1997). Once again, individual differences in patterns of attachment, like those classifications in the Strange Situation experiment, are not considered disorders themselves (unlike diagnosable psychopathologies). *However*, insecure attachments can increase a child's overall risk, in a nonlinear manner, for a diagnosable disorder (Zeanah et al., 1993), which can then increase the probability of later abuse of animals.

The Clinical Descriptors

Certainly a child's level of insecurity due to stress within a relationship can become so overwhelming that he or she begins to show serious behavioral disturbances and pathological symptoms. The DSM IV, TR addresses this issue in its taxonomy as Reactive Attachment Disorder of Infancy or Early Childhood (RAD), (313.89) (APA, 2000). It identifies children who exhibit pervasive and inappropriate behaviors in social relatedness that begin before age 5, and this disorder is associated with early pathogenic care (APA, 2000). RAD can be diagnosed as inhibited, which is characterized with fear, withdrawal, and ambivalence, or disinhibited, which is manifested by indiscriminate friendliness and the lack of selective attachment to someone for ongoing comfort (APA, 2000).

The esteemed developmental scientist Charles Zeanah and his colleagues created an alternative taxonomy that distinguishes several types of troubled attachments, including nonattachment, disordered attachment, and disrupted attachment, with subtypes within each category (Zeanah et al., 1993; Zeanah, Boris, & Lieberman, 2000). The predominate characteristic of nonattachment disorder is similar to RAD, where a child is indiscriminately social and does not demonstrate a preference for anyone in particular even when hurt or needy (Greenberg et al., 1997; Zeanah et al., 1993). The disordered attachment child personifies a secure base distortion, and he may not effectively utilize his parental secure base for comfort, or he may exhibit extreme inhibition, recklessness, or parental role reversal (Greenberg et al., 1997; Zeanah et al., 1993). The child with a disrupted attachment has experienced a loss of a primary caregiver and is dealing with grief reactions (Greenberg et al., 1997; Zeanah et al., 1993).

Within the disordered attachment profile, Zeanah describes a subtype called attachment disorder with self-endangerment. In this subtype, a child has a preference for an attachment figure but his anger and aggression (both verbal and physical) toward others, including the caregiver or even toward himself, interferes with his receiving comfort and security (Zeanah et al., 1993; Zeanah et al., 2000). Zeanah reports that children who are exposed to family

violence are more likely to raise their own emotional temperature and act out to gain attention from their unreliable caregivers (Zeanah et al., 2000). Without inhibitory controls and self-regulation, these children, like many other insecurely attached children, have a higher risk of abusing both animals and humans.

Pat Crittenden (1997) has also developed a descriptive continuum characterization of attachments which addresses how some children utilize anxious, coercive, and aggressive affective displays to achieve their goals, while others employ avoidant cognitively defended strategies. While the affectively coercive results in false cognition, the highly defended cognitive styles are handicapped with false affect (Crittenden, 1997). Her model, and others, demonstrate how integrated secure attachments guide children toward a path of increased self-confidence and empathy (Bowlby, 1988; Crittenden, 1997).

Part Three—Animals and Attachment: Putting It All Together
Life Scripting for Love

The devastating Tsunami wrecked havoc on millions of people in Indonesia, resulting in several hundred thousand deaths and homelessness for millions of survivors. Starvation and disease were rampant and grief filled the air. Despite these horrible conditions villagers in Khoa Lak sobbed with joy when a stranded dolphin, nicknamed Dolly, was rescued from a lagoon. She was loaded by crane onto a stretcher and taken 640m to the shore. "We couldn't let her die," said fisherman Pornsiri Thongsen (Crawford, 2005).

To serve animals in need allows us to resonate with that part within us that knows we are all somehow connected and we all share a common life force. Those who are judged securely attached start out in life being more aligned and connected to their sensitive caregivers and that prepares them to reciprocate care to others, including animals. This section will look at how modern researchers have clarified and built upon the key elements of attachment theory described in Parts One and Two regarding predictions of healthy functioning as contrasted with predictions of future violence and how attachment theory can interface with specific motivations to either support or abuse animals.

Secure and Sure

Although the origins of human altruism and morality are most likely embedded within the social and attachment processes that our animal ancestors have passed on to us, mature morality requires nurturance and learning in order to fully develop (Pennington, 2002; Ridley, 1996, 2003). To internalize moral behaviors we need to get outside of ourselves and see the other person's point of view and develop empathetic responses with people. This process, part of what Daniel Stern (1985) called intersubjectivity, is expedited with reciprocal imitated interactions about current or future feelings and intentions that the baby experiences with a sensitive attachment figure.

The usual blossom of this type of repeated positive interaction is empathy and compassion for others (Emde, 1996). And from this secure and exploratory base, the child attracts others, often with similar patterns. Therefore, the child generally tends to enjoy other people since his own empathy and caring is usually reciprocated. One might say that securely attached individuals are in harmony with the classic song lyrics, "People Who Love People." They internalize more positive beliefs and expectations about others' intentions and basic natures and feel more trusting and affectionate (Easterbrooks & Goldberg, 1990). It would be safe to assume that this platform of expressing compassion for humans could easily be extended to animals as it is consistent with an internalized caregiving behavioral system. It helps, of course, for adults to frequently model pro-social behaviors, such as the positive treatment of animals, so that children can observe and later practice similar behaviors (Bandura, Ross, & Ross, 1961). The mindset for caring starts early as the infant's brain aligns with the caregiver's brain.

Mirror Neurons, Brain Rhythms, and Attunement

In the beginning, the infant needs help with arousal regulation and the sensitive parent does just that. A lethargic infant can better pull himself out of a doldrum when he is appropriately stimulated into creative play by a supportive caregiver. Conversely, a crying infant can calm himself easier with a soothing parent's quiet voice or a gentle song or some rhythmic rocking. After a homeostatic balance is reestablished, the baby can better organize his thoughts and focus on the next learning task at hand.

That learning is facilitated by neural mechanisms called mirror neurons in the frontal lobes that allow an observed behavior or action to be directly simulated or replicated in our mind so that we can understand and respond to the actions, intentions, and mental states of others (Ramachandran, 2000; Goldman, 2005). It could be called monkey see, monkey do, but first it occurs in the observer's brain without the observer ever moving a finger, and then the observer feels and understands what it's like to be inside another, experiencing the other's intentions, actions, and emotions (Goldman, 2005; Ramachandran, 2000). This neural mechanism sheds light on intersubjectivity, imitation, language learning, and most importantly mindfulness or empathy (Goldman, 2005; Ramachandran, 2000). As I will soon discuss, maltreatment or damages to these cerebral structures may result in deficits in self–other differentiation, metacognition, rhythmic attunement, and compassionate care for others including animals.

So, valuable life lessons are constantly being acquired and stored in memory as the regulated rhythms of each event are being fed into the baby's brain. These rhythms need to be integrated with special attunement between the mother and baby's right orbitofrontal cortex (Schore, 1994). With an attuned right brain to right brain resonance, utilizing mirror neurons in the frontal lobes for imitative processing, the child develops his capacity for understanding his own and others' motivations, feelings, and intentions within a reciprocal process (Schore, 1994). After many similarly aligned experiences, these parent-assisted regulated rhythms will form a template or neural map that the developing child can use to regulate his own arousal levels without any outside assistance (Schore, 1994). The child will continue to directly utilize the mother for self-referencing (looking at how she reacts), especially in threatening situations, but gradually he will develop his own mental representation of the secure base when he is not with her (Emde, 1996).

As stated earlier, a newborn's expressions and sensory systems are designed to stimulate the caregiver to adequately respond and the empathetic parent will be genetically predisposed to reciprocate in a rhythmic synchronous "dance" with the baby. Developmental researcher Colwyn Trevarthan, who has used acoustic instruments to measure infant vocalizations, says that babies are like little jazz musicians who are able to creatively improvise the vocal, kinesthetic, and emotional responses contingent upon the caregiver's actions. When a singing caregiver takes a breath or pauses, an attuned baby inserts his vocalization or movement in a synchronous manner so that everything flows together (Pavlicevic & Trevarthan, 1989).

The importance of mutuality to a baby has been dramatically demonstrated in experiments where a mother is asked to make a still or blank face back to her engaging baby. With no stimulus feedback the baby is clearly upset and he makes attempts to reestablish a connection, but when nothing comes back his affect turns negative and he finally gives up and avoids all interaction (Striano, 2004; Tronick, Als, Adamson, Wise, & Brazelton, 1978). Babies and mothers establish synchrony only when a contingent stimulus response is available so they can play off each others' mutually rewarding positive responses. With good enough attunement and synchrony the baby develops self–other awareness (theory of mind) and higher levels of empathy. State matching promotes mutuality and empathetic responses.

Relationship experiences stimulate all parts of the brain and the synaptic strength of different neural pathways is formed early in the child's life depending upon the use it or lose it process of pruning and trophic factor reinforcement (LeDoux, 2002). If reciprocity and empathy are modeled by a sensitive caregiver then the integrated circuitry of the frontal lobes will coordinate other stimulated areas of the brain and lock in a template that promotes reflective thinking and compassion (Davidson, 2002; Post, 2003). The secure attachment patterns promote reflective thinking without a defensive or distorted posture since a secure base has been internalized.

Now, the full range of emotions, including the adaptive utilization of the affect *shame* for self-control, can be consciously experienced and the child has some internal source of modulation and balance (Robinson & Glaves, 1996; Schore, 1994). And it's within this interactive attachment process that the seeds of impulse control, emotional intelligence, and a conscience are planted (Goleman, 1995; Schore, 1994). "The right hemispheric orbitofrontal affect regulator performs functions that are essential to the adaptive moral functioning of the individual" (Schore, 1994, p. 353). In radical contrast, the psychopath does not have a secure attachment and has no trust, empathy, shame, or conscience (Hare, 1993; Magid, 1988). Many clinicians who have treated children with severe aggressive attachment disorders have noticed a pattern of unregulated behaviors that often starts with animal abuse and then progresses to human violence and criminal behavior (Magid, 1988). Their internal working models do not inhibit their aggressive acts.

On the other hand, securely attached children have developed an internal mental representation (IWM) that indicates their signals of need will be noticed and this ongoing support gives them a sense of potency. It's like having a permanent *home field advantage* in sports (Sroufe, 1988, 1997). Based on their previous experiences, securely attached children feel competent in their ability to effectively interact with others and to resolve problems and conflicts (Sroufe, 1997). A healthy caregiver supports a child's efforts to develop a unique personality (differentiation) while also gaining mastery skills on negotiating interpersonal relationships with practiced mutual collaboration and cooperation (i.e., integration) (Siegal, 1999). This relationship model promotes a proto self and later the development of a core self that is balanced, self-regulated, adaptive, and resilient (Siegal, 1999; Stern, 1985). When experimenters secretly placed a temporary rouge mark on a maltreated child's face, he tended to exhibit a neutral or negative feeling when noticing the mark in the mirror. But a securely attached toddler usually had a more positive self-appraisal on seeing the rouge mark (Gallup, 1994). The secure child can look in the mirror and see someone who is authentically valued and loved, based on his early reciprocal experiences with secure attachment figures (Easterbrooks & Goldberg,1990).

Secure Attachment, a Bias Buffer, and an Animal's Best Friend

If a child's early experiences are filled with caregiver availability and sensitivity, then that child's belief in his own inner worthiness and ability to successfully engage others in future relationships is likely to be positive and secure (McCrone et al., 1994). Children who are securely attached are more likely to approach problems in a balanced manner without being overly emotional or cognitively distant (Sroufe, 1997; Carlson, Sampson, & Sroufe, 2003). They manage their impulses with cool-headed behaviors and flexible adaptations despite high stress environmental challenges (Radke-Yarrow et al., 1995; Sroufe, 1990). And when stressors temporarily overwhelm them they tend to pick themselves up and rebound well, still confident in their core selves (Carlson et al., 2003; Sroufe, 1997). These talents, plus the ability to regulate and empathize with others, bodes well with peers and in sociometric studies they are viewed as popular children who are welcome into group activities (Carlson et al., 2003; Sroufe, 1997). They are creative at pretend play activities and seldom engage in aggression (Greenberg & Speltz, 1988; Sroufe, 1997). In fact, their early fantasy play (at 18 months) showed flexibility and balance, including positive resolution to negative themes (Carlson et al., 2003; Sroufe, 1997). Securely attached children tend to exhibit happiness, which acts as a protective mechanism that increases self-esteem and optimism while it inhibits conflict and aggression (Schultz, 2004; Seligman, 2002). These positive behavioral tendencies with peers bode well for animal/child interactions and increase the likelihood that the child will form healthy attachments to pets.

Strong resilient egos are developed in secure relationships, which allow children to interpret their social reality more accurately even when facing threatening conditions and negative self attributes (Mikulincer & Shaver, 2004). They are less likely to defensively distort or bias their perceptions of their own abilities (self-serving bias) or that of others (Mikulincer & Shaver, 2004). They are less likely to confuse dispositional and situational causes for problems and thus they commit fewer attribution errors (Mikulincer & Shaver, 2004). Secure individuals are more likely to seek out and incorporate the latest evidence when making judgments about others or situations even if the new information goes against their previously held conceptions (less confirmation bias) (Mikulincer & Shaver, 2004). A child's secure foundation allows him to not only reduce negative bias, but also to develop and store up good feelings, like in a bank account, and as Barbara Fredrickson (2001) says, to *broaden and build* upon his strengths to better actualize his potential.

Humans first evolved within small groups or tribes that formed tight in-group bonds for social and survival reasons (Kottak, 2002; Simpson, 1999). It's a natural tendency to believe that one's own familiar group is the best and this is at the root of our provincial ethnocentric beliefs (Kottak, 2002). But one of the benefits of being securely attached is to feel safe and confident enough to explore the unknown. This allows securely attached people to feel more curious than threatened whenever they encounter someone who is unfamiliar or an out-group member. And because they are secure inside, they have little need to vilify or aggress against someone outside their group in order to compensate for their own fearfulness or perceived inadequacies (Kottak, 2002). So, while inter-group biases have some innate evolutionary momentum because they have a self-serving protective function, researchers find that secure attachment counteracts this tendency and promotes tolerance toward strangers who are unfamiliar or who are different. It acts as a buffer against prejudice (Kottak, 2002; Simpson, 1999).

Social information processing theory tells us that how a child acts in any given social situation depends on how that child mentally processes that situation (Keiley, Howe, Dodge, Bates, & Pettit, 2001). If the child's sensory systems are processing accurately then the child is likely to make an adaptive socially congruent response. The attachment process that is secure not only helps organize and regulate early sensorimotor and physiological mechanisms, but it also provides a safe environment for the child to explore the mind of the caregiver and to recognize the power of his own mental transactions and intentional acts (McCrone et al., 1994). It's a sign of healthy adaptation and balanced awareness when a child is *on to himself and others* (Seeman, 1983).

With intersubjectivity, the secure child begins to see himself and others as possessing mental thoughts and feelings that can be intentional and consequential (Stern, 1985). This ability to empathize with others inhibits him from hurting others since he can mentally role reverse with their pain. The ability to engage in this meta-cognition allows the child to future-pace and ponder *as if* situations before they occur. He can also role reverse with the community at large (socialization) and imagine the personal pain of being censored by others. Thus the secure child can inhibit unwarranted aggression and is not motivated toward violent acts (Fonagy et al., 1997b). Overall, the secure child receives enjoyment from getting along with others and develops a repertoire of positive behaviors that are rewarding and simply incompatible with aggression and violence (Fonagy et al., 1997b; Kraemer, 1997).

This is especially relevant since most animals, especially dogs and cats, express both fear and pain in quite obvious ways. Therefore the same empathy that inhibits a child from hurting humans is likely to be extended to pets. As previously stated, children can identify with pets and often feel close to them both physically and emotionally (Ascione, 1998). Children can observe others using mirror neurons in their own prefrontal cortex and experience similar emotions of the observed object, which is likely to act as the neural mechanism for empathy (Goldman, 2005; Ramachandran, 2000). This means that their empathetic response not only inhibits them from hurting animals but it also helps motivate them toward assisting animals in need, especially if their immediate ecology supports animal care. Of course these moral behaviors are more likely to be associated with securely attached children who express normal pro-social adaptations. But what can be said about those children who are considered abnormal?

What Were You Thinking? Life Scripting for Hurting Animals and Humans

A man who attempted to shoot seven puppies was shot himself when one of the dogs put its paw on the pistol's trigger. The Escambia County, Florida Sheriff's Office reported that the man had already killed three of the dogs and was going to shoot the others because he wanted to get rid of all of them. According to the report he was holding two puppies, one in his arms and another in his left hand, when the dog in his hand wiggled and put its paw on the trigger of the .38 caliber revolver. The gun then discharged, hitting the man in the wrist. He was rushed to a local hospital and later charged with felony animal cruelty (Associated Press, 2004).

Most of us find ourselves rooting for the puppies. Justice deserved. If you were to meet someone who had just intentionally abused an animal you might want to say to him, "What were you thinking? Why in the world would you want to hurt a defenseless animal?" We must assume that the mental world inside the head of an abuser is different from the mental world of the non-abuser. We can easily describe the outcomes of abusers' distorted thinking when we observe the dysfunctional behavior patterns that show huge deficits in their morality, empathy, and compassion.

Sensitive contingent caregiving promotes secure attachments, which in turn increases the child's likelihood of developing a sense of morality, compassion, and balanced self–other interactions (Fonagy, Target, Steele, & Steele, 1997a). The normal process of human development involves the newborn child successfully moving through a number of stage-salient challenges, such as motor tasks, emotional self-regulation processes, autonomy, cognitive competencies, and all of those things that help someone become a highly adaptive and successful social being (Cicchetti et al., 2000; Manly, Jungmeen, Rogosch, & Cicchetti, 2001).

But there are many risk factors that can interfere with the normal progression of a child's development such as genetic anomalies, accidents, head injuries, and other natural occurrences (Cicchetti, 2003). And while *good enough parents* promote secure

attachments and less defensive thinking, suboptimal parenting (harshness, irregular responsiveness, distancing) can increase the probability of insecure attachment patterns being adopted that are more likely to reduce empathy for others and increase the probability of distorted thinking patterns, including those involving violence toward others (Fonagy et al., 1997a; Winnicott, 1965).

Maltreatment Promotes Insecure Attachments and Animal Abuse

One pattern many clinicians notice with children who abuse animals is that the early histories of these children are marked with suboptimal caregiving experiences (Magid, 1988). Suboptimal parenting in its most destructive form is called child maltreatment, which includes many different forms such as physical abuse, sexual abuse, neglect, and emotional maltreatment (Bolger & Patterson, 2001; Mrazek, 1993). For each broad area, such as sexual abuse, there are many subtype behaviors such as incest, exhibitionism, pornographic exploitation, and assault (Bolger & Patterson, 2001; Mrazek, 1993). Neglect, for example, can cover a parent's inadequate physical, educational, medical, or supervisory care of a child (Bolger & Patterson, 2001; Mrazek, 1993). In some cases the maltreatment is clear. The effects of physical abuse, such as bruises, lacerations, and burns, become obvious with even a cursory medical exam, although certain fractures can go undetected until the child receives X-rays. But the complexity of maltreatment is more evident when one looks at emotional abuse (such as verbal assaults or psychological abandonment), which does not present obvious physical scars but can still cause great harm to children (Bolger & Patterson, 2001; Mrazek, 1993). In one study of children ages 2 to 6, over 90% of those who were physically abused also suffered emotional abuse (Crittenden, 1994).

When you look into the face of either a small victim or an older victimizer you are looking directly at the personification of hurt … in the past, in the present, and often in the long-term future. Babies are born with physical and emotional needs that must be recognized, attended to, and regulated. Maltreated children have caregivers who have failed to regulate themselves and, therefore, they demonstrate major deficits in meeting the regulatory needs of the vulnerable infant (Dumas & Wekerle, 1995; McGee, Wolfe, & Wilson, 1997). What's at risk of being dysregulated is the infant's physiology, emotional affect, and behavioral conduct (Patrick et al., 1994;

Rogosch, Cicchetti, & Aber, 1995). For example, a baby experiences strong emotions, and it's useful for the infant to learn how to self soothe and lower his autonomic arousal during stressful situations in order to focus on his immediate needs. But in maltreatment the parent doesn't model how this is done and the early interpersonal transactions can set up a maladaptive regulatory model (Bolger & Patterson, 2001).

Parents who have lapses in their metacognitive ability to reflect on what others are feeling, especially regarding their own children's thoughts, are at increased risk of maltreating their offspring (Fonagy et al., 1995). The newborn sends out attachment cues but the maltreating caregiver is too unaware or too unwilling to attend to him in a sensitive synchronous manner. The lack of a sensitive consistent caregiving response increases the probability that the infant will not get his needs met and then feel invalidated, frustrated, angry, and confused. Early exposure of children to inter-adult anger is associated with increased levels of behavioral and emotional reactivity, including more problem-focused perceptions and aggressive actions (Cummings, Hennessay, Rabideau, & Cicchetti, 1994).

More importantly, maltreatment can compromise the child's ability to negotiate and complete existing and subsequent stage-salient developmental tasks for healthy, adaptive functioning (Cicchetti & Manly, 2001; McGee et al., 1997), and negatively "impact the information processing, appraisal, and emotional integration of experience crucial to this stage" (McGee, Wolfe, & Olson, 2001, p. 827). An important predictor of whether a child will develop psychopathology rests in how successful the child is in completing those expected species-typical developmental tasks such as attachment security and emotional regulation. Maltreatment can derail this and other sequential tasks that are important for normal development (Keiley et al., 2001).

So, maltreatment of children, especially physical abuse of boys, promotes emotional and behavioral dysregulation and lack of trust in caregivers (alienation), which then greatly increases the likelihood of antisocial, aggressive, and mean-spirited externalizing behaviors toward others (Cicchetti et al., 2000; Egeland, Yates, Appelyard, & van Dulmen, 2002). Maltreatment of children with its resulting negative sequelae and cumulative stressors can become a slippery slope into pathological outcomes for many children, including self-abuse, abuse of others, and the abuse of animals.

The chances of maltreatment for a child are greatly increased whenever a mother feels stressed and has a negative attitude about her pregnancy and/or rearing her children (Cicchetti & Walker, 2001; Mrazek, 1993; Susman, Schmeelek, Ponirakis, & Gariepy, 2001). Such attitudes may foreshadow other risk behaviors such as fetal abuse and neglect (drinking, smoking, not eating, etc.) (Mrazek, 1993; Cicchetti & Walker, 2001). Other stressors on parents such as poor health, lack of support and isolation, financial and employment problems, criminal histories, previous history of abuse, psychiatric disorders (affective or personality disorders, psychotic classifications) can all interact and/or produce a cumulative effect for undesirable outcomes (Cicchetti & Manly, 2001; Cicchetti & Walker, 2001; Mrazek, 1993; Wolf & McGee, 1994).

The specific maltreatment experiences and outcomes for each child are variable and contingent upon not only the child's preexisting physical and emotional health (Mrazek, 1993), but also many interacting potentially co-occuring factors such as onset, severity, chronicity, and developmental period (Cicchetti & Manly, 2001; Wolf & McGee, 1994), and the child's individualized coping mechanisms. (Clarification of each subtype can be assisted using The Maltreatment Classification System, MCS, and the Record of Maltreatment Experiences, ROME [Cicchetti & Manly, 2001]). Knowledge about each subtype factor sheds light on the maltreatment effect. For example, the chronicity of the maltreatment predicts strongly for later rejection by peers and aggression (Cicchetti & Manly, 2001). The onset and timing of physical maltreatment in a child's life relates to how a child internalizes or externalizes behaviors (Keiley et al., 2001). Neurological damage to the infant brain can be caused not only by shaken baby syndrome and blunt trauma to the head but also by the interactive effects of maternal stress or illness and other forms of maltreatment such as neglect, or other suboptimal parenting patterns (Sanchez, Ladd, & Plotsky, 2001). All development, of course, involves the interplay between nature and nurture.

Maltreatment Can Compromise Brain Circuits

The infant brain develops from both a genetic blueprint coded in the DNA as well as from the baby's neuronal responsiveness to environmental influences (Sesma & Georgieff, 2003). This openness or plasticity can be experience expectant where specific stimuli are needed for growth (such as with visual depth perception or language) as well as experience dependent, involving individualized learning and forming new synapses (Fox, Calkins, & Bell, 1994; Greenough & Black, 1994; Sesma & Georgieff, 2003). So, neural organization, development, and maturation are influenced by exposure to what occurs in the environment both before and after birth (Cicchetti & Tucker, 1994; Sesma & Georgieff, 2003).

If the child is exposed to stimuli that are threatening and the attachment figure is not considered a secure base for protection, then the risk of negative neurobiological events for the child increases as the fight/flight hypothalamic-pituitary-adrenal axis (HPA) goes into chronic protective action (Cicchetti & Manly, 2001). Ongoing stress, including maternal separation and other suboptimal caretaking, can elevate the HPA axis into hyperactivity, and with its accompanying changes in basal cortisol levels it can increase the probability of causing abnormalities in myelination, synaptic pruning, neurogenesis, and glucocorticoid actions (Bremner & Vermetten, 2001; Cicchetti & Manly, 2001; Heffelfinger & Newcomer, 2001). Maltreatment can disrupt these neurological processes and it has been associated with compromised regulation, hippocampal damage, and loss of learning and memory (Bremner & Vermetten, 2001; Cicchetti & Manly, 2001; Heffelfinger & Newcomer, 2001).

If the exposure to environmental stimuli and sensitive caretaking is severely limited and extended social isolation occurs, then neurological problems also become evident as was demonstrated by Harlow's deprived and emotionally damaged monkeys (Harlow & Zimmerman, 1959). Similarly, longitudinal studies by Zeanah and his colleagues of institutionalized children who currently reside in Romanian orphanages (where the physical and psychological care is suboptimal) also show an increased risk for both cognitive and affective disorders (Zeanah et al., 2003). In one PET brain scan study of the Romanian adoptees, the research team discovered less than normal metabolism in the orbitofrontal gyrus, the infralimbic prefrontal cortex, the various limbic structures (including the amygdala), and the lateral temporal cortex (Zeanah et al., 2003). Moreover, there was reduced glucose metabolism in the prefrontal areas such as the left frontal orbital cortex (Zeanah et al., 2003). Behavioral observations of these children (average age 8) showed problems with impulsivity and emotional regulation, cognition, and social relationships (Zeanah et al., 2003). And while

the effects of maltreatment vary from child to child, it appears that physical abuse promotes more uninhibited externalizing aggressive behaviors, while isolation and neglect increases the likelihood of low motivation and inhibited withdrawal (Crittenden, Claussen, & Sugarman, 1994).

And while studies of adoptees from orphanages demonstrate that most institutionalized children suffer deficits in multiple aspects of their development (attachment security, cognition, behavior, physical and socio-emotional growth), most are context sensitive and subject to later remediation and sustained recovery (Goldberg, 1999; Maclean, 2003). So, being institutionalized, by itself, does not guarantee later psychopathology although additional cumulative risks can certainly reduce the chances for a positive prognosis (Maclean, 2003). Continuing research on institutionalized children is needed to determine the extent of maltreatment to the brain and how sensitive neurological periods of growth are impacted as well as how windows of opportunity for repair can be implemented (Zeanah et al., 2003).

As previously mentioned, maltreatment can disrupt important brain circuits, like the orbitofrontal and ventromedial prefrontal cortex and other structures, which act in concert to clarify the emotional consequences of one's actions and act as an inhibitor when necessary (Pennington, 2002). Lack of inhibitory control and emotional regulation can then more easily lead to aggression against animals and people. Disorganized-disoriented insecure attachment patterns, which are more commonly seen in abusive parenting situations of children, show hyperarousal and dissociation, which can then become "imprinted into the developing limbic and autonomic nervous systems of the early maturing right brain" (Schore, 1996, p. 59). These structural changes can be enduring and can lead to inefficient non-coherent coping strategies with unpredictable relational outcomes (Schore, 2002). In short, maltreated children are at increased risk of acquiring neuropathological connections (Cicchetti, 2003).

Suboptimal parenting experiences can also change brain chemistries by altering neurotransmitter synthesis, transmitter receptor synthesis, and transmitter uptake systems (Sesma & Georgieff, 2003). One indicator of seratonergic function comes from measuring cerebrospinal fluid (CSF) levels and concentrations of a serotonin metabolite called 5-hydroxyindoleacetic acid (5-HIAA) (Markus, Kruesi, & Jacobsen, 1997). Although ranges and specific percentage levels are at best still correlative in nature, low 5HT seratonin levels have been associated with emotional regulation problems in insecurely attached children with conduct disorders who also have a higher propensity for expressing impulsive aggression (Pennington, 2002). There are also many transactional gene, brain, and environment correlations to consider (Fox et al., 1994). Genetic vulnerability, such as having two short forms of the serotonin transporter gene (# 17), coupled with suboptimal parenting can pose a significant risk for psychopathology (Hariri et al., 2002). Conversely, optimal parenting with one long form of the gene provide a far more optimistic life trajectory (Hariri et al., 2002) and, fortunately, single gene main effects are rare since so many other interacting genes buffer or accelerate the expression of complex behaviors like aggression. Of course, one of the most readily available solutions for reducing psychopathology resulting from a high-risk genetic vulnerability would be to substitute the maltreatment vector for sensitive and responsive caregiving.

Such sensitive caregiving could increase empathy for all children and even more so for those children who may have a special genetic propensity for loving others. Fricchione (n.d.) surmises that while athletic or musical prowess is an extra-genetic gift Mother Nature endows to some children, then why not assume that some other children possess a love prowess as well. Love encompasses many different dimensions within our affective self. Without our heartfelt loving emotions, our cognitions would be devoid of meaning and flavor. Our emotions help us perceive, appraise situations, and express regulated responses toward others (Curtis & Cicchetti, 2003). We attune and resonate with each other emotionally, and we integrate our cognitive thoughts using our emotions. Most pet owners are emotionally attuned to their animals as well, but sadly many others are not caring, largely because of their early emotional scars.

Masked Memories

When a child is exposed to traumatizing or intense negative affect and unresponsive care, then a disturbing internalized message is likely to develop. That message goes something like, "You are not worthy of positive attention and your signals won't bring someone who will support and comfort you" (McCrone et al., 1994). It's easy to see how this *no one is consistently there for you* message can distort a child's budding confidence levels, secure relationship

dialog, and development of self (McGee et al., 1997). Repeated negative interactions can send a scary message to the infant that he is on his own, which in turn can increase his fear and defensive responses. Maltreatment experiences like these are stored into a child's long-term memory, beginning with the subconscious motor and cognitive procedural memories which in turn later help organize the declarative symbolic memories (semantic and episodic) (McCrone et al., 1994). A deeply imbedded procedural memory of worthlessness, based upon thousands of painful motor interactions that usually are coupled with critical verbal assaults, can leave a vulnerable child with a lifetime of psychological scars and disorganized and distorted thinking patterns.

Problems arise when a child tries to process into a working memory some markedly contradictory interactions of self and other with multiple caregivers who present conflicting incomparable attachment models and inconsistent explanations for similar experiences (Adam, Sheldon-Keller, & West, 1995). Bowlby suggests that although multiple attachments models can be internalized, the child forms a hierarchy of the different caregiving models and chooses one as the primary internal compass within a specified context (McCrone et al., 1994). A child may lock in a negative procedural model of himself in relation to a maltreating attachment figure that is extremely traumatic. But to avoid internal anxiety and discomfort he may end up utilizing a more acceptable verbal declarative memory of himself to guide him.

Unfortunately, this new defensive model can mask the underlying unresolved pain and the incomplete termination and resolution of the past maltreatment issues can prevent new beginnings. The consequence of this defensive strategy is that he will likely be unaware of the internal incongruities between his different models that can in turn compromise his emotional security and perceptual accuracy in future relationships (McCrone et al., 1994). While the procedural memory of a securely attached child is associated with an ongoing secure base comfort and the knowledge that personal efficacy can handle stress and regulate one's emotions, the maltreated, insecurely attached child is more likely to compensate for perceived insecurities and construct adaptive defense mechanisms and be largely unaware he is using them.

Words and Empathy Escape Them

It's clear that animals would be safer if more people had more empathy and compassion for them, since empathy can act as an inhibiter of violence. Although pro-social cooperative behaviors can be genetically predisposed in humans, newborns do not automatically receive a mature empathetic response at birth. Empathy needs to be nurtured, and it begins to be developed through early experiences around the age of 2 and matures as children develop a *theory of mind* (Emde, 1996). This means that they can infer and ponder ideas about their own and others' mental states such as feelings and perceptions and the consequential behaviors and actions these might predict (Myers, 2002). As a child learns that others have minds and can infer different emotions, desires, beliefs, and intentions to what happens, then his curiosity motivates him to find out what makes a playmate sad, mad, or glad. With the assistance of language, he wants to know how he can get his brother to share or his mother to buy him a toy (Myers, 2002). It's this *taking the perspective of another* that allows a child to make assumptions and predict behaviors of both humans and animals.

Psychologist David Myers (2002) says that as part of this process of inferring behavior comes the ability to understand false beliefs, which is how Little Red Riding Hood saw through the wolf's ruse and ran away to safety. A child's ability to comprehend false beliefs to oneself and others is usually acquired around 4 years of age (Joseph & Teager-Flusberg, 2004). As caregivers model and encourage open dialogue, a child learns to talk about feelings and infer different internal state (IS) words that help develop more self-awareness and self–other differentiation (Cicchetti, Rogosch, Maughan, Toth, & Bruce, 2003). Children who are able to discuss the feeling states of themselves and others, even when others are not present, as well as how feeling states are both causal and consequential, are more likely to assume some responsibility and self-regulation for their actions (Cicchetti et al., 2003). With increased use of IS words come self-conscious emotions such as guilt, shame, and pride for social compliance and the ability to talk with playmates about their feelings in order to resolve problems (Cicchetti et al., 2003). And with a better understanding of self and others comes an increased likelihood of empathy and compassion (Cicchetti et al., 2003). This presupposes, however, that the child's parents have provided a nurturing environment for expressing internal state language and theory of mind.

But if the child is unable to rely on or predict the actions of the parent, then he will have a more difficult time organizing and regulating his emotional and cognitive responses. This is most likely to happen when a child's early learning experiences are from maltreating parents who model inconsistency, insensitivity, volatility, selfishness, fear, and suboptimal caregiving within a chaotic, stressful, and disorganized home environment (Beeghly & Cicchetti, 1994; Cicchetti et al., 2003). It's not hard to understand how maltreated children could experience confusion about inferring mental states in emotionally unstable parents and thus incur deficits in the use of positive internal state language, self–other differentiation, self-regulation, and empathy (Cicchetti et al., 2003; Zeanah & Scheeringa, 1997). And since effective communication depends upon each partner's meaningful cues and appropriate responses, the child without these skill sets is going to be at risk of feeling insecure and not very competent relating to others (Zeanah & Scheeringa, 1997). An ineffective caregiver also models for the infant that communication is not a reciprocal give and take flowing process but rather a frustrating assemblage of verbal assertions and unlistened to responses that seldom result in positive outcomes (Egeland et al., 2002; McCrone et al., 1994).

Words, especially positive words, are not part of the lexicon of maltreating caregivers. Early studies comparing non-maltreating parents to maltreating parents showed that the latter tended, when interviewed, to use fewer words to describe the emotions of their children (Beeghly & Cicchetti, 1994). When these parents talked with their children, they demonstrated lower levels of verbal interaction, less reciprocity, and more negativity (Beeghly & Cicchetti, 1994). Positive symbolic communication was not high on their list and not surprisingly their maltreated children subsequently displayed more negative self-conscious emotions (Cicchetti et al., 2003) and lagged behind on using advanced symbolic play with peers (Beeghly & Cicchetti, 1994).

Therefore, maltreated children living with volatile non-reflective caregivers may learn it is somewhat risky to explore the internal state words of self and others and even more risky to verbally express those inferred feelings or beliefs (Cicchetti et al., 2003; Crittenden, 1997). This stilted process can severely compromise the child's ability to achieve self-awareness and awareness of others and present more difficulties in obtaining theory of mind competencies (Cicchetti et al., 2003). Living with a non-reflective caregiver is like having to look into a mirror, but it has no return image for you. The child cannot see himself in the caregiver's eyes as a feeling, thinking person who is worthy and special.

And since severe maltreatment can influence developmental neurobiology (via experience expectant and dependent processes), it's possible that IS deficits are also correlated with structural and functional neuronal irregularities that result in pathological synaptic connections (Cicchetti et al., 2003). While not all children who suffer maltreatment demonstrate neurobiological problems, those who experience sexual and physical abuse encounter a higher risk and are more likely to compromise theory of mind abilities (Cicchetti et al., 2003). Maltreating parents do not demonstrate to children that reflective thought and self-talk promote self-understanding, self-regulation, and an increased sense of competency in interpersonal relationships.

Insecurity Breeds Bias and Distortion

A sensitive caregiver stimulates and encourages dialogue with the infant to nurture emotional openness, spontaneity, verbal fluency, and coherence in order to lay the building blocks for effective relationship communication and self-confidence in future relationships (McCrone et al., 1994). All these mastery skills enhance and reaffirm the child's positive internal working model. Securely attached children feel safe enough to explore and integrate challenging information about themselves or their close attachment relationships. Their self-worth has been validated within their caretaking experience and they can self-regulate and selectively exclude those signals from awareness which might overwhelm them or which cannot be readily assimilated (McCrone et al., 1994; West & Sheldon-Keller, 1994). It's like they have a dimmer switch to modulate their emotional enlightenment in order to flexibly respond.

But insecurely attached children whose history did not include sensitive caretaking tend to defensively exclude all information that reminds them of their painful fears concerning their attachment relationships and their perceived inadequacies (McCrone et al., 1994; West & Sheldon-Keller, 1994). Since they do not feel confident regulating their emotions they tend to utilize more of an on/off awareness switch. When it's switched *off*, it keeps them safe, but also in the dark about themselves and their relationship interactions. If the awareness switch were to be flipped *on* (by dropping their defenses), then they would feel anxiety and vulnerability and feel at risk of being emotionally overwhelmed, which sometimes occurs. There's no in-between modulation

and no secure mental representation or trusted caregiver who can offer them the confidence to directly confront and resolve painful issues. And since even minor environmental cues can appear threatening, their attachment system is chronically activated, and they remain defensive and emotionally fragile.

A maltreated child will use a variety of defensive measures to exclude emotional pain, including dissociation, repression, discounting, and specific denial of relevant input about attachment-related information (McCrone et al., 1994). His affective restriction has distanced him from truly understanding why he feels and acts the way he does (McCrone et al., 1994). Insecure individuals are more likely to defensively bias their social perception by bragging and making positive self-appraisals when confronted with parts of themselves they don't like in order to compensate for their perceived inadequacies. Their growth trajectory is compromised because they inflate their own worth to gain self-esteem and they refuse to accept critical feedback that might help them improve (Mikulincer & Shaver, 2004). Therefore, information coming in as well as going out is distorted and biased.

Specifically, anxiously attached individuals tend to commit a false consensus bias by thinking that other people are just like them in order to increase their sense of relative similarity and emotional closeness (Mikulincer & Shaver, 2004). Those with defensive avoidant attachment patterns bias their perceptions by projecting negative characteristics onto others while professing personal dissimilarity so they can make themselves feel superior and thus less vulnerable, which is called false distinctiveness bias (Mikulincer & Shaver, 2004). Both bias strategies serve to protect the user from having to directly confront feelings of not being wanted or worthy of love (Mikulincer & Shaver, 2004). This ongoing defensive protection robs them of congruent self–other awareness, clear thinking, and authenticity within relationships. This distorted cognitive process partially explains our earlier question about animal abuse, "What were you thinking?"

Awareness Deficits and Violence

The extent and quality of a child's intra- and interpersonal awareness and metacognition is influenced by the quality of his early attachment relationships (Fonagy et al., 1997). Insecurely attached children tend to have less self-reflective competencies than securely attached children, in large part because they had less early exposure to reciprocal intersubjective experiences that would have fostered metacognitive competencies (Fonagy et al., 1997). Awareness of self–other mental states, including emotions and intentions, can promote inhibition of violence and more social control as a person reflects upon and identifies with how the potential victim (whether it be human or animal) might feel and how his own actions might be interpreted by significant others in the community (Fonagy et al., 1997a; Fonagy et al., 1997b). Children with secure attachments utilize their metacognitive abilities to get along with others.

Those with limited mentalizing abilities are less likely to have clarity about emotions and intentions, including their own mental states, and with an impaired awareness, they cannot easily see themselves as being intentionally responsible for their own acts or how those actions might impact another (Fonagy et al., 1997). This distancing from how their actions might affect others is often accompanied by a corresponding devaluation or objectification of the person so they can justify victimizing him as if he were a non-living, non-feeling physical thing or object (Fonagy et al., 1997). Children over the age of 7 who view animals as non-living, non-feeling *objects* can more easily rationalize harming them. Secure attachment promotes what Martin Buber (1958) refers to as *I and Thou* relationships rather than *I and It* relationships. An insecure and defensive posture distorts a person's social perception and increases the chances for both interpersonal or inter-group conflict (Mikulincer & Shaver, 2004). Being defensive, judgmental, and insecure increases inter-group biases with vilification and prejudice toward anyone unfamiliar that belongs to an out group (Kottak, 2002; Mikulincer & Shaver, 2004).

Those who are classified with avoidant attachments tend to magnify small differences or create untrue negative projections about out group members so they can bolster their own self-worth (Mikulincer & Shaver, 2004). When confronted with pain or reminders of their own mortality, insecure individuals tend to judge others outside their group even more harshly and increase their own rigidity and cognitive closure (Mikulincer & Shaver, 2004). Insecure children who witness or experience maltreatment may learn to expect hostility in all relationships and thus develop hostile attribution biases about others, which, even in neutral situations, can result in preemptive aggressive strikes to defend against misperceived slights, (Fonagy et al., 1997; Keiley et al., 2001).

In-group/out-group biases cause much pain in the world and are genetically loaded survival behaviors that cannot easily be overcome without education, common purpose, and reflective thinking. Biased children, who previously had a negative experience with a pet and don't understand animals, may want to protect themselves, to appear powerful, or to get even, and they are especially dangerous for innocent animals. By observing and identifying with the similarities between animals and themselves, children can enlarge their self–other perspective and their ability to empathize and express increasing comfort with new stimuli and thus not automatically default into a defensive process (Pagani, Robustelli, & Ascione, in press). With supportive guidance and modeling, we can help a child move from a fear-based state of relationship disequilibrium to a more empathetic state of equilibrium and positive identification with others (this volume, pg. 247). Self-distortions lead to social awareness deficits and a higher probability of interpersonal conflict and violence. Insecurely attached individuals who have problems with self-regulation and self-reflection often approach problems with either volatile coercive emotions or defensive cognitive avoidance strategies (Crittenden, 1997; Sroufe, 1990; Mikulincer & Shaver, 2004).

Since mental representations and IS words are not their strong suit, children who have mentalization problems prefer to relate in a concrete physical manner, which for them can be more readily understood and manipulated (Fonagy et al., 1997; Zeanah & Scheeringa, 1997). Therefore, frustrations and perceived threats from unwanted ideas and symbolic representations can be resolved by acting out against their physical personifications (e.g., people, pets, property) (Fonagy et al., 1997). This is evident when children with aggressive attachment disorders vandalize a school or a church that has symbolic value, or when the ruthless Cambodian dictator Pol Pot ordered all intellectuals killed and extended his fear-based definition to anyone wearing glasses or anyone possessing books. As a result, millions of innocent people died in the killing fields. The disordered attachment patterns and hostile internal working models can guide aggressors toward violence with no inhibiting metacognitive thoughts about the consequences (Fonagy et al., 1997). Because aggressors feel insecure and powerless, they are more prone to displace the aggression they have for their insensitive caregiver toward a less threatening object such as a pet.

Of course, the chronic use of personal denial and other defensive measures to protect oneself from vulnerability take their toll and are akin to laying cement over hearty wild grass. In time, some sprouts (of the buried painful reality) will shoot up between the cracks and cause great discomfort. The unresolved past cannot be entirely blocked and it influences decisions in the present. Maladaptive coping mechanisms arise to quell the anxiety such as distortions, displacements (kicking the dog), and rationalization (the dog deserved it and it's not my fault). Human relationships also become maladaptive.

Without self-reflection and openness, a person is ill-suited to become genuinely intimate and vulnerable with someone else. Specifically, in personal relationships, he communicates a distorted reality through omissions, denials, and rigidity (West & Sheldon-Keller, 1994). He therefore has an impaired ability to accurately comprehend and assess his interpersonal experiences (Adam et al., 1995). In essence, he is unresolved about significant issues of loss, rejection, and abandonment in his life, and thus he remains incongruent, inauthentic, and in Martin Buber's (1958) terminology, *not transparently real*. These mental restrictions can be carried into adulthood and subsequently reflected as unresolved responses about his past as evidenced in the Adult Attachment Interviews (e.g., compulsive self-sufficient/dismissing attachment patterns, anxious/preoccupied patterns, etc.) (Main & Solomon, 1990; West & Sheldon-Keller, 1994).

So, within our child caregiver relationship lay the roots of our intra- and interpersonal functioning and awareness. Our attachment patterns set the emotional tone for how we relate to others including our expectations, our explorations, and our ability to trust and authentically love. And animals are therefore much less at risk around children who are securely attached and who are guided by internal working models coded with empathy and cooperation.

Part Four—Concluding Remarks
Our Common Ties With Animals

The fate of animals around the world rests upon the actions of *humankind*. How we develop into kind humans (humananus) or wise humans (homo sapiens) is a process that is not only important to the survival of animals but to the survival of all life forms on earth, including ourselves. As Mahatma Gandhi advised, "The greatness of a nation in its moral progress can be judged by the way its animals are treated" (Razdan, 2004, p. 72). If planet earth is 4½ billion years old, then what we think of as civilized modern humans have been occupying its surface for a relatively short period—approximately 0.0001% of the total time (Bryson, 2003).

But many scientists believe that some form of life has been replicating and evolving on this planet for almost 4 billion years (Bryson, 2003; Dawkins, 2004). And since humanity operates on a heritable continuum then we owe a great debt to those life forms that came before us that provided a genetic platform for our current existence. The renowned biologist Richard Dawkins proposed 40 different rendezvous points at which modern humans biologically intersect with other species (Dawkins, 2004). Suffice it to say that our basic human nature is the result of a long evolutionary journey from a large supporting cast, not the least of which are animals.

The more we understand our common bonds with animals the less likely we are to objectify them and see them as not worthy of our compassion and responsible stewardship. The human fetus possesses a rudimentary tail and gill slits, a spinal column similar to that of apes, and similar brain structures including spindle cells and many other shared biological forms (de Waal, 1996; Starr & Taggart, 1992). It's also important to note that humans possess some noncultural motivational tendencies and behavioral inclinations that are shared with non-human species like chimpanzees, dolphins, and other living creatures. Primatologist Frans de Waal (1996) has written extensively about how the human mind evolved from the past as it observed the phenomenon of animal attachment, maternal behavior, emotional contagion, reciprocity, exchange rules, sympathy, deceit, memory use, peacemaking, and more.

Animal expert Eugene Linden once described how Lincoln Park zookeeper Eric Meyers inadvertently dropped part of his hard-earned pay on the floor of the enclosure housing Koundo, a 611-pound adult male gorilla. To his horror, Koundo quickly picked up the dropped $50 bill and refused to give it up. Eric decided to outwit the gorilla so he went to the pantry and returned with a highly valued can of peaches that he could trade for the money. Koundo tore off a small piece of the bill to exchange for the desired fruit. Fearing that he would get his bill back in minute fragments Eric decided to increase the reward and he returned from the kitchen with more delicious food than the huge gorilla had ever been served before. Koundo paused, looked at the food, and then at the money, and quickly popped the bill in his mouth and ate it. Linden surmised that because of the offering of unprecedented rewards the gorilla knew that the human wanted that bill back badly and that it must be pretty special (Linden, 2002). Either Koundo thought that something so prized must be very delicious, and therefore worth consuming, or he wanted to assert his power with the frustrated zookeeper. Either way, this oppositional behavior is not too distant from what many human parents experience with their defiant children.

Our experience-expectant foundations for becoming human, including our predisposition for attachment and our proto empathetic responses, came from our genetic endowment and our animal predecessors (Kraemer, 1992; Shephard, 1998). Indeed, scientists cannot rule out that animals don't experience some form of emotional expression similar to empathy that can be directed across species (Preston & de Waal, 2002). In one celebrated case a female gorilla comforted and protected a small child who had fallen into a zoo enclosure (Preston & de Waal, 2004; Bils & Singer, 1996). There are also stories of dolphins pushing swimmers in trouble to shore and stories of dogs saving sleeping pet owners from deadly house fires or floods (Associated Press, 2005; Mita, 2004; Wynne, 2004). Primatologist Frans de Waal (1996) believes that we may occupy the top floor of the tower of morality but other species have previously provided the foundation and occupy some of the lower floors. Our connections run deep, but sometimes they can be rocky.

During the Middle Ages, when the ruling clergy did not want to risk offending God by harming any of his creatures, they held what they considered fair trials for law-breaking animals to judge them for their sins. In one case, rats were summoned to court for eating crops. The courts even appointed legal representation for the wayward rodents. The rats' clever lawyer said that the rats refused to obey the summons and come to court, because they were afraid they would be eaten by cats. The ruling clergy of the time obviously didn't understand that responsibility requires theory of mind (Wynne, 2004).

While in some ways animals are very much like us, there are other obvious ways that they are not like us. Animals are not as self-aware as we are, and they don't have our complex language, cultural skills, or abstract thinking abilities. de Waal (1996) cautions that we should not view them as simply primitive people in furry suits who must have the same legal status as humans. But a balanced perspective would require us to recognize both our similarities and our differences with animals and respect the thread of life connecting us all. In comparative terms, we need to realize that what makes us human, in the best sense of the word, is our consciousness of compassion coupled with our loving actions.

Momentum for Security and Compassion

In this chapter, I have looked at how both secure and insecure attachment processes can influence children's relationship compasses (internal working models). I reviewed how empathetic caregiver sensitivity and attunement promotes secure attachments and more positive outcomes for children including emotional regulation, congruent procedural memories, integrated brain functioning, accurate self-awareness (mindfulness), and, most notably, more empathy and compassion for others. I noted how secure attachment acts as a negative bias buffer and a probable life script for loving animals and other people.

And while we must always acknowledge the total ecological transactional nature of a developing child whenever we make assumptions (i.e., with no simple linear causal models), there are many positive corollaries that are associated with secure attachments. A securely attached mother who looks forward to having a child is more likely to activate her genetically predisposed caregiving behavioral system and exhibit healthy prenatal care before the birth of the baby and sensitive good enough mothering afterward. So, just having a positive maternal expectation is a foreshadowing boost toward security for the unborn offspring (Main, 1999). And if the secure attachment cycle passes onto a subsequent generation, then one might consider this as the action of a *friendly* ghost in the nursery.

It should not be surprising that there are so many good enough mothers out there. They have had a lot of momentum. Depending upon how one wants to view our humanoid predecessors, today's mothers are more than 3 million years old, and they are intrinsically motivated for contingent caregiving (Shephard, 1998). The baby's genes are also at work to make a connection. Trevarthan believes that embedded deep within the human embryo are intrinsic motivational factors that will pattern and imprint the infant's brain to seek emotional connections and emotional regulations within a caregiving environment (Trevarthan & Aitken, 1994). These genetic motives propel the newborn to imitate, reciprocate, and cooperatively learn the caregiver's thoughts, intentions, and feelings and to establish an internal working model to guide him (Trevarthan & Aikten, 1994).

With emotional regulation, intersubjectivity, and attunement comes awareness of self and others. This awareness of another person's needs forms the essential prerequisite for empathy, altruism, and compassion. With reflective reasoning about concepts previously experienced such as reciprocity and fairness the child discerns good from bad and incorporates an internal awareness of guilt and shame which then gives rise to a conscience (Kagan, 1984). The child tends to mirror the caretaker's rules and own a sense of moral responsibility to do the right thing for others (as it was done unto him). This empathetic thought process is referred to as the *moralization of attachment* (Stillwell in Fricchione, n.d., p. 13). With increased maturity the individual incorporates codified virtues, norms, and community standards and these norms can act to increase support for animal care and inhibit animal abuse.

Early in development the child internalizes his own worthiness as his attachment signals for belonging are repeatedly validated and reciprocated (McCrone et al., 1994). As he values himself more, he has less need to defensively compensate for insecurities by putting others down or negatively objectifying others in order to make himself feel good. Acquired intersubjectivity sets up a positive internal state (IS) dialog and a neural pattern for the child to become other-focused rather than defensively self-absorbed or narcissistic. He not only values his life but also the lives of others, and his circle of concern extends outward to more kinship connections. This same expansion of concern and lack of treating others as objects works to the advantage of animals who come into contact with a securely attached child or adult.

A secure child's early positive procedural memory template for how the world operates has been overlearned and is now largely out of consciousness but nonetheless useful as a potent motivator for altruistic acts. It seems that a preponderance of those brave individuals who risked their lives to hide Jews during WW II, or who helped Holocaust victims, did so without great personal deliberation or indecisiveness (Schloss, 2002). The personal stories of altruism mounted on the walls of the United States Holocaust Memorial Museum in Washington, DC, reveal a pattern where most of these heroes did not consider themselves as exceptionally courageous and they couldn't imagine themselves not acting as they did. Helping was almost automatic for them.

In studies comparing such helpers with similarly matched control groups researchers found that the altruistic individuals were more likely than the controls to have exceptionally close relationships with their parents (Oliner & Oliner, 1992; Rosenhan, 1970; Sober & Wilson, 1998). Elliot Sober, who analyzes variations in kindness and cruelty, speculates that such altruistic helpers also exhibit love to their own children (Sober & Wilson, 1998). It would not be surprising to find that these altruistically inclined individuals find it easy to extend their outwardly expanding compassion toward animals as well.

A Slippery Slope Toward Animal Abuse

In this chapter, I also looked at how suboptimal parenting, maltreatment, and genetic vulnerability increase the risks for insecure disordered attachments and more negative outcomes for children such as compromised brain circuits and problems with internal state language, emotional regulation, metacognition, and, most notably, reduced empathy and compassion for others. These children view the world differently, as if they are wearing glasses with incorrect prescriptions. These might be called 3D children as their intra- and interpersonal relationships are characterized by *Defensiveness* (of their own inadequacies), *Distortion* (of thoughts with attribution and negative bias), and *Dim Awareness* (of how to authentically relate to others). Although risk factors for violence do not have simple linear causes (as they are multidimensional and interactive), children with disordered attachment patterns are on a slippery slope toward animal abuse if their weakened powers of inhibition are overwhelmed by inner frustrations and/or outside pressures toward violence.

How these children got this way is in a general sense a reverse mirror image of the developmental trajectory securely attached children experience. And with all children their development starts before birth. There are fortunately relatively few types of congenital disorders (such as Rhett syndrome) where compromised brain functioning not only alters the normal intrinsic motivational drives to attach but also impairs the neural regulatory systems that organize imitative learning, sensory integration, language, and other factors that are critical for relating to others (Schore, 1996; Trevarthan & Aitken, 1994). Such a confluence of negative gene effects can result in reduced self–other awareness, communication deficits, and insecure attachment. More commonly though, relating disorders are the result of chronic maltreatment coupled with environmental stressors that make infant-brain to caregiver-brain intersubjectivity and emotional regulation difficult and this lack of attunement influences brain organization and ongoing relationship functioning (Schore, 1996; Trevarthan & Aitken, 1994).

Schore (1996) believes that unregulated stresses during critical growth periods of the orbitofrontal cortex are *source generators* of insecure attachments, which can compromise a child's corticolimbic regulatory circuits and thus predispose him to a higher probability of relationship maladaptation and psychopathology. Schore contends that altered orbito-prefrontal functions are part of all early forming psychopathologies because this area of the brain is involved in executive functioning and an individual's ability to discern the emotional states of others. Such lack of interpersonal awareness and dysregulation of emotion results in what Trevarthan calls an *empathy disorder* (Trevarthan & Aitken, 1994).

It's hard for a child to know about his own innate inner kindness or to be able to reflect upon others' mental states or to be able to imitate healthy adaptation responses when there is no healthy human caregiver consistently modeling such behavior. In other words, a slippery slope toward later animal abuse becomes more likely when a child's developing brain does not have a sensitive caregiver's brain there to contingently respond and initially regulate the emotional expressions and intrinsic motivations that normally lead to secure attachment. Regulation is a biological concept common in all life and, not unlike humans, those in the animal world also require it for proper adaptation.

The rhino population at Kruger National Park in eastern South Africa was in trouble. Someone was killing them and at first Park Rangers suspected poachers but the valuable horns were not removed. Then one ranger observed a young elephant deliberately "knocking over a rhino, trampling it and driving a tusk through its chest." Conservation vet Dave Cooper said: "There was a spate of killings and it was as if they were purposeful. The rhinos were ripped to pieces."

He explained that elephants and rhinos sometime clash in nature when provoked "but this sort of behavior when elephants actively go out and chase rhino, is totally abnormal." With time the story became more clear. The elephants were orphans and they were relocated to the Park with no adult supervision and they had become frustrated and angry.

The killings quickly stopped when Rangers put six mature large bull elephants in with the youngsters to model normal behavior and give needed interactive guidance (BBC News, 2000).

It's been said that wounded animals are dangerous yet our most psychologically wounded humans do the most damage to animals and then rationalize their cruelty by professing that they are *only human*. And while humans are complex creatures who can express good and bad or love and hate, it's the active quest for the internalized reward of goodness and love that distinguishes our species as humane (Schloss, 2002). Whenever humans needlessly inflict pain upon animals (not for a worthy purpose), it lowers the bar of moral behavior for the ones administering it.

It's believed that theory of mind and executive functioning abilities in humans were clearly established in our ancestors well before they drew animals on cave walls 40,000 years ago (Ridely, 2003; Siegal, 2003). And we assume that we have mentally and socially evolved since that time. But psychologically wounded children with disordered attachments who engage in angry aggressive actions toward humans (or animals) are simultaneously experiencing information processing biases or deficits that severely compromise their theory of mind abilities (Schultz, Izard, & Bear, 2004). With such distorted and defensive brain processing, these modern children forfeit any hard won evolutionary advances passed on by their forbearers. It's like the rage-filled teen who once said to me, "I've got half a mind to kill you," and I thought to myself, "Yes, at this moment, he is operating with only half a mind since his rational frontal lobes are not well activated." My task was then to reduce his emotional temperature enough to engage him in a positively distracting task so a more constructive dialog could ensue.

As stated earlier, Ascione (2005) concludes that children have many different motivations for hurting animals such as reenactment of a previous trauma, preemptive strikes, peer approval, monetary reward, rehearsal for future aggression, and much more. A child who hurts animals is more likely to be self-focused and lack empathy and compassion for humans as well, and these empathy deficits are correlated with disordered attachment patterns. So, for those children with motivations to hurt animals, one would expect to find a common association with insecure attachments. The angle of the slippery slope toward animal abuse will likely be correlated with the degree of the attachment disorder.

Healthy People Don't Abuse Animals

Healthy people have a moral awareness that guides them toward responsible and compassionate care toward animals and humans. Healthy awareness is nurtured within a secure attachment process that resonates with our deepest need to be connected with caregivers and then later to reciprocate loving care to others, including compassion for animals. We know that securely attached humans are capable of rising above rigid in-group favoritism and summary rejection of anything unfamiliar by feeling more secure and by integrating helpful new information into their lives (Mikulciner & Shaver, 2004).

What makes us morally healthy humans is our ability to consciously choose a more exclusive loving path apart from our base predispositions to help only ourselves, our kin, or our in-group members. Ernst Mayr (1997) considers such higher decision making as maybe the most important stage in our becoming human. Moral awareness is coupled with moral obligation, which, in order to be potent, must also be coupled with moral actions. Schloss states that "self differentiated love is the chief moral obligation of human beings and that only other-regarded love leads to fulfillment" (2002, p. 236). A healthy person's caregiving is expansive and not limited to just our species but extends outward to connect with other species. Therefore, our humanity is not only defined by our interactions with each other but with animals as well. In his *Lectures on Ethics*, Immanuel Kant said, "he who is cruel to animals becomes hard also in his dealings with men. We can judge the heart of a man by his treatment of animals" (1963, p. 143).

As animals continue to serve us they increasingly depend upon us for not only their quality of life but for their very survival on this shrinking planet. And the best way to promote the responsible treatment of animals is to rigorously promote the responsible treatment of human babies that someday will grow up and interact with animals. Good enough care for animals is largely the result of good enough care for humans. Parents can model responsible and compassionate care for animals and supervise how their children interact with pets. Seeing compassionate care predisposes others to imitate it and feel better about duplicating similar behaviors. There is a tendency for those who watch movies of Mother Teresa

to report more compassion for others, which may also increase their immune response (McClelland & Kirshnit, 1998). Likewise, Mikulincer & Shaver (2004) found that they could reduce inter-group bias and hostile responses of individuals of different nationalities by increasing individual attachment security. Positive results were obtained when they utilized priming techniques such as displaying security enhancing words like *love, hug,* or *proximity* or by showing positively regarded faces. Role training exercises that couple positively regarded child mentors with modern technology (such as computers) and child-directed movies also act as effective change agents for at-risk children (Magid, 1977).

These same attachment-anchored learning tools can also be implemented within the burgeoning fields of animal-assisted therapy (AAT) and animal-assisted activities (AAA), which this author believes should be incorporated within the traditional school curriculum. Lesson plans for understanding attachment in animals can increase a child's own personal understanding about how secure human attachment creates stability and mutual caregiving throughout the life cycle. We need more certificated college programs that can prepare teachers and counselors to utilize animals in their curriculum to actively engage students with *hands on* experiential life lessons. A useful teaching model differentiates positive engagement and positive disengagement activities from negative engagement and disengagement processes so that healthy self-esteem issues are enhanced for both the child and the caregiver (Magid, 1999).

Other efforts outside the school setting to educate children about the importance of having compassion for animals can also be highly effective. There are educational programs sponsored by the American Humane Association, the Delta Society, equine groups (Pony Club, NARHA, EFT), and many other groups that positively elucidate on the animal human bond. Many religious teachings promote human kindness toward animals. Having compassion for all living things is a core concept of the Buddhist faith and, as previously discussed in this chapter, empathy, altruism, and compassion correlate highly with secure attachment. Davidson (2002), who studies the impact of religious practices on emotional regulation and altruistic behavior, says that Buddhist caregivers teach children that all living things are worthy of compassionate care and that one can never be certain whether the next living thing they interact with could have been their mother in a previous life. Holding such an extensive empathetic view of life could increase empathy in the decision-making process when interacting with animals. The same attachment-caregiver system that elicits compassion for helpless babies can also be expanded to care for all suffering creatures (Gillath, Shaver, & Mikulincer, 2004).

In the first paragraph of this chapter a securely attached child said, "animals can feel pain." Perhaps we should equally state that animals are likely to also feel some semblance of pleasure, especially during times of play. Play is important for animals, and it is especially important for children in order for them to develop relational skills and to integrate the world around them (Pribram, 1999; Singer & Singer, 1990). What increases play activity in children is a secure attachment and freedom from fear of separation and danger. Post (2003) says love is the ingredient that allows children the freedom to play. And that's what animals and children need. More love and a safe place to play.

References

Adam, K. S., Sheldon-Keller, A. E., & West, M. (1995). Attachment organization and vulnerability to loss, separation and abuse in disturbed adolescents. In S. Goldberg, R. Muir, & J. Kerr (Eds.), *Attachment theory social, developmental, and clinical perspectives* (pp. 309–341). Hillsdale, NJ: The Analytic Press.

Ainsworth, M. D. (1990). Some considerations regarding theory and assessment relevant to attachments beyond infancy. In M. T. Greenberg, D. Cicchetti, & E. M. Cummings (Eds.), *Attachment in the preschool years: Theory, research and intervention* (pp. 463–488). Chicago: The University of Chicago Press.

Ainsworth, M. D. S., Blehar, M. C., Waters, E., & Wail, S. (1978). *Patterns of attachment: A psychological study of the strange situation.* Hillsdale, NJ: Erlbaum.

Ainsworth, M. D. S., & Wittig, B. A. (1969). Attachment and exploratory behavior of one-year-olds in a strange situation. In B. M. Foss (Ed.), *Determinants of infant behavior* (Vol. 4, pp. 129–173). London: Methuen.

American Psychological Association. (2000). *Diagnostic and statistical manual of mental disorders* (4th ed., text revision). Washington, DC: American Psychiatric Association.

Arluke, A., Frost, R., Luke, C., Messner, E., Nathanson, J., Patronek, G., et al., (2002). The health implications of animal hoarding. *Health and Social Work, 27*(2), 125–136.

Asicone, F. (1998). Children who are cruel to animals: A review of research and implications for developmental psychopathology. In R. Lockwood & F. Ascione (Eds.), *Cruelty to animals and interpersonal violence: Readings in research and application* (pp. 83–104). West Lafayette, IN: Purdue University Press.

Ascione, F. (2005). *Children and animals: Exploring the roots of kindness and cruelty.* West Lafayette, IN: Purdue University Press.

Associated Press. (2004, September 9). Pup shoots man, saves litter mates. Retrieved September 9, 2004, from http://cnn.usnews.printhis.clickability.com

Associated Press. (2005, January 21). All if forgiven: Chew happy dog saves owner in Spokane fire. *Seattle Post Intelligencer.* Retrieved March 8, 2005, from http://seattlepi.newsource.com/local/208835_dog21.html

Atkinson, L. (1997). Attachment and psychopathology: From laboratory to clinic. In L. Atkinson & K. Zucker (Eds.), *Attachment and Psychopathology* (pp. 3–16). New York: The Guilford Press.

Bandura, A. (1959). *Adolescent aggression: A study of the influence of child-training practices and family interrelationships, (A Psychology series).* New York: Ronald Press.

Bandura, A., Ross., D., & Ross, S. A. (1961). Transmission of aggression through imitation of aggressive models. *Journal of Abnormal and Social Psychology, 63*, 575–582.

BBC News. (2000, February 14). Elephants kill endangered rhino. Retrieved March 8, 2000, from http://news.bbc.co.uk/1/hi/world/africa/642731.stm

Beauchaine, T. P. (2003) Taxometrics and developmental psychopathology. *Development and Psychopathology, 15*, 501–527.

Beeghly, M., & Cicchetti, D. (1994). Child maltreatment, attachment, and the self system: Emergence of an internal state lexicon in toddlers at high social risk. *Development and Psychopathology 6*, 5–30.

Belsky, J., Steinberg, L., & Draper, P. (1991). Childhood experience, interpersonal development, and reproductive strategy: An evolutionary theory of socialization. *Child Development, 62*, 647–670.

Berman, W. H., & Sperling, M. (1994). The structure and function of adult attachment. In M. B. Sperling & W. H. Berman (Eds.), *Attachment in adults: Clinical and developmental perspectives* (pp. 1–28). New York: The Guilford Press.

Bierer, R. (2000). The relationship between pet bonding, self-esteem, and empathy in preadolescents. Retrieved July 28, 2005, from http://www.abramarketing.com/p/dogskids/abstract.html

Bils, J., & Singer, S. (1996, August 17). Gorilla saves tot in Brookfield Zoo ape pit. *Chicago Tribune*, p. 11.

Bolger, K. E., & Patterson, C. J. (2001). Pathways from child maltreatment to internalizing problems: Perceptions of control as mediators and moderators. *Development and Psychopathology, 13*, 913–940.

Bowlby, J. (1944). Forty-four juvenile thieves: Their characters and home life. *International Journal of Psychoanalysis, 25*, 19–52, 107–127.

Bowlby, J. (1969/1982). *Attachment and loss: Vol. 1. Attachment*. New York: Basic Books.

Bowlby, J. (1988). *A secure base: Parent-child attachment and healthy human development*. New York: Basic Books, Inc.

Bremner, J. D., & Vermetten, E. (2001). Stress and development: Behavioral and biological consequences. *Development and Psychopathology, 13*, 473–489.

Bretherton, I. (1995). The origins of attachment theory John Bowlby and Mary Ainsworth. In S. Goldberg, R. Muir, & J. Kerr (Eds.), *Attachment theory social, developmental, and clinical perspectives* (pp. 45–84). Hillsdale, NJ: The Analytic Press.

Bretherton, I., & Ainsworth, M. D. S. (1974). Responses of one-year olds to a stranger in a strange situation. In M. Lewis & L. A. Rosenblum (Eds.), *The origins of fear* (pp. 131–164). New York: Wiley.

Brofenbrenner, U. (1979). *The ecology of human development*. Cambridge, MA: Harvard University Press.

Bryson, B. (2003). *A short history of nearly everything*. New York: Broadway Books.

Buber, M. (1958). *I and thou*. New York: MacMillan.

Cain, A. (1983). A study of pets in the family system. In A. Katcher & A. Beck (Eds.), *New perspectives on our lives with companion animals*. Philadelphia: University of Pennsylvania Press.

Cairns, R. B., & Cairns, B. D. (2000). The natural history and developmental functions of aggression. In A. J. Sameroff, M. Lewis, & S. M. Miller (Eds.), *Handbook of developmental psychopathology* (2nd ed., pp. 403–429). New York: Kluwer Academic/Plenum Publishers.

Carlson, E., Sampson, M., & Sroufe, L. A. (2003). Implications of attachment theory and research for developmental-behavioral pediatrics. *Journal of Developmental and Behavioral Pediatrics*, 364–380.

Cassidy, J. (1999). The nature of the child's ties. In J. Cassidy & P. R. Shaver (Eds.), *Handbook of attachment theory, research and clinical applications* (pp. 3–20). New York: The Guilford Press.

Cicchetti, D. (2003). Experiments of nature: Contributions to developmental theory [Editorial]. *Development and Psychopathology, 15*, 833–835.

Cicchetti, D., Cummings, E. M., Greenberg, M. T., & Marvin, R. S. (1990). An organizational perspective on attachment beyond infancy: Implications for theory, measurement, and research. In M. T. Greenberg, D. Cicchetti, & E. M. Cummings (Eds.), *Attachment in the preschool years: Theory, research and intervention* (pp. 3–49). Chicago: The University of Chicago Press.

Cicchetti, D., & Manly, J. T. (2001). Operationalizing child maltreatment: Developmental processes and outcomes [Editorial]. *Development and Psychopathology, 13*, 755–757.

Cicchetti. D., Rogosch, F. A., Maughan, A., Toth, S. L., & Bruce, J. (2003). False belief understanding in maltreated children. *Development and Psychopathology, 15*, 1067–1091.

Cicchetti, D., & Sroufe, L. A. (2000). The past as prologue to the future: The times, they've been a-changin' [Editorial]. *Development and Psychopathology, 12*, 255–264.

Cicchetti, D., Toth, S. L., & Maughan, A. (2000). An ecological-transition model of child maltreatment. In A. J. Sameroff, M. Lewis, & S. M. Miller (Eds.), *Handbook of developmental psychopathology* (2nd ed., pp. 689–722). New York: Kluwer Academic/Plenum Publishers.

Cicchetti, D., & Tucker, D. (1994). Development and self-regulatory structures of the mind. *Development and Psychopathology, 6*, 533–549.

Cicchetti, D., & Walker, E. F. (2001). Stress and development: Biological and psychological consequences [Editorial]. *Development and Psychopathology, 13*, 413–418.

Crawford, C. (2005, January 9). Aid effort for animals. *Sunday Herald Sun.* Retrieved January 12, 2005, from http://www.news.com.au/story/0,10117,11891943-28477,00.html

Crittenden, P. M. (1997). Patterns of attachment and sexual behavior: Risk of dysfunction versus opportunity for creative integration. In L. Atkinson & K. Zucker (Eds.), *Attachment and Psychopathology* (pp. 47–93). New York: The Guilford Press.

Crittenden, P. M., Claussen, A. H., & Sugarman, D. B. (1994). Physical and psychological maltreatment in middle childhood and adolescence. *Development and Psychopathology, 6*, 145–164.

Cummings, E. M., Hennessay, K. D., Rabideau, G. J., & Cicchetti, D. (1994). Responses of physically abused boys to interadult anger involving their mothers. *Development and Psychopathology, 6*, 31–41.

Curtis, W. J., & Cicchetti, D. (2003). Moving research on resilience into the 21st century: Theoretical and methodological considerations in examining the biological contributors to resilience. *Development and Psychopathology, 15*, 773–810.

Darwin, C. (2002). *The expression of emotions in man and animals.* Oxford: Oxford University Press.

Davidson, R. J. (2002). Towards a biology of positive affect and compassion. In R. J. Davidson and A. Harrington (Eds.), *Visions of compassion* (pp. 107–130). Oxford: Oxford University Press.

Dawkins, R. (2004). *The ancestor's tale: A pilgrimage to the dawn of evolution.* Boston: Houghton Mifflin.

de Waal, F. (1996). *Good natured: The origins of right and wrong in humans and other animals.* Cambridge: Harvard University Press.

Diamond, D., & Blatt, S. (1994). Internal working models and the representational world in attachment and psychoanalytic theories. In M. B. Sperling & W. H. Berman (Eds.), *Attachment in adults: Clinical and developmental perspectives* (pp. 72–97). New York: The Guilford Press.

Dodge, K. A. (1991). The structure and function of reactive and proactive aggression. In D. J. Pepler & K. H. Rubin (Eds.), *The development and treatment of childhood aggression* (pp. 201–218). Hillsdale, NJ: Erlbaum.

Dumas, J. E., & Wekerle, C. (1995). Maternal reports of child behavior problems and personal distress as predictors of dysfunctional parenting. *Development and Psychopathology, 7*, 465–479.

Easterbrooks, M. A., & Goldberg, W. A. (1990). Security of toddler-parent attachment: Relation to children's sociopersonality functioning during kindergarten. In M. T. Greenberg, D. Cicchetti, & E. M. Cummings (Eds.), *Attachment in the preschool years: Theory, research and intervention* (pp. 221–334). Chicago: The University of Chicago Press.

Egeland, B., Yates, T., Appelyard, K., & van Dulmen, M. (2002). The long-term consequences of maltreatment in the early years: A developmental pathway model to antisocial behavior. *Children's Services: Social Policy, Research and Practice, 5*(4), 249–260.

Efrati, A. (2005). When bad chickens come home to roost, results can be good. *Wall Street Journal, 246*(10), pp. A1–A2.

Emde, R. N. (1990). The third phase of attachment research [Preface]. In M. T. Greenberg, D. Cicchetti, & E. M. Cummings (Eds.), *Attachment in the preschool years: Theory, research and intervention* (pp. ix–xii). Chicago: The University of Chicago Press.

Emde, R. N. (1996). Thinking about intervention and improving early socio-emotional development: Recent trends in policy and knowledge. *Zero to Three, 17*, 11–16.

Fisher, A. G., Murray, E. A., & Bundy, A. C. (1991). *Sensory integration: Theory and practice.* Philadelphia: F. A. Davis Company.

Fonagy, P., Steele, M., Steele, H., Leigh, T., Kennedy, R., Mattoon, G., et al. (1995). Attachment, the reflective self, and borderline states: The predictive specificity of the adult attachment interview and pathological emotional development. In S. Goldberg, R. Muir, & J. Kerr (Eds.), *Attachment theory social, developmental, and clinical perspectives* (pp. 233–278). Hillsdale, NJ: The Analytic Press.

Fonagy, P., Target, M., Steele, M., & Steele, H. (1997). The development of violence and crime as it relates to security of attachment. In J. D. Osofsky (Ed.), *Children in a violent society* (pp. 150–177). New York: The Guilford Press.

Fonagy, P., Target, M., Steele, M., Steele, H., Leigh, T., Levinson, A., et al. (1997b). Morality, disruptive behavior, borderline personality disorder, crime, and their relationship to security of attachment. In L. Atkinson & K. Zucker (Eds.), *Attachment and psychopathology* (pp. 223–274). New York: The Guilford Press.

Fox, N. A., Calkins, S. D., & Bell, M. A. (1994). Neural plasticity and development in the first two years of life: Evidence from cognitive and socioemotional domains of research. *Development and Psychopathology, 6*, 677–696.

Fraiberg, S., Adelson, E., & Shapiro, V. (1975). Ghosts in the nursery. *Journal of the American Academy of Child Psychiatry, 14*, 387–421.

Fredrickson, B. L. (2001). The role of positive emotions in positive psychology: The broaden-and-build theory of positive emotions. *American Psychologist, 56*(3), 218–226.

Fricchione, G. (n.d.) Human development and unlimited love. Retrieved March 30, 2004, from http://www.unlimitedloveinstitute.org/

Frost, R. (2000). People who hoard animals. *Psychiatric Times*, XVII(4). Retrieved August 8, 2005, from http://www.psychiatrictimes.com/p000425.html

Gallup, G. G. Jr. (1994). Self recognition: research strategies and experimental design. In S. T. Parker, R. W. Mitchell, & M. L. Boccia (Eds.), *Self-awareness in animals and humans: Developmental perspectives* (pp. 35–50). New York: Cambridge University Press.

Gillath, O., Shaver, P. R., & Mikulincer, M. (2005). An attachment-theoretical approach to compassion and altruism. In P. Gilbert (Ed.), *Compassion: Conceptualizations, research, and use in psychotherapy* (pp. 121–147). London: Brunner-Routledge.

Goldberg, S. (1999). Attachment and childhood behavior problems in normal, at-risk, and clinical samples. In L. Atkinson & K. Zucker (Eds.), *Attachment and Psychopathology* (pp. 171–195). New York: The Guilford Press.

Goldman, A. (2005). Mirror systems, social understanding and social cognition. Presented at the Interdisciplines, European Science Foundation conference "What Do Mirror Neurons Mean?" Retrieved January 25, 2005, from http://www.interdisciplines.org/mirror

Goleman, D. (1995). *Emotional intelligence*. New York: Bantam Books.

Gottlieb, G., & Tucker Halpern, C. (2002). A relational view of causality in normal and abnormal development. *Development and Psychopathology, 14*, 421–435.

Greenberg, M. (1999). Attachment and psychopathology in childhood. In J. Cassidy & P. R. Shaver (Eds.), *Handbook of attachment theory, research and clinical applications* (pp. 469–496). New York: The Guilford Press.

Greenberg, M., DeKlyen, M., Speltz, M., & Endriga, M. (1997). The role of attachment processes in externalizing psychopathology in young children. In Atkinson & K. Zucker (Eds.), *Attachment and Psychopathology* (pp. 196–222). New York: The Guilford Press.

Greenberg, M., & Speltz, M. (1988). Attachment and the ontogeny of conduct problems. In J. Belsky & T. Nezworski (Eds.), *Clinical implications of attachment* (pp. 177–218). Hillsdale, NJ: Lawrence Erlbaum Associates.

Greenough, W. T., & Black, J. E. (1992). Induction of brain structure by experience: Substrates for cognitive development. In M. R. Gunnar & C. A. Nelson (Eds.), *Minnesota symposia on CHILD PSYCHOLOGY: Vol. 24. Developmental behavioral neuroscience* (pp. 155–200). Hillsdale, NJ: Erlbaum.

Greenspan, S. I., & Lieberman, A. F. (1988) A clinical approach to attachment. In J. Belsky and T. Nezworski (Eds.), *Clinical implications of attachment* (pp. 387–424). Hillsdale, NJ: Lawrence Erlbaum Associates.

Hare, R. D. (1993). *Without conscience: The disturbing world of the psychopaths among us*. New York: Pocket Books.

Hariri, A. R., Mattay, V. S., Tessitore, A., Kolanchana, B., Francesco, F., Goldman, D., et al. (2002, July 19). Serotonin transporter genetic variation and the response of the human amygdala. *Science, 197*, 400–404.

Harlow, H. F., & Zimmerman, R. R. (1959). Affectional responses in the infant monkey. *Science, 130*, 421–432.

Heffelfinger, A. K., & Newcomer, J. W. (2001). Glucocorticoid effects on memory function over the human life span. *Development and Psychopathology, 13*, 491–513.

Janov, A. (2000). *The biology of love*. New York: Prometheus Books.

Johnson, M. H., & Morton, J. (1991). *Biology and cognitive development: The case of face recognition*. Oxford: Blackwell Publishing.

Joseph, R. M., & Teager-Flusberg, H. (2004). The relationship of theory of mind and executive functions to symptom type and severity in children with autism. *Development and Psychopathology, 16*, 137–155.

Kagan, J. (1984). *The nature of the child*. New York: Basic Books.

Kant, I. (1963). *Lectures on ethics* (L. Infield, Trans.) New York: Harper & Row.

Karen, R. (1994). *Becoming attached. Unfolding the mystery of the infant-mother bond and its impact on later life*. New York: Time Warner.

Keiley, M. K., Howe, T. R., Dodge, K. A., Bates, J. E., & Pettit, G. S. (2001). The timing of child physical maltreatment: a cross-domain growth analysis of impact on adolescent externalizing and internalizing problems. *Development and Psychopathology, 13*, 891–912.

Kohut, H. (1977). *The restoration of the self*. Madison, CT: International Universities Press.

Kottak, C. P. (2002). *Anthropology: The exploration of human diversity*. New York: McGraw Hill.

Kraemer, G. W. (1992). A psychobiological theory of attachment. *Behavioral and Brain Sciences, 15*, 493–541.

Kraemer, G. W. (1997). Social attachment, brain function, aggression and violence. In A. Raine, P. A. Brennan, D. P. Farrington, & S. A. Mednick (Eds.), *Biosocial basis of violence* (pp. 207–229). New York: Plenum Press.

Ledoux, J. (2002). *Synaptic self: How our brains become who we are*. New York: Viking.

Linden, E. (2002). *The octopus and the orangutan: More true tales of animal intrigue, intelligence and ingenuity*. New York: Dutton.

Maclean, K. (2003). The impact of institutionalization on child development. *Development and Psychopathology, 15*, 853–884.

Magid, K. (1977, May). Children facing divorce: A treatment program. *The Personnel and Guidance Journal*, 534–536.

Magid, K. (1988). *High risk: Children without a conscience*. New York: Bantam Books.

Magid, K. (1999). Engagement therapy. *Students At Risk, 2*(1), 1–4.

Main, M. (1995). Recent studies in attachment: Overview, with selected implications for clinical work. In S. Goldberg, R. Muir, & J. Kerr (Eds.), *Attachment theory social, developmental, and clinical perspectives* (pp. 45–84). Hillsdale, NJ: The Analytic Press.

Main, M. (1999). Attachment theory: Eighteen points with suggestions for future studies [Epilogue]. In J. Cassidy & P. R. Shaver (Eds.), *Handbook of attachment theory, research and clinical applications* (pp. 845–887). New York: The Guilford Press.

Main, M., & Solomon, J. (1990). Procedures for identifying infants as disorganized/disoriented during the Ainsworth Strange Situation. In M. T. Greenberg, D. Cicchetti, & E. M. Cummings (Eds.), *Attachment in the preschool years: Theory, research and intervention* (pp. 407–474). Chicago: The University of Chicago Press.

Manly, J. T., Cicchetti, D., & Barnett, D. (1994). The impact of subtype, frequency, chronicity, and severity of child maltreatment on social competence and behavior problems. *Development and Psychopathology, 6*, 121–143.

Manly, J. T., Jungmeen, E. K., Rogosch, F. A., & Cicchetti, D. (2001). Dimensions of child maltreatment and children's adjustment: Contributions of developmental timing and subtype. *Development and Psychopathology, 13*, 759–804.

Markus, J., Kruesi, P., & Jacobsen, T. (1997). Serotonin and human violence: Do environmental mediators exist? In A. Raine, P. A. Brennan, D. P. Farrington, & S. A. Mednick (Eds.), *Biosocial basis of violence* (pp. 189–205). New York: Plenum Press.

Marvin, R., & Britner, P. (1999). Normative development, the ontogeny of attachment. In J. Cassidy & P. R. Shaver (Eds.), *Handbook of attachment theory, research and clinical applications* (pp. 44–88). New York: The Guilford Press.

Mayr, E. (1997). *This is biology, The science of the living world*. Cambridge: Harvard University, Belknap Press.

McClelland D. C., & Kirshnit, C. (1998). The effects of motivational arousal through films on salivary immunoglobulin A. *Psychological Health, 2*, 31–52.

McCrone, E. R., Egeland, B., Kalkoske, M., & Carlson, E. A. (1994). Relations between early maltreatment and mental representations of relationships assessed with projective storytelling in middle childhood. *Development and Psychopathology, 6*, 99–120.

McEwen, B. S., & Seeman, T. (1999). Protective and damaging effects of mediators of stress: Elaborating and testing the concepts of allostasis and allostatic load. *Annals of the New York Academy of Sciences, 896,* 30–47.

McGee, R., Wolfe, D., & Olson, J. (2001). Multiple maltreatment, attribution of blame, and adjustment among adolescents. *Development and Psychopathology, 13,* 827–846.

McGee, R. A., Wolfe, D. A., & Wilson, S. K. (1997). Multiple maltreatment experiences and adolescent behavior problems: Adolescents' perspectives. *Development and Psychopathology, 9,* 131–149.

Mikulincer, M., & Shaver, P. (2004). Mental representations of attachment security: Theoretical foundation for a positive social psychology. In M. W. Baldwin (Ed.), *Interpersonal cognition* (pp. 227–265). New York: The Guilford Press.

Mita, A. (2004, November 27). Poachers kill "dolphins that saved swimmers." *The Scotsman,* Retrieved March 8, 2005, from http://news.scotsman.com/archive.cfm?id=1362192004

Mrazek, P. J. (1993). Maltreatment and infant development. In C. H. Zeanah, Jr. (Ed.), *Handbook of infant mental health* (pp. 159–170). New York: The Guilford Press.

Myers, D. (2002). *Exploring psychology.* New York: Worth Publishers.

O'Connor, T. G., Marvin, R. S., Rutter, M., Olrick, J. T., Britner, P. A., & The English and Romanian Adoptees Study Team. (2003). Child-parent attachment following early institutional deprivation. *Development and Psychopathology, 15,* 19–38.

Oliner, S. P., & Oliner, P. M. (1992). *The altruistic personality: Rescuers of Jews in Nazi Europe.* New York: Free Press.

Patrick, M., Hobson, R. P., Castle, D., Howard, R., & Maughan, B. (1994). Personality disorder and the mental representation of early social experience. *Development and Psychopathology, 6,* 375–388.

Patronek G. J. (1999). Hoarding of animals: An under-recognized public health problem in a difficult-to-study population. *Public Health Rep, 114*(1), 81–87.

Pavlicevic, M., & Trevarthan, C. (1989). A musical assessment of psychiatric states in adults, *Psychopathology, 22,* 325–334.

Pennington, B. (2002). *The development of psychopathology: Nature and nurture.* New York: The Guilford Press.

Perrett, D., & Puce, A. (2003). Electrophysiology and brain imaging of biological motion. *Philosophical Transactions: Biological Sciences, 358,* 435–445.

Piaget, J. (1972). *The psychology of the child.* New York: Basic Books.

Pipp-Siegel, S., & Pressman, L. (1996). Developing a sense of self and others. *Zero to Three, 17,* 17–24.

Polan, H. J., & Hofer, M. A. (1999). Psychobiological origins of infant attachment and separation responses. In J. Cassidy & P. R. Shaver (Eds.), *Handbook of attachment theory, research and clinical applications* (pp. 162–197). New York: The Guilford Press.

Post, S. G. (2003). *Unlimited love: Altruism, compassion and service.* Philadelphia: Templeton Foundation Press.

Preston, S. D., & de Waal, F. B. M. (2001). The communication of emotions and the possibility of empathy in animals. In S. B. Post, L. G. Underwood, J. Schloss, & W. B. Hurlbut (Eds.), *Altruism & altruistic love: Science, philosophy & religion in dialogue* (pp. 184–308). Oxford: Oxford University Press.

Pribram, K. H. (1999). Brain and the creative act. In M A. Runko & S. Pritzker (Eds.), *Encyclopedia of creativity* (pp. 213–217). New York: Academic Press.

Radke-Yarrow, M., McCann, K., De Mulder, E., Belmont, B., Martinez, P., & Richardson, D. T. (1995). Attachment in the context of high-risk conditions. *Development and Psychopathology, 7,* 247–265.

Ramachandran, V. S. (2000). Mirror neurons and imitation learning as the driving force behind "the great leap forward" in human evolution [Electronic version]. *Edge: The Third Culture.* Retrieved January 25, 2005, from http://www.edge.org/3rd_culture/ramachandran/ramachandran_p1.html

Razdan, A. (2004, March/April). Petropolis, *Utne Reader,* 72.

Ridley, M. (1996). *The origins of virtue.* London: Viking.

Ridley, M. (2003). *Nature via nurture.* New York: Harper Collins.

Robin, M., & ten Bensel, R. (1998). Pets and the socialization of children. In R. Lockwood & F. Ascione (Eds.), *Cruelty to animals and interpersonal violence: Readings in research and application* (pp. 105–120). West Lafayette, IN: Purdue University Press.

Robinson, J. A., & Glaves, L. (1996). Supporting emotion regulation and emotional availability through home visitation. *Zero to Three, 17*, 31–35.

Rogosch, F. A., Cicchetti, D., & Aber, J. L. (1995). The role of child maltreatment in early deviations in cognitive and affective processing abilities and later peer relationship problems. *Development and Psychopathology, 7*, 591–609.

Roisman, G. I., Padron, E., Sroufe, L. A., & Egeland, B. (2002). Earned-secure attachment status in retrospect and prospect. *Child Development, 73*(4), 1204–1219.

Rosenhan, D. (1970). The natural socialization of altruistic autonomy. In J. Macaulay & L. Berkowitz (Eds.), *Altruism and helping behavior* (pp. 251–268). New York: Academic Press.

Rutter, M. (1997). Clinical implications of attachment concepts: retrospect and prospect. In L. Atkinson & K. Zucker (Eds.), *Attachment and psychopathology* (pp. 17–46). New York: The Guilford Press.

Rutter, M., & Sroufe, L. A. (2000). Developmental psychopathology: Concepts and challenges. *Development and Psychopathology*, 12, 265–296.

Sanchez, M. M., Ladd, C. O., & Plotsky, P. M. (2001). Early adverse experience as a developmental risk factor for later psychopathology: Evidence from rodent and primate models. *Development and Psychopathology, 13*, 419–449.

Schore, A. (1994). *Affect regulation and the origin of the self: The neurobiology of emotional development*. Hillsdale, NJ: Lawrence Erlbaum Associates, Inc.

Schore, A. (1996). The experience-dependent maturation of regulatory system in the orbital prefrontal cortex and the origin of developmental psychopathology. *Development and Psychopathology*, 8, 59–87.

Schore, A. N. (2002). Dysregulation of the right brain: A fundamental mechanism of traumatic attachment and the psychopathogenesis of post-traumatic stress disorder. *Australian and New Zealand Journal of Psychiatry, 36*, 9–30.

Schloss, J. P. (2002). Emerging accounts of altruism: "Love creation's final law?" In S. B. Post, L G. Underwood, J. Schloss, & W. B. Hurlbut (Eds.), *Altruism & altruistic love: Science, philosophy & religion in dialogue* (pp. 212–242). Oxford: Oxford University Press.

Schultz, D., Izard, C. E., & Bear, G. (2004). Children's emotion processing: Relations to emotionality and aggression. *Development and Psychopathology, 16*, 371–387.

Seeman, J. (1983). *Personality integration: Studies and reflections*. New York: Human Sciences Press.

Seligman, M. E. P. (2002). *Authentic happiness*. New York: Free Press.

Sesma, H. W., & Georgieff, M. K. (2003). The effect of adverse intrauterine and newborn environmental on cognitive development: The experiences o premature delivery and diabetes during pregnancy. *Development and Psychopathology, 15*, 991–1015.

Siegal, D. J. (1999). *The developing mind: Toward a neurobiology of interpersonal experience*. New York: The Guilford Press.

Shephard, P. (1998) *Coming home to the Pleistocene*. Washington, DC: Island Press.

Silk, J., Nath, S., Siegel, L., & Kendall, P. (2000). Conceptualizing mental disorders in children: Where have we been and where are we going? *Development and Psychopathology, 12*, 713–735.

Simpson, J. A. (1999). Attachment theory in modern evolutionary perspective. In J. Cassidy & P. R. Shaver (Eds.), *Handbook of attachment theory, research and clinical applications* (pp. 115–140). New York: The Guilford Press.

Singer, D., & Singer, J. (1990) *The house of make-believe: Children's play and the developing imagination*. Cambridge, Massachusetts: Harvard University Press.

Sober, E., & Wilson, D. S. (1998). *Unto others: the evolution and psychology of unselfish behavior*. Cambridge, MA: Harvard University Press.

Solter, A. (1984). *The aware baby: A new approach to parenting*. Goleta, CA: Shining Star Press.

Sroufe, A. L. (1988). The role of infant-caregiver attachment in development. In J. Belsky and T. Nezworski (Eds.), *Clinical implications of attachment* (pp. 18–38). Hillsdale, NJ: Lawrence Erlbaum Associates.

Sroufe, A. L. (1990). Pathways to adaption and maladaption: Psychopathology as developmental deviation. In D. Cicchetti & S. L. Toth (Eds.), *Rochester symposium on developmental psychopathology series vol. 1* (pp 13–40). Rochester, NY: University of Rochester Press.

Sroufe, A. L. (1997). *Emotional development: The organization of emotional life in the early years.* Cambridge: Cambridge University Press.

Starr, C., & Taggart, R. (1992). *Biology: The unity and diversity of life* (6th ed.). Belmont, CA: Wadsworth Publishing Company, Inc.

Stern, D. N. (1985). *The interpersonal world of the infant: A view from psychoanalysis and developmental psychology.* New York: Basic Books, Inc.

Stillwell, B. M., Galvin, M., Kopta, S. M., Padgett, R. J., & Holt, J. W. (1997). Moralization of attachment: A fourth domain of conscience functioning. *Journal of the American Academy of Child Adolescent Psychiatry, 36,* 1140–1147.

Striano, T. (2004). Direction of regard and the still-face effect in the first year: Does intention matter? *Child Development, 75*(2), 468–479.

Sussman, E. J., Schmeelk, K. H., Ponirakis, A., & Gariepy, J. L. (2001) Maternal, prenatal, postpartum, and concurrent stressors and temperament in 3 year-olds: A person and variable analysis. *Development and Psychopathology, 13,* 629–652.

Thompson, R. A. (2000). Early attachment and later development. In J. Cassidy & P. R. Shaver (Eds.), *Handbook of attachment theory, research and clinical applications* (pp. 265–286). New York: The Guilford Press.

Thompson, R. A., & Raikes, H. A. (2003). Toward the next quarter-century: Conceptual and methodological challenges for attachment theory. *Development and Psychopathology, 15,* 691–718.

Trevarthan, C., & Aitken, K. J. (1994). Brain development, infant communication, and empathy disorders: Intrinsic factors in child mental health. *Development and Psychopathology, 6,* 597–633.

Tronick, E. A., Als, H., Adamson, L., Wise, S., & Brazelton, T. B. (1978). The infant's response to entrapment between contradictory messages in face-to-face interaction. *Journal of the American Academy of Child Psychiatry, 16,* 1–13.

Waddington, C. H. (1957). *The strategy of genes.* London: Allen & Unwin.

Werner, E. E., & Smith, R. S. (1986). *Kauai's children come of age.* Honolulu: University of Hawaii Press.

West, M. L., & Sheldon-Keller, A. E. (1994). *Patterns of relating: An adult attachment perspective.* New York: The Guilford Press.

Winnicott, D. W. (1965). *The Maturational Process and the Facilitating Environment.* New York: International Universities Press.

Wolf, D. A., & McGee, R. (1994) Dimensions of child maltreatment and their relationship to adolescent adjustment. *Development and Psychopathology, 6,* 165–181.

Wynne, C. D. L. (2004). *Do animals think?* Princeton, NJ: Princeton University Press.

Zeanah, C. H., Boris, N. W., & Lieberman, A. F. (2000). In A. J. Sameroff, M. Lewis, & S. M. Miller (Eds.), *Handbook of developmental psychopathology* (2nd ed., pp. 293–307). New York: Kluwer Academic/Plenum Publishers.

Zeanah, C. H., Mammen, O. K., & Lieberman, A. F. (1993). Disorders of attachment. In C. H. Zeanah, Jr. (Ed.), *Handbook of infant mental health* (pp. 332–349). New York: The Guilford Press.

Zeanah, C. H., Nelson, C. A., Fox, N. A., Smyke, A. T., Marshall, P., Parker, S. W., et al. (2003). Designing research to study the effects of institutionalization on brain and behavioral development: The Bucharest Early Intervention Project. *Development and Psychopathology, 15,* 885–907.

Zeanah, C. H., & Scheeringa, M. S. (1997). The experience and effects of violence in infancy. In J. D. Osofsky (Ed.), *Children in a violent society* (pp. 97–123). New York: The Guilford Press.

Law Enforcement Perspectives and Obligations Related to Animal Abuse

Lt. Sherry Schlueter

Who is responsible for the investigation of animal cruelty complaints? Is this a task law enforcement officers are expected or required to perform? If so, why is it so hard for law enforcement officers to do it? If it is not a police function, then whom should you call? And what can you do when everybody ignores your complaints and nobody is helping the animals? In this chapter, I will share my decades of experiences as a law enforcement professional dedicated to the protection of animals and vulnerable people. I will challenge perspectives that are obstacles to helping protect animals and their rights and that promote the effective enforcement of animal cruelty laws. Finally, I offer recommendations for fostering more humane community standards and guidelines for investigating crimes against animals.

Background

Written declarations of protection for animals have existed since the Puritans of the Massachusetts Bay Colony voted into their first legal code "The Body of Liberties" in 1641. Liberty No. 92 intended to prohibit any man from committing tyranny or cruel treatment to any animal usually kept for man's use, and was the first such law anywhere in the world. It was followed by Liberty No. 93, another first, intended to address treatment of animals being moved from place to place. It required cattle being led or driven a distance sufficient to cause them fatigue, illness, lameness, or hunger to be rested and refreshed (see *Cruelty Indivisible* by Unti, this text). These legal codes were progressive at a time when there were no common law protections afforded animals, and because animals were not generally thought of as beings worthy of concern as individuals, but were considered to be property of persons. So many centuries later, such uncharitable and ego-

centric views persist, coloring attitudes and perceptions that affect content and enforcement of law (Leavitt & Halverson, 1990, Chapter 1).

The United States of America became the first country in the world to formally legislate animal protection laws when New York enacted the first anti-cruelty statute in 1828. Every other U.S. state eventually followed, including the U.S. territory of the Virgin Islands, last, in 1921. However, just as incentives for passage of the legal code by the Puritans had religious undertones that included a desire to reduce the nuisance aspect of animal abuse and its resulting offense to the sensibilities of the citizens, current laws are not always about altruism toward animals, either. Some laws demonstrate a clear design to protect the "property rights" of "owners," not the animal victims themselves. Others are crafted to discourage interference with animal-based enterprises, or some other financially motivated endeavor cloaked under the guise of animal protection.

The good news is that one need only to look at animal protection laws in most progressive countries today to find that codified anti-cruelty measures applicable to many of the animal species living within do exist. These protections provide varying degrees of benefit to animals if well enforced. And therein lies the rub. In most places, including the United States, the issue is less about whether good laws exist to protect animals than about indifference toward these victims. Anemic community standards, underreporting of these crimes, delayed or non-existent investigations, and negligent enforcement efforts by authorities responsible for upholding such laws are what leave many animals in chronic jeopardy, states of suffering, and subject to cruel death.

Hence the focus of this chapter—law enforcement perspectives and obligations—is precisely those things, often influenced by the attitudes, expectations, and mandates of society, that determine which victims and what crimes receive attention and who and what get ignored. Dissatisfaction with the status quo led me to an unexpected career choice to try to change it.

A Personal Journey

I became a law enforcement professional when barely out of my teens. The decision stemmed from my experiences during the several years prior, while volunteering for the Humane Society of Broward County, Inc., in Fort Lauderdale, Florida, where I grew up. My volunteerism was focused on animal abuse and neglect issues, and I reported my concerns and observations to the appointed cruelty investigator. It was my youthful expectation that some positive difference in the lives of the animals involved would result. But I found myself constantly disappointed when nothing seemed to change for the better, so I began to initiate informal investigations on my own without the benefit of any authority, training, or enforcement powers. In February 1973, my unofficial efforts paid off when the Humane Society hired me to assume the humane agent position. Limited arrest powers and confiscation authority accompanied my successful statutory appointment by a circuit court judge.

Choices and experiences in youth proved to be good preparation for the challenges of the investigations that lay ahead. Summer vacations from junior and senior high school spent working with small-animal and large-animal veterinarians (with my sister, Shelly Schlueter, who became a most skillful and gifted wildlife rehabilitator), and a childhood enriched by the companionship of horses, cows, dogs, cats, various birds, turtles, rabbits, and sundry other rescued or adopted beings, provided useful knowledge about a wide variety of species. This advantage helped to qualify me for the judicial appointment and to establish credibility at an early age and stage in my professional life.

I knew from my several years of unofficial inquiries into animal abuse and neglect cases that the better the investigation, the better the case outcome. Skillful, lawful, objective investigations were the tool best suited to legally get suffering animals permanently out of jeopardy and into a better life. I learned everything I could about conducting quality criminal investigations, speaking frequently with experienced prosecutors, including the Broward State Attorney. They were helpful and appreciative

of my determination to approach these cases from a professional, rather than emotional, perspective. I met with many judges as well, most of whom were animal-friendly individuals, though there had not yet been much activity regarding animal cruelty cases in their courts. In fact, there had never been any jail time imposed in Broward County at that time for such offenses.

Though there was little available in the early 1970s, I read everything I could find about conducting animal cruelty investigations, and studied Florida law and U.S. constitutional law as suggested by the prosecutors. Without the benefit of formal training, but with an abundance of passion, energy, and resolve to improve the lives and safety of animals, my formal career began.

I worked for nearly 7 years in that capacity, but was routinely frustrated by the limitations of authority and the resultant need to call police officers or deputy sheriffs to crime scenes when prosecution was anticipated, backup help needed, or a search warrant indicated. I learned quickly that most "cops" knew little or nothing about existing statutes to protect animals, and that most had little interest in enforcing them. Procedurally, they were often less knowledgeable than I, and for the most part, far less motivated to expend much effort, as these non-human victims were not the priority to most officers that I saw them to be. There were always obstacles in filing cases with some prosecutors to whom these crimes and victims seemed invisible. Even the judiciary was a disappointment sometimes—there were judges who, no matter how compelling the case or evidence against the defendant, were reluctant to impose a criminal record on a perpetrator of "just animal abuse."

I decided that the solution to my position limitations was to become a deputy sheriff. I wanted to create the first animal-cruelty-specific unit within a law enforcement agency exclusively committed to conducting investigations of crimes against animals. I proposed this idea to the sheriff of Broward County, Robert Butterworth, a progressive-thinking former prosecutor and judge. As my work regularly received generous news media coverage and vocal support from the community, Sheriff Butterworth recognized the value of such an endeavor and hired me. I entered the Broward Police Academy in late 1979. After graduation in early 1980, I worked in a uniform road patrol capacity for 2 years, waiting for the opportunity to start the special unit. I continued to conduct animal abuse investigations daily on my off-duty hours, before or after working my regular patrol shift. In early 1982, I became a detective and was allowed to finally create the Animal Cruelty Investigations Unit.

It was a one-person investigative unit. I worked alone, even after earning promotion to sergeant in 1986. In mid-1987, two detective positions were finally added to the unit, confirming its worth to the agency and successful impact on the community. Over the years, the unit morphed intentionally several times to include agricultural crimes, criminal code violations, and the like, and I simultaneously performed supervisory duties for multiple other diverse units. Finally, in 1995, the Criminal Investigations Division (central detective bureau) agreed to allow me to modify the unit significantly to include crimes against vulnerable persons, after many years of demonstrating to the agency's upper echelon the similarities between the abuse, neglect, and exploitation of animals, children and the elderly. Each increase in the unit's scope helped attain greater credibility for the animal-crimes aspect, as it linked these investigations on an equal basis with crimes against vulnerable persons.

In 2000, upon promotion to lieutenant, a career-long goal was achieved with the creation of the Special Victims and Family Crimes Section, a crimes-against-persons-based section of the Sheriff's felony detective division (Regional Criminal Investigations Division). The Special Victims and Family Crimes Section was designed to effectively connect under one investigative umbrella all of the specialized units dealing primarily with crimes that stem from dysfunction within a family, and that result in inter-personal violence. My purpose was to provide a more comprehensive and holistic approach to these crimes, recognizing the obvious correlations between crimes against animals and crimes against persons, especially intra-familial-based crimes. The Special Victims and Family Crimes Section, therefore, is composed of the Abuse and Neglect Unit (abuse; neglect; and exploitation of animals, children, the elderly, and the disabled), as well as the Sex Crimes Unit, Missing Persons Unit, the Domestic Violence Unit, and the Victim Services Unit.

Many successes and disappointments have accompanied the hard-won transitions from circuit court–appointed investigative humane agent to Sheriff's lieutenant of detectives. There have been constant struggles and career progress-stymieing professional biases and prejudices endured due to my focus on animals, especially in the early years. It has never completely abated. Brothers and sisters in law enforcement sometimes lack appreciation for the need to address responsibly and with equal professionalism given other offenses, crimes against animal victims. The progressive work of the Federal Bureau of Investigation's Behavioral Sciences Unit in the 1970s and 1980s in studying and sharing chilling histories of animal torture and killing among dangerous, violent offenders (Lockwood & Church, 1996; Lockwood & Hodge, 1986) finally helped to capture the attention of people from a number of professional disciplines. The dedicated empirical work of the many individuals and organizations that followed provided more than anecdotal information of such connections, making progress within skeptical professions possible. As a result, it has become easier to convince those who do not care about animals as victims to at least give some consideration to the crime of animal cruelty—if only for the insight it may yield about the offender's possible capacity to commit human interpersonal violence (Lockwood & Ascione, 1998, Section 5, Criminology).

Perspectives

The following law enforcement perspectives about which I am most critical are certainly not universally held, as there are a great many compassionate, caring professional law enforcers who do take seriously crimes against animals. Their rewards have probably often been similar to mine—to risk the wrath of supervisors and the ridicule of colleagues, all for doing the right thing for animals and for the bravely insistent, complaining public who cares about them. But in my own experience, the following perspectives seem to be pervasive among the majority of law enforcement types whom I have encountered or heard about over my lifetime of work in this field. Readers of this Handbook may help to tip the scales in favor of animals through greater understanding of these issues, and by your demands for better performance from those who have the duty and the power to protect vulnerable others from those who would illegally harm, neglect, or kill them.

No Responsibility

Many law enforcement agencies and agents do not acknowledge that crimes against animals are within their sphere of responsibility to investigate and properly resolve. Additionally, most make no effort to ever try to prevent such crimes, although crime prevention should be an important goal of all enforcement agencies. These cases are, of course, within law enforcement purview by virtue of their status as criminal offenses. Just as age, race, sex, socio-economic status, religious affiliation, or any other "category" within which a human victim may be classified should not come into play when responding to a call for service, the victim's species should not be a factor in deciding the worth of a victim. In many communities in which animal sheltering or control organizations exist, however, police and deputies routinely absolve themselves of understood responsibility by relegating the matters to these primarily civilian animal-caring organizations. This is an unfair burden to place on those who may have neither sufficient training, funding, resources, nor even authority to assume such important tasks.

Even in communities where the law enforcement agencies and the animal entities have agreed to the separate assumption of functions, there should still be a shared responsibility for outcome. But in so many jurisdictions, even if police respond, they assume a secondary "assist-other-agency" role when called for help on a crime scene. Law enforcement professionals should rightfully take the lead in such matters, as they enjoy the power, authority, armed status, and training advantages many civilian investigators do not.

This pattern is also often seen in crimes against vulnerable persons, when civilian child or adult protective investigators from family services–type organizations call police for assistance. If the matter is criminal, regardless of whom the victim may be, the cops should assume the lead on the investigation of the crime. The humane investigator, or child or adult protective investigator, should handle his or her own investigative responsibilities connected to risk assessment, social services concerns, and transport and safe placement of the victim. Each should share his or her expertise and work together to improve the outcome. But routinely one will see law enforcers view their purpose as "standing by"—ostensibly to protect the civilian investigator in a sort of peacekeeper role only. That a cop would essentially abdicate his or her authority on a crime scene to a civilian has always surprised me. Though I understand that there is often an agreement in place concerning these crime-specific cases based on an expectation that the specialist has more expertise in the matter than the patrol officer, if a crime has been established, law enforcement officers should assume the lead in the criminal aspect of the investigation.

The expert civilians should address their own investigative and services-provision functions. In this way, the investigation will be a team effort with each responsible for and fulfilling his or her agency's own important, specialized roles.

Low-Priority Crime

Most agencies consider crimes-against-animals complaints to be low-priority calls, regardless of whether they are in-progress crimes, and no matter how violent. This is a mistake (Lockwood, 1989). Although it is common for humans to consider any crime against their own species to be of greater import than those against other species, this, too, is a mistake for reasons not the least of which is the biased attitude it conveys. Animal-related offenses may be higher crimes than other competing calls (felony versus misdemeanor; aggravated felony versus felony, etc.), may be crimes-in-progress calls (and thus likelier solved than a delayed call), and may be types of crimes considered predictive in nature. If one pays attention to such crimes occurring particularly in a dysfunctional intra-familial setting or in conjunction with other destructive behaviors, future animal abuse or neglect, as well as similar crimes against vulnerable human members of the household, may become potentially preventable if proper interventions are put into place.

If one looks objectively at them, many types of offenses targeting animals are no different than those targeting humans, and are often perpetrated by the same offenders for both. This can happen within the family or the target can be other vulnerable human or non-human beings outside of the family. Regardless, common sense would suggest that an escalation of any violence by a perpetrator creates heightened jeopardy for others under the control of, or in proximity to, the violent offender. In an effort to prevent or reduce crime and protect vulnerable others, authorities should consider such circumstances when assessing danger, risk, and even lethality potentials.

For people who care about animals as victims, I need not justify the necessity of a timely, dedicated response to any alleged abuse or neglect of an animal. For us anything less would be unthinkable. For those less concerned about animal citizens, it is important to point out that when animals are protected by law, it is the duty of law enforcers to investigate violations and to try to resolve these matters in the best interest of the victims. Officers should review their own oath of office, their own agency's mission statement, and other guiding principles to confirm this. I would be surprised if most did not discover that these responsibilities are not species specific. Law enforcers have little legal justification to decide which victims matter and which laws they choose to enforce, though many agencies will defend such positions by trotting out the "resources constraints" excuse. One's sworn duty, however, usually requires enforcement of laws—not just some of them, and protection of victims—not just the ones an individual or agency deems worthy. That should be at the heart of everything for which we stand.

Investigators considering prioritization of animal complaints would also do their human victims much good by familiarizing themselves with the abundance of anecdotal and empirical information that discusses demonstrated connections between crimes against animals and humans. It has helped me and others to gain insight into the psyche of people being investigated, and to potentially predict and therefore prevent in some cases, future criminal actions against a variety of possible victims.

Requires Specialist

There is little argument that most investigative specialists have more experience, knowledge about, and perhaps interest in the issues on which they focus than might a generalist. However, it is not true that expertise about the crime to be investigated is required or even necessary to be effective. Most animal abuse or neglect complaints can be satisfactorily resolved by an investigator who takes an interest in trying to determine whether a crime is occurring (or did occur), whether the victim is in foreseeable present or future jeopardy, and what the best course of action on behalf of the victim will be needed to resolve it. Does the animal in question have adequate amounts of nourishing food and potable water and access to necessary shelter? Is the animal provided frequent, positive social interactions, wholesome exercise, and space and opportunity for normal postural changes? Is he or she free from obvious signs or symptoms of physical abuse, psychological abuse, and medical or other neglect? Is the animal's environment reasonably clean, free of dangerous debris, and comfortable? Does he or she appear to be at immediate risk of harm, suffering, or cruel death?

In most situations, these are observable conditions and circumstances a relative novice could determine by visual inspection, discover through appropriate questioning, and confirm through follow-up measures. When one considers that law enforcement professionals have usually attended and graduated from a law enforcement academy or comparable formal instruction covering general, as well as some specialized, investigative training, it is hard to insist that only a "specialist" could work these cases. Is it preferable? Yes. Is it necessary? No. In fact, this holds true for most crimes.

Patrol-level uniformed officers conduct most initial investigations as the law enforcement agency's "first responder"—everything from a noisy party complaint to a multiple-victims homicide call. Once the initial investigation has established a need, a detective might be immediately summoned, or assigned after supervisory review of the circumstances. Either response would ordinarily follow the patrol officer's assessment and handling of the situation as best as he or she is able from a patrol-level capacity. Detectives are generally reserved for more complex cases requiring a lengthier investigation, when there is a complicated crime scene, or when multiple sworn statements need to be taken from suspects, victims, or witnesses. A detective would be preferred, as well, when search warrants or perhaps covert surveillance are needed, or more specialized knowledge, experience, or equipment indicated. Most animal abuse or neglect cases troubling society can be resolved at the road patrol level if investigated when issues first arise (e.g., dog without water, rabbit in cage without protection from the elements, skinny horses in a pasture, overcrowded animals in a pet shop). If addressed early on, corrective measures can be imposed to rectify the situation without the matter becoming complicated and without the animal victim continuing to suffer or becoming debilitated. If ignored until the animal is emaciated, severely compromised, or dead, the complexity of the case is heightened for the investigators. Worse, the victim, who should never have been left to suffer and decline to a serious degree, now may pay with his or her life. That is inexcusable.

No Real Victim

This is one of the most arrogant, biased positions an investigator can take. It reveals a lack of acknowledgment of the sentiency of the victim, an indifference to the effect the situation has on the complainant, and disregards the jurisdiction's standards and interest in protecting the well-being of society. For those unaware, it should be understood that usually the state/county/city or other body that enacted the law is the technical victim in an animal-based crime—the government represents the interests of the animal, as it is that government's criminal state statute (or county or municipal ordinance or code, etc.) that was violated. Even in criminal cases involving human victims, though the victimized person's name will appear in the "Victim" section of the police incident or investigative report documenting the matter, when the case is successfully filed, it is the government entity's name that appears on documents connected to the case, such as a subpoena. And it is the government entity's attorney (prosecutor) that represents its own, and thus the victim's, position. For example: *State of Michigan vs. John. M. Smith* (defendant), even though Mary Smith is the actual victim of the domestic abuse. Therefore, in a police or other incident report in which a non-human is the injured, dead, or suffering party, the Victim section might simply read, *State of Florida*, or, *Florida, State of, To Wit: one adult mixed-breed dog, "Jasper,"* or *City of Fort Lauderdale*, and other similar variations.

No Impact on Society

The lack of awareness such a position suggests is surprising under any circumstance, but appalling in the 21st century. With empirical and anecdotal examples that illuminate correlations that often exist between intentional animal cruelty and human interpersonal violence, such ignorance on the part of law enforcers is baffling (Ascione, 2001, 2005; Ascione & Arkow, 1999; Lockwood & Ascione, 1998). And with empathy, sympathy, and compassion for others at the very heart of civilized behavior, one would be a fool not to consider exposure to such violence to be at least potentially desensitizing, especially when segments of many cultures seem accepting of it. I believe that when needless cruelty, violence, and death are perpetrated upon the innocent, society suffers considerably both literally and figuratively.

For those indifferent to the plight of animal victims, it is important to recognize the psychological distress human complainants of these crimes often experience. Anguish, a sense of helplessness, and feelings of indignation, anger, worry, and fear are just some of the unpleasant emotions evoked when people of compassion and empathy witness or are otherwise exposed to animal suffering (Ascione, 2005). I have always considered such persons to be secondary victims of sort, much as we consider surviving loved ones of persons who commit suicide or who are victims of homicide to be secondary vic-

tims. Witnesses exposed to violence, suffering, or death who are not the targeted victim are often in as much need of crisis interventions as the primary (actual) victims.

No Budget

It is a rare and fortunate agency that enjoys adequate funding and other resources to carry out all aspects of its mission in comfort. The truth is, most entities, governmental as well as private, have resource limitations. Most must limit the scope of their preferred mission and activities to remain fiscally afloat. This is understandable. What are not acceptable, however, are decisions about priorities based upon faulty and or biased thinking. This is especially true in the profession of law enforcement, where the focus should be on protecting society's *most* vulnerable members *first*. No budget for animal abuse investigations? One doesn't need a separate budget for these crimes. Assign the cases to appropriate personnel for investigation as with any other crime. Expenses incurred during the investigations, such as for confiscation of animals (medical exam, board and care), can fall under the same budgetary category as do investigative expenses for other crimes (the dry-docking of a drug smuggler's confiscated boat, having a vehicular homicide suspect's car towed and stored, or paying a company to research and copy medical records on a crimes-against-persons case). Yes, it costs money to investigate these cases, the same as is true of any other criminal investigation.

If an agency is concerned about fiduciary responsibilities, it should pay attention to these complaints from the beginning. This may reduce annoying and costly repeat calls for service, help to prevent future, more complex crimes against at-risk persons and animals, and save someone, human or non-human, from needless pain and suffering. Any one of these beneficial outcomes will also likely save taxpayer dollars, something to which no one would object and that should help the agency in multiple ways in the long run.

Only Felonies Matter

It has long been my opinion that if agencies would take seriously and work enthusiastically complaints of a minor nature, most matters would never have the chance to rise to a felony (serious) level. This thinking was used as part of the strategy when creating my Special Victims and Family Crimes Section. It is similar to the progressive approach used in our agency-wide domestic violence program. The tactic involves comprehensive investigation of misdemeanor-level domestic (spouse/partner) abuse. Broward sheriff's deputies are required by policy (Sheriff's Policy Manual) to effect an arrest if sufficient probable cause to do so exists; to take photographs of even minor injuries; to obtain sworn tape-recorded statements on scene, if possible (preferably when the parties are most inclined to cooperate); to obtain the 911-dispatch call tape (tape-recorded call to the emergency telephone line of the law enforcement agency); and to send the completed case-filing investigative package to a domestic violence–specific prosecutor. Additionally, the victim must receive information on crime victims' rights and our agency also attempts to assign a victim advocate or to otherwise connect the victim to services that may be of benefit. It is believed that if this is done consistently as an aggressive standard policy or operational procedure, one will eventually see a decline in felony-level domestic cases involving these families. The tracking of repeat calls for law enforcement and even other public services (paramedics, firefighters) by geographic location, as well as by names of victims and offenders, can also be beneficial in getting important interventions into place where the need is greatest and the most good can be done (see *Counting Cruelty* by Lockwood, this text).

Nip it early on. This tactic works equally well on many other criminal matters (see *Counting Cruelty* by Lockwood, this text). What is important to recognize is that if domestic calls of a minor (misdemeanor) nature are handled seriously and professionally, with appropriate interventions put into place to educate victims and to offer batterers an opportunity to address productively the issues that have led them to harm those they are supposed to love and protect, perhaps the occurrence of felony-level domestic violence could be reduced. The same holds true for child abuse, elder abuse, and animal cruelty. Address it productively while still minor in nature, and in some cases it may never escalate to a felony level. Crime reduction. Crime prevention. Both are legitimate and preferred methods of policing in a modern, forward-thinking society. Smart law enforcers know this and practice it.

No Public Support/Waste of Resources

As one who experienced much public and media support, the benefits of which always extended to my agency and its successive sheriffs, it is my conclusion that people generally care about animals and their well-being. Even those who don't seek the companionship of animals usually want to see them treated fairly by others. I found it to be a rare individual who would criticize the use of law enforcement resources to help animals. In fact, I have seen public criticism more likely to surface when no one will do anything about reported animal abuse or neglect. Officers and agencies that do extend themselves to protect animals are often regarded as heroes by their citizenry, and may find it difficult to escape the positive attention of the news media eager to cover stories of interest to the majority of their readers, listeners, or viewers.

No Crime Prevention Value

My own experience has convinced me that early intervention, including education, often results in crime reduction or prevention. My experience also convinces me that intentional animal cruelty is often present where one also sees other dysfunction and violence within a family. I know from over 34 years of work in this profession that neighbors are often more inclined to report animal cruelty than other forms of suspected family violence. This is even true of other victims. Intimate partners or children of batterers who remain silent about their own victimization sometimes will report or talk about threats or violence targeting beloved animals. There are many reasons for this, but in this context it is a reminder that authorities should and must make a committed effort to respond to reported or suspected animal crimes. Doing so should benefit the animal victim and potentially any vulnerable humans under the control of the offender, if appropriate interventions and follow-up measures are put into place. The earlier this is accomplished, the better the crime reduction and crime prevention value (Ascione & Arkow, 1999).

It should not be overlooked that there are also crime detection opportunities afforded officers clever enough to use them. Many savvy suspects successfully thwart law enforcement access to their various criminal enterprises by concealing activities using foliage, fences, buildings, surveillance equipment, guard dogs, and so forth. When criminal activity is suspected, officers are often unable to adequately develop or demonstrate necessary *probable cause* to obtain search warrants or arrest warrants, because they have had no lawful access to the person or property in question. But many serious offenders keep dogs or other animals for protection ("attack dogs") or as personal companions, and certainly as "alarm systems." Animals can also be instrumentalities of crimes (game fowl, "fighting" dogs, etc.). Depending on the circumstances, officers can sometimes get on property or initiate contact with suspects under the authority to investigate animal issues, where they may not have been able to intrude otherwise. There are also opportunities to develop alliances with diverse enforcement agencies through advantageous use of animal welfare/animal cruelty laws. One might acquire intelligence on and evidence of other crimes that result in many beneficial outcomes. If such tactics are used, however, be sure to handle the animal issues used to gain access, both for the sake of the animals and to avoid legal and procedural challenges critical of the ploy.

Not Real Police Work

Being responsive to community concerns. Investigating complaints. Solving crimes. Arresting perpetrators. Bringing offenders to justice. Protecting society's vulnerable members. Reducing crime. Preventing crime. Detecting crime. These are exactly what real policing and good law enforcement are about. It is everything we do, and what we do best. Crimes are crimes. Victims are victims. Criminals are criminals. The species of the victim and the nature of the crime should not be determinants of what constitutes real law enforcement. The criminal actions and motivations of the perpetrator, the commission of a crime, and the victimization of an innocent should be.

Animals Are Property

At the time of this writing this is appallingly still true from a legal perspective (see *The Impact of Improved American Anti-Cruelty Laws* by Frasch, this text). But animals are also beings protected by law. The best laws don't excuse criminal behaviors based on the relationship or status of the perpetrator to the victim. Take child protection laws as an example. In some places, corporal punishment, which technically likely constitutes a crime (battery of the child), is usually permitted if imposed by a parent or guardian and if the purpose is solely disciplinary. But if the act becomes seriously injurious or excessive, or the motivation is one of retaliation, vindictiveness, or of a sadistic nature, the same act may then become criminal, and parents' or guardians' own children can be taken from them.

Society, through government or righteously indignant individuals, should protect animals from anyone who would unnecessarily or cruelly neglect, harm, or kill them—whether still considered property or not.

Law enforcers need to remember that just as it is not acceptable to excuse family violence with regressive rationalizations ("It's his wife—he can do what he wants," or "It's her child—we can't interfere"), it is equally wrong to excuse animal abusers because of their victims' unfortunate property status ("It's their cattle—they can starve them if they want," or "It's his dog, he can beat it if he wants"). If the laws or authorities in your community tolerate any of these defenses or positions, you need better laws and better law enforcers.

Obligations

The following suggested obligations are based on a presumption of the existence of enforceable laws and possession of sufficient authority to enforce them by those investigating crimes against animals. The international scope of this handbook presents challenges to discussion of specific police obligations. Law is an often imprecise rule of conduct subject to myriad interpretations and constant changes. Enforcement abilities affected by case-law decisions, jurisdictional issues, applicable policies and procedures, community standards, and societal and governmental priorities limit discussion of obligations to general concepts.

Know Your Laws

One of the first observations I made as a circuit court-appointed humane agent in the early 1970s was the utter ignorance of police officers and deputy sheriffs about the existence of state or even local laws that protected animals. In the hundreds of trainings of cops, animal control officers, and humane agents I have conducted since, and wherever I have traveled, this basic deficiency has held true. Most law enforcers don't know much at all about animal cruelty laws.

To be effective at their job, it is incumbent upon authorities to become at least familiar with the criminal laws they are expected to enforce. Otherwise they won't recognize crimes when they see them or be able to properly respond to complaints from the public about suspected violations. The onus is on officers, as well, to keep current about investigative and enforcement procedural issues, case-law decisions, and to know how to research that about which they are unfamiliar when working such cases (Lockwood, 1989).

It is imperative to understand terminology found in the laws and how such definitions will affect legal and investigative decisions. How the terms are defined—"animal," "owner," "cruelty," "neglect," "torture," "torment," "abandonment," "baiting and fighting," "overload," "overdrive," "necessary shelter," "unnecessarily cruel," etc.—must be understood to be effective. A firm grasp of search and seizure, rules of evidence, expectation of privacy, probable cause, and other critical procedural and federal constitutional issues will reduce chances of dooming a case because of mishandling. As important, such knowledge will minimize one's exposure to the serious legal consequences that haunt officers and their agencies when citizens' constitutional rights are trampled.

Be Objective

There is no place for bias or prejudice in the noble field of law enforcement. No matter our experiences, no matter our personal views—when investigating crimes, one must be fair and deal in facts. As earlier mentioned, the sex, race, nationality, social or economic status, occupation, ethnicity, religion, or species of any victim should not color one's attitude about response to or prioritization of a call for service. No justice can come from discriminatory attitudes or arrogant indifference. We are professionals who are legally bound to protect animals, people, property, and certain freedoms guaranteed by laws. To do so faithfully is our sworn duty.

Conduct Sound Investigations

Most investigations require certain basic steps to be taken to be able to draw truthful conclusions. These steps are rarely followed on animal crime cases, as officers either don't take seriously the need to work the cases for real, or they apply a different standard because they are on unfamiliar ground. Treat these as you would a crime-against-person investigation. If uncertain, mentally substitute a child or infirm adult as the victim, and follow a similar investigative pattern.

Talk to the complainant first, if possible. Canvass for witnesses. Establish the suspect's guardianship status (legal responsibility for the animals). Be observant and appropriately inquisitive. Be suspicious of answers that don't add up. Look at every animal on scene in the environment in which kept. Don't assume anything, and challenge and verify everything. Document your findings. Take photographs, tape recordings, or video recordings. Obtain sworn, recorded statements to lock in the testimony of everyone of value. Do a crime scene sketch, or call out your crime scene investigators for help in

processing the scene. Use search warrants where appropriate, and do everything else you would and should do on any other criminal investigation and crime scene.

If you are unfamiliar with the species with which you are dealing, it can be more challenging to know whether what you are observing is in the normal range or is criminal. Ask for help. There are animal-knowledgeable people in every community, most of whom would be flattered and eager to help. Species-specific expertise can come from veterinarians, civilian experts, or any credible person more knowledgeable than you. Most will come to your scene, if you can safely allow that, or can provide telephonic advice while you describe what you are observing.

Don't forget there are victims who may be in need of rescue and removal, whose bodies may yield valuable evidence, and who may remain in jeopardy from the suspect if not taken. Write property receipts documenting the animals you are confiscating. Make sure the seized victims receive an immediate medical examination and evaluation for evidentiary purposes, and are provided all required treatment and care.

Look objectively at every member of the household, regardless of which member is the reported victim or the reported perpetrator. That is one of the most import tasks of any investigation in which any form of abuse or neglect is alleged. Cross-report concerns if you don't possess the expertise or authority to handle that with which you are confronted or about which you are suspicious. Even investigators who fulfill their obligations to investigate reported crimes and to enforce laws often fail to recognize the importance of crime detection, reduction, and, most important, crime prevention.

Spend time on the scene to ask necessary questions and to probe beyond the superficial. Take a physical look at everyone in the household and responsibly assess observable circumstances and interpersonal dynamics. In many intra-familial crimes, the perpetrator may be someone other than the obvious choice, or there may be multiple perpetrators in the household. Likewise, if there is one victim, there are likely others. Trust your gut. Your instincts, training, and experience will help you to identify other at-risk family members or to discover those who are already victims about whom no one has yet reported. Your efforts on scene may make the difference in whether animals and people in that household lead lives of misery or lives of relative peace and comfort, free from the terror such jeopardy brings.

Don't be daunted by the prospect of conducting investigations regarding animal abuse or neglect. Though you may have received no specific training regarding crimes against animals, law enforcement professionals have received training in conducting investigations in general and probably some specific training in family crimes, especially domestic violence and child abuse investigations. Think in terms of what you should do and would do in any other criminal investigation. Animal abuse or neglect is a crime, and this is a criminal investigation. For some, it may be helpful to ask yourself, "What would I do if this victim were a child?" and then act accordingly. Likewise, humane or animal control officers should not be intimidated by the prospect of trying to evaluate jeopardy to human family members when encountering issues of concern. If you are competent to recognize cruelty, neglect, or abuse in animals other than your own species, you are certainly capable of recognizing at least the more obvious signs of the same in that of your own.

Resolve the Matter in the Best Interest of the Victim

Too often, law enforcers focus on the crime and the criminal, not on the victim. This is understandable, but reversed in importance and logic. If in doubt, consider the purpose of most laws. They are designed to protect innocent members of society. Think about your own training as law enforcement officers. What have you been told should be your priority if there is a critically wounded victim who needs immediate attention and you encounter his or her fleeing suspected perpetrator at the same time? Do you chase the bad guy, leaving the victim in crisis and vulnerable, or render aid first to the victim until relieved by someone competent? All aspects of policing and law enforcement are important, but none as important as the victims. So, regardless of pressure to generate impressive arrest statistics or an agency's focus on revenue-enhancing citation issuance, never lose sight about that which laws and enforcement agencies exist to accomplish. Victims come first. Look out for their best interests when deciding what actions to take or not to take. Ironically, in so many animal abuse and neglect cases, the suspect remains in the home, and the victim is hauled away, incarcerated behind bars, and often put to death. Or the suspect is cited, but the victim is left in the offending circumstances, probably to soon bear the brunt of the perpetrator's wrath your citation just ignited. Justice is not served in these instances, but perverted. Think about what is best for the victim, not what is expedient.

In considering options about whether to confiscate the animal or to try to achieve rectification of the problem and leave the animal on scene, consider:

Is the crime one of intent? If so, one should usually remove the victim and any other vulnerable or at-risk beings from the suspect at once. Delay could be disastrous, as the animals could be moved or hidden or destroyed before return. Stay on scene and wait for necessary help. Keep the perpetrator in view. If grounds exist for arrest, and there is no compelling legal reason to delay, do it then. If you need a search warrant to complete your mission, leave officers there to hold the scene while you prepare and obtain the warrant.

Was the crime committed due to ignorance? If so, determine whether the victim would ever be truly safe remaining there. For example, if a child threw kittens off of a roof, or put the hamster in the microwave, regardless of his or her level of understanding or intent to harm, no vulnerable being should be left there, including other animals, children, or infirm or disabled adults. (The interventions concerning such a dangerous and troubled child perpetrator are subjects for serious discussion in another forum by an appropriately qualified expert.) If a person, on the other hand, used minor poor judgment in a training method based upon bad advice from another, or didn't recognize signs of nutritional deficiencies or certain symptoms of illness because of unfamiliarity with the species and its needs, though you may well want to take appropriate legal action in response to any violation, it may not be necessary to remove the animal, unless its condition requires it or for evidentiary purposes, such as a medical examination to document an injury or illness. Whether or not to remove the victim in that circumstance would depend on the perpetrator's attitude toward the animal, the overall quality of the animal's life, and whether a sincere desire by the perpetrator to rectify the matter exists, and he or she could be trusted not to repeat that mistake or make others that would jeopardize the animal's safety and well being.

Was the crime committed as a result of financial constraints? If so, those circumstances must be carefully reviewed for determination of appropriate action. If, for example, the perpetrator lives on a fixed income, made efforts to try to get the animal veterinary care, and made whatever sacrifices to that end reasonably possible (offered items of value possessed as collateral; tried to borrow money from family or friends; offered to work off the bill), though the animal may need to be seized to receive the needed care, criminal sanctions against the caregiver may not be the best course of action. Regardless, ensure the victim gets what is needed. Then consider what is in his or her best interest, and act accordingly. If the choice is made to return the medically treated animal, remain available as a trusted resource the financially unable caregiver may call upon should the animal need help in the future. You can prevent much suffering and help a deserving person and his or her animal companion by such efforts.

If, on the other hand, the perpetrator uses low finances as a defense, but made no overt effort to secure help for the animal, proceed as you would on any criminal case and consider the animal at risk if returned to that situation.

Similarly, if you encounter a person suffering from a significant handicap or infirmity that limits his or her ability to perform certain necessary tasks to maintain an animal in good health and comfort, and this physical inability is the only reason the caregiver has allowed the animal to deteriorate (has become dirty, the hair coat is matted, nails have grown long, is not getting enough exercise) the investigator needs to determine what is in the animal's best interest and whether sanctions against the caregiver are warranted. Regardless, the animal needs help and cannot be left in such circumstances. The investigator may be able to find assistance for the caregiver through organizations or individuals that will make it possible for the animal to safely remain in the company of the caregiver, aided by others of greater physical ability who will perform necessary tasks to ensure the comfort and good health of the animal.

Where will the victim be safest? If confiscated, will he or she go to a better location than that from which taken? Some animal shelters and rescue environments are excellent. Unfortunately, in others the conditions are highly unsuitable. There may be contagious diseases present that could infect the victim. Some staff members may be ill-suited to perform compassionate work. The temperatures, lighting levels, unfamiliar sounds, smells, and noise levels in such facilities can be terrifying, overwhelming, and contraindicated for an already traumatized, debilitated victim. Do the very best you can to secure a safe, suitable environment for the victim's recovery and future. Contracting with private veterinary hospitals will help to ensure immediate, and therefore superior, evidentiary medical results in most

cases, as well as adequate environs for incapacitated and distressed animals. Twenty-four-hour access is essential—delay affects evidentiary value and validity, and further imperils the animal and the case.

If the removal is permanent, will the victim have a better future—a realistic opportunity for adoption to a kind and understanding caregiver and a safe, more enriched environment?

Is the victim a good candidate for adoption, or is it unsuitable or undesirable because of:

- age (geriatric)
- disability (severely psychologically damaged, or deaf and blind, or permanently non-ambulatory)
- serious medical conditions (contagious disease, cancer—is there a lack of funds sufficient to help the animal through recovery from severe debilitation)
- temperament (hyper-aggressive or withdrawn/fearful)

Does the victim have bonds with others who will be remaining on scene, or, if also confiscated, will likely be separated temporarily or permanently from one another? Do the very best you can to keep emotionally bonded animals together, just as one would strive to do for sibling children who have been removed from their home by authorities. Abused victims have suffered enough. Let's do our part to minimize trauma associated with our well-intentioned rescues and remedies.

Reduce and Prevent Crime Occurrence

To Serve and Protect—the motto and mission of so many agencies. What better way to accomplish this than to prevent crime from happening? It would be a rare individual who would not prefer to have been spared whatever unpleasantness or injury, regardless of how successful the investigative outcome. What community would rather measure the effectiveness of its policing agency by the number of crimes solved, as opposed to its crime reduction figures? Crime reduction spells real success. As mentioned in the previous section, early investigation of even minor animal abuse or neglect can often give one insight into the dynamics of the animal's family or psyche of the offender, if you just pay attention and remain alert and inquisitive. Such advantages offer opportunities for early intervention measures that may effectively reduce occurrence of future crimes against at-risk family members, including the animal victim. A mere direct encounter with a law enforcement officer often has a profound impact on a law violator or one contemplating such violations. One can optimistically suggest that the earlier such an encounter occurs, the better the chances he or she will deter from the questionable course of action, either because the educative effort or the intimidation factor was effective. Regardless, your mission is accomplished.

Recommendations

The following recommendations are offered to help officers make better decisions when working crimes-against-animals investigations, and to offer insight to civilians who rely on them to resolve matters of concern.

- If you work in a community that has low community standards for the keeping of animals, don't accept the "status quo" argument—"That's how we've always kept animals in our family/community." Nothing changes for the better until someone stands up for the weaker, the unheard, the powerless, and says, "This is not acceptable" and then does something to improve it. Look carefully at your laws—there may be more to work with there than you think, allowing you to flex your enforcement muscles for the good of your victims, agency, and community.
- When the matter of concern is not yet criminal, provide directives about changes you expect to see and give a specific time frame for improvement. Go back and recheck. Educate, guide, and encourage that the recommended changes be made. Remind citizens that you will keep coming back until circumstances improve. Most people don't want law enforcers coming to their property or workplace and will do whatever is necessary to avoid such contact. Be realistic in your recommendations, based on law, financial abilities, and reasonable standards. However, don't be afraid to challenge the norm—without such forward thinking and courage, change for the better would never occur.

   If, for example, the community standard is to leave farmed animals outside without access to protection from the elements, and your law doesn't require shelter, remind caregivers about the choices these species would have in nature and would likely avail themselves of if able. Remind caregivers of the financial investment in such animals, and of the economic gamble they take when conditions for the animals are substandard. Remind them these animals are owed at least as humane an existence as reasonably possible, considering that the caregivers' livelihoods depend on these animals and that they take everything that matters—freedom, choices, relationships, happiness, life—from them. Challenge people to be leaders in their communities by setting a better standard that others may emulate. Better care and more humane circumstances usually cost more to provide than substandard ones. Reward elevated behavior by providing some form of community recognition for the person or company that steps up to the challenge. Such considerations can make a huge difference in improving the lives of the many animals whose unfortunate existence is confined to those surroundings day after day.

   Don't forget to improve the deficient law. And if you are of the mind to do so, work to change the deficient ethics that allow such indefensible practices to ever exist. That is key to ending most of the suffering, pain, and death for the greatest number of animals.

- Law enforcement officers and concerned citizens can make a significant difference in the lives of domestic violence victims and their animals by recognizing that in many violent households, the batterer uses the beloved pets (or other dependant animals) as tools to control human family members. The batterer's threats toward, harm of, or even killing of the animals impacts the human victims' decisions about whether to flee abusive situations. Many are reluctant to leave and risk their own safety and that of their children when they realize the jeopardy their animals face if left behind. Most can barely locate safe shelters for themselves. Rarely would their animals be welcome there. Loyalty to and concern for their animals becomes a barrier to their own escape from violence. Cops and citizens who care about animals, children, or battered adults must help to ensure the availability of free, temporary safe housing for the animal members of the family. Getting such animals out before or simultaneous with the escape of the human members is an act of kindness that can be a significant factor in the emotional and physical well-being of animals, children, and victimized adults. (For information about starting a program or service, see Ascione, 2000, *Safe Havens for Pets: Guidelines for Programs Sheltering Pets for Women Who Are Battered*.)

- All law enforcement officers who make arrests and all correctional intake personnel or others in contact with arrested persons should make an effort to inquire of arrested persons, early on in the process, whether there are any dependant people (children, elders, or disabled persons) or animals left in the home, vehicle, warehouse, or other confined space for whom the arrested person is the sole or primary caregiver and provider of life necessities. Most arrested people who have small children home alone will reveal this information at the time of arrest, but not always. If the arrestee is very drunk or high on some mood-altering substance, he or she may not even remember such critical matters for some time. Others may be reluctant to say anything if there are already custody issues the new arrest may jeopardize or further complicate. Some remain mute, optimistic they will be released before any harm comes to their dependants.

    When the arrest occurs at the residence or another place where dependant family members are located, most officers take necessary steps to ensure the care of children or infirm, dependant adults in the home. However, in my experience, some officers do not make similar arrangements for dependant animals, or if they do anything, they call for the animal's removal by a government entity that may not hold the animal for the arrested person, effectively sealing the animal's fate. Less ethical officers seem to even enjoy making the loss of the animal part of the prisoner's "punishment" without regard for the traumatic and often life-ending ordeal created for the unfortunate animal who is perhaps the only innocent party of all involved.

I am aware of many occasions in which prisoners have tried to tell arresting officers of animals left at their small business, residence, or in a vehicle parked somewhere who will have no food, water, or ability to tend to their own needs in the absence of that caregiver. "Too bad you didn't think about that before you committed the crime" is an inexcusable attitude no law enforcement or correctional officer should ever display. Instead, arrangements should be made that will allow for the animal's needs to be met, and for his or her survival to be possible. I have found that if given the opportunity to participate in these arrangements and decisions, the prisoner will often come up with a reasonable solution that will be less work for the officer and provide a better outcome. Officers should remember that a certain liability attaches when he or she is made aware of dependant people or animals left in vulnerable circumstances when their primary caregiver is arrested. Should the officer not ensure reasonable arrangements are made, any suffering or death of that dependant may be attached to the officer and his or her agency. Remember that the arrested person is the only one society may have a right to punish. His or her family members, whether human or non-human, should not be part of that equation.

The tables turn, however, when it is the arrested person who fails to notify anyone about dependant others in need of care in his or her absence. As in the example above—a small child left alone, or an aged parent, or a pet about whom the prisoner tells no one—the responsibility for that deliberate omission is on the prisoner. Should any needless suffering or death come to the dependant, the prisoner should be charged with those crimes. Defeat the prisoner's likely defense that he or she told officers, but no one listened or acted. Make certain to ask the necessary questions, preferably both at the time of arrest and again at some point in the initial jail intake and/or orientation stages. It is best to get the process started early on, when there is sufficient time to make necessary arrangements before anyone has to suffer.

- Civilians who report animal abuse crimes that are ignored by investigators should know that as complainants or witnesses, they can go to the prosecutor's office (state attorney, district attorney, city attorney, etc.) of the jurisdiction in which the suspected crime is occurring. Try to meet with a case-filing prosecutor. Explain your suspicions, provide any evidence (photographs, tape recordings of the animal's cries during a beating, videotapes of the killing, veterinary exam results, etc.) and supply as much information as known about the suspect(s), other witnesses, and so forth. You may be able to swear out a complaint yourself, or the prosecutor may be able to initiate the law enforcement response you alone could not. Don't give up—you may be the victim's only voice and hope in the ordeal.

- I am aware that some of you, whether deputy sheriffs, police officers, or humane or animal control officers, live and work in very small or very rural communities where there may not even be an animal shelter, and where no money is allocated to provide services to animals, or perhaps to needy people for that matter. I am sympathetic to the frustrations you feel when you are unable to make the difference you desire because of these limitations. Know that anything and everything you do each day to intervene on behalf of innocent others and to encourage and educate people to improve the circumstances of those in their care does matter. That which you do is far better than doing nothing, and likely is making a much greater impact on lives than you will ever know. And for that, I gratefully salute you. You are somebody's hero every day.

- Below are some indicators of animal abuse, neglect, and cruelty that may be of use to investigators of these crimes:

  - **Animals in poor physical condition:** Low body weight, skinny, malnourished, emaciated, starving; dull-coated or dull-feathered; sores, loss of hair or feathers; dirty; matter in the eyes, nose; foul odor; excessive head shaking, scratching; depressed or lethargic; long or cracked hooves, long nails or beaks, long, broken, cracked, or missing teeth; cracked (turtle) shells, poor color of teeth, gums, coat, feathers, body (of fish).

  - **Animals excessively aggressive:** Lunging, snapping, snarling, growling; ears laid back; kicking; squawking.

  - **Animals excessively submissive:** Poor eye contact; head-shy; cowering; crawling, slinking; urinating; hiding; backing away.

  - **Inappropriate environment:** Excessive feces, urine present. Stall, cage, tank unclean. Marginal or no access to potable (drinking-quality) water, nourishing food, species-appropriate and weather-appropriate shelter; presence of odor, flies, maggots; exposed nails, sharp objects, live electrical wires, other dangerous conditions or objects present; no access to or limited diversions or "toys" (to reduce boredom, prevent depression, apathy); absence of (bird) perches of correct and varying sizes, placement, and numbers.

  - **Space, light, ventilation deficiencies:** Space too confining (doesn't allow comfortable sitting, standing, raising and lowering of head, turn-around and other normal postural changes); lack of wholesome exercise or exchange of air; over- or under-ventilated; long hours of darkness without light; long hours of light without quiet and darkness; lack of weather-appropriate shelter.

  - **Excessive numbers of animals for space and other resources:** *Private animal "hoarders"* (sometimes referred to as animal "collectors"). Example: Persons with about a dozen to hundreds of animals inside and/or outside of house—caged, tied, confined in bedrooms, bathrooms, in airline (transport) animal carriers, milk crates, etc., often identified as "rescued strays" by hoarder. *Also*, pet shops, farms, kennels, ranches, private breeders, or other animal-enterprise businesses where animals are considered commodities and are overcrowded and individual needs are not being met. Usually accompanied by filth, odor, and illness. Many "hoarders" are also responsible for the welfare of children or elders in their homes. Animal hoarders are surprisingly often connected to the professional human-caring and teaching fields (nurses, teachers, child or elder day care or home health care workers). Circumstances in hoarders' own homes should send up a "red flag" of alarm or concern regarding their other contacts with vulnerable people or animals outside of the home.

- **Cruel confinement:** Short tethering (tying); small cage, stall, or tank; tied on self-tightening chain or nylon "choker-type" collar; incompatible animals confined together or in close proximity; animals confined in hot cars; left in drafty or very cold or freezing locations; overloaded; overcrowded; left without shelter, access to food and/or water.

- **Lack of necessary medical care:** Sick, injured, or dying animals deprived of basic preventative and/or diagnostic care, required medical intervention, and pain-reducing measures; failure to euthanize (cause the humane death of) when medically indicated.

- **Species not permitted by zoning regulations:** Exotics, wildlife, farm mammals, or fowl in urban settings. (Potential for abusive confinement elevated due to attempts to hide or conceal the presence of the animal(s), including muffling of associated sounds. Often found in conjunction with ritual animal sacrifices.)

- **Evidence of ritualistic sacrifice:** Paraphernalia and accoutrements associated with Santeria, Voodoo, Satanism, etc. Also, species of animals used in ritual sacrifice are often not permitted in location (violate zoning laws, see above). Animals are often cruelly transported and cruelly confined and neglected prior to the ritual killing, which itself is generally done in a manner that causes suffering and does not attempt to minimize pain and suffering. (In some religions or cults, infliction of pain/suffering is a necessary element of the sacrifice and is the desired result. The "pursuit of religious freedom"—status *does not excuse or legalize* such cruelty, or any other violations of state laws.)

- **Poor general sanitation:** Urine, feces, filth, excessive clutter in house, yard. Poor personal hygiene of adults and/or children; animals and/or people dirty, malodorous; unbathed, ungroomed.

- **Evidence of animal baiting and fighting:** *Pit bull terrier* (and other types of) dogs confined separately from one another, bearing bite injuries, puncture wounds, or scars to heads, legs, faces, etc.; short-cropped ears, docked tails; or *male game fowl (roosters)* caged separately from one another, often denuded of feathers in chest, back, stomach, leg areas—spurs sharpened or removed to accommodate artificial spurs or gaffs to be attached. Birds may bear injuries (puncture wounds) to heads, eyes, faces, chests, etc. Often will find fighting pits/arenas, performance-enhancing drugs, herbs and vitamins, antibiotics, or other medications, agitation devices, endurance-building apparatuses, ledgers and/or journals, blood-sport magazines, fight or exhibition advertisements, photos, trophies, and so forth, on premises.

- **Financial inability:** Unable to afford animal food, veterinary care, or to meet other needs of animals. Often evident in association with human family members, as well, that is, bad teeth, untreated illnesses, no preventative care, minimal food, property in disrepair. Does not excuse neglectful practices, but compassionate nonpunitive remedies may be appropriate alternative to criminal intervention. All circumstances should be taken into account to achieve optimal outcome for animal and human family members.

- **Cruel or inappropriate "training" or "exercise" methods:** Animals tethered to treadmills. catmills, or hot-walkers to "build stamina"; or left clinging by the teeth off of or barely off of the ground to a tire or other device suspended from a rope or chain to "strengthen jaws"; or suspended with front legs off of the ground to punish; or thrown repeatedly into water, sometimes weighted down by a cement block or other weighted devise to swim or tread water for long periods of time; or forced to run alongside a bicycle, car, person on rollerblades or skateboard, or other moving vehicle to "build endurance." These are dangerous and unnecessarily cruel acts inconsistent with acceptable exercise or training of show, "working," performance, or any animals.

- **Absence of appropriate food for species kept on property:** Suggests animal(s) not fed regularly, or not fed species-appropriate, nourishing food in sufficient quantity. Circumstances often found in connection with absence of proper shelter, veterinary care, etc. Sometimes will find rotting produce, stale or molding breads/pastries obtained free from grocery stores as cheap inappropriate sources of feed for farmed animals, etc.

- **Bestiality:** Many states have no statute specifically prohibiting such aberrations (sexual act(s) by person upon or with an animal initiated by the person), but the physical and psychological suffering resulting from such exploitative and often injurious acts may qualify as a form of animal cruelty prosecutable under general animal cruelty statutes. Method(s) used to force animal to comply should be investigated, and evidence of injury to or suffering of the animal help to qualify the matter as abuse or cruelty, absent a specific law addressing such behavior (see *Bestiality and Zoophilia* by Beetz, this text).
- **Social isolation:** Animal(s) kept isolated from other animals or from human family members; ignored, left for long periods without attention, without inclusion or social contact. Results in depression, emotional distress, neuroses, extreme suffering, and ultimately the debilitation of health.
- **Excessive matting of hair coat:** Especially tangles found close to the skin causing pulling of skin, pain, irritation, sores and/or hair loss; or evidence of previous year's winter coat (heavier hair coat grown by the animal to protect against cold weather) present during later seasons (suggests no grooming or other skin/coat care).
- **Excessive loss of feathers:** Birds suffering excessive loss of feathers (beyond normal molting process) often associated with malnutrition, self-mutilation, and so forth. Causes should be investigated.
- **Inhumane transport:** On or within cars, trucks, trailers. Animals lack ability to make normal postural changes (turn around, sit, lie down without being trampled); standing or lying in urine or feces; overcrowding; conditions too hot or cold, no relief (excessively long travel without unloading, exercise, rest, food, water, and sleep).
- **Collars, harnesses, halters, bridles and bits, saddle cinches too tight or ill-fitting:** Causes acute and often chronic pain or injury.

  NOTE: Be alert especially for collars, ropes, or chains imbedded into the necks of tethered dogs or other animals, producing open necrotic flesh wounds accompanied by infection, foul odor, maggot infestation, etc. This is *not uncommon*. It most often occurs when a collar, halter, or harness is placed on a young animal who is still growing or gaining weight. Neglectful or indifferent people fail to notice or fail to intervene. Similarly, but usually with very specific intent to cause pain and suffering, rubber bands are placed around the necks or tails of animals—the device is almost undetectable (covered by hair), but very painful and injurious.

- **Parasite infestation:** *External*—fleas, ticks, mites, flies, other stinging/biting insects; *internal*—hookworms, roundworms, tapeworms, heartworms, etc. All are generally preventable and all cause unnecessary pain, suffering, illness, and sometimes even death.
- **Abandonment:** Short-term, long-term, or permanent desertion of animal; or failure to meet one's legal obligations for the support and care of the animal.
- **Human fascination with and/or enjoyment of live-feedings of mammals or small avian species to reptiles or exotics:** Creates potential for greater suffering of longer duration for the captive "prey" animal. Behavior of such people suggests lack of empathy and possible sadistic characteristics.
- **Evidence of dead animals, buried or unburied, on property:** Very likely especially with animal hoarders or poorly run animal-enterprise businesses, and abandonment situations. Check freezers, sheds, back rooms, etc.

References

Ascione, F. R. (2000). *Safe havens for pets: Guidelines for programs sheltering pets for women who are battered*. Logan, UT: Author.

Ascione, F. R. (2001). *Animal abuse and youth violence*. Bulletin. Washington, DC: U.S. Department of Justice, Office of Justice Programs, Office of Juvenile Justice and Delinquency Prevention.

Ascione, F. R. (2005). *Children and animals: Exploring the roots of kindness and cruelty*. West Lafayette, IN: Purdue University Press.

Ascione, F. R., & Arkow, P. (Eds.). (1999). *Child abuse, domestic violence, and animal abuse:*

Linking the circles of compassion for prevention and intervention. West Lafayette, IN: Purdue University Press.

Leavitt, E. S., & Halverson, D. (1990). *Animals and their legal rights, A survey of American laws from 1641 to 1990* (4th ed.). Washington, DC: AWI.

Lockwood, R. (1989). Cruelty to animals and human violence. Training Key No. 392. Arlington, VA: International Association of Police Chiefs.

Lockwood, R., & Ascione, F. R. (Eds.). (1998). *Cruelty to animals and interpersonal violence: Readings in research and application.* West Lafayette, IN: Purdue University Press.

Lockwood, R., and Church, A. (1996). Deadly serious: An FBI perspective on animal cruelty. *HSUS News (Fall)*, 1–4.

Lockwood, R., and Hodge, G. R. (1986). The tangled web of animal abuse: the links between cruelty to animals and human violence. *Humane Society News, Summer.*

Collaborating to Assess, Intervene, and Prosecute Animal Abuse: A Continuum of Protection for Children and Animals

Barbara W. Boat, Lynn Loar, and Allie Phillips

Introduction

Most mental health professionals, child protection workers, and prosecuting attorneys do not ask children or adults about their animal-related experiences or gather corroborating information about animal abuse (Bell, 2001; Nelson, 2001). This chapter provides a rationale for professionals working in each of these fields to assess for exposure to and perpetra-tion of animal abuse. In addition, we present specific assessment tools, describe the types of information that are most useful when collaborating across disciplines, and discuss how best to use this information in the respective practices of mental health, child protection, and prosecution. The Appendix contains the assessment tools referred to in the following vignette.

Case Scenario

Bobby is a 9-year-old Caucasian boy living with his mother and father and two younger siblings, a sister age 6 and a brother age 4, in a middle-class suburb. Bobby was referred by his pediatrician to psychologist Dr. Barbara Boat for a mental health assessment and counseling after Bobby presented with complaints of headaches and stomach aches. The pediatrician found no physiological cause for the child's complaints.

Bobby presented with a small cut over his right eye. Initially Bobby was reluctant to talk until Dr. Boat administered *The Childhood Trust Survey on Animal-Related Experiences*. Bobby revealed that there had been several pets in his family, including two dogs that lived outdoors and a suc-cession of cats. He added that "animal cops" had been to the house several times after complaints by neighbors about the treatment of the various animals. The first cat, a stray, arrived three years earlier. Bobby had formed a special attachment to this cat and named it Smokey, often seeking com-fort from the cat when his father yelled and was abusive. Bobby mentioned that the family pets hid whenever his father entered the room. Approxi-mately one year ago, Smokey defecated outside the litter box. Bobby's father then threw Smokey across the room. Smokey hit the wall, fell to the ground, and was unable to move. The father, still enraged, would not let anybody help Smokey. Later, when Bobby's mother made an effort to help Smokey, the father punched her in the ribs and then pulled a shotgun out from the gun cabinet in the family room and pointed it at her. Bobby said that his father was angrier than he had ever seen him. Smokey died 2 days later and Bobby did not know what happened to Smokey's body.

Two months later, the father bought a kitten for Bobby. The kitten was also scared of Bobby's father and ran away later that year. Another cat arrived but was run over by a car. Neither cat was special to Bobby. Bobby told Dr. Boat that if he loved something, his father would hurt it. Recently, the father showed Bobby how to shoot BBs at a stray cat that was hanging around the house, saying he was sick of cats and their fleas.

When asked about the cut over his eye, Bobby reluctantly disclosed that his father had thrown a plate in anger and when the plate shattered against the wall, a shard cut Bobby. Based on the concerning information obtained, Dr. Boat notified Child Protective Services (CPS).

Ms. Lynn Loar, a social worker at CPS, was assigned the case. Using the *Family-Based Risk Assessment* as a guide, Ms. Loar interviewed Bobby, his parents, and his teachers. Bobby's current teacher reported that he was alternately charming and angry, frequently complaining of psychosomatic ailments, and was twice stopped from roughly handling the classroom hamster. The teacher checked with Bobby's former teachers about abusive behavior toward pets and learned that Bobby had deliberately stepped on a gerbil in the second grade classroom.

Ms. Loar visited the home to assess risk. She substantiated the allegations of injury to the child, weapons in the home, the stray cat shot with BBs, and the poor condition of the two outdoor dogs. Ms. Loar urged the mother to call the police and report the domestic violence, and to call the municipal department of animal care and control to report the abuse of Smokey and the stray cats. The mother complied.

The police and animal control officer responded together. The father was arrested for domestic violence and cruelty to animals. During an interview with the arresting officers, the father denied killing or being abusive to Smokey or any other animal in the house, denied teaching Bobby how to shoot BBs at animals, and denied all abuse of Bobby and his wife.

Reports from all incidents were forwarded to prosecuting attorney Allie Phillips. Smokey's body was never located so a necropsy could not be performed. Attorney Phillips issued criminal charges for one count of felony child abuse, one count of felony domestic assault using a weapon, and one count of felony animal abuse causing the death of an animal. Attorney Phillips successfully used the *Pattern of Abusive Conduct* assessment to obtain convictions on all charges, including the killing of Smokey. Bobby, his siblings, and his mother are now at a safe and undisclosed family violence shelter.

The Mental Health Practitioner's Perspective

Mental health evaluators who work with children face two ongoing challenges. The first challenge is to gather as much relevant information as possible from the child in a timely, efficient, and effective way. The second challenge is to assess the child's risk for abuse or neglect and to design an effective intervention, which may necessitate using the services of a child protection agency and the courts. Most clinicians use a standard set of forms to gather data about the child client that covers a variety of symptoms and behaviors. Missing from this repertoire, however, is a systematic screening of the child for animal-related experiences. *The Childhood Trust Survey on Animal-Related Experiences* (Appendix A) provides a structured interview to complement existing assessment tools and elicit relevant information about exposure to and treatment of animals.

Reasons Why It Is Important in the Continuum of Protection for Children and Animals to Screen Routinely for the Child's Experiences With Animals

- Pets are part of the family. Nearly 75% of American families with school-age

children have at least one companion animal (Humane Society of the United States, 2004). Thus, mental health professionals who work with children will frequently encounter children who have had experiences with pets that share the child's family environment. Furthermore, in the United States, there is considerable monetary and emotional investment in a pet's welfare, reinforcing for a child that pets are considered to be part of the child's family. For example, in a recent survey of pet owners, 84% said they acquired their pet mainly for companionship, 83% referred to themselves as their pet's " mom" or "dad," 59% celebrated their pet's birthday, 90% would not consider dating someone who was not fond of their pet, and 52% believed their pet listened to them best, 93% were willing to risk their own life for their pet, and 53% were spending more on their pets now than they did 3 years ago (American Animal Hospital Association, 2004). A mental health professional who does not ask about animal-related experiences is missing potentially relevant information about a child's risk status.

- A second reason to inquire about the child's experiences with animals is that the behavior that harms the animal is the same behavior that harms the human.

From William Hogarth's *The First Stage of Cruelty*, illustrated in 1751 (Lindsay, 1979) to the FBI profiles of serial killers (Lockwood & Church, 1996), anecdotal and research evidence links acts of cruelty to animals with acts of cruelty to humans (Arkow, 1996; Felthous & Kellert, 1987; Kellert & Felthous, 1985). Research indicates that in homes where children are physically abused, pets are significantly more likely to be abused (DeViney, Dickert, & Lockwood, 1983). Furthermore, and importantly, inhabitants of these physically abusive homes were 10 times more likely to be bitten by the family dog. Mental health professionals should be aware of this important observation because currently, in the United States, dog bites to children ages 5 to 9 are determined to be a major public health problem (Centers for Disease Control, 2000; see *Animal Abuse, Cruelty, and Welfare* by Gullone and Clarke, this text). The statistics on dog bites are alarming. Fifty percent of dog bite victims are children under the age of 12, 70% of fatal dog bite attacks involve children, and dog bites are the third leading cause of emergency room admissions in children ("Task Force on Canine Aggression," 2001). The important point for mental health professionals is that, in some cases, dog bites to children that occur in the family home may be an indicator of a physically abusive or otherwise chaotic household. Furthermore, dog bites can be traumatizing to both the child and the caregiver (Bernardo, Gardner, & Amon, 1998; Bernardo, Gardner, O'Conner, & Amon, 2000; Rossman, Bingham, & Ende, 1997).

Because the behavior that harms the animal is the same behavior that harms the human, it is not surprising that research documents show that both children and animals are at risk in homes where there is domestic violence (Ascione, 1998; Ascione, Friedrich, Heath, & Hayashi, 2003). In one study involving 48 shelter programs, 85.4% of family violence shelter workers reported that women entering the shelter disclosed animal abuse in their home. In addition,

63% of the shelter staff reported that children spoke of animal abuse in their home (Ascione, Weber, & Wood, 1997). In two studies in different locales, the majority of pets in home where battering occurred were threatened with harm or actually killed by the batterer and the majority of children witnessed the abuse to the pet. In addition, in 21%–40% of these homes the children continued to be exposed to potential harm because their mothers remained in the home to protect the pet rather than seek safe shelter for themselves and their families (Ascione, 1998; Thomas & McIntosh, 2001). Just as the majority of children witness domestic violence, the majority of children also witness pet abuse (Ascione, 1998). Exposure to animal cruelty can have a significant impact on the developing child, including promoting desensitization and decreasing empathy; reinforcing the idea that the child, like the pet, is expendable; damaging the child's sense of safety and confidence in the ability of adults to protect him or her from harm; accepting physical harm as part of allegedly loving relationships; fostering the seeking of empowerment by inflicting pain and suffering; and leading to the imitation of abusive behaviors. Thus, mental health professionals urge pediatricians to assess for domestic violence and to ask mothers and their children about animal-related experiences (Boat, 2000).

Exposure to pet abuse in the context of domestic violence can also contribute to the recently documented neurobiological deficits occurring in children who witness domestic violence. One result is that the brains of children exposed repeatedly to traumas such as witnessing domestic violence are significantly smaller, resulting in serious problems in social, emotional, and intellectual functioning (De Bellis, 1999; De Bellis et al., 1999).

- A third reason for mental health professionals to ask about animal-related experiences is that children appear to be less likely to censor the information they give about their pets and thus inadvertently reveal incidents or settings that put them at risk for abuse or neglect. For example, when a 15-year-old boy was asked if there was a stressful time when his favorite dog was a source of comfort to him he replied, "Yeah. After my stepdad beats me my dog jumps up and licks my tears." The mental health professional had no idea that the boy's stepdad was beating him.

- Another reason to assess for animal-related experiences is that the child's experiences of attachment, loss, and coercion related to companion animals are potentially informative about a child's risk status. When a child reveals that he or she has a favorite pet, mental health professionals must be aware that caring about a pet can make the child more vulnerable to loss and threats of harm to the pet in order to coerce the child to comply with a demand. Examples of coercive threats include: "If you tell anyone what I did, I will kill your kitty." "If you don't have sex with me, I will take your dog to the pound and have it killed." "You have been a bad boy and to punish you, one of your puppies must die. You choose the puppy that I will kill or I will kill all of them." Mental health professionals must be aware if their child clients are experiencing similar threats.

- Finally, more potentially effective interventions for both children and animals can be informed by knowing and understanding the impact of the child's animal-related experience. Effective interventions utilize knowledge of animal-related experiences with the aim of reducing risk, addressing loss, and creating safe ways for the child to attach to another living being. One example is to report to humane authorities the animal abuse or neglect that the child has disclosed. Another intervention may involve consideration of the child's attachment to a pet if the child needs to be removed from an unsafe home and placed elsewhere. During a 911 call to report domestic violence, a terrified 6-year-old girl said to the dispatcher, "I think my cat's scared!" Her mother was murdered during the call ("Battered hearts," 1995). Hopefully the professionals who intervened to provide care for the girl were aware of her concern about her cat and aware that providing care for the child's cat was potentially an important therapeutic intervention.

Mental health professionals may need to develop a "safety plan for pets" in homes where abused or neglected children reside. Physically and sexually abused children have a higher incidence of abusive behavior to animals (Ascione, 2001), which can involve several different motivations including their lack of boundaries, witnessing and imitating violence toward animals, and a desire for revenge. Also, a sexualized abused child may seek sexual stimulation from a pet and experience a tragic end as illustrated by the following case: The mother of a 5-year-old girl had recently discovered that her child had been sexually molested for some time by a male neighbor. One day the mother was walking by the closed door of her child's bedroom and heard moaning sounds inside. Upon opening the door the mother discovered that her daughter had the family pet cat between her legs and the cat was licking the child's genitals. The mother was so distraught and enraged by this scene that she grabbed the cat and slammed the cat against the wall, killing the cat. Mental health professionals can anticipate and problem solve these situations with caregivers to make sure that neither child nor pet is harmed further.

A teenager who has been adjudicated for cruelty to animals may be remanded by the courts to perform community service at a humane society. However, mental health professionals should insist that no child or adolescent be in a humane society unless they are screened for animal-related experiences first. For example, an early adolescent boy was adjudicated for animal cruelty after setting fire to a kitten. He stated, "It was just a cat" and "I thought the cat was a stray." He also noted that his father "hated cats." However, the boy described having a favorite dog that was a source of comfort to him. This boy may be an appropriate candidate for supervised community service in an animal shelter. On the other hand, children who are fearful of animals or report no attachment to a pet or animal may be inappropriate for such a service slot. In addition, mental health professionals who may be involved in treatment recommendations must remember that humane societies are short-staffed and often unable to provide the supervision these referrals require.

The Childhood Trust Survey on Animal-Related Experiences

It is useful to have a set of questions available to guide the assessment of the child's experiences with animals. *The Childhood Trust Survey on Animal-Related Experiences* (CTSARE) is a 10-item screening questionnaire for children, adolescents, and adults that asks about experiences of attachment, loss, and fear in relationship to pets and other animals (see Appendix A). A longer version of the CTSARE has been adapted for use in several studies (Baker, Boat, Grinvalsky, & Geracioti, 1998; Flynn, 1999; Miller & Knutson, 1997). However, the validity and reliability of CTSARE have not been established. This instrument should be used as an interview guide and administered orally so the interviewer can use follow-up questions to obtain additional information as appropriate. The questions that are found in the CTSARE are described below and illustrated with Bobby's case.

- Questions 1 and 2 inquire about past and present ownership of pets. Data support that pets rarely survive more than 2 years in homes that are chaotic, have few resources, and have several risk factors for abuse or neglect (DeViney, Dickert, & Lockwood, 1983). Frequently, the inhabitants of these homes list many pets and a high mortality and turnover rate. When asked what happened to all the pets he had listed, one teenager shrugged and said, "I don't know. Either grandma got rid of them or they're dead." When several pets have "just disappeared," a caution flag should be raised that the family needs help. In Bobby's case, the therapist was alerted by the cats being short-lived and cats that just "ran away."

- Question 3 seeks information about whether the child has, or has had, a favorite pet as an indicator of attachment. Lack of any special relationship with a pet may signal a child who is divested from, or never formed, close relationships. Bobby decided that he could not invest caring feelings in a pet any longer because of the fear that his father would hurt the pet and, inevitably, pets would leave or die.

- Question 4 asks about a difficult or stressful time when a pet was a source of comfort or support. Children often readily disclose situations where they felt vulnerable, sad, or frightened when they are focused on their pet (Doyle, 2001). Bobby revealed both that he derived comfort from Smokey and that he was overwhelmed by witnessing Smokey being hurt and being prevented from assisting him. Bobby's psychosomatic symptoms appeared soon after this event.

- Questions 5, 6, and 7 address issues of the pet having been hurt, worries about something bad happening to the pet, and losing a pet. Responses to these questions can offer a window into the child's home environment and assist in focusing the intervention. Bobby's responses to these questions revealed not only his sad history of loss of pets and realistic fears that any new pet would be harmed by his father, but also his father's physical abuse of him and his mother.

- Questions 8 and 9: Seeing someone hurt an animal makes a significant impact on witnesses. Bobby's cat Smokey died after being thrown across the room by Bobby's raging father. Denying a child or adult the opportunity to help a favorite sick or injured animal is a potentially devastating experience. However, some children and adults do not consider harming a stray animal comparable to harming a family pet. Bobby admitted, with no show of remorse, to shooting BBs at a stray cat under his father's tutelage. He did not admit, or perhaps recall, deliberately stepping on the gerbil at school in the second grade or handling the hamster roughly in his current classroom. Interviewers must query other observers to get adequate information about the child hurting animals or pets, as commonly used instruments such as the Teacher Report of the Child Behavior Checklist for Children (Achenbach, 1991) do not include items on animal cruelty. However, teachers with classroom pets may observe harsh treatment of the animal. Other teachers may overhear a child talking about seeing or committing cruel acts, or read about concerning behaviors around animals in the writings of their students. Such observations warrant further inquiry.

- Question 10 underscores the need to know if a child has ever been badly frightened or hurt by a pet or other animal. The trauma of being chased, pinned, or bitten by a dog can shape a lifelong, negative response to dogs. This question also can reveal a home or neighborhood where a child may be at greater risk to be harmed by an animal. Examples of such neighborhoods include the child having access to dogs that are chained outdoors, dogs that are running freely, and the presence of higher risk dogs such as pit bulls.

As a mandated reporter, Dr. Boat was required to refer Bobby to Child Protective Services. She shared her concerns about the safety of people and the animals in the family with both Lynn Loar and with Bobby's mother. Bobby's mother was initially very concerned about losing Bobby and his siblings. However, with support, she seemed relieved that there might be an intervention to stop the violence in the family.

The Child Protective Services Perspective

Tasks of the Child Protective Services Worker

Child Protective Services (CPS) investigates allegations of abuse or neglect to minors when it receives reports either from mandated reporters or concerned citizens. Both law enforcement agencies and CPS respond to reports of harm. As governmental agencies, both are limited in scope and cannot take preventive action except in exigent circumstance. Reports must specifically explain what jeopardizes the child's safety or welfare. It is not enough for the reporter to describe a chaotic or alcoholic family or harm to another, human or animal, in the home. Rather, the reporter must make the risk to the child clear, and present the additional information to support the parent's ability or inability to recognize risk and protect the child from harm. Dr. Boat referred Bobby because she observed an inflicted injury, was told of additional physical abuse, and diagnosed emotional abuse from Bobby's account of witnessing his father's abuse of his mother and Smokey.

Reporters of suspected child abuse or neglect should keep in mind that CPS can only intervene when the child's welfare is at risk. Therefore, they should begin their report by describing the child, his age and specific vulnerabilities, and the incident that precipitated the report. Reporters should add relevant information about patterns of abusive or negligent behavior, especially any recent abusive or neglectful treatment of other siblings in the home. Reporters of suspected child abuse and neglect should also comment, when appropriate, on the parents' ability or inability to recognize the harm to the child in order to inform the development and implementation of a plan to protect the child from future harm.

Although it may seem logical that a child would be at risk in a home that is unsafe for animals, this in itself is not sufficient for CPS to respond. Reporters must make the specific risk to the child clear. *The Family-Based Risk Assessment* (Loar & Colman, 2004) contained in Appendix B provides a tool to assess risk for all living beings in the home and to make explicit who is at immediate risk in which situations.

CPS cannot act preventively, nor can it get involved with families who do not wish to receive services unless the problems are severe and directly compromise the welfare of the minor children in the home. CPS is a governmental agency that is intruding into a family's privacy and thus its scope is statutorily limited. CPS's dual mission is to protect minors and preserve families. At times these two goals are mutually exclusive and greater weight must be given to the child's safety. Furthermore, CPS workers have limited time to gather information about their clients and can only force involvement in serious situations. These limitations often frustrate concerned relatives and professionals involved with troubled families. Anguished relatives are exasperated when CPS says the situation is not serious enough for them to get involved. Domestic violence professionals and substance abuse treatment providers are often frustrated when, on occasion, CPS removes the child of a battered woman or a relapsing addict. As a result, CPS workers must learn interview techniques that quickly elicit relevant information and also build collaborative relationships with other professionals who are involved with the family and will report their concerns.

The Childhood Trust Survey on Animal-Related Experiences (Appendix A) facilitates the gathering of relevant information for CPS workers by beginning with questions that are neutral and easy to answer and then focusing on areas of concern. The CPS worker who asks the children and the non-offending parent about the welfare of animals in the home is also apt to be seen as empathic and caring—as well as smart—for bringing up such a painful and distressing topic. If the worker knows local resources for companion animals—for example, safe haven programs that provide emergency shelter for pets so families can enter battered women's shelters—and has a good relationship with the local animal control officers, otherwise-reluctant families may well cooperate with the CPS worker.

Collaborations with animal control officers and prosecutors of animal cruelty cases can facilitate CPS involvement if they focus on the dangerous behavior of the adult and how that dangerous behavior jeopardizes the safety of all living beings who, in the normal course of activity, trigger these behaviors. Further, a CPS worker presenting to the Juvenile Court a ruling from a criminal court that a person was found too dangerous to be allowed to have a dog would be in a stronger position to advocate for increased protections for the minor children in that person's care.

However, CPS workers (and others) must be mindful of their role and its limitations. They are not mandated to report cruelty to animals or domestic violence in most jurisdictions, and confidentiality requirements, along with their agency's policy, may preclude contacting the police and animal control. In the vignette, the worker encourages Bobby's mother to contact these authorities herself, and that is generally what CPS workers must do unless the offender poses immediate danger to him/herself or other humans.

Using the Family-Based Risk Assessment to Document Risk to All Living Beings in the Home

The *Family-Based Risk Assessment* (Loar & Colman, 2004) is designed to help professionals determine the dangerousness of a potential offender in a particular family situation involving children, dependent adults, frail elders, animals, and other members of the household. *The Family-Based Risk Assessment* considers which factors are most likely to act as triggers for a particular individual and the probability that other family members will activate these triggers. Realistically evaluating triggers and assessing how likely they are to be activated by others in the home points out risks and steps to take to protect potential victims from getting hurt.

For example, some people are easily provoked by noise while others might be indifferent to noise but be very aggravated by messiness or demands for assistance. A number of people find normal behaviors such as crying, barking, or whining highly stressful. High frequency, intensity, and duration of stressful behaviors can increase the probability of violence. Thus, the chronically noisy child or pet could be at greater risk in one home than in another. Each family has its own unique combination of stressful circumstances that contributes to the degree of risk for violence.

Larger social, economic, and environmental factors affect risk as well. Psychosocial and economic impoverishment creates a context in which a potential abuser is less able to inhibit aggression. Sleep-deprived parents caring for a colicky and constantly crying infant who live in a nice home in a quiet neighborhood and who can afford a babysitter pose less risk to their infant than do sleep-deprived parents who live in a run-down apartment in a dangerous neighborhood and who cannot afford in-home help.

The professional assesses the family's risk based on six common individual and family (including companion animals) behaviors that can act as triggers for abusive behaviors. These "triggers" are explained in detail in Appendix B. The trigger behaviors assessed are:

- noisiness
- messiness
- disobedience
- eating difficulties
- toileting difficulties
- level of activity and need for supervision

The professional assesses to what degree each behavior is a trigger for the offender, and scores the offender from 1 (minimally reactive) to 5 (extremely reactive) for each trigger. Then the professional assesses and scores from 1 to 5 each family member and companion animal for the likelihood that they will demonstrate any of these trigger behaviors, and who is most likely to be at risk for which behavior. The chart at the end of the risk assessment allows the professional to assess the offender and each animal, child, person with a disability, elder, and adult partner in the home on a grid. That grid makes patterns clear and demonstrates how known abusive behavior toward a companion animal indicates risk for certain human cohabitants and why.

In Bobby's case, the referral indicated that the father was extremely reactive to messiness, especially toileting accidents, and disobedience. The CPS worker would want Bobby's mother and teachers to describe how noisy, messy, and disobedient Bobby tended to be, along with his behavior at meal times, bathroom habits, and level of activity and need for adult supervision. By noting the correspondence between Bobby's father's greatest areas of reactivity and Bobby's most trying behaviors, and the father's known violent behavior in response to those triggers, the worker can reasonably assess risk to Bobby.

The animal control officer can assess risk to the companion animals, factoring in their quirks, noisiness, messiness, and the like. The mental health professional working with Bobby and his mother can use the information on the grid to help the mother focus on areas of greatest risk in order to be more effective in protecting Bobby. Together, the mental health professional and the mother can design a treatment plan that will address areas of greatest vulnerability. The mental health professional working with Bobby's father can use the chart to teach coping skills to the father and depersonalize his sense of being wronged and deliberately provoked by what are, actually, just the annoying behaviors that all living beings tend to do.

The Prosecuting Attorney's Perspective

When a prosecuting attorney pursues a child abuse or family violence case that contains contemporaneous allegations of criminal charges or animal abuse, the prosecutor is in a unique position to gain valuable information regarding the dynamics of abuse within the family. Possessing such information will aid in properly prosecuting the offender, tailoring appropriate plea agreements and sentencing terms, and making provisions to enhance the safety of the family and its companion animals.

In addition, the animal abuse charges will assist the prosecutor in protecting and helping child victims or witnesses. Children who have been abused or who have witnessed family members or pets being abused need appropriate assessment and treatment. Failure to provide such interventions may result in the child becoming a part of the criminal justice system as a juvenile or adult offender (Ascione, 2001).

Understanding the Serious Connection Between Animal Abuse, Child Abuse, and Domestic Violence

Most law school curricula do not prepare attorneys to recognize the pattern of abusive conduct involved in co-occurring animal abuse, child abuse, and domestic violence. Many prosecutors feel helpless and ineffective in cases involving family violence due to a lack of cooperation from victims and/or recurring incidents despite court intervention. When family violence includes animal abuse, especially if the assailant has killed or mutilated a pet, or threatened to injure or kill a pet, the lethality risk for all in the family may increase (Boat, 1999).

Prosecutors must take seriously all cases that involve charges or allegations of animal abuse because abusing an animal may be contemporary with, or a precursor to, more serious future abusive conduct (Arkow, 2003). A study conducted by the Humane Society of the United States in 2001 involving 1,677 official and unofficial reports of intentional cruelty against animals discovered that 89% of those cases also involved males perpetrating domestic violence, 67% of those cases involved coexisting child abuse, and 50% of the cases involved coexisting elder abuse (Arkow, 2003; see *Counting Cruelty* by Lockwood, this text).

One of the first studies to address the link between child abuse and animal abuse discovered that 88% of homes with physically abused children also had abused or neglected pets (DeViney, Dickert, & Lockwood, 1983). Due to the alarming connection between family violence and animal abuse, prosecutors must be aware of animal abuse occurring within homes for several reasons: (1) Animal abuse displays serious antisocial behavior by the offender (whether child or adult); (2) animal abuse is a relatively common occurrence in the lives of many children; (3) animal abuse witnessed by children has potential negative developmental consequences for the child; (4) animal abuse is related to interpersonal and family violence; (5) the well-being of companion animals is at risk in violent homes; and (6) if violence to animals is reduced, this could help achieve a less violent society for children and adults (Flynn, 2000).

Prosecutors not only have the mandate to represent and protect the people of their community in criminal cases, but the duty to reduce the likelihood of future criminal conduct through tough stances on crime and sentencing issues.

Prosecutors are accustomed to the fast pace of the court system and often do not have sufficient time to effectively analyze and process a criminal case. In particular, misdemeanor criminal charges (which encompass many forms of animal abuse and domestic violence charges) are quickly processed through the court docket due to case overload and minimized by time constraints on prosecutors. Prosecutors, nevertheless, need to take time to assess family violence cases that involve animal abuse, as well as cases that solely charge animal abuse, to prevent future occurrences of violence. A dismissive attitude regarding animal abuse allegations or charges does a disservice to the abused animals, as well as to children and domestic partners who witness the abuse or are abused themselves. In the United States, all states now have statutes that protect animals from abuse, cruelty, and killing. Therefore, if prosecutors take an appropriate stand on animal abuse cases, the prosecutors may help protect the physical and mental well-being of the children and domestic partner and interrupt the cycle of violence within the family. This stance is consistent with the prosecutor's mandate to protect the community and reduce the risk of future violence (see *The Impact of Improved American Anti-Cruelty Laws* by Frasch, this text).

In Bobby's case, a prosecuting attorney should take seriously the multiple allegations of animal abuse as depicted in Bobby's interview with Dr. Boat as well as the corroborative evidence obtained by CPS, law enforcement, and animal control officers. Bobby informed Dr. Boat that "animal cops" had frequented their home for several years because neighbors complained about his father's treatment of the family pets. A prosecutor should attempt to locate any reports or citations involving Bobby's father. Having this information available in a criminal prosecution is essential to documenting the past history of violence by Bobby's father. Some evidence of prior violence may be admissible as "prior bad acts" or "other acts evidence" to help gain a conviction against Bobby's father (Federal Rules of Evidence 404(b)).

The prosecutor should charge *all* offenses to address *all* dimensions of the father's violent behaviors. Ignoring the multiple allegations of animal abuse in Bobby's case would enable the offender to continue to terrorize his family members through abuse of any pets or other animals. Furthermore, the father could continue to model abusive behaviors for Bobby who already is harming animals.

The Prosecutor's Role on a Multi-Disciplinary Team

In states that require multi-disciplinary teams (MDTs) to investigate child abuse or domestic violence allegations, the prosecuting attorney is often designated to lead the team based upon the premise that investigations conducted by the team may be serious enough to result in criminal prosecution. As such, cases must be legally sound and consist of legally obtained evidence in order to survive the high-level burden of proof in criminal trials. Although prosecutors do not have investigatory powers, prosecutors still need to have a broad-based understanding of the complexities of investigating child abuse and domestic violence cases that also involve animal abuse. The diverse composition of an MDT provides the broad knowledge base required to handle these cases most effectively. However, most teams do not include an expert on animal welfare. Prosecutors should take the initiative to include

animal welfare professionals (such as animal control officers, forensic veterinarians, and/or humane society professionals). Animal welfare professionals can provide essential information to effectively prosecute a criminal case.

One example of an MDT that includes animal welfare professionals is the Domestic Violence Enhanced Response Team (DVERT) in Colorado Springs, Colorado. Developed in 1992, DVERT works collaboratively with state and federal law enforcement agencies, prosecutors, animal welfare professionals, human services, probation agents, child advocacy centers, schools, and hospitals to intervene and advocate for safety of the entire family. The mission of the Domestic Violence Enhanced Response Team is to address domestic violence:

- by enhancing the safety of high-risk-for-lethality victims, to include children and animals;
- by ensuring appropriate containment of high-risk offenders;
- by facilitating local community oriented policing initiatives;
- by providing specialized training locally and nationally; and
- by supporting communities seeking to develop and sustain similar collaborative efforts.

DVERT is a comprehensive program that receives referrals, works confidentially with families through victim advocates, conducts home visits with child and animal welfare professionals, assesses safety of the victim and family, provides educational materials and information, assists with support during criminal prosecution and victim relocation, and provides continues criminal and advocacy case management for the victimized family. DVERT works closely with appropriate agencies to refer allegations of child or animal abuse and also receives assistance to remove family members, including companion animals, from abusive environments. DVERT also coordinates a program to provide low-cost or no-cost apartments to displaced victims and their families.

Other collaborative MDTs such as those in Wayne County, Michigan, and Lucas County, Ohio, cross-train animal control officers, humane society investigators, police officers, child protective services workers, and

Cross draining vs Cross reporting

domestic violence professionals on how each can recognize and document all signs of abuse or neglect occurring within a home. Animal abuse or neglect is often more visible because it occurs outdoors and can be viewed by concerned neighbors, whereas child abuse and domestic violence more often occur within the private confines of the home. My experience as a prosecuting attorney has been that people tend to more readily report concerns of animal cruelty than suspected child abuse, neglect, or domestic violence because of the visibility of animal abuse. However, it also appears that some concerned citizens are aware of the link between animal abuse, child abuse, and domestic violence. Several citizens have called me to seek advice about reporting suspicions of child abuse or domestic violence after they witnessed the abuse or neglect of pets in a particular family. Prosecutors are in a unique position to educate professionals and citizens and to encourage cross-reporting.

Animal welfare professionals are often the first emergency responders to have contact with a family that may be suffering from other forms of violence in the home. Training animal welfare professionals to recognize child abuse or neglect or domestic violence facilitates earlier reporting and better documentation of what may be occurring in the home. Similarly, if law enforcement is called to a domestic violence scene or child protective services receives a complaint, these responders should be trained to look for evidence of abused or neglected animals and to report this information to designated animal humane agents.

MDT members must be aware that reports of child abuse and neglect are mandatory and they are provided immunity and confidentiality for reporting. However, in most states, reports of domestic violence and suspected abuse or neglect of animals are not mandated and therefore not necessarily protected. Memoranda of understanding between agencies can indemnify reporters of abuse and neglect and should be developed by MDTs. Some states mandate partial cross-reporting in these areas. For example, in California, humane society and animal control officers are mandated reporters of suspected abuse and neglect of children, elders, and dependent adults. In Colorado, veterinarians are mandated reporters of suspected child abuse or neglect, and in Maine and Ohio, county humane agents are mandated reporters of child abuse and neglect. In 2006, West Virginia passed legislation that requires domestic violence, adult protective services, and animal welfare investigators to report suspected

child maltreatment. States that require all persons (including animal welfare professionals) to report suspected child abuse are Delaware, Florida, Idaho, Indiana, Kentucky, Maryland, Mississippi, Nebraska, New Hampshire, New Jersey, New Mexico, North Carolina, Oklahoma, Rhode Island, Tennessee, Texas, Utah, and Wyoming.

Veterinarians are mandated reporters of suspected animal abuse in Arizona, California, Illinois, Kansas, Minnesota, Oklahoma, Oregon, West Virginia (including humane officers), and Wisconsin. Veterinary technicians are also mandated reporters of suspected animal abuse in Oregon. States that have discretionary reporting of suspected animal abuse and provide civil protection for reporters include California (any employee of child/adult protective services), Colorado (veterinarians), Georgia (veterinarians), Maine (veterinarians, medical professionals and social workers), Maryland (veterinarians), Massachusetts (veterinarians), Rhode Island (veterinarians), and Vermont (veterinarians).

Prosecutors should contact their state prosecuting attorneys association and take steps to propose legislation in states that do not presently mandate reporting of animal abuse by law enforcement and child and adult protective services workers. Animal control officers should also be mandated to report suspected abuse or neglect of children, frail elderly, and dependent adults.

Family Safety Issues

The prosecutor should be aware of shelter options for battered women, their children, and their pets. If private housing with family or friends is not available, options to place companion animals in a safe shelter situation should be explored. If companion animals can be removed safely from the home, abused domestic partners and children are more likely to leave the abusive home. Removing the family pets as pawns from the abuser will allow the entire family (including pets) to remain safe before, during, and after criminal prosecution of the offender (Ascione, 2000). The Humane Society of the United States initiated a *Safe Havens for Animals* program and maintains a list of animal shelters, animal care and control agencies, veterinary clinics, and private boarding kennels that will assist in housing companion animals when a family flees an abusive home.

Gathering Corroborating Evidence

Prosecutors should ensure that MDT members are cross-trained on types of evidence to look for in cases that involve allegations of animal abuse along with child abuse and/or domestic violence. Such evidence can include:

- Animals left outside without sufficient food, water or shelter
- Animals that appear emaciated
- Animal hoarding (possession a large number of companion animals; inability to provide even minimal standards of nutrition, sanitation, shelter, and veterinary care, with this neglect often resulting in starvation, illness, and death; denial of the inability to provide this minimum care and the impact of that failure on the animals, the household, and human occupants of the dwelling (Illinois statute 510 ILCS 70/2.10; see *Animal Hoarding* by Patronek, this text)
- Filthy house that contains animal feces in the living areas
- Injuries on the animals (which might be evidence of organized animal fighting or other forms of abuse)
- Frightened or cowering animals (which may be a result of abuse)
- Aggressive animals
- Areas in the home (particularly in basements) that appear to be set up for animal fighting
- Abusive attitude or language used by adults or children in the home toward the family pet in the presence of MDT members
- Comments by adults or children that indicate a lack of compassion for the pet

Prosecutors should require that an animal welfare professional be contacted immediately if there are any concerns about an animal's health or safety. The subsequent veterinarian's examination may produce corroborating evidence of animal abuse or neglect. Crime scene investigations should include videotapes or photographs of the home as well as evidence listed above. These tapes and photographs will allow the prosecutor to view the home and search for additional corroborating evidence that was not seized (see Appendix C for further information on gathering corroborative evidence).

Forensic Interviews With Allegedly Abused Children

If a child discloses information regarding his/her own abuse or witnessing of abuse of a family member and there is a companion animal in the home, a person trained in conducting forensic interviews should explore whether the child has witnessed animal abuse or suspects the animal has also suffered abuse. When children have experienced physical, sexual, or emotional abuse, or have witnessed abuse of a parent or sibling, they may have difficulty discussing these traumatic issues with a stranger who is conducting a forensic interview. In the rapport-building stage of the interview, children may more readily talk about their pet than about themselves. Therefore, asking children a few simple, open-ended questions about their pets will likely get the interview off to a good start and provide valuable forensic information. Examples of such questions are provided in *The Childhood Trust Survey on Animal-Related Experiences* (Appendix A).

If the forensic interviewer learns that a child has a special attachment to a companion animal, the interviewer can explore that relationship to make the child comfortable during the interview. For example, Bobby was reluctant to speak with Dr. Boat about his father's abuse until she asked about family pets, whose maltreatment was of great concern to Bobby. During this process the interviewer may learn that the animal has been threatened, abused, or neglected. This information may offer law enforcement an opportunity to gather corroborating evidence. Bobby's disclosures prompted a search for the remains of Smokey, the cat.

Criminal Charging Decisions, Plea Negotiations, Sentencing and Probation, and Court-Ordered Counseling

Prosecutors are ethically bound to issue criminal charges only when there is sufficient evidence of criminal wrongdoing. Prosecutors seek testimony from domestic partners, children, neighbors, veterinarians, the accused, and others involved with the family regarding dangerous behavior. Prosecutors also rely on photographic and/or videotaped evidence showing the condition of the home and all victims. Prosecutors should charge any and all crimes that have sufficient evidence to support the criminal charge. When multiple forms of abuse occur in the home, all abuse should be considered when criminally charging the offender. Prosecutors often fail to criminally charge animal abuse crimes or summarily dismiss animal abuse charges in order to obtain a guilty plea to a more "serious" human abuse charge. Deeming animal abuse as a "lesser" criminal offense does a disservice to the entire family, including pets and the offender, in stopping the cycle of violence.

Of particular importance to prosecutors is whether an offender has a pattern of abusive conduct. When criminal offenders enter the court system on charges of family violence, prosecutors often hear that this was the first time the abuse occurred along with promises that the abuse will never happen again. The background of the offender should be investigated thoroughly to uncover prior incidents or reports of violence to humans or animals. Information about prior incidents of abuse will greatly assist the prosecutor in issuing criminal charges and negotiating resolution of the charges. In Bobby's case, his father had a concurrent history of animal cruelty and physical and emotional abuse of his son and wife. This pattern of abusive conduct should strengthen the prosecutor's position in criminally charging the offender, obtaining a conviction, or negotiating a plea and sentence.

In some situations, prosecutors may uncover a unique pattern of abusive conduct by an offender that may be admissible as similar acts evidence. Federal Rules of Evidence 404(b) provides:

> Evidence of other crimes, wrongs, or acts is not admissible to prove the character of a person in order to show action in conformity therewith. It may, however, be admissible for other purposes, such as proof of motive, opportunity, intent, preparation, plan, knowledge, identity, or absence of mistake or accident, provided that upon request by the accused, the prosecution in a criminal case shall provide reasonable notice in advance of trial, or during trial if the court excuses pretrial notice on good cause shown, of the general nature of any such evidence it intends to introduce at trial.

For example, if an offender has been criminally charged with child abuse or domestic violence and the offender has targeted the family pet in order to gain silence or compliance from the child or adult victim, this information may be admissible at trial to demonstrate the offender's motive and pattern of conduct. If the primary allegation in a criminal complaint involves child abuse or domestic violence and includes allegations of animal abuse, the prosecutor should request further information from family members or the family veterinarian to determine if there is evidence to support an animal abuse charge. Even if the information cannot support a criminal charge, prosecutors should consider such information when negotiating a plea agreement. Criminal

cases that have an underlying suspicion of animal abuse should have plea agreements or sentencing terms that contain sufficient safeguards for the entire family, including companion animals. The terms should include appropriate counseling and probationary terms for the offender that address issues of animal abuse, child abuse, and/or domestic violence.

When requesting specific probationary terms for the offender, prosecutors must be vigilant to ensure that the offender is not assigned to do community service at an animal shelter or with animals. As demonstrated in the following case example, mandating a convicted animal abuser to perform community service involving animals may not only result in community outrage, but create another tragedy. Community service is not a replacement for counseling and treatment. Anger management, empathy, and compassion counseling must be delivered in a professional setting. It is important to recognize that the anger management counseling typically ordered for offenders convicted of child abuse or domestic violence rarely addresses the abuse of the family pet or how the offender leverages power and control by threatening, injuring, killing, or getting rid of the pet. However, when prosecutors pursue convictions or guilty pleas to animal abuse charges, the Court can then order comprehensive, abuse-specific treatment for the offender that addresses all manifestations of the offender's abusive behaviors.

In sum, prosecutors should not be quick to dismiss the animal abuse charges as the "less serious" charges in cases of family violence. Rather, prosecutors should attempt to obtain guilty pleas on the charges of animal abuse along with appropriate guilty pleas to child abuse and/or domestic violence so the Court can order the offender to have no contact with animals, participate in abuse-specific counseling, and tailor other appropriate probationary terms.

In our scenario, Bobby's father was appropriately charged and prosecuted on all abuse in the home. The court ordered intensive counseling and tough probationary terms. Concerns about the father's pattern of animal abuse led to protective orders for the remaining family pets as well as for Bobby and his mother. In the interests of their immediate safety, Bobby and his mother moved into a domestic violence shelter and the humane society took custody of the outdoor dogs and placed them in adoptive homes. The father will not be able to manipulate his wife or son by threatening to harm the dogs if the dogs remain out of the home.

Case Example

An example of a cooperative effort to gather evidence for purposes of criminal prosecution occurred in a case when I was an assistant prosecutor. Four individuals, three males and one female, all between the ages of 17 and 18, were convicted of felony animal abuse involving the killing, mutilation, and torture of animals. The investigation began as a simple retail fraud involving the theft of developed photographs from a local store. When responding police officers seized the photographs as evidence in the retail fraud investigation, they observed that the photographs depicted some of the teens engaging in sexual acts with cats and dogs. The teens admitted that the dogs and cats belonged to the female teen in the group. A search warrant was obtained for the female teen's residence where she resided with her mother and stepfather. The family pets depicted in the photos were taken into protective custody by animal control and given veterinary examinations to determine whether abuse has been perpetrated.

What initially appeared to be a routine retail fraud investigation turned in to a multi-suspect, multi-victim, and multi-jurisdictional investigation into animal torture rituals by the teens. The teens admitted to police officers that they had recently purchased a rat at a local pet store for the sole purpose of eating it. The teens unsuccessfully hung the rat, but then strangled, killed, and disemboweled the rat, then fried and ate the rat. The teens then nailed pieces of the rat to a cross with "repent" written on it. The teens further admitted to finding a large bird, later identified as a Muscovey duck, and torturing the duck with a machete. The duck was killed after 10–12 attempts to cut off the duck's head. The teens drew a pentagram on a wall with the duck's blood. The investigation also showed that the teens had gone to a neighbor's property and killed their African goose with a pitchfork and also killed a brown Leghorn Rooster. The teens had been scared away from killing some goats at the neighbor's property when the neighbor caught the teens hanging around and dressed in black Gothic attire.

Due to the cooperative effort in gathering significant photographic and testimonial evidence of multiple crimes of animal abuse, all four teens pled guilty to the original charges of felony animal abuse and were sentenced in ranges from 3 to 6 months in jail plus an additional 2 to 5 years of probation. As a result of the thorough investigation and gathering of evidence, I was able to convince the court of the seriousness of the felony animal abuse charges and

not succumb to pressure that my victims were "only animals." At sentencing, I advocated on behalf of the tortured animals and educated the judge on the connection between animal abuse and other human violence. I requested the maximum sentence under the sentencing guidelines in order to send a strong message to the teens and members of the community that torture of animals would not be tolerated. I also hoped to prevent these teens from engaging in future, and possibly escalating, violence against living beings.

Of particular interest in this case is that two of the four teens admitting during pre-sentencing interviews that they were physically and emotionally abused by their parents as younger children, and one teen admitted to being physically and sexually abused by both of his parents as a young child and that both parents were still incarcerated as a result of that abuse. Moreover, between the time of arrest and conviction all four teens were released on bond by the court. During this interim, one teen admitted he tortured and killed a cat and a chicken. I emphasized the abuse histories of the teens and the ongoing perpetration of animal cruelty during sentencing to encourage the judge to impose appropriate counseling and interventions to end the cycle of violence for these teens.

One lesson learned by the investigators in this case came prior to the issuance of criminal charges. The officers who had taken the dogs and cats into protective custody decided to return them to the female teen without consulting with the prosecutor's office. Working together as an MDT and maintaining an open dialogue would have prevented these companion animals from returning to an abusive environment. Nonetheless, at sentencing I successfully obtained a court order to prohibit the female teen to possess, or be in the vicinity of, animals during her 5-year term of probation. Consequently, the family pets (which fortunately had not been harmed further) were removed again and placed for adoption. It is important to understand that leaving the pets in the home imperiled both the animals and the teenager as she could have been charged with additional counts of abuse if she had continued to harm her pets.

Other Case Examples Showing the Link Between Animal Abuse and Human Violence

In Brooklyn, New York, James Whalen pled guilty to beating and killing his ex-fiancée's cat after his fiancée terminated their relationship. The 9-pound cat named Darwin was beaten to death by Whalen with his bare hands in April 2004. According to news reports, Whalen's ex-fiancée stated that Whalen had injured Darwin previously, but that no action was taken at that time. On March 11, 2005, Whalen was sentenced pursuant to a plea agreement to five years' probation, no jail, and continued alcohol abuse and anger management treatment.

On March 8, 2003, in Wilkeson, Washington, Steven L. Paulson, age 20, and Troy L. Loney, age 18, shot a dog (believed to be a homeless Siberian Husky) repeatedly with a bow and one arrow. According to charging papers filed in Pierce County Superior Court, the defendants roped the dog to a tree and took turns shooting him. He was struck by the arrow at least 10 times before he died. Afterwards, the men allegedly threw the body into a nearby creek. Volunteers had to search for the body. Initially, police did not arrest the pair, but during their arraignment on April 2, 2003, which drew 90 activists from as far away as the Canadian border, the Prosecutor asked the Judge to jail both immediately because he said they were a danger to the community. The men were jailed by the Judge in lieu of $5,000 bail. Paulson and Loney were subsequently found guilty of felony animal cruelty for torturing and cruelly killing a defenseless dog and were sentenced on October 1, 2003. Both men had prior convictions: Loney was convicted of child molestation at age 13 and Paulson has been convicted of assault, robbery, mischief, and forgery. The Judge sentenced both defendants to 8 months in the Pierce County jail, 8 to 10 weeks of mental health treatment, and fines of $1,500 and 240 hours of community service at the Humane Society of Tacoma and Pierce County. The community service factor of the probationary order came under severe scrutiny because it placed convicted animal abusers in the presence of animals. The defendants were released one month and two months early, respectively, due to "overcrowding." Loney served 81 days in jail; Paulson served 50 days.

In State v. Pugsley, 911 P.2d 761 (1995), the defendant was convicted of raping both his minor daughters and sentenced to life terms and a 20-year indeterminate term, with a 10-year minimum period of confinement. In affirming the conviction and sentence, the Idaho Court of Appeals noted, "On one occasion, he forced himself on his daughter while her younger sister was in the room. Pugsley threatened to kill his daughters if they told of the abuse. Pugsley was also convicted of raping his half sister. Evidence adduced during the two trials indicates that Pugsley raped another of his half sisters and that he reinforced his threats against his youngest daughter and a half sister by killing animals in front of them."

In State v. Twist, 528 A.2d 1250 (Me. 1987), the appeals court affirmed child sexual abuse convictions of the defendant who molested five children, including two of his own children. The court commented on the severity of the abuse, including psychological trauma to the children, in addressing whether the children would testify in open court by mentioning that the children saw the defendant kill their cat by burning it in an oven followed by his threat to shoot them if they told about the abuse.

Cases that involved threats to kill pets in order to silence child sexual abuse victims include Murphy v. Mersbacher, 697 A.2d 861 (Md. 1996) (one abuse victim was told that her dog would be killed if she disclosed the abuse); State v. Swanson, 2 NCA 777; 1993 Neb. App. LEXIS 117 (Neb. App. 1993) (the victim was reluctant to disclose the abuse, because her father "said he would kill my dog Lucky and chop me and my mommy and the furniture up with his ax."); and State v. Foster, 915 P.2d 567 (Wash. Ct. App. 1996) (the victim delayed disclosing abuse because the defendant threatened to harm the victim, as well as her dog, and the victim witnessed the defendant slam a sliding glass door on the dog).

Conclusion: None of Us Does This Job Alone

"Enhancing our awareness and knowledge about the relationship between violence to animals and violence to children provides a unique opportunity to enhance our services to both" (Boat, 1999). It is important to educate all child abuse, animal abuse, legal, and family violence professionals about the links among abuse of animals, children, and domestic partners, the importance of gathering relevant information using tools such as those discussed in this chapter, and the value of collaboration among professionals. Providing a continuum of protection for children and animals will enhance the safety of family members, the prosecution of the abuser, and provision of appropriate interventions.

References

Achenbach, T. M. (1991). *Manual for the Child Behavior Checklist/4–18 and 1991 Profile*. Burlington, VT: University of Vermont, Department of Psychiatry.

American Animal Hospital Association. (2004). Pet owner survey. Retrieved January 15, 2005, from http://www.aahanet.org

Arkow, P. (1996). The relationship between animal abuse and other forms of family violence. *Family Violence and Sexual Assault Bulletin, 12*(1–2), 29–34.

Arkow, P. (2003). *Breaking the cycles of violence: A guide to multi-disciplinary interventions.* Alameda, CA: Latham Foundation.

Ascione, F. R. (1998). Battered women's reports of their partners' and their children's cruelty of animals. *Journal of Emotional Abuse, 1*(1), 119–132.

Ascione, F. R. (2000). *Safe havens for pets: Guidelines for programs sheltering pets for women who are battered.* Logan, UT: Author

Ascione, F. R. (2001). Animal abuse and youth violence. *OJJDP Juvenile Justice Bulletin,* Washington, DC: U.S. Department of Justice.

Ascione, F. R., Friedrich, W. N., Heath, J., & Hayashi, K. (2003). Cruelty to animals in normative, sexually abused, and outpatient psychiatric samples of 6- to 12-year-old children: Relations to maltreatment and exposure to domestic violence. *Anthrozoös, 16*(3), 194–212.

Ascione, F. R., Weber, C. V., & Wood, D. S. (1997). The abuse of animals and domestic violence: A national survey of shelters for women who are battered. *Society and Animals, 5*(3), 205–218.

Baker, D., Boat, B. W., Grinvalsky, M. D., & Geracioti, T. (1998). Interpersonal and animal-related trauma experiences in female and male military veterans: Implications for program development. *Military Medicine, 163*(1), 20–25.

Battered hearts: A story of family violence (p. 49). (1995). S.A.F.E. Place, Battle Creek, MI.

Bell, L. (2001). Abusing children-abusing animals. *Journal of Social Work, 1*, 223–234.

Bernardo, L. M., Gardner, M. J., & Amon, N. (1998). Dog bites in children admitted to Pennsylvania trauma centers. *International Journal of Trauma Nursing, 4*, 121–127.

Bernardo, L. M., Gardner, M. J., O'Conner, J., & Amon, N. (2000). Dog bites in children treated in a pediatric emergency department. *Journal for the Society of Pediatric Nurses, 5*, 87–95.

Boat, B. W. (1999). Abuse of children and abuse of animals: Using the links to inform child assessment and protection. In F. R. Ascione & P. Arkow (Eds.), *Child abuse, domestic violence, and animal abuse: Linking the circles of compassion for prevention and intervention.* West Lafayette, IN: Purdue University Press.

Boat, B. W. (2000). Links among animal abuse, child abuse and domestic violence. *Social Work and the Law, 35.*

Boat, B. W. (2000). Children exposed to domestic violence. In R. C. Baker (Ed.), *Pediatric PRIMARY CARE: Well-child care* (pp. 236–239). Philadelphia, PA: Lippincott, Williams & Wilkins.

Centers for Disease Control. (2000). Healthy people 2010: Animal control. Retrieved May 25, 2004, from http://www.healthypeople.gov

De Bellis, M. D. (1999). Developmental traumatology: Neurobioligical development in maltreated children with PTSD, *Psychiatric Times, 16*, 11.

De Bellis, M. D., Keshavan, M. S., Clark, D. B., Casey, B. J., Giedd, J. N., Boring, A. M., et al. (1999). Developmental traumatology part II: Brain development. *Society for Biological Psychiatry, 45*, 1271–1284.

DeViney, E., Dickert, J., & Lockwood, R. (1983). The care of pets within child abusing families. *International Journal for the Study of Animal Problems, 4*, 321–329.

Doyle, C. (2001). Surviving and coping with emotional abuse in childhood. *Clinical Psychology and Psychiatry, 6*, 387–402.

Felthous, A. R., & Kellert, S. R. (1987). Childhood cruelty and later aggression against people: A review. *American Journal of Psychiatry, 144*(6), 710–717.

Flynn, C. P. (1999). Exploring the link between corporal punishment and children's cruelty to animals. *Journal of Marriage and Family, 61*, 971–981.

Flynn, C. P. (2000). Why family professionals can no longer ignore violence toward animals. *Family Relations, 49*, 1, 87–95.

Humane Society of the United States. (2004). Animal cruelty and family violence: Making the connection. Retrieved June 13, 2004, from http://www.hsus.org

Kellert, S. R., & Felthous, A. R. (1985). Childhood cruelty toward animals among criminals and noncriminals, *Human Relations, 38*, 1113–1129.

Lindsay, J. (1979). *Hogarth: His art and his world.* New York: Taplinger Publishing.

Loar, L., & Colman, L. (2004). *Teaching empathy: Animal-assisted therapy programs for children and families exposed to violence.* Alameda, CA: Latham Foundation.

Lockwood, R., & Church, A. (1996). Deadly serious: An FBI perspective on animal cruelty. *HSUS News*, HSUS, 2100 L Street, Washington, DC, Fall.

Miller, K. S., & Knutson, J. F. (1997). Reports of severe physical punishment and exposure to animal cruelty by inmates convicted of felonies and by university students. *Child Abuse and Neglect, 21*, 59–82.

Nelson, P. (2001). A survey of psychologists' attitudes, opinions, and clinical experiences with animal abuse. Unpublished doctoral dissertation. Wright Institute Graduate School of Psychology, Berkeley, CA.

Rossman, B. R., Bingham, R. D., & Emde, R. N. (1997). Symptomology and adaptive functioning for children exposed to normative stressors, dog attack, and parental violence. *Journal of the American Academy of Child and Adolescent Psychiatry, 36*, 1089–1096.

Task Force on Canine Aggression. A community approach to dog bite prevention. (2001). *Journal of the American Veterinary Medical Association, 219*, 1733–1749.

Thomas, C., & McIntosh, S. (2001, June 7). *Exploring the links between animal abuse and family violence as reported by women entering shelters in Calgary communities*. Paper presented at Our Children, Our Future: A Call to Action, International Conference on Children Exposed to Domestic Violence, London, Ontario, Canada.

Appendix A

The Childhood Trust Survey on Animal-Related Experiences

The Childhood Trust 10 Screening Questions for Children, Adolescents and Adults on Animal-Related Experiences

1. **Have you or your family ever had any pets?** .... Y   N

	How many?			How many?
a. Dog(s)	_____			
b. Cat(s)	_____	**f.** Turtles, snakes, lizards, insects, etc.		_____
c. Bird(s)	_____	**g.** Rabbits, hamsters, mice, guinea pigs, gerbils		_____
d. Fish	_____	**h.** Wild animals (describe) _____		_____
e. Horse(s)	_____	**i.** Other (describe) _____		_____

2. **Do you have a pet or pets now?** .... Y   N

	How many?			How many?
a. Dog(s)	_____			
b. Cat(s)	_____	**f.** Turtles, snakes, lizards, insects, etc.		_____
c. Bird(s)	_____	**g.** Rabbits, hamsters, mice, guinea pigs, gerbils		_____
d. Fish	_____	**h.** Wild animals (describe) _____		_____
e. Horse(s)	_____	**i.** Other (describe) _____		_____

3. **Did you ever have a favorite or special pet?** .... Y   N

What kind? _____

Why was the pet special? _____

_____

4. **Has a pet ever been a source of comfort or support to you—even if you did not own the pet? (e.g., When you were sad or scared?)** .... Y   N

How old were you?
a. Under age 6   **b.** 6–12 years   **c.** Teenager   **d.** Adult

Describe the pet and what happened _____

_____

_____

5. Has your pet ever been hurt? .... Y   N

What happened? (describe) _____

_____

_____

   a. Accidental? (hit by car, attacked by another animal, fell, ate something, etc.)
   b. Deliberate? (kicked, punched, thrown, not fed, etc.)

6. Have you ever felt afraid for your pet or worried about bad things happening to your pet? (describe)
.... Y   N

_____

_____

Are you worried now? .... Y   N

**7. Have you ever lost a pet you really cared about? (e.g., Was given away, ran away, died or was somehow
killed?)** .... Y   N

What kind of pet? _____

If your pet died, was the death:

a. Natural	**b.** Accidental	**c.** Deliberate	**d.** Cruel or violent
(old age, illness, euthanized)	(hit by car)	(strangled, drowned)	(e.g. pet was tortured)

What happened?

_____

_____

_____

Was the death or loss used to punish you or make you do something? ....Y   N

How difficult was the loss for you?
  a. Not difficult   **b.** Somewhat difficult   **c.** Very difficult

How much does it bother you now?
  a. Not at all   **b.** Somewhat   **c.** A lot

How did people react/what did they tell you after you lost your pet?
  a. Supportive   **b.** Said it was your fault   **c.** Punished you   **d.** Other_____

How old were you?
  a. Under age 6   **b.** 6–12 years   **c.** Teenager   **d.** Adult

8. Have you ever <u>seen</u> someone hurt an animal or pet? .... Y   N

	How many?		**How many?**
a. Dog(s)	_____	**f.** Turtles, snakes, lizards, insects etc.	_____
b. Cat(s)	_____	**g.** Rabbits, hamsters, mice, guinea pigs, gerbils	_____
c. Bird(s)	_____	**h.** Wild animals (describe) _____	_____
d. Fish	_____	**i.** Other (describe) _____	_____
e. Horse(s)	_____		

What did they do ?

a. Drowned
b. Hit, beat, kicked
c. Stoned
d. Shot (BB gun, bow & arrow)
e. Strangled
f. Stabbed

g. Burned
h. Starved or neglected
i. Trapped
j. Had sex with it
k. Other (describe) _____

Was it
a. accidental?   b. deliberate?   c. coerced?

How old were you? **(circle all that apply)**
a. Under age 6   b. 6–12 years   c. Teenager   d. Adult

Were they hunting the animal for food or sport? .... Y   N
Did anyone know they did this? .... Y   N
What happened afterwards? _____

---

9. **Have <u>you</u> ever hurt an animal or pet?** .... Y   N

How many?		**How many**
a. Dog(s) _____	f. Turtles, snakes, lizards, insects etc. _____	
b. Cat(s) _____	g. Rabbits, hamsters, mice, guinea pigs, gerbils _____	
c. Bird(s) _____	h. Wild animals (describe) _____ _____	
d. Fish _____	i. Other (describe) _____ _____	
e. Horse(s) _____		

What did you do ?

a. Drowned
b. Hit, beat, kicked
c. Stoned
d. Shot (BB gun, bow & arrow)
e. Strangled
f. Stabbed

g. Burned
h. Starved or neglected
i. Trapped
j. Had sex with it
k. Other (describe) _____

Was it
a. accidental?   b. deliberate?   c. coerced?

How old were you? **(circle all that apply)**
a. Under age 6   b. 6–12 years   c. Teenager   d. Adult

Were you hunting the animal for food or sport? .... Y   N
Were you alone when you did this? .... Y   N
Did anyone know you did this? .... Y   N
What happened afterwards? _____

---

10. **Have you ever been frightened—really scared or hurt by an animal or pet?** .... Y   N

What happened? _____

Are you still afraid of this kind of animal or other animals? .... Y   N
(Describe) _____

(Optional)

Demographics

Date: _____   **Current grade or highest grade completed:** _____

Date of birth: _____   **Gender: Male** _____ **Female** _____

Age: _____ _____
         (years)   **(months)**

Maternal level of education (highest grade completed) _____

Appendix B
The Family-Based Risk Assessment

The Family-Based Risk Assessment considers which factors are most likely to act as triggers for a particular individual and the probability that other family members and companion animals will activate these triggers. Realistically evaluating triggers and assessing how likely they are to be activated by others in the home points out ways to prevent potentially dangerous situations from worsening and steps to take to protect potential victims from harm.

Assess the family's risk based on six common individual and family behaviors:

- noisiness
- messiness
- disobedience
- eating difficulties
- toileting difficulties
- level of activity and need for supervision.

Assess to what degree each behavior is a trigger for the potential offender, to what degree the behavior is evident in the household, and which household member is most likely to be at risk for each behavior.

Step one: Assess the potential offender's likely response to these six triggers.

Fill out the potential offender reactivity assessment, the left column of the chart on page 414, scoring the potential offender on a scale from 1 to 5 on his or her reactivity to each of six common behaviors.

"1" indicates this individual finds the behavior minimally annoying.
"5" indicates that it could be dangerously annoying.

With a reactivity rating of 1 to 5 in each category, a potential offender would have a Personal Reactivity Rating between 6 and 30.

Step two: Assess the degree to which these triggers might be present in the household by looking at the likely behavior of children, dependent adults, frail elders, animals, and other members of the household.

To do this:

- Make a list of all human and animal members of the household on the chart on page 414. Include all children and pets.

- Include other potential victims who reside in the home either permanently or temporarily, like an aging parent who lives in the guest room over the garage or another relative needing assistance while recuperating from an illness. Domestic violence of any sort can put even able-bodied adults in harm's way.

- Consider the frequency, intensity, and duration of the behaviors of the potential victims, scoring them using a scale of 1 to 5.

"1" indicates minimally provocative behavior.
"5" indicates maximally provocative behavior.

- Score each member of the household on each behavior, then add the scores of the members of the household together. Next, multiply the cumulative score for each category by the potential offender's reactivity rating.

- Look at the resulting totals for high and low risk for individuals, for behaviors, for times of the day (such as meal times), and for a total indicating overall risk of violence.

Family-based risk assessment definitions:

1. Noise.

- animals
  Unaltered cats howl when in heat, a sound many people find dismaying or even chilling. To some, it sounds like a child's cry. Some dogs bark only occasionally—when somebody comes to the door, for example, while others bark more often, at any movement outside the house; still others seem to bark almost constantly. While this may not matter to people who are comparatively indifferent to noise, the noise-sensitive person finds this very trying behavior. Noise complaints are among the most common and frequent that animal control agencies receive. *Score each animal for how noisy it is.*

- children
  Children tend to be very noisy people: crying, whining, complaining, playing

FAMILY RISK CHART

POTENTIAL OFFENDER

POTENTIAL VICTIMS

SCORE

Triggers	Reactivity Rating	Animal A	Animal B	Child A	Child B	Child C	Adult Partner	Other Adult	
Noise	___	___	___	___	___	___	___	___	___
Messiness	___	___	___	___	___	___	___	___	___
Disobedience	___	___	___	___	___	___	___	___	___
Eating Problems	___	___	___	___	___	___	___	___	___
Toileting Problems	___	___	___	___	___	___	___	___	___
Requirements for supervision	___	___	___	___	___	___	___	___	___
Total Risk Score	___	___	___	___	___	___	___	___	___

Add the score of all the potential victims together, then multiply that number by the potential offender's Reactivity Rating for each trigger to obtain scores.

Degree of isolation: _____

Economic consideration: _____

Comments: _____

_____

noisily, banging things, dropping things, and colliding with things. Some learn that they only get attention from their parents when they make a considerable amount of noise; the annoyed adults unwittingly reinforcing the behavior they abhor. *Score each child for noisiness.*

- people with disabilities, frail elders
Hearing loss afflicts a considerable percent of the aging population as well as a smaller segment of the general population. Aging friends or relatives may play the television very loudly, often to the point of causing pain to others around them. Those sensitive to noise may become uncomfortable at home because the aging parent, now living in the spare bedroom, blasts the television all day. They may notice their own tempers flaring more quickly and small irritants appearing larger. In addition, helpers may need to shout and repeat everything several times to be understood. This can add considerably to stress levels. *Score each disabled adult or frail elder for hearing loss and resultant noisiness.*

- adult partners
Adults make noise, especially when using a vacuum cleaner, washing machine, or other household appliance. Talking on the phone, nagging, or yelling at others may also activate triggers. Partners may have unrealistic—or at least unfulfilled—expectations of peace and quiet on demand. They may interpret noise as provocation worthy of retaliation, even if the noise is moderate and in response to normal boisterousness from young and energetic children or animals or hearing loss of older relatives. *Score the noise level of the adult partner and factor in the general level of noise in the home and environment.*

2. Messiness, disregard for or destruction of property.

- animals
Animals do not share human regard for possessions. Cats see drapes and couches as fine things to scratch their claws against—and scratching claws is necessary to keep nails trim. Smart cat owners understand that cats scratch of necessity and the best way to protect the drapes and

the couch is to provide something the cat will prefer to scratch. Pet supply stores sell carpeted cat trees; they go up higher than the average couch and have a better nap than most drapes. Providing a more attractive alternative to the cat solves the problem; families without these alternatives are likely to find scratched furniture, curtains, and other household property.

Dogs, especially teething puppies, like to chew things. People who give their dogs rawhide to chew are nonetheless surprised that their dogs demolish leather shoes they leave lying around. From the dogs' perspective, leather is leather and their human cohabitant generously provides a variety of types and textures. The easy solution is to shut the closet door so the dog cannot get at the shoes and to give the dog non-leathery things to chew like nylon bones and densely stuffed Kongs™ (a chew toy).

With a few simple changes, families can avoid much destructive behavior by pets. However, many pet owners blame their animal for bad behavior. Having decided that the behavior was bad, they then feel justified in punishing it. *Score the animals' messy or destructive behavior, factoring in mitigations like cat trees and nylon bones and noting their absence as contributing to risk.*

- children
Children are messy and clumsy. They drop and spill things. They also enjoy fingerpainting, splashing in puddles, and other messy activities. They are too young to appreciate the value of an expensive vase on a small table and to steer clear of it while enthusiastically if imprecisely careening down the hallway on a tricycle. With good intentions but poor understanding of developmental stages, some parents decide to teach young children not to touch fragile and valuable objects instead of simply putting them safely out of reach. The young child's take on the situation is of being tantalized and constantly tempted. Intermittent if not frequent failure of impulse control is normative for children. A wiser parent would baby- and toddler-proof the home and generally keep treasured or valuable objects in safe and inaccessible places.

Score the messy or neat tendencies of the child and factor in the number of toys and the number of parts they contain. A spilled set of Legos or a 1000-piece puzzle looks messier than a Gameboy left on the table.

- people with disabilities, frail elders

People with poor coordination or ambulation may also find navigation difficult. Weak or tremulous hands mean that things will inevitably if unintentionally get dropped and broken. Difficulty walking and the use of assistive devices mean more room is required than most floor plans provide for doorways, hallways, and bathrooms. Without wide openings, someone using a walker is likely to scratch the molding in doorways and other narrow passages.

Score the disabled adult or frail elder based on strength and coordination, and the presence or absence of canes, walkers, wheelchairs and other devices that tend to require more space than is available in the average home.

- adult partner

Partners often differ in their needs for tidiness and orderliness. Even if they agree on standards of neatness and cleanliness, they are apt to disagree on the division of labor and the specific value of the other's personal and cherished property. Thus, one partner may keep personal items neat but neglect household chores, while another might clean the car but ignore spills in the kitchen. An adult partner is at greater risk of triggering the potential offender's rage when power is not shared in the relationship, when individual rights and preferences are generally not honored, and when the more powerful partner's expectations include maid and other services. Mess may then be misinterpreted as a deliberate provocation, and a violent reaction felt as justifiable retaliation. The potential offender often chooses to destroy the things lying around or to shatter a treasured object such as a family heirloom to show his or her power to hurt.

    In the clinical literature on domestic violence, injuring or killing the family pet is discussed under the rubric of destruction of property. While true, the pet as a sentient being represents more than that. Violent adults may kick or throw a pet against the wall and refuse to let anybody help it. Thus, the family watches in horror as the pet suffers and dies a few days later. Family members identify and foresee their own fates in the pet's agony and death. Their pain goes beyond the sense of loss triggered when a treasured heirloom is thrown against a wall and breaks into pieces.

    Another important point to consider is how the pet entered the family. Instead of chocolates or flowers, the remorseful gift accompanying the batterer's tearful apology may be a kitten and the words, "Honey, I don't know what came over me. I'll never do that again. To show you how much I love you and want us to be a family, I've brought you this kitten. We'll care for it together." The pet thus represents all the optimism and hope for the future that the human victim clings to.

Score this category on general demands for tidiness, the presence of valuable and treasured objects, the presence of and past history of pets living and dying in the home, the number of people in the home (four children inevitably create more disarray than two do), and the egalitarian or unequal division of labor in maintaining the home and its contents.

3. Disobedience, disrespect, noncompliance with rules, directions.

- animals

People say "sit" or "come" and expect the animal to comply. They tug vigorously on the leash expecting the animal to learn to walk without pulling. To humans the point of the talking or pulling is obvious. But to the animal, the message is indecipherable. For the animal to understand what is being asked and to learn to comply with the request, these behaviors must be taught in a variety of settings with clear and predictable directions and reinforcement. It is far easier to get a dog to come when called indoors, for example, than outdoors where competing smells, distractions, and food sources abound. Some pet owners mistake inadequate training for disobedience.

Score this based on the animal's compliance and the owner's flexibility.

- children

Children test limits to learn about themselves, other people, and the world around them. Limit testing is a normal—if trying—behavior, more intense at some stages (the "terrible twos" and the teens) than others. Adults sometimes have developmentally inappropriate expectations, expecting a young child to remember things or draw on life experience as though they were older. For example, a 3-year-old has an attention span of roughly three minutes. So, if a parent tells that child 20 times in an hour not to go near a hot coffee pot, that child is actually fully compliant for his or her developmental stage. Few parents who tell their 3-year-old something every three minutes also marvel at their child's flawless compliance. Rather, based on their own memory and attention span, they interpret the brevity of their child's retention as disobedience and respond angrily or punitively.

Score this based on the child's tenacity in testing limits and the adult's realistic or unrealistic appreciation of developmentally appropriate expectations.

- people with disabilities, frail elders

People with disabilities or infirmity due to age may need assistance, even attendant care. Does this mean they should not get to make decisions for themselves? In some cases, when the impairment is cognitive, it does for safety's sake. But, what of the aging parent who moves in with an adult child after breaking a hip and does not do as told? Should the desire of an adult to make his or her own decisions be interpreted as disobedience? Does the adult child repeat the words remembered from his or her teenage years, "When you're under my roof, you'll do as I say"?

Such constraints naturally may elicit noncompliance. Loss of autonomy and the need for assistance are problematic enough without having to risk abuse when asserting oneself.

Score the empathy and flexibility of the caregiver as well as the vigorousness of the recipient's desire for autonomy. Take into account collusion between genera-

tions, as when a grandparent will seek to undermine a parent's authority with a child in the home.

- adult partners

Some adults agree with their partner's right to make all the rules; others are overtly or covertly defiant. A partner may be at risk by breaking the rules, whether intentionally or not.

Score the rigidity of the rules, the frequency or infrequency of tolerated exceptions, and the partner's ability to fulfill the potential offender's expectations for respect, obedience, and compliance with rules.

4. Eating difficulties or quirks.

- animals

Cats are notoriously picky eaters for reasons largely having to do with their dietary and digestive needs. However, the cat owner who sees yet another can of food go uneaten after sitting untouched for hours can easily misinterpret the cat's refusal to eat as defiance. This behavior is a common source of frustration for owners who, believing the cat is deliberately ignoring the food, fail to understand the cat's delicate dietary and digestive needs.

Dogs get into trouble for the opposite reason: they eat everything. Scavengers and omnivores by nature, they delight in food old and new, moldy and fresh, the not-yet-eaten and the already excreted. The dog owner who opens the oven, takes out a chicken, and then momentarily abandons it to answer the door is likely to find a happy dog and an empty platter back in the kitchen. Unless the owner has invested substantial time teaching the dog impulse control around food using increasingly large and tempting challenges, the empty platter represents predictable behavior, not a bad dog. The empty platter indicates that more training is needed, that food should be put in inaccessible places, and that the problem of the consumed chicken was caused by the person's failure to exercise hypervigilence around coveted food.

Score the availability of generous enough amounts of fresh and appropriate food so the animal is not unduly hungry, the animal's drive and determination to hunt for extras, and the vigilance of the pet owner in putting things away.

- children
Children control so little in life that they readily seek to control what they eat. They may develop quirks to feel in charge, eating the same food for lunch every day for three months, only to say they hate it the first day of the fourth month. They may eat carrots or apples if they are sliced a certain way, but not another, or they may refuse to eat foods that "touch" (e.g., peas roll that into mashed potatoes on a plate). Some parents understand their child's need for control and the advantages of choosing battles wisely; others take this behavior as an affront or a challenge and turn mealtimes into battlegrounds and power struggles.
Score the child's need for self-determination; the level of risk increases with the parent's need to control what the child eats and to attribute motives like disrespect to quirks.

- people with disabilities, frail elders
Some adults find eating difficult. They may have trouble chewing or swallowing; they may have ill-fitting or uncomfortable dentures, or their hands may tremble making it hard to cut food or manage utensils. What used to be a pleasurable half hour for the family to eat and socialize may become, through age or disability, a labor-intensive hour, generating frustration, spills, and despair.

Other adults need to be fed. When people feed children, they know their children will soon eat independently, outgrowing the need for mealtime assistance. When people feed adults, however, they foresee—realistically—that demands will continue indefinitely and may even increase. People who offered to help a relative for a short while may feel trapped when that relative's health deteriorates rather than improves and the need to provide assistance increases.
Score the level of assistance needed. Assess whether help is needed to cut or feed food, prepare special meals, or clean up messiness from feeding difficulties. Base this score on the level of repugnance or disgust

the caregiver experiences and reaction to increased dependency.

- adult partners
The adult partner may be at risk in this category not because of eating quirks but because of his or her role in food preparation. A controlling partner may make exacting demands on the timing, quality, and service of meals.
Score the potential offender's level of expectations and willingness to adjust expectations downward when other demands press.

5. *Toileting or housebreaking accidents, incontinence; hygiene and grooming.*

- animals
Cats tend to be fastidious, only avoiding litter boxes when the cat is ill or bothered by something or when the box dirty. People may misconstrue the cat's illness or their own failure to clean the litter box as the cat's misbehavior.

Dogs surpass humans in some physical capabilities such as hearing and sense of smell. But they are similar to humans in needing to relieve themselves a few times during the day. Yet owners will take a dog out in the morning to relieve itself, go to work for the day, and return 10 hours later angry about a wet spot on the carpet—even though they themselves have gone to the bathroom two or three times during the day at work. This problem is simply a question of owners overestimating the dog's physical capacity.

Other toileting accidents may be due to improper or inconsistent training, failure to notice the dog's behaviors indicating a need to go out, insufficient time outdoors, or illness, particularly urinary tract infections. Some submissive and frightened dogs also urinate as one of their submissive behaviors. Scaring this dog will only increase the urinating indoors.
Score the owner's realistic or unrealistic expectations and willingness to provide clean litter boxes, sufficient training, and frequent enough opportunities to go out.

- children
Most parents look forward eagerly to the day their child will outgrow the need for

diapers. This day usually arrives when the child is between 2½ and 3, although some children, particularly boys, wet the bed until they are older. Added pressure to toilet train children at an early age is put on parents by child care programs that only accept toilet trained children. Some children, due to illness, disability, emotional distress, or physical or sexual abuse are incontinent longer, particularly at night.

Parents are not always charitable with a child who wets the bed and may take it as an affront to their capacity as parents. This is especially likely if the parent was also a bed wetter and was humiliated or punished for the same behavior. Instead of engendering compassion, the memory increases the risk that the humiliated parent will repeat the abusive behavior with the bed-wetting child. Doubts about one's ability to control oneself can be projected on others, particularly when memories of self-regulatory failure are vivid and hurtful.

Score the parent's history of enuresis and emotional trauma sustained in childhood and the age of the child and current frequency of toileting accidents.

- people with disabilities, frail elders
  Some people with disabilities need toileting assistance throughout their lives, perhaps because of incontinence or needing help transferring from a wheelchair to a toilet seat. Some people become incontinent as they age. Incontinence is the single biggest trigger for elder abuse and the most common reason cited by family members for institutionalizing an older relative. This dependency takes a great toll on the caregiver and increases risk for the person with the disability. Even if an attendant provides the help, attendant care is poorly paid and poorly supervised, increasing the risk of both physical and sexual abuse by caregivers.
  Score the level of assistance needed with toileting, frequency of needing to relieve oneself, screening and supervision of staff (if applicable), and other control issues around bodily functions, appearance, and access.

- adult partners and teenage children in the home

Adult partners and teenagers are probably not incontinent, but they may, through hygiene or grooming, trigger control issues. They may dress or wear makeup in ways that seem sexy or provocative.
Score the level of control attempted by one adult over another's appearance, grooming and hygiene.

6. **Need for supervision due to level of activity or maturity.**

- animals
  People tend to fall in love impulsively with a cute and bouncy puppy without realizing the puppy's level of energy and need for supervision and exercise. Puppies chew and explore constantly, requiring as much baby-proofing as a toddler. Older dogs are more mellow, happy to go for a run and to take a nap. Shelter staff may recommend that busy people select an older dog, but this advice usually goes unheeded.
  Score the animal's and human's levels of energy and the time the human allocates to exercise and recreate with the animal.

- children
  Because young children have enormous amounts of energy and little sense of safety, they must be supervised at all times. Always on the go, children require a high degree of attention. Parents, meaning well, think getting a puppy for their young child would be nice—the child and puppy can grow up together and their comparable energy will allow them to play enjoyably together. These parents ignore shelter warnings that young children and animals may double, not halve, the need for attention.
  Score the caregiver's willingness and level of energy to keep up with the child all his or her waking hours.

- people with disabilities, frail elders
  People who have limited mobility or energy place demands on caregivers to get things for them and help in a variety of ways. They may also have bells to ring to summon help—and may ring them often. Particularly stressed are the people simultaneously supervising young and energetic children, a new puppy, and a bedridden in-law in the spare bedroom, bell ever at the

ready to summon a glass of juice or the newspaper.

- adult partners

  Demands of infants and people who are ill, frail, or disabled take precedence over the demands of teenagers and able-bodied adults. An insecure partner may be provoked when others come first, seem "more important" and more worthy of care and attention.

  Score the number of competing demands and the potential offender's relative ability or inability to yield center stage to the needs of others.

  Consider two additional factors as you score family-based risk in each category:

1. Isolation

   Isolation is the biggest generic risk factor for abuse and neglect. Abuse and neglect take place at home in private when nobody outside the family is watching. Reducing isolation is the single most useful intervention.

   Assess risk by calculating time the family is alone, and the availability and involvement of friends, relatives, and neighbors from work, school, church, or other organizations.

2. Impoverishment

   While poverty does not cause abuse, economic hardship reduces ways to minimize risk. An overwhelmed parent with disposable income can place the dog in a kennel for a few days, hire a housekeeper and a babysitter, or bring in a nurse's aide for a disabled or elderly relative. Though stressed, and now the employer of a small staff, this person can carve out a few moments to regroup and delegate a number of tasks, especially those he or she finds most onerous or off-putting. Without money to hire help, people get pushed beyond their limits when forced to handle multiple and seemingly endless demands.

   Assess existing level of demands, use of support services, ability to pay for additional help, and the availability of reduced fee and volunteer services in the community.

Appendix C

A Prosecutor's Checklist of Abusive Conduct Toward Animals

Individuals Who Can Provide Information:

- Teachers (observed behaviors of children around classroom animals)
- Neighbors (neighbors often observe animal abuse and neglect that occurs outdoors)
- Friends
- Animal control and humane society officers (citations for an unlicensed or dangerous dog, neglect, abuse)
- Family members
- Protective Services (adult and child)
- Mental health professionals
- Law enforcement officers
- Veterinarians

Documented Behaviors of Children:

- Rough handling of companion animals (throwing, kicking, pulling appendages, pulling out or cutting whiskers)
- Yelling at animals
- Shooting weapons or throwing rocks, etc., at animals
- Trying to run over animals with bicycles or other vehicles
- Stealing pets from neighbors
- Bragging about injuring or killing animals (whether true or not)
- Feeding toxic substances to animals
- Injuring, killing, or attempting to kill animals
- Ritually torturing and/or killing animals
- Using animals to kill other animals
- Leaving companion animals without appropriate food, water, or shelter
- Using companion dogs to fight other dogs or animals
- Killing an animal to rehearse the child's own suicide or homicide
- Killing an animal before an abusive adult can do so
- Abuse-reactive behavior (e.g., repeating their own abuse with an animal)

Documented Behaviors of Adults:

- Rough handling of companion animals (throwing, kicking, pulling appendages, pulling out or cutting whiskers)
- Yelling at animals
- Threatening to injure or kill animals in front of children or family members
- Shooting weapons or throwing rocks, etc., at animals
- Trying to run over animals with vehicles
- Stealing pets from neighbors in retaliation for other incidents
- Feeding toxic substances to animals
- Injuring, killing, or attempting to kill animals
- Ritually torturing and/or killing animals (i.e., gang initiation)
- Using animals to kill other animals
- Leaving companion animals without appropriate food, water, or shelter
- Using companion dogs to fight other dogs or animals
- Using companion animals as coercion and control in domestic violence and child abuse scenarios
- Owning a vicious dog

Gathering Corroborating Evidence:

- Behavior of companion animals in the home (aggressive, vicious, or cowering)
- Veterinary records (establish a history of abuse or neglect through injuries, malnutrition, emaciation)
- Necropsy reports (if an animal was killed) to determine cause of death and document prior injuries
- Availability of food, water, and shelter for each pet
- Observations by police, animal control officers, or others regarding treatment of pets and attitude of the owner toward the pet
- Prior visits to the house by animal control to check on the welfare of pets
- Complaints by neighbors concerning the welfare of pets
- Prior citations or criminal complaints against the owners for animal-related violations of law

Assessing Children's Experiences With Animal Cruelty: Assessment, Treatment, Community Needs, and Policy Considerations

Shari Lewchanin and Mary Lou Randour

Introduction—Why Focus on Children

The importance and the long-term implications of the link between animal cruelty and other forms of interpersonal violence have been well-established and documented earlier in this publication and elsewhere (Arkow, 1997; Ascione, 2004; Lockwood, Arluke, & Ascione, 1999; Lockwood & Hodge, 1986). Why is it important to focus on young children? It will be argued here that adult animal cruelty probably begins in childhood. The roots of later interpersonal violence may be first apparent as early as the preschool years. Very early intervention may be our best hope of preventing violent behavior from escalating.

This chapter offers an overview of the importance of a child's relationship to animals and research on children's experiences with animal cruelty. Models of assessment and intervention are also suggested. In addition, the importance of community education is discussed. Lastly policy considerations are discussed, with a focus on the implications of how juvenile crime statistics are collected.

A young child's experience with animals, particularly family pets, can be seen as a microcosm for how the child learns to relate to others. The foundation of mature adult relationships is laid in early childhood, ideally, first with the child's experiences with loving caregivers, then with the objects that the child begins to love. Children practice relating and loving with favorite dolls, toys, and stuffed animals. Children identify with animals in their innocence, unconditional love, and even in their helplessness and total dependency on adults. How children see animals treated reflects how they come to believe they will be treated as well by those who are bigger, stronger, and more powerful. It is no accident that stuffed animals often become the child's first external transitional love object. How many parents have spent anguished hours late at night searching for that lost loved doll or animal toy without which the child is inconsolable? And how many of us mature adults still have, in the attic perhaps, a box of favorite stuffed animals that we just cannot part with?

It is possible that children who have difficulty attaching to favorite toys may present with later attachment concerns. Children who mistreat their toys, dolls, and stuffed animals may be demonstrating issues with power and control over those who are smaller and weaker. There is a continuum of love objects ranging from toys, to stuffed animals and dolls, to live animals, to other children, and eventually to other adults. These are the relationships in which children learn how to handle strong feelings. Affection, responsibility, anger, disappointment, pain, loss, and power can all be seen in the way children treat the things, pets, and people important to them. In addition, what children observe and experience regarding how the adults in their lives treat their love objects—also things, pets, and people—presents lifelong lessons to the child. It is crucial that children learn to form early, solid empathic connections.

It is very difficult for most of us to accept that anyone would deliberately and intentionally hurt an animal. It is even more difficult to believe that young children, even pre-school age children, can be guilty of animal cruelty, yet there are numerous research studies that have documented that this is a real concern. In discussing animal cruelty, this chapter adopts the following definition: "Animal cruelty is defined as socially unacceptable behavior that intentionally causes unnecessary pain, suffering or distress to and/or death of an animal" (Ascione, 1993). This behavior goes beyond the common pulling of a cat's tail or petting a puppy too hard. Animal cruelty is not normal, regardless of the age of the child.

Children's' Experiences With Animal Cruelty

Cruelty to animals may be one of the first conduct disorder symptoms to be seen in young children (see *Conduct Problems and Cruelty to Animals in Children* by Dadds, this text). As our interest in the early identification of those children who may grow into later violent offenders against people increases, the connection between early symptoms of violence directed at animals and possible later violence directed at people becomes even more salient. In preschoolers, cruelty to animals may be the first warning sign that something is wrong in the child's life. It may be that the child is a direct victim of abuse or neglect, an indirect victim having witnessed violence toward people or animals, or it may be an early warning sign that the child is developing antisocial behaviors. In 1987, the American Psychiatric Association in its Diagnostic and Statistical Manual recognized animal cruelty as an important indication of a child's mental health status (American Psychiatric Association, 1987). The International Classification of Diseases also views animal cruelty as an aspect of antisocial behavior (World Health Organization, 1996).

A study by Achenbach, Howell, Quay, and Conners (1991) examined the frequency with which caregivers reported an incident of "behavior cruel to animals" in a sample of children 4–16 years of age who had been referred to a mental health clinic. The results indicated that the frequency of such behavior for boys ranged from 34% for 4 to 5 year olds to 18% for 10 to 11 year olds. For the sample of girls referred for treatment, the percentages were smaller, but still surprisingly high, ranging from 7% to 18%. The reported rates of animal cruelty for children over 4 years old were very similar to those rates reported for vandalism. However, animal abuse may be exhibited at even younger ages. Larzelere, Martin, and Amberson (1989) studied a sample of children under 2 years from pediatric clinics, and found that parents reported a 5% rate of animal cruelty during the one month prior to the completion of the questionnaire.

Like other covert behaviors such as vandalism and fire setting, it is likely that animal cruelty in young children is underrated by the adults in their lives. Offord, Boyle, and Racine (1991) compared the reports of caregivers and adolescents ages 12 to 16 years old. The male teenagers admitted to 3.8 times more instances of cruelty to animals

than their caregivers reported. Girls acknowledged hurting animals 7.6 times more often than their caregivers reported. Frick et al. (1993) conclude that for parents reporting developing conduct disorder symptoms in their children, the age of 6 1/2 years seems to be the median age at which hurting animals appears. This is earlier than bullying, cruelty to others, vandalism, or fire setting.

The significance of addressing early aggressive behavior cannot be overemphasized. "The Pittsburgh Study," funded by the Office of Juvenile Justice and Delinquency Programs, is an ongoing longitudinal study of the causes and correlates of antisocial behavior that began in 1987. The longitudinal research from the Pittsburgh Youth Study showed that the development of disruptive and delinquent behavior takes place in a progressive fashion, adding weight to the argument that early identification of animal cruelty in children is essential. Youth exhibit less serious problem behavior first, and then gradually advance to committing more serious, disruptive, and delinquent behavior (Kelley, Loeber, Keenan, & DeLamatre, 1997). In addition, a recent analysis of these data determined that cruelty was one of four factors associated with the persistence of aggressive and criminal behavior (Loeber, 2004).

The literature also indicates that young children have been involved in the criminal justice system due to their abusive behavior toward animals. A recent analysis of prosecuted animal abuse cases during the period 1975–1996 indicated that children as young as 9 have been prosecuted, and that approximately 27% of the offenders were under the age of 18 (Luke, 1997). As law enforcement and juvenile justice systems professionals know, only a fraction of animal abuse cases ever are prosecuted, and the minimum age of eligibility for prosecution varies from state to state. A recent study in Maine (Righthand, Welch, Carpenter, Young, & Scoular, 2001) reviewed case records of adjudicated juvenile sex offenders in the state correctional system. For 15% of the males, there were indications of animal cruelty mentioned in the records even when this was not a focus of initial inquiry. In a companion study, Righthand et al. (2001) looked at the records of juveniles who were known to have committed sexual offenses, but were not necessarily known to the correctional system. An even larger number of these male juveniles, 26%, were found to have histories of cruelty to animals. In addition, 32% of these males were found to have engaged in fire setting.

Research studies have documented that children who are exposed to domestic violence or who are victims of physical or sexual abuse have been found to hurt animals. Children may mistreat their pets or other animals as a result of the mistreatment they themselves are experiencing. DeViney, Dickert, and Lockwood (1983) studied a sample of 53 families in which child abuse had been substantiated by the state child protective program. Of family members interviewed, 25% acknowledged that they or another member of the household had injured their pets at some time. Caseworkers directly observed animal abuse or neglect in an additional 38% of the families, which was either underreported or not reported in the interview. In addition, approximately a third of the abused children were found to have hurt the family pet, and in 14% of the cases, the child was reported to be the sole animal abuser. When children hurt animals, something is wrong in their lives. When the children's caregivers do not respond appropriately, something is wrong in the family. The response of the adult caregiver is crucial.

In a landmark study, Ascione (1998) interviewed women who were victims of domestic violence and had sought shelter. Of the 38 women he studied, 74% had pets. Of these, 71% reported that their violent partner had threatened to hurt or kill their pets. In addition, 32% of the women indicated that their children had hurt or killed family pets. In a later study, Ascione (2000) found that 54% of the women interviewed reported that their partners had actually hurt or killed their pets. In the earlier study, Ascione (1998) also found that concern for the welfare of their animals was reported as a deterrent to seeking shelter by 18% of the women. This is a powerful lesson in the ways that abusers may use threats of violence or actual violence to intimidate or control their victims. This dynamic extends to child physical and sexual abuse as well as domestic violence. Threats of harm to loved pets are sometimes used to guarantee the silence of the victims.

Exposure to mistreatment of animals may affect children in powerful ways. It may promote desensitization to the pain and suffering of a living creature and damage the capacity for developing empathy. It may give children the idea that they, like their pets, are not important, are expendable. It damages the child's sense of safety and confidence in the ability of adults to protect them from harm. It can lead to the idea that physical harm in allegedly loving relationships is acceptable. It can encourage children to seek power by inflicting pain and suffering on those

who are smaller, weaker. Abusive behaviors can be learned and imitated. These are dangerous lessons.

Children who may be at risk of hurting animals include victims of physical and or sexual abuse, witnesses to domestic violence, and witnesses to adults abusing animals or displaying a lack of compassion to the pain and suffering of animals. It is important to pay attention to how a child treats the family pets. If the child does accidentally harm an animal it is important to determine whether he or she feels remorse or regret for the actions. The child's response to the vulnerability and dependency of family pets is also an important factor. The child's reaction to the loss or death of family pets is also indicative of his or her ability to form loving attachments to animals. When children hurt something they care about, or should care about, such as a favorite toy, doll, or stuffed animal, we need to pay greater attention. When a child hurts a living creature, we really need to pay attention. The child is letting us know that something is wrong in his or her life. We need to find out what that is. Is the child in danger? Are others in the child's home in danger? What has gone wrong in the child's course of development? These are but a few of the critical factors in an assessment of a child who hurts animals. In fact, it may be important to assess experiences with animals for any young child entering the mental health system, even those who do not present with behaviors indicative of animal cruelty.

Assessment

Researchers in the field of animal cruelty have identified numerous motives underlying this disturbing behavior (Ascione, 2001; Ascione, Thompson, & Black, 1997; Kellert & Felthous, 1985). It is tempting to try to reduce these to several typologies based on the age of the abuser, the type of the abuse, whether the abuse is in reaction to victimization, etc. However, the assessment approach offered here suggests that this may be premature and perhaps overly simplistic. It may be dangerous to presume that because young children are developmentally immature, their abusive behavior toward an animal is based on innocent curiosity. Instead, we stress that it is very important to assess what a child's intentions were. We have found that in a clinical interview setting even children as young as 3 can answer our questions as to why they did what they did. Often those who do take childhood animal cruelty seriously make the assumption that a child who hurts animals does so based on ignorance or lack of information, and will benefit from spending time volunteering at an animal shelter where they can learn to interact with animals in a more humane manner. However, this is not always effective. For example, a child who abuses animals based on curiosity or ignorance may benefit from humane education. Yet this intervention is clearly not appropriate for a child whose animal cruelty is motivated by sexual arousal. We have learned that we must not make assumptions about why children do what they do, and what they need to stop doing it.

As we learn more about children who hurt animals, it may be determined that there are clusters of motivational factors, and that such clusters may respond to similar types of intervention. At this point in our research into these issues we would urge that all childhood animal cruelty be taken seriously, that a professional assessment be conducted that takes all possible motivations for the behavior into consideration as a guide toward determining the most effective treatment response.

We would urge that the time to conduct a clinical assessment of a child who hurts an animal is soon after such an incident first occurs. Lewchanin and Zimmerman (2000) have developed an extensive clinical interview format that is modeled after a program for assessing juvenile fire setting (DiMillo, 1996). DiMillo has developed an excellent protocol for interviewing children and their caregivers that provides a useful model for assessing a child's relationships with animals as well. The connection between childhood animal cruelty and fire setting has been an area of research interest for some time. As early as 1966, Hellman and Blackman (1966) looked at the possibility that animal cruelty, fire setting, and enuresis together might constitute an important "triad" of behaviors that could be predictive of adult violence. Subsequent research (Heath, Hardesty, & Goldfine, 1984) has suggested that enuresis might be the least predictive of these behaviors, and that an important connection might exist between animal cruelty and fire setting. In current clinical practice many mental health professionals view these two behaviors as having similar underlying clinical dynamics.

The assessment developed by Lewchanin and Zimmerman (2000) includes the chronological and developmental level of the child, environmental influences, current family functioning, as well as peer, cultural, and other influences. The interview protocol includes questions regarding the child's experiences and perceptions of animals (Boat, 1994) as well as the family's messages and modeling about human and animal treatment. The specific details of who, what, when, where, why, and how the incident of animal cruelty occurred, the number and severity of past incidents, and the extent to which the child demonstrates empathy for animals are also assessed. For example, caregivers are asked how they found out about the incident of animal cruelty, and how they responded. They are asked how they think the child got the idea to do this behavior. Questions include the child's reaction to being confronted about the behavior. Questions are asked as to how conflict is resolved in the home, and how the child is disciplined. In addition caregivers are asked about the family's experiences with pets, and how animals are treated in the home.

It is beyond the scope of this chapter to provide a detailed analysis of this assessment protocol; however, it can be summarized as covering four major areas.

1. The severity of the animal cruelty.
2. The level of the child's culpability (i.e., the extent to which the child can be held accountable).
3. The level of resilience of the child.
4. The level of readiness for change of the child and of the caregivers.

Measures of severity include the Children and Animals Assessment Instrument (Ascione, Thompson, & Black, 1997), the Factors in the Assessment of Dangerousness in Perpetrators of Animal Cruelty scale (Lockwood, 1998), as well as a summary scale developed by the authors. Culpability is measured by an adaptation of the Juvenile Culpability Assessment (Hindman, in press), which was designed for use with youth who act out sexually. Resilience is assessed based on the work of Steven and Sybil Wolin, (Wolin & Wolin, 1993) who define resilience as "the capacity to bounce back, to withstand hardship and repair yourself." The authors have developed a measure based on the work of the Wolins. Readiness for change is a concept developed by Prochaska, Norcross, and DiClemente (1994) and his colleagues. They suggest that change is a developmental process, in which people pass through several distinct stages. Intervention must be geared to the specific developmental stage in the change process in order to be effective. In addition, a checklist of motivations for animal cruelty is included.

Results of all of the previous measures can then be put together in a Summary Grid (see Appendix), which shows the relationship between severity, culpability, resilience, and readiness for change, both for the child and the caregivers. It should be stressed that it is the relationship between these measures that should direct treatment, not just any one single measure or concept. A case example: A 12-year-old child with mental retardation has killed a family pet, a gerbil, by squeezing it too hard. She has minimal understanding of the nature and consequences of her behavior and has minimal insight and desire to change. The behavior was motivated by curiosity and lack of understanding of the impact on the animal. She had no apparent intention to cause harm. However, the child has parents who clearly understand the situation as one of ongoing danger and are committed to provide appropriate education and supervision of any contact this child might have with animals. These are parents who immediately and without external pressure sought help. This assessment would result in a Summary Grid in which the Severity rating is high, Culpability is low, Resilience is low, Child's Readiness to Change is low, and Parent's Readiness to Change is high.

The intervention suggested by such a pattern would focus primarily on the parents, assisting and supporting them in their efforts to supervise and monitor the child's behavior and contact with animals. The child could be provided with humane education, such as that offered in *Teaching Compassion* (Raphael, Colman, & Loar, 1999). They define such education as "lessons that teach respect, responsibility, and compassion for all life" (p. 8). This program includes lessons on the connection between children and animals, pet care, pet overpopulation, habitat loss, the question of hunting, and animal neglect and abuse. The child's response to such a program would determine the extent to which she could safely have contact with animals.

Another case example: A 4-year-old child has committed a minor act of animal cruelty. He was caught attempting to take a goldfish out of its bowl to play with it. He is motivated by curiosity and lack of awareness of the impact of his behavior on the animal. The child is very bright and highly resilient, and has had minimal exposure to animals of any kind. Both the child and his parents are extremely distressed at what he had done, and both reacted with a high degree of motivation to make sure nothing like this happens again. They also immediately contacted the child's pediatrician for help for the

situation. Here the Severity rating is low, Culpability is low, Resilience is high, and both the Child's Readiness to Change and the Parent's Readiness to Change are high.

These parents would be supported in their concerns and attempts to provide more supervision for the child. In addition, because of the child's lack of exposure to animals and stated interest in learning more about animal care, this child could participate in a humane education program, which could be followed up with an opportunity to spend some time helping out at an animal shelter in an age-appropriate manner.

Another case involves a 12-year-old girl who stood on her porch and threw rocks at a neighbor's bird feeder until she had killed one of the feeding birds. She then put the bird in a box and presented it to her father, a veterinarian. The neighbor complained to the father, who scolded her, but did nothing else. The child had been in trouble before for bullying younger children in the neighborhood, and was suspected of setting several minor fires at home and at school. This child was unable to give a reason for this behavior, other than that she was "bored." She showed minimal remorse, and seemed unconcerned that she had killed the bird. Results of the interviews with her and her father indicated that she had a long history of mistreatment of family pets; however, these behaviors were minimized by her and her father. This would be a situation where the Severity is high, Culpability is high, Resilience is moderate, and Readiness to Change, for both parent and child, are low. In this case intervention would need to begin with the parent, who needs assistance in recognizing that his child is exhibiting some serious behavior problems.

These are only a few of the numerous patterns that would evolve from the information gathered in the assessment process. Each situation is unique, and will require an individually designed intervention program.

Treatment

The most difficult part of working with a child who hurts animals may be in identifying and referring the child and family to treatment in the first place. As has been argued throughout this chapter, taking this problem behavior seriously is often the major obstacle. Both the assessment and the treatment of children who hurt animals is really quite straightforward. The skills required to intervene with these children should be within the clinical repertoire of any well-trained child mental health professional. Once the child is involved in mental health assessment and treatment, the process may not be all that difficult. We are not suggesting that the clinician needs to do anything all that radically different, only that the child's abusive behavior toward animals be viewed as the primary focus of intervention. Certainly, if it is determined that the child is not safe in a home due to physical or sexual abuse, or neglect, then child protective services needs to be involved immediately. If family violence is occurring, then this needs to be addressed as well. Once human safety issues are assessed and resolved, then the animal cruelty behaviors need to be prioritized and addressed. Rather than viewing animal cruelty as a part of the background of the child's problems or as a result of some other emotional issues, it should be seen as the starting point of treatment.

There are several components of intervention that need to be considered in approaching intervention with a child who has hurt an animal. These factors include:

1. Mandate or leverage for intervention. In other words, who is urging treatment? Is it the community police, the court, the school, the day care program, the babysitter, or the family? In other words, who in the child's life is concerned about the child's behavior toward animals? The agent of intervention and their associated leverage is likely to be a critical factor in the success of the outcome.

2. Safety issues. As a result of the comprehensive assessment process, is the child in danger? Are other adults in the home in danger? Are animals in the home in danger at the hands of the adults? The assessment may lead to referrals to child protective services, adult protective services, domestic violence programs, or animal control agents. In the case of domestic violence, it is particularly important to be sensitive to victim safety issues, and not report without the victim's consent. As previously discussed, these interventions need to take priority before the child's problematic behavior can be effectively addressed.

3. Containment issues. Are animals in the home in danger at the hands of the child? There may be necessary restrictions on contact with animals including supervision, limited access, or, in the case of older offenders, restraining orders or termination of rights to have animals. A critical factor is whether the adults in the child's life are willing to ensure

that animals in the home are safe, and that the child does not have unsupervised access to animals in the neighborhood. In working with a young child, work with their family will be crucial in making certain that they are able and willing to set appropriate limits on the child's behavior. As indicated in the previous section on assessment, the family's willingness and readiness to make the necessary changes are a key component of the success of intervention.

4. Restitution issues. These may take the form of financial restitution or interpersonal restitution. Is there any way the child can compensate for the harm they have caused? Although restitution is a concept usually applied to adult offenders, it can be very therapeutic for juvenile offenders to experience the process of trying to make up in some way for the harm or damage that they have done.

5. Educational needs. Following the assessment, it will be determined what the child and perhaps the caregivers need in the way of education about the care and treatment of animals. Education may take the form of humane education and/or animal-assisted therapy, among other approaches, to enhance empathy.

6. Skills training. The assessment may identify other educational needs of the child, such as life skills education, social skills training, anger management training, and conflict resolution skills. These may focus on the reduction of negative behaviors and deficits, as well as efforts to increase and build on the child's assets.

7. Psychotherapy. The results of the assessment may identify more intense psychological needs of the child that may indicate treatment for post-traumatic stress disorder, anxiety and mood disorders, affect dysregulation, attachment issues, and conduct disorders ranging from mild to the more psychopathological.

There is a clear need for treatment models to address the specific needs of children who hurt animals. Although at least 27 states have provisions in their animal anti-cruelty laws that either recommend or mandate counseling for youthful offenders (see *The Impact of Improved American Anti-Cruelty Laws* by Frasch, this text), there are few published treatment programs. An excellent program, *AniCare Child* (Randour, Krinsk, & Wolf, 2001), has been developed by the Doris Day Animal Foundation and Psychologists for the Ethical Treatment of Animals as a response to changes in the state animal cruelty laws.

AniCare Child offers practical assessment and treatment strategies for counselors and others working with at-risk children and children identified as engaging in animal cruelty. It focuses on two goals of treatment, the development of self-management skills and the development of empathy, by providing exercises, projective materials, and clinical case examples. In addition to its use with identified and at-risk children, the *AniCare Child* approach encourages all professionals working with children and families to make assessments of a child's and family's relationship to animals a routine part of any formal or informal evaluation, just as questions of substance abuse and family violence are routinely included in screenings of children and families.

In summary, not all juvenile animal cruelty behaviors have the same etiology, motivation, meaning, or severity. Animal cruelty by a child is not simply a form of conduct disorder. Assessing animal abuse may uncover domestic violence, intimidation, threats, or child abuse and/or neglect. It may mean that the parents need help in supervising, setting limits, and practicing positive parenting skills. (see *Collaborating to Assess, Intervene, and Prosecute Animal Abuse* by Boat, Loar, & Phillips, this text). Animal cruelty rarely happens in isolation. Moreover, no treatment is likely to be effective if the child is still in a dangerous situation, is continuing to be abused, or still feels threatened or unsafe. Treatment is not likely to be effective if the child's caregivers continue to allow the child to be abusive to animals or people. Children who hurt animals must be given a clear and direct message by their families and by our culture that this behavior is not acceptable.

In recent years, we seem to have become reluctant to tell children that they are doing something wrong or bad. As the anthropologist Margaret Mead (1964) pointed out, societies are based on their ability to define and restrict deviant behavior. Martin Seligman, past president of the American Psychological Association, has cautioned against overvaluing self-esteem at the expense of self-control (Seligman, Reivich, Jaycox, & Gillham, 1995). Now we appear reluctant to judge a child's behavior as wrong. Perhaps we have valued enhancing self-esteem at the cost of tolerating deviant behavior. Yet a child who hurts a defenseless animal should feel bad. This is an example of a situation in which a child should feel shame and remorse over his or her behavior. Defining and restricting this behavior is how the family and the larger culture help the child to become positively socialized.

The Need for Community Education

The previous discussion suggests that there is a great deal of work to be done in educating both the lay and professional community about animal cruelty in general and in particular the significance of this behavior in very young children. The experiences of one volunteer coalition will be discussed briefly in an attempt to illustrate how such efforts might proceed.

In 1996, a countywide task force on the connection between child abuse, domestic violence, and animal cruelty (referred to as the LINK) was established by a group of volunteers in York County, Maine. This group consisted of representatives of child protective services, the local humane society and animal shelter, the county domestic violence program, animal control officers, and the county child abuse and neglect council. Over the years this group has focused its attention on educating the professional and lay community about the link between child abuse, domestic violence, and animal cruelty. A mission statement evolved that read, *"To educate the community about the connection between animal cruelty, child abuse, domestic violence, and other forms of interpersonal violence. To encourage all members of the community to be able to recognize and respond effectively to all types of violence."*

Public awareness efforts have included distributing brochures to schools and parent–teacher organizations throughout the county, and including information fliers in the monthly bills for television service going out to over 10,000 homes countywide. Presentations have been made to numerous professional groups, including a daylong conference with Dr. Randall Lockwood, workshops at the annual child abuse prevention conference, training for school social workers, university social work classes, local school systems, and hospital staffs. Cross training has also been emphasized. This involves reaching out to professionals in several areas of violence prevention or intervention and inviting them to participate in training together. These have included the state animal control association, the county collaborative on juvenile fire setting, and joint training of domestic violence shelter and animal shelter staff. The task force has also tried to reach out to groups that might come into contact with young children who are struggling with this problem, such as day care providers, visiting nurses, and child protection workers.

In general, most community and professional groups have been very receptive to initial educational efforts on the LINK. Most of these groups have immediately grasped the importance of the connection between various forms of violence, as well as the need for coordinated intervention by the appropriate community agencies. A great deal of progress has been made in terms of getting information out to the community in general, and the professional community in particular. The coalition was instrumental in establishing a "safe haven" (Ascione, 2000) program, in conjunction with the domestic violence shelter, that offers women temporary foster care for their pets if this has been a barrier to leaving a violent living situation. In addition, as a direct result of the coalition's efforts, the concept of the LINK is now incorporated into many other types of trainings offered throughout the state, such as those conducted by domestic violence programs, other county child abuse and neglect trainings, humane society trainings, and trainings for animal control officers. This small group of volunteers has become a model for groups throughout the state.

However, there have often been subtle and not so subtle indications that many people, even seasoned professionals, do not really want to listen to information about animal cruelty. Mental health professionals with extensive experience seem more at ease hearing about abused children and women, yet have been traumatized hearing about abused animals. We have heard feedback that indicates mental health professionals "don't want to hear about this awful stuff." In particular, we have noticed that as long as the offender against animals is an adult, the audience appears to be much more receptive to the idea of intervention, especially by law enforcement. It has been more difficult to gain acceptance of the need to hold children accountable for their violent behavior toward animals.

Shortly after its inception, the coalition conducted an informal survey of a number of mental health clinicians, from both mental health agencies and private practice. Of the 29 who responded to the mailed survey, 42% indicated that they are willing to work with children who hurt animals, and 48% indicated they would see adolescents with this behavior problem. In addition, 60% indicated that they would like additional training on the LINK. These results were encouraging, but not indicative of an overwhelming number of professionals willing to serve as treatment resources.

When we attempt to stress the need for intervention when the offender is an adolescent, or a young child, there is much more denial that younger offenders could engage in such dangerous and offensive behavior. Time and time again, we have been questioned by audiences as to why we are getting so worked up over children pulling puppies' tails! When we respond by explaining that we are talking about much more serious forms of cruelty, there is a disconnect on the part of the listener. They cringe when we give the example of a child dousing a cat with gasoline and setting it on fire. "How could such a young child do such a thing?" This is not unlike the response to hearing that a young child, perhaps a 5 year old, has engaged in serious sexual abuse of another child. People just don't want to hear about this material! And yet, one of the most critical messages regarding children and animal cruelty is that when a young child is exhibiting such behaviors, something is seriously wrong.

Recently a family court judge shared with one of the authors (Lewchanin) a case in which a 3-year-old girl had climbed up on a counter and shoved the family cat into the microwave oven. When the judge inquired as to what the parent had done in response to this, she was told "I'm sure the child didn't mean to do that"! Very young children are exhibiting behaviors that are far beyond the norm, and parents are in shock and denial. And these children are apparently not being brought to the attention of the mental health system.

It is curious to note the rarity with which children are brought into a clinical setting for behavior that is cruel toward animals. Some states have enacted legislation that requires psychological evaluation for adults convicted of animal cruelty, while other states have imposed this requirement only for juveniles (Humane Society of the United States, 1999). Maine has legislation that states that the court "shall order" counseling for juveniles convicted of animal cruelty. Yet informal discussions with colleagues suggest that this is a rare event. One of the authors (Lewchanin), who has a reputation for interest in this area, has to date not received a single referral of a child for concerns around animal cruelty.

Clearly, mental health providers are struggling with these issues. We have been invited in for initial presentations, but we have not been invited back for ongoing collaboration and case conferencing.

We have provided information as to how to report animal cruelty and how to refer children and families for help, yet cases are rarely reported and, as previously discussed, children are rarely referred. For a long time it has been argued that people need to know about the LINK so that early intervention can occur. We are now faced with developing additional strategies for addressing the community and professional denial that even a very young child can engage in behaviors that are horribly violent. Unless we can reach their caregivers, families, pediatricians, day care providers, religious educators, and the community as a whole, the future developmental course for young children who hurt animals is likely to be a rough one.

Policy Considerations

As previously noted, too often the courts, mental health professionals, parents, educators, and other community leaders either do not recognize the significance of childhood animal cruelty for the child and society, or they fail to act on the information they have. This section will examine how a larger context of policy and practice influences the attitudes and actions of various professional groups. In particular, this section will examine: (1) federal funding of research on animal cruelty; (2) federal and state crime data reporting systems; and (3) professional standards for, and government oversight of, counselor training.

Federal Funding of Research on Animal Cruelty

The research and practice community has made considerable progress in acknowledging the seriousness of childhood animal cruelty. As previously mentioned, many states now either mandate or permit counseling for juvenile offenders. However, there remains a serious lack of funding for research on animal cruelty, even though animal cruelty is an important aspect of the larger problem of youth violence and delinquent youth.

In the 1980s, there was growing alarm among juvenile justice agencies about the rapid increase in youthful violence. Responding to this legitimate concern, the federal government, as well as private agencies, directed funding to conduct research on the causes and correlates of youth violence and to evaluate what types of intervention were most successful.

One well-known group of studies on the causes and correlates of delinquency began in 1987, headed

by teams at the University at Albany, State University of New York; the University of Colorado; and the University of Pittsburgh. These three teams interviewed 4,000 participants at regular intervals at study sites of Rochester, New York; Denver, Colorado; and Pittsburgh, Pennsylvania.

As noted earlier, these well-designed and comprehensive studies provided valuable information to researchers, policymakers, and program planners by showing that "the development of disruptive and delinquent behavior by boys generally takes place in an orderly, progressive fashion, with less serious problem behaviors preceding more serious problem behaviors" (Kelley et al., 1997, pp. 1–2). After the government dedicated increased resources to the problem of escalating youth violence, the latest analysis of crime data shows a decline in juvenile crime (Snyder, 2003).

Even though many of these studies collected data on animal cruelty, it was not included in the data analysis or in the construction of developmental models. For example, The Pittsburgh Youth Study proposed a developmental pathway model, as well as an ordering of the various manifestations of disruptive and antisocial behaviors in childhood and adolescence, and the temporal sequence of developmental tasks relevant for pro-social development. In the construction of a developmental pathway model, the researchers used an earlier study by Frick et al. (1993), which produced a Multidimensional Scale of Disruptive Behavior (MSDB) with a destructive-nondestructive dimension and a covert-overt dimension. These two dimensions produced four quadrants: property violations (covert, destructive), aggression (overt, destructive), status violations (covert, nondestructive), and oppositional (nondestructive, overt).

In the MSDB developed by Frick et al., animal cruelty appeared in the higher end of the destructive pole, with "property violations," but very close to the "aggression" quadrant. The formulations provided by The Pittsburgh Youth Study (1997), however, did not include animal cruelty in their listing of component behaviors used to develop their conceptual model of covert, overt, and authority conflict categories, which formed the basis for the construction of their developmental pathways model.

Why does animal cruelty disappear as a factor in building models of disruptive behavior? It is a behavior identified by DSM-III-R, DSM IV, and DSMM IV TR as a symptom of conduct disorder; it is recognized as an early "marker" of troubled youth; it is associated with other forms of violence.

Additionally, animals play an important role in the lives of families and communities.

If the bad news is that The Pittsburgh Youth Study did not include the variable of animal cruelty in the analyses, the good news is that these data sets, and other longitudinal data sets, have information about animal cruelty that could be analyzed. For example, The Pittsburgh Youth Study asked questions about cruelty that included both cruelty to people and animals. The Montreal study, conducted by Richard E. Tremblay and colleagues, as well as the Christchurch School of Medicine longitudinal study in New Zealand, collected data about animal cruelty that as yet has not been analyzed (Broidy et al., 2003). Even if these studies contain only a single item that asks about animal cruelty, they still could provide valuable information. If single items produced similar results across studies, the resulting converging validity would offer strong support for the findings.

Secondary analyses of these data sets might yield information about the following questions. If animal cruelty is considered in the development of disruptive and delinquent behaviors, where does it appear in the sequence of the age of onset for these behaviors? Is animal cruelty associated with other behavioral problems, such as ADHD? Are the type, severity, and other characteristics of animal cruelty relevant to understanding the degree of risk the child faces? If animal cruelty were considered a crime of violence in the Multidimensional Scale of Disruptive Behavior, how would that affect its usefulness as a factor for understanding the development of disruptive and delinquent behavior?

Crime Data Reporting Systems

The Statistical Briefing Book (SBB) developed by the National Center for Juvenile Justice for the Office of Juvenile Justice and Delinquency Prevention lists the following eight national data sets (retrieved June 25, 2007, from http://ojjdp.ncjrs.org/ojstatbb/): Census of Juveniles in Residential Placement, Monitoring the Future: A Continuing Study of the Lifestyles and Values of Youth, Uniform Crime Reporting Program; National-Incident Based Reporting System, National Longitudinal Survey of Youth 1997, National Youth Risk Behavior Survey, National Crime Victimization Survey, and National Child Abuse and Neglect Child Data File.

Five of these data sets are considered here: Census of Juveniles in Residential Placement, the Federal Bureau of Investigation's Uniform Crime Reporting Program and National-Incident Based Reporting System, National Crime Victimization Survey, and the National Child Abuse and Neglect Data File. All of these databases either contain unanalyzed information about animal cruelty or have categories of questions to which a question about animal cruelty would have relevance and add important information.

Following are examples of how animal cruelty might be added to the analysis of some of these data sets or added to the instrumentation.

Census of Juveniles in Residential Placement. The Census of Juveniles in Residential Placement (CJRP) was administered by the U.S. Bureau of the Census for the Office of Juvenile Justice and Delinquency Prevention (OJJDP) for the first time in 1997, replacing the Children in Custody (CIC) census. The CJRP, conducted biennially, records the most serious crime committed by each juvenile in residential placement. The Offense Code Card uses five categories: Offenses Against Property, Offenses Against Persons, Drug-Related Offenses, Offenses Against the Public Order, and Probation or Parole Violation. One of the subcategories under Offense Against Public Order is "Other public order offenses" (retrieved June 25, 2007, from http:ojjdp.ncjrs.org/ojstatbb/Cjrp/pdf/CJRP1999form.pdf).

At present, animal cruelty is recorded in "Other public order offenses," making it impossible to retrieve the data on the rate of animal cruelty among juvenile offenders in residential placement. Again, there is vital information that is lost by not having animal cruelty reported in a way in which the data can be retrieved and analyzed. One possible remedy would be to assign animal cruelty to its own subcategory within the "Offenses Against the Public Order" category.

The Three Crime Data Collections Systems of the Federal Bureau of Investigation: (1) Uniform Crime Reporting Program, (2) National Incident-Based Reporting System, and (3) "National Indices Initiative." The Federal Bureau of Investigation (FBI) has administered the Uniform Crime Reporting Program (UCR) since 1930. The purpose of this data collection system is to obtain nationally representative estimates of the level and change in level of crimes reported by state and local police organizations. Crimes in the UCR are placed into two categories: Part I, which include the most serious crimes that constitute the Crime Index; and Part II crimes, such as fraud, vandalism, drug abuse violations, curfew, and loitering laws. The manual sent by the FBI to local and state law enforcement agencies instructs them to record contact with juveniles in the same way as they would for adults, although adults and juveniles will be processed differently in the court system (Federal Bureau of Investigation, UCR Handbook, personal communication).

As reported in the SBB, "The amount of data on juveniles in the UCR is quite limited. Coverage problems in the system further limit the usefulness of the available data. Moreover, because the system is jurisdiction-based rather than incident-based, the data cannot be manipulated extensively to provide estimates useful in national estimation or policy research" (retrieved June 25, 2007, from http://ojjdp. ncjrs.org/ojstatbb/Compendium/asp/Compendium. asp?selData=3).

The FBI sought to address some of the short-coming of the UCR system with the development of the National Incident-Based Reporting System (NIBRS). NIBRS entails an incident-based reporting rather than jurisdiction-based, or summary, reporting. It provides more complete information on crimes, victims, and offenders than UCR. Implementation has been slow and to date only 18% of local and state police agencies participate, covering only a minority of the U.S. population. Although NIBRS' coverage is quite limited, it is an improvement, enabling the analysis of incidents of juveniles as victims or offenders, the relationship between offender and victim, the number of offenders and victims, the severity of injury, incident setting, weapon and substance abuse, and incident timing. The improvement made by NIBRS would have been enhanced if this system had assigned animal cruelty crimes as a separate category so they could be retrieved and analyzed (retrieved June 25, 2007, from http://ojjdp.ncjrs. org/ojstatbb/Compendium/asp/Compendium. asp?selData=4).

Currently, the FBI is developing a third version of the crime data collection system, referred to as the "national indices initiative." This new initiative is in the strategic planning stages of development with approximately 20 local, state, and federal agencies participating in a pilot project. This latest version of the FBI crime report data collection system "is envisioned as a national repository of incident/case report information that would yield expanded details concerning a subject's criminal history, known associates, employment/trade, modus operandi,

etc." (M. D. Kirkpatrick, personal communication to Honorable Paul Sarbanes, September 10, 2003).

Animal cruelty is a crime in every state and, as noted, some acts of animal cruelty are a felony in 43 states and the District of Columbia. Animal cruelty also is linked to other crimes, including child abuse and spousal abuse. Yet there is no category except "other" for local and state police agencies to report data on animal cruelty crime, making its future retrieval and analysis impossible.

Assigning animal cruelty a separate category in the FBI's crime data collection system could be added without any additional costs to local police agencies. As police agencies convert from UCR to NIBRS, or adopt the forthcoming national indices system, this new category could be incorporated into the system and absorbed in the general costs entailed in converting to a new system.

Although they have made no commitment to do so, the Federal Bureau of Investigation recognizes that the inclusion of animal cruelty as a separate category in the national indices initiative would add considerable data analysis capabilities. "(V)ariables such as felony animal abuse arrests could be linked with a vast array of other statistics to develop useful demographic information" (M. D. Kirkpatrick, personal communication to Congressman Chris Van Hollen, May 5, 2003).

There also is Congressional interest in the FBI making this change. In response to an effort initiated by the Doris Day Animal League, the House Committee on Appropriations passed out of committee a report with the following language:

N-Dex.- The Committee understands that the FBI is currently developing an information sharing system called the Law Enforcement National Data Exchange (N-DEx). Once implemented, the N-DEx will deliver enhanced analysis of criminal justice data, improving law enforcement's ability to detect, investigate, link, predict, prevent, and solve crimes and report statistics. The Committee believes that N-DEx should be capable of reporting on the incidence of animal cruelty crimes. Further, the Committee directs the FBI, in coordination with the Criminal Justice Information Service Division's Advisory Policy Board (APD), to provide a report to the Committee on the advantages and disadvantages of adding animal cruelty crimes as a crime category in the Uniform Crime Report.

The report shall discuss adding animal cruelty crimes as a category for State and local agencies that are implementing the National Incident-Based Reporting System (NIBRS) in the future. The report shall also make recommendations concerning whether animal cruelty should be considered as a crime against society as opposed to a crime against property. The Committee directs this report to be submitted within 180 days of enactment of this Act. (House Report 108–576, second session, Departments of Commerce, Justice, and State, the Judiciary, and Related Agencies Appropriations Bill, Fiscal Year 2005)

The National Crime Victimization Survey. The National Crime Victimization Survey (NCVS), a nationally representative sample of approximately 49,000 households, obtains information on the frequency, characteristics, and consequences of criminal victimization in the United States. Crimes are categorized as "personal" or as "property." Vandalism is one type of property crime covered by NCVS (retrieved June 24, 2007, from http://ojjdp.ncjrs.org/ojstatbb/Compendium/asp/Compendium.asp?selData=7).

In the "Household Respondent's Vandalism Screen Questions," question 46b asks, "What kind of property was damaged or destroyed in this/these act(s) of vandalism? Anything else?" One of the possible responses to question 46b is "Animal (pet, livestock, etc.)." The following question 46c asks, "What kind of damage was done in this/these act(s) of vandalism? Anything else?" Again, one of the responses is "Injured or killed animals" (retrieved June 24, 2007, from http://www.icpsr.umich.edu/NACJD/NCVS/#About_NCVS).

Although data about the rate of injured and/or killed animals are not presently analyzed in the NCVS, it is possible for those data to be extracted from the current NCVS database (T. Zelenock, personal communication, April 9, 2004). As there are currently no statistics on the rates of animal cruelty, a very useful first step would be to analyze the NCVS for this information.

Expanding the reach of the National Child Abuse and Neglect Data System Child File Including animal cruelty as a variable in these data sets would offer more information on at-risk youth, families, and perpetrators, and could guide intervention efforts. For example, the National Child Abuse and Neglect Data System Child File is a national data collection and analysis program on child abuse and neglect. The Children's Bureau in the Administration for Children and Families maintains the national data collection and analysis program (retrieved June 25, 2007, from http://ojjdp.ncjrs.org/ojstatbb/Compendium/asp/Compendium.asp?selData=7).

One of the areas of interest addresses caretaker risk factors; for example, for the primary/family caretakers, data is sought on the presence of substance abuse, mental or physical disability, emotional disturbance, domestic violence, financial strain, and inadequate housing (retrieved June 25, 2007, from http://www.ndacan.cornell.edu/NDACAN/Datasets/Abstracts/DatasetAbstract_NCANDS_Child_File.html).

As animal cruelty frequently overlaps with both child abuse and spousal abuse, separate questions about the presence and type of animal abuse by primary/family caretakers would add useful information. The more serious degrees of animal injury could indicate advanced pathology and a more lethal situation; identification of members who are participating in animal cruelty also could help identify the extent to which children in the family have been affected by their abuse and are now externalizing that experience. If animal cruelty is present, other resources in the community could be mobilized that would add to the efforts being made to protect children and families. Animal control officers, many of who are now trained to recognize and report child abuse, could coordinate visits with child protective service agencies, offering the family greater coverage.

State Juvenile Justice Agencies. The data collection by state agencies of juvenile crime statistics mirrors the FBI's approach to collection and recording animal cruelty arrests. Despite the utility of animal cruelty as a marker for the development of delinquent behavior and its association with other risk factors, such as family violence, state systems do no collect juvenile crime statistics on animal cruelty. For example, in the State of Maryland, juvenile crimes are organized into four categories: (1) Person-to-Person Offenses, (2) Property Offenses, (3) Alcohol & Drug Related Offenses, and (4) Uncategorized Offenses. Specific subcategories of the "Uncategorized Offenses" include conspiracy, loitering, motor vehicle/traffic violations, pager at school, telephone misuse, and tobacco violations, but not animal cruelty (Maryland Department of Juvenile Justice, 2002).

A preliminary review of the data collection of state agencies could not identify any state that collects or reports animal cruelty as a separate category in its juvenile crime data. An examination of the FBI Arrest Statistics for juveniles for the years 1994–2001 reveals a total of 6,896 per 100,000 and the number of arrests within "All other offenses" include 1,205 per 100,000, or 17.47% of all arrests for juveniles in this time period, making it the subcategory with the largest number of arrests in the entire crime index (retrieved June 25, 2007, from http://ojjdp.ncjrs.org/ojstatbb/ezaucr/).

Presumably some proportion of those arrested for "All other offenses" committed acts of animal cruelty, yet because of the way in which juvenile crime statistics are ordered, there is no way to determine this. The lack of such information has at least two important consequences. First, not reporting animal cruelty crimes among juveniles implies that these behaviors are not important, which contradicts evidence that they are. Second, lack of information about the demographics and other factors associated with animal cruelty restricts the ability to identify at-risk youth as early as possible and to design the most effective interventions for them.

Professional Standards and Government Oversight of Mental Health Professionals. Standards for the licensure and re-licensure of mental health professionals—psychologists, social workers, marriage and family counselors, and counselors—are typically established by state government, often working in cooperation with professional associations. Some states now require the inclusion of courses on family violence, sexual abuse, and substance abuse as part of required coursework leading to a degree in a mental health profession. For example, the California Business and Professional Code (2002) states:

> This bill will require any applicant for licensure as a psychologist who began graduate study on or after Jan. 1, 2004 to complete a minimum of 15 contact hours of coursework in spousal or partner abuse assessment, detection, and intervention strategies. … Additionally, on January 1, 2004 this new law will require all licensed psychologists who began graduate study prior to January 1, 2004 to take a course in spousal or partner abuse assessment, detection and intervention strategies for his or her first renewal after the

operative date of this new law. This is a one-time renewal requirement (Senate Bill No. 564, Chapter 481).

In Florida, psychologists seeking license renewal must take one hour of domestic violence coursework (Chapter 64B19–12 FL Administrative Code).

Not all states specify coursework in family violence, as California and Florida do. An opportunity exists for coalitions of domestic violence, child protective services, and animal protection groups to propose amendments to legislation in states where there is no such specification, so that family violence, including animal abuse, is added to the requirements for licensure and re-licensure of mental health professionals.

Related to this needed change in professional standards and licensing is the need for relevant state agencies to establish standards for, and provide oversight of, counseling programs that have been certified to assess and treat juvenile animal cruelty. Government oversight of treatment programs for batterers provides a framework for how this could be accomplished. The certification of batterer treatment programs occurs at the state level and every state maintains its own system. In California, the Department of Probation certifies programs, whereas in Michigan, it is a governor's task force that established batterer intervention standards, and in Massachusetts the Department of Public Health is the agency responsible.

Adding coursework on the assessment and treatment of animal cruelty to these educational standards could be a powerful tool for changing the attitudes and behavior of the mental health profession toward animal cruelty.

The legitimacy of animal cruelty as a serious behavior that needs to be addressed by the mental health profession will not be achieved until it is included as a required subject in the training and retraining of this professional community.

Additionally, this change in professional standards also would ensure that counselors are appropriately trained. Although it is important for the courts, prosecutors, and others in the juvenile justice system to recognize the importance of treating juveniles who engage in animal cruelty, it also is important that counselors be trained. The mental health profession has long accepted the significance of animal cruelty as a symptom, but it mostly neglected to recognize the importance of directly addressing animal cruelty as a behavior.

Discussion

In his review of animal abuse and youth violence, Ascione (2001) notes the value of national data collection systems in the area of child abuse and neglect, but observes, "it is not clear how animal abuse offenses could be incorporated into the existing categorization (person, property, drug, public order) of juvenile arrests" (p. 10). The Office of Juvenile Justice and Delinquency Prevention (OJJDP) provides a slightly different list of categories. OJJDP's "crimes and behavior youth may be arrested for" are violent crimes, property crimes, other crimes (non-indexed by the OJJDP), and status offenses. Some of the "other" non-indexed crimes are loitering, suspicious behavior, and vagrancy; animal cruelty is not on the list within any of OJJDP's categories (retrieved June 25, 2007, from http://ojjdp.ncjrs.gov/ojstatbb/ezacjrp/pdf/CJRP2003form.pdf).

The Pittsburgh Study observes a difference between the juvenile justice community and mental health practitioners as to what constitutes disruptive behavior. Citing the American Psychiatric Association, Kelly et al. (1997) note that mental health practitioners consider a range of diagnostic labels as disruptive child behaviors, including conduct disorder, which may involve aggression toward people and animals. Contrasted to the mental health community, which recognizes animal cruelty as an indicator of conduct disorder, juvenile justice practitioners define delinquent and disruptive behaviors as property crimes, violent crimes against persons, sale or alcohol or drugs, illegal possession of weapons, and status offenses.

The failure to develop categories that include the collection, retrieval, and analysis of data on animal cruelty crimes could be easily resolved. There are at least two ways to accomplish this goal.

The first approach would entail an updated and enhanced legal definition of property. David Favre (2000) of the University of Michigan Law School observes, "As property laws are a human construct and not an inherent characteristic of physical objects, there is always conceptual space for innovation" (p. 2). In a carefully articulated legal argument, he makes the case for animals being assigned a qualitatively different position within property law. Such a "special designation" of animals as property would satisfy the concerns expressed by Alex Foster, Assistant State's Attorney for Montgomery County, Maryland. At a sentencing hearing for a person convicted of felony animal cruelty, Mr. Foster urged the judge to ignore the recommendation of the sentencing guidelines. He noted that because animals were categorized as property, the formula used underestimated the seriousness of the crime. Mr. Foster noted, "Animals are not human beings, of course. However, they are also not just property. They are sentient beings, so that cruelly injuring and killing an animal has a different motivation and consequence" (Alex Foster, personal communication, January 15, 2003).

Another approach is to adopt the three categories of crime offered by NIBRS, which are (1) Crimes Against Persons, (2) Crimes Against Property, and (3) Crimes Against Society (retrieved June 25, 2007, from http:www.fbi.gov/ucr/nibrs/manuals/v1all.pdf).

There are several advantages to this approach. First, the Federal Bureau of Investigation, which often sets the standard for law enforcement, established this framework. Second, the framework has been in operation for over 15 years so it has been tested. Finally, the category of "Crimes Against Society" would be the most logical place for crimes of animal cruelty. Like other crimes in that category—drug use, disorderly conduct, and non-violent family offenses—animal cruelty is a crime that often reflects distress in families and communities. In addition, classifying animal cruelty under "Crimes Against Society" would recognize that the neglect, injury, and killing of a sentient creature, albeit a being legally defined as property, are actions that are qualitatively different from other destructive acts against property.

Summary

The subjects of this chapter—the assessment and treatment of children's experiences with animal cruelty and what the community and policy responses are to that area of behavior—underline the necessary interaction between these topics. In fact, these four topics—assessment, treatment, community needs, and policy responses—form an interactive loop, each feeding and building on one another. Clinicians recognize the fluid categories of assessment and treatment, with assessment being an ongoing enterprise in the therapeutic relationship and treatment being initiated with the first contact with the client. The same holds for the needs for community education and policy responses. As community education on the significance of animal cruelty grows, in turn the community influences policy decisions. The increase in enhanced penalties for animal cruelty in many states is one example of this. Conversely, as policy changes are instituted that reflect an appreciation of the importance of animal cruelty, the community at large is affected. In 2003, the Florida animal cruelty statute added mandatory counseling for children adjudicated for animal cruelty. As a result of that policy change, service providers began to request training in juvenile animal cruelty so that they could feel equipped to handle the cases to which they had been referred.

There is a benefit for all relevant parties—mental health, community groups, and policy makers—to both understand the significance of animal cruelty for animal and human welfare and also how effectively assessing and treating animal cruelty depends on informed communities and responsive policies.

References

Achenbach, T. M., Howell, C. T., Quay, H. C., & Conners, C. K. (1991). National survey of problems and competencies among four-to-sixteen year olds. *Monographs of the Society for Research in Child Development, 56,* Serial No. 255.

American Psychiatric Association. (1987). *Diagnostic and statistical manual of mental disorders* (3rd ed.). Washington, DC: Author.

Arkow, P. (1997) The relationship between animal abuse and other forms of family violence. *The Latham Letter, 18*(1).

Arluke, A., Levin, J., Luke, C., & Ascione, F. R. (1998). The relationship of animal abuse to violence and other forms of antisocial behavior. *Journal of Interpersonal Violence, 4*(9), 963–975.

Ascione, F. R. (1993). Children who are cruel to animals: A review of research and implications for developmental psychopathology. *Anthrozoös, 6,* 226–247.

Ascione, F. R. (1998). Battered women's reports of their partners' and children's cruelty to animals. *Journal of Emotional Abuse, 1,* 119–133.

Ascione, F. R. (2000). *Safe havens for pets: Guidelines for programs sheltering pets for women who are battered.* Logan, UT: Author.

Ascione, F. R. (2001). Animal abuse and youth violence. *Juvenile Justice Bulletin.* Washington, DC: Department of Justice, Office of Justice Programs, Office of Juvenile Justice and Delinquency Prevention.

Ascione, F. R. (2004). *Children and animals, kindness and cruelty.* West Lafayette, IN: Purdue University press.

Boat, B. W. (1994). *Boat inventory on animal-related experiences.* Cincinnati, OH: University of Cincinnati, Department of Psychiatry.

Broidy, L. M., Tremblay, R. E., Brume, B., Ferguson, D., Howard, J. L., Laird, R., et al. (2003). Developmental trajectories of childhood disruptive behaviors and adolescent delinquency: A six-site, cross-national study. *Developmental Psychology, 39,* 222–245.

Census of juveniles in residential placement. Compendium of National Juvenile Justice Data Sets. Retrieved on June 25, 2007 from http:ojjdp.ncjrs.org/ojstatbb/Cjrp/pdf/CJRP-1999form.pdf

Deviney, E., Dickert, J., & Lockwood, R. (1983). The care of pets within child abusing families. *International Journal for the Study of Animal Problems, 4,* 321–329.

DiMillo, J. (1996). *Children and fire—A bad match: A juvenile firesetter intervention program.* Jerry DiMillo, Publication Officer, Portland Fire Department, Portland, Maine.

Easy Access to Census of Juveniles in Residential Placement. Retrieved on June 25, 2007http://ojjdp.ncjrs.gov/ojstatbb/ezacjrp/pdf/CJRP-2003form.pdf

Easy Access to FBI Arrest Statistics: 1994–2004. Retrieved on June 25, 2007 from http://ojjdp.ncjrs.org/ojstatbb/ezaucr/

Favre, D. (2000). Equitable self ownership. *Duke Law Journal, 50*(2), 473–492.

Federal Bureau of Investigation. UCR Handbook, personal communication.

Frick, P. J., Van Horn, Y., Lahey, B. B., Christ, M. A. G., Loeber, R., Hart, E. A., et al. (1993). Oppositional defiant disorder and conduct disorder: A meta-analytic review of factor analyses and cross-validation in a clinical sample. *Clinical Psychology Review, 13,* 319–340.

Heath, G. A., Hardesty, V. A., & Goldfine, P. E. (1984). Fire setting, enuresis and animal cruelty. *Journal of Child and Adolescent Psychotherapy, 1,* 97–100.

Hellman, D. S., & Blackman, N. (1966). Enuresis, firesetting, and cruelty to animals; A triad predictive of adult crime. *American Journal of Psychiatry, 122,* 1431–1435.

Hindman, J. (in press). *Juvenile Culpability Assessment,* second revision. Baker City, OR: Alexandria Associates.

Humane Society of the United States. (1999). First Strike Campaign. Washington, DC: Author.

Kellert, S. R., & Felthous, A. R. (1985). Childhood cruelty toward animals among criminals and noncriminals. *Human Relations, 38*, 1113–1129.

Kelley, B. T., Loeber, R., Keenan, K., & DeLamatre, M. (1997). Developmental; pathways in boys' disruptive and delinquent behavior. *Juvenile Justice Bulletin*. Washington, DC: Department of Justice, Office of Justice Programs, Office of Juvenile Justice and Delinquency Prevention.

Larzelere, R. E., Martin, J. A., & Amberson, T. G. (1989). The toddler behavior checklist: A parent-completed assessment of social-emotional characteristics of young preschoolers. *Family Relations, 38*, 418–425.

Lewchanin, S., & Zimmerman, E. (2000). Clinical assessment of juvenile animal cruelty. Brunswick: ME: Biddle Publishing Company and Audenreed Press.

Lockwood, R., & Hodge, G. R. (1986, Summer). The tangled web of animal abuse; The links between cruelty to animals and human violence. *The Humane Society News*, 1–6. Washington, DC: The Humane Society of the United States.

Lockwood, R. (1998). *Factors in the assessment of dangerousness in perpetrators of animal cruelty*. Washington, DC: The Humane Society of the United States.

Luk, E. S. L., Staiger, P. K., Wong, L., & Mathai, J. (1999). Children who are cruel to animals; A revisit. *Australian and New Zealand Journal of Psychiatry, 33*, 29–36.

Maryland Department of Juvenile Justice. (2002). Annual statistical report, fiscal year 2000. Annapolis, MD: State of Maryland.

Mead, M. (1964). Cultural factors in the cause and prevention of pathological homicide. *Bulletin of the Menninger Clinic, 28*, 11–22.

National Child Abuse and Neglect Data System Child File. Compendium of National Juvenile Justice Data Sets. Retrieved on June 25, 2007 from http://ojjdp.ncjrs.org/ojstatbb/Compendium/asp/Compendium.asp?selData=8

National Crime Victimization Survey. Compendium of National Juvenile Justice Data Sets. Retrieved on June 25, 2007 from http://ojjdp.ncjrs.org/ojstatbb/Compendium/asp/Compendium.asp?selData=7

National Crime Victimization Survey Resource Guide. Retrieved on June 25, 2007 from http://www.icpsr.umich.edu/NACJD/NCVS/#About_NCVS

National Data Archive on Child Abuse and Neglect. National Child Abuse and Neglect Data System (NCANDA) Child File. Retrieved on June 24, 2007 from http://www.ndacan.cornell.edu/NDACAN/Datasets/Abstracts/DatasetAbstract_NCANDS_Child_File.html

National Incident Based Reporting System: Volume 1, Data Collection Guidelines. Retrieved on June 25, 2007 from http://www.fbi.gov/ucr/nibrs/manuals/v1all.pdf

National Incident Based reporting System. Compendium of National Juvenile Justice Data Sets. Retrieved on June 25, 2007 from http://ojjdp.ncjrs.org/ojstatbb/Compendium/asp/Compendium.asp?selData=4

Offord, D. R., Boyle, M. H., & Racine, Y. A. (1991). The epidemiology of antisocial behavior in childhood and adolescence. In D. J. Pepler & K. H. Rubin (Eds.), *The development and treatment of childhood aggression* (31–54). Hillsdale, NJ: Lawrence Erlbaum Associates.

Prochaska, J. O., Norcross, J. C., & DiClemente, C. C. (1994). *Changing for good*. New York: Avon Books.

Randour, M. L., Krinsk, S., & Wolf, J. L. (2001). *Ani-Care child: An assessment and treatment approach for childhood animal abuse*. Washington, DC: The Doris Day Animal Foundation and Psychologists for the Ethical Treatment of Animals.

Raphael, P., Colman, L., & Loar, L. (1999). *Teaching compassion: A guide for humane educators, teachers, and parents*. The Latham Foundation for the Promotion of Humane Education.

Righthand, S., Welch, C., Carpenter, E. M., Young, G. S., & Scoular, R. J. (2001). *Sex offending by Maine youth: Their offenses and characteristics*. Unpublished documents, Maine Departments of Corrections and Human Services.

Seligman, M. E. P., Reivich, K., Jaycox, L., & Gillham, J. (1995). *The optimistic child*. New York: Houghton Mifflin.

Snyder, H. N. (2003). Juvenile arrests 2001. *Juvenile Justice Bulletin*. Washington, DC: Department of

Justice, Office of Justice Programs, Office of Juvenile Justice and Delinquency Prevention.

Statistical Briefing Book. Retrieved on September 20, 2004 from http://ojjdp.ncjrs.org/ojstatbb/

Uniform Crime Reporting, Summary Reports of Offenses and Arrests. Compendium of National Juvenile Justice Data Sets. Retrieved on June 25, 2007 from http://ojjdp.ncjrs.org/ojstabb/Compendium/asp/Compendium.asp?selData=3

Wolin, S. J., & Wolin, S. (1993). *The resilient self: How survivors of troubled families rise above adversity*. New York: Villard.

World Health Organization. (1996). International Classification of Diseases.

Appendix

Summary Grid Presentation:

	Severity (Lockwood, Ascione)	Culpability (Hindman)	Resilience (Wolin)	Child's Readiness to Change (Prochaska)	Parent's Readiness to Change (Prochaska)
HIGH ↑					
⎪					
LOW					

The Relation Between Psychiatric Disorders and Human–Animal Interactions: A Japanese Psychiatric Perspective

Akimitsu Yokoyama*
Teikyo University of Science & Technology Department of Animal Science

Introduction

Scientific studies over the past 50 years have gradually revealed contributions of animals and pets to the positive mental and physical health of humans. In the present day, Animal-Assisted Therapy/Activity (AAT/A) is used in a variety of situations. The studies in this scientific area originally began in Western countries where humans' close relations with animals were present, and these studies are now widespread all over the world. In addition to positive relations with animals, studies have recently revealed relations that have negative aspects as well. The following is an outline of a case of a man whom the current author met in his clinical experience.

He was a 56-year-old local public servant suffering from paranoid schizophrenia. When he was 52 years old, his wife had uterine cancer surgery and, since then, he started claiming, "My wife has a love affair" and "The meal is added with a poison." After his father died the following year, his persecution mania symptoms deteriorated and he occasionally had quarrels with his colleagues at his workplace. When he had his first medical examination at a psychiatric clinic at age 53, he did not admit that he had a mental disorder and he believed that his family members attempted to oust him from his house (his explanation was convoluted and difficult to understand). The prescription of haloperidol alleviated his symptoms so that he was able to return to his workplace. However, his symptoms deteriorated again, and he presented with insomnia, fretfulness, and inactivity. He eventually divorced his wife and quit his job two years later. Since then, his mental state had been stabilized with a small amount of antipsychotic

drugs, but he began having auditory hallucinations in the following year. These included "Somebody is singing in my head" and "I hear a rumination of my voice." Simultaneously, a depressive symptom emerged so that his physician recommended that he be hospitalized.

However, he refused to be hospitalized because he took care of a dog at his home: He lived in solitude and did not have any acquaintances that he could ask to take care of his dog. He reported that his dog was a 10-year-old Shih Tzu. He used to like the dog, but stopped doing so around the period when his father died. Still, he took good care of his dog and he went walking with his dog everyday.

His physician was unable to convince him to be hospitalized because of the presence of his dog. Instead, the physician tried to adjust his medication, but the man's symptoms of an auditory hallucination and depression kept intensifying. In the next several months, this patient attempted suicide by swallowing a large amount of organophosphorous pesticide and he was transported to an emergency hospital. Since then, he has been institutionalized in a psychiatric hospital. It is unknown what happened to his dog. (Yokoyama, 2000a, pp. 84–86)

This case study shows that (1) this patient's dog was a partner in his life after he divorced his wife and was the only one who motivated this inactive patient to go outside his house, and (2) his responsibility to take care of his dog kept intensifying his symptoms (there is certainly a problem in this society which did not enable this patient to leave his dog in someone else's care but it is beyond the theme of this article). If he only thought of his own situation, he could have been hospitalized earlier by renouncing his responsibility to take care of his dog. But this might have resulted in animal abuse or neglect. Nonetheless, it is not reassuring that he had attempted suicide but did not commit animal abuse.

In clinical settings, there are some cases where, whether consciously or unconsciously, particular abnormal behaviors and symptoms can be seen as ways of self-protection, preventing other destructive behaviors such as depressive symptoms, suicide, and harmful behavior toward others.

As I have shown, relations with animals are two sides of the same coin, and the positive and negative sides mingle with each other. Thus it is necessary to have a clear grasp of the comprehensive picture, particularly, in psychiatric clinical settings.

The author of this chapter, as a psychiatric clinician who has been closely involved with AAT/A addresses a variety of perspectives that may disentangle the complex relation between psychiatric disorders and human–animal interactions, including animal abuse. In addition to the empirical data, there are many hypotheses derived from the author's own clinical experiences. To begin, a clinician must start with considering how to deal with an immediate incident of animal abuse contrary to some recommendations in animal abuse research. The main purposes of this chapter are to facilitate the work of professionals involved with animal abuse by (1) suggesting new perspectives in order to develop this scientific area and (2) describing ways to more effectively intervene with and treat animal abusers. Hopefully, this will encourage more professionals to collect empirical data on these issues in Japan.

The Relation Between DSM-IV-TR Psychiatric Disorders and Animals

Because a psychiatric disorder is difficult to measure and express as objective data (unlike blood assays, for example), there had not been any standard for its diagnosis in the early history of psychiatry. In other words, the same psychiatric disorder used to be categorized differently depending on the professionals who diagnosed. In the present day, there are some standards used internationally that facilitate data collection for psychiatric symptoms and treatments. The two standards most commonly used in clinical settings are the Diagnostic and Statistical Manual of Mental Disorders (DSM)

developed by the American Psychiatric Association (APA) (2000) and the International Classification of Diseases (ICD) developed by the World Health Organization (WHO) (2004). DSM is a diagnostic standard for psychiatric disorders only whereas ICD is used for all known diseases and disorders (Chapter V is for Mental and Behavioral Disorders). The current version of ICD is ICD-10 updated in 1990.

DSM is also intermittently updated. There were DSM-I (1952), DSM-II (1968), DSM-III (1980), DSM-III-R (1987), and DSM-IV (1994), and the latest version is DSM-IV-TR (2000).

The DSM method of classification is called an operational diagnostic system and is based on symptomatologic examination. Some critics argue (Kutchins & Kirk, 1997) that DSM's classification system lacks considerations of knowledge of psychopathological and etiological hypotheses that psychiatry has long established (e.g., it is difficult to describe psychogenic depression due to a pet loss). Although the human mind is extremely deep and complex and the borderlines between psychiatric disorders are sometimes ambiguous, this clear and distinct classification system allowed professionals to create a common language across schools and years of experience so that it opened the door for better diagnostic standards in psychiatry.

The primary characteristic of DSM is a multiaxial approach. Briefly, its five axes are:

Axis I: Clinical Disorders and Other Conditions That May Be a Focus of Attention
Axis II: Personality Disorders and Mental Retardation
Axis III: General Medical Conditions
Axis IV: Psychosocial and Environmental Problems
Axis V: Global Assessment of Functioning

When applying this, for example, to the diagnosis of the male patient in the case study previously described, the following classification results:

Axis I: Schizophrenia (paranoid type)
Axis II: None
Axis III: None
Axis IV: Divorce and resignation
Axis V: 30/100

DSM has several problems such as the absence of cultural considerations, but it allows professionals to objectively classify psychiatric disorders in narrow and broad categories, and its authors continuously strive to collect field-test data in support of the categories and as a basis for future revisions. Studies in animal abuse require a comprehensive picture depicting the relation between psychiatric disorders and human–animal interactions, and DSM is a particularly useful tool for that purpose. The following subsections correspond with DSM-IV-TR classifications of disorders and the potential relations between each psychiatric disorder and animal-related issues are examined.

1. Disorders Usually First Diagnosed in Infancy, Childhood, or Adolescence

It is often difficult to diagnose in this category because it is extremely broad. Also, the development of certain abilities, for example, sympathy, depends on age. Still, the frequency with which people are involved with animals is high in these developmental stages and, therefore, it is necessary to have a diagnostic and intervention perspective utilizing this characteristic.

First, there are some cases where mental retardation leads to animal abuse due to a deficiency in mental ability (this is similar to cognitive disorders). With pervasive developmental disorders including autistic disorder and Asperger's disorder, some animal abuse is related to children's general aggressive behaviors due to their stubbornness and inflexibility (this is similar to obsessive-compulsive disorder). The more severe cases may result from attention deficit and disruptive behavior disorders, including conduct disorder and oppositional defiant disorder. Conduct disorder, particularly, is seen as a previous stage of antisocial personality disorder, and its diagnostic criteria include "Has been physically cruel to animals" (see *Conduct Problems and Cruelty to Animals in Children* by Dadds, this text).

On the other hand, AAT/A appears to be most effective in these developmental stages because (1) children are often interested in animals, (2) nonverbal communication rather than verbal communication is used in relations with animals, and (3) children can subdue their tension in clinical settings because the necessity of standing face to face with counselors is minimized. In fact, AAT/A is experimentally used today for learning disabilities due to Down syndrome (Limond, Bradshaw, & Cormack, 1997) as well as pervasive developmental disorders (Martin & Farnum, 2002; Redefer & Goodman, 1989) and even conduct disorder (Gullone, 2003). Furthermore,

there are possible positive effects of AAT for separation anxiety disorder, selective mutism, and reactive attachment disorder of infancy or early childhood.

2. Delirium, Dementia, and Amnestic and Other Cognitive Disorders

Dementia, such as Alzheimer's and vascular types, is characterized by disorganization in the abilities people have had. The primary symptoms are amnesia and cognitive disturbance(s) (i.e., aphasia, apraxia, agnosia, and/or disturbance in executive functioning) and it may lead to animal neglect due to the loss of ability to take care of pets. The symptoms can also include hoarding behavior (see *Animal Hoarding* by Patronek, this text).

Particularly, the symptoms of frontotemporal dementia (e.g., Pick's disease) such as cognitive dysfunction and focal symptoms rarely emerge in the early stages but the change in personality and lack of restraint take place without the patient admitting that he or she suffers from a psychiatric disorder, and these characteristics sometimes lead to impulsive aggressive behavior.

There have been many experiments with pharmacotherapy as well as non-pharmacotherapy for dementia. However, researchers have not yet found a decisive method to eliminate symptoms. For example, dementia is accompanied by a decline in mental functioning, reduction in the range of social functioning, decline in intelligence due to lack of use, and psychiatric symptoms such as delusions, hallucinations, depressive mood, and disturbances of sleep as well as behavioral symptoms such as aggressive assault, agitation, wandering, and disquiet.

AAT/A has been applied to dementia. There are some reports in which AAT/A alleviated the patients' dementia, but it is probably more appropriate to interpret it as "the normal functioning they had possessed reemerged due to the alleviation of various psychiatric symptoms even though dementia itself is not cured." Similarly, it may delay the development of dementia even though it is difficult to completely check its development. For example, Richeson (2003) reports that the use of AAT/A for aged patients suffering from dementia at a nursing home reduced their frequency of agitated behaviors and also improved their social interaction. Dogs and cats are not the only animals that have been used to assist in the interventions. For example, Edwards and Beck (2002) report that patients suffering from Alzheimer's disease gained weight with exposure to an aquarium.

The Japanese Psychogeriatric Society collected articles published between 1990 and 2001 through MEDLINE, PsycLit, and CINAHL, and examined the methods and outcomes of non-pharmacotherapy for dementia of the Alzheimer's type (Nagata, 2005). As a result, the two most recommended approaches (Rank A) were training and rehabilitation for memory and reality-oriented therapy; music therapy or the use of music was placed on Rank B. Cognitive rehabilitation, intervention, management, training, memory aids, recollection methods, AAT/A, and light (phototherapy) therapy were placed on Rank C. This ranking was partly attributed to the small number of research studies conducted. Yet there is no firm evidence for the positive effect of AAT/A, for example, for Alzheimer's disease, which is only one form of many known dysfunctions in humans.

3. Mental Disorders Due to a General Medical Condition

The co-morbidity of depression and anxiety is common among progressive physical diseases including cancer, dementia, cerebral vascular disorder, and traumatic brain injury (for which rehabilitation has some positive effects). For instance, Akechi et al. (2003) report that 12.8% of 1,721 patients with cancer were diagnosed as having major depression. Galynker et al. (2000) examined 44 inpatients in an intensive rehabilitation unit who were transferred from the general surgical and internal wards due to having a bone fracture, a tumor, or cerebral vascular disorder. They report that 36% had a cognitive disorder and 14% had severe depressive symptoms. Furthermore, the researchers found an association between those psychiatric symptoms and the length of hospitalization. Similarly, Shah, Evans, and King (2000) examined 78 inpatients in a rehabilitation unit for the aged and reported that 28 (35.9%) had depression and 15 of those experienced anxiety. Twenty-one (41.0%) had severe cognitive disorders and 14 of those had depression. There were only 33 (42%) who suffered neither from cognitive disorders nor depression.

One of the targets of AAT/A in the hospital, rehabilitation center, and nursing home for the elderly is mental problems due to physical disease (Johnson, Meadows, Haubner, & Sevedge, 2003; Velde, Cipriani, & Fisher, 2005). For example,

there is a report showing a negative correlation between depression among patients suffering from AIDS and the presence of pets they own (Siegel, Angulo, Detels, Wesch, & Mullen, 1999). Similarly, the positive effect of AAT/A was reported among patients who were depressive and/or easily irritated due to the stress from a speech impediment following treatment for laryngeal cancer (Yokoyama, Kamijo, Arisawa, & Sakae, 1997). In addition, there are many cases where people having physical disabilities in vision, hearing, and physical functions develop some psychiatric symptoms such as depression (De Leo, Hichey, Meneghel, & Cantor, 1999). Assistance dogs are considered to have an important role for providing their owners with positive effects on their mental health as well as their physical health (Allen & Blascovich, 1996; Guest, Collis, & McNicholas, 2006).[1]

4. Substance-Related Disorders

Although the effects vary depending on the substances, drug users often show dependence, abuse, intoxication, and withdrawal symptoms. Those substances also increase the users' impulsivity and reduce self-control over aggressive behaviors. Moreover, substance-related disorders sometimes show co-morbidity with delirium, dementia, psychotic disorders, mood disorders, and anxiety disorders. Furthermore, it is not uncommon that delusions with persecutory content and the change into irritable personality characteristics due to organic changes in the brain with repeated use of drugs lead to self-destructive behaviors as well as aggressive behaviors toward others. There is a possibility that animals become targets of aggression as well. Those substances include both legal and illegal drugs, and the use of legal drugs on animals should be considered. Buchta (1988) warns of such possibilities, in which children who receive drugs from their parents to use themselves may feed the drugs to animals.[2]

Moreover, Arluke, Levin, Luke, and Ascione (1999) report that the rate of being arrested for drug-related problems among people who were charged with animal abuse was three times higher than for a comparison group with no reported animal abuse. Thus, animal abuse may be a risk factor for substance-related disorders.

Effective treatment for this clinical population includes some supporting organizations such as Alcoholics Anonymous in addition to individual and group psychotherapies. However, recidivism is high. A research team at Northwestern University points out that the inclusion of AAT/A in an intervention program for substance-related disorders may increase the participants' motivation for and compliance with treatment (Jenuwine & Lyons, 2004).

In the current author's own clinical experience, a patient with a history of alcohol abuse developed binge drinking behavior after the patient's dog was killed in a traffic accident when he went walking with his dog. This can be seen as due to pet loss. This patient eventually succeeded in ceasing drinking behavior after obtaining a new dog (Yokoyama & Kimura, 2002).

5. Schizophrenia and Other Psychotic Disorders

The primary symptoms of schizophrenia are divided into positive symptoms such as hallucinations and delusions and negative symptoms such as blunted affect and avolition (i.e., lack of volition). As Kraepelin called this psychiatric disease *dementia praecox* or premature dementia, the progressed form of negative symptoms and dementia are alike. Thus, as AAT/A is applied to dementia, it is also applied to schizophrenia. For example, Barak, Savorai, Mavashev, and Beni (2001) report the positive effects of AAT/A on enhancing socialization, ADLs (Activities of Daily Living), and general well-being among aged patients suffering from schizophrenia. Similarly, there is a report that AAT/A was effective in reducing anhedonia (i.e., the inability to experience pleasure) among patients chronically suffering from schizophrenia (Nathans-Barel, Feldman, Begqer, Modai, & Silver, 2005). Furthermore, dogs are utilized as a part of the Schizophrenia Treatment and Education Program (STEPS) for patients learning how to manage stress, cope with troubling symptoms of their illness, and develop social skills at Christian Hospital Northeast in St. Louis (Bender, 2004). On the other hand, it is likely inappropriate to use animals in intervention when hallucinations and delusions are highly active.

Hallucinations and delusions are the main characteristics of positive symptoms and are typically associated with humans: hearing an intrusive human's voice or thinking that someone has malicious intentions toward patients. For example, even when the patient is under the delusion of hearing a dog's bark, he generally thinks "'someone' is 'using the dog' or 'intentionally having the dog bark'" and does not think that the dog itself has malicious intentions. Thus, there exists an *auditory delusion* such as "hearing the *dog's voice* as if it were the *human's*"

but there rarely are *auditory hallucinations* such as "a dog directly *talks* to the schizophrenic patient by using the *human's voice*." However, Dening and West (1990) sorted out the very few cases of the latter form of hallucinatory voices from animals and proposed calling them "Dolittle phenomena." These researchers argue for four characteristics in this phenomenon: (1) it is unrelated to the diagnosis (note that many patients in their report were diagnosed as schizophrenic), (2) it becomes an indication of a severe psychiatric state, (3) the patients frequently show risky behaviors, and (4) the patients often dislike talking about this experience. In the total of 22 cases from Denning and West's study, Sasaki et al.'s (1996) study, and the current author's own clinical experience (Yokoyama, 2000b), there are some cases of aggressive behaviors toward others but there is no case where the patients assaulted the "talking" animals. This can be seen as ambivalence (i.e., living in the world of hallucinations and delusions), which is a characteristic of schizophrenia. However, the fact that Dolittle phenomena are extremely rare suggests that people unconsciously distinguish between humans and animals, and is worthy to note.

The psychotic disorders include chronic tactile hallucinations and delusion of parasitosis (also called Ekbom symdrome) in which patients often believe that tiny vermin and parasites have malicious intentions. There is no report that those patients talk about malicious attacks by larger animals such as dogs. However, there are some reports in which the dog-owning patient argued that the dog had infected the patient (Bers & Conrad, 1954; Leder, 1967; Siegel, 1994 [The last reference is about a patient having a cocaine-related disorder and the more appropriate diagnostic category in which the patient should be placed is "Substance-Related Disorders."]).

6. Mood Disorders

This classification includes disorders associated with emotions such as depression and mania. There is a report that AAT/A was applied for depression based on the observation that some patients reported feeling better when they were with animals or pets (Antonioli & Reveley, 2005). According to psychiatric recommendations, however, the primary interventions are pharmacotherapy and the rest from routine activities and duties. Psychotherapy and cognitive therapy certainly have some degree of positive effect but they should be applied after the depressive symptoms are somewhat alleviated. One special form of intervention is electroconvulsive therapy (ECT). There is a report that the use of an aquarium had a positive effect in the alleviation of anxiety toward ECT (Barker, Rasmussen, & Best, 2003). Similarly, there is a report that interaction with dogs facilitated the alleviation of a dread of ECT (Barker, Pandurangi, & Best, 2003).

The primary characteristic of mood disorders is a violent fluctuation in emotions. In the author's own clinical experience, a pet-owning female patient suffering from bipolar mood disorder felt annoyed by the need to care for the pet while under a depressive mood and then blamed herself for not taking care of her pet once her depressive symptom was alleviated (Yokoyama,1996). This case may have led to animal/pet neglect. There exist double suicides among family members in Japan and some pets are included (i.e., killed) because they are seen as family members. Particularly, some pet-owning patients suffering from *typus melancholicus* (one of its characteristics is the feeling of strong responsibility) kill their pets when they commit suicide. On the other hand, there are some cases where the presence of pets kept people with suicidal thoughts from actually committing suicide.

Concerning the relation with pet loss, DSM ambiguously deals with cases of clinical depression following bereavement. One of the reasons behind its ambiguity is the extremely complex nature of the reaction to bereavement. Many people, following the death of parents, have episodes of major depression while some present symptoms of adjustment disorders (although DSM's criteria for adjustment disorders do not include a reaction to the bereavement). The situational factors related to the death of the beloved may complicate the course of psychiatric disturbance: witnessing of a brutal slaughter, for example, may lead to the post-traumatic stress. Furthermore, the personality, experience, and available support that the survivors have also have a strong impact on the degree of their ability to surmount the given difficulties. The author's own clinical experience clearly shows the occasional necessity of pharmacotherapy and psychotherapy for patients suffering from major depression following pet loss (Yokoyama, 2001).

7. Anxiety Disorders

Anxiety disorders overlap with so-called "neurosis" in many aspects. Psychotherapy has been the primary form of intervention although pharmacotherapy is currently becoming popular. Morita therapy (its name originating from Dr. Morita,

who created this psychotherapy in the 1920s in Japan), has been applied to anxiety disorders. This form of psychotherapy emphasizes the removal of attempts to intentionally deal with one's own symptoms, the desire for living that people have already had, and the actualization of having a life as he or she is. As a part of treatment in Morita therapy, the patients take care of animals such as dogs and chickens (Nakamura, 2006).

The presence of assistance dogs in interventions is thought to be one form of psychotherapy or thought to augment the effect of psychotherapy for an attack seen in panic disorder, social anxiety disorder, and generalized anxiety disorder and for a reaction to trauma seen in post-traumatic stress disorder (PTSD) and acute stress disorder. For example, Lefkowitz, Paharia, Prout, Debiak, and Bleiberg (2005) point out the merits of applying AAT/A for survivors of sexual assault suffering from PTSD. Similarly, Greenbaum (2006) lists the reasons for the positive effect of animals used by crisis intervention teams. Greenbaum notes the following roles played by animals: "establish rapport, building bridges, have the animals act as symbols, shift the focus of attention off the individual, normalize the experience, act as a calming agent, have animal as objects of attachment, give support, serve as a catalyst for movement, [and] identify stress in individuals" (pp. 52–54).

The specific phobias include the animal type in addition to the natural environment type, blood-injection-injury type, and situational type. DSM-IV-TR states that the animal type "should be specified if the fear is cued by animals or insects [and] [t]his subtype generally has a childhood onset" (APA, 2000, p. 445). It is thought that phobias eventually are alleviated if they had begun before the age of 20, whereas they last longer if they began after that age. According to Hoffmann and Human (2003), the preceding research revealed that 12% to 68% of people having animal phobias could not explain or remember why they did so. The study done by these researchers shows that those people tend to pay attention to the specific parts of animal (e.g., size, eyes, and teeth) rather than an animal as a whole. They also report that 25% of people having a dog phobia in their study had more than one dog. In general, behavioral therapy is the primary intervention for phobias, and it includes modeling and systematic desensitization. The symptoms of a phobia require that one have an unusual, often irrelevant, fear toward a specific object, and it disturbs one's life in an attempt to avoid that fear.

Thus, a specific phobia is essentially different from a mere fear of the animal. It is possible that some people having an animal phobia abuse a specific animal due to their extreme fear of the animal. Furthermore, an injury resulting from being bitten by an animal sometimes results in PTSD and acute stress disorder. For example, Peters, Sottiaux, Appleboom, and Kahn (2004) report that among 22 children who received minor surgical treatment at the emergency room after being bitten by dogs (see *Collaborating to Assess, Intervene, and Prosecute Animal Abuse* by Boat, Loar, and Phillips, this text), 12 of them presented the symptoms of PTSD, but none received psychological support.

Obsessive-compulsive disorder (OCD) is also one form of anxiety disorder. It is not rare that people having OCD compulsively wash their hands with such obsessions as, "They may get infected by dogs" (De Silva & Rachman, 1998). In fact, the Yale-Brown Obsessive-Compulsive Scale, a scale designed by Goodman and his colleagues as a diagnostic tool for the severe form of OCD and receiving an international consensus, includes an item noting an excessive concern with animals including insects (Goodman, Price, & Rasmussen, 1989a, 1989b). Moreover, Baer (2001) points out that a list of negative thoughts as a form of obsession includes hitting a dog while driving a car, worrying that one may have sexual intercourse with animals, worrying about one actually wanting to have intercourse with animals, and worrying about staring at a dog's genital area. In another aspect, Lemelson (2003) introduces a case where a 44-year-old male in Bali compulsively checked the carcass of chickens on the street (this male did not collect animals although he presented the symptoms of hoarding). In contrast, there are some reports in which living with a cat as a "dirty" animal (Ando, Ichida, & Kondo, 1998) and walking on the "dirty" street with a "dirty" dog (Schwartz, 1996) played a role in facilitating the alleviation of OCD symptoms. These cases are thought of as a kind of exposure therapy. Some researchers argue that animal hoarding may be associated with OCD from the perspective of hoarding as an obsession toward a collection (Frost, Steketee, & Williams, 2000; see also *Animal Hoarding* by Patronek, this text) and this issue is examined in a later section.

8. Somatoform Disorders

Somatoform disorders include somatization disorder, which is characterized by making multiple somatic complaints without any medical problem, and hypochondriasis, which is characterized by having the irrelevant fear and belief that one suffers from a disease. These people are convinced they are ill rather than being factitious (lying about symptoms) so that some of them begin doctor shopping if their claims are unaccepted. Whether these symptoms are extended to the inclusion of pets is discussed in the following section on factitious disorders.

Although there are few studies focusing on an association of indefinite complaint and chronic pain with pets, Hirsch and Whitman (1994) examined the association between patients' claiming chronic pain such as headaches and living together with pets, children, and adults. They report that there was no strong association between "they claim/they do not claim" and "living together/not living together."[3]

An imaginary pregnancy is also included in this category. Chowdhury, Mukherjee, Ghosh, and Chowdhury (2003) report that there were 7 cases (6 males and 1 female) where they claimed that they were pregnant with puppies after touching or being bitten by dogs in India.[4]

9. Factitious Disorders

Patients with factitious disorders intentionally and consciously create (or feign) the symptoms of illness, and those symptoms can be psychological and physical. Munchausen syndrome by proxy (MBP) is classified in this category and patients diagnosed as having this syndrome intentionally injure people other than themselves (or simulate illness) in order to get attention from others. Many cases involve mothers injuring their children but Munro and Thrusfield (2001) report that the victims can be animals as well. It is possible that a circumstance in which "well-intentioned" animal welfare volunteers are involved with long-lasting animal hoarding is similar to MBP involved with animals because animal hoarders can get attention from others by the intentional continuation of hoarding.

Is it possible that people genuinely, not factitiously, believe and keep arguing that others (e.g., children or pets) have a disease? There are some cases of excessively anxious parents in pediatric clinics. According to Schreier (2002), there are cases of pediatric condition falsification (PCF) but not MBP (e.g., parents who go doctor shopping with a belief that their children are not being accurately diagnosed) and neither PCF nor MBP (e.g., a cultural creed that there is a risk in medical care) so that there is a necessity to distinguish MBP from other similar cases. In the case of PCF but not MBP, it is necessary to consider the presences of delusion, hypochondiasis/somatization, and personality disorder, and there may be cases where the strength of identity with the object (child/pet) is involved. In the case of pets, there is currently no report about excessively anxious pet owners. Nonetheless, the medical records of veterinarian shopping are scarce when pets are involved, unlike in pediatric clinics, and the excessively anxious pet owners simply may not have come to the surface. Thus, it is recommended that this be considered in future clinical research.

10. Dissociative Disorders

Dissociative disorders are characterized by occasional disturbances or losses in consciousness, memory, identity, and perception and include dissociative amnesia, dissociative fugue, and dissociative identity disorder (DID; formerly called multiple personality disorder).

The imaginary companion, or a fanciful playmate, is a common experience in infancy and it generally disappears by the time children reach adolescence. The imaginary companion can be a person, a doll, or an animal.[5] One of the diagnostic criteria for DID is "[i]n children, the symptoms are not attributable to imaginary playmates or other fantasy play" (APA, 2000, p. 529), but Nakagawa et al. (2006) report two cases in which a person kept having the imaginary companion until adolescence; one presented hallucinations and delusions whereas another developed DID (the imaginary companions in both cases were not animals).

The phenomenon of "possession" does not exclusively occur with patients with dissociative disorders and a metamorphosis delusion is, to be exact, not synonymous with the phenomenon of possession. They are discussed as part of dissociative trance disorder in this chapter even though their symptoms are often reported in patients having schizophrenia or mania. The symptoms seen in phenomenon of possession and metamorphosis delusion actually reflect the culture where those terminologies are used (Dening & West, 1989) and, therefore, those symptoms help describe the perspectives toward animals in given cultures. For example, Western countries have a term, *lycanthropy*, or metamorphosis into a wolf, whereas Japan has a term, *alopecanthropia*, or being possessed by a spirit of a fox. The idea of a continuous relationship between animals and human beings led to the idea of being possessed by animals in Asian countries, including Japan, whereas

the idea of a discontinuous relationship led to the idea of metamorphosis in the West (Takahata, Shichida, & Uchikata, 1994). Nakamura (1984) compares folk tales between Japan and Western countries and points out that the metamorphosis from the specific animal to human, which never shows up in the Western folk tales, is actually the mainstream in Japanese folk tales. Nakamura suggests that a difference in a sense of distance toward animals is due to religious and dietary cultural differences.

Despite the fact that the cause of DID is still unclear, almost all patients suffering from DID have traumatic experiences in childhood, and many traumatic experiences are associated with child sexual abuse, particularly incest. The DSM-IV-TR only uses "personality" to describe alters that emerge in DID, but "animal" alters may emerge in some cases. For example, Arisaka, Suzuki, and Ohara (1983) report a case of a 15-year-old Japanese female who presented a variety of personalities, including alters of other humans, a fox, and a dog, besides her own personality. These authors considered this case a reactive psychosis. Hendrickson, McCarty, and Goodwin (1990) examined five cases where animal alters had emerged and pointed out that "animal-like behaviors have been described in abused children as well as in adults with multiple personality disorder" (p. 220). They stated:

> In some cases, the development of the animal alter could be traced to childhood trauma involving 1) being forced to act or live like an animal, 2) witnessing animal mutilation, 3) being forced to engage in or witness bestiality, or 4) experiencing the traumatic loss of or killing of an animal. (p. 218)[6]

11. Sexual and Gender Identity Disorders

The presence of pets at home is sometimes related to sexual dysfunctions. Beck and Katcher (1996) report a case in which a couple could not have sexual intercourse because there were dogs and cats in their bedroom.

Bestiality (see *Bestiality and Zoophilia* by Beetz, this text) is classified in the category of Paraphilia Not Otherwise Specified, and some researchers have recently revealed a link between bestiality in childhood and adolescence and interpersonal violence (Hensley, Tallichet, & Singer, 2006). In addition, there is a risk for bestiality to lead to the spread of zoonotic infections.

Finally, it is necessary to pay attention to some criminal cases where people who are pedophiles utilize children's interests in animals by telling them, for example, "Do you want to come see my puppies?" in order to entice them to a secluded location.

12. Eating Disorders

Eating disorders include anorexia nervosa and bulimia nervosa. There are multiple factors contributing to their development but many researchers suggest that there is a strong association of family dynamics with eating disorders (Minuchin, Rosman, & Barker, 1978). Yokoyama and Todoroki (2004) examined relationships between eating disorders and the presence of pets generally seen as family members, by administering surveys about pets to 136 outpatients. Results showed that 21 individuals were classified as having eating disorders. These outpatients' characteristics included the following: (1) although they had fewer experiences rearing dogs and cats than outpatients having other forms of psychiatric disorders, a high proportion of them had cats and dogs at home when the surveys were administered and, moreover, many of them had experiences of rearing other pets than dogs and cats (this may have resulted from a relatively lower average age for this group); and (2) although a higher proportion of them answered, "they like animals" than outpatients having schizophrenia, a lower proportion of them had positive relations with animals than outpatients having other forms of psychiatric disorders. From his own experience, the current author feels that girls having eating disorders tend to want to have future careers in settings of nursing, the theater, and animal-related professions. This may be attributed to a characteristic of people with eating disorders in that they do not have close relationships with significant others even though they wish to have them. In addition, there are many cases in which people having eating disorders do not want to go out or socialize after binge eating, because they think they are obese or because they lack the motivation to physically move about. In the author's own clinical experience, there was a patient who could not take care of the pet after binge eating.

On the other hand, Frankel and Halmi (2003) report on a 16-year-old boy suffering from anorexia nervosa who was given the role of rearing a family dog after leaving the hospital, and they argue that their "[r]esearch on pet therapy has demonstrated that providing care to a pet is similar to promoting care of one's self" (p. 1058). Similarly, in the current author's own clinical experience, there was a case of a patient with bulimia nervosa who became able to go to a course of pet training, go walking, and eventually go to a part-time job after rearing a dog according to a firm treatment plan made together with the patient's family members and the physician in charge (Yokoyama & Kimura, 2002).

The following is a unique case study reported by Bruch (1971) of a 12-year-old male diagnosed with anorexia nervosa at the incipient stage but then diagnosed as having atypical symptomatology over three years:

> The illness began with his superimposing a reducing regimen on his dog whom he felt was "too fat" and not "frisky" enough to win when racing against the dogs of other boys in his neighborhood. He became so insistent and anxious about reducing the dog and made such frightful scenes whenever the parents tried to feed it that finally the dog was given away. The boy became quite depressed about losing his dog and now worried that he himself was too fat; he went on a diet and then stopped eating. (p. 38)

This case study implies processes such as obsession and guilt and it suggests that this form of animal abuse does occur.

13. Sleep Disorders

It is suggested that one of the merits of having pets at home is to regulate circadian rhythm. Yet a research team at the Mayo Clinic Sleep Disorders Center in 2002 reported that 52% of 300 patients having sleep disorders had more than one pet, with approximately 60% of those pet-owning patients leaving their pets in their bedrooms while they were asleep. The sleep of 53% of those pet-owning patients was found to be disturbed somehow by their pets (1% were found to be disturbed in that way for more than 20 minutes, on average, every night). In addition, it is reported that the dogs owned by 21% of them and cats owned by 7% of them snored (Mayo Clinic news, 2002). It is also possible that not only animal snores but barking by dogs in the neighborhood can disturb a circadian rhythm.

The hypnagogic (prompting sleep/dreaming) hallucination, one of the symptoms in narcolepsy, is characterized by its verisimilar contents and its occurrence when people are half-awake just after they start falling asleep. Some people who experience this form of hallucination report that bears or snakes assaulted them in their hallucinations.

14. Impulse-Control Disorders Not Elsewhere Classified

In pyromania, it is necessary to consider the possibility in which pyromaniac people set animals on fire as well as the association between incendiaries and animal abuse. In trichotillomania, people having a strong identity with animals may pull out the animal's fur as an extension of pulling out their own hair. Repetitive self-mutilation can result from multiple factors (e.g., borderline personality disorder) and, for example, Ascione (2005) introduces a case of a child, an abuse victim, who made an animal scratch him as a way of self-mutilation.

The most controversial disorder in this category is intermittent explosive disorder. The diagnostic standards for this disorder are described as:

A. Several discrete episodes of failure to resist aggressive impulses that result in serious assaultive acts or destruction of property.

B. The degree of aggressiveness expressed during the episode is grossly out of proportion to any precipitating psychosocial stressors.

C. The aggressive episodes are not better accounted for by another mental disorder (e.g., antisocial personality disorder, borderline personality disorder, a psychotic disorder, a manic episode, conduct disorder, or attention-deficit/hyperactivity disorder) and are not due to the direct physiological effects of a substance (e.g., a drug abuse, a medication) or a general medical condition (e.g., head trauma, Alzheimer's disease). (APA, 2000, p. 667)

Some animal abusers behaviors are not extreme enough for the abusers to be diagnosed as having personality disorders and also they show neither "continuous" aggressive behaviors nor "continuous" interpersonal violence typically seen in people having some forms of personality disorders; therefore, their problems do not come to the surface as the social problems. Thus it is recommended that consideration be given to creation of a new subcategory of intermittent explosive disorders or even a new category, such as "habitual animal abuse." The details of this proposal are examined in a later section.

15. Adjustment Disorders

Adjustment disorders result from a variety of stresses in given situations, and symptoms emerge in emotions and behaviors. Yet a definition of stress varies from culture to culture and from region to region. According to the Social Readjustment Ratings Scale by Holmes and Rahe (1967), in the United States the highest stressful events were the death of spouse, divorce, living apart, detention, and death in relatives. On the other hand, the same type of study conducted in Japan found the death of spouse, bankruptcy of company to which one belonged, death in relatives, divorce, and living apart as most common (Natsume, Murakami, & Fujii, 1988). These two studies did not include the death of a pet in choices.

If an association between relations with animals and adjustment disorders is discussed, it may be related to the following: (1) some situations (e.g., starting to rear a new pet or a pet becoming sick) become stressful enough to make pet owners develop adjustment disorders, and (2) due to these symptoms, animal abuse (e.g., destructive behaviors) emerges.

One's own pet may be a source of stress but so are the cries, smell, and fur of other pets in neighborhood. It is not uncommon that a quarrel about a neighbor's dog escalates into a fight involving some lethal weapons. Namba, Kuwano, and Schick (1986) compared the kinds of sounds that annoyed people the most across Japan, West Germany, the United States, China, and Turkey. The outcome revealed that pets could be a source of din. In addition, they report that Americans were the most sensitive to the sounds made by pets and it may explain why the laws about dins made by pets (noise ordinances) are strict in the United States. Animal hoarding is perhaps the ultimate form of nuisance associated with animals and neighbors are the most affected by the unsanitary conditions (Patronek, 1999).

This category of disorders indicates that "[t]he symptoms do not represent Bereavement" (APA, 2000, p. 683) so that a reaction to a general pet loss should not be included in this category. However, there is no clear definition of a reaction to bereavement and whether or not a reaction to a pet loss should be included in adjustment disorders may depend on the given culture. In addition, some cases where an unusual behavior (e.g., repetitive harassment of a veterinarian) is presented in a reaction to the death of a pet may be included in the subtype of With Disturbance of Conduct.[7]

16. Personality Disorders

Personality disorders (PDs) are not diseases but unbalanced personalities due to their extreme nature and are classified into Axis II in DSM (only mental retardation other than PDs is classified into Axis II). Thus, a different point of view is required when discussing PDs unlike other psychiatric disorders previously mentioned. Moreover, there are three clusters in PDs.[8]

> Cluster A (appearing odd or eccentric): Paranoid PD, Schizoid PD, and Schizotypal PD
>
> Cluster B (appearing dramatic, emotional, or erratic): Antisocial PD, Borderline PD, Histrionic PD, and Narcissistic PD
>
> Cluster C (appearing anxious or fearful): Avoidant PD, Dependent PD, and Obsessive-Compulsive PD

One caution is that although some characteristics seen in each PD also exist in everyone's personalities so that people tend to think that PDs are extensions of normal personalities, people must have trouble in social settings due to their personalities, or sometimes even conspicuous anguish due to the difficult situations their personalities have led to, in order to be diagnosed as having PDs. More precisely, people having PDs cannot improve their lives because acting out with their rigid personalities is the only way of behaving of which they are capable. They cannot modify their ways of behaving and thinking, unlike what normal people do while going about their lives.

Antisocial PD is not the only disorder most closely associated with animal abuse. As shown in DSM-IV-TR (APA, 2000, pp. 701–702), people having antisocial PD are very likely to commit crimes. Even though these diagnostic criteria do not indicate animal abuse, a significant number of studies clearly demonstrate an association between the present and/or past experience of animal abuse and violent criminal behavior (Schiff, Louw, & Ascione, 1999; Wright & Hensley, 2003). Besides antisocial PD, some PDs classified in Clusters A and B sometimes lead to a variety of crimes. Johnson et al. (2000) indicate that the risk of violent behaviors in adolescence or early adulthood would increase if one had tendencies toward paranoid PD, narcissistic PD, or passive-aggressive PD in adolescence (this study excluded antisocial PD).

In the current author's own clinical experience, a 27-year-old female having borderline PD presented unstable emotions, chronic feeling of emptiness, depressive mood, unstable self-image, deficiency of self-control over impulsivity (e.g., binge eating and substance abuse), repetitive self-mutilation, deficiency in anger management, paranoid ideation over her boyfriend, dissociative symptoms (e.g., paralysis of her hands), and animal abuse (Yokoyama, 1998). This female patient reported the following about a kitten: "I kept hitting it until my hand swelled because I was angry," "I confined it in a box and did not feed it," "I forced it to take a shower and hanged it," "I burned it to death by putting it a plastic bag with hot air from a drier machine." She described her feelings at the time: "I did not have any feeling about it" and "I thought I would be in trouble if this is known to my parents or veterinarians." She later reminisced about her past experience by saying, "I thought I did the same thing as my mother had done to me."

In general, people having PDs come to a hospital not because of their PDs themselves[9] but because of other troubles they have. Borderline PD is probably the most common PD seen in clinical settings because its symptoms include binge eating, suicide, and drinking, and therefore the family members or partners of the people having borderline PD often visit a hospital for a consultation. Antisocial PD is often diagnosed in the correctional system after a person is incarcerated for committing a crime.

Psychotherapy and cognitive-behavior therapy are often applied for the intervention but the positive outcome is not easy to accomplish because the symptoms are resistant to improvement, the treatment becomes lengthy, and the patients having PDs do not easily admit their PDs. However, although these patients may commit animal abuse, there is also a report that the use of AAT/A with a cat for a patient having borderline PD facilitated the extinction of behavioral problems (Sato, Miyazaki, Senjo, & Tanaka, 2003).

17. Other Conditions That May Be a Focus of Clinical Attention

Other conditions become known when diagnosing psychiatric disorders. These conditions may or may not have strong associations with Axis I disorders. If these conditions do, they should be written down in Axis I. If not, they may be written down in Axis IV.

Because DSM-IV-TR does not use the terminology "psychosomatic disorder" in the same way as neurosis, it utilizes a category of Psychological Factors Affecting Medical Condition. There are many patients who present physical symptoms associated with stress and, therefore, require a psychosomatic disorder-like consideration. These symptoms include peptic ulcer disease, asthma, essential hypertension, and diabetes. They are also closely associated with lifestyle-related disease following an accumulation of unhealthy coping with stress. There are many studies showing that the presence of pets has some positive effects on the prevention of these symptoms (Friedmann & Thomas, 1995; Saito, 2001).[10]

Here I focus on the associations of animals with these other conditions. First, Relational Problems include problems in a parent–child relationship, with a spouse, and companions, but if there is an index for relations with animals, then "overprotection" and "improper rearing" may be included in this category. Second, Problems Related to Abuse or Neglect include child physical abuse, child sexual abuse, child neglect, physical abuse of adults, and sexual abuse of adults. However, neither psychological abuse nor neglect of the aged is included in this category. Animal/pet abuse as an action should probably be placed here. Third, Additional Conditions That May Be a Focus of Clinical Attention include adult antisocial behaviors and child or adolescent antisocial behaviors excluding those behaviors due to psychiatric disorders. For example, smuggling of pets by adults, illegal dog fighting by adolescents, and animal abuse due to curiosity by children should probably be included here. A reaction to bereavement is finally discussed here. However, the object of the bereavement is limited to humans and "lost or missing" animals or "euthanasia" of pets is not mentioned at all. Instead, it is stated that there are differences across cultures. In addition, people must keep having depressive symptoms for at least two months after the loss in order to be diagnosed as having major depression.[11, 12]

For convenience, psychosocial and environmental stressors in Axis IV are further subcategorized (see APA, 2000, pp. 31–32). Although even these subcategories do not include a statement about pets, clinicians can record anything that they think may be associated with the psychiatric disorders. For example, significant events that happened within the past year, or even beyond the past year if necessary, may be recorded. Thus it is recommended to record not only issues in human relationships such as past interpersonal violence and a history of being a perpetrator/victim of abuse but also issues

in relation to animals such as animal abuse, animal hoarding, improper relation with animals, and the death of beloved pets because it is known today that relations with animals are closely associated with psychiatric disorders.

The commonalities across most of the psychiatric disorders are that (1) pets tend to be neglected when the symptoms take a turn for the worse; (2) supplemental therapy such as AAT/A is absent or, at least, not the primary treatment choice; (3) it is necessary to consider the flow (e.g., fluctuating or progressive) of long-term psychiatric disorders when animals are involved because it is routine to take care of pets (it is preferred to have a third party such as a family member play this caretaking role); and (4) the more stress builds, the more likely that symptoms may take a turn for the worse, and the more likely animal abuse may occur. It is thought that living in solitude presents fewer checks against animal abuse.[13, 14, 15]

The introduction of a pet into a family not only has a direct influence upon circadian rhythm and a sense of responsibility but also frequently has an influence upon the balance of the family dynamics. In the current author's own clinical experience, there were cases where patients having eating disorders or borderline PD mentioned that their mothers' meddling became less intrusive after the introduction of pets (symptoms in both cases improved), because the attention from family members shifted from patients to pets (Yokoyama and Kimura, 2002). Levinson and Mallon (1997) bring up a similar case study and point out that the introduction of a pet into a family diverted humans' attention from each other, had some positive effect in reducing the mother's desire to control the patient, and therefore, it seems, eased the tension in the atmosphere at home. In addition, the use of animals has some positive influences upon the caregivers (Fritz, Fraver, Hart, & Kass, 1996). On the other hand, the use of animals may have a negative influence upon family dynamics. There is a case where a person having mental retardation began envying a pet for monopolizing the attention of family members and bullied the pet.

A Proposal for Classification of Animal Abuse

In order to objectively measure childhood animal abuse, Ascione, Thompson, and Black (1997) created the Children and Animals Assessment Instrument

(CAAI) and Guymer, Mellor, Luk, and Pearse (2001) refined the CAAI into the Children's Attitudes and Behaviors Toward Animals (CABTA) assessment. CABTA includes items such as "severity, frequency, duration, recency, diversity of animals harmed, intention to cause harm, covertness of the abuse, whether it was performed with others or in isolation, and whether the child displayed empathy for animals who were harmed" (p. 1059). These items are essential in order to categorize the basic data (see also *Animal Abuse, Cruelty, and Welfare* by Gullone and Clarke; *Conduct Problems and Cruelty to Animals in Children* by Dadds; and *Collaborating to Assess, Intervene, and Prosecute Animal Abuse* by Boat, Loar, and Phillips, this text).

Ascione (2005) applied the classification system for fire setting in order to classify childhood animal abuse into three categories (see Table 1). Here, I focus on my own clinical experiences with personal opinions from a variety of studies and reports in order to discuss the Pathological Animal Abuse category in detail, including adults whose behavior fits this category.

First, there are cases where people having mental retardation or dementia are probably classified into the Exploratory/Curious Animal Abuse category because they were unable to intellectually understand animal abuse. There are some steps in the understanding of animal's reactions from subtle indications, clear unwillingness, and showing signs of pain, and it is essential to examine at what level a person understands, given certain forms of cognitive disability.

The category of Delinquent Animal Abuse is complex and it also can be seen for those delinquents who are struggling to balance out a desire for belonging with a group and empathy for animals and a sense of guilt over animal abuse as well as shame and self-reproach (some researchers studying delinquency suggest that the number of delinquents who cannot even maintain relationships with other delinquents has increased). However, those delinquents are unaware, whether temporarily or not, that they will eventually face a deadlock by being unable to maintain such a relationship with a delinquent group because such a human relationship also requires a balance between empathy, a sense of guilty, self-reproach, and shame. Also factors such

Table 1   Proposed Classification System for Childhood Animal Abuse (Ascione 2005)

(1) **Exploratory/Curious Animal Abuse**	Children in this category would likely be of preschool or early elementary school age, poorly supervised, and lacking training on the physical care and humane treatment of a variety of animals, especially family pets and/or stray animals and neighborhood wildlife. Humane education interventions (teaching children to be kind, caring, and nurturing toward animals) by parents, childcare providers, and teachers are likely to be sufficient to produce desistence of animal abuse in these children. It should be noted that age alone should not be the determining factor in including children in this category. For example, CD symptoms may have an early developmental onset and, as noted earlier, cruelty to animals is one of the earliest CD symptoms to be noted by caregivers.
(2) **Pathological Animal Abuse**	Children in this category are more likely to be older (though, as noted above, not necessarily) than children in the Exploratory/Curious group. Rather than a lack of education about the humane treatment of animals, these children's animal abuse may be symptomatic of psychological disturbances varying in severity. For example, studies have tied childhood animal abuse to childhood histories of physical abuse, sexual abuse, and exposure to domestic violence. Here, professional, clinical intervention is warranted.
(3) **Delinquent Animal Abuse**	Youth in this category are most likely to be adolescents whose animal abuse may be but one of a number of antisocial activities. In some cases, the animal abuse may be a component of gang/cult-related activities (e.g., initiation rites) or less formal group violence and destructiveness. The associated use of alcohol and other substances may be implicated with these youth. These youth may require both judicial and clinical interventions.

as valor, ritual, or masculine spirit may obscure one's individual behaviors.

The problematic category is Pathological Animal Abuse. For example, there are many animal abuse cases where such actions of abusers are not serious enough to result in diagnoses of PDs or other psychiatric disorders. These actions should not be classified into the other two animal abuse categories, but it is also difficult to determine whether they should be placed in this pathological animal abuse category.

A research team led by the current author conducted survey research about animal abuse cases across 862 veterinary hospitals in Japan (Yokoyama & Japanese Animal Hospital Association, 2006). Having taken a general view of the outcomes, the justifications for animal abuse were classified into three categories according to the following keywords: unintentionally, due to frustration, and for diversion.

Unintentional Animal Abuse

This includes a case where the perpetrator said, "I hit my dog because he made a careless mistake/had a toilet accident." This was the most common justification in the survey research. A style of dealing with mental conflict by including attributions and problem solving generally promotes self-control over impulsivity but, in this case, the impulsive behavior takes place before the mental conflict does. Thus those people regret and are guilty about behaviors they have just engaged in and some of them bring the animals to veterinary hospitals. Nonetheless, they often repeat this sequence. They may also present this impulsivity toward humans.

A goal of intervention for unintentional animal abusers is to enable their mental conflict and problem solving to take place before their impulsive behavior does. The most appropriate intervention is perhaps cognitive-behavioral therapy in which a therapist helps a patient to think about instances of unintentional animal abuse as well as similar cases and to consider alternative, non-abusive responses. If unintentional animal abuse is to be included in DSM, then it probably will be classified into Impulse-Control Disorders.

Animal Abuse Due to Frustration

This includes a case where the perpetrator may say, "I hit my dog back at home when I get frustrated at my workplace." A mental conflict seems to be little involved when one displaces one's negative emotions by hitting others. Also, it is not impossible

for the person to hit others even when he or she is not frustrated. There may be reverse cases as well: the frustration comes out of the displacement. In addition, there may be some degree of self-control over impulsivity because of selecting the object for the displacement and, therefore, there could be an ability to plan. It is also possible that the fixation of this behavioral pattern further decreases the mental conflict that is experienced.

A goal of intervention during psychotherapy for this type of animal abuser is probably to enable abusers to objectively understand their negative emotions. If this type of animal abuse is to be classified into DSM, then it is perhaps placed in Adjustment Disorders. But the current author reluctantly diagnoses in this way because the diagnostic criteria for adjustment disorders must include a clear stressor, while the individual's unbalanced personality weighs more heavily than stress for this type of animal abuse.

Animal Abuse for Diversion

Some abusers may state, "I divert myself by bullying animals." This type of animal abuse is clearly different from the two categories previously mentioned because the goal is to obtain "pleasure" rather than coping with negative emotions. Animal abusers in this category have a high level of self-control over impulsivity for seeking pleasure and they also have capabilities to plan and to devise ways to achieve the greatest pleasure. Moreover, the seriousness of this type of behavior progresses over time because these people are not satisfied by the same pleasure and seek more intense ones. A trigger can be mere frustration. Also, the object can shift from animals to humans.

Animal abuse for diversion probably should be classified into psychopathy or antisocial PD. A goal of intervention is to remove the "pleasure," but it is very difficult to achieve because of addiction to the pleasure. If an animal abuser of this type admits to having some psychiatric disorder, then treatments like ones used for drug addiction (e.g., self-support group) may be effective. The three categories mentioned in this section are summarized in Figure 1 with some additional information.

In addition, Puri, Baxter, and Cordess (1995) suggest a diagnostic system using a multiaxial approach in pyromania (see Table 2). This system focuses on risk factors for the increase in the motivation for pyromania from a point of view of the intervention rather than the motivation itself. It is highly recommended that a

Figure 1 A Draft of the Classification System for Animal Abuse Based on Motivation

	IM	MC	PL	SF	RE	DE	AA	Intervention
Unintentional	3	3	0	3	2	1	1	Control of impulsivity
Due to frustration	2	2	2	2	2	2	3	Understanding of negative emotions
For diversion	1	0	3	0	3	3	3	Removal of pleasure

Note 1: Impulsivity (IM); Mental Conflict (MC); Pleasure (PL); Situational Factor (SF); Recidivism (RE); Deterioration (DE); Association with Arson (AA)

Note 2: 3 = Strong Association; 2 = Moderate Association; 1 = Weak Association; 0 = No Association

Table 2 Diagnostic Axes for Fire Setting (Puri, Baxter, and Cordess 1995)

Predisposing factors
  Psychiatric, e.g., schizophrenia
  Psychological, e.g., history of sexual abuse
  Psychosocial, e.g., social isolation.

Precipitating factors
  Psychiatric, e.g., problem drinking
  Psychological, e.g., death of mother
  Psychosocial, e.g., care worker on leave.

similar diagnostic system to Puri et al.'s be developed for animal abuse in order to provide information for where to begin the intervention. In short, when animal abuse cases are brought into the clinical settings, the recommendations are:

1. Collection of basic information such as patient gender, age, abuse severity, frequency, and duration
2. Attention to three keywords (i.e., unintentionally, due to frustration, and for diversion)
3. Psychiatric, psychological, and psychosocial assessments using the multiaxial approach for both predisposing and precipitating factors

Besides these three recommendations, it is expected to be beneficial to share information among various professionals involved with the case (e.g., social workers, teachers).

Examination of Animal Hoarding From a Psychiatric Point of View

The chapter authored by Patronek in this handbook provides extensive coverage of animal hoarding. Here, the current author's opinions as a psychiatric clinician are offered. His research team, including staff in the Environmental Health Bureau in Nara, Japan, continually conducts research at the setting of animal hoarding cases by interviewing animal hoarders.[16] A research team led by Patronek classified animal hoarders into (1) overwhelmed caregiver, (2) rescuer hoarder, and (3) exploiter hoarder (Patronek, Loar, & Nathanson, 2006), and this seems applicable in Japan as well. In viewing animal hoarding cases from the perspective of psychiatric diagnosis, there are some patterns.

First, some animal hoarding is associated with dementia if hoarders are elderly. These hoarders had been able to take care of animals well but as the symptoms of dementia progress, proliferation of animals and neglect are likely to take place. Also, physical decrepitude may prevent them from properly rearing animals. In addition, some people having dementia develop a collecting mania. Second, some hoarders have mental retardation. In this case, some people develop their animal hoarding habit after bereavement for family members who did not allow animal hoarding. Third, some psychological factors such as experiences in childhood or experiences of stressful events are associated with animal hoarding. These animal hoarders sometimes mention the triggers such as, "I started after my mother died" and "I started after I got divorced" so that those psychological factors may explain animal hoarding. However, they may be mentioning these triggers as justifications for animal hoarding.[17]

The rest of the cases are difficult to diagnose. Still, some researchers recently argued for a strong association between OCD and hoarding. This possibility is discussed next.[18] It is argued that approximately 20% to 30% of people having OCD present compulsive hoarding (Frost, Steketee, & Greene, 2003). On the other hand, the current author has seen few cases of OCD associated with hoarding although he often sees patients having

OCD (he sometimes see cases of dementia and schizophrenia associated with hoarding). Thus, it seems that those people having OCD associated with hoarding may not seek medical examinations. The diagnostic criteria for OCD in DSM-IV-TR state that, "[t]he obsessions or compulsions cause marked distress . . ." (APA, 2000, p. 463), and note with a seemingly strained statement at the end, "Specify if: With Poor Insight: if, for most of the time during the current episode, the person does not recognize that the obsessions and compulsions are excessive or unreasonable" (p. 463). Few people having OCD associated with hoarding come to clinical settings possibly because they do not feel any mental anguish.[19] In other words, there seem to be two types of OCD (i.e., with the presence/absence of mental anguish) and hoarding is thought to be the one with absence of mental anguish.[20, 21]

Recent studies using neuroimaging devices have been elucidating the distinction between these two types of OCD. For example, Anderson, Damasio, and Damasio (2005) compared 13 participants who started presenting collecting behavior after traumatic brain injury with 73 participants absent of such a behavior through high-resolution, three-dimensional MRI. In their outcome, all 13 participants in the former group were shown to have damage in the medial frontal region. A study on the symptom provocation paradigm with functional magnetic resonance imaging (fMRI) done by Mataix-Cols et al. (2004) indicates a distinct pattern between the paradigm associated with hoarding and the symptom-provocation paradigm associated with cleaning and checking.[22] Nakao (2006) classified OCD into neurotic-OCD and organic-OCD models. The former model is a core group and its symptoms are formed by neurotic anxiety. In the brain, the thalamus, anterior cingulate gyrus, caudate nucleus, and orbital frontal cortex form an OCD loop and may be a factor in obsessions .(e.g., fear of contamination and fear of harming others), compulsive behaviors (e.g., cleaning and checking), and anxiety. The neurotic-OCD model has an organic abnormality in the brain regions forming an OCD loop. The primary symptom is not always anxiety and can be special forms such as hoarding and obsessional slowness (i.e., spending an excessive time for compulsive behavior). This model also frequently has co-morbidity with tics, Tourette, or Trichotilomania and it is

hypothesized that its co-morbidity contributes to resistance to treatment.

Next, when a clinician observes animal hoarding behavior itself, he or she thinks there may be a probable association with personality disorders.[23] The clinician may especially consider delusions, isolation, odd beliefs, and obsessions seen in PDs in Cluster A and obsessive-compulsive PD.[24] In fact, a 60-year-old female having schizotypal PD, who is introduced in an article by Allen Frances, a Chairman of the DSM-IV Take Force, and Ross (2000), lived in solitude with 13 cats and her apartment was full of odds and ends that she had long collected. Nonetheless, the diagnostic criteria for schizotypal PD do not mention hoarding or collecting at all but only mention odd beliefs and odd thinking and speech. Thus, the association between PDs and hoarding is discussed below.

The co-morbidity of OCD with some PDs is not uncommon.[25] Particularly, PDs in Cluster C are strongly associated with OCD. For example, according to a study by Samuels, Nestadt, and Bienvenu (2000) with 198 patients suffering from OCD, 36.6% had co-morbidity with Cluster C whereas the percentages were 4.4% with Cluster A and 12.9% with Cluster B. However, their outcome is confounded because people classified into Cluster C are anxious and this study was done with treatment-seeking patients. Also people who fit the organic-OCD model who do not feel anxious may not have been included in this study. In addition, the patients having co-morbidity of OCD with Cluster A, particularly with schizotypal PD, are less likely to expect hopeful outcomes from the interventions (Baer et al., 1990; Orloff et al., 1994).

In a narrower focus on OCD hoarders, Frost, Steketee, Williams, and Warren (2000) show that people in an OCD hoarder group were older; had higher scores on measures of anxiety, depression, and family and social disability; and had higher rates of dependent PD and schizotypal PD than people in an OCD non-hoarder group, anxiety disorder group, and control group. However, the characteristics of animal hoarders that the current author's research team studies are different from the ones of participants in Frost et al.'s because participants in the latter study are collected from a self-help support group for problems with clutter/hoarding and from OCD treatment facilities. Concerning hoarding and anxiety, Claiborn (n.d.) states:[26]

More commonly, hoarders have anxiety when their hoard is threatened in some way. . . . people who are not distressed by a behavior are unlikely to seek help in changing it. Finally, the individuals, who report they don't fit the model described above, are individuals who are highly motivated to change their hoarding. They are involved in a support group and committed to changing. They seem to represent a minority of hoarders for whom hoarding is no longer a "successful compulsion." (9–11)

In short, there are possibilities that OCD hoarders, unlike OCD non-hoarders, have organic abnormalities in their brains and coexist with schizotypal PD characteristics. And those hoarders may be the group of people who have rarely shown up in the general psychiatric clinical settings, although they may have shown up in the court.

There are many convincing points in studies on animal hoarders. Yet there are a couple of unconvincing points as well. The first one is the fact that some hoarders collect animals while others do not. The second is the fact that animal hoarders are completely indifferent to the collected animals: they do not name the collected animals; they are indifferent when those animals get sick; and they do not dispose of the carcasses of dead animals. Although whether hoarders collect animals or not may depend on their intentions, these intentions are not convincing enough to elucidate their complete indifference displayed by seeing animals as "odds and ends." It is not about whether or not people having OCD or schizotypal PD can see living organisms as nonliving organisms (there is no diagnostic criterion related to this). Even when their indifference was pointed out at the interviews in the animal hoarding cases, as a part of study by a research team led by the current author, their reactions were still indifferent and they made noncommittal answers without being serious. Thus they acted as if they were not seeing the collected animals. Some animal hoarders were beside themselves when being questioned persistently but they looked frustrated by persistently being asked about something that, for them, was irrelevant, rather than being ashamed or angry.

It is possible to reason that they are indifferent to the collected animals because they are able to see those animals as "things." Still, how can it be possible to equate the "moving" and "reacting" animals with nonliving items such as junk? One of the hints appears in recent studies indicating that there are disturbances in cognitive performance and working memory among people having schizotypal PD (Mitropoulou et al., 2005; Voglmaier et al., 2000). If the disturbances in brain function (Dickey et al., 2003; Levitt et al.,, 2002) lead to disturbances in cognition and memory, then the animal hoarders' indifference may be explainable by suggesting that they are totally controlled by hoarding because they are not capable of finding a better solution to organizing their thoughts by comparing them with their past memory and experience, and seeking a more effective, current solution.

Brand New Type of Animal Abuse

Ascione (2005) introduces an association between abuse and technology such as the Internet. As in most Western countries, there are no precise statistical data for how many animal abuse cases exist in Japan. The students at Teikyo University of Science & Technology (where the current author has a faculty position) reviewed 92 animal abuse cases in Japan from January 2000 to April 2006, and they found that there was a sudden increase in 2002. This can probably be attributed to the *Kogenta-chan Jiken* (*Kogenta*'s case) which took place in May 2002.

Kogenta-chan Jiken is a case in which a kitten was abused and eventually slaughtered as a live broadcast on a bulletin board system on the Internet. The criminal was a 27-year-old unemployed male. This man spent 4 hours at night cutting, with scissors, the ears and tail of a kitten he picked up somewhere and killed it by fastening its neck to a string (he confessed that he had abused a hamster as well). He was taking pictures while he was doing such things and posted them on Internet with the title, "A live broadcast for slaughtering a kitten." This man was arrested and prosecuted in August of the same year and was sentenced to 6 months in prison ("Broadcasting Cat," 2002; "Broadcasting Kitten," 2002). This criminal case occupied the attention of many people in the public sector. This slaughtered kitten was named *Kogenta* and a signature-collecting campaign took place. This case eventually led to a revision of the Animal Protection and Control Law in June 2005.

What this case suggests is that it is very easy to broadcast images and video clips of animal abuse through the Internet (and it may become a further reinforcement or pleasure for people doing that).

Answers to the question, "Why would someone want to proudly display those distressing images?" are no better than conjecture, but may be complicated by a desire to exercise power over the weak as well as a desire to be recognized by others. It is recommended that surveillance over the Internet and a reporting system be established since those actions "behind closed doors" may become public due to scientific technology.

Another criminal case in Japan was associated with the Internet. A 44-year-old male calling himself a web designer was arrested for abusing his dog. According to an investigation, he purchased a Labradoodle puppy via the Internet and then broke its leg bones and left this puppy in a garbage dump near his house. The puppy had been abused since the day this man received it. Then it was found that three abused beagles were left in the same garbage dump, so that it was suspected that the same man purchased those dogs only to abuse them. He may have also been implicated in other criminal cases ("The Arrested," 2005; "The Violation," 2005).

What this criminal case suggests is that people can purchase animals very easily without meeting a sales agent. This case was discovered only because he left a puppy alive in the garbage dump, but if he had killed and disposed of this puppy, no one was going to notice, even if he had abused and slaughtered hundreds of animals. In addition, one of the characteristics of this criminal case is that he had a plan to abuse, rather than engaging in animal abuse impulsively (since he reportedly purchased the animals with the expressed purpose of abusing them).

An irony is that even though it was the Internet where *Kogenta-chan Jiken* took place, it was also the Internet users' outrage that prompted a revision of the Animal Protection and Control Law. Furthermore, according to the study done by students mentioned at the beginning of this section, the number of reported animal abuse cases has decreased since 2003, suggesting that interests of people in public very easily change (decreased attention) or that the outcome of this case deterred other perpetrators of animal abuse.

In another technological development, studies about the use of "pet robots" as a substitute for AAT/A (since animals often are not permitted in medical facilities in Japan) have recently emerged (Wada, Shibata, Saito, & Tanie, 2004; Yokoyama, 2005). Researchers suggest that there are some special advantages of pet robots (e.g., capability to work in an aseptic room in a pediatric ward). There is also a report in which children

thought that these robotic pets may be capable of some emotions, although children did not see pet robots as living organisms (Melson, Kahn, Beck, Friedman, & Roberts, 2004). Furthermore, in cloning technology, there is a movement toward the production of a pet having the same genetic background as a deceased pet, a potentially lucrative new enterprise.

Nevertheless, there is a possibility that people, especially children, may become confused about the concepts of living organisms and death because of the technology of pet robots and cloned pets which, in turn, may have some impact on human relationships as well as relations with animals. Researchers have to consider questions such as, "What if people come in touch only with robots, but not living organisms, throughout childhood?" or "What if children are given the cloned pets immediately after the bereavement of beloved but deceased former pets?"

A Cue for the Practical Use of Scientific Knowledge About Animal Abuse: The Present State in Japan and a Challenge

The topic of cultural differences was intentionally minimized thus far in this chapter focusing on psychiatry in order to make discussions applicable to varied cultures and countries. This section, however, discusses the present state in Japan and a challenge to Japanese professionals as a cue for the practical use of scientific knowledge about animal abuse in communities.

The study of animal abuse in Japan is in its infancy (see also *Animal Abuse* by Maruyama and Ascione, this text). Neither research on animal abuse nor data on the effects of intervention exists. The following are some of possible reasons for this:

1. Historically, the Japanese were agricultural tribes, so that their personal relations with animals, which played important roles in hunting and in stock-farming, were unnecessary. Thus pets were considered an accessory rather than valued family members and the animal protection movement was not common (i.e., there were few people arguing from the standpoint of the pet) compared with the West.

2. People do not enter homes with their shoes on in Japan and pets were kept outside. This prevented physical and, perhaps, psychological proximity between Japanese people and pets.

3. Addressing problems about child abuse and domestic violence is recent compared with the situation in the West.

4. The animal protection and child welfare movements collaborated early in Western history whereas there is no foundation where those two movements were aligned in Japan.

In contrast, the prevalence of animal abuse may be low in Japan since the prevalence of violent crime such as murder is extremely low when one examines international data.[27] Yet animal abuse, such as the *Kogenta-chan Jiken* case, exists and it is discussed frequently today as a sign of juvenile delinquency (see *Animal Abuse* by Maruyama and Ascione, this text). Although statistical data on animal abuse certainly do not exist, animal abuse simply may not have come to the surface because no one paid attention to or reported it. The incidence rate is increasing recently, as has occurred for child abuse and domestic violence, but this may represent a greater willingness to report abuse, a true increase in incidence rates, or both.

Smaller families (low birth rate), nuclear families, late marriage, growth of an aging society, and population concentrated in cities are becoming more prevalent today in Japan. Simultaneously, the number of pet owners is annually increasing and the number of pets outside the house is decreasing. These phenomena spur the tendency to see a pet as a family member so that the psychological distance between humans and pets may be decreasing. This proximity with a pet is likely to produce a therapeutic-like positive effect. On the other hand, it may increase the opportunities for negative outcomes such as animal abuse and pet loss.

The current author, who has long studied the human–animal bond, has promoted the study of animal abuse, which is common in the West, and helped this topic to take root in Japan where there is no historical foundation for it. I translated a chapter, "The Abuse of Animals and Human Interpersonal Violence" authored by Ascione in the book *Child Abuse, Domestic Violence, and Animal Abuse: Linking the Circles of Companion for Prevention and Intervention* (Ascione and Arkow, 1999), and then I published the translated article in the *Japanese Journal of Addiction and Family*. This opportunity triggered an invitation to Ascione to be a visiting professor at Teikyo University of Science & Technology for a month-long series of

meetings in Japan during May 2006. I carefully considered ways to make this event as effective as possible and executed the following plans during a year of preparation:

1. Translation and publication of Ascione's book *Children & Animals: Exploring the Roots of Kindness & Cruelty* (2005/2006) in Japan prior to the invitation.

2. Utilization of the format of a symposium in Ascione's lectures in order to make the audiences think about and consider their own standpoints rather than providing them information in a single direction (e.g., teacher to student).

3. Designing some symposia for professionals specializing in specific areas and allowing them to discuss each area in depth (e.g., veterinarians, psychiatrists, child welfare professionals).

4. Lecturing for future professionals (students) in each area at universities.

5. Gathering as many data as possible related to animal abuse and associated topics in Japan prior to the invitation.

6. Opening symposia in as many major cities in Japan as possible.

7. Preparing Ascione to discuss an analysis of tendencies in the perpetration of felonies involving animal abuse, child abuse, and domestic violence in Japan and asking him for advice about similarities and differences in their characteristics and interventions between Japan and the West.

8. Asking representatives from each area to gather together and open a meeting for collaborative work, with Ascione as an advisor, on the final day.

These plans were challenging because those who had had an interest in the scientific study of animal abuse prior to the meetings were only a small portion of people who were involved with animal issues. However, the problems associated with animal abuse do not exist independently and it had been suggested that it has such a strong association with human welfare, medical treatment, crimes, and education that it was obvious that there would be no opportunity for successful intervention unless professionals in each area worked collaboratively.

These plans resulted in 20 symposia and approximately 3,000 attendees over the course of a month. There were sessions about animal-assisted education and animal hoarding besides animal abuse and interpersonal violence. There were also separate, special sessions for audiences from psychiatry, education, the judiciary, child abuse, domestic violence, veterinary medicine, animal protection, as well as the public. The lectures at universities took place in the areas of veterinary medicine, psychology, social service, and animal nursing. Also, symposia were held in many major cities across Japan from Sapporo to Kumamoto. In addition, there were some news reporters for newspapers and periodicals as well as interviews. I now share some of my impressions of the entire symposium tour:

- Many professionals had some awareness of a possible association between animal abuse and interpersonal violence but their knowledge did not go beyond that point.
- There was also attendance by leading figures whose areas of study corresponded to the topics of meetings. They began grasping the importance of studies in animal abuse, and they shared passionately, listened, and discussed various opinions and experiences from their professional settings during the meetings.
- Some politicians who attended the symposia made comments such as, "I was involved with developing a bill about child abuse and I was also involved with a revision of the Animal Protection and Control Law. But I never thought that these two were associated with each other."
- Some people involved with animal protection and welfare, at times, tend to deliver public messages that are exaggerations, such as "Those children who abuse animal will be criminals" (and the mass media publicizes it) whereas professionals who were seriously involved with child abuse and pediatric care were worried about the negative consequences of such labeling. Accurate data on these issues (e.g., the percentage of animal abusers who go on to commit other crimes) are not available in Japan. The need for accurate information to share with the public was stressed and could serve as a foundation for more balanced messages and more collaboration among agencies.
- Professionals in each area focused on their own intricate jobs and this situation

prevented them from broadening their points of view. Given this difficulty, their explanations for the merits of their areas in company with scientific knowledge and data are essential for promoting a collaborative structure. The possibly effective explanation for people involved with animal protection and welfare is, for example, "Animal abuse behind the scenes can be discovered by employing multiple numbers of staffs for the simultaneous participation of people involved with human issues. That allows not only the salvation of victimized animals but also the identification and treatment of animal abusers." On the other hand, the explanation for people involved with human issues can be, for example, "Information from the scenes of animal abuse will be available due to the participation of people involved with animal issues which, in turn, potentially leads to the discovery of unknown child abuse, domestic violence, or elder abuse cases and the prevention of crimes."

- It was very difficult to collect data about a history of animal abuse on the human side partly because of the privacy issue. It is especially difficult to surmount obstacles stemming from the judicial system. Also, the laws for animal protection and welfare in individual nations are intimately related to an ability to secure data. In other words, a view of animals in a given culture based on the law in that nation has a strong impact on an ability to have a comprehensive view of the animal abuse issue.
- The translation and publishing of Ascione's book prior to the invitation were very effective as a source of information for audiences. Also, although the current author had spent a year to prepare for that invitation, it was still insufficient to lay the groundwork for people from each professional area to address these issues with the same intensity and depth.

This opportunity certainly established a tentative foundation for assessment of and intervention for animal abuse problems in Japan. But it is still uncertain whether this foundation will keep flourishing. The most difficult issue is to assist people from each area to work collaboratively and, therefore, it is essential for those grasping a broad view of the problem to play a role of steadfast coordinator in order to make study in this area take root and flourish.

Conclusion

This chapter has discussed the relations between psychiatric disorders and human–animal interactions as well as concrete challenges for this area of study taking root in Japan. The shortest track for improving the situation is for professionals to take the appropriate action (e.g., pharmacotherapy, psychotherapy, and psycho-educational therapy) when faced with any situations involving psychiatric disorders. Such action may lead to an end of animal abuse or may require AAT/A. The strategies for dealing with psychiatric disorders themselves fill the scientific literature but the problem is that few professionals are aware of the fact that animals are closely connected with psychiatry. Many animals are present around people all the time so that people should pay more attention to them. It is my hope that information in this chapter becomes useful to help achieve this goal.

Finally, one more thing should be mentioned from a psychiatrist's point of view. Because issues about animal abuse have seldom been discussed in the scientific literature, each professional now has to face and consider a new point of view that differs from the preexisting perspectives. At the same time, those professionals will have to collaborate with other professionals from a totally different area. One possible negative consequence, then, is burnout: Professionals involved with animal-related issues may burn out if they become involved with human-related issues such as child welfare. Burnout is a situation in which a variety of symptoms (e.g., unable to take appropriate actions, languor, and isolation) emerge due to the excessive amount of stress (an issue that may also affect animals used in AAT/A). It often happens to professionals involved with humans (e.g., nurses, clinicians, caregivers, social workers, and teachers), particularly to highly motivated people. The more closely involved the person is, the higher at risk he or she may be, and so it is crucial to consider the psychological health of each individual involved with cases during cross training or cross reporting and during the process of developing and implementing collaborative programs to address animal abuse.

Acknowledgments

I appreciate Frank Ascione's invitation to me to author this chapter and thank Toshikazu Kuroda, also at Utah State University, for his translation.

Notes

*The author of this chapter is a Japanese psychiatrist with a long-term interest in the human–animal bond and is also a director of The Society for the Study of Human Animal Relations (HARS) in Japan. He discusses issues from his own clinical experience as well as experiences that were shared by audiences from psychiatry, education, judicature, child abuse, domestic violence, veterinary medicine, and animal protection, as well as the public during a month-long series of meetings in Japan during May 2006 (Editor commentary).

1. There is also a report that a dog may be able to anticipate an epileptic seizure. According to Kirton, Wirrell, Zhang, and Hamiwka (2004), out of 45 children with epilepsy having dogs at home, dogs of 20 children presented some actions (e.g., licking children's faces or being immobile) just before the epileptic seizures took place. Those researchers state that "[v]isual cueing on subtle early seizure behavior has been suggested as the mechanism for seizure anticipation, whereas olfactory sensation seems less likely" (p. 2305). Given the possibility that falling down due to epileptic seizures may be preventable and the finding that approximately half of the patients with epilepsy show neurotic tendencies, which is strongly associated with biases toward seizures and their unanticipated occurrence (Kogeorgos, Fonagy, & Scott, 1982), a "seizure-alert dog" as a new type of assistant dog may be a hopeful development.

2. Delirium, as one of the symptoms seen in alcohol-related disorders, often includes visual hallucinations in which an infinite number of small organisms (e.g., mice, bats, and small insects) move around the room or on the bed and tactile hallucinations in which a snake slithers into the bed or insects creep about the entire body.

3. The data in their study can be interpreted in multiple ways. For example, "There is no strong association because pets have positive therapeutic effect," "People present symptoms because pets are stressors," "People having these

symptoms tend to want to have pets," or "There is no association." In addition, some recent studies have yielded outcomes that contradict the notion, "Pets have a positive effect" (Daly & Morton, 2003).

4. The terminology *imaginary pregnancy* is almost synonymous with *delusions of pregnancy*. Female patients comprise most of the cases and it is often seen in patients with chronic schizophrenia in clinical settings. Out of seven cases reported by Chowdhury et al., two cases involved OCD, one case anxiety-phobic locus, and three cases were without any other psychiatric disorder. Cultural thinking is suggested to have a strong influence, and it is similar to the cultural difference in the sense of distance toward animals discussed in the section of dissociative disorders.

5. Like the imaginary companion, dreams involving animals decrease in frequency. According to a study by Van de Castle (1983), the frequencies of having dreams involving animals in the ages of 4–5, 6–7, 8–9, 10–11, 12–13, and 14–16 and college students are 39.4%, 35.5%, 33,6%, 29.8%, 21.9%, 13.7%, and 7.5%, respectively. The kinds of animals included are dogs, horses, and cats.

6. Hendrickson also points out that "[i]n addition to childhood memories of animals, other clues for therapists are 1) feeling like an animal or identifying oneself with an animal, 2) hearing animal calls inside one's head, 3) fear of animals, 4) excessive protective involvement with a current pet or other animal, 5) cruelty to animals, 6) reports of conversations with pets, 7) animals as protectors, guides or guards, and 8) animal-like behavior, such as scratching, crawling, licking or eating like an animal" (p. 220).

7. In this connection, there are some OCD cases where patients not only think they are filthy but also think their family members are filthy as well (Narita, Nakamura, & Mizuno, 1994). There are also some cases where the same symptoms emerge among the same group members of induced psychotic disorder and mass hysteria. It is possible that these symptoms may be associated with animals (e.g., having an obsession such as "Pets are filthy as well" or claiming that they have the same symptoms as pets do).

8. In addition to the PDs included in DSM-IV-TR, passive-aggressive PD, depressive PD, and sado-masochistic PD are under discussion.

9. The incidence rate of PDs varies depending on the studies. One of the examples is 13.4% according to a study by Torgersen, Kringlen, and Cramer (2001) who recruited 2053 people in Norway. The three highest ones are avoidant PD (5.0%), paranoid PD (2.4%), and schizoid PD (1.7%). In addition, 0.7% was reported for antisocial PD and 0.6% for schizotypal PD. Zimmerman, Rothschild, and Chelminski (2005) recruited 859 psychiatric outpatients in Rhode Island and the total incidence rate for the main 10 PDs was 31.4% and 45.5% if one includes PD not otherwise specified. The three highest rates were avoidant PD (14.7%), borderline PD (9.3%), and obsessive-compulsive PD (8.7%). In addition, 3.6% was reported for antisocial PD and 0.6% for schizotypal PD.

10. There are some reports showing that the rate of allergic patients was lower if people lived with pets in childhood (Hesselmar, Aberg, Eriksson, & Bjorksten, 1999; Ownby, Johnson, & Peterson, 2002). This may be associated with exposure to allergens.

11. This category stipulates some hints for determining deviant grief reactions to the death of the beloved from what is considered normal. These are "1) guilt about things other than actions taken or not taken by the survivor at the time of the death; 2) thoughts of death other than the survivor feeling that he or she would be better off dead or should have died with the deceased person; 3) morbid preoccupation with worthlessness; 4) marked psychomotor retardation; 5) prolonged and marked functional impairment; and 6) hallucinatory experiences other than thinking that he or she hears the voice of, or transiently sees the image of, the deceased person" (APA, 2000, p. 741). Both normal and deviant grief reactions are actually seen in clinical settings and these are useful for distinguishing normal grieving reactions from the symptoms of major depression.

12. Li, Precht, Mortensen, and Olsen (2003) examined 21,062 parents who lost their children and 293,745 parents who had not in Denmark. They report that "[t]he death of a child is associated with an overall increased mortality from both natural (e.g., cancer, disease) and unnatural (e.g., accident, suicide) causes in mothers, and an early increased mortality from unnatural causes in fathers" (p. 363). It is

understandable that the increased rate of parental deaths immediately after the death of children was due to stress but, about the fact that it remained high for so long, the authors suggest that "[s]tress also affects lifestyle—e.g., by increasing smoking and alcohol intake, altering dietary patterns, and reducing physical activity—which could increase the risk of mortality from both natural and unnatural causes" (p. 365). Although there have not yet been any reports about the long-term influence of the pet's death upon the pet owner, its influence upon lifestyle (e.g., ceasing to go for a walk or less conversation among family members) is likely, as in the case of the death of children.

13. Concerning whether there is a preference for the kind of animals or a history of animal care depending on the form of psychiatric disorder, a research team led by the current author did not find any strong associations (Yokoyama & Todoroki, 2004). A history of animal care is probably involved with haphazard factors and how people are involved with animals is perhaps more important than whether they have/had them or not.

14. The use of assistance dogs is being tested with certain psychiatric disabilities. There are some cases in which a dog has a very positive influence on the pet-owning patient in the clinical setting. But the current author is concerned that a patient may not be able to take care of a dog when the patient has active symptoms.

15. While writing this chapter, the current author actually became confused by the definition of psychiatric disorder itself. What makes or defines a disorder? There is a variety of concepts of psychiatric disorder but it possibly reaches a point where "The disorder is what a person and/or others (including the society) suffer from." In the case of depression, one suffers from it; he or she probably suffers from the inability to function in society; one's inability to function adds more burden to others so that others suffer as well. In the case of mania, people around the person having mania suffer. Ultimately, the psychiatric disorder requires that one and/or others suffer. In childhood animal abuse, it seems that no humans (except, perhaps, the animal's owner, if there is one) directly suffer from it. However, it

may have resulted from a history of being a victim of abuse. Also childhood animal abuse, in the long run, may bring troubles such as committing a crime or having to commit a crime. Thus the way we assign the term "psychiatric disorder" may need to be reconsidered. Furthermore, is it also appropriate to call it a "psychiatric disorder" in cases where neither humans nor animals suffer and there is no long-term negative consequence? Bestiality, for example, may be one example. Leaving cases where bestiality is associated with violence or abnormal behavior toward others aside, should it still be called a psychiatric disorder if bestiality does not result in physical harm to the animal? (There are certainly cases where animals feel pain and suffer or even cases where they are killed by acts of bestiality. But what if they are not harmed? What if an adult having no other problems has sexual intercourse with the pet?) Children are society's responsibility whereas pets are the individual pet owner's responsibility, although some people may protest. As long as pets are the property of individual pet owners, society cannot effectively guarantee animal welfare. The definition of the animal depends on the culture and the value of the animal may change in extreme situations such as natural disasters (as in the case of the Kobe earthquake) or wars. The inclusion of these issues makes this discussion endless but it is recommended that we keep in mind that the inclusion of animals in the criteria for psychiatric disorders may be as important as considering cultural and religious factors.

16. Nara is a unique city in Japan for its active intervention in animal hoarding present within the city. The leaders are two veterinarians belonging to the Environmental Health Bureau and the research team is involved with many cases of animal hoarding. Its motto is "It is a start to secure the trust from animal hoarders by frequent visits instead of using a compelling intervention" (the current author really respects their effort of making frequent visits to the scenes even on holidays). There are some cases where they spend several years to solve problems in a case but there are steadily fruitful results.

17. Grisham, Frost, Steketee, Kim, and Hood (2006) showed that 22 out of 51 patients having compulsive hoarding had experienced an event that triggered their behavior. Also, these 22 patients

tended to have a later onset of hoarding compared with the remaining participants.

18. Thobaben (2006) listed anorexia nervosa, bipolar disorder, dementia, depression, impulse-control disorders (e.g., impulsive buying or stealing), personality disorders, schizophrenia, and social phobia other than OCD in which compulsive hoarding may be seen.

19. There are certainly cases where OCD hoarders suffer from their own behavior. In a case introduced by Schwartz (1996), a woman in her 50s, who lived with her husband only, kept hoarding useless junk and her house was full of it. She also described animal hoarding behavior by mentioning that her house was shrouded in odor from 16 cats and 4 dogs urinating and defecating behind the accumulated junk. At the same time, however, she mentioned that she was unable to invite any visitors because it was embarrassing and that it was as if she was in a prison. Her symptoms eventually were alleviated after she attended a mutual support meeting for OCD, but until then her OCD hoarding had lasted for 10 years.

20. Wu and Watson (2005) found checking rituals and contamination as the core symptoms of OCD do not inter-correlate with hoarding and suggested that, ". . . we must be careful not to prematurely classify hoarding among the core symptoms of OCD" (p. 916).

21. People with hoarding behavior that includes obsessive shopping often come to hospitals for their financial problems and it is different, in some aspects, from other hoarding behaviors including hoarding many animals (from the current author's experience, most cases are involved with picking up abandoned or stray animals, neglecting to sterilize or neuter animals, and the common justification is, "in order to save animals"). Oniomania or obsessive shopping is not included in DSM-IV-TR but it is associated with dependence or addiction so that it may be classified into a category of the Impulse-Control Disorders. On the other hand, Ratey and Johnson (1997) introduced the case of a 30-year-old female having OCD with oniomania who mentioned that some ideas stuck in her thoughts: Her thought about a quarrel with her husband continually reoccurred and she was unable to stop it; her thought about a desire to have a puppy repeated itself in spite of

already having one dog and three cats at home. In the current author's own clinical experience, there was an elderly female, who used to be a judge, who had purchased numerous puppies over a period of time. The sanitary conditions were extremely bad (e.g., carcasses were left in a yard). She purchased another puppy immediately even after a government agency took live puppies away from her for their protection. This case illustrates that oniomania can be associated with animal hoarding, especially, if there is no financial problem.

22. Studies using high technology such as fMRI are elucidating characteristics of a variety of psychiatric disorders even more clearly. For example, a study comparing the reactions to some stimulus between patients having OCD and patients having small animal phobia (both disorders are classified into Anxiety Disorders in DSM-IV-TR) through fMRI suggests differences in regions of the brain that are involved (Martis, Wright, McMullin, Shin, & Rauch, 2004). In PTSD (also classified into Anxiety Disorder in DSM-IV-TR), the anterior cingulate cortex has been implicated (Yamasue et al., 2003). The progression of these studies on brain function perhaps will have a strong impact on the classification system for psychiatric disorders as well as for interventions.

23. Schizophrenia should be considered as well. However, animal hoarders interviewed by the current author have never shown any clear positive symptom such as hallucinations and delusions and the symptoms of those animal hoarders are relatively stable over time. On the other hand, their symptoms may be due to schizophrenia presenting primarily negative symptoms (and even hoarding behaviors). It is also possible that schizotypal PD and schizophrenia are within the same spectrum. Poyurovsky, Weitzman, and Weitzman (2004) present a model for schizophrenia/OCD spectrum disorders and it includes a category of "OCD+schizotypal PD" (see Figure 2).

24. Harada, Sato, Kobori, and Kachikura (2006) introduce a case of a female, in her 30s, who had co-morbidity of borderline PD and OCD. Her symptoms included the following: spending a long time praying for the spirits of each dead pet; obsessive thoughts that something ominous

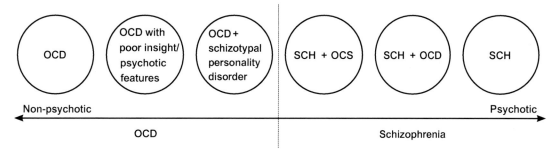

Figure 2 A model for schizophrenia/OCD spectrum disorders (Poyurovsky, Weitzman, and Weitzman 2004)
OCS = obsessive-compulsive symptoms: **SCH** = schizophrenia.

might happen to currently alive pets as well as the spirits of dead pets if she did not conduct compulsive behaviors; washing her hands repeatedly in order to prevent filth, excreta, oil, or detergent from getting into a goldfish tank (she even instructed her mother to do the same thing); having many goldfish without setting aquatic plants or pebbles in the tank but placing the entire responsibility for the actual care on her family members; frequently staring at the tank for a long time in order to check the health condition of those goldfish; and stubbornly refusing a family member's suggestion to release goldfish into a pond (some of these symptoms overlap with animal hoarding). Her symptoms were resistant to pharmacotherapy but cognitive-behavioral therapy produced some improvement.

25. The co-morbidity between OCD and obsessive-compulsive PD is so low (Mavissakalian, Hamann, Abou Haidar, & de Groot, 1993) that it is better to think that these two are independent of each other.

26. A logic of "Going to a hospital leads to abandonment of a collection" is similar to a logic of "Going to a hospital leads to being forced to be fat" seen among patients having eating disorders. Just as interventions to modify family dynamics and lifestyle rather than focusing on body weight frequently have some positive effects on patients with eating disorders, intervention in other aspects may be more effective than focusing on hoarding behaviors themselves in the treatment for hoarders.

27. For example, very rarely are cases of human sexual relations with animals such as bestiality reported in Japan according to the research reported by people involved with veterinary medicine (Yokoyama & Japanese Animal Hospital Association, 2006). This may be a characteristic of Japan. However, there is not much discussion on "bestiality" itself in veterinary medicine in Japan so that there is a possibility that it is overlooked (e.g., a veterinarian does not suspect the presence of bestiality even if there is a laceration in the vagina or the anus).

References

Akechi, T., Nakano, T., Akizuki, N., Okamura, M., Sakuma, K., Nakanishi, T., et al. (2003). Somatic symptoms for diagnosing major depression in cancer patients. *Psychosomatics, 44,* 244–248.

Allen, K., & Blascovich, J. (1996). The value of service dogs for people with severe ambulatory disabilities: A randomized controlled trial. *The Journal of the American Medical Association, 275*(13), 1001.

American Psychiatric Association. (2000). *Diagnostic and statistical manual of mental disorders, text revision* (4th ed.). Washington, DC: Author.

Anderson, S. W., Damasio, H., & Damasio, A. R. (2005). A neural basis for collecting behaviour in humans. *Brain, 128,* 201–212.

Ando, K., Ichida, M., & Kondo, M. (1998). 強迫神経症の一治療例―治療過程におけるネコの役割― [A case study of obsessive compulsive disorder: Some role of a cat during the treatment]. *精神神経誌 [Psychiatria et Neurologia Japonica], 100*(8), 537.

Antonioli, C., & Reveley, M. A. (2005). Randomised controlled trial of animal facilitated therapy with dolphins in the treatment of depression. *British Medical Journal, 331*, 1231–1234.

Arisaka, M, Suzuki, Y, & Ohara, K. (1983). 多彩な動物が表意した1症例 [A case report on delusion of possession by many kinds of animals]. *Japanese Journal of Clinical Psychiatry, 12*(11), 1433–1438.

Arluke A., Levin J., Luke C., & Ascione F. (1999). The relationship of animal abuse to violence and other forms of antisocial behavior. *Journal of Interpersonal Violence, 14*, 963–975.

The arrested male puppy abuser: He actually purchased a puppy with the "sole intention of abuse" [逮捕された子犬虐待男　実は…「虐待目的」で犬購入]. (2005, July 20). *ANN News.* Retrieved July 20, 2005, from http://www.tv-asahi.co.jp/ann/news/web/index.html

Ascione, F. R. (2005). *Children & animals: Exploring the roots of kindness & cruelty.* West Lafayette, IN: Purdue University Press.

Ascione, F. R. (2006). *子どもが動物をいじめるとき　動物虐待の心理学.* [Children and animals: Exploring the roots of kindness and cruelty.] (A. Yokoyama, Trans.). Tokyo, Japan: Being Net Press. (Original work published 2005)

Ascione, F. R., & Arkow, P. (1999). *Child abuse, domestic violence, and animal abuse: Linking the circles of companion for prevention and intervention.* West Lafayette, IN: Purdue University Press.

Ascione, F. R., Thompson, T. M., & Black, T. (1997). Childhood cruelty to animals: Assessing cruelty dimensions and motivations. *Anthrozoös, 10*, 170–177.

Baer, L. (2001). *The imp of the mind: Exploring the silent epidemic of obsessive bad thoughts.* New York, NY: Dutton/Penguin Books.

Baer, L., Jenike, M. A., Ricciardi II, J. N., Holland, A. D., Seymoour, R.J., Minichiello, W. E., et al. (1990). Standardized assessment of personality disorders in obsessive-compulsive disorder. *Archives of General Psychiatry, 47*, 826–830.

Barak, Y., Savorai, O., Mavashev, S., & Beni, A. (2001). Animal-assisted therapy for elderly schizophrenic patients: A one-year controlled trial. *The American Journal of Geriatric Psychiatry, 9*, 439–442.

Barker, S. B., Pandurangi, A. K., & Best, A. M. (2003). Effects of animal-assisted therapy on patients' anxiety, fear, and depression before ECT. *The Journal of ECT, 19*(1), 38–44.

Barker, S. B., Rasmussen, K. G., & Best, A. M. (2003). Effect of aquariums on electroconvulsive therapy patients. *Anthrozoös, 16*(3), 229–240.

Beck, A., & Katcher, A. (1996). *Between pets and people.* West Lafayette, IN: Purdue Press.

Bender, E. (2004). Schizophrenia patients empowered to take charge of illness. *Psychiatric News, 39*(5), 43.

Bers, K, & Conrad, K. (1954). Die chronische taktile halluzinose. *Fortschritte Neurologie, 22*, 254–270.

Broadcasting cat abuse photos on the Internet: Sending the papers pertaining to a case of the suspected man to the public prosecutors office in Fukuoka [猫虐待の写真をネットで公開、容疑の男を書類送検　福岡]. (2002, May 22). *Asahi Shimbun, Evening Edition*, p. 14.

Broadcasting kitten abuse photos on the Internet: A 27- year-old man was found guilty of a crime at Fukuoka district court [子猫虐殺をネットで中継　27歳男に有罪判決　福岡地裁]. (2002, October 21). *Mainichi Newspapers Evening Edition*, p. 9.

Bruch, H. (1971). Anorexia nervosa in the male. *Psychosomatic Medicine, 33*(1), 31–47.

Buchta, R. (1988). Deliberate intoxication of young children and pets with drugs: A survey of an adolescent population in a private practice. *American Journal of the Diseases of Children, 142*, 701–702.

Chowdhury, A. N., Mukherjee, H., Ghosh, K. K., & Chowdhury, S. (2003). Puppy pregnancy in humans: A culture-bound disorder in rural West Bengal, India. *International Journal of Social Psychiatry, 49*(1), 35–42.

Claiborn, J. (n.d.). *Hoarding—A successful compulsion.* Retrieved August 5, 2006, from http://www.ocfoundation.org/1005/m110a_004.htm

Daly, B., & Morton, L. L. (2003). Children with pets do not show higher empathy: A challenge to current views. *Anthrozoös, 16(4)*, 298–314.

De Leo, D., Hichey, P. A., Meneghel, G., & Cantor, C. H. (1999). Blindness, fear of sight loss, and suicide. *Psychosomatics, 40*, 339–344.

Dening, T. R., & West, A. (1989). Multiple serial lycanthropy. *Psychopathology, 22*, 344–347.

Dening, T. R., West, A. (1990). The Dolittle phenomenon: Hallucinatory voices from animals. *Psychopathology, 23*, 40–45.

De Silva P., & Rachman, S. (1998). *Obsessive compulsive disorder: The facts.* New York, NY: Oxford University Press.

Dickey, C. C., McCarley, R. W., Voglmaier, M. M., Niznikiewicz, M. A., Seidman, L. J., Demeo, S., et al. (2003). An MRI study of superior temporal gyrus volume in woman with schizotypal personality disorder. *The American Journal of Psychiatry, 160*, 2198–2201.

Edwards, N. E., & Beck, A. M. (2002) Animal-assisted therapy and nutrition in Alzheimer's disease. *Western Journal of Nursing Research, 24*(6), 697–712.

Frances, A., & Ross, R. (2000). *DSM-IV-TR case studies: A clinical guide to differential diagnosis.* Washington, DC and London, UK: American Psychiatric Publishing, Inc.

Frankel, G. J., & Halmi, K. A. (2003). An adolescent with anorexia nervosa and gastrointestinal stromal tumors. *The American Journal of Psychiatry, 160*, 1056–1059.

Friedmann, E., & Thomas, S. A. (1995). Pet ownership, social support, and one-year survival after acute myocardial infarction in the cardiac arrhythmia suppression trial (CAST). *The American Journal of Cardiology, 76*, 1213–1217.

Fritz, C. L., Fraver, T. B., Hart, L. A., & Kass, P. H. (1996). Companion animals and the psychological health of Alzheimer patients' caregivers. *Psychological Reports, 78*(2), 467–481.

Frost, R. O., Steketee, G., & Greene, K. A. I. (2003). Cognitive and behavioral treatment of compulsive hoarding. *Brief Treatment & Crisis Intervention, 3*, 323–337.

Frost, R. O., Steketee, G., & Williams, L. (2000). Hoarding: A community health problem. *Health and Social Care in the Community, 8*(4), 229–234.

Frost, R. O., Steketee, G., Williams, L. F., & Warren, R. (2000). Mood, personality disorder symptoms and disability in obsessive compulsive hoarders: A comparison with clinical and nonclinical controls. *Behaviour Research and Therapy, 38*, 1071–1081.

Galynker, I., Cohen, L., Salvit, C., Miner, C., Phillips, E., Focseneanu, M., et al. (2000). Psychiatric symptom severity and length of stay on an intensive rehabilitation unit. *Psychosomatics, 41*, 114–120.

Goodman, W. K., Price, L. H., & Rasmussen, S. A. (1989a). The Yale-Brown Obsessive Compulsive Scale. I. Development, use, and reliability. *Archives of General Psychiatry, 46*, 1006–1011.

Goodman, W. K., Price, L. H., & Rasmussen, S. A. (1989b) The Yale-Brown Obsessive Compulsive Scale. II. Validity. *Archives of General Psychiatry, 46*, 1012–1016.

Greenbaum, S. D. (2006). Introduction to working with animal assisted crisis response animal handler teams. *International Journal of Emergency Mental Health, 8*(1), 49–64.

Grisham, J. R., Frost, R. O., Steketee, G., Kim, H., & Hood, S. (2006). Age of onset of compulsive hoarding. *Anxiety Disorders, 20*, 675–686.

Guest, C. M., Collis, G. M., & McNicholas, J. (2006). Hearing dogs: A longitudinal study of social and psychological effects on deaf and hard-of-hearing recipients. *Journal of Deaf Studies and Deaf Education, 11*(2), 252–261.

Gullone, E. (2003). The proposed benefits of incorporating non-human animals into preventative efforts for conduct disorder. *Anthrozoös, 16*(2), 160–174.

Guymer, E. C., Mellor, D., Luk, E. S. L., & Pearse, V. (2001). The development of a screening questionnaire for childhood cruelty to animals. *Journal of Child Psychology and Psychiatry, 42*, 1057–1063.

Harada, S., Sato, H., Kobori, O., & Kachikura, R. (2006). 統合失調症、境界性人格障害と強迫性障害 [Schizophrenia, borderline personality disorder, and obsessive-compulsive disorder]. In S. Harada (Eds.), 強迫性障害治療ハンドブック [A Practical guide for the treatment of OCD] (pp. 307–334). Tokyo, Japan: Kongo Publisher.

Hendrickson, K. M., McCarty, T., & Goodwin, J. M. (1990). Animal alters: Case reports. *Dissociation, 3*(4), 218–221.

Hensley, C., Tallichet, S. E., & Singer, S. D. (2006). Exploring the possible link between childhood and adolescent bestiality and interpersonal violence. *Journal of Interpersonal Violence, 21*(7), 910–923.

Hesselmar, B., Aberg, N., Eriksson, B., & Bjorksten, B. (1999). Does early exposure to a cat or dog protect against later allergy development? *Clinical and Experimental Allergy, 29*(5), 611–617.

Hirsch, A. R., & Whitman, B. W. (1994). Pet ownership and prophylaxis of headache and chronic pain. *Headache: The Journal of Head and Face Pain, 34*(9), 542–543.

Hoffmann, W. A., & Human, L. H. (2003). Experiences, characteristics and treatment of women suffering from dog phobia. *Anthrozoös, 16*(1), 28–42.

Holmes, T. H., & Rahe, R. H. (1967). The social readjustment rating scale. *Journal of Psychosomatic Research, 11*, 213–218.

Jenuwine, M. J., & Lyons, J. S. (2004). Short-term animal assisted group therapy with adolescent girls in residential substance abuse treatment. *10th International Conference on Human-Animal Interactions Conference Handbook*, 63.

Johnson, J. G., Cohen, P., Smailes, E., Kasen, S., Oldham, J. M., Skodol, A. E., et al. (2000). Adolescent personality disorders associated with violence and criminal behavior during adolescence and early adulthood. *The American Journal of Psychiatry, 157*, 1406–1412.

Johnson, R. A., Meadows, R. L., Haubner, J. S., & Sevedge, K. (2003). Human-animal interaction: A complementary/alternative medical (CAM) intervention for cancer patients. *American Behavioral Scientist, 47*, 55–69.

Kirton, A., Wirrell, E., Zhang, J., & Hamiwka, L. (2004). Seizure-alerting and -response behaviors in dogs living with epileptic children. *Neurology, 62*, 2303–2305.

Kogeorgos J., Fonagy, P., & Scott, D. F. (1982). Psychiatric symptom patterns of chronic epileptics attending a neurological clinic: A controlled investigation. *The British Journal of Psychiatry, 140*, 236–243.

Kutchins, U., & Kirk, S. A. (1997). *Making us crazy: DSM-the psychiatric bible and the creation of mental disorders*. New York, NY: Free Press.

Leder, H. (1967). Bemerkungen zum problem des dermatozoenwahns [Some remarks on the problem of dermatozoic hallucinations]. *Psychiatrie Neurologie Und Medizinische Psychologie, 19*, 210–215.

Lefkowitz, C., Paharia, I., Prout, M., Debiak, D., & Bleiberg, J. (2005). Animal-assisted prolonged exposure: A treatment for survivors of sexual assault suffering posttraumatic stress disorder. *Society & Animals, 13*(4), 275–295.

Lemelson, R. (2003). Obsessive-compulsive disorder in Bali: The cultural shaping of a neuropsychiatric disorder. *Transcultural Psychiatry, 40*(3), 377–408.

Levinson, B. M., & Mallon, G. P. (1997). *Pet-oriented child psychotherapy* (2nd ed.). Springfield, IL: Charles C. Thomas, Publisher.

Levitt, J. J., McCarley, R. W., Dickey, C. C., Voglmaier, M. M. Niznikiewicaz, M. A., Seidman, L. J., et al. (2002). MRI study of caudate nucleus volume and its cognitive correlates in neuroleptic-naive patients with schizotypal personality disorder. *The American Journal of Psychiatry, 159*, 1190–1197.

Li, J., Precht, D. H., Mortensen, P. B., & Olsen, J. (2003). Mortality in parents after death of a child in Denmark: A nationwide follow-up study. *Lancet, 361*, 363–367.

Limond, J. A., Bradshaw, J. W. S., & Cormack, K. F. M. (1997). Behavior of children with learning disabilities interacting with a therapy dog. *Anthrozoös, 10*, 84–89.

Martin, F., & Farnum, J. (2002). Animal-assisted therapy for children with pervasive developmental disorders. *Western Journal of Nursing Research, 24*, 657–670.

Martis, B., Wright, C. I., McMullin, K. G., Shin, L. M., & Rauch, S. L. (2004). Functional magnetic resonance imaging evidence for a lack of striatal dysfunction during implicit sequence learning in individuals with animal phobia. *The American Journal of Psychiatry, 161*, 67–71.

Mataix-Cols, D., Wooderson, S., Lawrence, N., Brammer, N., Speckens, A., and Phillips, M.L. (2004). Distinct neural correlates of washing, checking and hoarding symptom dimensions in obsessive-compulsive disorder. *Archives of General Psychiatry, 61*, 564–576.

Mavissakalian, M. R., Hamann, M. S., Abou Haidar, S., & de Groot, C. M. (1993). DSM-III personality disorders in generalized anxiety, panic/agoraphobia, and obsessive-compulsive disorders. *Comprehensive Psychiatry, 34*, 243–248.

Mayo Clinic news (2002, Summer). Dog tired? Mayo research suggests it could be your pooch. *Inside Mayo Clinic, 7*, 14.

Melson, G. F., Kahn, P., Beck, A., Friedman, B., & Roberts, T. (2004). Children's understanding of robotic and living dogs. *10th International Conference on Human-Animal Interactions Conference Handbook*, 71.

Minuchin, S., Rosman, B. L., & Barker, L. (1978). *Psychosomatic families: Anorexia nervosa in context*. Cambridge, MA: Harvard University Press.

Mitropoulou, V., Harvey, P. D., Zegarelli, G., New, A. S., Silverman, J. M., & Siever, L. J. (2005). Neuropsychological performance in schizotypal personality disorder: Importance of working memory. *The American Journal of Psychiatry, 162*, 1896–1903.

Munro, M. H. C., & Thrusfield, M. V. (2001). "Battered pets": Munchausen syndrome by proxy (factitious illness by proxy). *Journal of Small Animal Practice, 42*, 385–389.

Nagata, H. (2005). アルツハイマー型痴呆の診断・治療・ ケアガイドライン：非薬物療法ガイドライン [Diagnosis, treatment, and care guide line of Alzheimer disease: The guide line of nonpharmacologic therapy]. *Japanese Journal of Geriatric Psychiatry, 16-1*, 92–109.

Nakagawa, H., Enatsu, I., Takagi, T., Hayashi, K., Iwasaki, S., & Watanabe, K. (2006). 青年期に至るまでImaginary　Companionが存続した2例 [Two cases of the continuance of imaginary companions in adolescence: The clinical features of the imaginary companions]. *Japanese Journal of Clinical Psychiatry, 35*(7), 1017–1025.

Nakamura, K. (2006). 神経症圏障害の森田療法の原則 [The principle of Morita therapy for applying to neurotic disorders]. *Japanese Journal of Clinical Psychiatry, 35*(6), 709–714.

Nakamura, T. (1984). *日本人の動物観-変身譚の歴史 [Japanese thinking of Animals: The history of folk tale related with metamorphosis]*. Tokyo, Japan: 海鳴社 [Kaimeisha].

Nakao, T. (2006). Biology of obsessive-compulsive disorder: An integrated model of clinical and neurobiological findings. *Japanese Journal of Clinical Psychiatry, 35*(6), 835–841.

Namba, S., Kuwano, S., & Schick, A. (1986). A cross-cultural study on noise problems. *Journal of the Acoustical Society of Japan, 7*, 279–289.

Narita, Y. Nakamura, Y., & Mizuno, N. (1994). *強迫症の臨床研究 [Clinical study of obsessive-compulsive disorder]*. Tokyo, Japan: 金剛出版 [Kongo Publisher].

Nathans-Barel, I., Feldman, P., Begqer, B., Modai, I., & Silver, H. (2005). Animal-assisted therapy ameliorates anhedonia in schizophrenia patients: A controlled pilot study. *Psychotherapy and Psychosomatics, 74*(1), 31–35.

Natsume, M., Murakami, H., & Fujii, H. (1988). 勤労者におけるストレス評価法（ 第1報 ） [Assessment method of stress with working people: First report]. *Journal of Occupational Health, 30*, 266–279.

Orloff, L. M., Battle, M. A., Baer, L., Ivanjack, B. S., Pettit, A. R., Buttolph, M. L., et al. (1994). Longterm follow-up of 85 patients with obsessive-compulsive disorder. *The American Journal of Psychiatry, 151*, 441–442.

Ownby, D. R., Johnson, C. C., & Peterson, E. L. (2002). Exposure to dogs and cats in the first year of life and risk of allergic sensitization at 6 to 7 years of age. *The Journal of the American Medical Association, 288*, 963–972.

Patronek, G. J. (1999). Hoarding of animals: An under-recognized public health problem in a difficult-to-study population. *Public Health Reports, 114*, 81–87.

Patronek, G. J., Loar, L., & Nathanson. J. N. (2006). Animal hoarding: structuring interdisciplinary responses to help people, animals and communities at risk. *The Hoarding of Animals Research Consortium*. Retrieved September 18, 2006, from http://www.tufts.edu/vet/cfa/hoarding/

Peters, V., Sottiaux, M., Appleboom, J., & Kahn, A. (2004). Posttraumatic stress disorder after dog bites in children. *The Journal of Pediatrics, 144*, 121–122.

Poyurovsky, M., Weitzman, A., & Weitzman, R. (2004). Obsessive-compulsive disorder in schizophrenia, clinical characteristics and treatment. *CNS Drugs, 18*, 989–1010.

Puri, B. K., Baxter, R., & Cordess, C. C. (1995). Characteristics of fire-setters: A Study and proposed multiaxial psychiatric classification. *British Journal of Psychiatry, 166*, 393–396.

Ratey, J. J., & Johnson, C. (1997). *Shadow syndromes*. New York, NY: Pantheon Books.

Redefer, L. A., & Goodman, J. G. (1989). Brief report: Pet-facilitated therapy with autistic children. *Journal of Autism and Developmental Disorders, 19*(3), 461–467.

Richeson, N. E. (2003). Effects of animal-assisted therapy on agitated behaviors and social interactions of older adults with dementia. *American

Journal of Alzheimer's Disease and Other Dementias, 18(6), 353–358.

Saito, T. (2001). The relationship between keeping a companion animal, instrumental activities of daily living and use of antihypertensive drugs: A study of Japanese elderly living at home. *9th International Conference on Human-Animal Interactions Abstract Book*, 85.

Samuels, J., Nestadt, G., & Bienvenu, O. J. (2000). Personality disorders and normal personality dimensions in obsessive-compulsive disorder. *The British Journal of Psychiatry, 177*, 457–462.

Sasaki, Y., Oikawa, A., Takeuchi, J., Suzuki, H., Sakai, A., Mita, T. (1996). 動物に関連した病的体験を持つ症例の臨床的検討 [A clinical study of the cases with animal-related psychopathological experiences]. *精神医学 [Clinical Psychiatry], 38*(1), 49–54.

Sato, Y., Miyazaki, T., Senjo, M., & Tanaka, R. (2003). 動物介在療法が著効を示した難治性境界性人格障害の一例 [A case of refractory borderline personality disorder improved with animal assisted therapy]. *精神医学 [Clinical Psychiatry], 45*(6), 659–661.

Schiff, K., Louw, D., & Ascione, F. R. (1999). Animal relations in childhood and later violent behaviour against humans. *Acta Criminologica, 12*, 77–86.

Schreier, H. (2002). Munchausen by proxy defined. *Pediatrics, 110*(5), 985–988.

Schwartz, J. M. (1996). *Brain lock*. New York, NY: HarperCollins Publishers, Inc.

Shah, D. C., Evans, M., & King, D. (2000). Prevalence of mental illness in a rehabilitation unit for older adults. *Postgraduate Medical Journal, 76*, 153–156.

Siegel, J. M., Angulo, F. J., Detels, R., Wesch, J., & Mullen, A. (1999). AIDS diagnosis and depression in the multicenter AIDS cohort study. *AIDS Care, 11*(2), 157–170.

Siegel R. K. (1994) *Whispers: The voices of paranoia*. New York, NY: Crown Publishers.

Takahata, N., Shichida, H., & Uchikata, I. (1994). *憑依と精神病 [Hyôi and mental disorder]*. Hokkaido, Japan: 北海道大学図書刊行会 [Hokkaido University Press].

Thobaben, M. (2006). Understanding compulsive hoarding. *Home Health Care Management & Practice, 18*(2), 152–154.

Torgersen, S., Kringlen, E., & Cramer, V. (2001). The prevalence of personality disorders in a community sample. *Archives of General Psychiatry, 58*, 590–596.

Van de Castle, R. (1983). Animal figures in fantasy and dreams. In A. H. Katcher & A.M. Beck (Eds.), *New perspectives on our lives with companion animals* (pp.148–173). Philadelphia, PA: University of Pennsylvania Press.

Velde, B. P., Cipriani, J., & Fisher, G. (2005). Resident and therapist views of animal-assisted therapy: Implications for occupational therapy practice. *Australian Occupational Therapy Journal, 52*, 53–50.

The violation of the animal protection law: A man was arrested on suspicion of puppy abuse at Sakura police station in Chiba [動物愛護法違反：子犬虐待、 容疑で男逮捕‐‐佐倉署／千葉]. (2005, July 20). *Mainichi Newspapers Morning Edition in Chiba*, p. 23.

Voglmaier, M. M., Seidman, L. J., Niznikiewicz, M. A., Dickey, C. C., Shenton, M.E., and McCarley, R. W. (2000). Verbal and nonverbal neuropsychological test performance in subjects with schizotypal personality disorder. *The American Journal of Psychiatry, 157*, 787–793.

Wada, K., Shibata, T., Saito, T., & Tanie, K. (2004). Effects of three months robot assisted activity to depression of elderly people who stay at a health service facility for the aged. *System Integration Division Annual Conference*, 2709–2714 (CD-ROM).

World Health Organization. (2004). *International statistical classification of diseases and related health problems, tenth revision* (2nd ed.). Geneva, Switzerland: Author.

Wright, J., & Hensley, C. (2003). From animal cruelty to serial murder: Applying the graduation hypothesis. *International Journal of Offender Therapy and Comparative Criminology, 47(1)*, 71–88.

Wu, K. D., & Watson, D. (2005). Hoarding and its relation to obsessive-compulsive disorder. *Behaviour Research and Therapy, 43*, 897–921.

Yamasue, H., Kasai, K., Iwanami, A., Ohtani, T., Yamada, H., Abe, O., et al. (2003). Voxel-based analysis of MRI reveals anterior cingulate gray-matter volume reduction in posttraumatic stress disorder due to terrorism. *Proceedings of the National Academy of Sciences of the United States of America, 100*, 9039–9043.

Yokoyama, A. (1996). *アニマル・セラピーとは何か* *[What is an animal assisted therapy and activity]*. Tokyo, Japan: 日本放送出版協会 [NHK Book].

Yokoyama, A. (1998). 動物虐待が見られた境界性人格障害の一例 [A case study of borderline personality disorder conducted with animal abuse]. 第*20*回比較心身症研究会要旨集 *[The 20th Japanese Comparative PSD Association Abstract Book]*, 6–13.

Yokoyama, A. (2000a). Comparison between two different cases of having a pet when patient must be hospitalized. *Japanese Journal of Human Animal Relations, 8*, 84–86.

Yokoyama, A. (2000b). 動物に対して妄想を持った4症例 [Case study of four patients with delusion toward animals]. *動物観研究会公開ゼミナール2000発表要旨集 [Open Meeting 2000: Association for Thinking of Animals Abstract Book]*, 11–12.

Yokoyama, A. (2001). いわゆる「普通の」ペット・ロス [So called 'common' symptom after pet loss]. *どうぶつと人 [Human and Animals], 9*, 45–52.

Yokoyama, A. (2005). The trial of RAA/RAT in the clean room at the pediatrics ward. *The Society of Instrument and Control Engineers Annual Conference 2005*, 2346–2349 (CD-ROM).

Yokoyama, A., & Japanese Animal Hospital Association. (2006). 動物病院における故意的外傷 (NAI: non-accidental injury) 調査結果報告 [The debrief report: The research of non-accidental injury (NAI) observed in veterinary hospital setting]. *Japanese Animal Hospital Association News Letter, 225*, 8–9.

Yokoyama, A., Kamijo, M., Arisawa, S., & Sakae, K. (1997). 精神症状に関してアニマル・アシステッド・セラピーを施行した癌患者2例 [The case study: Animal assisted therapy to two patients with cancer who have psychiatric problems]. *第16回比較心身症研究会要旨集 [The 16th Japanese Comparative PSD Association Abstract Book]*, 16–17.

Yokoyama, A., & Kimura, Y. (2002). 新たにペットを飼うことによって精神症状に良好な変化が見られた症例の検討 [The case study of the patients whose psychiatric symptom were improved after keeping dogs]. *第26回比較心身症研究会要旨集 [The 26th Japanese Comparative PSD Association Abstract Book]*, 7–12.

Yokoyama, A., & Todoroki, K. (2004). 精神疾患患者におけるペット飼育の分析–摂食障害との比較から–[The analysis of the rate about keeping pets among psychiatric patients: By comparison with that rate of eating disorder patients]. *動物観研究 [Thinking of Animals-Perception, Concept and Attitude], 8*, 45–48.

Zimmerman, M., Rothschild, L., & Chelminski, I. (2005). The Prevalence of DSM-IV personality disorders in psychiatric outpatients. *The American Journal of Psychiatry, 162*, 1911–1918.

Animal Abuse:
The Continuing Evolution of Theory, Research, and Application

Frank R. Ascione

The contributors to this handbook have provided a comprehensive exploration of the landscapes of theory, research, and applications related to animal abuse and cruelty to animals. In this chapter, I illustrate the continuing evolution of scholarly work on these topics by highlighting recent additions to the literature and the emerging research horizons that draw us to even more refined examination and understanding of animal abuse. New scholarly efforts related to animal abuse topics now appear in the literature with remarkable frequency and during the time between completion and publication of this handbook, my attempt to update will, no doubt, be out of date. My apologies to the reader!

The late Ken Magid (personal communication, June 19, 1998) once shared an image with me, an image I believe he attributed to Einstein, of our current knowledge represented by a circle embedded within an infinite space representing everything not yet known. As our knowledge increases, it touches and illuminates more and more of what is yet to be known. As with most scientific endeavors, as our understanding of the phenomenon of animal abuse increases, we are led to ask new questions and to reframe old questions in the context of advances in related scientific fields.

Conceptualizations of Animal Abuse

The definition of animal abuse continues to be constructed by historians, cultural observers, and other social scientists. Nell (2006) examines the general topic of cruelty and Munro (2005) prompts a consideration of whether or not our conceptions of cruelty to animals have been too narrow, especially in empirical studies of animal abuse. One additional example of the construction of animal abuse is McMillan's (2005) thoughtful treatment of the

emotional maltreatment of animals, a topic that begs for research analysis. McMillan's analysis suggests that we need to know much more about animals who live in violent human environments and how their physical and emotional health is affected by aggression between humans (e.g., child maltreatment, domestic violence, abuse of the elderly).

The history of the animal welfare movement in the United States, focused on the 19th and early 20th centuries, is addressed in two contemporary analyses of humans' relations with their companion animals (Grier, 2006; Mason, 2005) and complements a recent encyclopedia entry on one of the oldest animal welfare organizations in the United States, the American Humane Association (Ascione & Arkow, in press). A novel and intellectually rich set of historical and cultural analyses of the roles of animals in Japanese society has also recently been published (Pflugfelder & Walker, 2005). Our understanding of animal abuse in different societies can only be enhanced by appreciating the roles that different species of animals have had in the past as well as their more contemporary roles in human social groups.

Diversity in the Forms and Functions of Animal Abuse

Recent studies of animal abuse add to our understanding of the topography of animal abuse and the demographics and personality characteristics of perpetrators. Henry (2004a, 2006) has conducted compelling research with college students tying animal abuse to attitudes toward the humane treatment of animals, empathy, delinquency, and histories of trauma. The forms that animal abuse may take are explored by Tallichet, Hensley, and Singer (2005), and Tallichet and Hensley (2005) consider how the species of animals who are abused may be related to perpetrators' rural or urban upbringing.

A number of studies have highlighted the significance of being exposed, during childhood and adolescence, to others committing acts of animal abuse (Henry, 2004b; Thompson & Gullone, 2006). Such exposure has been related to college students' reported history of perpetration of animal abuse (Henry, 2004b) and adolescents' attitudes toward the humane treatment of animals (Thompson & Gullone, 2006). In the field of developmental psychopathology, increased concern has emerged about the effects of exposure to community violence on young people's mental health (Brandt, Ward, Dawes, & Flisher, 2005). Unfortunately, assessments of exposure to community violence do not include questions about violence to non-human animals that children and adolescents may have witnessed in their homes or neighborhoods. Clearly, this issue warrants further investigation.

Psychological and Psychiatric Explorations

Given our society's concern with antisocial behavior, it is not surprising that the study of conduct disorder continues to be a major focus of research on developmental psychopathology. Recent reviews have examined the relation of conduct disorder to conceptualizations of psychopathy (Vaughn & Howard, 2005; Vien & Beech, 2006) with special emphasis given to youth who display what have been termed "callous and unemotional traits," traits suggestive of deficits in empathy (Kotler & McMahon, 2005; Raine et al., 2006). Dadds, Whiting, and Hawes (2006) have examined callous/unemotional traits in a normative sample of children and found that such non-empathic traits are related to higher scores on Dadds' measure of cruelty to animals (see *Conduct Problems and Cruelty to Animals in Children* by Dadds, this text). In Raine et al.'s analysis, proactive (instrumental) and reactive aggression are distinguished based on the authors' belief that understanding the motivations for aggression may enhance our understanding of its differing etiologies and recommendations for intervention. These sentiments have been echoed in the area of animal abuse in a study by Hensley and Tallichet (2005), who call for more attention to the motivations underlying animal abuse. The proactive/reactive distinction might also be fruitfully applied to cases of animal abuse.

In this same vein, research on animal abuse could be informed by recent developments in the study of the developmental psychobiology of aggression and violent behavior. Chapters included in a volume edited by Stoff and Susman (2005) address genetic, hormonal, and neurotransmitter influences implicated in aggression as well as developmental models that have relevance for understanding animal abuse (e.g., early onset/life course persistent antisocial behavior versus adolescent-limited antisocial behavior). One of the challenges to understanding animal abuse is that the preponderance of research has relied on cross-sectional or retrospective methods. One of my hopes is that future studies of animal abuse will employ longitudinal methods that will allow us to better understand developmental sequences in the emergence of animal abuse with respect to other forms of antisocial behavior (e.g., interpersonal violence, property destruction, sex offenses).

Animal Abuse and Other Antisocial Behaviors

The study of fire setting has clear relevance for our understanding of animal abuse. Dadds and Fraser (2006) recently published an analysis, with a normative sample of children, demonstrating a positive correlation, for boys, between fire setting and cruelty to animals. Similar findings have been reported by Becker, Stuewig, Herrera, and McCloskey (2004) with a sample of adolescents exposed to domestic violence. Fire setting and animal abuse may both result in potentially devastating costs (in terms of destructiveness and human/animal suffering), both may be perpetrated covertly, and their assessment requires that we develop appropriate ways to query young people about acts they perpetrate away from the eyes of parents, guardians, and other concerned adults. For example, Dadds et al. (2006) found that parents underreported children's cruelty to animals when compared to their own children's self-reports.

Bullying has been the focus of concerted research efforts for more than three decades (for a recent overview, see Smith, Pepler, & Rigby, 2004). These efforts provide a number of models for assessment, prevention, and intervention that could be applied to the study of animal abuse. Childhood bullying and animal abuse share a number of qualities. Both involve power differentials between perpetrators and their victims and both may be predictive of other antisocial behaviors in later developmental periods. Baldry (2005) has pioneered exploration of the relations between bullying and animal abuse in a sample of Italian children, and similar research is being pursued by an Australian research group (E. Gullone, personal communication, August 3, 2006).[1]

Bestiality continues to be a controversial topic. A book edited by Beetz and Podberscek (2005) provides a comprehensive treatment of this topic, including historical and legal analyses, the relation of bestiality to aggression and violence, and consideration of bestiality as a sexual orientation (especially in cases where animals are not *physically* harmed). Hensley, Tallichet, and Singer (2006), in their study of incarcerated men, demonstrate that bestiality is related to crimes against humans. A soon to be published encyclopedia on interpersonal violence will include an entry on bestiality (Ascione, in press c) suggesting a greater willingness in the scholarly community to address the significance of human sexual activity with animals.

Animal Abuse in Violent Human Environments

Animal abuse in the context of domestic violence (Ascione, in press a, d, e) continues to receive extensive research attention, perhaps due to the diversity of forms animal abuse may take in families suffering from intimate partner violence. Batterers may engage in animal abuse for a variety of motivations (Fitzgerald, 2005), there are cases where women who are battered are coerced into animal abuse by their partners (Loring & Bolden-Hines, 2004), and children exposed to domestic violence have been found to be more likely to abuse animals than nonexposed children (Ascione et al., in press; Currie, 2006; Duncan, Thomas, & Miller, 2005).

A substantial minority of women who are abused report that concern for their pets' welfare affected their decision making about leaving an abusive partner (see Ascione, 2007, for a summary of this research) and a number of collaborative programs now exist to shelter pets of women who are battered (Ascione, in press d Carlisle-Frank & Flanagan, 2006). Threats or harm to pets have been reported by women who are abused (Walton-Moss, Manganello, Frye, & Campbell, 2005) and women seeking protective orders from courts (Logan, Shannon, & Walker, 2005). Maine recently became the first state to include the welfare of pets in protective orders sought by women who are battered (Zorza, 2006);

Vermont and New York recently passed similar legislation. It has been remarkable to witness this area of inquiry move from anecdote to empirical research to social policy change in such a relatively brief period of time.

Animal Abuse: Sentinel for Children at Risk?

Interest in animal abuse continues in the fields of child welfare and clinical child and adolescent psychology and psychiatry. Fine's (2006) handbook includes chapters related to these topics and the potential relation between animal abuse and child maltreatment has been acknowledged and is receiving attention in the research community (Ascione, in press b; Duncan, Thomas, & Miller, 2005). Recently, a case study appeared that noted the diagnostic significance of both actual and symbolic animal abuse (Shapiro, Prince, Ireland, & Stein, 2006) and the value (and challenges) of implementing cross reporting between animal welfare and child welfare agencies has been explored by Zilney and Zilney (2005). Although some skeptical voices have been raised about the significance of the overlap between child welfare and animal abuse (Gough & Stanley, 2006; Piper & Myers, 2006), a compelling case has been made for the potential fruitfulness of collaboration between child and animal welfare agencies (Becker & French, 2004, 2006).

Forensic and Veterinary Applications

Animal abuse is receiving greater attention in the field of forensics. Haden and Scarpa (2005) discuss animal abuse in the context of forensic evaluation of criminals and a landmark book on veterinary forensic medicine, the first of its kind, has just been published (Sinclair, Merck, & Lockwood, 2006). Interest in animal abuse within the veterinary community is high. In the United States and Canada, veterinary periodicals have included articles on animal abuse reporting laws, ethical responsibilities to report animal abuse, confidentiality and liability issues, and veterinary testimony about animal abuse in court cases (Babcock & Neihsl, 2006; Jack, 2005). A veterinary periodical has recently highlighted, with a cover story, the issue of animal abuse from the perspective of the veterinary practitioner (Lofflin, 2006), including an update on the issue of animal hoarding (Patronek, 2006).

The topic of animal abuse, first illuminated by philosophical analysis, is now a field enjoying vibrant research conducted from basic and applied scientific perspectives. During the first 75 years of the 20th century, a mere handful of studies had been published on this topic. Since then, scholarly activity on animal abuse issues has dramatically increased. The contributions to this handbook clearly demonstrate how animal welfare and human welfare are intertwined and illustrate the challenges to studying a phenomenon that is at times hidden, but when uncovered is emotionally disturbing to most human observers. It is my hope that this handbook will serve as a useful reference for professionals as well as an encouragement to students and young scientists to devote their scholarly expertise to enhancing our understanding of animal abuse. Animal and human victims are depending on our collective success in these efforts.

> Effective violence prevention must begin with perpetrators, not victims. If the upstream approaches to violence prevention advocated by the public-health model are to be effective, psychologists must be able to provide violence prevention workers with a fine-grained understanding of perpetrator gratifications. This is a distasteful task that will compel researchers to interact with torturers and abusers . . . It is nonetheless an essential step in developing effective strategies for the primary prevention of violence. (Nell, 2006, p. 211)

Note

1. An important paper on this topic was just published by Henry and Sanders (2007).

References

Ascione, F. R. (2007). Emerging research on animal abuse as a risk factor for intimate partner violence. In K. Kendall-Tackett & S. Giacomoni (Eds.), *Intimate partner violence*. Kingston, NJ: Civic Research Institute, 3-1–3-17.

Ascione, F. R. (in press a). Animal/pet abuse. In C. Renzetti & J. Edleson (Eds.), *Encyclopedia of interpersonal violence*. Thousand Oaks, CA: Sage.

Ascione, F. R. (in press b). Animal abuse and child maltreatment occurrence. In C. Renzetti & J. Edleson (Eds.), *Encyclopedia of interpersonal violence*. Thousand Oaks, CA: Sage.

Ascione, F. R. (in press c). Bestiality. In C. Renzetti & J. Edleson (Eds.), *Encyclopedia of interpersonal violence*. Thousand Oaks, CA: Sage.

Ascione, F. R. (in press d). Sheltering of domestic violence victims' pets. In C. Renzetti & J. Edleson (Eds.), *Encyclopedia of Interpersonal Violence*. Thousand Oaks, CA: Sage.

Ascione, F. R., & Arkow, P. (in press). American humane association. In C. Renzetti & J. Edleson (Eds.), *Encyclopedia of interpersonal violence*. Thousand Oaks, CA: Sage.

Ascione, F. R., Weber, C. V., Thompson, T. M., Heath, J., Maruyama, M., & Hayashi, K. 2007. Battered pets and domestic violence: Animal abuse reported by women experiencing intimate violence and by non-abused women. *Violence against Women 13*, 354–373.

Babcock, S. L., & Neihsl, A. (2006). Requirements for mandatory reporting of animal cruelty. *Journal of the American Veterinary Medical Association, 228*, 685–688.

Baldry, A. C. (2005). Animal abuse among preadolescents directly and indirectly victimized at school and at home. *Criminal Behaviour and Mental Health, 15*, 97–110.

Becker, F., & French, L. (2004). Making the links: Child abuse, animal cruelty and domestic violence. *Child Abuse Review, 13*, 399–414.

Becker, F., & French, L. (2006). Response to "Forging the links: (De)constructing chains of behaviours." *Child Abuse Review, 15*, 188–189.

Becker, K. D., Stuewig, J., Herrera, V. M., & McCloskey, L. A. (2004). A study of firesetting and animal cruelty in children: Family influences and adolescent outcomes. *Journal of the American Academy of Child and Adolescent Psychiatry, 43*, 905–912.

Beetz, A. M., & Podberscek, A. L. (Eds.). (2005). *Bestiality and zoophilia: Sexual relations with animals*. West Lafayette, IN: Purdue University Press.

Brandt, R., Ward, C. L., Dawes, A., & Flisher, A. J. (2005). Epidemiological measurement of children's and adolescents' exposure to community violence: Working with the current state of the science. *Clinical Child and Family Psychology Review, 8*, 327–342.

Carlisle-Frank, P., & Flanagan, T. (2006). *Silent victims: recognizing and stopping abuse of the family pet*. Lanham, MD: University Press of America.

Currie, C. L. (2006). Animal cruelty by children exposed to domestic violence. *Child Abuse and Neglect, 30*, 425–435.

Dadds, M. R., & Fraser, J. A. (2006). Fire interest, fire setting and psychopathology in Australian children: A normative study. *Australian and New Zealand Journal of Psychiatry, 40*, 581–586.

Dadds, M. R., Whiting, C., & Hawes, D. J. (2006). Associations among cruelty to animals, family conflict, and psychopathic traits in childhood. *Journal of Interpersonal Violence, 21*, 411–429.

Duncan, A., Thomas, J. C., & Miller, C. (2005). Significance of family risk factors in development of childhood animal cruelty in adolescent boys with conduct problems. *Journal of Family Violence, 20*, 235–239.

Fine, A. H. (Ed.). (2006). *Animal-assisted therapy: Theoretical foundations and guidelines for practice* (2nd ed.). San Diego, CA: Academic Press.

Fitzgerald, A. (2005). *Animal abuse and family violence: Researching the interrelationships of abusive power*. Lewiston, NY: Edwin Mellen Press.

Gough, D., & Stanley, N. (2006). Making and understanding the links. *Child Abuse Review, 15*, 155–158.

Grier, K. C. (2006). *Pets in America: A history*. Chapel Hill, NC: University of North Carolina Press.

Haden, S. C., & Scarpa, A. (2005, Summer). Childhood animal cruelty: A review of research, assessment, and therapeutic issues. *The Forensic Examiner*, 23–32.

Henry, B. C. (2004a). The relationship between animal cruelty, delinquency, and attitudes toward the treatment of animals. *Society and Animals, 12*, 185–207.

Henry, B. C. (2004b). Exposure to animal abuse and group context: Two factors affecting participation in animal abuse. *Anthrozoös, 17*, 290–305.

Henry, B. C. (2006). Empathy, home environment, and attitudes toward animals in relation to animal abuse. *Anthrozoös, 19*, 17–34.

Henry, B. C., and Sanders, C. E. (2007) Bullying and animal abuse: Is there a connection? *Society and Animals, 15*, 107–126.

Hensley, C., & Tallichet, S. E. (2005). Animal cruelty motivations: Assessing demographic and situational influences. *Journal of Interpersonal Violence, 20*, 1429–1443.

Hensley, C., Tallichet, S. E., & Singer, S. D. (2006). Exploring the possible link between childhood and adolescent bestiality and interpersonal violence. *Journal of Interpersonal Violence, 21*, 910–923.

Jack, D. C. (2005). "Good Samaritans": A legislative solution for mandatory reporting of suspected animal abuse. *Canadian Veterinary Journal, 46*, 539–540.

Kotler, J. S., & McMahon, R. J. (2005). Child psychopathy: Theories, measurement, and relations with development and persistence of conduct problems. *Clinical Child and Family Psychology Review, 8*, 291–325.

Lofflin, J. (2006). Animal abuse: What practitioners need to know. *Veterinary Medicine, 101*, 506–518.

Logan, T., Shannon, L., & Walker, R. (2005). Protective orders in rural and urban areas: A multiple perspective study. *Violence against Women, 11*, 876–911.

Loring, M. T., & Bolden-Hines, T. A. (2004). Pet abuse by batterers as a means of coercing battered women into committing illegal behavior. *Journal of Emotional Abuse, 4*, 27–37.

Mason, J. (2005). *Urban animals, sentimental culture, and American literature, 1850–1900*. Baltimore, MD: Johns Hopkins University Press.

McMillan, F. D. (2005). Emotional maltreatment in animals. In F. D. McMillan (Ed.), *Mental health and well-being in animals* (pp. 167–179). Ames, IA: Blackwell Publishing.

Munro, J. (2005). *Confronting cruelty: Moral orthodoxy and the challenge of the animal rights movement*. Leiden, Netherlands: Brill.

Nell, V. (2006). Cruelty's rewards: The gratifications of perpetrators and spectators. *Behavioral and Brain Sciences, 29*, 211–224.

Patronek, G. J. (2006). Animal hoarding: Its roots and recognition. *Veterinary Medicine, 101*, 520–530.

Pflugfelder, G. M., & Walker, B. L. (Eds.). (2005). *JAPANimals: History and culture in Japan's animal life*. Ann Arbor, MI: University of Michigan Press.

Piper, H., & Myers, S. (2006). Forging the links: (De)constructing chains of behaviours. *Child Abuse Review, 15*, 178–187.

Raine, A., Dodge, K., Loeber, R., Gatzke-Kopp, L., Lynam, D., Reynolds, C., et al. (2006). The Reactive-Proactive Aggression Questionnaire: Differential correlates of reactive and proactive aggression in adolescent boys. *Aggressive Behavior, 32*, 159–171.

Shapiro, H. L., Prince, J. B., Ireland, R., & Stein, M. T. (2006). A dominating imaginary friend, cruelty to animals, social withdrawal, and growth deficiency in a 7-year-old girl with parents with schizophrenia. *Journal of Developmental and Behavioral Pediatrics, 27*, 231–236.

Sinclair, L., Merck, M., & Lockwood, R. (Eds.). (2006). *Forensic investigation of animal cruelty: A guide for veterinary and law enforcement professionals.* Washington, DC: Humane Society Press.

Smith, R. K., Pepler, D., & Rigby, K. (Eds.). (2004). *Bullying in schools: How successful can interventions be?* Cambridge, UK: Cambridge University Press.

Stoff, D. M., & Susman, E. J. (Eds.). (2005). *Developmental psychobiology of aggression.* Cambridge, UK: Cambridge University Press.

Tallichet, S. E., & Hensley, C. (2005). Rural and urban differences in the commission of animal cruelty. *International Journal of Offender Therapy and Comparative Criminology, 49*, 711–726.

Tallichet, S. E., Hensley, C., & Singer, S. D. (2005). Unraveling the methods of childhood and adolescent cruelty to nonhuman animals. *Society and Animals, 13*, 91–107.

Thompson, K. L., & Gullone, E. (2006). An investigation into the association between the witnessing of animal abuse and adolescents' behavior toward animals. *Society and Animals, 14*, 221–243.

Vaughn, M. G., & Howard, M. O. (2005). The construct of psychopathy and its potential contribution to the study of serious, violent, and chronic youth offending. *Youth Violence and Juvenile Justice, 3*, 235–252.

Vien, A., & Beech, A. R. (2006). Psychopathy: Theory, measurement, and treatment. *Trauma, Violence, and Abuse, 7*, 155–174.

Walton-Moss, B. J., Manganello, J., Frye, V., & Campbell, J. C. (2005). Risk factors for intimate partner violence and associated injury among urban women. *Journal of Community Health, 30*, 377–389.

Zilney, L. A., & Zilney, M. (2005). Reunification of child and animal welfare agencies: Cross-reporting of abuse in Wellington County, Ontario. *Child Welfare, 84*, 47–66.

Zorza, J. (2006). Maine's encouraging law protecting animals in domestic violence situations. *Domestic Violence Report, 11*, 65, 78.

Contributors

Phil Arkow is interim director for Human-Animal Bond Programs at the American Humane Association, the nation's oldest federation of child and animal protection organizations. He chairs the Latham Foundation's Animal Abuse and Family Violence Prevention Project, and he lectures internationally to cross-train employees of animal shelters, child protection agencies, domestic violence prevention programs, and veterinarians to recognize and report family violence. He teaches a distance-education certificate course in Animal-Assisted Therapy/Activities through Harcum College and a similar campus course at Camden County College. He has authored or edited numerous articles and nine key reference books on the human-animal bond, humane education, animal-assisted therapy, violence prevention, and animal shelter management. He has served with the American Veterinary Medical Association, the Delta Society, the National Animal Control Association, and the American Association of Human-Animal Bond Veterinarians.

Frank R. Ascione is a professor in the Department of Psychology and adjunct professor in Family and Human Development at Utah State University. He has co-edited two books: *Cruelty to Animals and Interpersonal Violence: Readings in Research and Application* (1998) and *Child Abuse, Domestic Violence, and Animal Abuse: Linking the Circles of Compassion for Prevention and Intervention* (1998), and authored *Safe Havens for Pets: Guidelines for Programs Sheltering Pets for Women who are Battered. Children and Animals: Exploring the Roots of Kindness and Cruelty* is Dr. Ascione's latest book, published in 2005 by Purdue University Press. He was selected to receive the 2001 Distinguished Scholar Award from the International Association of Human-Animal Interaction Organizations and the International Society for Anthrozoology. He serves on the editorial boards of *Anthrozoös* and *Aggression and Violent Behavior.*

Andrea M. Beetz, Dipl.-Psych., Ph.D., works as a psychologist in research on attachment, emotional intelligence, and human-animal interactions. She received her degrees from the University of Erlangen-Nuremberg, Germany, and conducted several research projects in the United States at the University of California, Davis; Utah State University, Logan, Utah; and in the UK at the University of Cambridge. Her research was supported by several scholarships from German foundations including the German Academic Exchange Service (DAAD) and the German Research Foundation (DFG). She has published and presented her research at several international conferences. The focus of her current work in human-animal interactions is the application of attachment theory to human-animal relationships, the development of emotional intelligence and empathy, the evaluation of projects in Animal-Assisted Therapy and Education, and correlates of animal abuse. In 2006, she established a research group on human-animal relationships at the Department of Education of the University of Erlangen, Germany.

Barbara Walling Boat, Ph.D., is associate professor in the Department of Psychiatry and director of The Childhood Trust at Cincinnati Children's Hospital Medical Center. She conducts research, training, and treatment in the area of childhood trauma and maltreatment with specific interest in links among animal cruelty, child abuse, and domestic violence. She is clinical supervisor for the Trauma Treatment Training Center, which offers training in evidenced-based interventions for traumatized children and their families including Parent-Child Interaction Therapy and Trauma-Focused Cognitive Behavioral Therapy. She also conducts an intervention for teens adjudicated for domestic violence called the Strategic Humane Interventions Program (SHIP), which was developed by Lynn Loar. The Program teaches teens and their caregivers to "clicker train" homeless shelter dogs to enhance their adoptability and to interact more effectively with each other using positive reinforcement skills.

John Clarke received a Ph.D. in Psychology from the University of Sydney by examining the developmental experiences and crime scene behaviors of sexual homicide offenders, rapists, and non-sexual homicide offenders from an offender profiling perspective. He has also completed studies looking at psychopaths in the workplace, criminal profiling, serial rape, animal cruelty offenders, and sexual homicide crime scene analysis. He consults for corporations experiencing problems with a suspected workplace psychopath, as well as working with victims of workplace psychopaths. He has also consulted for the New South Wales (NSW) Police in developing offender profiles for homicide (sexual and non-sexual), child abuse, pedophilia, stalking, and serial sexual assault cases amongst others. He has commented on criminal psychology and workplace psychopaths in print media, radio, and television both in Australia and overseas. He is also the author of three books: *Touched By The Devil* (2001 with Andy Shea), *Working With Monsters* (2005), and *Pocket Psycho* (2007).

Mark Dadds is professor of Psychology at the University of New South Wales, Sydney, Australia, and senior research fellow of the National Health and Medical Research Council of Australia. He directs several national intervention programs for children, youth, and their families at risk for mental health problems. These programs have been implemented in each state in Australia and in Canada, the United States, Belgium, and Holland. In the last decade, he has been awarded more than $4 million in research funding for his work in clinical child and family mental health. He has been national president of the Australian Association for Cognitive and Behavioural Therapy, director of research for the Abused Child Trust of Queensland, and a recipient of several awards including the Australian Psychological Society's awards for Early Career Research in 1991 and the Ian Matthew Campbell Award for Excellence in Clinical Psychology in 2005.

Jane A. Eberle, M.Ed., is a school psychologist in the Seattle Public Schools. During her 28 years with Seattle schools, she has been the coordinator of Psychological Services and supervisor of Special Education. She earned her master's degree in school psychology at the University of Washington in Seattle. She also serves as the assistant to the editor for the journal *Violence and Victims*, an internationally distributed research journal devoted to theory, practice, and public policy related to perpetrators, victims, and the trauma associated with interpersonal violence. She has been recognized as the School Psychologist of the Year in the State of Washington and chairs the assessment review committee for the Washington State School Psychologist Association. Her current research interests include the development of school-based interventions for youth with emotional and behavioral disorders, adult outcomes associated with of learning disability, and developmental perspectives on violence and victimization.

Catherine A. Faver, Ph.D., LMSW, is professor of social work at the University of Texas-Pan American. Her scholarly work on animal abuse and family violence is published in social work and interdisciplinary journals. Currently, she is investigating animal welfare issues in the Texas-Mexico border region. As co-founder of a local coalition of animal welfare and human services professionals, she is active in community efforts to prevent and end violence. She earned her Ph.D. in Social Work and Sociology at the University of Michigan and her MSSW at the University of Texas at Arlington. She has held faculty appointments at the University of Tennessee from 1983 to 2002 and the University of Texas at Arlington from 1979 to 1983.

Clifton P. Flynn is professor of Sociology at the University of South Carolina Upstate where he has taught since 1988. He is the past Chair of the Section on Animals and Society of the American Sociological Association. He serves on the editorial boards of both *Society & Animals* and *Anthrozoös*. In 2001, his Animals and Society course was chosen as the "Best New Animals and Society Course" by the Humane Society of the United States and was featured on "The Osgood File" on CBS radio. He has written numerous articles on animal abuse and its relationship to family violence.

Pamela D. Frasch is an attorney and vice president of Legal Affairs for the Animal Legal Defense Fund. In that capacity, she oversees and develops ALDF's Criminal Justice and Litigation Programs. The Criminal Justice Program assists prosecutors and others in law enforcement in their efforts to investigate, prosecute, and sentence animal abusers. The Litigation Program seeks to bring civil actions to advance and protect the interests of animals in the legal system. In addition to her duties with the Animal Legal Defense Fund, she is the co-author of the premier American legal casebook in the field, *Animal Law, Cases and Materials* (3rd Ed., 2006), and is an adjunct professor of Law at Northwestern School of Law of Lewis & Clark College where she teaches survey and advanced courses in animal law. She is also the author of Oregon's first felony anti-cruelty law and the author or co-author of numerous articles in the field.

Eleonora Gullone is associate professor in the School of Psychology, Psychiatry, and Psychological Medicine at Monash University in Australia. She earned her Ph.D. in 1993 for her work on children's fears which involved a 3-year follow-up examination from childhood through to adolescence. Since then, she has continued to extensively investigate the emotional development of children and adolescents with a continued focus on fear and anxiety. Her work has also focused upon important contextual contributions to children's development, most particularly, attachment and parenting. She is in the distinguished position of having earned several competitive large grants for her research. In the past 6 years, she has extended her research interest to human-animal and human-nature interactions with a view to promoting positive relationships, thereby decreasing animal cruelty and environmental destruction. In 2002, her significant contribution to the discipline of Psychology was formally recognized when she was elected to Fellowship of the Australian Psychological Society. Further reinforcing her contribution to the discipline are her publications, which exceed 80 published works in refereed journals of significant international standing.

Shari Lewchanin, M.S., Psy.D., has been a clinical psychologist in private practice in Kennebunk, Maine, for the past 25 years, specializing in treating child and adult victims of physical and sexual abuse. In addition, she has provided consultation and training to school systems, mental health centers, and hospitals on trauma and forensic issues related to child abuse. She is a founder of the York County Coalition Against Violence, a multidisciplinary taskforce addressing the link between animal and interpersonal violence, and past president of the Board of the York County Child Abuse and Neglect Council. She has consulted on board management, strategic planning, program evaluation, designing fundraising strategies, personnel policy development, visioning, and leadership coaching for non-profit agencies. In addition, she is a senior consultant with Miller Consultants, where she has worked in researching the change process in organizations, change management, conflict management, and program development and evaluation She is the co-author with Ellen Zimmerman of two books related to children and animal cruelty: *Community Intervention in Juvenile Animal Cruelty* and *Clinical Assessment of Juvenile Animal Cruelty.* She has also published numerous articles in a variety of professional journals.

Lynn Loar, Ph.D., LCSW is the president of the Pryor Foundation. A social worker with expertise in abuse and neglect across the lifespan, she provides training and technical assistance to mental health, human service and animal welfare agencies, law enforcement, and educators about neglect, abuse, and violence involving children, elders, dependent adults, people with disabilities, domestic violence, and animals. She has designed and implemented training and treatment programs that teach gentleness and empathy to child victims of abuse and neglect and their families, including the Strategic Humane Interventions Program [SHIP] (2001–2004). She is the co-author with John H. Weakland of *Working with Families in Shelters: A Practical Guide for Counselors and Child Care Staff*, and with Libby Colman, Ph.D., of *Teaching Empathy: Animal-Assisted Therapy Programs for Children and Families Exposed to Violence.*

Randall Lockwood, Ph.D., has degrees in Psychology and Biology from Wesleyan University in Connecticut and a doctorate in Psychology from Washington University in St. Louis. He is currently senior vice president for Anti-Cruelty Initiatives and Legislative Services for the American Society for the Prevention of Cruelty to Animals. He regularly provides training on animal cruelty issues for law enforcement, social service, mental health and veterinary professionals. His articles have appeared in many scholarly and popular publications. *Cruelty to Animals and Interpersonal Violence*, co-edited with Dr. Frank Ascione, was published in 1998 by Purdue University Press. His most recent works are *Forensic Investigation of Animal Cruelty: A Guide for Veterinary and Law Enforcement Professionals* written with Leslie Sinclair, DVM, and Melinda Merck, DVM, and *Prosecuting Animal Cruelty Cases: Opportunities for Early Response to Crime and Interpersonal Violence,* both published in 2006.

Ken Magid (1946-2005), psychologist, documentary filmmaker, film director, newspaper columnist, reporter, and author was affiliated with the Developmental Psychobiology Research Group at the University of Colorado's Health Science Center in Denver and Red Rocks Community College in Lakewood, Colorado. He was co-author of the widely acclaimed book, *High Risk: Children Without a Conscience* (1989). From 1992 to 1994, he was clinical director of the High Risk Child Foundation. His documentary, entitled "Child of Rage," was sold to HBO and aired nationally. It was nominated for an ACE award and was co-sponsored by the National Association for the Prevention of Child Abuse. A highly respected clinician, he was well-known for his work on attachment processes and developmental psychopathology. Much of his career was spent working with psychologically wounded youth, yet he always maintained a vision for healing and peace through his efforts at positive life coaching. He was a member of the American Psychological Association and the National Register of Health Care Providers in Psychology.

Roland D. Maiuro, Ph.D., is the clinical director of the Seattle Anger Management, Domestic Violence, and Workplace Conflict Programs, adjunct research scientist for the Albert Einstein Health Care Network, and a clinical research affiliate for the Drug and Alcohol Abuse Institute at the University of Washington. He was a Henry Rutgers Scholar at Rutgers University, and he earned his doctoral degree in Clinical Psychology at Washington University in St. Louis. He has received the Social Issues Award from the Washington State Psychological Association for his research on domestically violent men and the Gold Achievement Award from the American Psychiatric Association for program development, teaching, and applied research in the areas of anger and interpersonal violence. He has published extensively in the areas of domestic violence, anger, stress, and coping and has recently co-edited the books *Psychological Abuse in Violent Domestic Relations* with K. Daniel O'Leary and *Stalking: Research Perspectives on Perpetrators and Victims* with Keith Davis and Irene Hanson Frieze. He is currently editor-in-chief for *Violence and Victims,* an internationally distributed research journal devoted to theory, practice, and public policy related to perpetrators, victims, and the trauma associated with interpersonal violence.

Mika Maruyama is a doctoral candidate in Psychology at Portland State University. Her research focuses on child-animal interaction and its effects on children's cognitive development; humane education as an intervention and prevention of future violent behaviors; and relationships between children's cruelty toward animals and its social or cultural factors, including domestic violence, child abuse, and school violence. Her studies have been conducted both in Japan and the United States, including the effects of animals in the classroom on children's empathy, Japanese children's experiences of animal cruelty and their attitudes toward animals, Japanese batterer intervention programs, and men's reports of violence.

Camilla Pagani is a psychologist who works as a researcher at the Institute of Cognitive Sciences and Technologies of the Italian National Research Council. She collaborated for some years with Francesco Robustelli in a research project on education against violence; the aims of the project being conducting research on violence-related issues and trying to get the results of scientific research on violence translated into concrete intervention at the educational, social, and political level. In this context, she organized conferences, held refresher courses for teachers, and gave lectures to principals, teachers, students, and convicts. She has carried out research in the following fields: children's attitudes toward death, the role of psychology in addressing the problem of existential suffering, social conflict resolution, cross-cultural relations, and human-animal relations particularly with regard to children's attitudes and behaviors toward animals. She has recently written a book with Francesco Robustelli on teachers' attitudes toward immigrant pupils' attending Italian schools in mainstream classes.

Helen Margaret Christina Munro qualified in Veterinary Medicine from the University of Glasgow, Scotland, in 1966. Her first year after graduation was spent as house physician in the Department of Veterinary Medicine at Glasgow University Veterinary School, after which she lived and worked for several years in differing parts of the world: Kenya, Hong Kong, and Fiji. She began specialization in Veterinary Pathology in 1974 at Edinburgh University Veterinary School and spent 15 years in the industry, where she became head of Pathology for Syntex Research Scotland. In 1995, she returned to academia as a research fellow in Edinburgh University Veterinary School. Her particular area of study is the difficult subject of deliberate physical abuse (non-accidental injury/NAI) in companion animals. Acknowledged as the first person to describe the "Battered Pet Syndrome" and to describe the differentiation of accidental and deliberate injury in animals, she lectures widely to veterinary and medical audiences. Her extensively published work highlights the similarities between physical abuse of companion animals and children. She has held the offices of president of the Scottish Metropolitan Division of the British Veterinary Association, member of Council and Executive Committee of the Royal Zoological Society of Scotland, and treasurer of the Society of Companion Animal Studies.

Gary Patronek received a degree in Veterinary Medicine from the University of Pennsylvania in 1984. After a short stint in private practice, he became the director of the Chester County SPCA in West Chester, Pennsylvania. While in that position, he supervised a group of cruelty investigators and first encountered animal hoarding, then known as collecting. He later pursued a Ph.D. in Epidemiology in the Center for Human-Animal Bond at Purdue University, where he conducted some of the first epidemiological studies of pet relinquishment and animal shelter population dynamics. He became a faculty member at Cummings School of Veterinary Medicine at Tufts University in 1996, and from 1997 to 2003, he was the director of Tufts Center for Animals and Public Policy, where he also supervised the graduate program in Animals and Public Policy. His academic and research interests include the link between human and non-human animal health and welfare, including the sentinel value of animal abuse for human violence. While at Tufts, he began academic research into the problem of animal hoarding and founded the Hoarding of Animals Research Consortium (HARC) to bring an interdisciplinary approach to the study of this novel form of animal neglect. He currently works in the private sector in medical communications.

Allie Phillips is the director of Public Policy for the American Humane Association and manages the Washington D.C. office. She was previously employed as a senior attorney with the National District Attorneys Association's National Center for Prosecution of Child Abuse in Alexandria, Virginia, and was an assistant prosecuting attorney in Michigan for approximately 8 years. Her most recent publication is entitled *Establishing Pet-Friendly Disaster Shelters: The Human-Animal Bond is Important,* in State Bar of Michigan Animal Law Section Newsletter, Fall 2006. She received her Juris Doctorate *cum laude* from University of Detroit Mercy School of Law.

Dr. Anthony J. Pinizzotto received a B.A. in English from De Sales University, an M.A. in Forensic Psychology from John Jay College of Criminal Justice, an M.A. in Theology and Pastoral Counseling from De Sales Graduate School of Theology, a Ph.D. in psychology from Georgetown University, and a post-doctoral M.S. in Clinical Psychopharmacology from Alliant University. He completed a clinical internship at Bellevue Hospital in New York City in Psychiatric Emergency and Evaluation. He was an instructor in the Department of Psychology at Georgetown University. He is a senior scientist currently assigned to the FBI's Training Division, Behavioral Science Unit (BSU), where he teaches courses in clinical forensic psychology and the psychology of violent behavior. He currently serves as an Advisory Board member of the National Consortium for the Study of Terrorism and Responses to Terrorism (START). He has lectured throughout the United States, Canada, Switzerland, Italy, and the UK on the topics of law enforcement safety, criminal investigative psychology, personality assessment, the psychology of interview and interrogation, hate-related crimes, sensory distortions involved in critical incidents, forensic hypnosis, and deviant social groups. He is the author of numerous articles reflecting his research in these fields of study and investigation. He has been recognized by the courts as an expert witness in cases involving child exploitation and pornography.

Dr. Mary Lou Randour is the professional outreach coordinator for the Animal Fighting/Animal Cruelty Campaign of The Humane Society of the United States. She is a psychologist who was a practicing clinician for 17 years, received post-graduate training at the Cambridge Hospital at Harvard Medical School and the Washington Psychoanalytic Institute, and holds the position of adjunct assistant professor of Psychiatry at the Uniformed Services University of the Health Services. She offers training seminars to law enforcement and court personnel, mental health professionals, educators, animal control and humane society officers, and advocates for domestic violence victims and child protective service workers. The training seminars address the link between animal abuse and human violence as well as the assessment and treatment of animal abuse committed by children and adults. In addition to offering workshops and seminars, she identifies legislative and policy opportunities that address this important link and organizes efforts in support of them. She is the author of *The Empathy Connection,* first author of *AniCare Child: An Assessment and Treatment Approach for Childhood Animal Abuse*, and second author of *The AniCare Model of Treatment for Animal Abuse*, which is designed for use with adults. She also is editor of one book and author of two; her latest one is *Animal Grace.*

Pooka Rastaman completed his undergraduate work in animal psychology at the University of Washington–Tacoma Branch and is now employed as a research assistant and consultant in Seattle. His interests include the positive effects of animal-assisted therapy, particularly for those with a history of attachment, autism, and externalizing disorders. His areas of ongoing research include the relationships between sibling order, disability status, and social and emotional attachment processes.

Francesco Robustelli is a researcher at the Institute of Cognitive Sciences and Technologies of the Italian National Research Council. He was a research associate at the Albert Einstein College of Medicine of the Yeshiva University in New York and professor of Comparative Psychology at the La Sapienza University in Rome. He has carried out research in the following fields: comparative psychology, memory, learning, the relationship between biological evolution and cultural evolution, people's attitudes toward death, cross-cultural psychology, aggression, education against violence, and human-animal relations. He is also the Italian representative of an international United Nations Educational, Scientific, and Cultural Organization (UNESCO) network for education against violence. The theoretical framework of this network is the *Seville Statement on Violence*, a scientific document that maintains that the fundamental causes of human violence are not biological but sociocultural. He has recently written a book with Camilla Pagani on teachers' attitudes toward immigrant pupils' attending Italian schools in mainstream classes.

Sherry Schlueter has been involved in animal rights, animal liberation, and environmental protection efforts since her youth. She has worked both personally and professionally all her adult life on these and other social justice causes. She entered the law enforcement profession to protect animals and created the first animal cruelty-specific detective unit established within a law enforcement agency. Her concern for the safety and protection of society's most vulnerable human and non-human members was the impetus to form a law enforcement detective section to deal comprehensively and holistically with crimes against animals, children, disabled, and elderly persons; sex crimes and domestic violence victims; and abducted and missing persons, and to provide victim services to them. She has authored successful local and state legislation, including the original Florida felony aggravated animal abuse statute. She personally founded private programs to meet critical needs of jeopardized animals and their guardians for whom no government programs existed. These financial safety nets ("Fund for Abused Animals and Companion Animal Rescue Effort") provide emergency veterinary care and safe-housing to abused, neglected, and abandoned animals, and facilitate rescue of those living at risk in violent homes. Her "Animal Abuse Reward Fund" encourages the reporting of such crimes.

Bianca Snowflake completed her undergraduate work in Animal Psychology at Wayne State University in Detroit and is now employed as a research assistant and consultant in Seattle. Her interests include the positive effects of animal-assisted therapy, particularly for those with a history of attachment, autism, and internalizing disorders. Her current areas of research include canine-human relationships across breeds and service adaptations within the urban setting.

Dr. Elizabeth B. Strand is the founding director of Veterinary Social Work (VSW) at the University of Tennessee College of Veterinary Medicine. Founded in 2002, VSW is a partnership program between Colleges of Veterinary Medicine and Social Work designed to enhance, support, and inform both professions. She is a licensed clinical social worker, experienced family therapist, Grief Recovery Specialist, and a Mindfulness-Based Stress Reduction Teacher. She also is trained as a Rule 31 Mediator, Child and Adult Anicare Animal Abuse Treatment counselor, and a Compassion Fatigue Specialist. She holds a Doctor of Philosophy in Social Work. Her service work centers around anti-animal abuse and anti-racism efforts. Her interest areas include the link between human and animal violence, animals in family systems, the scholarly and practice development of Veterinary Social Work as a sub-specialty of social work practice, communication skills, conflict resolution, and mediation in animal welfare environments, and stress management techniques. Her professional mission is to encourage the humane treatment of both people and animals and to care for those professionals who care for animals.

Dr. Bernard Unti is senior policy adviser and special assistant to the CEO and president of The Humane Society of the United States (HSUS). He earned his Ph.D. in U.S. History from American University, writing a dissertation on organized animal protection in the United States before World War II. He is the author of

Protecting All Animals: A Fifty-Year History of The Humane Society of the United States (2004). He has been a regular contributor to The HSUS's public policy series, *State of the Animals,* and has written widely on animal protection as an historical and contemporary phenomenon.

Akimitsu Yokoyama was born in Hiroshima in 1963 and is a 1990 graduate from University of Occupational and Environmental Health, Japan. He is a practicing psychiatrist who conducts research about the relation between humans and animals (AAA/T, pet loss, animal abuse, the thinking toward animals) from psychiatric view. He has written many articles and books about this field in Japan and is a leader in Japan in promoting the scientific study of animal abuse issues. He is currently an assistant professor at Teikyo University of Science & Technology and is director of the Society for the Study of Human Animal Relations (HARS).

NAME INDEX

Names in italics appear in reference lists.

A

Aber, J. L. 355, 372
Aberg, N. 462, 467
Abou Haidar, S. 468
Abrahamson, S. 186, 196
Abrams, D. 135, 152
Abromaitis, S. M. 118, 127
Achenbach, T. 114, 120, 124, 146–7, 186, 196, 397, 406, 424, 437
Adam, K. S. 357, 361, 366
Adams, C. 33, 35, 48–9, 165, 171, 184, 196, 211, 217–9
Adams, D. 247, 262
Adamson, L. 352, 373
Adelman, S. A. 152
Adelson, E. 346, 369
Adnkronos 250, 262
Agnew, R. 118–9, 125, 158, 166–71, 177, 196, 252, 262
Ainsworth, M. D. S. 135, 147, 337, 340, 343–5, 348, 366–7
Aitken, K. J. 373
Akami, R. 300
Akami, T. 300
Akechi, T. 444, 465
Albee, E. 206
Albert, A. 133–4, 147, 159, 171
Alexander, M. 107
Alger, J. M. 166, 171
Alger, S. F. 166, 171
Alison, L. 209, 220
Allen, K. 296, 299, 373, 444
Als, H. 352, 373
Alvarez, W. A. 207, 217–8
Amberson, T. G. 424, 438
American Academy of Pediatrics Committee on Infant and Pre–School Child 46

American Animal Hospital Association, 394, 407
American Humane 33, 46, 175–6, 178, 193, 196
American Medical Association 34, 36–7, 46, 48–50, 109, 150, 333, 469
American Psychiatric Association (APA) 5, 125, 145, 147, 181, 202, 218, 282, 299, 424, 436–7, 442
American Veterinary Medical Association 33, 38–9, 46–8, 109, 236, 408, 476
Ammerman, R. T. 152
Amon, N. 395, 407
Anderson, R. K. 49, 208, 220, 456
Ando, K. 447, 465
Andronico, M. P. 125
Angulo, F. J. 444, 470
Antonioli, C. 445, 466
Aoki, H. 280, 286, 299
Appelbaum, P. 152
Appelyard, K. 355, 368
Appleboom, J. 447, 469
Arakawa, K. 274, 299
Arisaka, M. 448, 466
Arisawa, S. 444, 471
Arkow, P. 1–2, 5, 25–8, 31–2, 34, 36, 38, 40, 42, 44–50, 171, 189–90, 196–8, 269–70, 294–5, 298–9, 311–2, 331, 400, 407
Arluke, A. 22–3, 24–5, 88, 106, 114–5, 125, 134, 148, 155–60, 162–6, 169, 171, 185, 232–3, 238, 256, 261, 313–5, 331
Aronson, J. 151, 239
Arrigo, B. A. 326, 331
Arseneault, L. 149
Ascione, F. R. 1, 2, 4, 22–8, 32, 103–4, 120–1, 125, 159, 162, 171, 179–82, 185–7, 189, 196–8, 216–9, 231, 247, 251–3, 260–5, 269–70, 272, 274, 246, 278, 280, 282, 284, 286, 288, 290, 292, 298–9, 311–3, 331–3, 366, 380–1, 473–4, 436–7, 457–61, 475–6

SUBJECT INDEX